John Selden and the Western Political Tradition

Legal and political theorist, common lawyer and parliamentary leader, historian and polyglot, John Selden (1584–1654) was a formidable figure in Renaissance England, whose true importance and influence are now coming to be recognized after many years of neglect. *John Selden and the Western Political Tradition* highlights his crucial role in the development of early-modern political ideas such as modern natural law and natural rights, the role of national identity and tradition, Church and State, and the impact of Jewish ideas on Western political thought. Selden's political ideas are analyzed in comparison to those of his contemporaries Grotius, Hobbes and Filmer, and the book demonstrates how these ideas informed and influenced the more familiar works of later thinkers such as Burke. Taking into account the sophistication of his ideas and his impact on later political thought, a new interpretation of Selden is proposed, as an important thinker of the Anglo-American constitutional tradition.

Ofir Haivry is the co-founder and currently Vice President of the Herzl Institute of Jerusalem, a research institute and training center in the fields of Jewish political thought, Jewish philosophy and political Hebraism. He is also Director of the Herzl Institute's National Strategy Initiative.

John Selden and the Western Political Tradition

OFIR HAIVRY

The Herzl Institute

CAMBRIDGE
UNIVERSITY PRESS

University Printing House, Cambridge CB2 8BS, United Kingdom

One Liberty Plaza, 20th Floor, New York, NY 10006, USA

477 Williamstown Road, Port Melbourne, VIC 3207, Australia

314-321, 3rd Floor, Plot 3, Splendor Forum, Jasola District Centre, New Delhi - 110025, India

79 Anson Road, #06-04/06, Singapore 079906

Cambridge University Press is part of the University of Cambridge.

It furthers the University's mission by disseminating knowledge in the pursuit of education, learning and research at the highest international levels of excellence.

www.cambridge.org
Information on this title: www.cambridge.org/9781108978125
10.1017/9780511894923

First published 2017
First paperback edition 2021

A catalogue record for this publication is available from the British Library

Library of Congress Cataloging in Publication data
NAMES: Haivry, Ofir, author.
TITLE: John Selden and the western political tradition / Ofir Haivry.
DESCRIPTION: Cambridge, United Kingdom : Cambridge University Press, 2017. | Includes bibliographical references and index.
IDENTIFIERS: LCCN 2016053734 | ISBN 9781107011342 (hardback)
SUBJECTS: LCSH: Selden, John, 1584–1654. | Political science – Great Britain – History – 17th century. | Politicians – Great Britain – Biography. | Scholars – Great Britain – Biography. | Great Britain – Politics and government – 1603–1714. | BISAC: POLITICAL SCIENCE / History & Theory.
CLASSIFICATION: LCC DA390.1.S4 H35 2017 | DDC 942.06092 [B]–dc23
LC record available at https://lccn.loc.gov/2016053734

ISBN 978-1-107-01134-2 Hardback
ISBN 978-1-108-97812-5 Paperback

Dedicated to my Parents
Rosa and Yoseph Yedgar
With Love and Gratitude

Contents

Illustrations are to be found between pp. 240 and 241.

Preface

The beginnings of this book go back to more than a decade ago, when I first encountered the name of John Selden while working on the political thought of Edmund Burke. A passing reference in Burke's *Reflections on the Revolution in France* pointed to someone who, I soon found out, was considered by his contemporaries, as well as by several succeeding generations, a giant of seventeenth-century law, letters and politics. Except for his important activities as a politician and lawyer, Selden had also authored a large number of works, some of massive girth, which had a significant impact on contemporaries, among them several of the most significant figures of English intellectual history.

Nevertheless, it soon transpired that Selden – who in his own time was regarded as the most learned man in an unusually learned age, and of no less intellectual significance than contemporaries Grotius and Hobbes – had gradually receded from view, into the province of specialized academics only. As I found out, while books and articles devoted to either Grotius or Hobbes easily count up in their thousands (in the case of the latter, probably tens of thousands), the most generous tally of modern research directly addressing Selden would not add up to more than two digits. Even this modest total includes the products of a mini-revival of interest in Selden, spearheaded by J.G.A. Pocock, D.S. Berkowitz and R. Tuck, which has all but doubled the number of such titles in the last thirty years or so.

More curiously, even among this relatively meager number of scholarly works, the verdict on Selden's ideas and significance diverges sharply. Some regard him as a learned and appealing figure, but without any lasting effect on intellectual history; others assign him with a far more durable, albeit largely unnoticed, legacy in political thought and practice.

There are several reasons for this long neglect of Selden and his ideas. For one, on the most practical level, the access to many of his most important works, which were written in Latin, is seriously restricted by the lack of translations into English, let alone of critical editions or accessible formats. Work on translating some of these writings is currently underway, but it will take many more years until there is adequate access to all of Selden's important intellectual products. Also challenging is the character of Selden's work, combining an exceptionally large output with a vast array of sources from very different disciplines, so that those wishing to approach his work must grapple with unusual methodological hurdles. The fantastic reach of Selden's output has made it very difficult for even the best of scholars to encompass it, so that the first (and to date only) general study reviewing all of his works appeared only in 2009, the product of many years of work by G.J. Toomer. Finally, it seems that reigning intellectual fashions, favoring more outspoken and provocative thinkers, also had their role in making Selden's ideas less appealing to scholars for a long time, although this too may now be changing.

This picture is slowly being transformed, with new editions of several of Selden's important books now in the making, many more scholars and students interested in his works than ever before, and a renewed interest in the relevance of his ideas, even pertaining, for example, to the growing likelihood of possible maritime conflicts in the China Sea, of all places.

As anyone in this line of work knows, embarking on serious historical study means that for a sustained period you end up spending far more time with your subject than on any other thing. This may prove to be more or less fortuitous, depending on the contents of your research. Luckily for me, working on the life and ideas of John Selden, I found myself in the presence of a captivating figure, intellectually stimulating and rewardingly complex, as well as, one might add, of a generosity of spirit that is somewhat rare in his own time or since. I have thoroughly enjoyed the time spent in his company; something that I hope the following pages will convey.

Acknowledgments

Any work such as this one entails by its very nature many intellectual and personal debts, which it is my pleasant duty to acknowledge to the best of my ability. Throughout the long years it has taken to complete, this work has not received sustained institutional support, but it has gained much from the relatively small but resolute circle of those interested in the ideas of John Selden, so that "The fewer men, the greater share of honor." First, I owe thanks to the work of those whose writings on Selden cleared the intellectual path I have entered, without which my own journey could not have begun. Among these stand out the works of Pocock, Berkowitz, Tuck, Sommeville, Toomer, Caruso and Rosenblatt, most of whom I have known only through their works – but the latter two I had the opportunity to personally meet, and to benefit from their knowledge and ideas about Selden. Others with whom, to my great profit and pleasure, I have discussed more at length (especially during several conferences on Political Hebraism held in the last decade) some of the issues treated in this book include Paul Rahe, Gordon Schochet, Eric Schliesser, Mordechai Feingold and Peter Wyzner as well as Steven Grosby, who, on top of his intellectual input, has also been a constant source of encouragement and support. One of the few opportunities that researches on such topics have to interact with others of their small sect are conferences devoted to the subject, and I take this opportunity to thank the friends from the Institut Michel Villey at the University of Paris II Pantheon-Assas, and especially Professor Denis Baranger, who graciously invited me to their 2010 conference on Selden – who would have thought to find a whole score of Seldenians in Paris? In this context I must mention what is one of the most curious coincidences that I have ever witnessed: to the best of my knowledge, in the last centuries there have been only two academic conferences devoted wholly to John Selden – and both took place, independently of each other, in Paris and Oxford, during the very same week of June 2010! As it happens, I was one of those few who managed to attend the first one as well as the last day of the second one, therefore meeting virtually every living scholar working on John Selden.

As for the actual turning of my studies into this book, my thanks go to the openness and advice (and patience) of the good people at Cambridge University Press, and especially so to the two anonymous readers whose comments contributed significantly to the structure and contents of the final version, as well as to Lewis Bateman, without whose persistent trust in the subject and the author this book would never had made it to print.

My warmest thanks go to my good friends and co-founders at the Herzl Institute: Yael Hazony, who helped especially with access to ongoing translations of Selden's works; Meirav Jones, fellow revivalist of Political Hebraist studies; and, of course, Yoram Hazony, for more than two decades my closest intellectual fellow, partner in philosophical entrepreneurship and chief understander, with whom I learned much more than I can ever fully acknowledge.

Finally, to my family, who, as these things go, have a share in many things large and small which made it possible to bring this work to fruition. To Yoseph of blessed memory and Rosa, may she long live: my parents, who along the years gave me all their support, both material and spiritual. Last but not least, to my share in the world to come: my children Netanela and Yonatan; their love is ever my sustenance.

Note on the Text

TRANSLATIONS

While working on this book, I have consulted drafts of the exceptional, as yet unpublished, translations by Peter Wyzner of *Jure Naturali* and *Synedriis*, as well as other translations of sections from these and from other Selden texts. However, in several places I have altered the wording of these translations, where I wished to emphasize Selden's use of a particular terminology or preferred a more literal rendition of a passage. Therefore, all responsibility for the quality or accuracy of translated Selden texts quoted lies with me alone, unless otherwise noted.

DATES

In Selden's days, England used the Old Style reckoning in which the year started on 1 April, rather than the New Style now used, starting on 1 January. Thus, a date referred to at that time as 2 February 1614 would be today 2 February 1615. In order to avoid confusion, all dates given in the book are New Style, starting the year on 1 January – unless otherwise noted.

Abbreviations

ABBREVIATED SELDEN NOTATION

For abbreviated titles referenced repeatedly by book and chapter number, I have used a merged abbreviations style including title, book and chapter; thus, for example, *Jure Naturali* book 2 chapter 5 appears as JN b2c5; *Mare Clausum* book 1 chapter 8 appears as MC b1c8.

Selden's *Table-Talk* is organized according to subject headings rather than numbered chapters, with some headings having several numbered sections. I have therefore abbreviated it by title followed by subject heading and, where relevant, section number, thus: *Table-Talk*, subject heading "Money," section 2, appears as TT "Money" sec. 2.

OTHER ABBREVIATED TITLES

DNB – *Dictionary of National Biography*, Leslie Stephen et al., eds., 63 vols. (1885–1900)

ODNB – *Oxford Dictionary of National Biography*, C. Matthew & B. Harrison, eds., 60 vols. (Oxford University Press, 2004)
HOPO – *The History of Parliament: The House of Commons, 1604–1629*, A. Thrush and J.P. Ferris, eds. (Cambridge University Press, 2010) accessed through www.historyofparliamentonline.org.

I

Introduction: "Glory of the English Nation" – The Life, Works and Ideas of John Selden

I.I INTRODUCTORY

"The Great Light of the English Nation is now estinguished" – with these words a London weekly named *The Faithful Scout* announced, on 8 December 1654, the recent death of John Selden.[1] This was not some isolated comment, for the great scholar and parliamentarian who died on 30 November, two weeks short of his 70th birthday, had been praised in his lifetime with extraordinary tributes by many prominent men of that age. An oft-repeated phrase was "Glory of the English Nation," while some other acclaims about him were: "a very great man, in my judgment" (Hugo Grotius), "Law book of the Judges of England, the bravest man in all languages" (Ben Jonson), "noble genius" (Peter Paul Rubens), "the learnedest man on earth" (John Lightfoot), "the glory of the men of culture and their chief ornament" (Edward Pococke), "the chief of learned men reputed in this land" (John Milton) and, most amusingly, "our honored teacher and sage, rabbi Selden" (J.S. Rittangl).[2]

---

[1] *The Faithful Scout*, issue 204 (8 December 1654) a London weekly, appearing 1651–1655 and specializing in military news, "impartially communicating the most remarkable passages of the armies, in England, Scotland, and Ireland."

[2] "Glory of the English nation" (*Anglorum gloria genus Selden*) is often attributed to Grotius describing Selden, but G.J. Toomer thinks it an apocryphal exaggeration by Anthony Wood of other comments by Grotius. However, William Burton (1609–1657), in his *A commentary on Antoninus* (1657), remarks on p. 194 that Selden was regarded by Grotius as "that glory of our nation" (while repeatedly referring elsewhere to "the All-knowing Mr. Selden"), indicating that the attribution to Grotius was already current less than three years after Selden's death, apparently preceding Wood. For Grotius' "Seldeno, quod vir meo judicio maximus" see letter of February 1639, from Grotius to Francis Junius, quoted in J.G. Toomer, *John Selden: A Life in Scholarship* (Oxford University Press, 2009) p. 515 note 179; and Grotius also described Selden as "the best of men and a very brave citizen" ("virum optimum ac civem fortissimum") in a letter of September 1630, from Grotius to Peiresec, in Hugo Grotius, *Briefwisseling Van Hugo Grotius*, B.L. Meulenbroeck ed. (The Hague: Nijhoff, 1964) vol. iv p. 261. Jonson quoted in G.H. Herford,

Selden continued to be read and praised, in England and abroad, well into the eighteenth century. In late seventeenth-century England, prominent figures such as Sir Robert Atkyns and William Atwood seriously addressed Selden's ideas, while his name evidently carried a reputation eminent enough for the Secretary of the Admiralty and noted diarist Samuel Pepys to invent an acquaintance, and for the literary imposture *Johannis Seldeni Angli Liber de Nummis* to be published in 1675 under false attribution to him. A generation later, Selden was still honored as "The immortal glory of Britannia" by J.F. Budde, who in 1695 published an abridgment of his *Jure naturali*; and even as late as 1725, he was reputed by G.B. Vico, to be one of the "three princes" of natural law (with Grotius and Pufendorf). These latter words of praise came from erudite and baroque writers, who were increasingly untypical of their period, for Selden's ideas and style were going out of fashion, not being attuned to the simpler truths and clear-cut vogue of the new "age of reason." In the foremost monuments of Enlightenment culture, like Diderot's and d'Alembert's *Encyclopedie*, Selden, unlike Hobbes, Grotius or Leibnitz, is usually not judged as important enough to deserve a separate entry; he is treated in a sub-subject, and is valued negatively as having failed to strictly and rationally deduce either the natural law or natural morality. Selden was too elaborate and measured a thinker for the straightforward enthusiasms of the enlightenment, and his repute gradually receded into obscurity, persisting for the most part among devotees of English history and law. Thus, whereas Selden's contemporaries like Grotius and especially Hobbes enjoyed continuous interest in their ideas, with the books devoted to them since their death easily numbering in the hundreds and even thousands, all books devoted to Selden would have, until relatively recently, barely summed up to double digits. Nevertheless, after a long eclipse, interest in him and his works has been growing once more, with the number of books published on Selden in the last three decades or so easily outstripping everything published on him in the previous three centuries.[3]

Ben Jonson (1925) vol. i p. 149; Rubens in R. Saunders Magurn, *The Letters of Peter Paul Rubens* (Evanston: Northwestern University Press, 1955) p. 332; Lightfoot quoted in G. Parry, *The Trophies of time* (Oxford University Press, 1995); Pococke's comment occurs in the preface to his *Specimen Historiae Arabum* (1649) and appears in Arab letters; Milton from his *Areopagitica*, (1644); Rittangl, originally in Hebrew "*morenu harav rav Seldenus*" is in a 1641 letter to Selden from J.S. Rittangl, Extraordinary Professor of Oriental Languages at Konigsberg University, quoted in Toomer *Scholarship* pp. 626–629. There was much additional lavish contemporary praise, like the poet Robert Herrick declaring in 1648: "Live thou a Selden, that's a demi-god" in "To The Most Learned, Wise, And Arch-Antiquary, M. John Selden" in Robert Herrick, *Hesperides* (1648); Thomas Greaves in a poem he sent to Selden probably in 1650, called him "glory of the literate nation" (gentis literatae Gloria) and Edward Reynolds, Vice-Chancellor of Oxford University in a letter of October 1648, addressed Selden as "the Honor of this nation for learning." See *Joannis Seldeni Jurisconsulti Opera Omnia tam edita quam inedita* David Wilkins ed., 3 vols. (1725) vol. 1 tome 1 pp. xxxviii–xxxix.

[3] For Atkyns and Atwood see Chapter 3; Pepys implied in his diary (such as the entry for 29 November 1661) that he had been personally acquainted with Selden as a very young man, but

Regardless of how his repute fared in later ages, in his own time Selden's standing was such that, no sooner had he died than, from competing ideological quarters came efforts to enroll him among their supporters. The materialist philosopher and ferocious anti-clerical Thomas Hobbes claimed there had been a strong affinity between them, and reported a version of Selden's deathbed scene that had him (naturally, on Hobbes' suggestion) turning out a priest who had come to hear his confession; the account of Selden's final days by the devout Archbishop and prodigious scholar James Ussher, who, although ailing, insisted on giving the eulogy at Selden's funeral on 14 December 1654, was the very reverse of Hobbes' one, having the dying man converse about scriptural passages and redemption, with Ussher and Gerard Langbaine, another clergyman-scholar.[4] Such conflicting depictions of Selden and his views did

later owned up to having invented this; the literary imposture was the issue in 1675, under Selden's name, of a book titled *Liber de Nummis*, which had been actually authored by the Italian Alessandro Sardi and published in 1579. Budde (Buddeus), a German philosopher and theologian, praised Selden and published an abridgment of his great work – "Synopsis juris naturalis et gentium juxta disciplina ebraeorum" within Ph. Reinhard Vitriarius' *Institutiones Juris naturae et Gentium* (1695). For Vico see his *The New Science* (Ithaca, NY: Cornell, 1984), pp. xxvii, 94, 124, 165. For a modern assessment of Selden as "undoubtedly the most erudite Englishman of his day" see A.B. Ferguson, *Clio Unbound* (Durham, NC: Duke University Press, 1979), pp. 117–118. For the *Encyclopediestes*' attitude to Selden see S. Caruso, *La miglior legge del regno* (Milano: Giuffre, 2001) pp. 941–942.

[4] The accounts of the relationship between Selden and Hobbes are exceptionally divergent. Aubrey, Hobbes' friend, related that the two only first met after Hobbes sent Selden a copy of his newly published *Leviathan* in 1651, and then developed a personal as well as intellectual affinity, reflected in Selden's alleged deathbed refusal of confession on Hobbes' advice. See John Aubrey, *Brief Lives*, R. Barber ed. (Boydell, 1982) pp. 161, 283. Aikin contests this account, relating that Selden, approaching his end, discussed with Ussher and Langbaine his state of mind, relaying to them the passage most on his mind was from scripture – Epistle to Titus II 11–14, the import of which is redemption to all who live virtuously, with Ussher even reporting that Selden actually turned out Hobbes when his comments became irritating. J. Aikin, *The Lives of John Selden and Archbishop Usher* (1812) pp. 151–152. Cause for suspecting the Hobbesian account is the identity of the priest supposedly turned out by Selden on Hobbes' urging being none other than Richard Johnson, Master of the Temple Church – on Selden's death, soon afterward, it was the same allegedly spurned Johnson who brought Selden to burial in the church and addressed the mourners.

R. Tuck, *Hobbes* (Oxford University Press, 1989) pp. 31–32 credits the Hobbesian account, while to P. Christianson, "Selden, John" in *Oxford Dictionary of National Biography* (Oxford University Press, 2004) – henceforth Christianson "Selden" ODNB – the account is suspect. Christianson suggests the two were probably at least superficially acquainted since the 1620s when both attended meetings of the Virginia Company governing body, and remarks that after the presentation of the *Leviathan* "Hobbes struck up a somewhat quarrelsome friendship" with Selden. Perhaps we should not read too much into Selden's eminent good nature and toleration of those with ideas different from him. The fact that many who knew Selden well, such as Hale, Ussher, Langbaine and Clarendon, were prominent anti-Hobbesians and believed Selden's views close to theirs, points at the least to his not being an obvious Hobbesian. Moreover, at least two additional, apparently reliable, reports indicate a more strained relationship. The first is from Hale, who is recorded as asserting that Selden was a decided adversary of Hobbes' opinions, and

not emerge only after his death, for even while alive he was often sought after and courted by opposing political factions. In 1642, King Charles I seriously considered Selden for the post of Lord Keeper of the Great Seal, while about a decade later it was Oliver Cromwell who reportedly wanted Selden to draft a new constitution for England. It says a lot about Selden, as well as his ideas, that the two defining figures of the political conflict of that age both regarded him as someone whose adherence to their government could legitimize their version of the English constitutional tradition.

The high esteem Selden enjoyed from such opposing personalities and factions should not lead one to conclude that he was timid or duplicitous in airing his ideas. For, while he lived in dangerous times, and certainly did advise and practice prudence where possible, his public writing and speaking over decades meant that his main ideas were quite well known. Moreover, he did not shirk from presenting these ideas, often before overwhelmingly dissenting audiences, entering into many an ideological and political controversy. His outspokenness led repeatedly to interrogation and imprisonment under the monarchy, and to purge and political suspicion under the interregnum.

Thus, the wide respect and esteem Selden enjoyed among opposing factions and ideologies were no result of dissimulation and equivocation. Rather, there was a combination between, on the one hand, his ideas, that were by their nature adaptable to different (though certainly not all) interpretations of mainstream English constitutional terminology and institutions, and, on the other hand, his character, which was by all accounts an uncommonly pleasant and generous one. Selden's conviviality and personal generosity are well attested, as are his willingness to cooperate politically with bitter former adversaries, his lack of interest in exacting personal revenge from those who had wronged him, and his even more evident aversion to the taking of lives as the price for political defeat. Hence, without hiding his own ideas, he had the ability to remain on good terms, and even collaborate, with those with whose opinions he disagreed.[5]

The diverging assessments of Selden in his own time have persisted in later scholarship, with widely contrasting appraisals of his political ideas and intellectual influence. In current scholarship some describe Selden as a natural lawyer and others as a historicist conservative; some have him a confused Grotian, others an anti-Grotian; some view him as a bridge towards Hobbes,

---

as having witnessed their clash of opinions as so fierce as to drive the latter from the room; see J.W. Warter, *Appendiciae et Pertinentiae; Or parochial fragments relating to the parish of West Tarring...* (1853) p. 85; the second is an anecdote about Selden siding with those who derided Hobbes' claim to be able to square the circle: "Mr. Joyner says that, Mr. *Hobbs* us'd to say that Mr. *Selden* understood nothing of mathematicks, which Mr. *Selden* being inform'd off, he reply'd that if Mr. Hobbs understood no more mathematicks than he did Law, he understood nothing at all of them." See M. Feingold, "John Selden and the nature of seventeenth-century science" in M. Feingold (ed.) *In the presence of the past* (1991) pp. 61–62.

[5] D.R. Woolf, *The Idea of History in Early Stuart England* (Toronto University Press, 1990) p. 207.

others as totally irrelevant to Hobbes' ideas; some regard him as a significant figure of modern constitutionalism, others as only of peripheral importance.[6]

This book aims to put some of these differences to rest by presenting an extensive account of Selden's political ideas and suggesting their significance for both his own time and subsequent political ideas and practices. It will propose that Selden's main political preoccupation was the safeguarding and strengthening of the English tradition of government, from serious intellectual (and later actual) threats from both within and without. In this concern, he was hardly alone in his time or later, although he certainly had an important role in a number of junctures decisive for the development of the English constitution. However, the singular feature of his work – what sets him apart from so many others – was that in his attempt to reinforce the English political tradition he directed his exceptional scholarship to call upon ideas and traditions that were not only outside it, but indeed seemed completely foreign to it. Moreover, the staggering scale of Selden's scholarly output, in both quantity and quality, meant that the scope and depth of these efforts was unrivalled. This character of his work had the twin effects of, on the one hand, putting much of his output outside of the reach of even most educated readerships, and on the other hand of supplying to those who could use them a wide range of resources in support of a vision of constitutionalism which had a major role (often by indirect and surprising avenues) in the development of the political thought and practice of English-speaking countries. The influence of Selden's ideas on the constitutional views of such figures as Clarendon, Hale and Edmund Burke makes him a founding figure of what we may term the traditionalist approach to constitutionalism – of continuity through change – that to this day exerts a strong influence on the political thought of the UK, the US and other countries.[7]

In particular, this book will attempt to show that Selden's efforts to muster a vast array of texts and ideas from outside the English tradition, especially from those of the Jewish legal tradition, supplied for the first time a wider, comparative and comprehensive theoretical framework for the justification of English (and indeed any) constitutional and legal particularism – that, up to that point, had been made only on internal, sometimes literally insular, arguments. On top of this effort, which was what we would today call theoretical and

---

[6] See Caruso's excellent overview of contrasting views of Selden in current scholarship, in Caruso *Miglior* pp. 15–16.

[7] Clarendon and Hale will be discussed later in this volume. As for Burke, J.G.A. Pocock and I. Hampsher-Monk are among those who indicate that Selden's ideas had a significant influence on Burke, although they do not develop the point. Hampsher-Monk claims Burke supports a "Seldenian natural rights theory" which regards natural rights as being given up on entering society "and thereafter irrelevant" – completely different from theories like those of the Levellers or Locke, in which men even within civil society "retain some natural rights." See I. Hampsher-Monk, "John Thelwall and the eighteenth-century radical response to political economy" in *Historical Journal* 34/1 (March 1991) pp. 9–10; and I. Hampsher-Monk, *A History of Modern Political Thought* (Oxford: Blackwell, 1992) pp. 46, 270 note 28, 272.

comparative, Selden also attempted another no less ambitious objective: to show that the Jewish sources he was studying were an integral part of western and English legal and moral thought; as much as, and perhaps more than, the Greco-Roman and even many Christian ones.

Selden devoted his efforts especially to the justification of customary laws in general and the English Common Law in particular, as well as to issues of church and state, and of political and judicial assemblies, which he regarded as interconnected. Consequently, for all the stupendous variety of sources and subjects he treated, a number of main themes prominently recur in his works: the keeping of contracts as a basis for society and politics, the limits of self-referring reason, the role of national identity and the process of continuity through change.

1.2 SELDEN'S WORLD

One of the unusual features of John Selden's life was that – as the great polymath of his age, unsurpassed in his erudition in England and perhaps in Europe, who had mastered some two dozen languages ancient and modern – as far as is known he never left England, and in fact spent almost all of his life within a day's ride from the city of London. This contrast between the relatively confined geographical area within which his life transpired, and the extraordinary reach of his studies and activities, was not lost on contemporaries like Ben Jonson, who as early as 1614, in a commendatory epistle prefixed to the first edition of the *Titles of Honor*, addressed his friend as: "You that have been ever at home, yet have all countries seen."

Thus, we can easily trace almost all of Selden's adult life within a relatively small area of today's central London, from the Palace of Westminster in the west to the Tower of London in the east, spanning only some two and a half miles. Let us then, before proceeding to relate of his life and times, briefly draw within this area the places of importance to him, so that, as events and places unfold, we will be able to orientate ourselves within this world.

Entering this perimeter, traveling from west to east, we start with Westminster Abbey where, in its Jerusalem Chamber and King Henry VII's chapel, during the 1640s, convened the Westminster Assembly of Divines, of which Selden was a member; while nearby, facing the great west door of the Abbey, there then stood a complex of buildings consisting of the Abbey's ancient Gatehouse, where a jail operated, within which Selden would be imprisoned in 1630–1631 as a result of his parliamentary activities.[8]

---

[8] There used to be gates around the Westminster Abbey precinct, along the line traced by today's Great College Street. A south entrance remains today on Tufton Street, while long gone are the main gate to the north and a postern gate to the east (where today stands a statue of King George V). On the west side, near today's memorial to the Crimean War, stood the Gatehouse, part of which was used as a prison, where Selden was for a time jailed. Incidentally, another part of the

Adjacent to these, where today's Houses of Parliament stand, was the "palace" of Westminster, in the seventeenth century an eclectic conglomerate of buildings housing, among other things, a number of law courts (where Selden only rarely appeared, for his practice focused on consulting and drawing contracts), and the two Houses of Parliament, where Selden sat as a MP in the 1620s and 1640s. Stuck between these, occupying part of the site of today's House of Lords, stood a large private residence with a garden going down to the river, home to Selden's patron and friend, the scholar Sir Robert Cotton, who owned what was probably the best library in England of those days, Selden's access to which had a decisive impact on his scholarship.[9]

Proceeding eastwards, we first encounter the royal palace of Whitehall, where Selden had an important audience with King James I following the controversy surrounding the publication of the *Historie of Tithes*; then, continuing through the Strand, we would pass by the sites where the town houses of many great nobles of that time stood (some of them Selden's customers, supporters and political allies), like Bedford House, Somerset House, Arundel House and so on. Continuing eastwards, to where the Strand meets Fleet Street, we would arrive at the heart of legal London, composed of communities where lawyers trained, lived and practiced – not only the four Inns of Court, which survive to this day with the traditional authority to create barristers, but also many others, now long gone, which had more restricted functions as places of residence or training only. At the corner of Fleet Street and Fetter Lane there stood one such establishment, Clifford's Inn, where Selden first resided in 1603 on coming to study law in London, and then turning southward we enter the precinct of the Inner Temple, where Selden received his legal education, practiced as a lawyer and was eventually raised, in 1632, to the dignity of Master of the Bench – member of the governing body of the Inn. Within these precincts, just on the banks of the Thames, overlooking the still extant and beautiful gardens of the Inner Temple, among a complex of chambers and residences called "Paper" buildings, we would find one erected by Selden's friend, Edward Heyward, and on its top floor an apartment and chamber to which Selden moved sometime after 1610, and resided for most of his life.[10] Adjacent to the east side of the Paper

---

Gatehouse, the porter's lodge, served as Sir Robert Filmer's town house at least until early 1630; while by 1628, Ben Jonson too lived nearby in a house located over the passage leading from the old palace to the churchyard.

[9] The library in Cotton's house was a large but narrow room, some 26 feet long and only 6 feet wide, with the books situated in rows at the two sides of a tight middle passage, each row headed by a brass bust of a Roman emperor by which the row was called and books were located. The room contained some additional objects like old swords, Dr. Dee's instruments, and various curious artifacts.

[10] By about 1610, Heyward had erected within the Inner Temple precinct a building consisting of sixteen chambers, where on the top story he and Selden shared rooms until about 1620, when Heyward left and Selden took over the whole suite. The structure known as Heyward's Building overlooking the Temple Gardens is no more, but its location is to this day occupied by the "Paper Buildings" housing lawyers' chambers.

buildings, just outside the Inner Temple grounds, there stood the Carmelite friary house and garden, known as Whitefriars, a former monastery, and in Selden's days the London residence of the Earl and Countess of Kent, the latter of whom Selden was so close to that, after the Earl's death in 1639, he moved in with her and they possibly even married, so that on her death in 1651 he inherited her personal property, including the lease on the Carmelite house.[11] One more adjacent site meriting mention is the ancient Temple Church, standing to this day between the grounds of the Inner and Middle Temple, serving as the place of worship for the members of the two inns and the location where Selden himself was eventually buried – his simple black tombstone can still be observed there near the southern gate, through a glass slab on the floor. Moving eastwards again we would pass by St. Paul's Cathedral and enter a far less reputable area, the Cheapside, where streets named Milk Street, Bread Street, Fish Street and so on testify to its commercial and raucous character. Among its lanes were situated taverns such as the Mermaid and the Three Cranes, where poets, playwrights and actors fraternized in evenings of food and drink, and Selden, especially in his younger days, spent many a convivial evening in the company of friends such as the poets Ben Jonson, Michael Drayton and John Donne. Leaving Cheapside eastwards again we would arrive at the Tower of London, the city's ancient eastern limit, and another one of the jails where Selden was imprisoned for some months in 1629–1630. Finally, backtracking briefly to London Bridge and crossing the Thames, then continuing southwards for about half a mile, we would arrive at the Marshalsea Prison, yet another place where Selden was imprisoned, in 1631–1632.

Aside from this London world, one can point to only a handful of other places of any importance in Selden's life – all of them in southern England: the hamlet of Salvington (today a neighborhood within the town of Worthing) where he was born and lived as a youth, and the nearby city of Chichester, where he attended grammar school, both in Sussex; the universities, of Oxford where he studied at Hart Hall (now Hertford College) between 1598 and 1602, and Cambridge, where he sometimes visited in his scholarly pursuits; and finally Wrest Park in Bedfordshire, some fifty miles north of London, the country seat of the earls of Kent, where he stayed for extended periods between 1624 and 1639.[12]

---

[11] Whitefriars was a precinct or "liberty" on the site of the former house of the "Fratres beatae Mariae de monte Carmeli," the Carmelite aka White Friars – from their white habits. Founded in 1241, it grew to eventually cover the whole area from the Thames northwards almost to Fleet Street, bounded on the east by Whitefriars Street and on the west by Temple Lane. At the dissolution of the monasteries, King Henry VIII granted the site to private individuals and within a short period the monastic buildings had been for the most part replaced by small courts and alleys. The house of the Countess of Kent and later of Selden occupied the site of the friary's main house and garden, most adjacent to the Inner Temple precinct.

[12] To the above, two more venues might perhaps be added: Theobald's, the country residence of King James I, just west of London, to where Selden was summoned and twice appeared before the king, following the controversy surrounding the publication of the *Historie of Tithes*; and

1.3 BEGINNINGS: 1584–1601

John Selden was born on 16 December 1584 at Lacies Farm, Salvington, a hamlet in the parish of West Tarring, near the coastal town of Worthing, Sussex, not far from Brighton. Selden's father, also John, was a local yeoman (small independent farmer) and "minstrell," who succeeded in marrying above his class, to Margaret Baker, only daughter and heir of Thomas Baker from nearby Rustington, from a knightly family, who brought with her a good estate.

On his father's side, Selden came from an undistinguished family. The parish records of fifteenth- and sixteenth-century southern Sussex villages (especially between Chichester and Brighton) like Binsted, Rustington, Angmering, Patching, Goring, Tarring, Wiston and Upper Beeding, are full of Selkedens, Selkdens, Seldons and Seldens, minor farmers and artisans all, none, it appears, of any particular prominence.[13] They are recorded as being christened, married and buried, or mentioned for such minor occurrences as a small contribution to the church or some slight moral transgression. As for Selden's more immediate family, we know from his own testimony that his grandfather, one Thomas Selden, probably a farmer of quite modest means, was born in 1541 and lived to the age of 70 – long enough to see his son become a prosperous farmer with considerable landed property, as well as to witness his grandson's rise by 1611 from modest farm beginnings to Oxford, the Inns of Court and the ranks of published scholars.[14]

On his mother's side, Selden's family roots were altogether more prominent, and may have had a role in assisting his rise. His grandfather, Thomas Baker, was reputedly related to the family of knightly landowners from eastern Sussex and western Kent, whose most prestigious member had been Sir John Baker

Great Tew, in Oxfordshire, residence of Lucius Cary, Second Viscount Falkland, where Selden is reputed to have sometimes attended the literary circle gathered there, although exact details are scarce.

[13] There have been various proposals for the origin of the surname, most often connecting it to some Saxon or Norse word. A more prosaic provenance would be an alteration of the name Eklesdon (Eccleston), the medieval Sussex hamlet near Angmering, where as early as the mid-fourteenth century a number of Selkedens and Selkedons are recorded as taxpayers (and at the center of the area where subsequent records of Seldens are most concentrated). Incidentally, in the sixteenth century, "selden" was a common variant spelling for the word "seldom."

[14] On Selden's father rise to prosperity, from owning an estimated 8 acres in 1581, to some 81 acres in 1609, See D.S. Berkowitz, *John Selden's Formative years* (Washington: Folger Press, 1988) pp. 13–14. Aubrey describes Selden's father as "a yeomanly man, of about forty pounds a year" while Warter *Appendiciae* pp. 79–80, claims that in a survey of 6 James I (1609) the annual value the land owned by Selden's father was assessed at 23 pounds and 8s. About the middle of these two estimates seems the correct amount, as in the early seventeenth century an acre yielded an average annual income of something like 8 shillings (there were 20 shillings in a pound), so that by the later years of John Selden senior, his annual income would amount to around 32 pounds a year – a steep increase from the about 3 pounds he was assessed as earning in 1581. In any event he comfortably exceeded the 40 shilling minimum annual income necessary for the parliamentary franchise, enabling one to vote in elections for county seats.

(d. 1588) of Sissinghurst, Kent, Speaker of the Commons and Chancellor of the Exchequer in the mid-sixteenth century. The Bakers were also connected to the powerful Sackville family, owners of extensive landed properties in Kent and Sussex (including at Wiston, Buckhurst, Lewes and East Grinstead), and from 1604 earls of Dorset, who might have had a hand in assisting Selden's early educational and professional path. To the best of my knowledge, Selden's possible connection with the Sackvilles has not as yet been commented on, and although its full extent may never be definitely established, it is worthwhile to point out a number of certain facts, which suggest something more than a coincidence. We know for a fact that the Sackvilles and Bakers were related: Edward Sackville (c. 1590–1652), Fourth Earl and his brother Richard (1589–1624), Third Earl, were the sons of Robert Sackville (1561–1609), Second Earl of Dorset, whose parents were Thomas Sackville (1536–1608), First Earl of Dorset, and his wife Cecily Baker, daughter of the abovementioned Sir John Baker – to whom Selden's maternal grandfather, Thomas Baker (d. 1598), was reputedly related. Although we are unsure about Selden's exact family relationship to the more prominent Bakers, Selden was evidently aware and proud of this Baker heritage, since he mentions it in a short autobiographical fragment he penned (intended as his funeral inscription), and later considered a coat of arms that was a version of the one displayed by the Sissinghurst Bakers.[15] Moreover, as Robert Sackville – who became Second Earl in 1608 – had been educated at exactly the same institutions which Selden eventually attended, Hart Hall, Oxford, and then the Inner Temple (to which Sir John and other Bakers were also connected), it seems possible that some degree of patronage from the Bakers and Sackvilles played a role in enrolment and funding at these institutions. The Sackvilles certainly had a lot of influence and patronage in Sussex, with Robert Sackville, for example, a Justice of the Peace and MP for Sussex in successive parliaments until 1607, providing in his will for establishing an almshouse (which still exists as Sackville College) at East

[15] Toomer correctly notes that we have no positive proof of the connection between Selden's Bakers and the Sissinghurst Bakers. However, in light of Selden's typical fastidiousness as to the veracity of his claims, his assertion of this connection in his autobiographical sketch as well as his intended adoption as his coat of arms of a version of the Baker's one, indicates that he certainly believed the connection to be true enough. See Toomer *Scholarship* p. 1 note 4, and 828–829; Berkowitz *Formative* pp. 13–14. Berkowitz finds the coat of arms displayed in: E. Cartwright, *The Parochial topography of the rape of Bramber in the western division of the county of Sussex* (1830) p. 266. It is possible that Selden's maternal grandfather, Thomas Baker, could have been the son of one of Sir John's three brothers (Thomas, Robert and James), thus making John Selden a third-degree cousin of the Third and Fourth Earls of Dorset. But even if the family connection was farther removed, the period offers many examples of rather tenuous and distant familial relations forming the basis for connections of fidelity and patronage. For example, the considerable assistance given by the future Fourth Earl of Dorset, Edward Sackville, while a member of the House of Commons in the 1621 Parliament, to his second-degree cousin, Sir Sackville Crowe, or the bringing about of the election of his third-degree cousin, John Sackville, and later his son Edward, as representatives to Parliament from East Grinstead.

Grinstead. Finally, we also know that at some point in his lifetime, Selden became so close a friend of Edward Sackville, the Fourth Earl, as to describe him in his *Vindiciae* of 1653 (a short time after Sackville had died) as "the earl, ever my great friend" (comes mihi semper amicissimus). Since the financial means necessary to fund Selden's fees and upkeep along the years at Chichester, Oxford and London, until he became financially independent, were not inconsiderable, and it is not known how much of it could have come from his parents, various conjectures have been offered as to the identity of the benefactors who sponsored his education. The evidence for familial bonds, institutional links and close personal acquaintances, points to a Baker–Sackville connection as a plausible candidate for this role.[16]

Young John apparently showed early potential to rise above the life of a farmer, and it is reported that at age 10 he inscribed the door-lintel of his parents' house with the Latin inscription "Honest friend, welcome, walk in and repose; Thief, get thee hence, to thee I'll not unclose" (Gratus, honeste, mihi, non claudar initio sede que bis, Fur, abeas; non sum facta solute tibi). At any event, he was sent as a boy to be educated at the Prebendal grammar school at Chichester Cathedral, and then in 1598 went on to Oxford's Hart Hall (now Hertford College), at first informally and then from 1600 as officially enrolled.[17]

We know very little more of certainty about Selden's early life or his relationship with his family. His parents apparently both died between 1610 and 1616; he had two brothers (George and Henry) who died in infancy and a sister, Mary, who grew to maturity and married John Bernard, a farmer and musician of Goring-by-Sea not far from Salvington (and similarly, long since engulfed by Worthing). The couple had six children who grew up to adulthood, and Selden was aware of these six nephews and nieces, to the extent that he bequeathed to each in his will 100 pounds: a nice sum, but unexceptional considering his vast wealth.[18]

---

[16] Two additional possible Baker connections are epigrams by a William Baker, appended to the 1610 *Jani Anglorum*, and a 1635 poem by (perhaps the same) William Baker on the freezing of the Thames, appearing in Selden's correspondence. The nature of Selden's connection with these is unknown to me. David "Brother Augustine" Baker, a Benedictine monk and scholar who corresponded with Selden, was of Scottish origins and not connected to the Kent Bakers.

[17] See G.W. Johnson, *Memoirs of John Selden, and notices of the political contest during his time* (1835) p. 34, where Johnson claims to have personally inspected and transcribed the inscription on the lintel in August 1834, and gives it as actually "Gratus honeste mih no clavdar inito sedelo / Fvr abeas: no sv facta solute tibi" (one wonders if this was the inspiration for the inscription fixed by J. R.R. Tolkien in his *The Lord of the Rings* on the Westgate of Moria: "Speak friend and enter"). At the Prebendal, Selden could have been acquainted with William Juxon, two years his senior, and future Archbishop of Canterbury. The Master at Chichester School, Hugh Barker (d. 1632), who later became a civil lawyer, from 1607 practicing at Doctors Common and was Dean of the Court of Arches, must also have had a role in Selden's entering Oxford, for he was tutored there by Barker's brother Anthony as well as by John Young, both Fellows at New College.

[18] Warter *Appendiciae* pp. 79–80, claims Selden's mother Margaret died in 1610, and Selden's father John died in 1616. See also Berkowitz *Formative* pp. 13–14. A sum of 100 pounds in 1654

There are two episodes, of uncertain reliability, which are nevertheless worth reporting, as they may throw some light not only on this early period of Selden's life, but also on some aspects of his subsequent outlook. The first is an anecdote reported secondhand by John Aubrey, from Sir Robert Cotton's wife, according to which as she was one Christmas dining at Edward Alford's house in Sussex, with the young student John Selden as one of those at the lower end of the table, someone asked who the young man was, and the reply came "his son that is playing on the violin in the hall."[19] If true, this episode situates the early Selden as a young man whose talents are raising him to partake in the table of rich and influential patrons, as well as points to an early connection with the Cotton family that would be significant to his later life. However, the episode also draws attention to the evident fragility of Selden's social status, as one who was earning his place at the table of the gentry only through his talents, and at little distance in place and standing from where his father supplied the entertainment.

The second episode is reported by Selden himself, but its biographical import is unclear. The *Table-Talk* reports Selden remarking (in the section on Money): "Money makes a Man laugh. A blind Fidler playing to a Company, and playing but Scurvily, the Company laught at him; his Boy that led him, perceiving it, cry'd, Father let us be gone, they do nothing but laugh at you. Hold thy Peace, Boy, said the Fidler, we shall have their money presently, and then we will laugh at them."[20] It is tempting to add this episode to the previous one, and picture young Selden as witness to his father's being derided by his audience. Although many of the episodes reported in the *Table-Talk* are biographical, we have no way of knowing if this one conveys something Selden himself experienced (or indeed if his father ever became blind). Nevertheless, even if the event related is not strictly speaking biographical, and Selden only relays of some other blind fiddler and his boy being mocked by their audience, it certainly has the ring of

would be worth more than 15,000 pounds in today's terms. The six children of Selden's sister were: John Bernard of Goring, Thomas Bernard of Goring, Mary Bernard who married Robert Douglas of Goring, Joan Bernard who married Edward Mansfield of Ham (between Angmering and Rustington), Susan Bernard who married John Bode of Wiston (in mid-Sussex), and Sarah Bernard who married James Chapman of Ifield (in northern Sussex).

[19] Aubrey, who reports the story, gives it as taking place at the house of "Sir Thomas" Alford but no person of substance by such name is known to have existed in Sussex at the time, so it seems a mistake for Edward Alford (1565–1631), owner of Offington House near Worthing, not far from the Selden farm. He was a prominent local leader in Sussex and seems to have been an ally of the Earls of Dorset and Arundel who assisted his retaining of the title of deputy lieutenant for Sussex in the mid-1620s. He had a distinguished parliamentary career, some of which coincided in time, as well as political positions, with Selden's. Alford was a prominent defender of the privileges of the Commons throughout the 1620s, and in 1628 among the first to propose (on 6 May) that instead of merely confirming Magna Carta, Parliament proceed by a Petition of Right. See R. Zaller, "Edward Alford" in ODNB (version retrieved 12 March 2013); Toomer *Scholarship* p. 3; Aubrey *Lives* p. 282.

[20] TT "Money," and for context see also M.P. Parker, "'To my friend G.N. from Wrest': Carew's secular Masque" in C.J. Summers and T.L. Pebworth (eds.) *Classic and Cavalier* (Pittsburg University Press, 1982) pp. 178–180.

touching a nerve. The story seems to reflect, at some level, Selden's own experience, as a fiddler's son elevated by his talents to a place among the powerful, but always wary of their fickle natures and suspicious of their precarious favors. His career will show him, despite easily congregating with the rich and mighty, always maintaining a level of detachment, repeatedly declining honors offered and keeping himself very much his own man, steadily building up his assets until he became very wealthy indeed, but always valuing above all his independence.

1.4   LAWYER AND SCHOLAR: 1602–1619

In 1602, Selden left Oxford without formally graduating (quite common at the time, among those not embarking on an academic or clerical career), and went on to London to acquire a legal education in the Common Law, a system very much unconnected to the learning in the universities. The Common Law was taught and practiced by a number of self-governing associations, congregating around inns and self-contained precincts in a small area of London, sometimes referred to as England's Third University, where lawyers trained and lived.[21] Some of the inns were places of residence or training only; others were designated as Inns of Chancery (each attached to an Inn of Court), where the rudiments of the legal profession were acquired; and finally there were the four Inns of Court, the only ones with the authority to create barristers, who are the lawyers permitted to appear before all Common Law courts, and to give specialist legal advice (unlike attorneys and solicitors, who are permitted to solicit customers and to appear only in the lower courts). Selden initially entered Clifford's Inn (an Inn of Chancery), and in May 1604 was admitted into the Inn of Court to which the former was attached, the Inner Temple.[22]

The Inns of Court of Selden's days were self-governing associations, with three grades of membership: students, also called Fellows, and after a certain

---

[21] See George Buc, "Third Universitie of England" in John Stow, *Annals* (1615). Selden himself wrote that "the study of common law hath no place in our Universities of Oxford and Cambridge because another university (the Inns of Court) is appointed for it," see cols. 1891–1892 of "Notes" on Sir John Fortescue's *De laudibus legum Angliæ* and Sir Ralph de Hengham's *Summæ magna et parva* (1616) in *Opera Omnia* vol. 3 tome 2 cols. 1883–1906.

[22] The Inns of Chancery and the Inns of Court apparently developed during the thirteenth century, when two events destroyed the previous system of legal education, that had been carried out in the city of London, primarily by the clergy: First a decree by Henry III, that no institutions of legal education could reside within the City of London itself, and second a papal bull that prohibited clergy from teaching law to laymen. As a result, lawyers settled in what was then an area immediately outside the City precincts, and close to Westminster Hall (where Magna Carta had provided for a permanent court). They inhabited "hostels" or "inns," which were named after their landlords or locality. By Selden's time the practice of training barristers in the Inns of Chancery was dying out, and by 1642 it had ceased completely, with those Inns becoming only associations and offices for lawyers, and gradually disappearing. See J. Megarry, *Inns Ancient and Modern* (Selden Society, 1972) pp. 13–17, 30–35.

period also referred to as Inner Barristers; who after being called to the bar on
Call Night, became Utter (or Outer) Barristers, those commonly referred to as
barristers; the most prominent among whom, usually after having served some
time as Reader (lecturer), might become Masters of the Bench or benchers. After
a century of steep rise in numbers, from a total of about 50 active barristers in
1520s England, by James I's time, each Inn of Court was composed of about
180 students, 60 utter barristers, and 20 benchers (totaling altogether about
700 students, 250 barristers and 80 benchers in the Inns of Court). The
benchers, appointed for life, constituted the supreme and self-electing
governing body of each Inn, while the practical government of the Inns was
carried out by a regularly called council – at the Inner Temple termed
"Parliament"– composed of the present benchers and headed by an annually
elected treasurer from among them.[23]

The method of Common Law education at the time was primarily oral, and
consisted mainly of Readings and Disputations. Readings were series of lectures
devised as expositions of the statutes, presented at certain times by prominent
barristers selected by the inn for the task; organized in a chronological sequence
starting with Magna Carta, students were exposed to all important statutes
during their years of study at the inn – with a sequence completed, it started
anew. Disputations, or Moots, were trial-like debates in which participants
tested their skills to argue points of law.[24]

In addition to these formal elements, law students could augment their
education by viewing actual trials in the courts, by reading legal literature and
by studying in groups. In effect, they were for the most part left to their own
devices, as to the quantity and quality of their studies, so that their schooling
could be quite diffuse and protracted. The average period of study seems to have
been about seven or eight years, but in many cases students spent shorter or
longer periods at the inns, never going on to formally complete their studies and
become barristers, especially when (such as near contemporaries young Robert
Filmer or Henry Grey, future Earl of Kent), they were heirs to an estate, coming

---

[23] Selden was admitted as a student in 1604, called to the bar in 1612, and appointed to the bench in
  1632 – by the latter appointment he also became a formal member of the Inner Temple
  "Parliament," but he seems to be recorded as actually participating only in the "Parliament"
  session held on 6 February 1645. See Megarry *Inns* pp. 13–17, 30–34.
     Most estimates put the numbers of barristers by the 1620s as more than 250, perhaps as high
  as 500; in any case, a steep rise from about 50 a century earlier. But it seems that all these new
  barristers did not lack employment, since the number of suits also rose steeply, for example,
  almost quintupling the number of suits in King's Bench, between 1563 and 1580. Indeed, there
  were those who regarded the expansion in the reach of the law and the lawyers as an important
  contribution to bringing about the Civil War. See A. Cromartie, *The constitutionalist revolution:
  An essay on the history of England 1450–1642* (Cambridge University Press, 2006) pp. 178–179.
[24] Megarry *Inns* pp. 19–20, 30–35; G. Burgess, *Absolute Monarchy and the Stuart Constitution*
  (New Haven: Yale University Press, 1996) pp. 62–63, and J.H. Baker, *The third University of
  England – the Inns of Court and the Common Law Tradition* (Selden Society, 1990) pp. 6–9.

to the inns to acquire some legal knowledge and cultural polish, but with no intention of ever practicing law.[25]

These circumstances meant that Selden had much time to devote to activities other than formal studies. He was eventually 'called to the bar' – licensed to argue in all law courts as barrister – in June 1612, and started to practice law. Seldom appearing in court, and sometimes giving chamber counsel, he was apparently particularly good at conveyancing – the transferring of legal property from one to another, by the often arcane rules and procedures of English law. In the event, this turned out to be a quite lucrative career choice.[26]

However, Selden evidently used up much of his time as a novice to gain an extraordinarily wide erudition, in matters legal and not, which enabled him while still formally a student, to pen a number significant works of scholarship. As early as 1605 (aged barely 21 years), Selden already appeared, along with Cotton and Camden, on the guest list of the party held to celebrate Ben Jonson's release from imprisonment, for his part in writing the play *Eastward Hoe!* (a satire including anti-Scottish remarks, that offended King James). Obviously, by this time the young student had already been recognized to be of such parts as to be invited to sit at one table with some of the greatest men of letters in the land. Some minor texts of his appeared in print by 1607, but his emergence as a significant writer came in 1610, when he published two works: *Jani Anglorum Facies Altera* (The Twofold Face of the English Janus), discussing laws of pre- and post-Norman Britain, as well as *The Duello, or Single Combat*, a tract on the trial by duel. The publication of these works marked Selden as a young talent on the rise, and the mixture they displayed, of legal erudition with an irrepressible interest in other, sometimes far-ranging learning, became a characteristic trait of his work.[27]

While at the Inner Temple, Selden naturally made acquaintance with a number of students who were to go on to distinguished legal careers, some of which were to intertwine with his. Most prominent among these were: Henry Rolle, later Lord Chief Justice of the King's Bench; Sir Edward Littleton

---

[25] A German lawyer who visited the Inns of Court in 1598 noted that in many cases the students were applying themselves to subjects such as philosophy, theology and medicine, far more than to the law. Toomer *Scholarship* p. 9, and W.R. Prest, *The Rise of the Barristers: A social history of the English Bar 1590–1640* (Oxford University Press, 1986) pp. 201–202.

[26] Aikin *Lives* pp. 3–4; TT "Law" sec. 3 mentions one case where Selden did appear in court, as counsel for an English merchant who sued the king of Spain for costs – which Selden won by having the Spanish king formally declared by the court an outlaw, prompting the Spanish Ambassador Gondomar to pay the sum owed (thus the case occurred between 1613 and 1622, when Gondomar resided in London).

   Most barristers also pleaded at least once or twice in their career before the Star Chamber court (between 1603 and 1625 more than 1200 lawyers did so). Selden apparently did so twice, but neither appearance was remarkable. See T.G. Barnes, *Shaping the Common Law: From Glanvill to Hale, 1188–1688* (Stanford University Press, 2008) p. 253.

[27] C. McEachern, *The poetics of English nationhood, 1590–1612* (Cambridge University Press, 2007) pp. 174; Toomer *Scholarship* pp. 817–820.

(descendant of the judge and legal scholar, Thomas de Littleton of *Tenures* fame), afterward Lord Keeper of the Great Seal; Sir Edward Herbert, afterward Attorney General; and Sir Thomas Gardiner, afterward Recorder of London.[28] However, the most significant bond forged with a fellow student was that with Edward Heyward, as far as we know the closest friend Selden ever had. A young gentleman of means, by 1610 Heyward had erected within the Inner Temple precinct adjoining the garden a four-story building, with the top one having a little open gallery to walk in, looking towards the garden.[29]

For about a decade the two friends shared the top floor premises, until on 18 June 1620, on Heyward's leaving, Selden petitioned the Inner Temple's governing "Parliament" for permission to retain sole use of the whole chamber and garret, since "albeit it were a double chamber yet it was but little and had but one bedchamber in it." The petition was granted, and Selden remained henceforth a formal resident of the chamber for the rest of his life, even when, in his later years, actually living at nearby Whitefriars.[30] Selden dedicated to Heyward as "most beloved friend and chamber-fellow," both editions of his *Titles of Honor* (1614 and 1631), and the book certainly fulfilled the hope he expressed for it: "And if it have the Fate of a long life, it will returne me a large Retribution by transmitting the memorie of our Friendship to Posteritie."[31]

Together with Heyward (who prefixed some lines to Jonson's *Works* of 1616, and verses before Drayton's *The Barons Wars* of 1619), Selden also participated in a literary circle which included most of the prominent men of

---

[28] Johnson *Memoirs* pp. 39–41.

[29] Aubrey *Lives* p. 282. In May 1609, a license was granted to Edward Heyward and others to erect what became known as Heyward's Building, located roughly on the site today occupied by number 1 Paper Buildings. The dimensions of Heyward's Building were 88 feet long by 26 feet broad and four storys high. The Inner Temple "Parliament" records attest that the building became cause of endless complaints, about its alleged weakness and ugliness, as well as about its blocking the air and the view to the garden and river, and so on. It is unclear how accurate these complaints were, but in April 1629, the Inner Temple Parliament resolved to pull down the buildings as soon as the vested interests of the builders and the tenants could be acquired. 25 years later, when Selden died, they were still standing.

[30] The Whitefriars had numerous intriguing connections to Selden. Between about 1608 and 1628 the mansion house of the old Whitefriars priory was rented from its lease-owner Lord Buckhurst (courtesy title of Edward Sackville, later Fourth Earl of Dorset), by Michael Drayton who operated there a roofed theatre, staging among other plays Jonson's *Epicene*. Moreover, in May and June 1614, it appears from the records of the Inner Temple, that one of the walls of the Whitefriars had been found to have made "encroachments" upon the grounds of the Inner Temple precinct, and one of those appointed to report upon it was Selden's friend Heyward – finding that the wall was to be "amended" with the owners of Whitefriars to bear the cost. Considering that Whitefriars priory was later purchased by the Countess of Kent, and at her death inherited by Selden, one cannot but wonder about the full nature of the dealings concerning the property and involving Sackville, Drayton, Heyward, Lady Kent and Selden.

[31] *Titles of Honor* (1631) – henceforth abbreviated as TH from the dedication to Edward Heyward, not paginated.

letters of the day, with some of whom he created strong and lasting friendships. Foremost among these was Ben Jonson, for whose *Volpone* Selden composed an introductory poem, "Carmen Potrepticon," as early as 1607. Others whose connection to Selden is well attested were Michael Drayton, to whose *Poly-Olbion* of 1612, an 18-song poetic historical and geographical survey of England, Selden wrote lengthy "Illustrations"; William Browne, a member of the Inner Temple, to whose *Britannia's Pastorals* of 1613 Selden contributed commendatory verses in Greek, Latin and English; and Thomas Farnaby, to whose edition of Lucan's *Pharsalia* of 1618 Selden wrote commendatory verses. It appears that he had a love of poetry, and John Suckling included his name in his 1637 poem 'A session of poets' – but little of Selden's verses survive, and what there is suggests that it was one literary field where his gifts were, at best, modest.[32]

Another prominent man of letters, with whom Selden became acquainted early on, and who remained a lifelong friend and companion in scholarship, was James (later Archbishop) Ussher, one of the most learned figures of the age. It appears that it was from Ussher that Selden began, in around 1609, to seriously learn the "Eastern tongues," Aramaic, Arabic, Syriac and of course Hebrew, that would form the glory of his scholarship.[33]

The names noted above hardly exhaust the scope of Selden's intellectual circle, which included at least some acquaintance with many other figures of literary London, often consorting at such Cheapside taverns as the Three Cranes, the Mitre and the Mermaid, in the latter of which, on the first Friday of the month, met the more or less formal "Fraternity of Sireniacal Gentlemen." Some of those he was acquainted with were John Donne, Samuel Daniel, Augustine Vincent, Robert Phelips, Edmund Bolton, William Oughtred,

---

[32] An example of Selden's poetry, are verses he penned, together with others, within the commendatory verses prefacing William Browne's poem, *Britannia's Pastorals* (1613). In Selden's case there are four pages (unpaginated) consisting of three texts, a 16-line Greek "Anacreonticum," a 41-line Latin "Ad amaris numina," and the following 10-line English poem:

> So much a Stranger my *Soueror Muse*
> Is not to Love-straines, or a Shepwards Reed,
> But that She knowes some Rites of *Phoebus* dues,
> Of *Pan*, of *Pallas*, and hir Sisters meed.
> Reade and Commend She durst these tun'd essaies
> Or *Him that loues her* (She hath ever found
> Hir studies as one circle.) Next She prayes
> His Readers be with *Rose* and *Myrtle* crown'd!
> No *Willow* touch them! As His *Baies* are free
> From wrong of Bolts, so may their Chaplets bee.

[33] Toomer *Scholarship* p. 23. During the sixteenth century the teaching of Hebrew was established in most European universities. In Oxford a Hebrew chair had been founded in the 1540s by Henry VIII; thus Selden could have picked up some Hebrew while a student there, but there is no direct evidence for it, and his early dealings with Hebrew sources clearly show it was at best a slight acquaintance. See Toomer *Scholarship* p. 42 and Parry *Trophies* p. 114.

William Austin, Francis Beaumont, Samuel Purchas, Edward Herbert (later Lord, of Cherbury), William Camden and Sir Robert Bruce Cotton.[34]

The last of those named was to have probably the greatest impact on Selden's subsequent life and career. Quite early into Selden's arrival as a student to the inns (they may have been acquainted even earlier, through mutual Sussex connections), his abilities had been recognized by the wealthy and learned Cotton. A generation older than Selden, and an established scholar and antiquary, Cotton employed the young newcomer to copy and summarize records needed for the elder scholar's studies. Thus started a personal and intellectual association by which Selden became closely attached to Sir Robert and his family, benefiting from his patronage and wide network of connections, as well as gaining access an inestimable library, the richest in England of that time. Cotton probably had some role in introducing Selden to the literary circles he was a part of, including many of the former members of the Society of Antiquaries, who were still occasionally meeting to informally exchange historical ideas and information.[35]

The extent of the two men's affinity is attested in their close and long cooperation thereafter. Selden dedicated his *Historie of Tithes* (1618) to Cotton, and the two men were prominently employed by the House of Commons during the 1620s to search records and report about parliamentary precedents. The high point of their personal, intellectual and political collaboration was probably the 1628 Parliament when, together with a number of Commons' leaders, they advanced the line advocated by Selden and Coke (in a planning meeting convened at Cotton's house), that the

---

[34] Jonson jocularly proclaimed: "Your Three Cranes, Mitre, and Mermaid men! Not a corn of true salt, not a grain of right mustard amongst them all." See Christianson "Selden" ODNB. John Donne, for example, mentions in a letter from c. 1623, his conferring with Selden about them both paying together eight pounds, to discharge from arrest John, the son of their mutual friend Sir Henry Goodyere. See Letter LXXII in *The Works of John Donne* (1839) vol. vi pp. 389–390. Selden's involvement with these literary circles means that he was also quite likely acquainted, at least to some degree with another participant, William Shakespeare. Until his retirement in 1611, Shakespeare was living in London and still active as playwright, actor and part-owner of the theatrical company known as the King's Men. He owned a share of the Blackfriars indoor theatre, as well as a house nearby, and was on close terms with Jonson, appearing as actor in at least one of the latter's plays staged in this period, *Sejanus* (performed 1603). But no positive proof of acquaintance between Selden and Shakespeare has emerged as yet.

[35] The Society of Antiquaries was active between 1588 and c. 1605, disseminating continental historical techniques and ideas among English scholars. The bulk of the Society's members were lawyers, and most of the questions it debated were in some way related to the history of English law. The Society petitioned successively Queen Elizabeth I, and later King James I, for a royal charter but were refused by both, in the latter case apparently because of fear that their enquiries into the past might drift into "matters of state." Selden, although never a member of the society, became part of the circle of cosmopolitan scholarship and informal meetings formed by former members of the society, like Cotton and Camden. See Woolf *Idea* p. 206; I. Donaldson, *Ben Jonson: A Life* (Oxford University Press, 2011) p. 360; G. Burgess, *The politics of the ancient constitution* (Macmillan, 1992) pp. 58–59; Toomer *Scholarship* pp. 139–140.

foremost issue should be the reassertion of the ancient laws and liberties of Englishmen. The passing in Parliament of that seminal English constitutional document, the "Petition of Right," was the eventual result – although it also resulted in the incarceration of Selden and the sealing of Cotton's library, probably hastening the latter's death in 1631. Selden's connection with the Cotton family and library continued after Sir Robert's passing, as he was given free access to it by Sir Robert's son, Thomas, from 1633, when the library was reopened. From 1643 to his death, at the time of the Civil War and interregnum, Selden became the prominent defender of the library, fending off attempts to seize its contents and safeguarding it for the Cotton family while allowing access to younger scholars such as Meric Casaubon and Gerard Langbaine.[36]

It is obvious that, regardless of his building up a lucrative law practice, Selden continued to devote much of his energies to scholarship – in what he called the "breathing times" from the "so different studies of my Profession." What had started as a student activity continued in later years as a steady stream of works, of growing erudition and significance. *Titles of Honor* (1614) dealt with the origin and nature of titles and dignities, *Analecton Anglo-Britannicon* (1615 – but

---

[36] Johnson *Memoirs* pp. 39–40; Toomer *Scholarship* pp. 25–28. Indicative of Selden's use of the library, is a list among the Harleian manuscripts in the British Library, recording a loan of printed books made by Cotton to Selden, on 2 February 1622. Many of the books remaining in Selden's library for good – whether as a gift from Cotton, or for other reasons. The list shows the wide variety of Selden's interests at that time. It includes a number of collections of laws from across Europe, such as some volumes of Spanish laws (in Spanish), a volume of Portuguese laws (in Portuguese) a Dutch Ordinance of 1543 as well as a Dutch dictionary and a "placard of the stats generall in France" from 1581. Also included are three books dealing with the history and institutions of the Church (on the College of Cardinals, on Provincial and General Councils and on the correspondence of Peter Damian), and two on Roman institutions (a book on the magistrates of the Roman Republic and a history of the Roman Forum). In addition there were two volumes binding together a number of works originally published separately, one volume comprising seven works mostly on various aspects of the institution of monarchy (but also including Guicciardini's *Sententiae*, in Italian), among which one deals specifically with the Lex Regia; and another volume collecting four works on disparate subjects (a history of Sicily, a consolation of Queen Catherine Medici on her husband's death, a verse work on living a life of right reason and virtue, and *Clandestinis matrimoniis*, a work by Hervetus on clandestine matrimony). Finally, there was Porphyry's *De abstinentia de esu animalium* (on abstinence from animal food). On top of displaying Selden's wide range of scholarly interests, as well as his exceptional grasp of languages, there are two aspects of the list which it is tempting to connect to his later political and personal activities. First, it is quite obvious from the works listed that in the legal sphere, Selden was at this stage particularly interested in constitutional issues, pertaining to legislative institutions and legal codes in various countries, as well as particular political institutions in state and church, such as kingship, the college of Cardinals and the magistrates of the Roman republic. It is not very hard to see the connection to the issues that would preoccupy him as MP throughout the 1620s. Considering his alleged secret marriage to the Countess of Kent later in life, it is also suggestive that he borrowed, among other works, one on clandestine marriage. See C.G.C. Tite "A 'Loan' of printed books from Sir Robert Cotton to John Selden" in *The Bodleian Library Record* 13/6 (April 1991) pp. 486–490.

composed c. 1607) was an account of pre-Norman British history, and he added his own learned "Notes" to a new edition of the fifteenth-century legal treatise by Sir John Fortescue, *De laudibus legum Angliae* published together with Sir Ralph de Hengham's *Summae* (1616).[37]

As his scholarly repute spread, Selden also developed his impressive network of connections with leading intellectual figures of the time, at home as well as abroad. These included, among many others, in Britain, Lancelot Andrewes, Roger Dodsworth, Peter Turner, John Bainbridge, James Howell, Patrick Young and Edward Pococke; in Europe, Thomas Erpenius, Francis Junius (the younger), Ludovicus de Dieu, Nicholas Peiresc, Daniel Heinsius, Marin Mersenne, Claudius Salmasius and Gerardus Vossius.[38]

An apposite illustration of Selden's intellectual world, at the meeting point of renaissance and modernity, as well as of his diverse and far-ranging social network, was his acquaintance with two of the most famous seventeenth-century physicians: Robert Fludd (or Floyd, 1574–1637) and William Harvey (1578–1657).[39] Fludd, a famous physician and chemist who also earned a notorious reputation for his embracing of astrology, his interest in the occult and his apology of Rosicrucians, cured Selden in 1613 of a serious illness.[40] Harvey, physician to Kings James I and Charles I, and the first to accurately

---

[37] TH (1614) in the dedication to Edward Heyward, not paginated. It appears that Selden was collecting material for his "Notes" on Fortescue and Hengham by the summer of 1616, however he did not edit or have anything to do with the text, only supplying the notes and a short introduction. See Toomer *Scholarship* p. 176.

[38] In addition to corresponding with these scholars on a wide range of topics, Selden also exchanged books and manuscripts with many, and his house became a required stop for foreign scholars visiting London. An amusing episode is recounted of an occasion when the Dutch scholar Vossius came to pay a visit to Selden, and was climbing the stairs to his study in Heyward's Building, when Selden, deeply engaged in some research, called to the Dutchman from the top of the stairs, telling him he was not at leisure to receive visitors and be interrupted. See Aikin *Lives* p. 160. Obviously Vossius did not regard the incident as offensive, for the two remained good friends for decades.

[39] Another physician known to have treated Selden was Samuel Turner, who is reputed to have cured him of a dangerous swelling in his throat by making him smoke tobacco with amber. See Toomer *Scholarship* p. 327 note 115.

[40] Selden reported his having been freed from a dangerous sickness "by the Bounteous humanitie and advise of that learned Phisician Doctor *Robert Floyd* (whom my Memorie alwaies honors)[.]" See TH (1614) from the dedication to Edward Heyward, not paginated. Fludd obviously reciprocated this high esteem, for in his unpublished treatise "The Philosophicall Key" composed around 1619 to defend himself from accusations of atheism and dark practices, he mentioned that his "Worthy freends, Mr Dr. [Launcelot] Andrews, and the most learned Gentlemen of the Inner Temple, Mr Seldein" could testify to his having completed his manuscript *Historia Macrocosmi* as early as 1611 – and thus not resulting from recent influence of the sinister Rosicrucians. Indeed, among books owned by Selden now held in the Bodleian library is a copy of Fludd's *Historia*, bearing on the leaf facing the title page, in Selden's handwriting: "Ex dono autoris Viri doctissimi, humanissimi, & de me optime meriti." See Feingold "Selden" pp. 70–71, and J. Sparrow, "Documents and Records – The earlier owners of books in John Selden's library" in *The Bodleian Quarterly Record* 70–71/6 (1931) p. 268.

describe (and prove) the circulation of the blood, was connected to a hilarious episode recounted in the *Table-Talk*, telling of his cooperation with Selden in dealing with a gentleman who believed he was possessed by devils.[41] The two physicians might seem to stand respectively for renaissance mysticism and clear-headed rationalism, but were in fact far more similar and complex figures than may at first appear. The two intellectual strands they represent were at this time closer and more intertwined than they later became, sharing many characteristics and concerns. Harvey, regardless of his theoretical innovation, resolutely opposed the new chemical and experimental turn medicine was taking in his days, preferring instead the traditional and holistic approach of Aristotle, Cicero and Avicenna; while Fludd, for all his interest in mystical and occult matters, was also intensely involved in innovative chemical and magnetic experiments, and was also among the first persons to correctly hypothesize the circulation of the blood.[42]

---

[41] See Woolf *Idea* pp. 212–213 and TT "Devils" sec. 3: "A person of Quality came to my Chamber in the *Temple*, and told me he had two Devils in his Head [I wondered what he meant] and just at that time, one of them bid him kill me, [with that I begun to be afraid, and thought he was mad] he said he knew I could cure him; and therefore entreated me to give him something; for he was resolved he would go to no body else. I perceiving what an Opinion he had of me, and that 'twas only Melancholly that troubl'd him, took him in hand, warranted him, if he would follow my directions, to cure him in a short time. I desired him to let me be alone about an Hour, and then to come again, which he was very willing to. In the mean time I got a Card, and lap'd it up handsome in a Piece of *Taffata*, and put Strings to the *Taffata*, and when he came, gave it to him to hang about his Neck, withal charged him, that he should not disorder himself neither with Eating or Drinking, but eat very little of Supper, and say his Prayers duly when he went to Bed, and I made no Question but he would be well in three or four Days. Within that time I went to Dinner to his House, and ask'd him how he did? He said he was much better, but not perfectly well, or in truth he had not dealt clearly with me. He had four Devils in his Head, and he perceiv'd two of them were gone, with that which I had given him, but the other two troubled him still. Well, said I, I am glad two of them are gone, I make no doubt but to get away the other two likewise; so I gave him another thing to hang about his Neck. Three Days after he came to me to my Chamber and profest he was now as well as ever he was in his Life, and did extreamly thank me for the great care I had taken of him. I fearing lest he might relapse into the like Distemper, told him that there was none but my self, and one Physician more in the whole Town that could cure the Devils in the Head, and that was Dr. *Harvey* (whom I had prepar'd) and wish'd him if ever he found himself ill in my Absence, to go to him, for he could cure his Disease as well as my self. The Gentleman lived many Years and was never troubled after."

In the *Diis Syriis* of 1629, Selden described the procedure for making a magician's amulet for curing fever, which was quite similar to the one he described performing in the *Table-Talk*: writing abracadabra repeatedly on a square piece of paper in a pyramid, then folding the paper so that it cannot be read and stitching it together with white thread, and then wore over bosom on a linen cloth for nine days. See *Diis Syriis* (1629) b1c2.

[42] Francis Bacon and John Dee (who, like Bacon, proposed a theory of experimental science), were additional figures linking both traditions. See S.L. Collins, *From Divine Cosmos to Sovereign State* (Oxford University Press, 1989) pp. 138–139. For some of the experiments performed by Fludd, see his account in R. Fludd, *Mosaicall Philosophy* (1659) pp. 252–259. On Harvey see also N.G. Siraisi, *Avicenna in Renaissance Italy* (Princeton University Press, 1987) p. 353

Up to this point, Selden's career had been one of quiet, scholarly pursuits and legal practice. By 1617 he had certainly built up enough of a reputation to be numbered among the prominent men of letters of the day, whose names were considered among those who would form an English Royal Academy.[43] The year saw a steady succession of works by Selden. Two smaller works of the same year were *A Brief Discourse Touching on the Office of Lord Chancellor of England* (presented to Francis Bacon upon his appointment to that office), and the very short piece (two pages long) "of the Iewes sometimes living in England," appearing within a book by Samuel Purchas, in such adulterated form that it caused a quarrel between the two, and ended their former friendship.[44] A far more substantial work was *De Diis Syriis* (1617, on which he had been working at least since 1613), an erudite study of the ancient deities of the near east, which was the origin for Selden's scholarly reputation among continental intellectuals, and was for a long time his most famous work abroad, although it is also probably the one among his works whose reputation has endured the least. Soon after its publication, Camden sent copies of the work to the continent, and it rapidly earned praise among such as Sirmond and Peiresec in Paris (who started a correspondence with Selden), as well as Aleandro and Cardinal Cobelluzzi (Librarian of the Vatican) in Rome. Selden was thus established as one of the few English scholars of repute in the European-wide republic of letters, whom scholars coming to London would call upon as a matter of courtesy.[45]

However, the next year marked Selden's abrupt emergence into the limelight of public controversy, and in dramatic fashion at that, as a result of his

---

and G. Clarck, *A History of the Royal College of Physicians of London* (Oxford: Clarendon, 1964) vol. I p. 302.

[43] In 1617, the impoverished scholar Edmund Bolton composed a proposal which he presented to King James I, for establishing an "Academ Roial" which would gather the great scholars, poets and artist, of the age (termed by Bolton "Essentials"), of which he named 84 to be among the founders – with Selden one of them. It was to be a house of wisdom presided by the English Solomon. King James, impressed and flattered by the proposal, pledged his support, but the project did not materialize before his death in 1625. Although he left specific instructions for his son to complete the task, Charles I had no interest in it, and it quietly died away. Donaldson *Jonson* pp. 365–366.

[44] The short piece "of the Iewes sometimes living in England" appeared (together with two poems penned by Selden) in the third edition of the successful compendium by Samuel Purchas, *Purchas, his Pilgrimage* (1617) – not to be confused with the similarly titled but different works *Purchas, his Pilgrime* of 1619 and *Purchas, his Pilgrimes* of 1625. In 1626, the year he died, Purchas published, the fourth and final edition of the *Pilgrimage*. See E. Fry, "Selden, John" in DNB (1897) vol. 51 pp. 212–224, and T. Brook, *Mr. Selden's Map of China* (Bloomsbury Press, 2013) pp. 130–131.

[45] Toomer *Scholarship* pp. 211, 251–252. Describing the drawbacks of the *Diis*, Toomer notes that instead of a coherent theory of religious origins, Selden offers a number of differing and inconsistent theories, and the same is true about his attitude to the rabbinical explanations, at times dismissing them as null, at others accepting them when it suits him. See Toomer *Scholarship* pp. 254–255.

publishing of the *Historie of Tithes*, probably his most famous work during his lifetime. The book, written mostly between September 1616 and September 1617 (except chapter 2, the section on Jewish tithes, on which Selden had compiled notes as far back as 1614), for all its avowal of being merely a scholarly examination of the historical practice and jurisdiction of tithes, unequivocally claimed that for Christians, these were not a divine injunction but only positive law. Not surprisingly, this position provoked fierce protestations and written attacks from churchmen, even while it was circulating in draft form, in late 1617. Selden quickly prepared an answer to the criticism, in a "Review" which he annexed to the printed edition, as he described it there:

After some few Copies, thus halfe printed and halfe writen, were dispersed, and since the various Censure of vnequall Readers, (some of them cauilling at such Passages in it, as the Autor at first thought, and not without cause, had been enough cleered) this short *Reuiew* is now added[.][46]

After its initial publication in early 1618, the *Historie of Tithes* was reprinted at least four more times in the same year, and caused much commotion especially among bishops – with apparently one bishop only, Lancelot Andrewes, pleased with it, regardless of his own doctoral dissertation having claimed tithes were due by divine right. Soon a number of bishops issued summons ordering Selden to appear before them, which he duly ignored. But the protests eventually reached James I, and Selden was summoned to appear before the king – who, it appears, had until then never even heard of him. In mid-December 1618, Selden traveled to Theobald's (country residence of the king, just west of London), where he had the first of three interviews with James I. The king took pleasure in displaying his own erudition in discussions with Selden about the book, and required him to write "palinodes" (penitential compositions) on three matters dear to James, which had come up incidentally in the *Historie of Tithes* (the meaning of the number 666, Calvin's opinion of Revelation, and that Christ's birthday was 25 December) – which Selden soon delivered, together with an apologetic *Of my Purpose and End in Writing the Historie of Tithes*. A second meeting took place in early 1619, at Whitehall, near the time of Selden's appearance before the Court of High Commission and the Privy Council. He had no option but to submit to these circumstances, but he carefully worded his apology so as to avoid admitting anything in the book was untrue, and expressed regret only for "the error which I have committed in publishing the Historie of Tithes." Selden thus escaped trial or imprisonment, but his book was suppressed, and he was forbidden to publish anything more on tithes. However, following a number of printed attacks on him, most prominently by Sir James Sempil (a Scottish friend of the king) and Dr. Richard Tillesley (Archdeacon of Rochester and royal chaplain), Selden chose to interpret "publishing" as meaning only putting to print, and he composed an

---

[46] *Historie of Tithes* p. 449, and see Toomer *Scholarship* pp. 261–262.

answer to the two, which he circulated in manuscript copies (including one in his own hand, now kept in the National Library of Wales). In his defense, Selden stressed that he had recanted only the publication of the book, not its truth, and singled out for rejection Tillesley's claim, especially galling to a common lawyer, that Selden had personally submitted and admitted his guilt before the Court of High Commission (the supreme ecclesiastical judicial body in England, which eventually Selden would have a role in abolishing, in 1641). The proximity to the king of the two authors of the attacks, should have given Selden pause to consider the favor their writings enjoyed at court. The king was incensed when he learned of the circulating manuscript by Selden, and at a third meeting, held at Theobald's, he harshly reprimanded Selden for composing and circulating the response, threatened him with imprisonment if he should express himself again in any way on the subject, and encouraged another royal chaplain, Richard Mountagu, Archdeacon of Hereford (and later Bishop of Chichester and then Norwich), to write a third attack on the *Historie*.[47]

The incident certainly did not do much for Selden's love of the clergy, and various claims have been raised since (by Peter Heylyn, among others), tracing from this time on, an allegedly anti-clerical and anti-episcopal slant in his views. It is, however, better to keep in mind that, on the one hand there were various anti-clerical utterances by Selden before this incident (indeed, in the *Historie* itself), and that on the other hand, later in life, though far from an enthusiast of clergy or episcopacy, Selden never became a decided enemy of either, even when

---

[47] Toomer *Scholarship* pp. 304–310; R. Zaller, *The discourse of legitimacy in Early Modern England* (Stanford University Press, 2007) p. 347; Aikin *Lives* pp. 25–28; and Christiansen "Selden" ODNB. Though Selden much later remembered Jonson (and Heyward) to have been with him at the first of the meetings with the King, I. Donaldson points out that Jonson was at that time in Scotland, and therefore, if he accompanied Selden to Theobald's, that must have been at the latter meeting. See Donaldson *Jonson* pp. 362–363.

The most important answers to Selden's *Historie of Tithes* were Sempil's, Tillesley's – who claimed, among other things that Selden had recanted his views before the Court of High Commission (whereas in fact Selden only expressed regret for publishing the book, but in no way disowned the views in it) – and Montagu's, but there were at least two more attacks, in 1623 and 1627 and some additional ones in later years. Regardless of King James' prohibition of Selden from publishing or even circulating manuscripts on the matter, Selden nevertheless did circulate privately among close friends and acquaintances manuscript copies of replies, some of which have survived. See Woolf *Idea* pp. 231–233.

However, Selden very likely allowed himself at least a small measure of satisfaction, when some years later he had a role in turning the tables on Montagu, who had described the writer of the *Historie of Tithes* as no less than an "emissary of the Prince of Darkness": in 1629, while an MP Selden was appointed by the Commons to investigate and decide "whether Mr. Montagu be a lawful bishop or no" after the latter had been accused that some of his writings were theologically suspect and tending to Arminianism. It appears that Selden actually approached the issue without undue vengefulness, and with the goal of finding a solution that would avoid further escalation. He succeeded in this goal, inasmuch as Montagu remained a bishop, but not without some squirming on the latter's part – he had to apologize for suspect writings and disclaim Arminianism. See R. Barbour, *John Selden: Measures of the Holy Commonwealth in Seventeenth-century England* (Toronto University Press, 2003) pp. 163–164.

the political circumstances made this very much profitable. On a personal level, Selden always expressed his esteem and friendship with prominent clerics such as Bishop Andrewes and later Archbishops Ussher, Williams and Laud, and he did not refrain from lending them what support he could, when they ran afoul of political authorities. In fact, Williams and Selden, who were close contemporaries, became friends as well as longtime political allies. On the level of political principles, when in the early 1640s the political circumstances reversed and made it quite advantageous to be numbered among the enemies of episcopacy and the established church, Selden actually was one of the minority in Parliament who remained a steady supporter of episcopacy (albeit a reformed one), of the presence of clerical representation in Parliament, and even of tithes (as long as they were based on human laws), while opposing "root-and-branch" schemes of radical reform in church and state.[48]

Before proceeding with the narrative of Selden's life, two more important points should be made about the *Historie*. The first is that the book, as well as both the *Treatise* and the *Diis*, from the same period, display the growing place that oriental sources, and particularly Hebrew ones, were taking in Selden's scholarship. The second is that the *Historie* is apparently the first work of its kind in the English language to use the term "History" to describe not an individual, a war or a country but rather a practice or institution; that is, a social history. Although Selden's was certainly not the only one responsible for what D.R. Woolf described as the "marriage of erudition with history," his concept of history had an important role in altering the common usage of the term by contemporary and later writers, so that by the 1630s, the terms "antiquarian" and "historian" came to be often used synonymously.[49]

In 1619, Selden attempted to publish the *Mare Clausum*, a work answering Grotius' *Mare Liberum*, and claiming for England the sovereignty over the northern sea, which he had been encouraged to compose by figures at court. He conveyed a copy of the book to the Earl of Pembroke, who apparently appreciated it and attempted to gain publication permission, but to no avail. It emerged that the Marquess of Buckingham was blocking the publication of the work, out of fear it might have adverse effects on England's foreign policy. More than 15 years were to pass before circumstances allowed for publication of the book, in updated form.

This episode marked Selden's first brush with Buckingham, a figure that was to become central to much of his public efforts and concerns in the next decade.

---

[48] For the claim that Selden became a decided anti-clerical after 1619 see Aikin *Lives* p. 34. D.R. Woolf points out that, ironically, when Selden returned to the issue of tithes in the 1650s, he defended their continuance albeit on grounds of custom and positive law. Thus his own position, that tithes were not divine but human law, remained the same, but the terms of public debate had changed. See Woolf *Idea* p. 234.

[49] Woolf *Idea* pp. 239–240. See also Toomer *Scholarship* p. 262; P. Christianson, *Discourse on History, Law and Government in the public career of John Selden, 1610–1635* (Toronto University Press, 1996) p. 197.

George Villiers (1592–1628) was one of the most successful court favorites in English history, ascending at dizzying speed from the moment in 1614 when, as a minor gentleman, he caught the eye of King James I to the successive titles of Knight, Baron, Viscount, Earl, Marquess and eventually, from 1623, Duke of Buckingham – becoming thus the highest-ranking peer outside the royal family. Trained from early age to the life of a courtier, and combining courtly abilities with a fetching physical presence, Villiers evidently excelled at his craft. He amassed within a short time not only great titles and vast riches, but also the decisive influence over political appointments and policies, and even achieved the unheard-of feat of retaining his position as chief favorite of James I with his son Charles I as well. However, Buckingham also combined his undoubted courtly talents and his unbounded ambitions, with less-than-modest political and diplomatic abilities and, what was even worse, a vanity that made him unable to recognize these limitations. The result was that he embroiled James and Charles in a succession of botched schemes at home and abroad, which together with the natural resentment at his meteoric rise (especially among the older peerage), turned him into a figure of public detestation. By the mid-1620s he was solidly identified with the infamous image of the grasping royal favorite, traditionally suspected of malevolent influence and nefarious intentions – a focal point for the mounting resentments and fears about constitutional and religious policies.[50]

1.5 PARLIAMENTARIAN: 1620–1629

With the controversy surrounding the *Historie*, Selden, who had been until that time a scholar and erudite, known mainly within legal and literary circles, was catapulted at once into the center of the public arena, where he was to gradually increase his involvement during the following decade. It was to bring him the mixed blessings of reputation and persecution – being numbered among the leaders of the parliamentary opposition to the king, as well as earning two bouts of imprisonment – and to witness a corresponding decline of his scholarly production. This made the 1620s by far the most intellectually unproductive

---

[50] Villiers was reputed "the handsomest-bodied man in all of England," and suspicions about the nature of his relationship with King James circulated at the time, and have continued since. See Godfrey Goodman, Bishop of Gloucester, quoted in P. Gregg, *King Charles I* (Berkeley: California University Press, 1984) p. 49.

In foreign affairs Buckingham spearheaded a bumbling and ultimately unsuccessful attempt to arrange the marriage of then Prince Charles to the Spanish Infanta and led two failed naval enterprises against Spain as well as two botched attempts to take part in internal French military clashes, the latter ending in spectacular defeat. At home he was involved in James' and Charles' clashes with Parliament, and especially in the latter's reign, although actually preferring a line of accommodation, he became the lightning-rod for parliamentary resentment at royal policies, so that in both 1626 and 1628, he was saved from impeachment only by Charles' suspension of parliamentary proceedings.

period of his adult life, so that aside from writings prepared for Parliament or in Parliament, the meager scholarly harvest of the whole decade were a prefatory letter to Augustine Vincent's *A Discouerie of Errours in the First Edition of the Catalogue of Nobility* (1622), the editing and notes to a twelfth-century English history, Eadmer's *Historiae Novorum* (1623), the catalogue and description of the Earl of Arundel's marbles and antiques collection, *Marmora Arundelliana* (1628), and a revised second edition of his *Diis Syriis* (1629).[51]

However, this period also saw Selden gaining acquaintance with a circle of the most prominent noble families in England of the time. It is quite likely that Cotton had a role, at least in the initial contacts of Selden with the Earls of Kent, Henry and Elizabeth Grey (more about this below); and the same is probably true for his acquaintance with Thomas Howard, Twenty-First Earl of Arundel. Cotton was connected to both Earls, themselves brothers-in-law, through the formidable sisters Alathea and Elizabeth Talbot, married respectively to Howard and to Grey.[52]

Arundel was the most significant early aristocratic patron of Selden's. An eminent collector and builder, whose collection of ancient inscriptions was the one that Selden described in the *Marmora Arundelliana*, the two had many other interactions, including Selden's involvement in the efforts to settle the complex disputes over the Talbot inheritance (due to Arundel's wife Alathea and her sisters), to finding precedent for titles, and possibly assisting the 1622 restoration of Arundel to the office of Earl Marshal forfeited by his father's attainder. Moreover, it appears that Arundel also had a role in recruiting Selden to advise Parliament in 1621 on various matters, and in procuring Selden's first parliamentary seat in 1624.

Other aristocratic figures who became close to Selden, and shared at least some of his scholarly pursuits were Edward Conway, from 1631 Second Viscount Conway, who had a particular interest in English literature, with many literary connections and a book collection in London and Ireland that came to number more than 10,000 volumes; and Henry Bourchier (or Bourgchier), a wealthy landowner who in 1638 became the Fifth Earl of Bath, a patron of Ussher, and in 1630 close enough to Selden as to offer to stand bail

[51] Selden inspected Arundel's marbles with the assistance of Richard James, librarian to Robert Cotton, and of Patrick Young, royal librarian to whom the *Marmora* was dedicated – regardless of the fact that the latter was a prominent protégé of Bishop Montagu. See Aikin *Lives* pp. 65–67, 371.

[52] It appears that Cotton was not only acquainted but also related to both the Earls of Kent and of Arundel. The brothers, Henry Grey (1541–1615), Sixth Earl, and Charles Grey (1545–1623), Seventh Earl, of Kent, married respectively Mary Cotton (daughter of Sir George Cotton of Combermere) and Susan Cotton (daughter of Sir Richard Cotton of Bedhampton, Hampshire). Mary was definitely if distantly related to Sir Robert (both descended from one William de Coton). It is unclear if there was a familial relationship between Susan Cotton (mother of Henry Grey, Eighth Earl of Kent) and Sir Robert, but it seems not unlikely. In addition, Thomas Cotton, the son of Sir Robert, married Margaret Howard, cousin (through her father, Lord William Howard) of Thomas Howard, Earl of Arundel.

in order for him to be released from imprisonment. One more prominent aristocratic figure with whom Selden shared literary interests was his near contemporary and eventual friend (and, as noted above, possible distant family relative), Edward Sackville, from 1609 styled Lord Buckhurst, who upon his brother's death in 1624 became Fourth Earl of Dorset. He was an MP for Sussex in 1621, active in the Virginia Company, became a Privy Councilor in 1626 and from 1628 was Chamberlain to Queen Henrietta Maria. Sackville was trusted by the royal family to the degree that his wife Mary was appointed governess of the prince of Wales and the Duke of York (later Kings Charles II and James II), and his chaplain Brian Duppa became tutor to the princes, well as chaplain to the king. Politically, Sackville was for the most part a supporter of Charles I's policies, even controversial ones such as the Forced Loan and the Personal Rule, albeit usually sounding a tone that was tactically more cautious and moderate. This moderation brought, in the late 1630s, a decline in his influence with the king (whose sound judgment he increasingly questioned), as more bellicose voices were in the ascendant, and Sackville was unsuccessful in opposing what he regarded as Wentworth's political excesses and in his attempts to defend Bishop Williams from being brought to trial by Laud in February 1639. Dorset was also a prominent patron of literature, owning for many years the lease to the premises where the Whitefriars theatre was situated and obviously involved in its operations, for in 1629 he was the force behind the moving of its company close by, to the Salisbury Court Theatre, which he erected on the grounds of his own Dorset house. In this context, Sackville was also instrumental in the arrest, trial and severe sentencing of William Prynne, for his attack on theatrical performances by women (perceived as directed against the Queen).[53]

The aristocrats in the former group were only intermittently involved in public affairs (Arundel and Dorset more than others), and devoted their energies mostly to artistic and literary pursuits, as collectors of art and patrons of men of letters. Thus their connections with Selden were centered primarily on shared intellectual and artistic interests, as well as on legal services he provided some of them. The close ties Selden forged with this group probably facilitated the far more political connections that he built with a number of additional aristocratic figures, which were to be crucial to the public role he would play in coming decades. Prominent among these were the members of the Herbert family, William Herbert, Third Earl of Pembroke (married to a third Talbot sister, Mary), his brother Philip, Earl of Montgomery (and in 1630

---

[53] As mentioned above, Selden was certainly aware of his maternal grandfather, Thomas Baker's purported family ties to Sir John Baker and thus, however distantly, to the Sackvilles. Curiously, considering that Selden published in 1610 his short tract *Duello*, Edward Sackville himself participated soon after in one of the most notorious duels of the seventeenth century, in September 1613, which resulted in his killing of Edward Bruce, Lord of Kinloss. On Dorset see D.L. Smith, "The Fourth Earl of Dorset and the Personal Rule of Charles I" in *Journal of British Studies* 30/3 (July 1991) pp. 257–287.

successor to William as Fourth Earl of Pembroke), as well as other members of the clan, like Lord Edward Herbert of Cherbury (who defended Selden during the *Historie* controversy, and remained a lifelong friend, appointing him one of his executors), and his cousin Sir Edward Herbert, closest to Selden and connected to him by literary and legal ties, since their student days at the Inner Temple.[54]

Another aristocratic clan with which Selden became acquainted following the *Historie* controversy were the Digbys: John Digby, First Earl of Bristol, his son the mercurial George, to whom Selden became for a time a kind of mentor, and their relative, the learned Sir Kenelm Digby (with whom Selden corresponded and exchanged books), as well as Francis Russel, Fourth Earl of Bedford and George's father-in-law. Bristol and Bedford were in the early 1640s leaders of the moderate parliamentarians, and for a time political allies of Selden.[55]

A third aristocratic connection, and the most politically significant one in the long term, was that formed by Robert Devereux, Third Earl of Essex to whom Selden supplied important legal services (on his part, Devereux was another one of those offering to stand bail for Selden in 1630), and his brother-in-law, William Seymour (also related to the Sackvilles, his brother Edward (d. 1618) having married Anne, sister of the Third and Fourth Earls of Dorset). Seymour, from 1621 Second Earl of Hertford, became Selden's foremost political ally during the 1620s, and continued to maintain close political, business and personal ties with him, throughout his life. Selden's election to Parliaments in 1626 (for Great Bedwyn), and 1628 (for Ludgeshall) was certainly due to Hertford's influence, and in the Commons he collaborated closely with the small but effective Seymour connection, which included MPs Francis Seymour and Edward Kyrton, respectively brother and steward to the Earl. In the 1640s Hertford gradually moved away from his previous opposition to the king's policies and became close to Charles I, so that by the beginning of the Civil War he had been created a Marquess, and written to Selden urging him to join the king's side at York. Selden's answer, an extant letter he wrote Hertford in

---

[54] It has been suggested that Selden's first election to Parliament, for Lancaster in 1624, was procured through the Herberts. See Christianson *Discourse* p. 92.

[55] John Digby (1580–1653), was imprisoned between 1624 and 1628. His son George (1612–1677), appeared before the Commons in 1624, when only 12 years old, to plead for the release of his father, and made a great impression (though the father was not then released). George, from 1641 Baron Digby and from 1653 Second Earl of Bristol, grew up to be a learned and talented if controversial figure. His correspondence with Selden, who possibly heard the boy's speech before the Commons, testifies to their warm relationship, which included lending and purchasing books. In a letter from 1637 Digby wrote to Selden: "For you beinge the person of all I knowe, that I reverence and value most, I shall not glorye soe much in anybodyes good opinion of mee." In the 1640s Digby was at first a moderate parliamentarian, but eventually became a leading royalist and a close advisor to Charles I. After the defeat of royalist forces he escaped to France, and was close to Charles II, but lost favor after converting to Catholicism. He wielded only little influence after the Restoration, but was instrumental in the fall of Clarendon.

June 1642, clearly shows his anxiety to persuade his friend that the decision to decline the invitation was justified. During the Civil War Hertford rose for a time to be a prominent military commander of the royalist forces, as well as guardian to the Prince of Wales (who, as Charles II, restored in 1660 his former guardian to the title of Duke of Somerset, forfeited in 1552 by his great-grandfather). Nevertheless, Seymour always remained a moderate royalist, seeking throughout the conflict a compromise settlement, and kept unofficial contacts with his brother-in-law Essex, by this time a prominent parliamentary commander, and probably also with Selden, who was always close to both. Hertford was the most prominent nobleman to remain with the king after his imprisonment, until his execution in 1649. After the regicide he retired from active politics, but his connection with Selden if anything only strengthened, mainly in legal matters having to do with the share of Essex's inheritance due to the latter's sister (Hertford's wife). When bankrupt interregnum governments greedily eyed the properties of royalists as prime targets for financial extortion, Selden, as a trustee of the Essex estate, employed his legal abilities and the public prestige he still retained to protect the inheritance of his now politically discredited ally. Documentary evidence shows that Hertford and Selden continued to cooperate until very near the latter's death, and in his will he bequeathed to Hertford a "Christall Cabinett." On her part, Hertford's wife Frances, in her own will, bequeathed to her daughter-in-law Sarah "my Box of Rarities that Mr. Selden gave me."[56]

The full nature and extent of Selden's relationships with England's leading noble families has been hardly looked into, and it is probable that a systematic inquiry will shed light on more unknown aspects of his activities and ideas. This is certainly not the place to carry out any such exhaustive study; however, even the most cursory glance at materials connected with Selden, to be found in Britain's National Archives, will show documents such as: a letter of 1618 informing Elizabeth Grey that judges were conferring about her inheritance; a draft from 1631 written in Selden's hand for a letter from the Countess of Kent to the Earl of Clare; a copy made for Selden of a judgment given in 1568, showing the Earl Marshal to have the authority to cancel false pedigrees

---

[56] See T. Page Johnson (ed.), *Sir Orlando Bridgeman's Conveyances* (1725, 5th edition) vol. I p. 147. In the Early seventeenth century the family of the Earl of Hertford, had a significant influence in determining MPs from Wiltshire seats, so that Francis Seymour (brother of the earl) sat for the County in the Parliaments of 1621, 1625, 1628 and the Short Parliament of 1640; Francis' son, Charles, sat in the short Parliament for Great Bedwyn, also in Wiltshire; and Edward Kyrton, steward to the Earl sat for Ludgershall in 1624, Marlborough in 1626, and Great Bedwyn in 1628–9. It appears that by the Long Parliament of 1640 the family had lost much of its erstwhile influence in the region, since no Seymour was elected from Wiltshire County, Ludgershall or Great Bedwyn. Francis only gained a seat through another Wiltshire constituency, Marlborough, and Kyrton sat for Milborne Port in Somerset (perhaps through Digby's influence). Selden was not elected to the Short Parliament, and sat in the Long Parliament for Oxford possibly as result of a deal between Pembroke and Laud.

(Arundel was restored in 1622 to the dignity of Earl Marshal forfeited by his father).[57] As is to be expected, a significant part of the documents, both in quantity and quality, are those relating to the involvement of Selden, as a trustee of the estate, in the inheritance arrangements for the estate of Robert Devereux, Third Earl of Essex.[58]

Thus, what had probably been at most intermittent relationships with aristocratic figures, relegated mainly to literary interests or legal practice, became a far closer cooperation, after the *Historie* controversy had shown that Selden was able and willing to bring his substantial scholarly capabilities to bear on current affairs. Also to this period, we should probably date the beginning of the close personal relationship between Selden and the Grey Earls of Kent, to whom he became legal advisor, protégé and friend – especially so of Elizabeth, the future Countess of Kent, who became his closest noble benefactor, devoted friend and eventual companion.[59] The earls of Kent were among the most ancient of English peers, the family sitting in Parliament since 1290, but also by the seventeenth century among the poorest of them, with an annual income from their land rentals, of less than 1800 pounds in 1602 (while the income of the richest peers was on average some 15,000 pounds a year) – therefore, most of the Earl's and Countess' income during this period apparently originated from Elizabeth's share of the massive Talbot inheritance. While Henry Grey (1583–1639) had sat in the Commons twice and from 1623 sat in the House of Lords, he left neither in Parliament nor in other activities any notable impression. Lady Elizabeth was clearly the more forceful personality among the couple, who impressed contemporaries accordingly. The Greys were permanent fixtures at King James I's court, especially so Lady Elizabeth, who at least since 1609 had been a member of Queen Anne's household, and became between 1617 and 1625 chief lady-in-waiting to the Queen. However, after the accession of King Charles

---

[57] All three at Lambeth Palace Library, MS 3513. Selden might have had a role in preparing the groundwork for Arundel's restoration as Earl Marshal, and perhaps his involvement in this is responsible for his being granted an annuity of 50 pounds by the Earl. See Toomer *Scholarship* p. 313.

[58] See especially Longleat House, Devereux papers, De/Box XV/5 and Seymour papers SE/Box XVI.70–72.

[59] Elizabeth (1582–1651) was the daughter Gilbert Talbot, Seventh Earl of Shrewsbury. In 1601 she married Henry Grey, but the couple had no children. She was well educated, with a keen interest in medical recipes (a famous collection of which she had produced for her use, also contributing to it some material), and in languages, especially Italian and French. Her Italian instructor dedicated to her the poetry book *Rime di Antimo Galli All'Illustrissima Signora Elizabetta Talbot-Grey* (1609) – describing scenes from court life, it consists of a long 124-stanze poem on occasion of a masque of January 1609, as well as numerous shorter "Sonetti, Madrigali, E Canzoni." Often at court from a young age, Elizabeth participated in state ceremonies and court masques, performing among others in Ben Jonson's *Masque of Queens* of 1609, and (with her sister Alathea) in *The Speeches at Prince Henry's Barriers* (aka *The Lady of the Lake*) of 1610, celebrating the investiture of Henry Stuart as Prince of Wales, as well as Samuel Daniel's *Tethys Festivall*, also of 1610, where Elizabeth preformed as the "Nymph of Medway." See J. Considine, "Grey, Elizabeth" in ODNB.

in 1625, the couple lost any significant influence at court and thereafter attended only rarely. Moreover, in 1627 Earl Henry was one of the "Refusers" who resisted the King's Forced Loan, and as consequence he was stripped of the lord-lieutenancy of Bedfordshire, which he had held since 1621. During Charles I's Personal Rule the Kents' position at court was somewhat rehabilitated, although they continued to attend only sporadically, with Henry restored to the lord-lieutenancy in December 1629 and present at the 1634 Garter installation, while Countess Elizabeth was singularly honored at the christening ceremony of James Duke of York in 1633 by being chosen to carry the infant to the font.[60]

Although Selden might have been independently acquainted with Henry Grey, his near contemporary and around 1610 a fellow student at the Inns of Court, it appears that their close acquaintance dates from about 1619, with Selden gradually becoming regular legal advisor and agent for the Greys. The relationship, both professional and personal, intensified after Grey succeeded his father as the Eighth Earl of Kent in 1623, and from this year onwards, Selden spent extended periods (usually summers) with the Kents at their country residence, Wrest Park in Bedfordshire.[61]

The Kents remained steadfast friends and supporters of Selden through the years, even between 1629 and 1632, when he was imprisoned and under a political shadow. When an outbreak of plague in London meant Selden was permitted to leave his jail in the capital for a time, they succeeded in having him reside at Wrest; later, Elizabeth was apparently the main force behind bringing her brothers-in-law, the Earls of Arundel and Pembroke, to procure from the king Selden's final release from imprisonment. It seems that an added incentive for this intercession was the Earls' need for Selden's good services in releasing the tangled Talbot inheritance, by virtue of his combination of a good relationship with them

---

[60] See L. Stone, *The Crisis of the Aristocracy, 1558–1641* (Oxford: Clarendon, 1965) pp. 760–761 and Parker "Wrest" pp. 172–173 and 190 note 23.

    Henry Grey was an MP in 1601 (for Tavistock) and 1614 (for Bedfordshire), in the first owing to the influence of his neighbor the Third Earl of Bedford, in the second owing to his cousins the Saint John's. From 1623, having ascended to the earldom, Grey sat in the Lords, but in neither house did he leave any notable impression – either because interested in other pursuits or because of a withdrawn personality.

[61] See Christianson "Selden" ODNB, and R. Tuck, "'The Ancient law of Freedom': John Selden and the English civil war" in J. Morrill (ed.), *Reactions to the English Civil War 1642–1649* (Macmillan, 1982) pp. 238–239. It appears that Selden's presence at Wrest Park was so habitual as to have a room permanently assigned to him there. An article by James Collett-White about the seventeenth-century history of the old house at Wrest Park (demolished 1830), appearing in vols. 22–23 of *The Bedfordshire Magazine*, mentions "Mr. Selden's Chamber" describing its content as: "A bedstead, Feather bed and boulster, a pillow, 2 blanckettes, a green Rugg, Curtens, double Vallens, tester and head peece and Counterpane of a stripestuff, the Chamber hung with Tapestry Hangings, 5 old red cloth stooles, an Irish stich Couch, 2 High Velvett stooles, 1 leather Chair, a pair of Anirons with brass nobbs." We have no way of knowing which items, if any, were in the room in Selden's time, including the green carpet.

all and his prominent expertise in conveyancing of property. After Henry Grey's death in 1639, as he was childless, Wrest and the title passed on to a distant cousin, while Elizabeth and Selden moved to reside permanently at Whitefriars (the lease of which the Countess personally owned). Thereafter they lived together as one household at Whitefriars, and were possibly married there in secret. In 1651, shortly before her death, Elizabeth succeeded in her own right to the title of Baroness Furnivall, which had been in abeyance since her father's passing in 1616 – we may suppose Selden, with his expertise in titles and honors, had his part in securing her the title, perhaps a kind of parting gift to a loyal friend and companion. When the Countess died, she bequeathed her considerable personal property, including the lease on Whitefriars, to Selden, so that he continued to reside in their house until his own death there in 1654.[62]

An excellent illustration the close relationships Selden had developed by the mid-1620s with the higher aristocracy and clergy, inextricably combining personal, business and intellectual aspects, is a 1626 short letter of his to Cotton, that it is worthwhile to bring here in its entirety:

Noble Sir,
Had I not thought with assurance to have seen you again long ere this, you had long since heard from me, that so my service might have been presented to you & I might also have received the comfort of your being well. Till Saterday [sic] we dispatched not my L. of Kents office. Now that is done, I shall soon come up again. My L. of Lincoln [Bishop Williams] remember[e]d you especially when I was w[i]th him the last week at Bugdon [aka Buckden, residence of the Bishops of Lincoln], where he lives finely within doores & without, and deserves the love & honor of good men. My Lady of Kent presents you w[i]th a red deere py[e], by this bearer. For she gave it [to] me to send you. And w[i]th it, you have the entire affection of

Sept. 25,   Your most acknowledging
1626   servant
Wrest in Bedf. J. Selden

Since I wrote this, I heare of the losse of my L. of Winchester [Bishop Andrewes]. His lingering sicknesse hath, together w[i]th his age, made his best friends the easier take it, I doubt not. It was rather Nature then death that took him away, if they might be divided in him. I hartily wish his library may be kept

[62] From about 1620 Elizabeth became very close to Selden, and they spent long periods together, even while her husband was alive (with some claiming that Henry acquiesced in all aspects of their relationship). The rumor that after Henry died in 1639, Selden and Elizabeth, after moving in together, were also married in secret, is given credence by the Countess' description of herself in her will as "late wife" rather than as "widow," of Kent. See Stone *Crisis* pp. 760–761; Berkowitz *Formative* pp. 283–284; and Christianson "Selden" ODNB. Perhaps we may attribute to these circumstances Selden's remark, recorded in TT "Marriage" sec. 1 "Of all Actions of a man's life, his Marriage does least concern other people, yet of All actions of our Life, 'tis most meddled with by other people."

together, at least till we may see it. Something I have in it that I value much &
something els[e] of slighter moment. That which I would take care of for my
self, is an Armenian dictionary; I neuer saw other copy, & my L. borowed it of
me some two yeeres since. a Cedrenus also he hath of mine, w[hi]ch I must
render to Mr [William] Boswell. These two I would not willingly loose. What els
his library hath of mine, is of no great moment, but I shall know it when I come
into mine own where I have something also that was his. I shall soon see you I
hope now; though if it please you to write, I shall receive it, before I shall
see you.[63]

The letter clearly shows Selden was by this time managing (probably legal)
business for the Earl of Kent, as well as living for extended periods at their Wrest
residence. Indeed, it displays almost familiar relationships between Selden,
Cotton and the Kents, as Selden discusses with Cotton their shared concern
for the fate of Andrewes' library, while also sending him a red-deer-pie prepared
by the Countess of Kent (reputed a connoisseur of foods and medicinal
remedies). The letter also reveals the close relationship Selden had developed
with the two bishops who had interceded in his favor following the publication
of the *Historie* – staying with Williams at his residence, and mutually
exchanging rare books with Andrewes.

Another mark of Selden's rising social standing at this period, is his entering
into involvement in the affairs of the Virginia Company, which had been
chartered in 1606 to establish a colony in America (and would be forcibly
dissolved by King James in 1624). Selden appears in the company records in
1620 as an "adventurer free" (shareholder) of the company, whose prominent
shareholders included the Earl of Pembroke (one of the largest investors),
Edward Herbert, Edward Sackville Lord Buckhurst, Sir Robert Cotton and
Sir Edwin Sandys (elected in 1619 as Treasurer – which was the chief
executive officer). Selden was no mere shareholder, for on top of being
retained as feed counsel of the company around 1620–1622, and serving as a
member of the advisory committee for "the drawing up of the Patent touching
the Contract to be made with his Ma(jes)tie for the sole Importac[i]on of
Tobacco," he was also an advisor on revising the company's charter, and
involved in what a 1620 pamphlet, written to impress the public with the
better management of the company, termed as its new "Orders and
Constitutions" drawn after Sandy's election. In another 1620 publication the
company asserted that in the new colony "the laudable forme of Justice and
government used in this Realme [has been] established and followed as neere as
may be," and Selden served as advisor on drafting the "Ordinance and
Constitution" of the Virginia colony – promulgated in 1621 and one of the
most significant early American constitutional documents. Selden's
collaboration with Sandys seems to have extended beyond company matters,

[63] See Letter from Selden to Cotton, Wrest Sept. 25, 1626, in Toomer "Correspondence."

and James I suspected the company leadership in fact doubled as a nucleus for parliamentary opposition to his policies.[64]

Selden's growing involvement in public matters, together with his attempts to continue some scholarly pursuits on top of his legal practice, obviously left him very little time or inclination to attend to other responsibilities. Thus when selected in 1623 by the members of the small Lyon's Inn as their Reader (that is, as lecturer to new students), he repeatedly declined the appointment. The response of the Inner Temple "Parliament" to what it regarded as a dereliction of communal duty came in November 1624, when Selden was fined 20 pounds, and disqualified from ever becoming Reader or Master of the Bench, as well as from participating in the common meals with the inn members in their hall (he was restored to common meals in June 1625, but not then from his disqualification as bencher). We may give here, at the point he rose to public prominence, the description of Selden's physical appearance in his mature years, as given by Aubrey, and borne out by extant portraits: very tall for the period (about 6 feet of height) and rather lean, with a sharp oval face, a long nose and somewhat bulging gray eyes – all in all, a notable figure, if a far from handsome one.[65]

Obviously, the controversy surrounding the *Historie* had revealed to a wide audience Selden's ability, and willingness, to turn his considerable scholarly capabilities towards issues with political relevance. This was especially significant in early-modern England's public culture, where historical precedents and records wielded extraordinary authority, and therefore influenced political deliberations. Finding precedents was as effective as parliamentary legislation, as a way of establishing a rule or institution, but with the added benefit that it did not need the assent of political opponents. Thus the assertive Parliaments of the early seventeenth century were

---

[64] See S.M. Kingsbury (ed.), *The Records of the Virginia Company of London* (Washington, 1906), vol. i p. 395, vol. ii p. 98; W.S. Craven, *The Virginia Company of London, 1606–1626* (Williamsburg, Virginia 350th celebration corporation, 1957) pp. 28–29; N. Malcolm, "Hobbes, Sandys and the Virginia Company" in *Historical Journal* 24/2 (1981) p. 307; Toomer *Scholarship* p. 320; Berkowitz *Formative* p. 57. In the summer of 1620 King James I opposed the re-election of Sandys as treasurer of the Virginia Company, indicating instead some acceptable other names including the previous Treasurer Smythe, and Sir Thomas Roe. See in *A Short Collection of the most remarkable passages from the Originall to the Dissolution of the Virginia Company* (1651) pp. 7–8. Sandys therefore withdrew his candidature, but remained a leading figure in the company, by engineering the election as his replacement in the treasury, of his ally Henry Wriothesley, Third Earl of Southampton. In February 1621 Sandys prepared, with Selden's assistance, a new patent whereby the title of the chief official was to be changed from treasurer to governor, and in the following June he laid before the company his "Propositions considerable for the better managing of the business of the company and advancing of the plantation of Virginia" see in *Abstract of Proceedings of the Virginia Company* (Richmond, Virginia, 1888) vol. I pp. 79–86.

[65] "He was very tall, I guess about six foot high; sharp oval face; head not very big; long nose inclined to one side; full popping eye (gray)." Aubrey *Lives* p. 283.

increasingly seeking precedents for their political claims, in the parliamentary rolls lodged in the Tower of London. At the same time, King James was also employing scholars to comb records, in order to unearth precedents for non-parliamentary ways to raise revenue (one result of which was the revival of the order of baronets).[66]

Against this background, Selden's expertise in legal scholarship was soon enough seized upon as a significant asset, in early 1621, when the House of Lords, drafted him to assist its activities. First Selden produced together with Henry Elsyng, the Clerk of Parliament, a draft roll of standing orders, and later, following a motion by the Earl of Arundel about many privileges anciently belonging to the House of Lords, that "by disuse and want of putting in practice are now almost lost," the peers created a Committee for Privileges, to establish and formally record their rights and procedures. The committee employed Selden to produce such a record, and the result was the House of Lords' *Book of Precedents* (or *Book of Privileges*), designed as a handbook for the peers as individuals as well as when assembled as a body in Parliament – the original copy was kept in the House of Lords for reference, and is there to this day. A version of the treatise was printed in 1642, when of renewed relevance, under the title *The Priviledges of the Baronage in England* (other works with similar names have nothing to do with Selden). Its most consequential section dealt with precedents of the Lords' judicial functions (including the procedure of impeachment), undoubtedly assisting in the successful effort of the 1621 Parliament, to revive them after a long hiatus. The revived judicial authority of the Lords was immediately exercised to prosecute notoriously rapacious monopolists Sir Francis Mitchell and MP Giles Mompesson, as well as the Lord Chancellor, Francis Bacon, Viscount St Alban. On the encouragement of Sir Edwin Sandys the Commons too attempted to assume a judicial role by passing judgment on a barrister named Edward Floyd (or Flood) for having spoken disparagingly of the Princess Elizabeth of Bohemia and her husband the Elector Palatine – respectively daughter and son-in-law of King James. But after a conference of both Houses of Parliament failed to agree on a judiciary role for the lower house, a solution was reached by the Commons annulling their decision, while the Lords assumed the judgment upon themselves.[67]

---

[66] Zaller *Legitimacy* pp. 583, 604.

[67] Christianson *Discourse* pp. 88–90. Ironically, the now forcibly unemployed Bacon was later in the same year aided by Selden in research and consultation for gathering sources for a history of Henry VII. In 1617 Selden had dedicated *A Brief Discourse Touching on the Office of Lord Chancellor of England* to Bacon on his appointment to that office, but at that time the two were not personally acquainted. Later they developed an obviously cordial relationship, since a version of Bacon's will named Selden as a literary executor, whose advice was to be sought concerning publications or suppression of manuscripts. There are even claims that Selden's report to the Lords in 1621 was so worded by him as to obliquely assist Bacon in his plight, but the evidence for this is indecisive. See Toomer *Scholarship* pp. 322–324 and Aikin *Lives* pp. 13–14.

In June of 1621, after Parliament had been adjourned, warrants were issued for the arrests of Henry Wriothesley, Third Earl of Southampton, Sir Edwin Sandys and Selden. As the warrants had been issued on the orders of the king "for special causes & reasons of state knowne unto himself" and no public charge was ever presented, various conjectures have been since offered as to the reason for the imprisonment. Some suggest Selden's assistance to the Lords in establishing their judicature, others for some possible involvement in the attempt to vest a power of judicature in the Commons, or perhaps connected to the three men's involvement in the Virginia Company. Possibly it was a combination of several, or the cause might have been altogether different, but we shall apparently never know for sure.[68]

Fortunately for Selden, he was treated quite courteously by his jailer, Sir Robert Ducie, the Sheriff of London, and though his papers were temporarily sequestered, he had access to a manuscript of Eadmer's medieval *History* so that he could occupy himself in his captivity with preparing the work for publication (it was printed in 1623). It appears that the intervention of Lancelot Andrewes, Bishop of Winchester, as well as of John Williams, recently appointed as Bishop of Lincoln and as Lord Keeper of the Great Seal, obtained for Selden a release after about five weeks. When the same Parliament later reconvened, it was the Commons who now sought Selden's assistance for preparing their Protestation of 18 December 1621, in which they asserted "that the liberties, franchises, privileges, and jurisdiction of Parliament are the ancient and undoubted birth-right and inheritance of the subjects of England," against the king's demand that they refrain from discussing matters bearing on foreign policy. The protestation so enraged James I that he dissolved Parliament at once, and erased the text of the Protestation from its journal with his own hands. Happily, from Selden's perspective, this time he was not implicated in the fracas, and no arrest or imprisonment followed.[69]

Evidently the services that Selden supplied to Parliament as an advisor had not gone unnoticed, for when the next Parliament was elected, powerful patrons assisted his finding a seat in it. He initially sought a place as representative for Nottingham, where the Earls of Shrewsbury (related to the Kents and Arundels), had some influence – but obviously not enough, since the corporation there rejected Selden's application. Instead he was elected for

---

[68] The affairs of the Virginia Company seem to me the most likely cause for the imprisonment. As noted above, Selden was a close collaborator of Sandys in the affairs of the Virginia Company, just when it entered a course of collision with the American policies of James I in 1620–1621, and it was in June 1621 that Sandys, after learning of the king's opposition to his re-election as treasurer, ensured the election in his stead of his close friend and ally Wriothesley.

[69] See Christianson "Selden" ODNB; Toomer *Scholarship* pp. 320–326, and Zaller, *Legitimacy* p. 748 note 179. See also Richard Hutton, *The Diary of Sir Richard Hutton 1614–1639*, W.R. Prest ed. (Selden Society, 1993) p. 39.

Lancaster on 2 March 1624 (possibly through the help of Arundel or Pembroke), and made his maiden speech in the Commons on 18 March.[70]

In the 1624 Parliament, Selden sat in various committees, and was consulted on a number of matters where his experience in finding legal precedents was necessary, so that he produced, for example, the precedents which assisted Carew Raleigh's (son of Sir Walter) restitution bill, as well as finding support for the claims of three Buckinghamshire boroughs that had petitioned for the restoring their ancient rights of electing MPs. However, he was not a particularly prominent member of this Parliament, probably due to a combination of his status as a novice in the House of Commons, together with the fact that, relative to many Parliaments before and after it, this one was devoid of serious conflicts with the crown. One of Selden's few notable interventions was in a debate on a bill to abolish all trial by battle, on 8 May, when (undoubtedly also as the author of a book on the subject, the *Duello*) he warned that this was "an ancient fundamental law not to be taken away with a breath without commitment." Perhaps Selden's most prominent activity in this Parliament was his stand with the minority in the Commons which opposed Buckingham's drive for a war with Spain. When a speedy decision on supplies for the war was demanded, Selden rose to speak, arguing that although he will not speak to the merit of the great matter discussed "being so young a parliament man," he nevertheless noted that his acquaintance with the journals of both Houses of Parliament showed him such an important business had never been so precipitated. He was appointed with Cotton to search for precedents on the appointment by Parliament of treasurers of war. On April 1, when he tried to oppose on technical grounds Buckingham's proposed appointment of Secretary of State Sir Edward Conway (father of Selden's friend, the future Second Viscount Conway) to a committee that would draft the public justification for the conflict with Spain, the house promptly overruled him. One last significant activity of Selden in this Parliament was his objection to what he regarded as politically motivated allegations against his ally and friend Lord Keeper Williams (who was increasingly in conflict with Buckingham), concerning some dispute of the latter with Lady Darcy, but his intervention on this matter was accused of partisanship and interrupted.[71]

---

[70] Parliamentary seats for the borough of Lancaster were traditionally controlled by the Chancellor of the Duchy of Lancaster. In 1624 Thomas Fanshawe, an Inner Templar and former auditor for the Duchy, and Sir Humphrey May, the Chancellor, were returned. When May chose to sit for Leicester, where he had also been elected, Selden was selected to replace him – probably on the advice of Pembroke or Arundel (especially in light of Selden's cooperation with the latter in matters of privilege in 1621), since both peers, like May, were political adversaries of Buckingham. See P. Watson & R. Sgroi, "May, Humphrey" in A. Thrush and J.P. Ferris (eds.) *The History of Parliament: the House of Commons 1604–1629* (2010 – retrieved 27 October 2014, www.historyofparliamentonline.org/volume/1604–1629/member/may-humphrey-1574–1630) henceforth HOPO. See also *Records of the Borough of Nottingham*, W.L. Stevenson ed. (1882) vol. iv p. 387; Christianson *Discourse* pp. 92–96.

[71] P. Hunneyball, "Selden, John" entry in HOPO (2010 retrieved from internet 27 October 2014).

Selden was apparently not a member of the short-lived 1625 Parliament, but he entered the 1626 Parliament, after being elected for two seats, Ilchester (controlled by Sir Robert Phelips) and Great Bedwyn, (controlled by the Seymours) and chose to sit for the latter.[72] In this Parliament he cooperated closely with the Seymour connection in the Lords and the Commons, as well as with other MPs like his friend Dr. Samuel Turner, in opposition to the court and especially to Buckingham. His activities in this Parliament marked Selden's emergence, together with Eliot and Pym, to the first line of parliamentary figures, assisted by the fact that the king had disqualified six "sticklers" among the established parliamentary leaders – among them Coke, Phelips, Wentworth, as well as Sir Francis Seymour – by the ploy of appointing them to honorary offices that precluded holders from sitting in the Commons. Coke, regardless of his having been appointed Sheriff of Buckinghamshire (required by ordinance to reside in their shire), attempted to challenge the exclusion ploy, by having himself elected MP for Norfolk, and Selden took a leading role in supporting his attempt. Selden's first recorded speech of this Parliament addressed this issue, and he later challenged the validity of the ordinance that had been approved by the Lords only, while the majority of the Commons was far more nervous about such a course – but on 9 June he succeeded in convincing the Commons to at least grant Coke parliamentary immunity until his status as a member was resolved. These activities of Selden were apparently coordinated with a parallel effort by his ally in the Lords, the Earl of Hertford, to prevent the king's attempt at barring Bishop Williams and the Earl of Bristol from taking their seats in the upper house. However, this wrangling about excluded members soon took second place to a wider conflict that was emerging between Parliament and the King. At first Parliament prepared a remonstrance of grievances to be addressed, but as it soon transpired that King Charles' dismissive attitude to it made such an effort a dead end, another course of action had to be sought. It thus came to be that the defining feature of the 1626 Parliament was the crystallization of the now usual grievances about the crown's demand for subsidies, and the complaints about unapproved taxation, into an attempt to impeach the royal favorite, the Duke of Buckingham.[73]

---

[72] Ilchester had long lost its parliamentary representation, and was only re-enfranchised in 1621, perhaps with Selden's assistance, after proof had been obtained of it having been represented in the past. The seat came to be under the influence of Phelips. See A. Davidson, "Phelips, Sir Robert" in HOPO (2010 – retrieved from internet 6 April 2015).

[73] Among Edward Littleton's papers, there is a draft of the 1626 remonstrance, addressed to Selden, many of whose words are taken virtually without alteration from the 1621 Commons protestation that James I had torn with his own hands from the Journal of the House of Commons – and that Selden seems to have had a hand in composing. See J. Sommerville "Parliament, Privilege, and the Liberties of the Subject" in J.H. Hexter (ed.), *Parliament and Liberty* (Stanford, California University Press, 1992) pp. 71–72.

It was against this background that Selden emerged into to a leadership position in the Commons, in no small part due to his track record of antagonism to Buckingham. It appears that Selden had a major role in preparing the remonstrance of grievances, and when that course failed, he was appointed by the Commons to be one of the managers of Buckingham's impeachment. Selden must have drawn some pleasure from being assigned specifically the fourth and fifth charges (out of 13) against the Duke – those having to do with the latter's "not guarding the seas," and apparently based at least partially on materials from Selden's *Mare Clausum*, which some years before the Duke had prevented from being published.[74]

Another important development Selden had a role in was his leading part in the attack against the Court of High Commission (before which Selden himself had been forced to appear in 1619). In 1625, Sir Robert Howard (Arundel's cousin), had been examined and excommunicated by the Court of High Commission for his adultery with Lady Purbeck, wife of Buckingham's brother (and daughter of Coke). Howard had nominally been a Member of Parliament when tried, so that the trial was formally a breach of parliamentary privilege, and Selden argued that if the Commons failed to act on this issue, they would create a precedent putting all of them in danger of future prosecution. He demanded that not only the verdict against Howard be voided, but also that the lay members of the court be questioned, and if need be punished, by Parliament. Selden's position ultimately carried the day, and after the lay members of the Court of High Commission were instructed to declare the sentence void or face punitive measures, the verdict was annulled in June and the precedent that Parliament may overturn a judgment of the Court of High Commission was clearly established.[75]

Parallel to his leading role in the Commons, it appears that Selden also had a significant, if more covert role, in the important developments in the House of Lords during that same Parliament. On 4 March 1626, at the king's instruction, the Earl of Arundel had been detained, at first in the Tower and later under house arrest, reputedly because of the secret marriage of the Earl's son to Elizabeth Stuart – against the king's wishes and without his authorization. However, there is convincing evidence that the real motivation for the arrest was the major role that Arundel was playing in the opposition to Buckingham, and in the attempt to impeach the Duke. Arundel was a prominent stickler for the rights and privileges of the peerage, and on 9 February he had taken the initiative to have the Clerk of Parliament read aloud before the Lords all the standing rules and orders of the upper house, which had been formulated on his initiative in 1621 with Selden's assistance. Moreover, on 20 February, when the issue of the habitual absence of many peers was raised, it was Arundel who moved that the Committee for Privileges, on

[74] Toomer *Scholarship* pp. 326–327; Johnson *Memoirs* pp. 119–120.
[75] Hunneyball "Selden" HOPO.

which he sat, "meet and consider of a newe order" for dealing with the problem. The result was a far-reaching motion for reforming the system by which peers had been hitherto able to amass an unlimited number of proxy-votes from those members who were not attending the House of Lords. The system had enabled the court to create a bloc of votes which usually managed to control the upper house by a combination of the Lords on the Privy Council, the bishops' mostly following the king's wishes, and the proxies. On 25 February the House of Lords voted on a reform, formulated by the Earl of Hertford and the Viscount Saye and Sele, that would enable in the future only a maximum of two proxies per peer, and it eventually passed with a narrow margin in favor, supplied by Arundel (and his four proxies...). Regardless of the fact that opposition peers like Arundel and Pembroke did lose some of the proxies they used to hold, the court was hit far harder, with Buckingham having held 13 proxies (out of a nominal membership of about 125 Lords). The reform effectively broke the stranglehold that the court had had on the upper house for a generation, and the effects were evident soon enough, since already on 4 March, the Lords gave permission to the Commons to proceed with the impeachment of Buckingham. The arrest of Arundel on the very same day could only raise suspicions as to its connection with political events, and while his personal attitude in detainment was one of outward passivity, the peers were soon clamoring that precedents showed the imprisonment of the Earl at the time of Parliament was a breach of privilege, so that on 18 April they unanimously voted to demand his release. The king attempted to delay his answer while parliamentary business continued, but on 2 June the Lords decided they would hereafter conduct no other business until Arundel's release (following the lead of a similar step by the Commons that had brought about the liberation of Eliot from imprisonment). On 5 June Arundel was released, and effectively advanced the precedent for the right of peers to attendance without restraint, which would be formally recognized with the eventual readmission of the long-excluded Earl of Bristol and Bishop of Lincoln (John Williams) in the next Parliament of 1628. With the break-up of the proxy-based stranglehold by the court and the House of Lords' newly found control of its membership and attendance, a truly "newe order" had indeed emerged, heralding what was to become an increasingly assertive and unpredictable upper house, in the Parliament of 1628–9 and even more so in the 1640s. The exact role Selden had in the emergence of this "newe order" is hard to reconstruct, but his long-standing alliance with Arundel on matters concerning the privileges of the upper house, the crucial importance that mustering precedents had in establishing the peers, right of attendance, and the leading place taken in the proxy reform and in Arundel's release, by Hertford, closest ally of Selden – all point to the latter having had in these matters, at the very least an important advisory role, and perhaps more.[76]

[76] See especially V.F. Snow, "The Arundel Case, 1626" in *Historian*, 26:4 (1964) pp. 337–347.

The impeachment of Buckingham was stopped dead in its tracks, by the king's abrupt dissolution of Parliament in June 1626. But far from resolving the conflict, this stratagem only succeeded in covering it up, so that it continued to simmer and gain steam while concealed from view. In the wake of the 1626 dissolution of Parliament Eliot was arrested, and it appears that, with others, Selden was in some danger of suffering the same fate. The Attorney General, Sir Robert Heath, demanded from a number of MPs, including Selden, information about the charges that had been in preparation against Buckingham. Selden's reply was a letter dated 21 June 1626, in which, by a mix of evasion and insolence he declined to answer Heat's questions. He then found it expedient to withdraw from the capital to another prolonged stay at Wrest Park with the Kents, in this case leisure undoubtedly married to prudence.[77]

Failure to obtain funding through Parliament forced the Privy Council to seek out other means by which to raise the money, troops and supplies needed to continue the ongoing struggle against the Habsburgs and their new French allies, that produced the Anglo-French War of 1627–1629. The result was the so-called Forced Loan, and when in the fall of 1627, five men imprisoned for refusing to "lend" their money to the king petitioned the court of King's Bench for bail through a writ of *habeas corpus* (and thus for being tried under Common Law), the court assigned counsel for each of the five, with Selden ordered to represent Sir Edmund Hampden. This case, which became known as the Case of the Five Knights' (or Darnel's), was a highly unusual one for Selden, since most of his legal career involved property law and he seldom appeared personally in court. Indeed, as far as we know, this was the only high-profile case with criminal implications that he ever handled (and one of only two of his cases for which copious evidence survives). In this hearing, with wide-ranging constitutional ramifications he approached his argument not only as an advocate but also as historian and constitutionalist. Selden brought precedents and technical arguments to defend his client, but he also acknowledged that ultimately the case would be decided by the meaning ascribed to the statutory foundations upon which the issue turned. He argued that imprisonment without trial was against the spirit of the "statute of Magna Carta," which stated that no free man shall be imprisoned but by "legem terrae" (the law of the land), a term that, he argued, should be understood to mean "due course of law." Selden proposed to the court that from this meaning it followed that imprisonment was to be had only "either by presentment or indictment."

Another sign of Selden's growing stature in Parliament was his retention as counsel by the Lords in the hearings on the proper descent of the earls of Oxford, when Robert de Vere argued (ultimately successfully) that he should be recognized as Nineteenth Earl and heir to his second cousin, the Eighteenth Earl. See on this Selden's mentioning of his discovery of "three Sonnes at once which are omitted in the descents of that most noble Family" of the earls of Oxford, in his prefatory letter to Augustine Vincent's *A Discoverie of Errours in the First Edition of the Catalogue of Nobility* (1622), 8 of 11 pages, not paginated.

[77] Barnes *Shaping* p. 172.

The court did not accept this interpretation, and the judgment went against the five, but even more ominously, Chief Justice Hyde stated that, if no cause for the imprisonment had been declared, then "it is to be presumed to be for matter of state," something which took it outside the authority of the court. Obviously such a view opened the door for an unforeseeable authority of arbitrary imprisonment that would be outside the jurisdiction of the courts, under a blanket "matter of state" justification. Such arguments on top of allowing for unrestricted arbitrary imprisonment undoubtedly also reminded Selden of his own arbitrary imprisonment under similar pretenses, a few years earlier.[78]

In the spring of 1628, only a few months after the court's ruling in the Five Knights' Case, a new Parliament convened and swiftly took up the case as emblematic of the problems of extra-parliamentary taxation and unlawful imprisonment – widely regarded as the marks of arbitrary government, hiding behind "matters of state." It was in this context that Selden came to the fore in the Parliament of 1628–1629 and established himself as one of the commanding figures in the Commons, second only to Eliot. Elected for Ludgershall in Wiltshire, again thanks to the influence of the Earl of Hertford, Selden swiftly secured a formidable reputation, as reflected in the words of no less a parliamentarian than Phelips, who only two weeks into the new Parliament referred to him, on 31 March 1628, as one "who never mistakes or so seldom as no man can do less."[79]

Even before the new Parliament assembled, there were widespread expectations that it would bring to a head a whole set of issues that had been brewing for a number of years. These expectations were translated into the election to it of prominent parliamentarians like Phelips and Coke, who had been barred from standing in 1626. Thus the 1628 Commons leadership, combining the returning old hands and the new guard that had emerged in their absence, was one of the most impressive groups to ever assemble together in the long history of English Parliaments.

On 13 March 1628, four days before the opening of the new Parliament, a strategy meeting of the Commons' leadership was held in Sir Robert Cotton's house, apparently including besides the host (MP for Castle Rising, and probably also his son Thomas, elected to one of two St. Germans seats in the Eliot influence) and Selden, also Sir Edward Coke, Sir John Eliot, Sir Robert Phelips, Sir Thomas Wentworth and his brother-in-law Denzil Holles, as well as John Pym. The meeting endorsed the course advocated by Selden and Coke, that the first and foremost issue of the session should be the reassertion of the ancient laws of the country: what would eventually become the "Petition of Right."[80]

---

[78] Barnes *Shaping* pp. 172–174. See also Christianson "Selden" ODNB.
[79] Hunneyball "Selden" HOPO; J.P. Sommerville, *Royalists and Patriots: Politics and Ideology in England 1603–1640* (Longman, 1999, 2nd edition) pp. 203–204.
[80] Fry "Selden" DNB and Toomer *Scholarship* pp. 328–329.

In the new Parliament Selden was named as member of fifty-seven committees and six subcommittees, ranking among the top-five committeemen. In addition, his ninety-eight recorded speeches in the House of Commons and in the Committee Of The Whole, as well as twenty-six additional speeches in the conferences of the two houses, helped to secure him a clear position of leadership. On 27 March he rose to speak on the issue of arbitrary imprisonment following from the Five Knight's Case, stating that

> I profess, though once I was of counsel and then spoke for my fee for the gentlemen in their *habeas corpus*, yet now I speak according to my knowledge and conscience to discharge a duty to my country.

He then went on to attack the arguments from reason of state, proposing that although, as he testified about himself, "I understand not matters of state," nevertheless in his view "[n]o matter of state can alter the law." Ingeniously, the reason he gave for this apparently startling assertion was the very indefinite nature of "reason of state" – since such matters are by definition not to be known or meddled with by subjects, they cannot be used in the regular law courts, since they may become "a word for any king to try the courage of his judges, and to suppose there is a cause of state, when perhaps there is no cause[.]" Moreover, acknowledging that the language and the issues were being drawn based in part on foreign examples, he employed his extraordinary erudition to turn the tables on those who proposed the relevance of such examples. He declared that as the king's supporters "tell us of foreign government," where a right of arbitrary imprisonment exists, he had seriously looked into this, and "I had read histories and lately for this purpose (for you know where I made use of them in abundance)," with the result being he had become convinced that, at least formally, "[i]n point of law there is no prince in Christendom that claims this right."[81]

On 4 April the Commons carried a motion by Coke to request a conference with the Lords concerning "certain ancient and fundamental liberties of England," and deputized four of their number as representatives – Coke himself, Dudley Digges, Edward Littleton and Selden. The speeches each of the four made at the conference, which took place on 7 April, reportedly consisted of one sheet of paper for Digges, 9 sheets of for Coke, 12 sheets for Littleton, and a full 60 sheets for Selden. The later presentation in the Commons, orchestrated by the four, of the conference with the Lords is often regarded as one of the constitutional high points of the "common law mind" in action – and the conference indeed opened the way for a grand restatement of

---

[81] Berkowitz *Formative* pp. 142–143; Barnes *Shaping* pp. 172–174; and Christianson *Discourse* pp. 161–162. The 1628 Parliament also showcased the talents and effectiveness of the small but disciplined Selden-Seymour connection. The 191 speeches made by Selden, Seymour and Kyrton, outnumbered the 174 speeches made by the whole of the 24 MPs identified as Buckingham's network. Proportions were similar for committee memberships, with the 24 Buckinghamites' 106 committee memberships barely outnumbering the 3 Seymourites' 101.

rights and liberties of Englishmen, that was intended to put to rest fears of arbitrary government, and offer the opportunity for a renewed atmosphere of trust between King and Parliament.[82]

Between 26 April and 7 May, as the houses debated various ways by which to ensure the liberties of Englishmen, the reports show Selden to have become unusually silent, only seldom and laconically intervening in the debates. It appears that this resulted from his disagreement with the rest of the parliamentary leadership about what kind of document they should pursue – while Selden (with Eliot) preferred a bill of rights that would enter the statute book, but also necessitate a frontal confrontation with the king, for most of the leadership, including Wentworth, the Seymours and Digges, a petition that would formally restate existing rights would suffice.[83]

In the event, the course agreed upon was a petition, as a document that could more easily muster the agreement of both houses, and the king. After rounds of wrangling about the wording, including arguments from natural law, political theory and English tradition, a document was agreed upon, that would be a reiteration of the "substance of Magna Carta and the best of those laws concerning the liberty of the subject in their person and goods." After much debate in the House of Lords, including such "tongue-combat [as] was never heard in the Upper House," the opposition peers, among whose leaders were prominent Selden allies such as John Williams Bishop of Lincoln and John Digby Earl of Bristol, recently released from imprisonment and reinstated as members of that house, convinced a majority of the peers to support the petition. A restating of constitutional principles as supreme over the king's will and even over the developments of legal practice, the petition was ratified by both houses on 26–27 May. The king, reluctant about what he saw as unnecessary binding of his hands, gave a vague wording to his acceptance of the petition on 2 June, but the houses demanded full ratification according to the traditional formula for a parliamentary bill, "soit droit fait comme est desire" and the king finally relented and supplied this on 7 June. The ratification of the petition was met with widespread relief, and the ringing of church bells as well as the lighting of bonfires was reported.[84]

However, exactly as Selden had feared when he preferred a bill to a petition, just as the ratification had been granted, disagreements appeared about its legal

---

[82] Burgess describes the presentation as the clearest example of the "common law mind" in action, when under pressure. See Burgess *Absolute* pp. 205–206.

[83] Berkowitz *Formative* pp. 164–171. Coke's position is unclear, with Berkowitz thinking Coke was closer to Selden's preference for statute, while Christianson conjectures Coke tended more towards Wentworth and the Seymours. See Christianson *Discourse* pp. 128–129, 133, 147–148.

[84] Berkowitz *Formative* pp. 160–199 – especially 166–167, 171, 191. On the debate about the petition in the Lords, the role of Lincoln and Bristol, and the careful coordination of opposition leadership in both houses see J. Stoddard Flemion, "The struggle for the Petition of Right in the House of Lords: The Study of an Opposition Party Victory" in *The Journal of Modern History* 45/2 (1973), pp. 193–210, and especially pp. 197–201, 203–204, 207–209.

status and interpretation. Thus, the agreement that was supposed to heal the rift in the relationship between King and Parliament only served to exacerbate it. As complaints against the activities of the government were rapidly building up again in Parliament, the king intimated that it should desist from attacks on Buckingham or face prorogation. The result was the very opposite of what the king had intended, and the Commons erupted in an uproar against what they regarded as a threat to their fundamental freedom of speech. On 11 June 1628 the House of Commons constituted itself into a Committee Of The Whole, to decide on an appropriate course of action, and an anonymously authored poem of the period "Upon the nameinge of the Duke of Buckingham the Remonstrance" opens its description of the session with the lines:

> Excuse me Eliott if I heare name thee
> the tyme requires itt since fewe honest bee
> and learned Selden for thy pregnant witt
> to be then named lett itt not seeme unfitt
> I shall not spare to put you two in one,
> since honest Longe hath made the motion
> tis due you to the world be understood
> more then Roomes Cato, hee who dust be good[85]

Sir Edward Coke made a motion that the Commons should acquaint the king of their opinion that Buckingham was the cause of the misgovernment, and Selden seconded the motion, proposing a declaration against the Duke, which was passed by acclamation. On 26 June, less than two weeks after the ratification of the petition that should have restored the peace between Parliament and King, the latter saw no other alternative than proroguing Parliament.[86]

After the shock of Buckingham's assassination on 23 August, many hoped that the relations between King and Parliament could be set on better tracks, now that what was widely regarded as the malign influence of the Duke had been removed. The King reconvened Parliament in early 1629, probably expecting that with the most polarizing figure in government gone, royal policies might receive a better parliamentary reception. However, as the session progressed, any such expectations turned out to be misplaced, and what unfolded instead was a series of successive clashes between King and Parliament. On 22 January an MP and merchant named John Rolle (brother of Henry, the Inner Templar friend of Selden, and later Chief Justice of the King's Bench) informed the Commons that his goods had been seized in the

---

[85] "Upon the nameinge of the Duke of Buckingham the Remonstrance" in BL MS Harley 6057, fols. 52v–53v.

[86] Aikin *Lives* p. 63. Incidentally, during the 1628 Parliament Selden was again required by the Lords as counsel, this time to assist in the case of Lady Purbeck, Buckingham's sister-in-law and Coke's daughter (in connection with the case of Sir Robert Howard which he had treated in the 1626 Parliament).

autumn, as he had refused to pay Tunnage and Poundage. Since the time of the seizure coincided with what had been intended to be a session of Parliament (but had not in fact been convened), a debate ensued about the question if this consisted a breach of parliamentary privilege, with Selden leading among those keen to pursue the issue. The Commons constituted themselves as a Committee Of The Whole for Merchants, and a number of debates and subcommittees followed, attempting to establish various aspects of the issue, mainly if the "custom farmers" (or "customers" – that is, those who were collecting the custom payments under a contract with the state) had confiscated the goods on their own authority or on behalf of the crown. On 19 February Selden insisted that the matter of the customers' possible breach of privilege in confiscating the property of MPs be looked into immediately, warning "if not they will come shortly and take the mace from before you, and say they have a commission for it." On the next day, Selden conducted a close examination of the customers' contract and concluded that according to its terms they were not in fact acting directly on behalf of the king. This seemed to divert the issue from a direct confrontation with the crown, and finally with some hesitations the Commons ratified on 23 February the proposition that privilege should be granted to Rolle's property. However, the King's reaction, taking responsibility for the customers' actions and commanding Parliament to desist from pursuing the matter, undermined Selden's whole strategy, and although he proposed that, like any other court, Parliament should proceed in its business regardless of royal commands, the Commons refused to follow him on this course.[87]

Nevertheless, this momentary setback did not derail the general course of the session, progressing as it was towards a total clash with the king. Eventually, on 2 March 1629, Eliot brought forth a strongly worded protestation in three articles denouncing Tunnage and Poundage, as well as alleged dangerous intentions by the government in matters of religion, and accusing innovators in religion and government of being capital enemies to the kingdom and commonwealth – thus he firmly establishing the connection between religious and political issues, that would come to shake England to its core in the middle decades of the century. Eliot claimed that while

---

[87] Hunneyball "Selden" HOPO. The importance of the John Rolle incident is in its presenting of Selden's clear belief in a division between persons and functions of institutions, even between the person of the king and his officers or courts of law. Selden refused to regard acts of the parliamentary committee censuring the officers a challenge to the person of the king: he regarded the question before the Commons as one of mere judicial proceedings, and accordingly held that Parliament had the privilege, no less than any other court at Westminster, to proceed in its judgment notwithstanding whatever command it may receive, for even the king could not pre-empt the course of law, nor judge a case directly. This view was something Charles I (and later Hobbes) absolutely denied, and the Commons at this point relented. Selden's view was a constitutionalist and impersonal one, Charles' view was one of fusion between king and office, and of supremacy of his will. See discussion in Zaller *Legitimacy* pp. 694–695.

Buckingham was dead, "he lives on in the Bishop of Winchester [Richard Neile] and my lord treasurer Weston" who were spearheading the dangerous intentions of the government. As Speaker Finch, according to the wish of the king, refused to put the motion to the vote, and attempted to adjourn the meeting, with dissolution expected in its trail, the Commons erupted in shouts, with a clear majority of members supporting the protestation to be read and put to the vote. Selden rose to speak for the only time on that day, and while he disassociated himself from the ferocity of the personal attack against Weston, he criticized on constitutional grounds Finch's stance, and moved that Eliot's paper be read before the house. When the Speaker refused to relent, what followed was no less than constitutional breakdown: with the House of Commons in an uproar, two MPs (Denzil Holles and Sir Walter Long) forcibly held the Speaker in his chair, thus denying him the possibility of stopping the session by leaving; Meanwhile, to prevent the entrance of the king's message announcing adjournment of the session, some other MP (apparently Miles Hobart) bolted from within the doors of the hall. The text of Eliot's Protestation was then put to the house, but as he had just destroyed the pages of his protestation in desperation at the Speaker's refusal to put it to the vote, it was now presented to the Commons from memory, and between the banging on the doors of Black Rod, the officer sent by the king to announce the adjournment of the house, on the one side, and the loud complaints of the Speaker at being forcibly held in his chair, on the other side, the protestation was passed by acclamation, as the session closed. It would be the last meeting of the Commons for more than a decade, for on 10 March, by the highly unusual procedure of coming to the House of Lords without sending for the Commons, Charles dissolved Parliament and began a decade-long attempt to rule without it.[88]

Through the 1620s, Selden had proceeded by degrees to become one of the most prominent figures in Parliament, first as an advisor, then as a prominent MP and finally as a Commons leader in 1628–1629. His abilities as both learned lawyer and effective political operator made him an indispensable figure in Parliament, and one of the main architects of the Petition of Right. His performance in this latter Parliament was undoubtedly the high point of his career as MP and political leader. But his (eventually justified) misgivings about passing a petition instead of a bill, and the tumultuous end of Parliament in 1629, showed the limitations of the English constitutional tradition as it was then. Without shared political foundations and rules, the constitution could not function, and complete political breakdown would follow, as England was to learn to its own cost, in blood and fire. In his *Table-Talk*, the dilemma at the basis of the conflict, the inadequacy of legal rules that are not backed by political institutions, was plainly addressed by Selden:

---

[88] Berkowitz *Formative* pp. 233–237.

The King's Oath is not security enough for our Property, for he swears to Govern according to Law; now the Judges they interpret the Law, and what Judges can be made to do, we know.[89]

1.6 "PLACES NEVER BEFORE TRODDEN BY THE FOOT": 1630–1639

The chaotic collapse of the parliamentary session on 2 March 1629 had exposed a constitutional impasse that Charles I now set out to resolve, and for the next 11 years he attempted to do without Parliament altogether, in what became known as the period of Personal Rule. On 3 March, warrants were issued for the arrest and confinement in the Tower of nine members of the Commons, regarded as leaders in the events that had prompted the dissolution: Selden, Sir John Eliot, Sir Peter Heyman, Sir Miles Hobart (or Hubbard, his son married Hampden's daughter), Sir Walter Long, William Coryton, Denzil Holles, William Strode and Benjamin Valentine (elected for one of the two St. Germans seats controlled by the Eliot family).

Shortly after being arrested, they were examined, but refused to answer questions regarding acts done in Parliament. There ensued a battle of wills between, on the one side, the prisoners, who insisted they had done nothing wrong and that if there were accusations against them, these should be judged by the courts, and on the other side, the king, who insisted that as the price for their release they should acknowledge they had done wrong, and submit to his mercy. The stakes of the struggle of wills are reflected in a proclamation issued by the king on 27 March, threatening with punishment anyone caught spreading dangerous rumors about the legitimacy of Eliot's three resolutions put before the Commons in its tumultuous final session. Obviously, it reflected the fear that popular support for the prisoners, might threaten public order.[90]

The king wished to try the prisoners on a charge of treason, but Attorney General Heath, after holding a conference with the judges of Star Chamber, could not find a way to charge any of the prisoners directly with such an offense as defined by law, and finally concocted an accusation under more indefinite terms. Heath also discovered that on 27 February 1629, the Friday before the contentious session, a group of Commons' leaders, including Selden, Eliot, Coryton and others, had dined together at the Three Cranes tavern, and he attempted to find out if parliamentary strategy had been discussed – since by occurring outside Parliament, it was liable to trial – but failed to uncover anything of the sort.[91]

---

[89] TT "The King" sec. 6.
[90] J. Reeve, "The Arguments in King's Bench in 1629 concerning the Imprisonment of John Selden and Other Members of the House of Commons" in *Journal of British Studies* 25/3 (July 1986) pp. 264–287. See especially pp. 265–267.
[91] On 18 March a committee of the Privy Council questioned Selden about the Three Cranes dinner. He conceded his attendance there with Eliot and others, but insisted no parliamentary business had been discussed. See Berkowitz *Formative* pp. 236–238.

On 1 May, some two months after imprisonment, Heath finally put his case before the Star Chamber, while petitioning the court to allow the accused free access to counsel. Selden immediately retained as counsel his Inner Templar friend Sir Edward Herbert, and instead of adopting a defensive stance and answering Heath's accusations, he went on the offensive, applying to the Court of King's Bench for a writ of Habeas Corpus (a move in which he was swiftly joined by five others among the prisoners). Selden was demanding the court to execute what he regarded as the most fundamental principle of the English legal system, which he held to be enshrined in chapter 29 of the Magna Carta – to which he had appealed as counsel in Darnel's Case, and which he had a leading part in reasserting within Parliament's recent passing of the Petition of Right – no imprisonment without cause shown before a court. Since the crown refused to give up what it regarded as its prerogative of arbitrary imprisonment, this issue became the basis for all of the prolonged legal battle that ensued. Selden's move was in the short run successful, for it put the legal procedures for a time in two parallel tracks, being discussed before the more political court of Star Chamber (made up of privy councilors as well as Common law judges) as well as the Common law court of King's Bench (presumably more attuned to the prisoners' interests), and forced the crown to disclose the grounds of imprisonment. These grounds were defined as: "notable contempts" against the government, and "moving sedition." In effect, the accusation was that the nine had joined in an unlawful conspiracy to falsely allege the king and government were planning to trample the "liberties of the subject"; the legal and factual grounds for the accusation were at best tenuous, but the crown claimed it was "cause" enough to take it out of the scope of the Petition of Right; that is, it claimed a cause for imprisonment had been shown, and thus that there was no imprisonment without cause, therefore making an appeal to the Petition irrelevant to this case. On 15 May, the last day of the Easter term, the prisoners were brought before the King's Bench, and two new counsel retained by some of the prisoners appeared, Richard Aske and Robert Mason, both arguing that there was no Common Law crime of sedition, and even if there were, it was certainly not listed as a capital offense, so that the prisoners were bailable by Common Law, Magna Carta and the Petition of Right. For the crown Sergeant Davenport's answer was to concede that "[i]t has been said that *seditio* is not a word known in the law, and is always taken either adverbially, or adjectively, and is not a substantive" but then he added that "yet it is a substantive for the destruction of a kingdom" always ranked together with treason, rebellion and the like – in effect he attempted to claim the charge to be somehow both general and particular. The judges reserved their decision and remanded the prisoners to appear before them the first day of the new term, three weeks away.[92]

---

[92] Berkowitz *Formative* pp. 241–244; Reeve "Arguments" pp. 270–273.

During the three-week hiatus of the Common Law courts, the prisoners were brought before the Star Chamber, on 23 May. This time the counsel appearing for the prisoners were Bramston, Holt and Mason for Eliot, while Selden added to Herbert another eminent Inner Templar and friend, Thomas Gardiner. Eliot and Selden apparently divided the arguments between them, for their counsel argued on different grounds. Quite probably, Selden had had a major role in preparing his own defense, which was considerably longer and more elaborate than Eliot's. At any event Selden's counsel presented a plea and demurrer (refusal to answer the charges), indicating several errors in the information and claims presented by the prosecution, by which the whole case was to be regarded as void. For example, to the accusation of Selden's abetting in Hobart's alleged locking of the Commons' doors before Black Rod, his counsel answered that Selden never had the key to the doors, had not been notified that the king dispatched Black Rod, and in addition was neither the doorkeeper nor had any responsibility for keeping it open; and in any case, his counsel argued, the authority to punish any member of the Commons for offenses pertaining to that house was in the Commons only, and not in the Star Chamber or even the king.[93]

On 5 June, as King's Bench had reconvened, Selden, Hobart, Holles and Valentine were brought before the court. This time Selden employed as counsel another friend and even more eminent Inner Templar, Edward Littleton, who had collaborated with him in several Parliaments against Buckingham, and on the passing the Petition of Right. The two, probably England's most eminent practicing lawyers of that time, collaborated closely in preparing the argument; indeed, a brief for use in the hearing on which Littleton would base his arguments in court has survived, and its academic tone as well as its reliance on linguistic and terminological analysis seem to indicate that it was principally the work of Selden. The whole case, Selden and Littleton agreed, was to turn upon the Petition of Right, for if the crown's claim for a general and arbitrary detention was accepted, then the Petition would be in effect nullified. Consistent with this strategy, Littleton did not settle for a conventional examination of the alleged offense and whether it deserved bail, instead opting to make the case all about the Petition of Right, to which, he pointed out, the king had formally assented, thus making it into a statute. He ridiculed the claim of an ill-defined offense of sedition, asserting "[t]his is strange news to me, that there shall be an offense for which a man cannot be convicted." He challenged the crown to present a charge of treason, for then bail could legitimately be denied, but argued that if this was not the case, then according to law, as long as the offense was not a capital one, no freemen might be imprisoned without bail before conviction. In an oblique warning to the judges, he remarked that when

[93] Berkowitz *Formative* pp. 247–249. Selden and Eliot also claimed that they did not know if Parliament had been dissolved, prorogued or adjourned – obliquely censoring the unusual manner by which Charles had dissolved Parliament, appearing before the Lords only.

judges at the time of Richard II had bowed before outside pressure and given a distorted verdict, they had later been found traitors by Parliament. By the time Littleton concluded his argument, Hobart, Valentine and Holles had decided that it was so persuasive, and their case being the same as Selden's, that they too would too rely upon it, and waived the presentations that had been prepared by their own counsel. The strength of Littleton's argument unsettled Attorney General Heath to the degree that he took several days to prepare his rebuttal, and eventually presented it only after Selden had complained to the judges of undue delays. Heath requested the judges not grant bail, basing himself on two arguments: first he chose to contest the meaning of the Petition of Right, asserting that the king had explicitly declared he had given no new law but only reasserted old ones, and that anyway "a petition in Parliament is no law," so that the practice remained as it had been before the petition (that is, as he had stated it in 1627, allowing arbitrary imprisonment); secondly he maintained that the offense in question was a potentially capital one, for sedition may beget treason, and thus he was "confident that ye will not bail them[.]" He then added that before the judges reach a verdict, "first ye are to consult with the king, and he will shew you where the danger rests."[94]

Sensing the weakness of the crown's case, the king decided to apply direct pressure on the judges to reach the verdict he expected from them. On 9 June, some three months after the nine MPs had been imprisoned, as judge Richard Hutton describes in his diary, all 12 Star Chamber judges were summoned to Greenwich Palace, and one by one brought before the king for single consultation. The attempt was obviously to persuade them that Selden and the other prisoners could not be protected by parliamentary privilege. Seven of the judges, including Hutton, refused to budge, declaring their opinion that Star Chamber had no jurisdiction over parliamentary offenses. The king realized this avenue would not wield the results he expected and, fearing that this court would discharge the prisoners, he let the Star Chamber case lapse, while continuing proceedings against them in the court of King's Bench.[95]

When the judges of the King's Bench conferred on the case, they, like those of Star Chamber, could not fail to recognize where the law stood, and unwilling to uproot it at least in principle, they concluded that bail had to be granted. In order to save the king from embarrassment, they informed him in a letter of their intention so that he could take credit for it. Charles summoned these judges too to Greenwich and signaled his displeasure with them, but could not sway them from their conclusion. However, as the decision to grant bail was to be given on 25 June, the king's advisors concocted a new scheme to thwart the liberation of the prisoners – by failing to produce the prisoners before

---

[94] Berkowitz *Formative* pp. 250–255; Reeve "Arguments" pp. 273–281 (especially note 52). For the text of the brief, apparently drafted by Selden (Wilkins claims it was written entirely in Selden's hand), see *Opera Omnia* vol. 3 tome 1 cols. 1398–1954, and the preface.

[95] Hutton *Diary* pp. xxxi, 77–78.

the court they could technically circumvent the judicial process, while keeping to the letter of the law, leaving the imprisoned in jail at least until the end of the long summer recess. The prisoners were all moved to the Tower, which was not controlled by the authority of Common Law courts, and since on the day the prisoners had been scheduled to appear none of them was produced, the judges had an opening by which to evade the conflict of prerogative and law on a technicality, and granted no bail by keeping to the procedural letter of the law, at least until the end of the summer recess. This was a clear indication that in point of substance Selden's views had won the day, and the crown could now only avoid acknowledging it by resorting to absurd technicalities and subterfuges. A majority of judges in both Star Chamber and King's Bench, even when submitted to intense and direct pressure from their monarch, could not find a way in good conscience to deny that, in point of law, the courts had no jurisdiction over Parliament, and that Selden was correct in his understanding of the authority of the Petition of Right and of the right to bail. Although it did not seem so at the time, this too was a crucial stage in the emergence of the supremacy of Parliament and the securing of fundamental liberties of Englishmen; Selden's role in this development was decisive.[96]

During the summer recess, while the case continued to arouse public attention in England and abroad, the king's advisors concocted a new idea – that he should offer the prisoners bail, but as a matter of grace, not of right (a view similar to his understanding of the Petition of Right), thus enabling the prisoners to go free only if they submitted an apology and sought pardon from the king. Being informed of this new proposal, the judges realized that granting bail only of grace would in effect undermine bail as a right, and determined to offer the prisoners an additional option – possibility of bail by right, but with the caveat that this should be granted only with sureties for good behavior, a stipulation only required in cases of accusations for heinous crimes. On 3 October, days only before the courts' Michaelmas term started, the prisoners were brought before the judges one by one, not to the usual King's Bench venue at Westminster Hall, but to private chambers at Serjeant's Inn, and as bail on surety for good behavior was offered, one by one the prisoners refused (Long at first accepted, but on hearing his fellows' position he later joined them). On 9 October five prisoners including Selden appeared before the court, and were again offered bail on surety for good behavior. Their counsel this time, Mason, argued surety for good behavior was requested only for capital crimes, and accepting them would be greatly prejudicial to the prisoners. Selden, D.S. Berkowitz writes, must have watched in disbelief as the judges unmade all the rights and liberties of Englishmen into nothing, by thwarting the very purpose of the law with a technical perversion of it. He rose to address the court himself, remarking that aside from the legal problems the court's position created, the prisoners could not assent to the request without great offense to Parliament. It

---

[96] Berkowitz *Formative* pp. 255–259.

was, as he wrote recalling these events many years later in his *Vindiciae* (1653), "a prophetic sign to the more knowledgeable in the world of the most odious of law." The judges refused to budge from their position, so that an impasse had been arrived at, and the king had finally succeeded in having the prisoners where he wanted them – remaining in jail unless requesting his pardon, or conceding the point of right to bail without prejudice. The prisoners too understood the situation, and as it became clear that another Parliament would not be soon summoned, they had to resolve themselves either to remain in prison for an indeterminate period, or submit. By this time, four of the prisoners had been separately tried and sentenced: Eliot, Holles and Valentine were found guilty of "sedition," Long of having quit without authorization the place of his shrievalty, in order to sit in Parliament; they were all fined and imprisoned at the king's pleasure, not to be released without acknowledging their offenses, submitting to the king and being bound for good behavior. Coryton and Heyman had already submitted and been released by the end of 1629; Holles did the same in 1630, Hobart in 1631 (dying in a carriage accident shortly afterward) and Long in 1633. Eliot, Valentine and Strode refused to budge, the first dying in prison in 1632, the other two remaining formally imprisoned (although, by 1630, actually permitted to go about town as long as they returned to the jail by night) until released by the calling of a Parliament in 1640.[97]

Peter Paul Rubens, working at that time in London on painting the *Allegory on Peace and War* for Charles I, mentioned Selden's fate in two letters, lamenting that the latter's involvement in politics had landed him in jail, deflecting him from devoting himself completely to scholarship. A sentiment parallel to Oliver Goldsmith's bemoaning, a century and a half later, the political involvement of Edmund Burke, "[w]ho, born for the universe, narrow'd his mind / And to party gave up what was meant for mankind." In both cases, the critics missed the point that, for such men, "narrow'd" political involvement was a key component of their principles.[98]

While imprisoned, the nine MPs were treated with relative leniency, and even in the Tower permitted in many cases to receive visitors. At first denied access to their books and papers (especially galling for Selden), eventually permission was granted for them to receive a small number of books and writing paper. As early as 4 July 1629 Selden had written a note (still existing) to Robert Cotton, requesting to borrow for him the Talmud "in divers great volumes" from the

---

[97] Berkowitz *Formative* pp. 260–264; Christianson *Discourse* pp. 190–191; Aikin *Lives* pp. 73–74; Reeve "Arguments" pp. 282–285. Those who agreed to stand bail for Selden, if necessary, were the Earl of Essex and Sir Henry Bourgchier, as well as Robert and Thomas Cotton.

[98] See Berkowitz *Formative* pp. 260–261, and Oliver Goldsmith "Retaliation" (1774). It appears Rubens was in 1629 not only engaged in artistic endeavors, but also representing Spanish interests in London, and sending dispatches to Madrid about the English political situation. See R.M. Smuts, "The Puritan Followers of Henrietta Maria in the 1630s" in *English Historical Review* 93/366 (1978) p. 29.

library of Westminster Cathedral. On 29 July Selden's friend Sir Edward Herbert, who had been his counsel in this case, was allowed by the Privy Council to break the seal that had been placed since the imprisonment on Selden's study at the Inner Temple, and bring him a limited number of books (which had to be named), and he was also permitted to procure the prisoner 19 sheets of paper on which to write his annotations. Selden chose, on top of the Bible granted to everyone who would request it, a volume of works by the Hellenistic satirist Lucian of Samosata as well as the Jerusalem and Babylonian Talmuds (evidently Cotton had successfully borrowed the "great volumes" from Westminster) – under cover of the later "books" he had procured himself a whole library.[99]

While imprisoned, Selden was for a time embroiled in a curious episode that might have further exacerbated his position. On 5 November 1629 Sir Robert Cotton together with the Earls of Bedford, Somerset and Clare, as well as Oliver Saint John, were imprisoned for complicity in disseminating what was regarded as a seditious pamphlet, named *Propositions for His Majesties Service*, which Cotton was alleged to have authored and disseminated, with the collusion of Selden. For his defense against this obviously grave accusation, Selden retained as counsel Littleton, Gardiner, Mason and John Goad, and they completely refuted any involvement of his in this affair. Soon afterward, the pamphlet was discovered to be in fact a text composed by Robert Dudley 15 years earlier, in an altogether different context. The prisoners were therefore released, but as a clear mark of the great power now reputed to books, records and precedents in the English political scene, Cotton's beloved library remained sealed even after his release (probably contributing to his decline and death in May 1631). Fortunately for Selden, this episode concluded without additional negative repercussions on him; indeed, by the end of November 1629, through the pressures of friends and patrons, Selden had been transferred from the Tower to the friendlier environment of the Marshalsea prison, south of the Thames, where he was permitted to move about town during the daytime.[100]

On 29 May 1630, the same day the Dudley pamphlet case was finally dismissed outright by the king, to mark the safe delivery of his son (the future Charles II), the Inner Temple selected Selden as one of the Stewards for its annual Readers, Dinner – a clear sign of the Templars' stance towards Selden and his imprisonment. Also in May 1630, Selden and the other prisoners (excepting Eliot who remained in the Tower), obtained by way of the courtier Sir Tobie Matthew, the permission of the Lord Treasurer, Richard Weston

---

[99] Toomer *Scholarship* pp. 331–333, 804.
[100] It appears that the tract was first sent by Oliver Saint John to Bedford, who passed it to Somerset, from whom it reached Clare, who showed it to Cotton. At this stage Cotton (apparently contacting Selden for the purpose) started to write a refutation of the tract, believing it to be a recent political proposal prepared for Charles I. See Berkowitz *Formative* pp. 272–274, 280 and Hutton *Diary* pp. 78–79.

(soon to become Earl of Portland), to transfer to the more congenial premises of the Westminster Abbey Gatehouse, close by to Cotton's house as well as to Jonson's lodging at that time.[101]

Soon later, ostensibly to avoid a plague outbreak in the city, they were permitted to leave the prison for extensive periods. They visited Eliot still in the Tower,[102] and stayed at the houses of friends, Selden eventually residing with earls of Kent at Wrest Park through the summer. But in October, as the judges returning to London at Michaelmas term found out that Selden and others had been moved without their permission, they complained to the Lord Treasurer who had granted the move. The group was ordered back to the Gatehouse, and as the Lord Treasurer formally apologized to the judges, the other transferred prisoners (Hobart, Strode and Valentine) petitioned them to admit the removal. But Selden, barely veiling his scorn towards the judges that were holding him imprisoned without bail, against what they knew to be the law, waited until these had set out on their country circuits and petitioned the Treasurer only – with the result that he was denied his request and returned to the Marshalsea. This second stay at the Marshalsea was undoubtedly less unpleasant, since in July 1630 his friend and former counsel Sir Edward Herbert had been appointed Steward of that prison. Selden was eventually released from actual imprisonment in May 1631, after a request by the Earls of Arundel and of Pembroke, apparently orchestrated behind the scenes by the Countess of Kent, Elizabeth Grey.[103] In 1630, Elizabeth had filed a bill of complaint against her brothers-in-law, the Earls of Pembroke and of Arundel, claiming that they had short-changed her in the complex partition of the considerable Talbot inheritance, involving her and her two sisters – one married to Arundel, the second to Pembroke (since William Herbert, the Third Earl of Pembroke had died childless in April 1630, Elizabeth amended the suit to include his widow Mary, her sister, and his brother and heir, Philip the Fourth Earl). Selden, as an expert on conveyancing as well as a figure known and trusted by all involved, was drafted to help solve the complex legal tangle – which he eventually did, and in

---

[101] In 1628 Ben Jonson was briefly involved in a fracas concerning a poem glorifying Buckingham's murderer, which was found in the house where he lodged and which he was suspected of having composed (which he denied). By this time Jonson, impoverished and ill, was boarding with an old lady in a two-floor edifice formerly known as the Talbot, located between St. Margaret's Church and Henry VII's chapel, with one of the rooms over the passage leading from the old palace to the churchyard. The house belonged to the Dean and Chapter of Westminster Abbey, at this time Selden's friend, Bishop Williams. The location enabled Jonson to reach at a short distance Cotton's house, where he visited frequently and interacted with the men of letters he found there. By 1631 he had suffered a debilitating stroke after which he read with difficulty and seldom moved about, relying on assistance from old friends and patrons as he became increasingly infirm. See Donaldson *Jonson* pp. 401–405.

[102] Evidently Selden and Eliot remained close until the latter's death while still in the Tower: Selden not only visited Eliot in jail, but they also corresponded and even discussed political ideas – including a pamphlet that Eliot had written while in jail.

[103] Berkowitz *Formative* pp. 283–284.

1635 the suit was finally settled in Lady Kent's favor. In their request for his release, the Earls argued that they needed Selden's assistance in settling the suit, but that it would be somewhat unseemly for all involved, to have him appear in court as counsel while still formally jailed. The solution found was to release him on bail into the custody of his friends (thus circumventing the need for him to personally request bail for good behavior), with the liberty to appear before the courts, but with the condition of having to appear before the King's Bench court every October and January to renew the application for bail (curiously, his registered lodging for this purpose, instead of his own house, was at William Lee's, Stationer, in Fleet Street).[104]

During this period of conditional release, Selden was also retained in late 1631 as counsel in a trial where there was use for his unique expertise – this time concerning trial by duel. Donald Mackay, Lord Reay (or Rhea) had accused one David Ramsay of treason against the Scottish crown, and when the latter challenged him to a duel, Reay accepted. As duels had been proclaimed illegal by James I in 1613, to stop this one from taking place the two were confined to the Tower, and as the Common Law judges referred the matter to the jurisdiction of a special Court of Chivalry, one such court was composed especially for this case, with Selden retained as counsel for Reay. The court convened on 28 November 1631 presided by Robert Bertie, First Earl of Lindsay, created Lord Constable for the occasion, and by Thomas Howard, Earl of Arundel in his capacity as Lord Marshal. The court attempted to have the matter solved by deciding on the merit of case, and let evidential and legal arguments be presented for a number of weeks, almost until Christmas. As a clear decision by the court proved impossible to reach, the duel was given the go-ahead for 12 April 1632 in the Tothill Fields near Westminster, but under pressure from the bishops, King Charles eventually prorogued the day of trial and informed the judges that he had decided both men would be committed to the Tower until he would be persuaded they would not attempt anything against each other. By August both had been freed.[105]

Selden's final release from all restrictions came only after the intercession of Archbishop Laud, to whom he had become close. Selden presented to the king in the fall of 1634 a "most humble petition," written in his own hand: "Prostrating himself at the feet of your sacred majesty" and requesting to be discharged from

---

[104] Christianson "Selden" ODNB; Toomer *Scholarship* pp. 330–332, 390; Johnson *Memoirs* pp. 192–197; Aikin *Lives* pp. 79–80. See also Parker "Wrest" pp. 181,191 note 25.

[105] On top of its two presidents, the court consisted of an array of senior peers: Philip Herbert, Earl of Pembroke and Montgomery, Lord Chamberlain to the King; Edward Sackville, Earl of Dorset, Lord Chamberlain to the Queen; James Hay, Earl of Carlisle; James Graham, Earl of Montrose; William Douglas, Earl of Morton; Edward Cecil, Viscount Wimbledon; Thomas Wentworth, Viscount Wentworth; Henry Cary, Viscount Falkland; as well as Sir Henry Martin. Selden's expertise on these matters meant that in 1640, when the Long Parliament set up a committee to investigate abuses in the Court of Chivalry, he was selected to sit on it. See Barbour *Measures* pp. 170–173.

the continuance of bail. In February 1635 the king informed the judges that he had received Selden's petition and submission, and that he grants the request that he be wholly discharged and set free. For all the mortification the petition certainly brought Selden, he made sure (as he had in the case of the *Historie of Tithes*) not to actually admit in it any wrongdoing, and indeed the "submission" mentioned in Charles I's message does not appear in Selden's original handwritten petition, and seems to have been added later by a different hand. In any event, it is significant that Selden preferred to personally humiliate himself by requesting the king's grace rather than to request from the court bail with security for good behavior, which would have conceded the judges' reading of the right to bail.[106]

The abrupt dissolution of Parliament in 1629, and the following 11-year period known as the king's Personal Rule, made the 1630s an exceptionally quiet decade on the political front. During the first part of the 1630s the government was fairly successful in maintaining a high degree of effectiveness despite the lack of parliamentary funds, and in preventing or suppressing hostile views from emerging. In the latter part of the decade, however, beginning with the public attacks by Puritan clergyman Henry Burton on prelates in 1636, criticism of church and government again became vocal, and increased towards the end of the decade, until by 1640 public opinion was thoroughly aroused against the constitutional and ecclesiastical policies of the crown. These, together with a number of military upsets and a growing financial crisis, would spell the end of Charles I's attempt to rule without Parliament.[107]

This decade of political hibernation saw Selden's public position gradually restored with the Inner Temple, the royal court and even the church, while his scholarly reputation rose to new heights. As early as 1630, his appointment as Steward for the Readers' Dinner had indicated the favor Selden now enjoyed with the Inner Templars, and in November 1632, regardless of his being still formally under the judicial cloud of periodical applications for bail, the Inner Temple "Parliament" formally rescinded his eight-year disqualification from becoming a bencher and elected him a Master of the Bench, member of the Inn's 20-odd governing body. Soon afterward, he and his friend and erstwhile jailer, Sir Edward Herbert, were selected as the two representatives of the Inner Temple to the group of eight managers from the four Inns of Court,[108] who

---

[106] Berkowitz *Formative* pp. 288–290. There were rumors that the *Mare Clausum*, published in 1635 and dedicated to Charles I, had been the price for Selden's final release, but he always vehemently denied this. A careful reading of the book would reveal that he had not retreated from his stance on issues like his denial of the king's authority to impose payments without the concurrence of Parliament.

[107] Johnson *Memoirs* pp. 217–218, 249–251; M.A. Judson, *The Crisis of the Constitution* (New Brunswick, Rutgers University Press, 1988 – reprint of 1949 edition) p. 315.

[108] The representatives were Selden and Herbert for the Inner Temple, Edward Hyde and Bulstrode Whitelocke for the Middle Temple, William Noy (the Attorney General) and a Mr. Gerling for Lincoln's Inn, Sir John Finch and another (whose name is not recorded) for Gray's Inn.

were responsible for staging together, on Candlemas day of February 1634, the masque *The Triumph of Peace* before the King and Queen, at the Banqueting House (and again at the Merchant Taylors' Hall).[109]

One cannot avoid the impression that Selden's successive elections as Steward, bencher and finally as co-manager of the royal masque, when under a shadow of political displeasure and formal judiciary proceeding, were a statement by the Inns of Court, of support for Selden, both personally and as a public figure, as well as of disapproval for the manner in which he had been deprived of his liberty.[110]

Meanwhile, as part of the royal attempt to establish the Personal Rule, on a relatively wide base of support, a number of prominent members of the parliamentary opposition were brought to the government's side and promoted. Among these were William Noy, appointed Attorney General, Sir Edward Herbert, appointed Solicitor General, Dudley Digges, appointed Master of the Rolls, and – most important – Sir Thomas Wentworth, who was made Privy Councilor and Lord Deputy of Ireland, and eventually as Earl of Strafford became the dominant figure in the government. Even Littleton, Selden's friend who had been a key ally in parliamentary battles and collaborated on passing the Petition of Right, as well as appearing as counsel against Selden's imprisonment, was enticed to join the king's men, being made Solicitor General in 1634, Chief Justice of Common Pleas in 1640 and Lord Keeper of the Great Seal in 1641 (but remained a centrist, even as a royalist). It

---

[109] Masque was a courtly form of dramatic spectacle, popular in England in the first half of the seventeenth century. It developed from earlier forms of performance, and combining elements of dancing, use of masks and costumes, and mingling of actors and spectators, it became a magnificent and colorful spectacle. The actors personified symbolic and mythological figures, with great emphasis placed on music and dance. The most successful masques, such as *The Masque of Blackness* (1605), and *Pleasure Reconciled to Virtue* (1618), were produced by the collaboration of Ben Jonson as writer, with Inigo Jones, the theatrical architect, famous for his elaborate costume designs, settings and scenic effects. *The Triumph of Peace* was a "Masque, presented by the Foure Honourable Houses, or Innes of Court. Before the King and Queenes Majesties, in the Banquetting-house at White Hall, February the third, 1633 [1634]. Invented and written, By James Shirley, of Grayes Inne."

[110] The message conveyed by selecting Selden was consistent with the one behind the staging of *The Triumph of Peace* by the Inns, at ruinous expense: although the text is obsequious enough, there was in the whole production an undertone of defiance: the very magnificence of the lawyers' display, which went so much beyond the necessary as to seem to more than one to beggar the royal purse by comparison. Some themes of the performance were also understood as not too veiled criticism of royal policy, such as the initial procession including among buffoon-like characters one of a "Projector" with a bunch of carrots upon his head demanding a patent of monopoly which, Bulstrode Whitelocke reported, was clearly understood by the spectators as a message "covertly given to the King, of the unfitness and ridiculousness of these Projects against the Law" – following the repeated attacks on monopolists in the Parliaments of the 1620s. In the masque itself, Eunomia (Law) declares to her sister Irene (Peace) that "The world shall bring prerogative to neither. We cannot flourish but together." The message of the lawyers couldn't be clearer. See Zaller *Legitimacy* pp. 461, 467 and K. Sharpe, *Criticism and Compliment* (Cambridge University Press, 1987) pp. 215–218.

appears Selden was also among those whom the king tried to co-opt with promise of appointment, and for a time in the mid-1630s there was a persistent rumor that he was to be appointed King's Solicitor or Secretary of State. It appears Selden had no real interest in office or honor, but he possibly used the assumption he might be in order to lessen antagonism towards him and expedite his release. Indeed, since we learn from a letter by Selden of 1634 that he had to carry out discussions of public affairs under shelter of anagrams, we may assume that, regardless of his improved standing with the court, he entertained the possibility that some idea or action of his might yet again fall foul of government.[111]

A first sign of Selden's recovering reputation with the court in this period was his involvement in the attempt to incorporate the city of Westminster. In 1633, when a group of residents approached John Williams, who was Dean of Westminster (1620–1644, as well as Bishop of Lincoln since 1621) with a proposal to incorporate the local government, he supported their idea and proposed they draft an official petition to the king, with the advice of prominent lawyers, recommending three names: Selden, Sir Edward Herbert and the Westminster Recorder Robert Mason. It is unknown if Williams considered the irony of proposing as advisors to the incorporation of Westminster Selden, who had recently been released from incarceration in the Westminster Gatehouse, and two of his counsel concerning that very incarceration. The petition was indeed drafted, and the Earl of Pembroke submitted it to the king. Although incorporation would eventually be granted only in 1636, the fact that Williams (whose standing with the court at that time was not good) proposed Selden's name to draft the petition that Pembroke submitted, seems to indicate that the scholar's involvement in the initiative was, at the least, not expected to be an impediment.[112]

---

[111] It should be pointed out, that in many cases the attitude of the court towards those who had defied it was quite inconsistent. Jonson, while under suspicion that his play *Sejanus* had political overtones regularly continued to perform at court; Cotton, twice confined for alleged political offenses, was nevertheless appointed to a number of offices and even regarded a candidate for Secretary of State – and even in 1630, as his library was sealed by royal order, he was appointed to the royal commission on fees. See K. Sharpe, *Remapping early modern England – The culture of Seventeenth century politics* (Cambridge University Press, 2000) p. 318.

As for Littleton, regardless of his appointment as Lord Keeper his political leaning in the 1640s was regarded as ambiguous, and in 1642 he refused to put the Great Seal on the proclamation for the arrest of five members, and he also voted for the Militia Ordinance. However, he assured his friend Edward Hyde, that he had only taken the later step to allay the suspicions of the parliamentary party who were contemplating depriving him of the seal, and in May 1642 he delivered the seal himself to Charles at York, gradually regaining the King's favor, he died in 1645.

On Selden's use of anagrams see letter from Selden to Lord Conway, 10 August 1634.

[112] See J.F. Merritt, *The Social World of Early-Modern Westminster* (Manchester University Press, 2005) pp. 97–98. Recurring problems, with the governance of the town of Westminster, had brought on several attempts to incorporate it in the early seventeenth century, which met with the hostility of the clerical establishment of the Abbey, fearing a loss of its considerable local

A more significant sign of Selden's newfound favor at court was his appointment by the king as councilor to the English embassy at the imperial court in Vienna, intended to accompany Arundel who was being sent there – but Selden declined the appointment, giving as justification his tender health, bringing him to fear that such a journey might kill him. A more consequential development for Selden came in the same year, with the long-awaited publication of the *Mare Clausum*. After being barred from publication by Buckingham in 1619, Selden received permission to publish it in 1635 and he prepared an extensively rewritten version. The importance of the issues treated in the book, and the intellectual stature of the author, were such that, as word started to get around Europe that Selden was about to publish a riposte to the *Mare Liberum*, expectations began to build, with Grotius hearing about it in May, the Pope in June and Charles I receiving the completed version by August (it was finally published in November). The book's support for England's claims to the waters around it, and for the crown's maritime policies – building up a fleet to enforce England's dominion – together with the dedication to the king that it bore, raised accusations, mainly by those who opposed its doctrines, that the book had been set as the price for Selden's release – something he always explicitly and vehemently denied.[113]

This involvement in maritime matters was also the background to Selden's establishing of a close relationship with another Laud protégé of the period, Algernon Percy, Tenth Earl of Northumberland, who was appointed in 1636 Admiral of the "Ship-Money" fleet (and from 1638 Lord High Admiral of England). The pertinence of Selden's work to Percy's remit is evident in the new admiral's first assignment: an expedition in 1636 to force Dutch ships, fishing in waters over which England claimed dominion, to purchase an English fishing license or else their fishing nets be cut. Northumberland was probably the one who brought about in the same year Selden's nomination, together with Sir James Galloway and mathematicians Henry Gellibrand and William Oughtred (inventor of the slide rule), to a four-member committee charged with evaluating the claim, by one Captain Marmaduke Nelson, of having found a method of calculating longitude at sea. We have no information about the

powers and rights. The 1633 proposal of an incorporation of limited scope, that would preserve local Church predominance, met with the enthusiastic support of Williams.

[113] Brook *Map* p. 36. Significantly, in the "Ship-Money" Case, Selden's *Mare Clausum* was actually cited as authority for the imposition, by the crown's lawyers, Sir John Bankes and Sir Edward Littleton (Selden's friend and counsel). Indeed, I have found no proof of Selden ever opposing the Ship-Money imposition, and it may well be that, unlike other crown schemes for extra-parliamentary taxation, he saw this one as a legitimate measure. For, unlike other arbitrary impositions levied by the crown for unclear purposes and periods, this one was intended to directly provide the emergency funds necessary to hastily build up the English navy, in the likelihood of an imminent maritime conflict with the Dutch. Nevertheless, I have also not found any public expression of support by Selden for the Ship-Money. See R. Tuck, *Philosophy and Government 1572–1651* (Cambridge University Press, 1993) pp. 212–213.

work of the committee, but the claim was obviously found wanting, since more than a century passed before a reliable method of calculating longitude was established.[114]

On the clerical front, too, Selden's standing was much improved, as he came to enjoy the respect and patronage of William Laud, Bishop of London and later Archbishop of Canterbury, as well as in the 1630s the most potent figure in government alongside Strafford. Laud was a patron of scholarship and Chancellor of Oxford University, and he seems to have developed with Selden a relationship of genuine mutual esteem. He assisted in obtaining Selden's formal release from all conditions, interceded to improve his standing with the royal court, and even attempted to entice him to join government – to the extent that Peter Heylyn (Chaplain to King Charles and Laud's protégé) wrote, Selden had "grown into such esteem with the Archbishop that he might have chosen his own preferment in the court" had he not undervalued such employment "in respect of his studies." Selden reciprocated by dedicating to Laud in 1636 his publication in one volume of two works on Jewish inheritance law, the *Bona* and the *Pontificatum* (on which more later).[115]

Indeed, the most significant consequence for Selden of the political hiatus imposed on the country by the Personal Rule was the impact on his studies. He embarked on what was undoubtedly to be his greatest intellectual endeavor, and a feat unparalleled elsewhere in England or Europe of his age – a series of publications, some of them massive, devoted to looking at the main ideas of the Jewish legal tradition, in the manner usually employed to explore and consider mainstream ideas and texts of the western legal tradition. A project whose ambition was best expressed in the motto, from Lucretius, chosen by Selden for his seminal book, the *Jure Naturali*, "...places never before trodden by the foot...," or as we would put it today: to go where no one had gone before.[116]

As early in his career as 1608, Selden had displayed an interest in and detailed knowledge of Roman and Canon law, and this fascination with (and learning in) other legal systems, quite uncommon among the vast majority of common lawyers, became a defining feature of his scholarship. Indeed, later in his career Selden had acquired, uniquely in own his time and probably to this day, a monumental proficiency in a number of great legal systems – on top of

---

[114] Berkowitz *Formative* pp. 284–288; Toomer *Scholarship* pp. 390–392; Feingold "Selden" pp. 55–78. Northumberland was Selden's junior by some two decades, but they became political allies of sorts in the 1640s and 1650s (although Northumberland's positions were far more volatile), and close enough personally for the scholar to bequeath in his will to the Earl, a "bason and ewer of silver gilt," and to the Lord Admiral's son Joceline a fit gift – a "crystal ship or gally" and a square marble table.

[115] Berkowitz *Formative* pp. 284–288.

[116] Toomer *Scholarship* p. 819. The quote is from the Epicurean Roman poet Lucretius' *De rerum natura*, iv: "Avia Pieridum peragro loca nullius ante trita solo" usually rendered as "I wander afield, thriving in sturdy thought, Through unpathed haunts of the Pierides, Trodden by step of none before."

Roman, Canon and Common law, also European customs and statutes and eventually the Jewish legal tradition – surpassed by some as regards one system or other, but by none overall. He thus embarked now on what was to prove the most challenging and extraordinary among his voyages of intellectual discovery.[117]

Already, by the time he published the *Marmora Arundelliana* in 1628, one can find evidence of the direction towards which his intellectual interest was turning at this time, in a lengthy aside, several pages long, discussing ancient chronology and various ancient Samaritan and Hebrew texts (in the unpaginated preface "Editionis Ansa, Causa, Consilium"). But the idea for this great project, which would occupy him for the rest of his life and came to consist of the great bulk of his scholarly output, was apparently born sometime while he was imprisoned following the events of the 1629 Parliament. Selden subsequently claimed that while confined to the Tower he planned out a series of books on Jewish legal tradition. When the more lenient circumstances of his later imprisonment permitted this, he set out to fully carry out this plan.[118]

The first product of his direct venture into Jewish law, started in 1629, was Selden's 1631 *De Successionibus in Bona Defuncti, Seu Iure Haereditario ad Leges Ebraeorum*, a book on Jewish inheritance laws which he sardonically described in the preface as written while "enjoying the abundant leisure of prison" (dum tranquillo Carceris abundauimus Otio).There followed a few years later *De Successione in Pontificatum Ebraeorum* (1636, published together with a substantially revised version of *Bona*) on the historical succession and the legal privileges and requirements of the Israelite High Priests, which he had composed in the summer of 1634 while at Wrest. During this period, at least since 1631, Selden was also working on what would become *De Synedriis et Praefecturis Iuridicis Veterum Ebraeorum*, a book on the judicial and political councils of the ancient Hebrews, and by 1638

---

[117] Toomer *Scholarship* pp. 81, 818. Toomer proposes that among the attractions of the Talmud for Selden, the primary one was learning about a fourth system of law alongside the three ones he was familiar with, Roman, Canon and Common law – one which was far more self-contained than the other three, which notwithstanding their putative independent status and authority, had many recorded interconnections. See Toomer *Scholarship* p. 442.

[118] Although Selden undoubtedly started to work on *Synedriis* by the early 1630s, he later claimed that while in prison he planned the writing not only of the *Bona* (which he later actually wrote at the Marshalsea), but also the *Pontificatum*, the *Jure Naturali*, the *Uxor* and the second edition of the *Titles of Honor*. But Toomer suspects Selden's memory might have deceived him about the precise time he conceived these works. Toomer proposes that, regardless of later claims, Selden did not have the *Jure Naturali* in mind when he embarked on his program of writing works on Jewish law, and that the idea for this book came to him only in 1635, when preparing for publication the *Mare Clausum* – the work in which he first refers to Grotius' *Jure Belli*. His first mention of the *Jure Naturali* was in the 1636 edition of *Bona Defuncti*, where he refers to it as a book he is working on about the Jewish theory of the law of nations ("libris de Iure Gentium ad eorum placita"). See Toomer *Scholarship* pp. 447, 490.

he had completed a draft version of the book, although he did not publish it at that time.[119]

To this output we should also add two more works which reflect Selden's growing proficiency and interest in Hebraism: the second and extensively rewritten edition of the *Titles of Honor*, published in 1631, and the *Mare Clausum seu de Dominium Mari (Closed Sea, or of the Dominion of the Seas)* which, as mentioned, having been originally composed much earlier, finally appeared after a thorough revision in 1635. Although in both cases reworking a text composed much earlier and containing much else besides Hebraist materials, even a cursory glance at the published texts reveals they had profited considerably from ideas and sources connected with Selden's new exploration of the Jewish legal tradition.[120]

But the culmination of this period's work was undoubtedly the *Jure Naturali* (1640), his massive work on the Jewish version of natural law, intertwined with a comparative consideration of western legal traditions and philosophical ideas touching on this subject. Thus by the end of the decade Selden had produced a series of works on the Jewish legal tradition, of growing sophistication (and bulk...), with the *Jure Naturali* being in many ways his most mature, coherent and systematic work in this field – the result of prodigious scholarship applied without serious interruption over a decade of largely (if unwillingly induced) undisturbed work. In many ways the culmination of his life's work and mind, it is not a coincidence that the *Jure Naturali* contains what is by all accounts the most philosophically sophisticated and thoughtful portion of his whole output.[121]

Selden's Hebraist project is a staggering feat of scholarship, in both breadth and depth, successfully mastering so many texts of the Jewish tradition, not only in Hebrew, but even in the idiosyncratic Aramaic of the Talmud.[122] He was

[119] Toomer thinks Selden might have been working on *Synedriis* possibly even as early as 1629 (as implied in a letter from Henry Bourgchier to Ussher). The long gestation of the work meant that its plan and execution changed considerably until the eventual publication in 1650–1655. Toomer *Scholarship* pp. 692–693.

[120] *Mare Clausum* was originally produced as a work rebutting the maritime conflict arising from claims in Grotius' *Mare Liberum* (who had even undertaken a trip to London to resolve the dispute, but apparently he did not meet with Selden). The work was withheld from publication in 1619, but in the mid-1630s, with the maritime dispute erupting again, Charles I gave permission to publish the work, and Selden rewrote it and published it in 1635. See Fry "Selden" DNB.

[121] *Jure Naturali* was in complete form by June 1639, when it received permission to be published from Laud's chaplain, and it was in print by early 1640. Although he produced some more works in later years, this was in fact Selden's most comprehensive and mature statement of his ideas, for his latter Hebraist works either treated of less comprehensive matters (like the *Anno Civili*), or were in fact started earlier, though taking longer to complete, such as *Synedriis* on which he was working at least since 1631, with a first version of book I completed by 1638 (see Aikin *Lives* p. 146), although only printed in 1650, with book II printed in 1653 and book III uncompleted at his death.

[122] Selden might have picked up some Hebrew as a student in Oxford, and certainly learned the language (with Aramaic, and other "eastern" tongues) with Ussher from about 1609. By 1612, his "Illustrations" to Drayton's *Poly-Olbion*, shows clear improvement of his grasp of the

assisted in this achievement by his own collection of Hebraica, which was gradually built up until at his death it eventually comprised more than 700 manuscripts and rare books, the largest and richest such collection in England. His accomplishment becomes even more remarkable when one considers that, for all we know, he never had actual contact with any Jew, especially one who would have afforded him significant information about contemporary Jewish practices.[123]

In effect, Selden devoted the great bulk of his considerable scholarly efforts in the quarter-century from 1630 to his death to the study and publication of works on the rabbinical tradition. Concurrently with this dive into Hebrew scholarship, Selden for the most part gave up scholarly work on English law. Except for his masterful *Dissertatio Historica* upon the English medieval legal commentary *Fleta*, printed in 1647, and the occasional touching on English legal subjects in works otherwise directed, like the 1631 new edition of *Titles of Honor* and the *Mare Clausum*, there was nothing more from him of substance on English law. There were practical reasons that made such a choice advisable, such as the fact that for much of the period there was hardly any subject having to do with English law that was not fraught with political significance and danger. The obvious efforts required by his fascination with mastering the immense bulk and complexity of the Jewish tradition also played a part. It nevertheless appears that a full and convincing account of this momentous turn in his scholarship and interests is still lacking. In any case, it is probably telling of the author's pride in the uniqueness of his project, as well as of the public standing and financial affluence he had achieved (and perhaps also the tumultuous political circumstances of the next decades), that, starting with the *Jure Naturali*, all his substantial works were published without patron or dedication.[124]

Hebrew language, and Toomer asserts he could at this stage certainly read the Hebrew Bible, while his knowledge of extra biblical Jewish literature was still dependent on secondary sources like Ricius' *De Thalmudica doctrina Epitome*. Only towards the time of his publication of the *Historie of Tithes*, he displayed a clear grasp of rabbinic sources. Toomer *Scholarship* p. 120.

[123] Toomer *Scholarship* p. 445 and note 81. Toomer regards Selden's relative ignorance about contemporary Jewish practices as a weakness of his work. One of Selden's few sources on such practices was the 1616 *Riti Ebraici* by the Venetian Rabbi Leone Modena, describing the Jewish religion and rites, and composed at the request of the poet and scholar Henry Wotton, who was English ambassador to Venice. The *Riti* reached England in manuscript (it was printed only in 1637), and was consulted by Selden, who received his copy from William Boswell (Secretary to Herbert of Cherbury when ambassador in Paris), as attested by his mention of it and its author in both *Bona* (1631 edition, p. 60) and later also in the *Uxor* (where the printed edition of the *Riti*, which had meanwhile appeared, is also mentioned). In a letter to Selden of 1636, Boswell wrote that he was enclosing a copy of a letter from Leone Modena to him, in which the Rabbi asked Boswell for a copy of Selden's work where his name had appeared. We know that a Hebrew Bible inspected and signed by Modena reached Selden (perhaps through Boswell), and is now in the Bodleian. There is no evidence that Selden and Modena ever corresponded directly. See C. Roth, "Leone Da Modena and England" in *TJHSE*, 11 (1928) pp. 206–227, and C. Roth, "Leone da Modena and his English correspondents" in *TJHSE* 17 (1953) pp. 39–43.

[124] Barnes *Shaping* pp. 170–171.

There was, however, one instance in which Selden's scholarly work had a crucial role in legal developments of this decade. In 1637, all the judges of Ireland decided The Case of Tenures upon the Commission of Defective Titles, which invalidated tenures not explicitly set as hereditary, based on an interpretation of tenure which owed crucially to Selden. The judges brushed aside various previous legal sources on tenures, like Bracton, and decided the issue strictly upon interpretations of Feudal Law that had emerged in recent works of legal scholars. Explicitly addressing two important legal narratives, the judges rejected Spelman's theory in *Archaeologus in Modum Glossarii* (1626) that Feudal Law had been introduced to England only with the Norman conquest (suggesting a clear break from the past), and they embraced instead Selden's view in his 1631 2nd edition of *Titles of Honor*, according to which Feudal Law had been in continuous use since the Anglo-Saxon times (a change from the 1614 edition, where Selden too had argued feudal tenures had been introduced by the Norman conquest). The judges' acceptance, on this basis, of the argument for legal continuity also used Selden's interpretation of the ancient constitution to justify an extension of royal claims to invalidate tenures not explicitly hereditary – seriously undermining previously secure land tenures. This judgment prompted Spelman to reinvest serious efforts in establishing his interpretation as the correct one, resulting in his *The Original, Growth, Propagation and Condition of Feuds and Tenures by Knight-Service in England* (1639), which became the definitive treatise in England upon tenures and Feudal Law.[125]

By the end of the 1630s, Selden had completed the main outline of his great Hebraist project, as well as executed a great part of it. He would continue to work on aspects of it, as well as on a few other works, for the rest of his life; however, by the closing of this decade the extended period in which he was able to devote his time primarily to his scholarly pursuits was coming to an end. The setting for much of this work, and his personal and intellectual safe haven at Wrest Park, was no more, with the death of Henry Grey on 21 November 1639, when his cousin Anthony Grey, an octogenarian Puritan clergyman, became the Ninth Earl, and the widowed Countess Elizabeth moved out permanently to reside at Whitefriars in London, together with Selden. During the 1630s Wrest had been the center of a literary and artistic circle, alongside the more famous ones of this period, like the Tew circle (with which Selden is also sometimes associated) around Lucius Cary, Viscount Falkland, and the Welbeck circle (of which Hobbes was part) around William Cavendish, then Earl of Newcastle. The Wrest circle included in addition to Selden also Robert Cotton, the poets Thomas Carew, John Suckling and young Samuel Butler, as well as the brother miniaturists Samuel and Alexander Cooper (the latter apparently converted to

[125] See *The Case of Tenures upon the Commission of Defective Titles argued by all the judges of Ireland* (1637); Christianson *Discourse* pp. 296–298; K. Davis, *Periodization and Sovereignty* (Philadelphia: Pennsylvania University Press, 2008) pp. 53–55.

Judaism by 1646, when he traveled to the court of Queen Christina of Sweden). In Thomas Carew's nostalgic poem "To my friend G. N. from Wrest," probably completed just before Henry Grey's death, Wrest Park became a symbol of the social and cultural ideas thriving in that friendly environment, now threatened by dark political clouds gathering over the horizon, with a great storm brewing.[126]

1.7 "IN A TROUBLED STATE": 1640–1648

In 1640, Charles I's attempts to rule without Parliament came to an end, ruined by the King's inability, with the means at his disposal, to militarily break a rebellion that had erupted in Scotland. After calling a Parliament in the spring (of which Selden was not a member), the King failed in his attempt to receive from it funds without making political concessions, and he dissolved it after only three weeks. The King toyed with ideas for circumventing Parliament, such as the resurrecting of medieval institutions which would enable him to rule with the support of the peerage only, but he soon found out this avenue too was closed to him. A number of disaffected noblemen, with Bedford House as their headquarters, saw in the recent debacles in the war with the Scots the chance to advance their long-standing opposition to the King's policies, and on 28 August 1640 they issued a *Petition of Twelve Peers for the Summoning of a New Parliament*. In the weeks after the petition's issue, as copies of it were being circulated, it acquired 11 new signatories willing to add their names to it, amounting to 23 peers: close to a quarter of the entire English nobility (excluding the bishops). With such explicit dissent brewing even among peers, and no other viable option left, the King reluctantly agreed to convene another Parliament, in the autumn of 1640 – it was to be the longest and most tumultuous in English history.[127]

Selden was elected to the Long Parliament as one of the two representatives of the University of Oxford. His election, which was not formally contested, was reputed to have been obtained by "higher influence," with some proposing this influence to have been Archbishop Laud, the Chancellor of the University, while others propose it was instead Philip Herbert, Fourthe Earl of Pembroke, the former Chancellor, ousted by Laud but retaining much influence in Oxford

---

[126] R. Wilcher, *The Writings of Royalism 1628–1660* (Cambridge University Press, 2001) pp. 30–31. However disagreeable leaving Wrest might have been, Selden's and Elizabeth's residence at Whitefriars was certainly most pleasant, with a literate circle often attending, and around 1642 the addition to the household of a new cook, Robert May (1588–c.1664), one of the earliest English *chefs*, who would publish in 1660 *The Accomplished Cook*, the first extensive recipes book in English. See Stone *Crisis* p. 560.

[127] John Adamson, *The Noble Revolt: The Overthrow of Charles I* (Phoenix, 2009) pp. 62–63, 78. The original signatory peers were the Earls of Rutland, Bedford, Hertford, Essex, Exeter, Warwick, Bolingbroke and Mulgrave, the Viscount Saye and Sele, and the Barons Brooke, Mandeville and Howard of Escrick.

and supporter of anti-court candidates throughout England. Actually, as the
two were bitter opponents, and Selden was on good terms with both but a
political ally of neither, apparently what happened was somewhat different. In
the spring election to the Short Parliament the University had returned as
representatives Sir Thomas Roe (1581–1644), a centrist diplomat, and Sir
Francis Windebank (1582–1646), the Secretary of State: two distinguished
figures who seemed above the political fray. But as the November elections
neared, there arose strong opposition to Secretary Windebank as being too
identified with the royal policies and the Laudian church, so that a contest
arose for his seat. Against the Laudian-backed Windebank the substantial
Puritan contingent at the University, apparently with Pembroke's backing, put
forward as their candidate Sir Nathaniel Brent (c. 1573–1652), Warden of
Merton College and enemy of Laud. At some point of this bitter contest,
Selden's name was put forward as a moderate candidate, inimical to none,
and it soon transpired that majority support was indeed coalescing around his
candidacy, rather than either of the partisan options. Both Laud and Pembroke
had good personal relations with Selden, and presumably preferred him in the
seat instead of a candidate of the opposite side. Windebank was the first to
retreat, and rather than face defeat withdrew his name from the contest (he was
eventually elected for the pro-court Cornwall "safe seat" of Corfe Castle),
thereafter, the supporters of Brent seeing they were now in the clear minority,
gave up the struggle, so that in the end there apparently was even no need for a
formal vote, and Selden's election was uncontested. Oxford would not regret his
election, and he became for as long as he lived a remarkably effective defender of
the university, its faculty and its scholarship, during the Civil War and the
interregnum – even after he was purged from his parliamentary seat.[128]

---

[128] M.B. Rex, *University Representation in England* (G. Allen & Unwin, 1954) pp. 144–146, and
M.F. Keeler, *The Long Parliament* (Philadelphia: APS, 1954) p. 60. Selden is reputed by Rex to
have been one of the most important and effective University representatives ever. In the
difficult times ahead he consistently defended the interest of the universities (not only
Oxford) and their faculty, as well as of scholarship. During the conflict Parliamentary
Visitations at Oxford and Cambridge attempted to evict faculty deemed politically or religiously suspect, and appoint in their place candidates more desirable to the regime. Selden used
all means at his disposal, including personal influence, technical maneuvers and delaying
tactics, to forestall these activities, not only within Parliament and government but also within
Oxford's own "Parliament" – the governing council of the University. Even during the interregnum, when no more an MP and largely withdrawn from public affairs, he often successfully
defended scholars and libraries from Puritan zeal, and presumably it was no coincidence, that
Oxford retained as their counsel to judicially fight problematic measures Selden's good friend
Matthew Hale. Selden's perceived activities in this period are best illustrated by a royalist satire
of the period, purporting to be a speech by Pembroke, the old-new Oxford University
Chancellor and champion of Puritans, bewailing Selden's obstructionism of Puritan designs
on the University: "Selden did so vex us with his law and his reasons, we could get nothing
pass … that fellow is but burgess for Oxford, and I am chancellor, and yet he would have
the parliament hear his law and reasons against their own Chancellor." See Rex *University* pp.
171–172.

At the opening of the Long Parliament in November, Selden was one of the few among the old Parliamentary leadership remaining in the Commons. Coke, Eliot and Phelips had died; Wentworth and Littleton had gone over to the King and joined government. Selden was also close to many of the opposition peers, who at least initially had a major role in directing events, including the Earls of Bedford, Hertford, Bristol and Essex. Thus, this should have been Selden's hour of political dominance; but for a number of reasons, it was to be very much the opposite. First, this Parliament more than any previous one saw the emergence of large organized groups, akin to adversarial parties, and Selden, very much his own man and seeking for political compromise, was not very well suited to that kind of politics. Second, unlike previous Parliaments, this time religious controversies were a main point of contention: an arena in which Selden was not in the best position to lead. Also, in practical terms, whereas the preceding Parliaments had been led mainly from the Commons, the Long Parliament was led in its initial period by disaffected noblemen. But perhaps most important was that Selden's basic approach, of trying to salvage and reinforce what he understood to be the principles of the constitution, meant that his response to the crisis was essentially conservative and within the existing constitutional framework. He supported the removal of individuals from office, a general reassertion of the traditional laws and liberties, some reforms in church and in state (such as the abolition of religious and civil courts competing with those of the Common law), and especially the reinforcement of the role of Parliament, so that it would be impossible for kings to rule without it. In other words, he favored a reform of government, but one that would overall preserve the existing mixed monarchy and constitutional framework, and would be achieved through cooperation and negotiation. This put him at a disadvantage when so many others were intent on fundamentally transforming the system. It soon transpired that most of the Commons leadership was interested in much more far-reaching changes. Pym and Holles more moderate on political issues, were after a radical refashioning of the Church; Saint John and Strode, less interested in church reform, were after a radical refashioning of government on "Venetian" lines (that is, making the king merely the figurehead of a republic). Each group was willing to go very far to further their agenda, including asking for the heads of Laud and Strafford, although probably very few (like Haselrig and Marten) wanted a radical upheaval in both church and state to begin with. Moreover, as party lines hardened, many of those supporting moderate political and religious reforms, found their only alternative to the growingly radical demands for change, was to gather round the king in opposition to Parliament. This dynamic meant that Selden repeatedly found himself in the small minority, who were neither radicals in church or in state, nor willing to throw their lot unreservedly with the King.[129]

---

[129] Barnes *Shaping* pp. 172–174.

As Parliament convened, there emerged within the opposition two groups, one more moderate and initially dominant, led by the Earl of Bedford, and in the Commons by Pym and Hampden; another more extreme in its political demands, and initially weaker, led by the Earl of Warwick, and in the Commons by Saint John and the younger Vane. As the political clash exacerbated, positions hardened, and the moderate Bedfordians were again and again forced to follow radical courses of action. In early 1641 it seemed as if the time of the Bedfordians had come: after secret negotiations with the King and Queen, a number of leading opposition peers joined the Privy Council in the expectation that they would accede to office and help stem the more radical elements in Parliament – especially save the Earl of Strafford, who had become the lightning-rod for all grievances against the government's faults. Of the seven peers sworn in as councilors on 19 February, Bedford, Hertford, Essex, Bristol, Savile, Mandeville and Saye, the first four had strong links to Selden.[130]

But things did not turn out as expected, when among the growing fears of an imminent dissolution, the Bedfordians, despite their misgivings, found no other course than supporting the Attainder against Strafford, with only Digby breaking ranks and opposing the bill. On his part, Selden would have nothing to do with a course that would deny a man his right to a fair trial. He had personally suffered from such a predicament, and he was not about to inflict it on even his greatest enemy. When the Commons abandoned the impeachment procedure, introducing instead a bill of Attainder, intimating the death penalty by decree, Selden (together with Digby) left the Strafford prosecution team that he had originally been a part of.[131]

For all his evident hostility to the policies of Strafford, Selden categorically refused to allow a facile use of legal instruments for political ends, and with typical consistency he raised in the Commons the very same arguments that he had employed to defend himself when an attempt was made to indict him with treason, after the 1628–1629 Parliament: that treason had an exact definition in English law, and that nothing in what Strafford had committed could be legitimately construed as legal treason. The minority opposing the Attainder included staunch royalists like Endymion Porter, and Strafford's brother George Wentworth, as well as lawyers like Orlando Bridgeman and Edward Hyde who heeded Digby's specific appeal to them in his speech, to witness the injustice of proceeding in this way. After the failure of the impeachment on 10 April, the atmosphere within and without Parliament became intensely hostile, even threatening, towards those who opposed the bill of Attainder. The bill

---

[130] C. Roberts, *Schemes and Undertakings: A Study of English Politics in the Seventeenth Century* (Columbus, Ohio: State University Press, 1985) pp. 38–40.
[131] Johnson *Memoirs* pp. 249–251. See also C. Roberts, "The Earl of Bedford and the Coming of the English Revolution" in *Journal of Modern History* 49/4 (1977) pp. 600–616, especially 610–612.

came to the vote on 13 April 1641, and Pym, who had supported proceeding by impeachment, lost control of the house: bowing to the wish of the majority, he supported the Attainder. In the eventual vote, those in favor of Strafford's execution numbered 204, while those against numbered only 59, but the size of the majority is misleading, for less than half of the Commons actually attended the vote in this division, with many who opposed the bill (among them, for example, Hampden and Sir Henry Mildmay) choosing to withdraw from the house rather than join the small group of those who, by casting their vote against the Attainder, faced the ire of the majority and the wrath of the mobs in the streets outside. Selden was one of the few prominent reformers (like Edward Kyrton and Robert Scawen) who did not bow before the intimidating atmosphere, and cast their vote against the Attainder.[132]

Regardless of the vote in the Commons, the moderate parliamentarians still had in early May of 1641 seemingly good prospects of controlling political developments. The Attainder had not yet passed in the Lords, where moderates enjoyed wide support, and reports from the committee for Church reform meeting in Westminster Abbey's Jerusalem Chamber, and headed by Bishop Williams, were that it had achieved an impressively broad consensus for a modified episcopacy, including with such prominent Puritans as Edmund Calamy. However, a noxious combination of the increasing pressure from London mobs and Bedford's illness, which brought about his swift and unexpected death on 9 May, together with the discovery of a bungled royalist plot to take the Tower (and free Strafford), destroyed the moderates' hopes. The Attainder passed in the Lords on 5 May, the King, bowing to overwhelming pressure from all sides, signed it on 10 May (the act he most regretted for the rest of his life), and on 12 May, before a gigantic crowd, Strafford was executed. May 1641 seems to be the moment when there was a decisive shift of power in the parliamentarian reformist coalition, away from the more moderate Bedfordians (led in the Commons by Pym), who were still attempting to work within a model of mixed monarchy and ultimate cooperation from the king to achieve reformation of government; towards the aggressive Essex-Warwick group (led in the Commons by Saint John and Holles), with a far more "Venetian" republican agenda, aiming to create an aristocratic-led regime, that would leave Charles with the mere title of King, stripped of all real authority. The death of Bedford and the success of the Attainder brought in May and June 1641 desertions of moderate centrists towards both extremities. The Earls of Pembroke and of Northumberland (respectively Lord Chamberlain of the King's Household and Lord High Admiral) orbited towards the Warwickian hard-liners, while on the opposite front too, the ranks of royalist

---

[132] Adamson *Noble* pp. 253–255. On 3 May 1641, before the crucial vote in the Lords, a list of names of those, including Selden, who had voted against the Attainder in the Commons followed by the caption "this and more shall be done to the enemies of justice, afore written" was posted on a wall in Old Palace Yard, Westminster, with obvious intimidatory intent.

opponents to reform were swelling with such names as the Earls of Bristol and Hertford, Viscount Falkland, Lord Savile and Lord Digby (recently promoted from the Commons), as well as Hyde. Westminster politics was becoming more polarized than ever, and in effect Bedford's death accelerated the demise of the moderate mixed-monarchy center, in favor of an emerging royalist-republican polarity.[133]

Selden, too independent to become a fully-fledged member of the Bedfordian circle, had cooperated with it to further the many constitutional principles and political goals they shared. For a time, he still retained a relatively prominent Commons role, and there are reports that at this period, while the extremist wing of the Parliamentarians met at the houses of Saint John and Cromwell to plot their strategies, the moderates met in Selden's house (and sometimes in Pym's).[134]

But as moderates on both sides were drifting to more polarized positions of an all-or-nothing struggle, Selden became increasingly isolated in political terms, opposing the radical line in the Commons on the one hand, while refusing to go over to the growing ranks of hard-line royalist on the other. The leadership of the Commons had clearly moved from the moderates to the radicals, and while some of the former, like Pym, succeeded in riding the tiger, perhaps in the hope of later finding opportunities to revert to a more centrist course, the retirement from attendance of many other erstwhile moderates, like Digby, Hyde, Colepeper and Hertford, tended to strengthen the weight of the radicals. Selden remained steadfast in his views and his attendance, many times pretty close to a lone voice of moderation and adherence to legal principles and procedures. Not giving up on Parliament, but neither adopting a radical line, he was now found regularly on the side of those opposing the majority view. It was, in many ways his finest hour as a defender of the constitution: he had been in the small minority actually voting against the Attainder in the Commons; he opposed the ejection of bishops from the House of Lords, and then their complete abolition; he opposed in the Westminster Assembly as well as in Parliament the attempts to establish a Presbyterian English church; he consistently opposed the resort to armed conflict. A later remark in the *Table-Talk* articulated the reasoning behind his position on the demands for far-reaching reform in the church (which would similarly apply in the state):

Alteration of Religion is dangerous, because we know not where it will stay; 'tis like a *Milstone* that lies upon the top of a pair of Stairs; 'tis hard to remove it, but if once it be thrust off the first Stair, it never stays till it comes to the bottom.[135]

But this suspicion of radical change did not turn Selden into a wholehearted supporter of the king, as it did many other moderates who initially favored reforms. The increasing polarization of the debate, and the mounting suspicions as to hidden intents and projects of each side, contributed to an incandescent

---

[133] Adamson *Noble* pp. 309–312, 322.   [134] Fry "Selden" DNB.   [135] TT "Religion" sec. 6.

atmosphere, not only within the halls of Parliament but also in the streets, with many moderate MPs altogether ceasing to attend out of fear of the mob. By the end of 1641 the active membership of the Commons was well under half its number, and usually hovered around a quarter of it, while attendance in the Lords was proportionally only slightly higher. Charles and his two closest advisors at the time, Bristol and Digby, suspected that with the support of the radicals in Parliament then declining, a return *en-masse* of those members who had been abstaining from attendance (and which were assumed to be proportionally more supportive of the king than those attending), might tip the balance of parliamentary control in their favor, or at the least seriously unsettle the radicals. Therefore, in December 1641, the King issued to all absentee members of both houses, amounting to some 210 in number, a summon calling them to return to Parliament by 12 January.[136]

Pym and his allies, realizing their control of Parliament to be in jeopardy, upped the stakes and decided on an ugly course that would prop up their majority by combining mob intimidation with exclusion of members regarded as especially loyal to the crown, chief among them the bishops sitting in the Lords. On 28 December, mobs prevented twelve of the bishops from attending the session of the House of Lords, and a few days later, Pym cynically moved to impeach those very twelve for their absence, and the majority of the peers attending actually endorsed this measure. The next day Archbishop Williams protested that if the bishops were forcibly expelled by the rabble, their absence could render the House of Lords incomplete and its legislation invalid; the parliamentarian leadership's reaction was to jail him. In this poisoned atmosphere, the clash was quickly departing the bounds of Parliament: London mobs headed by apprentices were increasingly threatening those who opposed the parliamentary leadership, and as a reaction, on 30 December hundreds of students from the Inns of Court marched to the palace, pledging their allegiance to the king. Shortly afterward groups of soldiers started to assemble near the palace to defend the king, while trained bands of the local militia with Essex at their head gathered to defended Parliament. The conflict was becoming one of arms – indeed, by this time the terms Cavaliers and Roundheads started to circulate, describing respectively the disaffected royalist soldiers going about the city and the bands of pro-Parliament apprentices.[137]

Fearing that the exclusion of the bishops and the presence of mobs would thwart hopes to obtain a parliamentary majority that would support him, the King imprudently tried to force the hand of his opponents, and on 4 January 1642, accompanied by 400 swordsmen, came in person to the Commons, attempting to arrest five MPs that he accused of treason – Hampden, Holles,

---

[136] Adamson *Noble* pp. 420, 464.
[137] R. Digby Thomas, *George Digby: Hero and Villain* (Bloomington, Indiana: Author House Press, 2005) pp. 65–66.

Haselrig, Pym and Strode. The five, having been forewarned, made themselves scarce and could not be apprehended. But the King's unprecedented irruption into Parliament at the head of an armed cohort had disastrous consequences, for at once it destroyed his contention that he was the one defending the constitution against dangerous schemes and innovations. Many who had been drifting away from the opposition, recoiling from its increasing extremism, now rallied to it again. Parliamentary meetings were moved for the next week, from Westminster to Grocer's Hall in the City of London, and the protection of the nearby London trained bands. On 11 January 1642 the King himself, now fearing for his own safety, left London. In an essential sense, the Civil War had begun.[138]

There followed some months of tense maneuvers by both sides, each organizing itself and considering options, while exchanging public declarations, designed to gain higher moral and political ground and indicate the other side as responsible for the constitutional breakdown. Selden saw where this scuffle for supremacy between two sides was going, for without mutually agreed rules, a conflagration was inevitable, as he put it in colorful words, unflattering to either side:

The King and the Parliament now falling out, are just as when there is foul play offer'd amongst Gamesters, one snatches the others stake, they seize what they can of one another's. 'Tis not to be ask'd whether it belongs not to the King to do this or that: before when there was fair Play, it did. But now they will do what is most convenient for their own safety. If two fall to scuffling, one tears the others Band, the other tears his; when they were Friends they were quiet, and did no such thing, they let one another's Bands alone.[139]

First and foremost, as the moment of armed clash was approaching, both sides were attempting to claim the better legitimacy for their side in raising armed forces. Things came to a head on 5 March of 1642 when both Houses of Parliament agreed to issue a Militia Ordinance in order to raise a military force. It was customary for such parliamentary ordinances to go ahead with royal assent, but as that would obviously not be forthcoming this time, Parliament attempted to proceed without it. The King responded by attempting to raise troops directly on his part, through reviving the medieval instrument of a Commission of Array. There followed days of fierce parliamentary debates attempting to establish which of the two measures, if any, was to be regarded as lawful. It was only natural that in such a matter, great import was ascribed to Selden's opinion. In the debate on the Commission of Array, Selden declared it to be categorically illegal, in such terms as not only to convince Parliament, but

---

[138] It appears that King Charles' attempt to arrest the five members was foiled by the Queen's inadvertent divulging of the plan to her Lady of the Bedchamber, Lucy Hay, Dowager Countess of Carlisle, who passed the information to her cousin, Robert Devereux, Earl of Essex and a leader of the opposition. See Smuts "Puritan" p. 43, and Digby Thomas *Hero* pp. 65–71.

[139] TT "The King" sec. 7.

also many out of it (including some in the King's camp), of his opinion. The weight attributed to Selden's opinion in these circumstances is attested by Lord Falkland's writing, with the King's knowledge, of a letter to Selden, asking for the reasons of his view on this matter. Selden's answer made clear that he regarded the commission as illegal, but he also assured Falkland that as he similarly opposed the ordinance (although regarding it as less blatantly illegal than the commission), he would speak against it also, and expressed his confidence that it too should be defeated – thus denying either side a legal army without the other, and furthering the case of a peaceful settlement. As he promised, when the Militia Ordinance came to be discussed in the Commons, Selden rose to speak against it, and attempted to convince the members to defeat it. But his expectations about the way the vote on the ordinance would turn out proved misplaced. Too many parliamentarians felt things had gone too far to back down, and were now considering the prospect of military options, which for them overrode any fine points of law, so that on 15 March 1642, a majority of both houses supported the declaration that "the People are bound by the Ordinance for the Militia, though it has not received the Royal Assent."[140]

It is important to point out that the claim about Parliament's authority to summon an army by ordinance was not a claim to <u>legislative</u> authority, but to a <u>judicial</u> one. That is, that Parliament in its formal function as the highest of Common Law courts, could issue ordinances as judicial decrees. This was the claim that Selden regarded as being less illegitimate than the King's claim to sole authority by Commission of Array. It appears that both Lord Littleton and Chief Justice Bankes, then staying with the King, tended towards the opinion that the parliamentary ordinance could arguably be regarded as legitimate, and this was also to be the view of Philip's Hunton's *Treatise of Monarchy* (1643). Such view was opposed by most royalists, who held that in cases of constitutional impasse, it was the king who was to have residual authority over political issues. It was also opposed by the minority of parliamentarians (among them Saint John) who held that it was the Houses of Parliament who had residual political authority in a constitutional impasse, so that the claim to judicial authority was unnecessary. Both of these views about a "residual" legislative authority, implied that such an authority could in the last resort reside only in King or only in Parliament. While those preferring to claim judicial authority only for the ordinance tended to suspect that there was no such thing as a "residual" authority, in King or in Parliament alone, insisting

---

[140] Toomer *Scholarship* pp. 565–566; Aikin *Lives* pp. 115–116, 118–120; M. Mendle, "The Great Council of Parliament and the First Ordinances: The Constitutional Theory of the Civil War" in *Journal of British Studies* 31/2 (April 1992) pp. 133–162, and on Selden's position see especially p. 149. When the king published a rebuttal to Parliament's declaration that the Commission of Array was illegal, the parliamentary response was *A Second Declaration ... concerning the Commission of Array* (January 1643), ascribed in great part to Selden.

instead that legislative authority was only from King and Parliament, or not at all. That this was Selden's view is suggested by many of his comments, as well as by his actions in Parliament. He held that an irresolvable impasse can only be solved by finding an agreement between King and Parliament, otherwise "the decision is by arms" – because there can be no "third" to judge between the two sides.[141]

On 1 June 1642, Parliament passed nineteen propositions about the government of the country which, if approved, would in effect make it the supreme power in the land. The propositions were sent to King Charles at York, as a proposal for resolving the political crisis. On 21 June 1642 Charles reacted to the parliamentary document by issuing his *Answer to the Nineteen Propositions*, which rejected Parliament's proposal on the grounds of the principle "Nolumus Leges Angliae mutari" (We do not wish the Laws of England to be changed). It was not incidental that these were traditionally held to be the exact words by which the earls and barons of Henry III unanimously rejected proposals to change England's laws at the 1235 Parliament held at Merton, which resulted in what was regarded as the first English statute law. Charles was thus claiming for himself now, the mantle of defender of the traditional rights and liberties of the English.[142]

With issues and intentions now clear, the battle lines were drawn. In London, on 4 July 1642, Parliament created a Committee for Safety, to oversee military affairs. It consisted of five members from the Lords, and ten members from the Commons, of which Selden was not a member, reflecting his practical and ideological distance from the military course of things.[143] Meanwhile at York, by early July some 32 peers and many members of the Commons had joined Charles I, and were setting up the royalist military forces. Within a few weeks, standing armies had been formed and hostilities began to break out in different

[141] See TT "War" sec. 5; Cromartie *Constitutionalist* pp. 264–266. There are interesting parallels with the similar point James I made when explaining that there can be no "judge of the breake" of mutual promises made between king and people, and "none of them ought to judge of the other's breake." See James I, *The true law of free monarchies and, Basilikon doron*, D. Fischlin & M. Fortier eds. (Toronto, Center for Reformation and Renaissance Studies, 1996) pp. 76–80.

[142] Sir John Davies, *Irish reports* (1615) from "Preface," unpaginated. See also Cromartie *Constitutionalist* p. 65. The nineteen propositions demanded that the King's councilors and great officers, as well as the education and marriage of his children, should be approved by Parliament; that the Church of England would be reformed; and that the command of the armed forces and navy would be put under parliamentary control. In effect it put the government, the succession, the church and the military under sole control of Parliament, instead of the King. The King's *Answer* was thus essentially correct in claiming Parliament wanted to change the laws of England.

[143] From the Lords, the Earls of Essex, Holland, Northumberland, Pembroke as well as Viscount Saye and Sele; from the Commons, Nathaniel Fiennes, John Glynn, John Hampden, Denzil Holles, Henry Marten, Sir John Merrick, William Pierrepont, John Pym, Sir Philip Stapleton and Sir William Waller.

Tuck thinks it is most probable that the "Declaration of both Houses against the Commission of Array" of 1 July 1642, was substantially Selden's work. See Tuck "Ancient" pp. 150, 240.

parts of the country, even before either side had officially declared war. The formal declaration came on 22 August 1642, when Charles raised the royal standard at Nottingham.[144]

Even at this stage, moderates on both sides still hoped all-out war could be averted, and a settlement found within the constitutional framework. Among those around the King were the men closest to Selden, like Hertford and Hyde. The Earl of Dorset too, regardless of having been one to early prepare armaments for a possible conflict, nevertheless in the summer of 1642 was still searching, in letters to William Cecil, Second Earl of Salisbury, for a way out of the "labyrinth" of the current conflict that would not lead to "passinge the Rubicon." Regardless of his decided royalism, he rejected a solution that would entail a complete victory of one side, fearing that such a course would destroy the constitution, bringing about "an arbitrary government even on both sides," and he continued to search for a solution of "accommodation" with his contacts at Westminster. Other former moderates, like the Digbys, were moving towards the intransigent views of hard-line royalists like the Marquess of Newcastle.[145]

Meanwhile, in London a few moderate royalists like Edmund Waller, who had stayed on at Westminster, joined forces with longtime opponents of the king, like Harbottle Grimstone, Sir Benjamin Rudyard and Bulstrode Whitelocke, who were now increasingly voicing their desire for an accommodation that would avert war. At the Commons debate of 9 July 1642 Rudyard warned the house of the consequences of shedding blood, and Whitelocke quoted a warning proverb that proved prescient: "he that draws his sword against his prince, must throw away the Scabbard."[146]

Selden too was part of the same small group of those who believed everything should be tried to prevent armed conflagration. He consistently opposed the recourse to arms, and attempted to identify some path towards an agreed settlement. He repeatedly begged in the Commons his fellow parliamentarians to "think of some way of accommodating all matters of difference with His

---

[144] Wilcher *Writings* pp. 128–129, 170–172.

[145] D.L. Smith, *Constitutional royalism and the search for settlement c.1640–1649* (Cambridge University Press, 1994) pp. 96–97. Five wagon-loads of arms were seized from the Earl of Dorset's house at Knole in 1641, apparently purchased by him for the coming conflict, see Stone *Crisis* p. 222. After the king raised his standard and war erupted, Dorset wrote in August 1642 ruefully "All is lost, all is lost: soe lost as I would I weere quiet in my grave." D.L. Smith, "Sackville Edward" ODNB (accessed 12 March 2013). A good reflection of the differences of opinion in the royal camp about the course to be taken, is the short tract from late 1642, *His Majesties gracious answer to the different opinions of the Earles of Bristol and Dorset concerning peace and war. Wherein is intimated to all his loyall subjects the earnest desire he hath of a faire attonement betwixt himselfe and his high court of Parliament.* (1642) It addresses the views of the Earls of Bristol and Dorset, with the first proposing a more activist course of pursuing a victory in the field, while the second proposing a more accommodating policy and a peaceful settlement.

[146] Wilcher *Writings* pp. 128–129, 170–172; Barnes *Shaping* pp. 218–219.

Majesty," and on 9 July he was, with Strangeways a teller against the proposal to raise an army of 10,000 volunteers. The proposal was carried by 125 to 45, but whereas upon this defeat Strangeways promptly retired to his home and started to oppose the parliamentary side, Selden remained in Westminster, to lead the nascent peace party, with men like Rudyard and John Maynard.[147]

Selden's remarkable lack of personal animus or vindictiveness, reflected through the years by his willingness to uphold positions regarded as favorable to the King or to Parliament, on their merit rather than the profiting party, brought on recurring attempts by both sides to draw him firmly to their side, as well as suspicions as to his allegiance. His own view seems to have been that he did not feel himself obliged to either side, but only to what he believed was a constitution grounded on the twin principles of tradition and reciprocal collaboration. It is also likely that in such unprecedented constitutional circumstances, he was unsure about the import of many an event and incident, as they unfolded, and as to the preferable course towards the lesser of what he certainly regarded as two evils. Many of these concerns are displayed in remarks reflecting Selden's comments and insights about events from the time of the Civil War and interregnum, recorded in the *Table-Talk*. One such example:

In troubled Water you can scarce see your Face; or see it very little, till the Water be quiet and stand still. So in troubled times you can see little Truth; when times are quiet and settled, then Truth appears.[148]

Selden's position was obviously regarded as ambiguous enough for him to be considered by the royalists as a possible recruit to their side. As the King's men at York were organizing a government, it seems that Selden was seriously considered as Lord Keeper of the Great Seal instead of Littleton. But Lord Falkland and Hyde, who knew Selden well, both insisted (probably correctly) that he would absolutely refuse it. However, they still hoped to bring Selden to their side without offer of formal office. After Selden's answer to a letter written by Falkland, had shown him to be still insisting on his devotion to the King and to the cause of a peaceful settlement to the crisis, it was the turn of Hertford, the closest political ally Selden ever had, to write to him, proposing he join the King at York.[149] Men who were younger and more decided than Selden in their support for the King, like Robert Filmer and Roger Twysden, regarded themselves as too advanced in years to join the fray, and Selden certainly could be of no military value, serving only symbolic or advisory roles. Nevertheless, Selden felt he needed to justify his decision not to join the King, and applied himself to avert offending Hertford or the monarch with his answer. In his reply letter to Hertford, besides blaming his own infirm health

---

[147] Smith *Constitutional* p. 99.   [148] TT "Truth" sec. 3; Barnes *Shaping* p. 175.
[149] Tuck "Ancient" p. 137. In Milward's preface to the *Table-Talk*, he claims the Lord Keeper's position had been actually offered to Selden, but declined on grounds of ill health.

for making such a voyage inadvisable (the same grounds on which he had refused to join the 1636 embassy to Vienna), he also argued that he could far more assist the cause of the King and his reconciliation with Parliament, by remaining in London, where, he maintained, the real confrontation was to be fought. His subsequent activities demonstrate that he was indeed an unrelenting supporter of finding a peaceful solution to the conflict.

Selden's position in this case and others, could be seen as simply self-serving and dissembling; some of his contemporaries as well as later scholars certainly saw it in this light, especially among his clerical detractors, several of whom were recorded as saying of him "'twas true he was a man of great reading, but gave not his own sentiment."[150] However, the drawback of such evaluations is that they do not account for the fact that, aside from tactical ambiguities in various circumstances, Selden was overall not one to hide his views on important issues, even when it was far more advantageous not to be forthcoming about them. His activities during these years, in both Parliament and the Westminster Assembly, as well as his writings against divine tithes and later against Presbyterianism, amply attest to his decided stance on many contentious issues. Moreover, he seems to have never pursued in any substantial way preferment or honors, and indeed repeatedly refused these when offered to him. Evidently, many royalists who were close to him, like Falkland, Hertford and Hyde, believed Selden to be at most a reluctant follower of Parliament and accordingly attempted to bring him over to their side, first to York, and later on, to the Parliament summoned by the King at Oxford. They were right about his regarding Parliament's constitutional legitimacy as tenuous, but they failed to realize that he was even more reluctant to follow the King into completely uncharted constitutional waters. He regarded the King and his supporters as the primary "Incendiaries" who had set the country ablaze and were now conveniently adopting more moderate stances.[151]

Selden's choice to remain in London, and his regarding of the parliamentarian side as the one less blameworthy for the constitutional meltdown, did not mean he considered it to be without blame. Far from it, he was patently distressed at seeing the parliamentary party employing every trick in the book to fan the flames of the conflict, instead of pursuing a settlement. He

---

[150] Aubrey *Lives* p. 284.
[151] Selden's view of the King's responsibility for sparking the conflict is reported in TT "Incendiaries" thus: "Fancy to yourself a Man sets the City on Fire at *Cripplegate*, and that Fire continues by means of others, 'till it come to *White-Fryers*, and then he that began it would fain quench it, does not he deserve to be punish that fist set the City on Fire? So 'tis with the Incendiaries of the State. They that first set it on fire are now become regenerate, and would fain quench the Fire; Certainly they deserv'd most to be punish'd, for being the first Cause of our distractions." His frustration at the repeated failure of initiatives to reach a peaceful settlement in "Peace" sec. 2: "When a County-wench cannot get her Butter to come, she says, The Witch is in her Churn. We have been churning for Peace a great while, and 'twill not come, sure the Witch is in it."

articulated this dissatisfaction in several scathingly anti-parliamentarian comments recorded in the *Table-Talk*, such as:

The parliament party do not play fair play, in sitting up till two of the clock in the morning, to vote something they have a mind to: it is like a crafty gamester that makes the company drunk, then cheats them of their money: Young men and infirm men go away; besides a man is not there to persuade other men to be of his mind, but to speak his own heart; and if it be liked, so; if not, there is an end.[152]

It appears neither side in the conflict appreciated that Selden's adherence to the constitutional system was grounded on his understanding of it as based on the cooperation of King and Parliament, not on the capability of one side to dominate. Indeed, his view on this seems similar to that of Philip Hunton, who rejected claims by both parliamentarians on the one side and royalists on other side, that men choose so to say ideologically between the two camps, writing instead that since there was no obvious remedy to the constitutional crisis, every individual had to judge which side was most likely to restore the traditional functioning of the constitution.[153]

This meant Selden could never fully be neither a king's man nor a parliamentary one, but could and would assist the attempts at a constitutional restoration. As the King gradually adopted a position of defending the traditional constitution, Selden's remaining in London with his constitutionalist position and his insistence on an agreed resolution to the conflict made him into one of the few remaining "King's friends" in the capital, as Parliament was coming to be dominated by extremist positions. But he always resisted suggestions that he leave the capital, for in his view the desertion of Parliament by those who would support a compromise with the King only bolstered the position of the parliamentarian extremists. Again the *Table-Talk* records his view in colorful terms:

The King calling his Friends from the Parliament, because he had use of them at *Oxford*, is as if a Man should have use of a little piece of Wood, and he runs down into the Cellar, and takes the Spiggot, in the mean time all the Beer runs about the House; when his Friends are absent, the King will be lost.[154]

At length, Selden's premonitions were proven right, and as many moderates left London to join the King or to retire to their homes, by March 1643 the peace party lost the majority it had for a time enjoyed in the Commons, and by April, as negotiations with the King finally broke down, the radicals firmly gained the upper hand. A flurry of pamphlets advising radical policies ensued, and gradually small armed skirmishes

---

[152] TT "Parliament" sec. 8. See also sections 6 and 7.
[153] See D. Wootton "Introduction" in (ed.) *Divine Right and Democracy* (Harmondsworth: Penguin, 1986) pp. 36–37.
[154] TT "The King" sec. 8.

followed, until on 23 October 1643 a first major battle took place at Edgehill – the war had begun.[155]

As the conflict escalated, by successive waves of defections and expulsions, the Long Parliament purged itself from its more restrained elements. The process was evident not only among the backbenches, but among the leadership too. As the initial ascendance of peers like Bedford and Warwick waned, Pym and Hampden had come to the fore as the prominent leaders of Parliament, but by the end of 1643 both had died (respectively in June and December), and the stage was empty of almost all of the great names who had led Parliament hitherto. This effectively ended moderate leadership at Westminster, and together with the alliance with the Scots, that Pym orchestrated just before his death, a new, more intense and widespread stage of the war was ushered in. Some of the old guard that remained in the Commons, like Saint John and Holles had adopted militant attitudes, but the way had also been paved for the rise to prominence of far more radical figures, like Vane, Haselrig and Cromwell, and for the natural ascendance of military affairs. There gradually emerged among the parliamentarians three groups divided on the necessity of war, and the terms for its cessation, and although they are frequently described as "parties," this should not lead one to imagine any kind of unified political organization: a "war party" led by Cromwell, Vane and Haselrig, advocated an armed resolution to the conflict; a "middle group" made up for the most part of those uncertain about the best path to be followed, rather than a group with clear political goals, first headed by Pym and later by Saint John; and a "peace party," strongest in the Lords, where it was led by Essex, and with Selden a prominent figure in the Commons, it sought a settlement with the King at almost any price (even contemplating the abandonment of many of the nineteen propositions, and of the reforms in the church).[156]

Although after the victory of Marston Moor in July 1644, which made a settlement from a position of parliamentary strength seem likely, a number of MPs who had held more militant views, like Whitelocke and Holles, gradually came to embrace moderate positions and joined the peace party – especially the latter, who eventually came to lead it in the Commons – the group long remained in the minority. This was primarily due to the two parallel developments, of a steep decline in the political presence in Parliament of many moderates, especially in the House of Lords, now dwindled to a small number of mostly not very substantial peers (especially after Essex's death in

---

[155] D. Wootton, "From Rebellion to Revolution: The Crisis of the Winter of 1642/3 and the Origins of Civil War Radicalism" in *English Historical Review* 105/416 (1990) pp. 654–669, especially 658–660.

[156] D. Underdown, *Pride's Purge: Politics in the Puritan Revolution* (Oxford: Clarendon, 1971) pp. 45, 59–60, 63–64, 73.

1646), and the concurrent rise in political weight of the army and its political allies.[157]

Among these political developments, Selden proved as true to his words as to his own position. With each shift in parliamentary leadership towards militancy, he was becoming farther removed from the center of influence. Regardless, he never wavered from his position of constitutionalism and a consensual resolution to the conflict. Supporting Strafford's impeachment but not his attainder and execution; supporting church reform but not the abolition of the bishops or their exclusion from the Lords; consistently opposed to military measures leading to armed conflict, like the recruiting of an army, and both the Militia Ordinance and Commission of Array. It was also no coincidence that Selden was not a member of either of the two parliamentary committees set up to oversee the conduct of the war effort: the fifteen-member Committee of Safety (1642–1644), and the later, twenty-one-member Committee of Both Kingdoms (1643–1648). In the following years, he would continue to be found, time and again, among those who recoiled from militant policies: opposing the 1644 passing in Parliament of the bill of Attainder against Laud (by which the Archbishop was beheaded in January 1645), and repeatedly attempting to find some formula of compromise between the warring sides. Despite his political weakness in the mid-1640s, he did not relent from his parliamentary efforts. Selden continued to be active in the Long Parliament until Pride's Purge destroyed it, and although he spoke far less in the Commons after the outbreak of the war in 1642 than before, his name appears on committee lists of the years 1643–1648 with a regularity and a quantity similar to 1640–1642. He even subscribed to the Solemn League and Covenant in 1646 in order to continue in Parliament, hoping against hope that some settlement could be eventually reached, and consistently supported proposals for a negotiated peace.[158]

---

[157] Wilcher *Writings* p. 197. Some members the "old peace party" who had stopped attending the Commons by late 1644 were Hotham, Waller, Geoffrey Palmer, Norton Knatchbull and Harbottle Grimstone. Others, like John Maynard, Sir Benjamin Rudyerd, Sir John Coke, Simonds D'Ewes and of course Selden, remained in the Commons and continued to be active, led by Holles and joined by some others of formerly "middle group" views. See R.W. Harris, *Clarendon and the English Revolution* (Stanford University Press, 1983) pp. 130–131.

[158] Rex *University* p. 155. Selden's constitutionalist position in the conflict evidently seemed ambiguous enough to some. For example, an anonymous royalist satire of the 1640s resorted to Selden's reported relationship with Elizabeth Grey in order to snipe at "Grave Mr. Selden, who doth now repent / He ever search ye antiquities of Kent." See in Parker "Wrest" p. 174. While on the other hand, when in 1643 Edmund Waller's plot to organize a London rising that would restore Charles I to power and murder a number of his prominent adversaries, was exposed, Waller testified that he had tried to recruit Selden, coming one evening to the latter's study where he was conferring with MPs (and eminent lawyers) William Pierrepont and Bulstrode Whitelocke. When he sounded his idea to them in very general terms, they attacked it as treachery, baseness and an occasion for shedding of much blood, and he was much disheartened, and gave up involving them further in his programs. See Johnson *Memoirs* pp. 295–296.

Parliament was now dominated by two groups who together formed the bulk of the ascendant war party: the bigger group of "Presbyterians" and the more bellicose "Independents." The appellations of these groups drew from the prevalent religious identity of members, but although there was a degree of correspondence in this period between religious and political identities, it is important to stress there was never a complete correlation between the two, and men of different religious persuasions could be found in various political camps. Moreover, the personal composition of the Commons was changing. Until late 1645, the seats of some 200 MPs who had joined the King's side had been left vacant, but after the parliamentary victory at Naseby, writs began to be issued for elections to the vacant seats. The political affiliation of the newly elected tended preponderantly towards the Independents and support for the army, with many among them, like Fleetwood, Ludlow, Ireton and Hutchinson, names who would become famous in the interregnum. By the end of 1646 the number of newly elected "Recruiters" was some 235 out of a total of some 500, so that the composition of the lower house had changed dramatically. Never a party man, Selden had become by this stage not merely politically unaffiliated, but also quite distant from the main groups. He now came to head his own caucus of sorts – having remained a prominent figure in the Commons by virtue of his legal expertise, he led a small but effective contingent of lawyers remaining there, like Whitelocke and Pierrepont (who was closely related to Elizabeth Grey), as political moderates fighting tooth and nail in Parliament (and for some time also in the Westminster Assembly), any development they regarded as noxious to what was left of the law and the constitution. Reports from the early 1640s have the parliamentary "extreme advocates of change" meeting at the residences of Cromwell, Haselrig and Saint John, while the moderates met at the lodgings of Pym and of Selden. When Pym died, Selden's house remained the main meeting place for the small cohort of parliamentary moderates, most of whom were common lawyers.[159]

Even as the men of blood came to dominate the stage, Selden did not despair. He believed that in such troubled times, one should proceed cautiously and by degrees, sometimes giving in a little, but all the while patiently waiting for circumstances that permit an advance forward to his goal:

In a troubled State we must do as in foul Weather upon the *Thames*, not think to cut directly through, so the Boat may be quickly full of Water, but rise and fall as the Waves do, give as much as conveniently we can.[160]

---

[159] Pierrepont (1607–1678), prominent in the peace party was the second son of the Earl of Kingston, and doubly related to Elizabeth Grey – his Cavendish grandmother was sister to Elizabeth's mother, his Talbot grandfather was brother to Elizabeth's father – thus making him a kind of cousin-in-law to Selden. Johnson *Memoirs* p. 29, Tanner *Constitutional* pp. 134–135. See also TT "Peace" sec. 2.

[160] TT "Power, State" sec. 10.

Selden continued to attend the Commons, biding his time, and patiently went about "crossing the river" as conveniently allowed by circumstances. The waves indeed rose and fell with the fortunes of armies and parties, but Selden never lost sight of his goal – achieving a settlement of the crisis that would be within what we would today term as the constitutional framework.

As the Civil War raged, Selden's involvement in public affairs declined somewhat, while continuing to be active in defending scholarly interests from the depredations and persecution of wartime. He repeatedly foiled attempts to plunder libraries like Cotton House and Lambeth, and he opposed as best as he could the purges of faculty at Oxford and Cambridge who were judged by Parliament to be politically or religiously unreliable. For example, he successfully foiled the ejection of Thomas Barlow from his fellowship at Queen's College, Oxford, and probably had a role in securing the release from imprisonment of Robert Creswell a fellow of Trinity College, Cambridge. Indeed, grateful for his efforts on their behalf in those hard times, the fellows of Trinity College attempted to elect Selden in 1645 as their Master – even obtaining special permission from Parliament to elect a Master who was not a Fellow of the college – an honor which he nevertheless declined.[161]

There was nevertheless one major exception to the relative decline in Selden's activities in Parliament during the Civil War period – he remained consistently one of the most prominent speakers and operators in the debates regarding the future of church and state. He had argued vigorously in the Commons debates of 1641 and 1642, against the exclusion of bishops from Parliament and the abolition of episcopacy in the church. By early 1642 bishops had been excluded from Parliament, but the debate about abolishing the Episcopalian system in the church continued, especially as it was unclear what should replace it. In this confused state, a plurality of Presbyterians in the Commons, together with the necessity of a military alliance with the Scots, meant that a reform of the English Church along Presbyterian line became a definite possibility. A council of clergy and lay representatives, which became known as the Westminster Assembly of Divines, after the place of its meetings, was created to work out a church settlement. Originally composed of 121 divines as well as 20 members of the House of Commons and 10 of the Lords, to which a contingent of Scottish divines and lay representatives was also added, the Presbyterians among its membership enjoyed a clear majority. This composition, together with the terms of the "Solemn League and Covenant" to which the English Parliament had subscribed in September 1643, and which explicitly stated its goal as the bringing of the churches "in the three kingdoms to the nearest conjunction of uniformity" according to the examples "of the best reformed Churches," made an established Presbyterian English church appear the inevitable outcome.

---

[161] Ralph Browning, Bishop of Exeter and Vice-Chancellor of Cambridge, in a letter of January 1644, credited Selden with unspecified efforts to assist the University in those adverse circumstances. See Toomer *Scholarship* pp. 576–577.

However, they did not sufficiently reckon with the resolve and ability of Selden and the small group of like-minded members, who were determined to avert such an outcome. Initially assumed by many to be inordinately averse to the Anglican church, due to his former clashes on tithes and other issues, Selden ironically turned out to be in many ways its savior, as the most prominent, relentless and successful opponent in the Assembly as well as in Parliament, of establishing an English Presbyterianism.[162]

The Westminster Assembly, gathered by parliamentary ordinance on 12 June 1643, first convened on 1 July 1643, in the Henry VII Chapel of Westminster Abbey, but because of the cold there (even in summer!), later moved to the Jerusalem Chamber. On 12 October of the same year, the Assembly was formally charged by Parliament with devising a proposal for a settlement of the English Church. In December 1643 there arrived in London the contingent of Scottish Presbyterian commissioners and ministers, prominent among them Robert Baillie, who had been added to this English Assembly, with the obvious intent of leading England towards a Presbyterian system on Scottish lines. They immediately indicated their intentions by boycotting Pym's funeral, for they regarded him as having been a main obstacle to England's adopting of such a settlement. Mistaking Selden's former clashes with the Anglican establishment as indicators of anti-episcopalian leanings, Baillie had at first believed him to be a potential ally, even sending him a sermon of his on the advantages to England of a Presbyterian settlement, inscribed to "the most lernit [sic], his noble friend, Mr. Selden, in testimony of his high respect" adding (in Greek characters) "the future is invisible." As H. Trevor-Roper aptly remarked, for Baillie at least it was invisible indeed, since Selden rapidly emerged as the single most relentless and effective obstacle to the establishing of Presbyterianism in England. Soon in Baillie's eyes, it was first and foremost the "insolent absurdity" of John Selden, "head of all the Erastians," that brought to ruin all the plans for establishing an English Presbyterianism.[163]

The membership of the Assembly had a majority of Presbyterians (English and Scottish), a significant contingent of Independents (Congregationalists), and a small assortment of Episcopalians (most of whom, like Ussher, actually boycotted the Assembly), and of MPs of undefined religious allegiance. As the work of the Assembly progressed, the tiny contingent of Englishmen who were neither Presbyterians nor Independents, some of them clergymen like John Lightfoot and Thomas Coleman, others lawyers like Whitelocke and of course Selden, rose time and again before a vast majority of the Assembly and confounded grandiloquent declarations of Gospel truths, with objections that were often learned and challenging. Waves of sweeping Presbyterian orations

---

[162] J.H. Leith, *Assembly at Westminster* (Eugene, Oregon: WIP and Stock Publishers, 2008) pp. 24–27, 45–46.
[163] H. Trevor-Roper, *The Crisis of the Seventeenth Century* (Macmillan, 1967) pp. 291–293; Toomer *Scholarship* p. 569.

repeatedly broke over a barrier of concrete objections by Selden and his allies, followed by deafening silence. The inbuilt Presbyterian majority could not be defeated in an outright confrontation, but by contesting every initiative point by point, and by identifying and exploiting any dissension among the majority (between English Presbyterians and their Scottish counterparts, as well as between both of these and the Independents), their opponents succeeded in significantly grinding down the work of the Assembly, making what was expected to be a triumphal procession into an infuriating and exhausting snail-paced stagger. Baillie confided to his English ally, Francis Rous, that he was exasperated and astonished that "the wheels of the Lord's chariot should move with so slow a pace."[164]

Selden stopped attending the Assembly in the spring of 1644, apparently having concluded that he had better concentrate his efforts elsewhere. While his allies in the Assembly, like Lightfoot and especially Coleman, continued to obstruct the attempt to swiftly impose Scottish-style Presbyterianism, Selden concentrated on his parliamentary activity as well as his composing of Hebraist works like *De Anno Civili* (1644), *Uxor Ebraica* (1646) and *On the History of Presbyters*, a draft which was eventually integrated into the first volume of his *De Synedriis* (1650) – where he fulminated against Presbyterian pretensions. In March 1645, the demoralized Presbyterians suddenly found out that Selden and his allies had well used the time bought by their delaying tactics: a majority in Parliament had been convinced to pass a new Ordinance for Church Government, without deferring to the views of the Westminster Assembly. The Assembly reacted with a petition asserting that the Ordinance was in a number of points against the divine (that is, Presbyterian) dispensation of church government, and that they could not in conscience submit to it. The Commons created a Grand Committee to consider their response to the petition, and furious debates ensued until, on 17 April 1645, the Commons finally declared that to concede an autonomous Presbyterian church government would set aside the fundamental laws which devolve supreme jurisdiction on Parliament, and that they had no intentions "to part with this power out of the hands of the civil magistrate" since "the reformation and purity of religion, and the preservation and protection of the people of God in this kingdom, hath under God been by the Parliament, and their exercise of this power." Selden could not have put it better, and he probably didn't have to, since as a prime mover behind these parliamentary deliberations and declarations, we can suppose he had a central role in drafting them. As it turned out, Selden and his small group of allies had orchestrated what would prove to be a definitive victory over the Assembly, by convincing a majority in Parliament that any church government had to be subject to parliamentary supremacy. The church settlement eventually enacted in March 1646, followed these lines, stipulating the subjection of church judicial and

---

[164] Trevor-Roper *Crisis* pp. 291–292.

disciplinary powers to the authority of Parliament, thus neutering any independent clerical discipline, and making the nominal Presbyterianism of the settlement a dead letter.[165]

A prominent (but anonymous) Italian, versant in English politics, wrote around this time in his report about the debates at the Westminster Assembly, that he had met one "called Selden the Independent, and thoroughly a Churchman without a Church" (chiamato Seldenus Indipendente, e tutto interamente Echlesiastico sine Ecchlesia), an assessment of Selden's non-aligned religious stance, that was equally valid for his position among the political factions in Parliament. Essentially the same evaluation of Selden's position is conveyed by the satirical poem composed by John Cleveland about the Westminster Assembly:

> But *Selden* he's a Galliard [dancer] by himself;
> And well may be; there's more Divines in him,
> Than in all this their *Jewish Sanhedrim*[166]

Meanwhile, on the political front, as the military successes of the parliamentary armies dissolved the danger of a royalist victory, a growing antagonism emerged inside the alliance that had won the war: on one side the army and its mainly independent and sectarian supporters in Parliament led by Cromwell, who were becoming ever more politically intransigent, and on the other side the Presbyterians led by Denzil Holles, who were coming round to politically moderate positions (undoubtedly aided by their evident losing political ground to the Independents) and gradually converging in their views of a settlement with the peace party. In early 1647, the Scottish Presbyterian army delivered King Charles, who had turned himself over to their protection, into the hands of the English army. But this apparently decisive victory only served to exacerbate the fissions within the parliamentary camp. The English army and its supporters were finding themselves politically threatened by the convergence of the Presbyterians and their Scottish allies with the peace party, as well as with a newly resurgent royalism that was gaining popular support, as more Englishmen were learning the realities of living under the new "godly" regime. In June 1647, as the Presbyterians were approaching an understanding with the royalists about a settlement that would end the domination of politics by the army, the latter charged eleven leading Presbyterian MPs, headed by Holles with treason, and although the accusations were rejected by Parliament, upon the subsequent advance of the army towards London, the Presbyterian leadership saw it prudent to escape the city. Even with its parliamentary foes on the run, the army had to enter London in order to quell a pro-royalist move by the city council, and did so yet again only a few months later, as popular riots

---

[165] A.F. Mitchell & J. Struthers (eds.), *Minutes of the Sessions of the Westminster Assembly of Divines* (1874) pp. 209–210, 434–436.

[166] Toomer *Scholarship* p. 574; J.L. and S.D. (eds.), *The works of Mr. John Cleveland* (1687) p. 35.

flared up against the ordinance that (since 1644) had forbidden the celebration of Christmas day. In effect, a second civil war had started as a series of isolated and ultimately unsuccessful risings, reflecting the mounting popular dissatisfaction with the new political masters.[167]

One of the last prominent acts of Selden's political career was not incidentally connected to the last significant attempt for bringing about a consensual reconciliation between the King and Parliament, which he doubtless had a part in preparing. On 11 December 1647, Selden is recorded as having gone up to the House of Lords with a message from the Commons, desiring consent to four bills which were to be then presented to the King for his assent: concerning the management of the army and navy; justifying the proceedings of Parliament in the late war; concerning the peerage; and concerning the adjournment of both houses. The four bills clearly laid down the groundwork for a reconciliation with the King and the resuming of a united government for the country. Moreover, when the Scottish Commissioners expressed their desire to inspect these bills before they were approved, Selden again appeared at the bar of the House of Lords, with two resolutions from the Commons, rejecting the Scottish request, and vindicating the independence of Parliament from such outside interference. However, the King once again failed to seize the opportunity to end the conflict on reasonable terms, so that the initiative came to nothing.[168]

Within a growingly distrustful and conspiratorial political atmosphere, Selden stood out as a consistently clear and calm voice, adhering to his often unpopular principles, unceasingly "churning for peace," as he termed it. He continued to attend the Commons, and kept to his course of advocating an agreed constitutional settlement, while refusing to bind himself to one of the factions jostling for power. An anonymous pamphlet of August 1648, referring scathingly to the greed and dishonesty of Commons' members, had a good word only for Selden, describing him as one who "keepes his Conscience, and often dissents from the Votes of the House."[169]

Selden himself apparently did not regard his often confrontational and isolated position in the Commons as completely fruitless, believing that, after the din of a debate had settled and MPs had time to reconsider and digest the issues, they may at length come to think differently about them, so that in the long run his dissenting stance may be eventually vindicated. This is pretty much the import of his somewhat comical remark (and yet another of his beer metaphors about politics) on the subject in the *Table-Talk*:

[167] Wilcher *Writings* pp. 261–262. As early as 1644 Holles and Essex had attempted to impeach Cromwell, and shortly afterward the latter's supporters retorted by accusing Holles of secret communications with the King. Although both attempts failed, they speak volumes about the deteriorating state of the alliance between the Presbyterians and the army.

[168] Johnson *Memoirs* pp. 333–334.

[169] Quoted in Toomer *Scholarship* p. 566 and note 26. See also TT "Peace" sec. 2.

Dissenters in parliament may at length come to a good end, though first there be a great deal of do, and a great deal of noise, which mad wild folks make; just as in brewing of Wrest-Beer, there's a great deal of business in grinding the Mault, and that spoils a man's clothes that comes near it; then it must be mash'd; then comes a fellow in and drinks of the wort, and he is drunk; then they keep a huge quarter when they carry it into the Cellar, and a twelvemonth after it is delicate, fine Beer.[170]

At length, Selden's patience did produce a fine brew. By late 1648, weariness of war had set in and, combined with the widespread realization that rule by a coalition of soldiers and religious fanatics would be the worse outcome imaginable for England, a clear majority of the Commons came to the conclusion that a settlement with the King, as advocated by Selden and his allies of the peace party, would be the preferable resolution to the crisis. Holles and his allies were permitted to return to take their seats in the house, and the search for some kind of Presbyterian–Royalist settlement accelerated – at the very same time that the army was growing less and less willing to submit to the authority of Parliament. When Parliament appointed 15 commissioners, headed by Holles, to treat with the captive King at Newport, the army drafted and sent to the King its own document, known as the "Grand Remonstrance" as basis for a settlement – the division in the parliamentary camp had come fully to the fore. On 18 September 1648, King Charles rejected the army's "Grand Remonstrance" as basis for settlement, while giving conciliatory answers to the latest proposals from the parliamentary commissioners. To a majority of Parliament, a peaceful settlement of the conflict now seemed at long last within reach, and after additional maneuvers, on 5 December 1648 the House of Commons passed, by 129 to 83 votes, a resolution on allowing a vote about whether the King's answers to the latest proposal were sufficient basis for a settlement of the constitutional crisis. Though this resolution was only a procedural one, it showed there was now a solid majority for the "peace party" and for achieving a settlement with the King that would discard the demands of the army – in effect the House of Commons had voted for a Restoration. But it came too late, as well as 11 years too early, for neither the radicals nor the army would allow such a course at this time.

On the morning of the very next day, Wednesday, 6 December, Colonel Thomas Pride's regiment took positions on the stairs at the entrance to the Commons and denied access to incoming members that the army had decided were to be purged. Some 45 members were arrested (Strode and Prynne among them) and confined in a Westminster alehouse, aptly named *Hell*; most were released within a few days, but permanently barred from returning to Parliament. Many more stayed away, some of them, like Holles and Anthony

---

[170] See TT sec. "parliament" par. 4. It has been suggested that the term "Wrest-Beer" refers to "rest-beer," from the time it was allowed to lie before being used. But perhaps it only refers to a beer made at Wrest, the country house of the Earls of Kent, of which Selden was a regular resident.

Ashley Cooper, prudently fleeing London before the soldiers could lay hands on them. Formally secluded MPs, whether imprisoned or not, eventually numbered some 230 – about half of the pre-purge House of Commons. But the true membership of the new "Commons" was effectively even smaller than these numbers suggest, since another 86 members, who had not been formally secluded, abstained hereafter from attending in protest at the purge. There was now a new "House of Commons," created solely by the will of the army, and numbering about 155 members – less than a third of the pre-purge membership. It is unclear if, on the day of the purge, Selden was among those briefly arrested (unlikely), those turned away at the door, or those who sensed where things were going and chose to stay away to begin with. It is not even known for sure if he had participated in the crucial vote the previous day, although that is very likely. What is clear is that he was one of those formally secluded, since the army certainly could not count on him to do their bidding.[171]

On 4 January 1649, recognizing that even the few peers remaining in the House of Lords would not participate in the final destruction of the King and of the constitution, the purged "Commons" arrogated to themselves alone the "Supreme authority of this Nation." Thus was formed the creature that would come to be colloquially known as the "Rump Parliament" – reflecting its true nature of an arbitrary and shameless tyranny by a self-appointed group, masking itself under the name of Parliament.[172]

As the trial of Charles I began on 20 January 1649, it appears that Selden, like other prominent lawyers (such as Whitelocke), unwilling to be anywhere near such a cruel farce masquerading as judicial proceeding, retired from the capital. In an ironic twist, during the trial, which was conducted in Westminster Hall, Cromwell ordered the King to be kept next door, in none other than Cotton's house, the library of which had formerly been sealed by Charles' command

---

[171]   D. Underdown, in his study of the purge divides the 471 members of the House of Commons at the time into five groups: (R) revolutionaries, committed to the revolution of Dec–Jan 1648/9; (C) conformists, who did not commit formally but accepted the revolution *a posteriori* in February (after the King's execution); (A) abstainers, not formally secluded but voluntarily stayed away from Parliament until at least March; (S) secluded, formally purged from Parliament; (I) secluded and imprisoned in the purge. Selden is listed among the (S) group, of those formally secluded. See Underdown *Purge* pp. 151–153, 210–211, 385. See also I. Roots, *Commonwealth and Protectorate* (New York: Schocken, 1966) pp. 132–133. A letter of January 1651 mentions that the committee of the Rump going through the lists of secluded members, to decide which of them should be protected from new elections and which expelled, compiled a list of names to be referred to the whole Commons for further consideration, among those names Selden appears. See Underdown *Purge* p. 289.

[172]   Barnes *Shaping* p. 218. It appears Selden had these events in mind when he was recorded as remarking sardonically: "The House of Commons is called the Lower House, in twenty Acts of Parliament; but what are twenty Acts of Parliament amongst Friends?" See TT "House of Commons."

(with Selden having the key, since the war began). By 30 January the King had been tried, condemned and executed.[173]

The army and its political supporters had carried out a military coup, probably the first one of the modern era, by ejecting a majority of the Commons membership and later abolishing the upper house altogether, to create the "Parliament" they wanted but never succeeded (nor would succeed) in achieving through elections. Selden lived long enough to witness the successive constitutional dead ends of the interregnum: in March 1649 the Rump's formal abolition of monarchy and in May the declaring of England a Commonwealth; in April 1653 the subsequent forced dispersion of the Rump itself by Cromwell at the head of his soldiers, with the words "Depart, I say; and let us have done with you. In the name of God, go!"; and in December 1653 what Milton later described as the "scandalous interruption" in English constitutional history – the installing of the six-year Protectorate regime with Cromwell at its head. The "constitution" created to legitimize the new regime was the first written one in the English language, and it formalized military dictatorship. In effect, by the end of 1653 the republican movement had collapsed and, through Cromwell, monarchical rule had been re-established, without a formal monarchy. There was a search for an appropriate appellation for its head, some suggesting he actually be crowned King Oliver; others preferred General as connected to the Roman military tradition, and the eventual title of Lord Protector was an ambiguous one, selected from English history for periods of interregnum or incapacity of a king – although there were those who pointed out it was also a version of the title given to governors of ancient Israel, like Moses and Joshua, with some even suggesting that he should head a supreme political council formally called "Sanhedrin." By 1657, the monarchical transition was complete with Cromwell's second investiture as Protector taking place in King Edward's chair, royal paraphernalia used, and the settling of the title as hereditary in his family.[174]

The rebellion against the fear from an arbitrary monarchy had transformed itself by degrees into a rule of an arbitrary tyrant, governing through Major-Generals, with "Parliaments" summoned by at will and dispersed by the sword, legislation by executive ordinance, judges sacked summarily and permanent public unrest. The nature of the regime was perhaps most evident in the state funerals of the commonwealth, such as those for Isaac Dorislaus and Henry Ireton – stripped of all the old myths, pageants and images scorned by the Puritans, these became little more than military parades. Always rapaciously

---

[173] Gregg *Charles* pp. 433–435.

[174] Sharpe *Remapping* pp. 250–251, 257; P.A. Rahe, *Against Throne & Altar – Machiavelli and Political Theory under the English Republic* (Cambridge University Press, 2008) pp. 116–117, 217–218. In 1653 Cromwell's court even staged (regardless of the general ban on theatrical performances) the very royal event of a Masque named "Cupid and Death"; devised by Davenant, it was performed in honor of the Portuguese ambassador. See Sharpe *Remapping* pp. 248.

exacting and perennially bankrupt, it was a regime so despotic and illegitimate
that it began to quickly unravel immediately upon the death of Oliver
Cromwell, the only figure capable of balancing its factions and the army;
within a mere 18 more months, the monarchy had been restored.[175]

The political path followed by the two main political figures of the period is
instructive: Cromwell traveled all the way from backbencher opposition MP in
the long Parliament to general and dictator, from defender to destroyer of
English liberties; it was a trajectory opposite to that of Charles I, whose
actions and intentions initially set him as the foe of English liberties, but who
by degrees came to present himself and indeed to be widely perceived as their
guarantor and martyr, declaring at his trial: "I am entrusted with the liberties of
my people. I do stand more for the liberties of my people than anyone seated
here as a judge: Therefore show me by what lawful authority I am seated here
and I will answer it. Otherwise I will not betray the liberties of my people."
Sadly, he was to be proven right.[176]

A comprehensive assessment of Selden's parliamentary activities in the 1640s
shows him to have been very much consistent in his constitutional outlook
(especially considering the great transformations that so many others went
through). For all the many particular reverses he suffered, he was
extraordinarily tenacious in pursuing his long-term political goals. Against a
background of growing extremism and shifting positions Selden was one of the
few individuals who were consistently heard in support of finding a moderate
and agreed resolution to the conflict. Although almost always in a small
minority, his constant and relentless pursuit of his goals, together with his
skillful exploiting of tactical opportunities, eventually handed him victories in
his two main fields of parliamentary activity: in the matter of church and state,
he had a prominent role in preventing the establishment of a Presbyterian state
Church of England, and in convincing Parliament that any religious settlement
had to be subject to political authority; in the conflict between King and
Parliament, he and his allies ultimately won over the majority of the long
Parliament to their vision of a restored constitution, that would establish a
stable balance between King and Parliament, while preserving the reforms of
government achieved in 1640–1641. This latter parliamentary victory was for a

---

[175] Sharpe *Remapping* pp. 248.
[176] Roots *Commonwealth* p. 170; Barnes *Shaping* pp. 209–210. English radicalism, whether in
Puritan, army or Leveller guise, never came anywhere close to drafting the support of a majority
of the people who might be called to vote, however defined, and thus had to enact various
purges and disqualifications from political participation in order to prop up their ascendancy.
Their real political theory, was aptly described by Needham in *Mercurius Pragmaticus*
(November 1648): "That their own faction (whom alone they call the well-affected, and the
honest men, excluding all others) are the People…" and "That themselves are the only
competent judges of the people's safety…" and therefore "may drive on their designs against
all powers, and forms of government, and law whatsoever, under pretence of that old aphorism,
Salus Populi Suprema Lex." Underdown *Purge* p. 359.

time nullified by the army coup which turned England into an 11-year military dictatorship. But in the longer run, his constitutional ideas were those which won out in the eventual shape of the Restoration, so that, all things considered, the name of John Selden certainly deserves a place of pride among those responsible for salvaging the English Constitution and the Anglican Church, during their ordeal of Civil War and interregnum.

During this period of great political upheavals, in which Selden was so deeply involved, he produced relatively little in the way of scholarly output. He published two works which formed part of his great Hebraist project, *De Anno Civili et Calendario Veteris Ecclesiae seu Republicae Judaicae* (1644) a treatise on the Jewish calendar, and the *Uxor Ebraica seu de Nuptiis et Divortiis Veterum Ebraeorum* (1646) on Jewish marriage and divorce law. Selden also mentioned in the latter work that he was working on a text named *On the History of Presbyters and Presbyteries*, dealing for the most part with Church government and the practice of excommunication (both of obvious relevance at that period). However, even this circumscribed output is deceiving, for the *Uxor* was essentially completed and probably even circulating in manuscript (which Milton might have read) before Selden prepared his *Jure Naturali* for publication in late 1639 – thus the *Uxor* really belongs to his work of the 1630s. As for the *History of Presbyters*, Selden eventually inserted it together with other materials which he had been working on since the early 1630s into the first volume of *Synedriis* (1650). It might therefore be said that the relatively small *Anno Civili* was the only Hebraist work by Selden wholly produced in the 1640s.[177]

In addition to these Hebraist texts, Selden published in the 1640s three other works, none of them a major endeavor. Two works printed in 1642 were the small treatise on the *Priviledge of the Baronage of England*, written long before, it was published at this time in the context of constitutional debates about the composition and powers of the peers. In the same year, he also published a translation of a section from a chronicle written by Said Ibn Batriq, the tenth-century Patriarch of Alexandria, referred to after the Greek version of his name, as *Eutychius*. The chronicle supported Selden's portrayal of early Christianity as a developing religion, with strong roots in contemporary Judaism, and thus very different in its earliest form from what it later became – again an issue of obvious relevance at a time of debates about the future shape of the English church.[178] The last work Selden published in this decade, and probably the most consequential, was his learned "Dissertatio historica" prefacing the anonymous

---

[177] Toomer *Scholarship* pp. 692–693. About the *Uxor*, the time of composition and its circulation in manuscript which Milton may have seen and employed (and about a possible personal acquaintance between Selden and Milton), see M. Biberman "Milton, Marriage, and a Woman's right to divorce" in *Studies in English Literature 1500–1900*, 39/1 (1999) pp. 131–153, and see especially note 7.

[178] Toomer *Scholarship* pp. 613–614.

but influential medieval commentary on English law known as *Fleta*, in which he presented his ideas as to the place of Roman law in English legal history, as well as about the traditional and national character of English law.[179]

1.8 FINAL YEARS: 1649–1654

In early 1649 Selden's old world had come to an abrupt end. He and a majority of MPs had been purged from Parliament, the King had been executed, the English constitution was dead and some meaningless simulacra had been put in their place. There followed successive attempts at creating a stable new regime, first as a Commonwealth, then as a Protectorate, with brute military force being all the while, the real deciding power. There was neither an apparent prospect for a restoration of the old constitution, nor an appealing alternative to it. Selden certainly had no intention of playing a part in a Regicide regime effectively controlled by the army. From the time of King Charles' trial and execution, in 1649, Selden took no further formal part in politics. It appears that there was some indecision in the Rump about his seclusion, and later there were repeated attempts to co-opt him into the Cromwellian regime, by investing him with some political office, but Selden declined all such suggestions. The one office he had previously accepted, having been voted by the Commons in 1643 as "clerk and keeper of the records of the Tower," he kept for its obvious rewards in advancing and defending scholarship, but ceased to draw the pecuniary income derived from it.[180]

Another non-pecuniary appointment he kept, until resigning in 1652 due to his age and health, was not formally in the power of the government – that of a member of the Assembly of Governors of the Charterhouse Hospital (in effect an almshouse for destitute elderly gentlemen), which had been voted to him in 1645 by the other governors, upon Parliament's deposing of Sir Robert Heath from that body.[181]

Regardless of their former political divisions,[182] Cromwell apparently esteeming Selden's legal abilities, and certainly appreciating the legitimacy to his rule that such a prestigious name would bestow, repeatedly attempted to

[179] The *Fleta* owes its name to its supposed composition while its anonymous author was in the Fleet prison. Doubts have sometimes been raised against this claim, but Selden, who worked on a number of his books while imprisoned, believed otherwise and probably even felt some kinship with the author on account of their similar circumstances. Selden is sometimes erroneously claimed to have edited the text of *Fleta* accompanied by his "Dissertatio" – he explicitly made it clear that he only supplied the manuscript used by the printer, without having done any work with the printed text, the defects of which he in fact severely criticized. See Toomer *Scholarship* p. 198.

[180] Underdown *Purge* p. 289, and Fry "Selden" DNB.

[181] See Toomer *Scholarship* p. 567 and note 31.

[182] Cromwell and Selden, prominent respectively in the war and peace parties, were mostly on opposite sides of political issues (church and state was an exception), and in February 1648 there were even reports that Cromwell had moved (unsuccessfully) to expel Selden from the

draft the great scholar into the new regime. There were reports that Cromwell wanted Selden (together with Oliver Saint John) to compose a new constitution for the state, but this too failed to entice Selden – recognizing the true nature of the regime, he refused all entreaties to partake in the government of interregnum England. Selden is also reported to have rejected a less formal, but still prominent, service requested of him by the Cromwellian circle, when he was asked to write an answer to the enormously popular royalist tract *Eikon Basilike* – upon his repeated refusal, the task was assigned to Milton. Nevertheless, Selden did not actively oppose the regime, nor he denied it informal advice on specific issues, when requested of him, especially such as was having to do with his expertise in international law. There are no signs of Selden's objecting to the command by the Cromwellian Council of State, in 1652 in the context of the Anglo-Dutch war, that the regime's principal propagandist, the able and mercurial Marchamont Needham, translate into English and publish Selden's *Mare Clausum*, titled in English *Of the Dominion or Ownership of the Sea* (naturally omitting the original dedication to Charles I), and reserving 200 copies for the use of the Council. Selden also assisted the government on matters of dignity and precedence of ambassadors, and in December 1653, he was consulted by his Inner Templar friend Henry Rolle, by then a member of Cromwell's Council of State and the Chief Justice of the Upper Bench (the interregnum name for King's Bench), about the law-of-nations aspects of bringing a charge of murder against Don Pantaleon Sa, brother of the Portuguese Ambassador, for whom diplomatic immunity was claimed (Sa was eventually convicted and executed in July 1653).[183]

Regardless of his abstaining from any formal participation in the political life of the interregnum, it appears Selden retained a keen interest in the political and legal developments of the new government, as befitted his lifelong commitment to the laws and the constitution of England. In August 1651 a visitor found Selden's doors and walls plastered with the recent acts of Cromwell's regime, clear evidence that the house-owner continued to follow them intently.[184]

Many of his erstwhile patrons and friends, like the Earl of Bristol and his son George Digby, were now ruined or exiled by the war and its repercussions, while others, like the Earls of Hertford and of Dorset, retreated from politics after the purge and regicide (reportedly, after the King's execution, Dorset did not again set foot outside his house for the remaining three years of his life). In

---

Commons when the latter defended the King from accusations of having attempted to poison his father. See Toomer *Scholarship* p. 569.

[183] Aikin *Lives* pp. 144–145, Toomer *Scholarship* pp. 567–568. Indeed, a letter of 2 March 1654 to Bulstrode Whitlocke, then English ambassador to the Swedish court, is addressed by Selden to "the Lord Whitelocke Lord Embassador [sic] from the State of England & c. to Hir Ma[jes]tie of Sweden." The strangely pallid definition of England as a "State" may reflect both the new regime's unstable formal definition (the Commonwealth had become a de facto Protectorate in December 1653), as well as Selden's aversion to it.

[184] Toomer *Scholarship* p. 567.

any case, real political power was now wielded by the army, by Cromwell and his extended clan, and by sectaries and agitators, all of them groups for whom someone like Selden or his ideas could have little substantial value.[185]

His lifelong efforts to defend English constitutionalism had ended in what appeared to be total and final failure; he was in his late 60s, of delicate health, not under any threat and quite wealthy. It would not have been unreasonable to expect that, like many others whose lives and work had been disrupted by the conflict, he too would now retire from public affairs entirely, and as best he could privately enjoy his later years.[186]

But this was not the measure of the man. Instead of retreating into voluntary isolation, he set about this new world to aid friendship and scholarship wherever he could. For all his having retired from political activity and office, he retained prestige and influence with many, and found himself chief protector of men like Hertford and Ussher, who were politically distrusted and financially challenged, as well as a number of scholars at Cambridge and Oxford whose scholarship and livelihood were being curtailed because of religious or political suspicions. He defended, encouraged and assisted them when he could, in some cases even extending his own financial patronage to aid the efforts of scholars like Edward Pococke and Meric Casaubon.[187]

Selden also actively defended repositories of scholarship, like the records in the Tower or the libraries of the universities and of the Cotton family, from

[185] The true nature of the Cromwellian ascendancy is best exemplified by the extremely clannish character of the regime, which would have likely increased had it had more time to settle. Cromwell's clan (to whom Hampden and Saint John too were related) included aside from the Protector and his sons, Major-General Henry and future Protector Richard, also three of his brothers-in-law Major-General John Desborough, and the regicide Colonels John Jones and Valentine Walton; two sons-in-law, General Henry Ireton and Major-General Charles Fleetwood; one cousin, Major-General Edward Whalley and the latter's son-in-law, Major-General William Goffe. Thus, out of ten Major-Generals ruling England, four were related to the Cromwell clan, while the sole Major-General ruling Ireland, was Cromwell's own son...

[186] On the cult of friendship and retirement among cavaliers in the 1650s, brought about by the political collapse of royalism, see Wilcher *Writings* p. 245.

[187] Since the start of the Civil War Selden held the key to Cotton's library, and assisted the needs of older and younger scholars including Ussher and Meric Casaubon. See Woolf *Idea* p. 238. A 1653 letter from Selden to Thomas Cotton, concerning the attempt by the government to lodge people in Cotton's house, which Selden successfully opposed, shows the latter's still significant political clout.

Regarding Ussher, Selden shielded him from persecution during the Civil War, when the Archbishop was under a cloud of political suspicion; and when Ussher's library was confiscated by Parliament, Selden had it purchased as if for his own use, but actually preserving it for his friend; and in 1647 he succeeded in procuring for Ussher the lectureship at Lincoln's Inn. See A. Ford, *James Ussher* (Oxford University Press, 2007) pp. 267–268. As for Casaubon, he had apparently already benefited from Selden's assistance by 1643, when he dedicated to the latter his edition of Marcus Aurelius' *Meditationes*; but as Casaubon relates in a letter of 1650 to Ussher, in the late 1640s, when Selden had learned the young scholar was in dire financial necessity, in yet another example of his generosity, he swiftly presented him of his own accord with a considerable sum of money. See Aikin *Lives* p. 159.

rapacious or zealous attempts to tamper with them. Moreover, he now had much more time to devote to his studies again, and in his last few years he published a number of works. Some of these were relatively small things, such as a collection of ten English medieval chronicles which he edited together with Sir Roger Twysden (a close friend of Robert Filmer), the *Decem Historiae Anglicanae Scriptores* (1653), to which he also wrote a preface; and the *Vindiciae Secundùm Integritatem Existimationis Suae per Convitium de Scriptione Maris Clausi* (1653) a defense of his conduct against the accusation by the Grotian Theodore Graswinckel (in his 1652 *Maris Liberis Vindiciae*) that the *Mare Clausum* and its contents had been composed by Selden under duress. He also seems to have been working on a third, revised edition, of *Diis Syriis*, which he was preparing for publication in 1653, but died before having completed it.[188]

However, Selden clearly directed the bulk of his scholarly efforts in this period to the completion of his massive *Synedriis*, a study of the ancient Jewish judicial and political bodies that had swelled to cover many other issues – an effort on which he was working intermittently perhaps even since 1629, certainly since 1631. In the preface to the eventual first volume, Selden stated that he had completed a version in two books by 1638 (the first on the council's history and organization, the second on its judicial procedures), but later accretion of materials meant he had split the first book into two, with only the third coming to actually deal with the Great Sanhedrin (aka Synedrion). Originally conceived and titled as *A History of the Great Synedrion*, it eventually came to be named (as translated by Toomer) *On the Assemblies and Offices of the Ancient Jews which Dispensed Justice* (*De Synedriis et Praefecturis Juridicis Veterum Ebraeorum*). The principal reason for the accretion and changes seems to be the large section, occupying some two thirds of the first book (and probably intended originally to appear as a separate work), on the history and theories of excommunication, mainly among Christians, apparently prompted by Selden's confronting the issue in the 1640s in both the Westminster Assembly and in Parliament. Thus the preface to the first volume contains a strong and explicit attack on

[188] The actual full title of the *Vindiciae* is *Ioannis Seldeni Vindiciæ Secundùm Integritatem Existimationis Suæ: Per Convitium de Scriptione Maris Clausi, Petulantissimum Mendacissimm̀que Insolentiùs Læsæ in Vindiciis Maris Liberi Adversùs Petrum Baptistam Burgum, Ligustici Maritimi Dominii Assertorem, Hagæ Comitum jam Nunc Emissis*, dated May 1653, from Whitefriars, and it is dedicated to his friend and protégé John Vaughan. Although Selden explicitly denied in the *Vindiciae* any agreement on his part to publish the *Mare Clausum* in return for his release from bail, Toomer suspects there was some kind of informal agreement as a condition for Selden's release. See Toomer *Scholarship* pp. 390–391.
  As for the *Diis Syriis*, when Wilkins printed the *Opera Omnia*, he had the manuscript of a revised third edition of the *Diis*, so he integrated many of its changes into the version he published. These insertions escaped notice for centuries until G.J. Toomer spotted and detailed them. See Toomer *Scholarship* pp. 841–844.

Presbyterians, accusing them of criticizing the Pope for trying to assert a divine right to excommunicate, while attempting to arrogate to themselves that very same right. The second volume follows the judicial history of the Jews to the destruction of the temple, and the third volume is devoted to the Great Sanhedrin itself.[189]

Selden continued to correct and enlarge every volume of *De Synedriis* until its publication, and was working on the final third volume when he died. He managed to complete a large part of this last projected great work, publishing the first volume in 1650 and the second in 1653. As for the third volume, although by the time he died he had proceeded a great deal towards completing it, he did not actually achieve this goal, and what was published posthumously in 1655 bears the mark of an incomplete effort (especially in its latter sections), probably intended to be at least one-third longer.[190]

These last years were not especially easy ones for Selden. Some of his old friends were making themselves scarce or devoting their time to escaping the rapaciousness of a bankrupt and regicide regime; others had died or were ailing. In 1651 his companion, Elizabeth Grey, or, if they indeed had married, Elizabeth Selden, passed away; her funeral was an elaborate affair, apparently costing the staggering amount of some 1600 pounds – about the same as the annual rent yields of the Earls of Kent. Yet, for all the grief the Countess' death certainly gave him, and for all the harsh realities of interregnum England, with its violent upheavals and coarse public life, with the impoverishment in commerce and the arts, without theatre and without Christmas, there is no hint, in what he or others write about him, of despondency or gloom. Instead, he continued to work incessantly, to lend when possible an assisting hand to scholars and friends, and at Whitefriars, in Aubrey's words, he "kept a plentiful table, and was never without learned company[.]" Although Selden is recorded as remarking jocularly, "Old friends are best. King James used to call for his old shoes; they were easiest for his feet," he did in fact allow some newer friends to join his old ones. Among his cultured company were old hands like Heyward and Ussher, and newer ones, some younger than Selden by a generation or more, like the prominent Inner Templars Matthew Hale and John Vaughan, academics from Oxford and Cambridge like Gerald Laingbaine and

---

[189] Toomer *Scholarship* pp. 692–693. Toomer thinks that Selden originally intended the section on excommunication to appear as a separate work (promised in the *Uxor Ebraica*), named "On the History of Presbyters and Presbyteries" but eventually decided to insert it into the *Synedriis*.

[190] The third volume deals with the competence of the Great Sanherdrin, covering judicial matters as well as deliberative affairs (and matters mixing both), then going on to compare the proceedings of that body with those of Medieval English Parliaments. Based on Selden's stated intentions, the uncompleted parts of the book were planned to address such issues as the introduction of new laws (modifying sacred law), the role of the Shanhedrin in the trial of Jesus, and the functions of the Sanhedrin in the case that the Jewish state had embraced Christianity. See Toomer *Scholarship* pp. 763–764, 786.

Ralph Cudworth, as well as intellectuals like Marchamont Needham and a recent acquaintance named Thomas Hobbes.[191]

A reflection of this period of conviviality was the collection of sayings from Selden's conversations, recorded by Richard Milward and posthumously published as the *Table-Talk* (1689). Milward had been a member of the Whitefriars household and apparently prepared the collection for publication soon after Selden's death, for it is dedicated to the four executors of Selden's will, one of whom (Heyward) was dead by 1658. The *Table-Talk* apparently circulated for some years in manuscript form, but for unknown reasons, Milward, who became Canon of Windsor in 1666, failed to put the collection to print before his death in 1680. However, manuscripts survived, and eventually, through joint efforts of Charles Sackville, Sixth Earl of Dorset (grandson of Selden's close friend) and the scholar Thomas Rymer, it was finally published in 1689. Although Milward had been a member of the Whitefriars household for some two decades before Selden's death, the *Table-Talk* reflects for the most part conversations from the last decade of Selden's life. In Selden's own writings, the style is usually scholarly and dense, often demanding, with frequent and sometimes lengthy digressions, so that one suspects a tongue-in-cheek of his remark in *Synedriis*: "On the other hand, I am also going to insert now and then a number of asides and investigations which are related to my main theme[.]" The style of the *Table-Talk* is very much different, with many of the ideas that had been elsewhere articulated in a more elaborate and guarded manner now expressed in a colloquial style that is succinct and often pungent. This, ironically, made the book by far the most popular of Selden's works, widely read and held in high regard by such as Dr. Samuel Johnson and S.T. Coleridge, and often reprinted well into the 21st century; it created a roundabout avenue by which many of Selden's ideas continued to inform mainstream English public discourse, well after his public career and his scholarly works had become the province of specialists only.[192]

Characteristic is Selden's articulation of his view of earthly pleasures, one that is quite consistent with his own lifestyle. He neither regarded them as empty vanities nor adopted the sensualist and materialist outlook of some skeptics of his age. Rather he rejected a view that forgoes earthly pleasures altogether in favor of the promise of heavenly ones, proposing instead a divinely sanctioned

---

[191] See Stone *Crisis* p. 785; Aikin *Lives* pp. 146, 283; TT "Friends."

[192] For Selden on his own asides, see *Synedriis* b1 Praefatio. Selden would probably have found it sardonically amusing that, with the quirks of history, his great efforts of scholarship were gradually forgotten while a collection of his occasional comments (and not even from his own hand) is so long remembered. The *Table-Talk* has been repeatedly reprinted through the centuries, and a new (and scholarly) edition is now being prepared by J. Rosenblatt – it will reveal among other things the extent to which the collection owes to Selden's use of Jewish sources. The authenticity of the work, once disputed, is now generally accepted. See Barnes *Shaping* p. 167; Toomer *Scholarship* pp. 593–594.

duty to enjoy in their proper measure the earthly bounties men are trusted with, without losing sight of their limited and transitory nature:

> Whilst you are upon Earth, enjoy the good things that are here (to that end were they given) and be not melancholly, and wish your self in Heaven. If a King should give you the keeping of a Castle, with all things belonging to it, Orchards, Gardens, &c. and bid you use them; withal promise you that after twenty Years to remove you to the Court, and to make you a Privy Councellor. If you should neglect your Castle, and refuse to eat of those Fruits, and sit down, and whine, and wish you were a Privy Councellor, do you think the King would be pleas'd with you?[193]

Thus Selden seems to have lived even his last years with a serene disposition; conversing and corresponding with friends and scholars to the end, and clearly remaining intellectually active until the very last hours of his life. In July 1654 he was still writing to the French scholar P.D. Huet about a text by Vettius Valens; and on 10 November, less than three weeks before his death, he sent Bulstrode Whitelocke a message requesting him to come to his home and discuss some matter – although in this message, a tone of weariness is palpable, and one suspects Selden already knew his end was rapidly approaching. During the next few days, Selden occupied himself with the practicalities of his passing away, and there is a note from Langbaine to Pococke, from soon after Selden's death, in which the former mentions discussing with Selden, the day previous to his passing away, the provisions made in his will for one of the executors to take care of the translation of *Eutychius* by Pococke.[194]

Selden died on 30 November 1654 at his house in Whitefriars, and his funeral took place on 14 December. He was buried at night, allegedly after the "custom of the early Christians," which had been adopted among some prominent Englishmen of the seventeenth century. There was a torchlight procession from the Carmelite to the Temple Church, in which his body was accompanied by a great number of the most distinguished men of that day, parliamentarians, great officers of the state, benchers, men of letters as well as many others, and with them "all the judges were in mourning." Described as a spectacle "never again repeated in the Temple Church," if only for a short time, loyal royalist churchmen and fervent republican sectarians stood shoulder to shoulder – in the poisoned political atmosphere of that time, Selden was probably the only one who could bring together in one place so many prominent men of the most divergent persuasions. To a grave dug in the Church floor, Selden's coffin was committed "without prayer, song, or

---

[193] TT "Pleasure" sec. 4. His approach appears to draw much more from the Jewish tradition than the Christian one on such matters. Aubrey reported that Selden, though temperate in eating and drinking, was fond of saying jocularly "I will keep myself warm and moist as long as I live, for I shall be cold and dry when I am dead."

[194] For the letter to Huet see Woolf *Idea* p. 238 and note 114 there; the note to Whitelocke is in B. Whitelocke, *Memorials of the English Affairs* (1682) p. 590; for Langbaine's letter, see Johnson *Memoirs* p. 289.

ceremony," and upon it was deposited a thick slab of black marble, bearing the simple inscription, "Here lies the body of John Selden, who died 30 November 1654" (Heic jacet corpus Johannis Seldeni, qui obijt 30 die Novembris 1654). The Temple Church minister, Richard Johnson, briefly addressed the mourners, and then Archbishop Ussher preached a eulogy sermon, in which he praised Selden as so great a scholar that himself was "scarce worthy to carry his books after him."[195]

Most of his substantial earthly possessions Selden divided between four Inner Templar colleagues who he also made executors of his will – Rowland Jewkes (or Jewks) the elder as well as Hale, Vaughan and Heyward who have already been mentioned. As to his incomparable library, he directed the executors to dispose of it as they saw fit, after a quarrel about the lending of some books had caused him to retract his original intention of donating the whole to the Bodleian library of Oxford. The executors eventually did give most of the books (minus some mainly legal texts, which they kept for themselves) to the Bodleian, apparently the biggest single donation of books and manuscripts that the library would ever receive.[196]

It is unclear how much weight should be accorded to each of the differing versions of Selden's final hours. But Ussher's account of himself and Langbaine discussing with Selden a passage from the Epistle to Titus (II 11–14), that asserts "the grace of God that bringeth salvation hath appeared to all men" and is seen by some as implying redemption even to non-Christians, is certainly in line with Selden's recurring interest in the idea that virtuous men are rewarded with the world to come, regardless of their specific religious denomination. Early in his career, in the 1617 edition of *Diis*, Selden had rejected the notion, for which he found evidence in ancient Christianity (such as prayers for the souls of Plato and Plutarch), that virtuous non-Christians acknowledging the existence of one God, may be rewarded in the afterlife. By the 1629 edition of *Diis*, this passage was omitted, and a decade later when he completed the *Jure Naturali*, Selden had evidently changed his view, remarking that the Mishna (the compendium of Jewish oral law) while excluding some men from "future life," does explicitly award the pious among the gentiles a portion in the world to come (indeed, this is the justification for their keeping of the seven Noahide precepts); he also mentioned that some Christians shared this view. He was interested enough in this idea to repeat it approvingly in the *Table-Talk*.[197]

---

[195] F.A. Inderwich, "Introduction" in F.A. Inderwich (ed.), *A Calendar of Inner Temple Records* (1898) vol. II pp. cxx–cxxi. See also Aubrey *Lives* p. 221.

[196] Jewkes (1588–1666), who on his death was buried in the Temple Church near Selden, is not known to have been engaged in any substantial public or intellectual activity. See Brook *Map* p. 20.

[197] Toomer *Scholarship* pp. 220–221, 558. The passage from Titus, in the words of the king James' Bible: "For the grace of God that bringeth salvation hath appeared to all men; Teaching us that, denying ungodliness and worldly lusts, we should live soberly, righteously, and godly, in this present world; Looking for that blessed hope, and the glorious appearing of the great God and

Selden was certainly not an outwardly devout churchgoer; nevertheless, there is no evidence at all for accusations of duplicity or even impiety, such as were hurled at him by some clerical adversaries. From all we know of his public as well as his private views, Selden showed very little interest in formal doctrine and faith; however, he did concern himself with the public role of religion as well as with questions of the religious basis for the public keeping of, and the private motivation for, morality. His writings clearly display a persistent, if matter of fact, insistence on the necessary role of religion and morality to society. Such views were not uncommon even among patently anti-clerical writers, and cannot in themselves clear him from suspicions of regarding these as merely necessary tools of social control. However, a number of remarks by Selden distinctly express his own rejection of a merely expedient public morality, and the importance he ascribed to the sincerity and reality of moral motivation for the individual. This view can be certainly observed in his *Jure Naturali*, where he made clear that moral behavior, even on the individual level, can truly spring only from some genuine notion of providential justice.[198]

Yet again, he articulated this view in a more direct and pithy manner in the *Table-Talk*, when discussing moral honesty and its relationship with religion (and incidentally indicating his household might have owned a mastiff dog):

They that cry down moral Honesty, cry down that which is a great part of Religion, my Duty towards God, and my Duty towards Man. What care I to see a Man run after a Sermon, if he couzens and cheats as soon as he comes home. On the other side Morality must not be without Religion, for if so, it may change, as I see convenience. Religion must govern it. He that has not Religion to govern his Morality, is not a Dram better than my Mastiff-Dog; so long as you stroke him, and please him, and do not pinch him, he will play with you as finely as may be, he is a very good moral-Mastiff; but if you hurt him, he will fly in your Face, and tear out your Throat.[199]

For all his evident dislike of affected and hypocritical men of saintly pretensions, Selden is also firmly asserting that morality without religion is no

---

our Saviour Jesus Christ; Who gave himself for us, that he might redeem us from all iniquity, and purify unto himself a peculiar people, zealous of good works." Significantly this passage is also sometimes taken to indicate that the person of Jesus is not coterminous with God, but rather is a separate entity. This interpretation would fit with Selden's thorough examination in *Synedriis* (b2c4) of the only passage in the New Testament where the Three Persons of the Christian Divinity are explicitly mentioned. Albeit refraining from explicitly pronouncing on its authenticity, Selden's examination strongly suggests the passage is a later interpolation. To Toomer this "invites speculation as to its purpose," which he connects to speculations about the orthodoxy of Selden's Christianity. It thus seems quite possible that Selden personally held a non-denominational, perhaps even anti-Trinitarian, view of the deity. See Toomer *Scholarship* p. 731. On Selden's religious outlook see also Barbour *Measures* pp. 30–31.

[198] See Toomer *Scholarship* pp. 490–491 and note 8.

[199] TT "Moral Honesty" sec. 1. This remark might be also directed against Hobbes' ideas. Amusingly, Elizabeth Grey's armorial stamp exhibits a hound or mastiff dog located between the initials E and G.

morality at all, but merely a kind of feral self-interest. This insistence on the providential foundation for morality, as well as his emphasis (evident in other places too) on the importance of this foundation for one's duties not only towards God, but towards other men also, suggests that Selden, regardless of his personal indifference to fine doctrinal points, apparently believed in his own theory of morality, based on the existence of a deity and of some kind of "world to come."[200]

1.9 LEGACY

On the issue of the afterlife and providential retribution, as in others (like his treatment of the Jewish law of succession, or the importance he attributed to the duties owed to one's fellow man, on top of those owed to God), there is an obvious affinity between many of Selden's own ideas and similar notions found in the Jewish tradition. It is unclear if the affinity was mainly the result of his extended exposure to Jewish ideas and themes along the years, or rather if to begin with he was drawn to Jewish ideas when finding them congenial to his own previously held views. Probably there was some mix of the two, but the result was an evident similarity, often blurring in his writings the distinction between his own opinion and that of the Jewish sages.[201] Selden certainly found it prudent to explicitly clarify (in his dedication to Archbishop Laud of his 1636 edition of *Bona*) that his Hebraist work did not belong to the genre of the "deserters" (transfugae) who either convert to Judaism or use its ideas to rashly challenge well-established Christian practices, but rather to that of the "explorers" (exploratores), who remain true to their Christian faith while nevertheless aiding themselves when encountering obscure passages in the scriptures, with the light to be had by perusing the traditions of that "most noble nation" (gentis Nobilissimae) the Jews, "once privileged by direct divine illumination, without which it is certain that even those who are most learned in other respects, must stumble in darkness."[202]

---

[200] Another example of Selden's stressing the reciprocal duties between men, and his dislike of their frequent neglect by clergy, is: "The Things between God and Man are but a few, and those, forsooth, we must be told often of; but things between Man and Man are many; those I hear of not above twice a Year, at the Assizes, or once a Quarter at the Sessions; but few come then: nor does the Minister exhort the People to go at these times to learn their Duty towards their Neighbours. Often preaching is sure to keep the Minister in Countenance, that he may have something to do." TT "Preaching" sec. 10.

[201] In his two treatises on the Jewish law of succession from the 1630s, Selden noted how the customs and traditions of the Jews, like unwritten English Common Law, guided both the succession of the priests and their powers. See discussion in Christianson "Selden" ODNB.

[202] Toomer *Scholarship* pp. 442, 470; Christianson "Selden" ODNB. Selden's employment of the light metaphor in the context of the role of Jewish tradition (elsewhere compared by him to the use of the then newly invented telescope), is especially interesting since he uses of the same metaphor in his *Jure Naturali* discussion of tradition and the "active intellect," as the twin sources of individual human knowledge of divine things. In both cases it seems that Selden is

This affinity between Selden's ideas and the Jewish tradition is displayed most prominently and significantly in book I of his *Jure Naturali*, widely regarded as the most 'philosophical' of his writings. In this work, he presented and justified what he regarded as the Jewish theory of natural law. Although ostensibly asserting that he is reporting the view of the Jewish "Teachers" (Magistri), it is obvious that to a great extent he assimilated that view to his own theory – and was indeed treated as such by contemporaries as well as later commentators.[203]

This feature is typical of Selden's style, which in general is not philosophical in purpose or structure, as he overall preferred to weave his own views into his discussion of past events and ideas, rather than discuss them separately. This tendency was even more marked when he was touching on issues that were politically contentious, so that instead of making overt political statements in his works, he usually opted for placing evidence on record, while making certain that the material he makes available points in a particular direction. Nevertheless, despite Selden's avoidance of formulating a systematic and general philosophical theory, it would be a mistake to infer that he did not have one. Those who subscribe to this approach regard even book I of *Jure Naturali*, where Selden proposed a philosophical theory of natural law in which he evidently believed, as a controversialist appendage to his work, rather than its framework. However, I will attempt to show that Selden did in fact possess at least the broad outlines of a general theory of man and society which, although never systematically formulated, forms a coherent framework for his various scholarly writings (as well as, often, his political activities) in the fields of religion, philosophy, law and politics.[204]

Moreover, although Selden never composed a system of philosophy in the style of someone like Hobbes, or even a work laying out a systematic theory of natural law like Grotius' *Jure Belli*, he nevertheless did author works like *Mare Clausum* and the *Jure Naturali*, which treat one subject quite systematically and display throughout a coherent theoretical approach. More than this, in these works and others, a generally consistent outlook, whose theoretical outlines can easily be reconstructed is evident; one which presents a coherent approach to epistemological as well as moral and political issues, and which produces the basis for his theories of law and tradition, of church and state, and of constitutional government.

In this context it is worthwhile to observe that many contemporaries did regard Selden's ideas as consisting of an overarching theoretical approach. As will be detailed later in this book, a number of eminent English philosophers of the next

---

     implying for the Jewish tradition, because of its unique place as record of divine things, the role
     of a kind of intellectual agent unto the nations.
[203] See Toomer *Scholarship* pp. 493, 561.
[204] On Selden's style and his philosophical theory, or lack thereof, see Parry *Trophies* p. 98, and
     Toomer *Scholarship* pp. 817–818.

generation, like Ralph Cudworth and Richard Cumberland, saw it fit to address Selden's theory of knowledge, and upheld some parts of it while contesting others (especially the part implying the necessity of reliance on traditions, and in particular on Jewish ones). Indeed, regardless of the extremely wide reach of his scholarship, for the most part Selden's ideas were articulated in a way which placed them, to contemporaries' eyes, clearly within the mainstream of English political and juridical tradition. When the mainstream broke down during the Civil War and interregnum, while both sides resorted to violent means to resolve the impasse, many among both royalists and parliamentarians, who desired some form of eventual reconciliation and Restoration, looked to Selden and his ideas as an emblem of the possible settlement of the conflict. When Selden died in late 1654, the English constitution he had struggled to defend for all of his adult life seemed irretrievably shattered; but in little more than five years the regicide regime had collapsed and Parliament restored the old constitution, declaring that "according to the ancient and fundamental laws of this kingdom, the Government is, and ought to be, by King, Lords and Commons[.]"[205]

Several figures have been suggested as having been significantly influenced by Selden's ideas, including the members of the influential Tew circle (for which I have not found any substantial evidence). However, it appears that the two most consequential figures in England to have been directly influenced by Selden (both explicitly owned to this), were Edward Hyde and Matthew Hale. During the interregnum, the two could justifiably be seen as representing Selden's ideas both in the inner circle of royalists (of which Hyde was a leading figure), and at the higher levels of the Commonwealth (of which Hale was an eminent if grudging collaborator). At the Restoration, Hyde as Lord Chancellor (until 1667) and Hale as Chief Baron of the Exchequer and later as Chief Justice of King's Bench (until 1676) had crucial roles in fashioning the political and judicial system. But even more than their direct political and judicial activities, it was through their exceptionally successful historical writings, which shaped the ideas of generations of Englishmen, that they exerted a great influence on English political and constitutional thought down to the nineteenth century. Many of these constitutional ideas and practices (including their evident anti-Hobbesianism, and in Hale's case his belief in the *intellectus agens*) can be traced to Selden's influence, and there probably were many more that have not yet been identified. In later generations of English-speaking legal and constitutional thought, there has been much pointing out of avenues of Grotian, Hobbesian and Lockean influences, which there certainly were. The role of Seldenian ideas has been as yet relatively unexplored; however, what there is suggests a potentially rewarding field of inquiry.[206]

---

[205] *Journal of the House of Commons: Volume 8, 1660–1667* (1802) p. 8.
[206] See, for example, M.P. Zuckert, *Natural Rights and the New Republicanism* (Princeton, University Press, 1994) pp. xvi–xix, 4–8. Pocock *Ancient* pp. 172–173; Hampsher-Monk *History* pp. 46, 270 note 28, 272; Caruso *Miglior* pp. 943–945.

In the eighteenth century, Selden's books were still a required component of an educated Englishman's library, far beyond the circles of legal practitioners, and his ideas can be found reflected in the works of several important figures of political and constitutional thought, like Blackstone and Burke. His works were also to be found in the libraries of many among the American founding fathers, including Franklin, Jefferson and Adams. Although later on direct exposure to his ideas became increasingly rare, it appears that through more indirect avenues he still impacts even today's thinking about the American constitution, as well as about the supremacy of English laws against the jurisdiction of the European Union, the latter contributing to the 2016 "Brexit" referendum in which the UK voted to leave the EU.

One final field where Selden's work was influential, and is deserving of mention because of the recent resurgence of interest in his ideas, is International Maritime Law. Selden's major foray into international law was the *Mare Clausum*, defending the principle of ownership of tracts of sea, against Grotius' *Mare Liberum*, which argued for a complete freedom of the seas, since by their nature these cannot be practically bound or defended. These two books and their authors may be regarded as co-founders of modern international maritime law: their own generation and the successive one understood this explicitly, and read both authors on this together.[207]

Later international Law of the Sea was based on a combination of these two works, but for long tending far more to Grotius, since for centuries the technological limitations of enforcing dominion over the sea meant that practice restricted application of Selden's view mainly to the concept of the "territorial waters." Originally defined as three miles from the shore, it was eventually established as 12 miles – based on the capacity of land-based cannons to effectively enforce a zone of control – and remained in place until about 1985. However, in the last decades, as significant technological advances have made it

R. Tuck claims the key English followers of Selden, were the (mainly Oxfordian) intellectuals who regularly met at Lucius Cary, Second Viscount Falkland's "Tew circle," during the 1630s. The group consisted of men who for the most part came to support the royalist side in the Civil War, even though many had supported the opposition in the 1630s. Tuck claims the ideas of the circle mixed Seldenian and Grotian influences, with notions of the divine rights of kings. However, I have not found significant evidence of Seldenian ideas, and in any case it is a problem calling these Selden's followers, as they mostly died before him: Falkland and Digges in 1643, Chillingworth in 1644 (Hammond lived to 1660). Only Hyde is to be seen a Selden follower, but the two were part of the London intellectual and literary circles, and did not need Tew to connect them. See R. Tuck, *Natural Rights Theories – Their Origin and Development* (Cambridge University Press, 1979) pp. 101–118.

[207] See Brook *Map* pp. 14–15, 38. Brook argues that an entire new structure of law was needed to hold up the new order of things emerging from the age of great maritime discoveries, not least the new realities of seafaring in distant lands, and Selden was the man to do that because he did not simply juggle the enormous store of laws and precedents about which he knew more than anyone else, but also, through his dealings with the past, he was able to reflect and in a way to anticipate the future.

possible to establish far wider areas of maritime control and to exploit resources lying under the seabed, the ideas of Selden are definitely roaring back. An intense debate is now underway over sovereign-nation control of the seas, which is decidedly more Seldenian than Grotian. One important field in which the issue is increasingly relevant is the exclusive economic zones (EEZ), extending between 200 to 350 nautical miles offshore (depending on the underwater topography), which have been established as areas in which countries are permitted to exclusively exploit resources, such as is happening with the recent massive natural gas findings in the seabed of the eastern Mediterranean and elsewhere. There is also a growing debate about ownership of underwater tracts of the Arctic, where neither Russia nor Canada could make their current claims of sovereignty without relying on Selden's argument that it is reasonable to delineate sea boundaries. In the latter case, the argument for rights of ownership in the Arctic Ocean up to the North Pole, is being put forward by the spokesmen for the Sovereign of Canada, the current heir of Charles I, to whom *Mare Clausum* was dedicated. But perhaps the area where the debate is currently most contentious and belligerent, sometimes descending into downright saber-rattling, is the China Sea, where several nations, including China, Japan, Vietnam, the Philippines and others, are raising contesting claims to control large maritime areas and the supposed mineral deposits beneath them. Even in a cursory look at reports of this debate, the explicit role of ideas by a hitherto virtually unknown English lawyer immediately stands out: in *The Diplomat* of 11 July 2013, a report on the new Chinese naval theories carried the byline, "Beijing's efforts to impose a new normal on the South China Sea are more Selden than Zheng He or Grotius"; while the journal *Foreign Policy* of 16 May 2014, treating the conflict in the South China Sea, carried the byline, "This British lawyer [Selden] has been dead for 360 years. So why is he at the center of China's oil fight with Vietnam?" As we can see, the legacy of John Selden and his ideas, to this day, definitely still has its portion in the world.[208]

---

[208] A good summary of the issues involved, and of the practice accepted until about 1985, is B. Johnson Theutenberg, "Mare Clausum et Mare Liberum" in *Arctic* 37/4 (December 1984) pp. 481–492, while a good recent treatment of the current state of things and of Selden's role in it is Brook *Map* pp. xxii, 14–15, 36–38, 106–107, 114–120, 164–167. See also Barnes *Shaping* pp. 169, 253.

About Selden's role in the current China Sea conflict see J.R. Holmes, "China's New Naval Theorist" in *The Diplomat* (11 July 2013) byline: "Beijing's efforts to impose a new normal on the South China Sea are more Selden than Zheng He or Grotius"; K. Johnson, "Lord of the Sea" in *Foreign Policy* (16 May 2014) byline "This British lawyer has been dead for 360 years. So why is he at the center of China's oil fight with Vietnam?"; S. Grove and D. Cheng, "A National strategy for the South China Sea" *Backgrounder – The Heritage Foundation* (24 April 2014) argues: "in a throwback to the time of John Selden's Mare Clausum, China has claimed sovereign rights to the entirety of the SCS within a "nine-dash line" that encloses the sea, encroaching on China's neighbors." See also "Mapping China" in *The Economist* (18 Jan 2014).

2

Selden and the Early-Modern Crisis of Knowledge and Obligation

2.1 THE CRISIS OF KNOWLEDGE AND LEGITIMACY

The early seventeenth century witnessed the culmination of a far-reaching intellectual crisis. Doubts about long-accepted social, political and religious ideas had been gathering for a long time and were reaching breaking point. Indeed, there was a widespread realization that the whole system of knowledge, based on a version of Christian neo-Aristotelianism, which for some 400 years had dominated European universities – the 'schools' – was in danger of collapsing. These 'schools' had become an international intellectual monopoly, sometimes divided by doctrinal and professional interests, but united in a shared stock of ideas and vocabulary, named scholasticism.[1]

Several challenges to the Aristotelian tradition shook scholastic assumptions, from the neo-classicism of renaissance Italy, through the religious reformation in northern Europe, to the new advances in the natural sciences – converging by the end of the sixteenth century into a fundamental, systemic challenge. Francis Bacon, Galileo Galilei and René Descartes were some of the more prominent among those who articulated the significance and extent of the crisis, and who attempted to offer a new "world system" of knowledge and understanding, to replace the old one.[2]

While the onslaught of the revolt against Aristotelianism in the sixteenth and seventeenth centuries meant that Aristotle's teachings in the natural sciences suffered a terminal crisis and eventually a virtual extinction, his moral and political teachings, though undergoing a marked decline from their formerly

---

[1] See D.R. Kelley, *The Human Measure: Social Thought in the Western Legal Tradition* (Cambridge, Mass.: Harvard University Press, 1990) especially pp. 109–112, 131.

[2] Ferguson *Clio* pp. 384, 390; Rahe *Against* pp. 20–21. Probably most explicit in its intent is Galilei's *Dialogue Concerning the Two Chief World Systems* (*Dialogo sopra i due massimi sistemi del mondo*, Firenze, 1632), directly contrasting the old 'system' Aristotelian and Ptolemaic, with a new one, Copernican and Galileian.

hegemonic position, nevertheless survived, in both scholastic and non-scholastic versions. The pace, extent and character of the crisis of scholasticism are subjects of ongoing scholarly disputes, which will not be resolved here. It is however clear that, by the early seventeenth century the scholastic system faced serious challenges throughout Western Europe. Its ascendancy was certainly challenged, and in some places undone, while in most Catholic countries, and especially in France, it survived and even enjoyed something of a revival. Throughout the seventeenth century, fierce theological and philosophical controversies between scholastic Aristotelians and their opponents, be they Cartesians, Platonists or Ramists, bear witness to the still robust state of scholasticism in many countries, and its success in retaining hegemony within the universities throughout the century and beyond. An example is the Jesuits' *Ratio Studiorum* (1586), formal expression of their educational policies, which simply stated: "in logic, natural philosophy, ethics and metaphysics, Aristotle's doctrine is to be followed." For most French academics, publishers, readers and students, scholasticism was far from dead or dying; indeed the adoption of Aristotelianism as a mainstay of counter-reformation, especially by the ascendant Jesuits, meant the continued dominance by Aristotelians of the universities and colleges, and thus of the texts from which the educated drew their concepts and terminology. In other cases, scholasticism survived and even thrived in a modified form, that might be better termed "neo-scholastic," such as in Spain, where there was a self-conscious and successful attempt by jurists to synthesize the Roman legal texts with the moral theology of Thomas Aquinas, which gave rise to the new "school of Salamanca," among whose most prominent figures were thinkers of the stature of Vazquez and Suarez. In Germany, while in Catholic areas scholasticism was never under serious threat, in Protestant areas Lutheran theologians' rejection of all things Roman initially included scholasticism. Nevertheless, as the need rose to repel the undoubted allure of Jesuit second-scholastics ideas, many Lutheran theologians gradually adopted scholastic terminology and eventually gave birth to the seventeenth-century so-called Lutheran scholasticism. Thus scholasticism survived the reformation even in many Protestant countries, and indeed there was a widespread revival of interest in the writings of the scholastic theologians in the later years of the sixteenth century. However, this was not the case in Italy and England, where scholasticism had always been weaker, and more easily lost its hegemonic position, although by no means all its adherents.[3]

[3] H.V. Jaffa, *Thomism and Aristotelianism* (Westport: Greenwood Press, 1979 – reprint of 1952 edition) p. 4. The fate of early-modern Aristotelianism is the subject of a lively debate among scholars. A good example of the case for its complete collapse by the early seventeenth century is section IV (entitled "The End of Aristotelianism") of J.H. Burns and M. Goldie (eds.), *The Cambridge History of Political Thought* (Cambridge University Press, 1991), which includes chapters by R. Tuck, P. Burke and N. Malcolm. This approach has been vigorously contested, among others by P. Rahe, J. Sommerville, B. Tierney and P. Zagorin. Good examples of the latter

The scholastics were strongest in the established universities, and displayed two related tendencies: a reliance on authority of some major ancient text (mainly Aristotle, and the Corpus Juris Canonici, as well as Patristic writings and the Latin version of the scriptures), and a faith in the absolute truth of knowledge gained through rigorous logic. Scholastics had an optimistic view of human intellectual abilities, and assumed not only universal order, but the capacity of the human mind to substantially grasp it. Many scholastics were confident that complete knowledge was attainable by man, but by the sixteenth century, this had become in many cases an almost automatic rejection of new unauthorized ideas, as stated by the minor Aristotelian philosopher Ludovico Boccadiferro (1482–1545), when censuring a colleague for entertaining some novel notions: "Most of these new opinions are false. Were they true they would have been adopted by one of many wise men of past ages." But, while in most of Europe scholasticism had long since conquered all before it, in Italy there had been an especially robust native anti-scholastic resistance, virtually contemporary with the introduction of scholastic ideas to the peninsula – a resistance which crystallized early on, into a contesting approach that came eventually to be known as Humanism. Growing out of the self-rule of the late medieval city-states, especially in a class of notaries hired to write speeches and documents (known as *dictatores*), and naturally concerned with active life, rhetoric and society, it therefore argued for reassessing the importance of the "*studia humanitas*" – the "trivium" of scholastic university curriculum. The goal of medieval universities was to impart to students the basic philosophical framework (both moral and natural) necessary for later specializing in advanced disciplines like Theology or Law. Within the seven "liberal arts" into which this philosophical framework was subdivided, the "trivium," comprising the three literary and therefore human disciplines of grammar, rhetoric and dialectic, was traditionally regarded as more lowly ("trivial") than, and subordinate to, the higher "quadrivium" of four mathematical, and therefore natural disciplines (arithmetic, geometry, music and astronomy). By the early fifteenth century a number of these *humanisti*, challenged the scholastic hierarchy of ideas, arguing for the precedence of moral

view are J. Gordley, *The Philosophical Origins of Modern Contract Doctrine* (Oxford: Clarendon, 1991) pp. 122–133 and Zuckert *Natural* pp. 137–149. For France see A.C. Kors, "Theology and atheism in Early Modern France" in Grafton & Blair (eds.), *The Transmission of Culture in Early Modern Europe* (Philadelphia: Penn University Press, 1990) pp. 242, 245–246. For the Jesuits see A.C. Grayling, *Descartes* (Pocket Books, 2005) pp. 1–2. For Germany See Kelley *Human* pp. 161–162. For Scholasticism in Protestant countries see Cargill Thompson *Reformation* pp. 148–149. For Italy see G. Tomlinson, *Monteverdi and the End of the Renaissance* (Los Angeles: UCLA University Press, 1990) pp. 4–5. Tomlinson makes the important point that scholasticism was imported to Italy from France just before 1300, only a short time prior to the beginnings of Italian humanism. Thus in Italy scholasticism was not a long-established medieval mode of thought, but rather a renaissance phenomenon, from early on competing and coexisting with humanism.

and social philosophy over the natural philosophy preferred by scholastic Aristotelians. They found sources for what they sought not only in philosophical texts, but also in prose and poetry. Thus they rejected the approach to philosophy as a lone, abstract discipline, and preferred to combine it with Ciceronian eloquence and historical experience; essentially they rejected the scholastic ideal of the philosopher's secluded contemplative life, preferring instead the orator's public and active life. In the words of the jurist and playwright Pier Paolo Vergerio (1370–1445):

By philosophy we learn the essential truth of things, which by eloquence we so exhibit in orderly adornment as to bring conviction to differing minds. And history provides the light of experience – a cumulative wisdom fit to supplement the force of reason and the persuasion of eloquence.

The great changes wrought by humanists in the "trivial" studies together with the allied disciplines of history, poetry and moral philosophy, in effect destroyed the coherence of the conventional scholastic system and its classic seven liberal arts.[4]

The Italian resistance to scholasticism was aided by a revival of Greek letters in the peninsula, brought about by the progressive influx of Greek scholars fleeing the Turkish conquest of the Byzantine empire and a parallel import of Hebrew and Arabic-language texts brought by Iberian Jews (many of them outward converts to Christianity) escaping persecutions and expulsions in Spain and Portugal. In both cases, many of the ideas introduced, articulated a Platonism which seemed easier to harmonize with Christianity, than several of Aristotle's ideas. As early as 1367 the great poet Francesco Petrarca (1304–1374), regarded as one of the first humanists, expressed contempt for "the modern philosophic fashion" of the academic establishment's scholastic methods and its abuses of Aristotle, to which he preferred Plato. The eminent scholar and philologist Lorenzo Valla (1407–1457) mounted in his writings full-scale, often virulent attacks on scholasticism, proposing a new approach to human understanding based on rhetoric, grammar, and what was later to be called "philology," he upheld the value of history against the abstractions of the Aristotelians, "that peripatetic tribe, destroyers of natural meaning" which served only to corrupt and confuse. The medic and philosopher Pietro Pomponazzi (1462–1525) exposed serious conflicts between Aristotle's own ideas of the soul and the scholastic rendition of them. Many more examples can be brought to illustrate the robust anti-scholastic propensities in Italy, including the informal but influential platonic academy of late fifteenth-century Florence which counted

---

[4] D.R. Kelley, *Renaissance Humanism* (Boston: Twayne, 1991) pp. 74–75; Tomlinson *Monteverdi* pp. 4–6. Italian Humanists like Petrarca and Valla rejected (and often satirized) the contemplative-life model of the philosopher, disputing in the classroom, instead they embraced the active-life model of the orators, such as Cicero and Quintilian, performing in the forum and leading the people. See Kelley *Renaissance* pp. 34–39.

among its members Marsilio Ficino and Giovanni Pico della Mirandola; the
formal institution in 1578 at Ferrara by Duke Alfonso II, of the first university
chair in Platonic philosophy; the far-reaching stylistic innovations of the
composer Claudio Monteverdi (1567–1643), first of the great baroque
musicians and an inventor of the opera, anathemized by scholastic musical
theorists; and Galileo Galilei's complete theoretical rejection of Aristotelian
natural philosophy as fundamentally erroneous, undermining what was to
a great extent the cornerstone of the scholastic system.[5]

The Italian humanist critiques of scholasticism were joined throughout the
sixteenth century by a growing chorus from many other quarters, significantly
aided by the reformation, which, although shifting the humanist focus from the
study of man's glories to that of his shortcomings (while also reflecting the shift
of the movement from Italy to the countries of northern Europe), at the same
time allowed humanism to invade many universities, producing the beginning
of modern philological and historical criticism, and introduced such ideas far
more comprehensively into theological and political controversies. By the end of
the sixteenth century, the scholastic systemic crisis was evident.[6]

Renaissance anti-scholastic "anthropology" (a term coined in the sixteenth
century), focused on two interrelated, basic questions: the problem of free will
(that is, human free will versus divine foreknowledge), and the problem of
human knowledge (the epistemological capabilities and limitations of men).
For centuries the basis for human epistemology and psychology had been
Aristotle's *De Anima*, and its many commentaries, but it was increasingly
challenged by works like Valla's *On the True Good* (*De vero bono*, c. 1449)
and Pomponazzi's *On the Immortality of the Soul* (*De immortalitate animae*,
1516), which attempted to address in new ways the question of how the human
mind could ascend from sense experience, to a more general knowledge and
beyond, to true wisdom of things divine and human. These challenges
intensified as the sixteenth century progressed, with the revival and
dissemination (by the newly invented printing press) of ideas from ancient

---

[5] Kelley *Renaissance* pp. 40–41, 44; Kelley *Human* pp. 9, 29, 36 and Tomlinson *Monteverdi*
pp. 243–244, 246. The preference for Plato over Aristotle was evident in many of the prominent
figures of Italian humanism, like Petrarca, Pico and Ficino – in Petrarca's words, while Aristotle
was "praised by the bigger crowd," Plato was "the greater man." See Kelley *Renaissance* p. 9.
Monteverdi exemplifies the challenge posed even in the musical field by new ideas. His musical
innovations stirred great controversy between supporters of the established musical practice,
based on scholastic theories of perfect harmony, order and eternal truth, and those who favored
learning from practice and contingent realities, even when clashing with scholastic theory.
Monteverdi participated himself in the theoretical controversy, explicitly distinguishing between
the older style, which he termed "prima pratica," and his newer "seconda pratica." Although
professing (sincere) respect for the older style and even composing several works in it, his very
distinction of the two styles betrays a principle of cultural change, acknowledging the possibility
of future, better styles, including such that would regard his own work as imperfect. See
Tomlinson *Monteverdi* pp. 11, 13–14, 22–28.

[6] Kelley *Renaissance* pp. 69–70.

skeptical philosophy, and reports on the manners and customs of the inhabitants of newly discovered lands, like Francisco de Lopez de Gomara's *History of the Indies* (1552), as well as works like Montaigne's influential writings, drawing on both sources. By the early seventeenth century, Descartes was making explicit his aim to sweep away traditional Aristotelian science and metaphysics, replacing them with a purportedly clean, rational, mathematic-style, self-standing approach to the nature of things.[7]

Clearly, the scope of the challenge posed by anti-scholasticism, even upon the most fundamental beliefs, was not lost on the defenders of scholasticism. They recognized early on that new claims about human nature and knowledge challenged not merely established doctrines in some disciplines, but rather the foundations for every philosophical and theological scholastic certitude. Thus, in the seventeenth century, a number of Aristotelian writers against Descartes and Malebranche, warned (as it turned out, correctly) that whereas traditional scholastic learning had developed numerous proofs for the existence of God, the narrow and weak Cartesian proof of the existence of God was so feeble as to be no proof at all, and those who would depend on it would find themselves compelled to entertain nefarious consequences about the existence of the first being.[8]

However, it should not be concluded that disbelief was necessarily the main product of growing doubts about the possibility of proving by reason the existence of God. In fact, it appears that the more common reaction to growing doubts was not disbelief, but rather fideism – the epistemological position that faith is independent of reason, indeed often hostile to it. Both responses to increasing doubt grew together in the seventeenth century, with fideism apparently being the far more widespread option.[9]

Parallel to the injuries they inflicted to scholastic coherence, the humanists sought their own coherence that would unite the traditional "trivial" disciplines, with new ones like history and philology, by stressing the centrality of the art of language and linguistic communication to the human experience. Indeed, their growing realization that language was essentially conventional brought about a reassessment by humanists of all knowledge, even in the higher spheres of philosophy or theology, as somehow dependent on these conventional, and thus extra-, or even non-, rationally constructed foundations. Learned not by abstract *a priori* rules but by observation, the legitimacy of conventional knowledge was not its reliance on nature, reason or logic, but rather that it was based in custom and memory, acquiring its

---

[7] Kelley *Renaissance* pp. 46–48, 72–73, 116. All major and most minor western philosophers were translated and available in printed form by the end of the sixteenth century. Especially significant was the translation of classical skeptical texts. See Kelley *Renaissance* p. 123. On Descartes' aims see Grayling *Descartes* pp. 225–226.

   The wish to obtain a mathematical-style new philosophical and political system was also expressed by Grotius, Hobbes and Locke. See Gordley *Philosophical* pp. 132–133.

[8] Kors "Theology" pp. 249–251.   [9] Kors "Theology" pp. 259–261.

authority through the force of time and popular acceptance. Philologists like Valla, Cujas, Scaliger and Selden were disparagingly referred to by scholastics as "grammarians" – but on their part, they were actually rather proud of this propensity, and, as Scaliger wrote, would "be ashamed not to be such."[10]

As the effects of the great intellectual crisis rippled across Europe, and through the various disciplines, from natural philosophy to music, it was inevitable they would bear into the realm of political ideas as well. Early medieval political thought had been in the main Augustinian – holding human nature to be too corrupt for men to construct a just political society unaided, and thus finding the only just polity to be the church, and the Pope as Christ's vicar on earth, the sole possessor of legitimate political power. In the thirteenth century, rediscovery of Aristotle's political writings viewing men as political animals, capable of naturally erecting a just society, had led to the intellectual revolution culminating in St. Thomas Aquinas' monumental translation of Aristotle's ideas into Christian terms. His theory, which won over the universities and became the standard scholastic approach, regarded men's reason, instilled in them by God, as capable of erecting a legitimate political structure to cater for temporal needs, albeit leaving the church as necessary to cater for the spiritual needs which reason could not supply. Aquinas, and thus scholasticism, constructed a theory of natural law as reason, which allowed for a legitimate autonomous temporal political sphere, without relinquishing the ultimate supremacy of church authority. Those versions of Aristotelianism challenging this view were formally rejected and condemned (even for a time excommunicated) by mainstream scholasticism. Probably the most influential but also the most contentious among such views was Averroism (originating in the Islamic thinker Ahmad Ibn Rushd, aka Averroes, 1126–1198), which counted among its supporters such eminent figures as Maimonides (1135–1204, who connected it to prophecy) as well as the closest thing Selden had to an intellectual hero, Roger Bacon (c. 1214–c.1294, termed by later generations "Doctor Mirabilis"); it doubted the capabilities of the individual soul independent of divine illumination, proposing instead an outside illumination, termed *"intellectus agens"* (active intellect).[11]

During the sixteenth century, the wider intellectual crisis assisted the introduction into political though of instrumental "new paths," like Machiavelli's amoral politics or Bodin's indivisible sovereignty, which were incompatible with established constitutionalist assumptions, associated with the social and political ideas of the scholastics. That the new political terms an ideas were consciously connected by contemporaries the wider crisis in

---

[10] Kelley *Renaissance* pp. 78–79. See Selden's similar sentiment in *Historie of Tithes* (1618) Preface pp. xix–xx.

[11] Selden described this conflict of views at length, while making clear he sided with the Averroists, in both his *Jure Naturali* and *Synedriis*. See Toomer *Scholarship* p. 727. More generally on this debate see Sommerville *Royalists* pp. 13–15.

knowledge, is readily exemplified by Machiavelli presenting himself in his *Discourses on Livy*, as committed to innovation, in the manner of those who had discovered new continents, like Columbus and Vespucci. By the early seventeenth century a number of writers were attempting to outline a new system of politics, one that could also incorporate the new claims about the nature and scope of human knowledge. Such efforts were most evident in the (often connected) fields of "natural law" and "law of nations."[12]

An essential component of political thought, on both the formal and informal levels, was the legal framework of political society, and for most of medieval and early-modern western European society, this had been supplied by the system of "Roman" civil law (and its counterpart in the clerical sphere, Canon law). The "Roman" civil law system in the west was based upon the medieval recovery, study and commentaries, of the Romano-Byzantine codex assembled under the emperor Justinian in the fifth century, known as the Corpus Juris Civilis. Justinian's legal system was intended to fulfill a juridical ideal of "true philosophy," and as such it was the expression of the emperor's claim to universal authority: since he was "lord of the world" (dominus mundi), and of his intention that his law should be valid "for all time" (in omne aevum). Thus, for all its claims to represent the historical legacy of Roman law, Justinian's code had no intention of being bound by the past – for, as it aptly asked rhetorically, if the Corpus Juris was the expression of true and perennial principles, "how can antiquity interfere with our authority?" From the same premise it also followed that not only the past but also the future, the "vain discourse of posterity," was to be denied authority. By deeming itself perfect, the code purported to eliminate all legal contradictions (*antinomiae*), making unnecessary and indeed forbidden, any further judicial or academic "interpretation" or commentary. However, regardless of these stated intentions, as is natural (and the code itself admitted) new unforeseen circumstances arose, bringing forth "new forms." The need to address these

---

[12] Following Q. Skinner's famous thesis in *The Foundations of Modern Political Thought* (Cambridge University Press, 1978), that the great struggle in the middle of the sixteenth century (the heart of the conflict in the French wars of religion and the Dutch revolt) was over the constitutional structures which the major European states should take as their norms – R. Tuck argues that, inspired by the anti-constitutionalist *raison d'etat* literature, which flourished in the later sixteenth century, the first half of the seventeenth century witnessed the replacement of the older internal-constitutionalist struggle, by an attack on the very idea of constitutionalism and by attempts to replace it with an instrumental and modern politics. See Tuck *Philosophy* pp. xii–xiii. For the explicit attempts by several Dutch writers on politics in the second half of the seventeenth century, like Lambert van Velthuysen, De la Court and Spinoza to apply Descartes' philosophical methods to politics, which developed into anti-constitutionalist, pro-absolutist ideas. See E.H. Kossmann, "The development of Dutch political theory in the Seventeenth Century" in J.S. Bromley and E.H. Kossmann (eds.) *Britain and the Netherlands* (Chatto and Windus, 1960) pp. 99–102. More generally on the subject see H.A. Lloyd, "Constitutionalism" in Burns and Goldie *History* pp. 254–297; Kelley *Renaissance* pp. 52, 72–73. On Machiavelli see Rahe *Against* pp. 20–21.

new forms created the loophole through which technically illegal new interpretations were introduced, soon becoming a flood which, exactly as its authors had feared, overran the original code. An important motive for the attempt to make the code to stand outside of history, had been to make the emperor the only source of the law, and at the head of title IV of the code, appeared the formula: "Whatever the Emperor had decreed has the force of law [(quod principi placuit legis habet vigorem)], since by the royal law which was passed concerning his sovereignty [(maiestas)] the people conferred upon him all their own authority and power." This reputed "Royal Law" (Lex Regia), was the source for the argument, according to which, while political authority was conceded to have originally been with the people, by the said law it had been irrevocably transferred to the monarch.[13]

With the revival of Roman law studies in the Middle Ages, the mutual implications of the two sources of authority of the *Lex Regia* – the people as origin of authority and the ruler as its current recipient – were thoroughly explored, together with the thorny question of whether this law was indeed irrevocable or not. Most later civilians accepted the irrevocable interpretation, although there were some who expressed doubts as to this argument, on the basis of both the lack of actual records or testimony for such a momentous event, as well as by arguing it was impossible for the people to abdicate its authority in perpetuity. Thus Justinian's system became an important theoretical model for absolutist government, although one which was never fully carried out in medieval practice.[14]

As Roman imperial power had dissolved in Western Europe by the fifth century, there emerged since the eighth century at the latest, as a powerful cultural premise promoted by medieval jurists, the idea that there had been a "translation of empire" (translatio imperii) – by which imperial authority and

---

[13] J. Canning, *A History of Medieval Political Thought 300–1450* (Routledge, 1996) pp. 7–9.

Surprisingly, it appears that the Corpus Juris Civilis Roman law of contract was dissimilar from the Aristotelian concepts in every respect except one: the prominent jurist Gaius distinguished between contract and delict, just as philosophers distinguished between voluntary and involuntary commutative justice. According to Gaius obligations arise by contract (ex contractu) or by delict (offense – ex delictu), or by the analogy of contract or delict (quasi ex contractu and quasi ex delictu). Some modern scholars claim this is because Gaius had borrowed directly or indirectly from Aristotle. But even if he did, there was no further sign of Aristotelian materials in relevant Roman legal texts. See S.A. Siegel, "The Aristotelian basis of English law" in *New York University Law Review* 56/18 (1981) pp. 30–31.

[14] Canning *Medieval* pp. 9–10; Kelley *Human* pp. 53, 55–59, 132, 137. Although the time and circumstances of the allegedly irrevocable *Lex Regia* were not recorded, there exists (today in the Capitoline Museum) a copy engraved on a bronze tablet of emperor Vespasian's specific *Lex Regia* – the decree by which the Senate and people of Rome conferred on Flavius Vespasian imperial power. This tablet, long set in an obscure position in the church of Saint John in Lateran, was in 1346 moved and situated in the middle of the basilica by the populist leader Cola Di Rienzo. For Cola the text obviously represented the authority of the people to confer political power – the very opposite of the interpretation given to it by most commentators on Roman law. See Kelley *Renaissance* p. 11.

wisdom had been transmitted from the Roman emperors and Justinian, via the Carolingians to the medieval German emperors. By the late thirteenth century, the emergence of the Italian city-states, as well as some definite territorial states (like England and Sicily), created conflicts in political and legal thought, with the Imperial claims to universal jurisdiction. In order to express the sovereignty of territorial or local jurisdiction by kings and republics, medieval jurists developed the formula, originating around 1200 with Bologna canonists and with civilians like Azo: "the king in his kingdom is the emperor of his kingdom" (rex in regno suo est imperator regni sui); however, most civilians retained the view that, whatever *de facto* situation and practice was, *de jure* sovereignty remained with the emperor.[15]

For much of the early Middle Ages, Roman law in Western Europe was to a great extent buried under the Germanic judiciary customs of the kingdoms which had replaced the empire, and produced legal codes which were a mix of Germanic and Roman laws, like the *Lex Romana Visigothorum* and *Lex Romana Burgundionum*. As time passed the recovery of key parts of Roman law was gradually carried out, broadly speaking, in three methodological stages: the age of the Glossators roughly from Irnerius to Accursius (eleventh to thirteenth centuries), the age of the Commentators (or post-glossators) from Bartolus in the late thirteenth century to the end of the medieval period and beyond, and the age of Humanists from Alciato in the sixteenth century onwards.[16]

The first stage occurred from the late eleventh century, when jurists in Bologna, foremost among them Irnerius and Accursius, founded the school of Glossators, which recovered and wrote lengthy commentaries explaining and systemizing texts of Roman law. This recovery of Roman law texts, dovetailed the parallel completion by the Bolognese canon lawyer Gratian, in about 1140 of his *Decretum*, the nucleus for what will become the Corpus of Canon Law (*Corpus Juris Canonici*), which was constructed primarily on the basis of Roman law, as well as on biblical and Patristic sources. The decretalists, enjoying in some respects a freer hand than the civilian in emphasizing judicial authority over legislative interpretation, transformed the ancient notion of equity into wide powers of judicial discretion.[17]

---

[15] Canning *Medieval* pp. 83–84, 122–125; Kelley *Human* pp. 110–111. The translation of empire myth was so powerful that in 1202 when Pope Innocent III treated in his *Decretal Per Venerabilem* the right of the pope to decide between contenders to the imperial throne, he maintained this right derived from the pope's anointing and consecrating the Roman emperors, which had been translated from the Greeks (Byzantines) to the Germans in the person of Charlemagne. For this idea still persisting in the sixteenth century see Roberto Bellarmino, *De Transitu Romani Imperii a Graecis ad Francos* (1584).

[16] Canning *Medieval* pp. 6–7; Kelley *Human* p. 113.

[17] Kelley *Human* pp. 88, 111, 154. The famous account, about Roman law in the west having been only resurrected in 1135, after discovery in Amalfi of a text of the Digest, is a great exaggeration. In fact, that discovery came only as additional assistance, to efforts which had already recovered most of the Digest.

Thus, in the later middle ages, in parallel with the conquest of the universities by scholasticism through most of Western Europe, Roman law infused customary law and cohabited with it. Although nowhere was there a complete replacement of customary law by the Roman, in most places the ideas and schemes of Roman law influenced and even determined legal development. In Germany and France, customary law had held sway for much of the middle ages, but gradual Romanist incursions of legal terminology and procedures, as well as scholastic methods of education in the universities, eventually overwhelmed it. In 1495, there was a formal reception of Roman law in the courts of the Holy Roman Empire (and there were discussions about such a reception in Spain, France and even England). Although Germanic law remained operative in lower courts, and this reception was in many cases more procedural than substantive, the result was a general success of Romanist legal science and the corporate tradition of professional jurists. This success was achieved not just by the official judgments of imperial courts, but through the growing practice of sending cases to university scholars for advice. In France too, the Romanist and Feudist (or customary) schools continued to coexist and do battle, each becoming invested with a philosophical as well as political identity.[18]

It appears that early medieval civil law was surprisingly ignorant of the moral and political ideas of Aristotle. While there is some evidence of Aristotle's logical ideas, gleaned mainly from Boethius, none of the Glossators or even Accursius seems significantly acquainted with the Aristotelian works on metaphysics, ethics or politics that were setting afire the theological circles of the thirteenth and fourteenth centuries. Remarkably, the medieval jurists seem to have developed the role of consent in making contracts binding from reflection upon Roman legal texts and independently from the similar notion developed by late scholastic philosophical Thomists. By the mid-fourteenth century, the fit between legal and Aristotelian ideas about justice had become very close, so that there was a juristic quasi-scholastic variant, which nevertheless owed little to Thomism and did not bring about a reorganization of Roman law around Aristotelian principles.[19]

This juristic quasi-scholasticism incorporating the legal thought of the Corpus Juris into a philosophical conceptualization and apparatus, originated in France around the figure of Jacques de Revigny, but received its most notable development among Italian scholars of the fourteenth century, like Bartolus and Baldus, and became thus identified as "jurisprudence in the Italian style" (*mos*

---

[18] Kelley *Human* pp. 204, 231–232. The ideological contest is exemplified by two successive sixteenth-century presidents of the Parlement of Paris: Pierre Lizet, who described Roman civil law as "our common law" (notre droit commun), and restricted French law when contrary to it, and Christofle de Thou, who rejected the dominance of Roman law, and used the description of "our common law" for the customs and laws of the French.

[19] Gordley *Philosophical* pp. 3–4, 31–34, 41–42, 55, 67.

Italicum juris docendi, aka "Bartolism"). "Romanoid" rather than Romanist, it was self-sufficient, in that essentially it derived its authority neither from antiquity nor from the emperors but from its own construction of legal principles – that is, not from historical Roman law, of even the Corpus Juris Civilis, but from an idealized law of nations which it claimed to rest on Roman principles. As early as the fifteenth century, humanists like Valla had criticized the Bartolist style, its abstractions and its contempt for the authorities of antiquity. In the sixteenth century, the Italian scholar Andrea Alciato (1492–1550), though critical of Valla adhered to many of his misgivings about Bartolism, and developed a historical (rather than philosophical) approach to inquiring into the meaning of words, holding an entirely conventionalist view of language – "for whence should words arise if not from the custom of men?" His work was the main source for the development by his disciples in the University of Bourges, of the historical approach termed "jurisprudence in the French style" (*mos Gallicum juris docendi*, aka "Alciaism"). Devotees of the older Italian style, like the eminent jurist Alberico Gentili, disparaged the new ways of those he called the "Alciatei" as well as their philologist allies like Valla, for their alleged grammatical excesses drawn against the sober "interpreters of the law." The new style had three main ingredients: a new philology, intent on restoring classical words and meanings, a sense of historical change and context, and the idea of a "reform" of the ancient legal canon (thus becoming suspect of association with reformed religion). All three were not totally absent from the Italian method, but they received a far greater emphasis in the French one. The new style was formulated not only in occasional writings, but even in a formal statute issued by the Bourges University law faculty in 1584, on "The Order, Way and Rationale of Interpreting Laws." Ironically, it thus came to be that both the *mos Italicum* and the *mos Gallicum*, though certainly thriving in their country of appellation, actually originated in the other one: the "Italian style" with the Frenchman de Revigny, the "French style" with the Italian Alciato.[20]

At the juncture of this conflict between the two juridical styles, with the historical *mos Gallicum* gradually gaining the upper hand, there emerged a third powerful jurisprudential option. It began with the intellectual conversion of a French Sorbonne professor, Pierre Crockaert, who abandoned his former Ockhamite nominalism in favor of Thomism, and in 1512 started to develop a fully Aristotelian juristic framework, aided by his Spanish pupil the Dominican friar Francisco de Vitoria (1483–1546). When Vitoria returned to his native Spain and became a professor at the University of Salamanca, he founded there a new jurisprudential style, a so to say *mos Hispanicum*, which developed a scholastic basis for a system of law of nature and of nations. This "school of Salamanca" (from whence most its founding scholars came), also known as the "second scholasticism" (or "neo-scholasticism"), was created in

---

[20] Kelley *Human* pp. 128–130, 136, 187–188.

the main by Spanish Thomist scholars during the sixteenth century. Prominent among these were the Dominicans Friars de Vitoria and Domingo de Soto (1494–1560), the non-clerical jurist Fernando Vazquez de Menchaca (1512–1569), and the Jesuits Luis de Molina (1535–1600) and Francisco Suarez (1548–1617), as well as the Italian Jesuit and Cardinal Roberto Bellarmino (1542–1621). Their approach took as point of departure the discussion of human law in Aquinas' *Summa Theologica*, and tended to subsume law under theology and moral philosophy.[21]

Thus, by the early seventeenth century there were to be found in western Europe at least three substantial juridical-political approaches to society and state: the traditional scholastic approach, identified with Roman law and the Bartolist Italian style, an eminent proponent of which was the Italian Protestant jurist transplanted to England in 1580, Alberico Gentili; the historical approach, identified with humanism and the French style, eminent proponents of which were the Frenchman Jaques Cujas and the Italian Joseph Justus Scaliger; and the neo-scholastic approach of the Spanish-style Thomist school of Salamanca, eminent among whom were the Spanish Suarez and the Italian Bellarmino.

As we shall see, these various approaches had a substantial impact on early seventeenth-century legal and political thought, with later thinkers opposing or incorporating ideas from these earlier theories into their own systems. Hugo Grotius in particular, though clearly opposed to the excesses of late scholasticism, retained much of the Aristotelian apparatus, and followed close in the footsteps of the neo-scholastic Aristotelians (often citing them approvingly), becoming in many ways a bridge between the scholastic natural law theories and the modern (often termed "antique-modern") natural rights ones. The theory he developed shared earlier beliefs in the capabilities of the human mind to attain complete knowledge, while abandoning the reliance on ancient texts and authorities. Writers like Thomas Hobbes and Sir Robert Filmer, were far more dismissive of earlier theories (although Filmer, for one, tried to show that Aristotle was not adverse to his own theory). They rejected not only scholasticism or neo-scholasticism (and each devoted special efforts to rebutting the ideas of Bellarmino) but really the whole Aristotelian intellectual heritage as well as the historical school, and accordingly, they attempted to erect complete intellectual structures that would be alternative to the old theories.[22]

---

[21] Kelley *Human* pp. 159–160; Gordley *Philosophical* pp. 69–70. Among the assumptions of this new school was that although the authority of Roman law is of no small import, it does not necessarily override the usage and custom of a people.

[22] Canning *Medieval* pp. 186–187; Gordley *Philosophical* pp. 3–9, 71–73, 92–93 110–111, 121–124, 129–133. Gordley regards the theories of Grotius and his followers as "a rationalist version of Aristotle" and points out that today's contract law was originally founded on neo-scholastic Aristotelian ideas about virtue and the essence of things, which have long been discarded, yet no adequate substitute for them has been found in jurisprudence. In other words, in the tradition of Grotius, Pufendorf, Barbeyrac and beyond, sometimes called the

John Selden is a case in point, for a departure from Aristotelianism which does not reject everything Aristotelian. On the whole close to the historical school, Selden retained a significant (though measured) regard for ancient texts and authorities, while being quite skeptical of the capabilities of human reason, and he often articulated harsh assessments of both scholastics and neo-scholastics. But he was no dogmatic anti-Aristotelian, and certainly subscribed to several notions originating in the Aristotelian tradition, such as the "active intellect." His very much practical attitude is neatly encapsulated in a comment from the *Table-Talk*:

The Aristotelians say, All Truth is contained in Aristotle in one place or another. Galileo makes Simplicius say so, but shows the absurdity of that Speech, by answering, All Truth is contained in a lesser Compass; viz. In the Alphabet. Aristotle is not blam'd for mistaking sometimes; but Aristotelians for maintaining those Mistakes. They should acknowledge the good they have from him, and leave him when he is in the wrong. There never breath'd that Person to whom Mankind was more beholden.[23]

In any event, we should bear in mind that the Aristotelian epistemology did not reach the seventeenth century unchanged, but had been modified by different schools and traditions which formed around it, producing a complex conceptual mix. Well into the seventeenth century, not only Aristotle, but the many juristic, theological and overtly political works of medieval scholastics continued to be prime sources for discussion of political thought, as is evident in the writings of such as Vitoria, Bodin, Suarez Grotius and indeed Selden. Moreover, even most anti-Aristotelian authors of this period retained many of the terminologies and classifications of the Aristotelian inheritance, and often concepts and habits of thought as well.[24]

The result is a complex mix of Aristotelian and anti-Aristotelian ideas, even within the theory of single writers, with the Aristotelian framework being decidedly replaced, only well into the eighteenth century, and in some cases not even then. The transformation of methodological approaches is an excellent example of the complexity of this process taking place. Philosophers at the time of the scientific revolution, decried the deficient methodology which had made philosophy progress so little in the previous two millennia, and elaborated replacements to the existing, Aristotelian methodology, which would employ allegedly more reliable methods, based on the senses and experiments. Ironically for modern science, the most famous discoveries of the early scientific revolution, such as that the earth orbits the sun, and that a body in motion remains in motion, actually illustrated the fallibility of the senses and of experience. Even acceptance in the physical sciences, of the notion that

northern natural rights school, the neo-scholastic ideas persisted in somewhat modified form, to this day still effecting a significant influence on fundamental concepts and doctrines of private law – long outlasting the authority or even awareness of its Aristotelian origins.
[23] TT "Truth" sec. 1.   [24] Siegel "Aristotelian" pp. 30–31.

inferences from a properly conducted course of empirical research were truths rather than hypotheses, only firmly established itself from the mid-eighteenth century onwards.[25]

Nevertheless, outward similarities to Aristotelian concepts and the uneven reception of the new ideas, should not deceive us about the real and profound conceptual shift that the new approach envisaged. The new analytic–synthetic methodology fashioned during the seventeenth century was fundamentally different from what went on previously, and its application to the moral sciences substantially altered not only their content but also their structure. In Aristotelianism, moral sciences as practical sciences were inherently fallible and inexact, in contrast the acolytes of the new philosophy typically viewed the universe mechanically and held all subjects as exactly knowable; truths about nature and humans were accessible, and therefore "modern" moral sciences were to be regarded as inherently universal and infallible, as the physical sciences. The quality of the moral sciences was thus transformed – seventeenth-century thinkers who abandoned Aristotelianism in favor of the new model of knowledge claimed they were approaching moral inquiries in a geometrical and mathematical manner. Grotius, whose break with Aristotelianism was more moderate than others, still claimed to discern natural law by a "mathematical" method, Descartes wanted to replace Aristotelian science and metaphysics with a clean, rational, mathematic-style method, Hobbes asserted he was applying the mathematical method to moral philosophy, while Spinoza even entitled a treatise "Ethics demonstrated in the Geometrical Manner" in which, he declared, he would consider human desires and actions exactly as though he was concerned "with lines, planes and solids[.]"[26]

The great crisis of ideas was by no means a matter of mere intellectual, or even scientific concern. For, on the continent as well as in England, it also had a very real presence in the thoughts and acts of those involved in politics. The growing uncertainty it produced, about political authority, bought forth a flood of political schemes, contentions and demands, in which hope and fear intermingled. Broadly speaking, the tendency was for attempting to establish a system that would be more naturalistic, simple and direct than the ponderous complexities of the scholastics – many times in the form of quantifying and calculating conceits. For example, in the legal sphere, proposals abounded for a quasi-geometrical legal science and a jurisprudence that would dispense with conventional learning in favor of calculation and meditation. This tendency was evident not only among anti-Aristotelians, but even among the Spanish

---

[25] Siegel "Aristotelian" pp. 45–46.

[26] H. van Eikema Hommes, "Grotius' Mathematical Method" in *Netherlands International Law Review* 31/1 (May 1984) pp 98–106; Grayling *Descartes* pp. 225–226; Siegel "Aristotelian" pp. 46–48; Gordley *Philosophical* pp. 121, 132–133. Locke too, believed in a new moral philosophy, where measures of right and wrong could be made out by necessary consequences, as in mathematics.

neo-scholastics, who attempted a simplification of many aspects of the old scholasticism. Among the main products of these intellectual developments were the modern natural law and natural rights theories, drawing on strands of Greek philosophy, Roman jurisprudence, Thomist theology, and humanist scholarship, which were reinforced and transformed by the new mathematical philosophy of the seventeenth century; their structure owed in no small degree to Ramism and to Protestant neo-Aristotelianism. The foundations of this modern natural law were laid by the "second scholasticism" of Spanish Theologians, and by philosophical jurists such as Coras, Gentili, Bodin and Althusius.[27]

2.2 THE CRISIS OF POLITICAL OBLIGATION

Beyond the many and differing approaches proposed to address the political consequences of the crisis, the core issue was increasingly seen as one of political obligation: what are the nature and effects of an individual's duty to obey the commands of government. The discussion of obligation required inquiring into a number of concepts, connected with the nature of political society: consent and contract (both individual and collective), authority, pact, oath, trust, faithfulness (commitment). Such issues and concepts were most intimately bound with the intersection between the moral and political, and the legal dimension in which scholasticism was facing challenges similar to those it faced in other disciplines.

Significantly, the ideas of Aristotle and the classical ancient world (but as we shall see, Selden believed the ancient Jews were an exception) could be of only limited assistance to such concerns. The issue of political obligation, so central to consent and contract theories, is on the whole foreign to the approach of Aristotle and the rest of the ancient Greek and Roman thinkers, for whom questions of obligation or degree of subjection were no thematic part of political science. Thus a work of historical contractarianism like Philip Hunton's *A Treatise of Monarchy* (1643) reflects a clear disconnection from the political framework of classical Aristotelianism. Hunton's point is to establish a contracting power of human will which is not the power of each individual, so he establishes that future generations are bound by the past ones, who have contracted political society, and have no right to complain, even if "they or their ancestors have subjected themselves to such a power by oath or political contract." Therefore, a community has no universal power above what previous generations constituted, only whatever powers were established by the historical, particular "original contract and fundamental constitution of that state." The problem of obligation to political society (what Caruso terms "obbligazione sociale") was also the main issue that Selden set out to address by

---

[27] Kelley *Human* pp. 209–211, 215–216.

his political thought, for it was a problem which, he felt, had been inadequately addressed by contemporary theories both scholastic and Grotian.[28]

Although recent studies have demonstrated significant canonist, scholastic and conciliarist foundations for the modern articulation of political obligation and the emergence of ideas about individual natural rights, consent and contract, it was in the seventeenth century that the modern conceptions of political obligation emerged distinctly. These modern conceptions surfaced as a response to the perceived crisis of political obligation, effecting the transition from a world of stable status and hierarchy, to one far less secure and clear cut. The legitimation crisis directly triggered by the reformation and the outbreak of religious wars, illustrated the explosive potential of men acting on their conscience, and the claims of exceptions to the moral principle that promises should be kept. In England, several religious changes of course, and the dynastic uncertainty of the sixteenth century, added a starkly practical dimension to these issues.[29]

As a result, a rethinking of the basis for political association and political obligation was felt to be necessary, and many continental writers responded to the challenge by elaborating older concepts of natural law, from Aristotelian, Stoic and Canon law sources, into what scholars like R. Tuck and V. Kahn term a "minimalist" conception of natural law and right, centered on sociability, self-interest and self-preservation. As we shall see, it was in early-modern England that this European crisis of political obligation and the responses to it crystallized most dramatically, resulting in escalating ideological confrontations, a number of radical innovations in political thought, and eventually all-out armed conflict and constitutional collapse. One of the most important ideas touching on political obligation, to emerge from this process, was aptly described by Kahn as the concept of political society "made up of autonomous individuals who rationally consent to their self-imposed government." The importance of this particular concept (which she describes at this stage as "protoliberal") is that it has had an extraordinary impact on accounts of the history of political ideas to this day, articulating the widespread liberal notion of what political modernity, and what contract theory, mean.

---

[28] Philip Hunton, *A Treatise of Monarchy* (1643) pp. 7–8; Caruso *Miglior* pp. 659–660; Zuckert *Natural* pp. 64, 68–71. Zuckert thinks (p. 105) that Hunton's theory display signs of a Grotian influence, but in my view it is a far more Seldenian than Grotian theory.

[29] See Canning *Medieval* pp. 119–120; Collins *Cosmos* pp. 91–94, 103–109; Franklin *Constitutionalism* pp. 35–39; L. Gambino, *I Politiques e l'idea di Sovranita, 1573–1593* (Milano, Giuffre, 1991) pp. 104–105; V. Kahn, *Wayward Contracts: The Crisis of Political Obligation in England 1640–1674* (Princeton University Press, 2004) pp. 85–95. See also P. Riley, "How coherent is the Social Contract Tradition" in *Journal of the History of Ideas* 34/4 (October–December 1973) pp. 543–562, and especially pp. 545–546, where he points out that preoccupation with obligation is a post-reformation modern one (albeit with roots in medieval Christianity), for theories of political obligation are needed only when the duty to obey is in doubt – and for this reason in ancient thought, which considered political being as the highest end of man, obligation did not become a problem.

It should be nevertheless recognized (as Kahn does, though perhaps not forcefully enough) that there are serious limits to this projection of later liberalism onto the thought of the seventeenth century, and that the period actually witnessed various theories of obligation, contractual as well as others.[30]

Most important to this examination of the issues pertinent to political obligation, is to clarify that the term "contract theory" as typically employed is a misnomer, serving more to confuse than elucidate concepts. In effect "contract theory" covers over a number of very different views and theories, some of which, while employing certain contractual terms, are in fact substantially anti-contractual – especially so the "protoliberal" ones, regarding the consent of autonomous individuals as the basis for society. Thus, a study wishing to adequately evaluate seventeenth-century political thought in general, and that of John Selden in particular, needs to question many assumptions of this popular account, and in particular the connection it makes between contract theory and individual consent. Simply put, the widespread identification of contract theory and individual consent is not merely inexact, but essentially counter productive. It attempts to collapse into one, two concepts that are quite distinct, and ultimately antithetical: sovereign individual consent, as the basis of political order means, in the final analysis, the supremacy of individual will to enter or discharge obligations, since it makes that same individual will, the judge of its obligations; while contract, by any useful definition, means exactly an obligation undertaken, of which the individual will is *not* the final judge.[31]

This conceptual conflict was not lost on those "protoliberal" thinkers, who are regarded as the founding fathers of modern liberalism. Hugo Grotius (and later John Locke) acknowledged that the sovereignty of the individual's will and judgment, presents a problem for obligation, which he and many others since attempted to solve by identifying that will with rational thought. Thomas Hobbes, similarly acknowledging the problem, but being far less optimistic about the possible convergence of human will and reason, wrote in *De Cive* that individuals "give their consent out of hatred, fear, hope, love or any other passion, rather than reason" – so that his solution to the conflict was the identification of individual survival as the single overarching utilitarian interest within which will, passions and reason converge. In both cases, it is not contract but will, guided by reason or by self-preservation, that forms the

---

[30] Kahn *Wayward* pp. 1–3, 8–9, 13, 20–22, 33–34. See also W.A. Prior, "Hebraism and the problem of church and state in England, 1642–1660" in *The Seventeenth Century* 28/1 (2013) pp. 37–61, especially p. 38 where the "prevalent narrative" in the history of political thought emphasizing the rise of "secularism" and "the emergence of the 'state', governed by rational and philosophical principles" is criticized.

[31] Kahn *Wayward* pp. 8–9, 20–22. Kahn too acknowledges this conflict when she remarks that early-modern thinkers who emphasized consent to political contract as the criterion of legitimacy, also worried about the unreliability of the will.

basis for political society; in both cases, the alleged solution to the conflict of individual will and obligation was a patently uneasy one since, as both those favoring and those opposing such theories pointed out, they always retained in the individual will some residual, inalienable "right" to judge and execute, such as the right to determine when his life might be endangered and, most importantly, to act upon this judgment. Therefore, although some measure of initial individual consent to an obligation is necessary in all contractual undertakings, to perpetually subject the keeping of obligations to this consent means there is no binding contract at all.[32]

In a seminal essay on the history of contract in political thought, H. Hopfl and M.P. Thompson pointed out that accounts of the history of European contractarian thought followed for the most part in a track (set by Gierke, and followed by such as E. Barker and J.W. Gough) that was seriously distorted by a number of wrong assumptions. These assumptions were that contract should be assessed through juristic rather than historical tools (that is, through logic rather than contingency), and that a proper contract argument contained two components, a social contract and a contract of rulership. According to such accounts, contractual theories that do not display all the required components are to be regarded as incomplete versions of the standard contractual model, which allegedly emerged in the late sixteenth century, was radically challenged by Hobbes, and was finally destroyed in the eighteenth century.[33]

Far from accepting this account of contractarianism, Hopfl and Thompson propose not only a different account, but also suggest that many of the concerns and ideas which brought about the emergence of contract theory have not disappeared to this day, even if the terminology addressing them has changed. Therefore, instead of the strictly logical model of contract theory, they propose to allow for the historical variations and even contradictions that emerged in the actual use of the contractual terminology, by regarding it as "vocabulary" or "language" of contract. In effect, they acknowledge that political writings of the period employed a wide range of contractual synonyms, often related between them, each carrying with it particular connotations and consequences, such as: contract, covenant, compact, pact, paction, treaty, bargain and agreement, and of course their equivalents in Latin (foedum, pactum, pactio, contractus) and other vernacular European languages (bund, traicte, pacte).[34]

Allowing for the central place played in the history of political thought by the "contractual" model culminating in Hobbes, and regarded by many as the

---

[32] Kahn *Wayward* pp. 14, 20–21, 23. See also P. Riley "Coherent" pp. 552, 561.

[33] Gierke regarded Johannes Althusius as the first to have clearly articulated a theory of contract and identified its components (which appeared far earlier, but less articulated). Although other scholars have rejected Althusius as source for this theory, the scheme itself is usually followed. See H. Hopfl and M.P. Thompson, "The History of Contract as a Motif in Political Thought" in *American Historical Review* 84/4 (October 1979) pp. 919–923.

[34] Hopfl *Contract* pp. 927–928.

standard for contractual theory, it is nevertheless certainly not the only one. Rather, it was one of two identifiable and distinct contractual languages – albeit often overlapping in practice, as a result of the many possible reflections of the contract metaphor. The first of these languages, described by Hopfl and Thompson as "constitutional contractianism," stressed particular institutions and historical inheritances over universal propositions for all men and polities, employing terms as "fundamental law," "fundamental rights and liberties," "original contract," and "ancient constitution" (or "fundamental constitution"). Hopfl and Thomson claim that although casual references to contract can certainly be identified earlier, this contractarian language emerged within identifiable circumstances: political writings produced to discuss and legitimate Huguenot resistance to established authority in the wake of the St. Bartholomew Day massacre of 1572. Such writings as Francois Hotman's *Franco-Gallia* (1573), Theodore Beza's *Du droits des Magistrats* (1574), and "Junius Brutus'" (pseudonym, most probably of Philippe de Mornay), *Vindiciae contra Tyrannos* (published 1579, but written about the same time as the other two), employed contractual terminology in discussing political obligation, with the third especially making covenant central to the argument, and containing enough general formulations to be later re-employed by others. This contractual terminology long retained an association with religious-political strife from where it emerged, commending to many as antidote to its perceived consequences, the alternative of absolute monarchy – prominently so to Bodin; and the controversy surrounding these ideas informed the writings of authors like Althusius and Hooker. As circumstances changed and in 1584 Henry IV acceded to the French throne, contractual talk was jettisoned by prominent Huguenots: Hotman essentially recanting his *Francogallia* thesis about the popular origin of kingship, and Mornay abandoning the principle of popular sovereignty in favor of divine investiture of kings. But the ideas they articulated and disseminated, had already irretrievably spread beyond their circles – and were adopted in France by their opponents of the Catholic *Ligue*, and later in the Netherlands and in England too, when discussions of the relationship between ruler and ruled emerged.[35]

---

[35] Hopfl *Contract* pp. 929–934, 940–941. See also Gambino *Politiques* pp. 117–118. The *Vindiciae*'s view was based on a reading of the scriptural covenant, as model for the desirable political order, in which commonwealths are constituted by two covenants: the first between king and people (as co-signatories responsible for the conduct of each other) on the one hand, and God on the other; the second was a covenant between the king and the people's representatives. In the second covenant the king is the promisor, undertaking to rule justly and the people released from obedience if the king's rule is judged to be unjust, but the *Vindiciae*'s vision of the contractual obligation was limited to the actual practices of coronation oath and public acclamation, as practiced in France at that time, and in case of breakdown of the contract, he could only offer that its reconstitution by a renewed treaty acceptable to both sides, based on the "fundamental laws" of the French realm. Neither attempting to explain the authority of the fundamental laws, or their relationship to any natural rights (which he mentioned), he was not

Although long remaining vital and, especially in the English-speaking countries during the seventeenth century, dominant, with prominent exponents like Hunton and Bishop Burnet, this first language was eclipsed and almost entirely neglected by later scholarship, which devoted most attention to the second language. This second language, described by Hopfl and Thompson as "philosophical contactarianism" aims for a general theoretical model rather than one bound by circumstances, and employs terms such as "natural right," "natural liberty," "natural equality," "condition of nature," "consent" and "sovereignty." Among writers in this vein were Grotius, Hobbes, Pufendorf, Spinoza, Locke, Rousseau, Wolff and Fichte. In England during the 1640s, pro-parliamentarian writers articulated exceedingly blatant philosophical contractarian theories, a most eloquent spokesmen of which was John Milton, who in his *Tenure of Kings and Magistrates* (1649) denigrated inherited law and constitution as "gibberish," in effect collapsing the people's constitutive and governing powers into one ever-present power. It is a sobering lesson in the dangers of an excessive (complete absence seems hardly possible) projection into the past of later concepts that, as pointed out by Kahn, the conceptual division between the philosophical and constitutional versions of contractarianism has been curiously reproduced and augmented by later scholarship about the history of contractarianism – with the juristic-type analysis predisposed towards philosophical contractarianism, for a long time eclipsing the nature and role of constitutional contractarianism, whose role has only relatively recently been reassessed in historical accounts.[36]

For Hopfl and Thompson, most contractarians of both types believed that the foundation of political society was ultimately in consent not in covenant. However, there was a crucial difference between the "consent" meant by each approach, for when constitutional contractarians describe a contractual phase (or phases) to the creation of political societies, it is attendant on common consent and approval, either of the whole people or of some intermediate associations thereof – so that, Althusius wrote, when this "common consent is withdrawn from these covenants and stipulations, the commonwealth ceases to exist." The consent involved in this version was always one of collectives – associations, corporations and other groups, but never of individuals only. What such writers certainly did not contemplate was political society as an association of independent individuals equipped with natural rights. The notion of a pre- or post- political condition where men are free of political obligation was not in itself difficult to envisage, for it was a notion familiar from classical sources, but constitutional contractarians did not adopt it, possibly because

interested in the pre-covenantal condition, only with the actual laws and structures of the France of his day.

[36] Hopfl *Contract* pp. 929–934, 940–941; Zuckert *Natural* pp. 64–65, 69–71, 77–81, 106–108.

such a condition involved for them a number of problems that were too conducive to solutions of high-handed political authority.[37]

In contrast, the original association of independent individuals equipped with natural rights, was the very essence of philosophical contractarianism. Accounting for the manner in which the "modern" idea of society emerged, as a voluntary association of individuals enjoying certain "natural rights" is no mean task. The seeds for such a view were already present in the (especially late-) scholastic distinction, sometimes made, between the natural essence of government and the conventional legitimation of specific governmental forms or persons; as well as in the parallel but connected distinction between natural, paternal authority, and conventional, political authority. That by the early seventeenth century, these distinctions were becoming increasingly accepted is shown by Filmer's furious attack on them, as well as by many attempts, including those of Grotius and Hobbes (and Locke), to integrate and overcome them. Significantly, contractual notions played little part in this process, and were, it seems, the by-product of the emergence of the autonomous individual possessing natural rights and the need to somehow frame the relationships of such individuals within society. Thus, what are usually described as "protoliberal" contract theories or "philosophical" contractarian theories actually amount to theories of individual consent, and this book shall refer to them as such.[38]

In summary, we should admit that a true theory of contract is first and foremost one where the individual is not the paramount judge of his own political obligations. Moreover, as many discussions of social and political obligation pointed out, any contractual political theory has to account for actual obligations contracted over historical time, and the extent to which

---

[37] Hopfl *Contract* pp. 935–937. One of the most important classical sources for the origins of society was Cicero which in his works actually provided two differing accounts: in *De Inventione* he described men wandering in a state of nature until brought together by the eloquence of a single individual, and only then establishing communities, laws and tribunals – asocial individuals voluntarily subjecting themselves to a social order; a different account is supplied in his work most influential in this period, *De Officiis*, where men naturally associated together. For his influence of Grotius especially see Kahn *Wayward* pp. 34–35.

[38] Hopfl *Contract* pp. 935–937. By the early seventeenth century English separatists were making explicit analogies between their own groups and civil societies, and putting them into practice by congregations coming to America. By the 1640s both the Levellers and figures like Milton had arrived (in parallel or through some yet unknown connection) at a conjunction between individual natural rights and covenant (or "agreement"). Hopfl and Thompson claim that nothing like this conjunction (which Hobbes crystallized into a theory that quickly became a leading model of political argument), had been asserted before, and find it curious that it originated in separatist Christian congregations drawing analogies between themselves and civil societies, since they were voluntary associations of adults active within a wider already-established society. I think it less surprising, considering the actual analogy between on the one hand the autonomous individual of late scholastic and early-modern political thought choosing to enter society, and on the other hand the basic separatist notion of the autonomous Christian believer choosing his own congregation. See also Hopfl *Contract* pp. 938–940.

they bind not only the contractors but also their successors, sometimes over centuries. Therefore, a theory of binding contract not only takes away the individuals' completely independent power over political obligations contracted by him, but also address the extent and manner of his subjection to obligations entered in other times and places. Such theories of contract did indeed exist, in the form of constitutional contractarian theories, and a few of them addressed these issues exactly. As we shall see, John Selden's ideas articulated one such theory, emerging at least in part, in opposition to philosophical contractarian theories of individual consent, as well as to absolutist ones.[39]

2.3   THE CRISIS AND ENGLISH POLITICAL IDEAS

By the early seventeenth century, the nature and scope of the intellectual crisis as well as its repercussions on social and political ideas, were recognized far beyond scholarly circles only, and could be found in the wider cultural scene. One leading poet of the period (and later Bishop of Oxford), Richard Corbett, asked in a 1618 line "Say, shall the old philosophy be true?" A few years earlier, another poet and Selden friend, John Donne, beautifully rendered the effects of the old philosophy being replaced by a "new philosophy," bringing in its wake pervasive doubt, loss of coherence and the breakdown of social and political relations before a rising egotistical individualism, in his poem of 1611 "An Anatomy of the World," a few lines of which are worth recounting here:

> And new philosophy calls all in doubt,
> The element of fire is quite put out,
> The sun is lost, and th'earth, and no man's wit
> Can well direct him where to look for it.
> And freely men confess that this world's spent,
> When in the planets and the firmament
> They seek so many new; they see that this
> Is crumbled out again to his atomies.
> 'Tis all in pieces, all coherence gone,
> All just supply, and all relation;
> Prince, subject, father, son, are things forgot,
> For every man alone thinks he hath got
> To be a phoenix, and that then can be
> None of that kind, of which he is, but he.[40]

---

[39] Most accounts place Hobbes as the most significant figure in "philosophical contractarianism" but, as will become clear, I believe Grotius should be assigned a place at least as important, if not more. I will also argue that Selden should be regarded as an important figure in the "constitutional contractarianism" tradition.

[40] See discussion in N. Tyacke, *Aspects of English Protestantism c. 1530–1700* (Manchester University Press, 2001) pp. 230–231, 234–238.

The extent to which such themes were visible to the wider public in early-modern England is evident in the many Elizabethan and Jacobean plays, by Shakespeare, Jonson and others, touching on themes of political and social relevance, which were ingested by what was for its time probably the widest social spectrum exposed to considerations of public issues. The audiences to these plays in theatres like the Globe or the Blackfriars, included very much of the full social spectrum, going from "groundlings" paying a penny for the standing-only space in front of the stage, to wealthier individuals paying as much as half a crown to sit in the covered galleries (or sometimes, even on the stage itself); while for those who did not care for the raucous settings of public theatres, special performances were held in great aristocratic houses or sometimes even at the royal court. Thus the audiences exposed to the ideas presented in the plays included humble artisans and tradesmen, rich merchants and members of the gentry, as well as great aristocrats like the brothers William and Philip Herbert, respectively, Third and Fourth Earls of Pembroke (who sponsored the printing of the First Folio of Shakespeare's plays), and even the royal family including Kings James I and Charles I, who attended performances of such plays (the latter even annotating in his hand a copy of Shakespeare's *Works*). It has been pointed out that the Italian and Spanish settings of much of Elizabethan and Jacobean drama were not merely expedient fiction, but also a way to conveniently address republican and absolutist discourse. The same is true for plays set in ancient Rome, such as *Sejanus, his Fall* (staged in 1603, with Shakespeare as one of the actors), for which the author Ben Jonson was briefly arrested and questioned, on suspicion of alluding to the royal court. Even more popular and with added political ramifications, were plays situated within English history, which later in the century were to become progressively identified with political royalism, especially as the theatre was frowned upon by Puritans and eventually banned altogether during the interregnum. Indeed, even Shakespeare's only Scottish play, *Macbeth*, staged in 1606, was written most probably to honor England's new Scottish king against the background of the foiling of the "gunpowder plot," which intended to blow up King and Parliament on 5 November 1605 when King James was about to address the houses. The play described the dire results of murdering the "Lord's anointed," with a resulting bloodbath in which "Confusion now have made his masterpiece!" – bringing the people to pray for salvation from the "unnatural rebellion, usurpation and tyranny of ungodly and cruel men" until eventually order and peace are restored. A generation later just such a rebellion would bring about the regicide of Charles I, as well as the ensuing confusion and tyranny. Thus in 1660, at the restoration of theatrical performances, the prologue to the first play preformed at the revived Cockpit theatre declared: "They that would have no king, would have no play" for fear that "the ghosts of Harries and Edwards" would, out of the glory on stage, "teach the people to despise their reign."[41]

---

[41] Zaller Legitimacy p. 387; Sharpe *Remapping* pp. 135, 143–147, 247 and R. Harrison *Hobbes, Locke and Confusion's Masterpiece* (Cambridge University Press, 2003) pp. 1–3.

A prominent example of political themes thus raised in the theatre, was the play *Henry V*, performed on London stages several times in the first decades of the seventeenth century (and on 7 January 1605 at the royal court), in which many scenes directly address political ideas such as: The title to a crown being founded on the law of nature and of nations ("The borrow'd glories that by gift of heaven, By law of nature and of nations [be]'long, To him and to his heirs; namely, the crown" Act II scene 4); Diversity of purposes and activities combining into one common political consent ("For government, though high and low and lower, Put into parts, doth keep in one consent, Congreeing in a full and natural close, Like music." Act I scene 2); National identity and its relationship to political allegiance ("Of my nation! What ish my nation? ish a villain, and a bastard, and a knave, and a rascal? What ish my nation? Who talks of my nation?" Act II scene 2; and "You thought, because he could not speak English in the native garb, he could not therefore handle and English cudgel: you find it otherwise; and henceforth let a Welsh correction teach you a good English condition." Act V scene 1). However, perhaps most instructive for our present purpose, is the treatment of a possible conflict between private conscience and public duty, especially as it pertains to following the King's orders. When a disguised King Henry discusses with some soldiers the justice of the war they are fighting (Act IV scene 1), one of the soldiers answers that they do not know nor indeed should know about such things: "Ay, or more than we should seek after; for we know enough if we know we are the king's subjects. If his cause be wrong, our obedience to the king wipes the crime of it out of us." The disguised King Henry points out that such an approach dangerously blurs the distinction between men's public duty to the King, and their private morality: "Every subject's duty is the king's; but every subject's soul is his own." Another soldier agrees with Henry's view: "'Tis certain, every man that dies ill, the ill upon his own head: the king is not to answer it." As we shall see, such themes exactly troubled much of English political thought and action, throughout the seventeenth century.[42]

The English reaction to the great intellectual crisis of scholasticism and its repercussions in political thought was, in some important aspects, unusual. On the one hand, it appears that at Oxford and Cambridge there was a continuous and general decline of intellectual quality and accomplishments during the fifteenth and sixteenth centuries, as a result of which Aristotelian thought had fossilized far more than on the continent, and thus was less adept at developing adequate responses when the challenge of humanism gained strength. Undoubtedly, English scholasticism did not enjoy anything like the

---

[42] William Shakespeare, *The Chronicle History of Henry the Fifth* (printed 1600), and see below discussion in the section dealing with Filmer's ideas. C. McEachern claims that in this play, Shakespeare's treatment of the four captains as four nationalities, is predicting not the union of the four nations, but their continuing fractiousness. See McEachern *Poetics* p. 138. And for the meaning of term "nation" in this period see McEachern *Poetics* p. 1.

hegemony it had in many continental countries, but this is not to say that there was no Aristotelian impact in early-modern England, far from it there might even have been something of a minor revival in the late sixteenth century. It is certainly the case that even in the second half of the seventeenth century, many in England believed Aristotelianism to still enjoy a verbose and dogmatic stranglehold over the universities as well as learning more generally, to the extent they felt compelled to attack it in writings of various genres. One example is the anonymous manuscript "Ballad of Gresham Colledge" (c. 1663 – perhaps composed by Joseph Glanvill, author of the furiously anti-Aristotelian *Vanity of Dogmatism* of 1665), which praised the new "experimental" philosophy practiced in places like Gresham College of London, and protested against the Aristotelianism of the schools, with lines like:

> Oxford and Cambridge are our laughter;
> Their learning is but Pedantry.
> These new Collegiates doe assure us
> Aristotle's an Asse to Epicurus.

Another, no less caustic example, are the lines penned by John Dryden who, writing of Aristotelian scholary oppression, also clearly implied it carried with it a potential for political servitude:

> The longest tyranny that ever swayed,
> Was that wherein our ancestors betrayed
> Their free-born reason to the Stagyrite,
> And made his torch their universal light.[43]

An additional factor, contributing to the relative weakness of English Aristotelianism, was the character of the English church. As elsewhere, the reformation in England entailed an initial rise in hostility to scholastic learning that was identified with Romanism. But while in Germany educational reform by Melanchton and others reinstated a modified Aristotelian learning, in England there was nothing of the sort, and scholastic Englishmen, found themselves unassisted on the theological front.

But probably the single most significant factor contributing to the weakness of English scholasticism was the peculiar path followed by English law and the unusual prestige it enjoyed. Though for sure indebted in origin and history to many Romanist and Aristotelian ideas and practices, the Common law nevertheless developed within a course that set it on a very different path from those intellectual traditions. Studied and practiced outside of the two English universities, within those London Inns of Court that were sometimes collectively referred to as England's "Third University," it retained a markedly self-referential character, that only intensified after the reformation discredited

---

[43] D. Stimson, "Ballad of Gresham colledge [sic]" in *Isis* 18/1 (July 1932) pp. 105–109; "Epistle to Dr. Charleton" in *The Poetical Works of John Dryden* (1855) vol. II.

much of the established continental learning, as suspect of "papism." Not incidentally, the rise of English historical antiquarianism, with its affinities to humanism, was associated with London and with legal studies, rather than with England's universities. Thus, while in many countries the conflict was fought in the main between scholasticism (old and new) on the one side, and the "modern" theories on the other, the character and authority of England's peculiar legal and political tradition, meant that there was a significant third player at hand. But this third option, often presented by its supporters as alternative to the dichotomic struggle between scholastics and moderns, could also find itself as a minor insular protrusion being progressively crushed between two massive, colliding continental shelfs.[44]

The earliest legal treatises that Common law students could read were two medieval texts: *Tractatus de Legibus et Consuetudinibus Regni Angliae* (*Treatise on the Laws and Customs of the Kingdom of England*, c. 1188), commonly named after its presumed author "Glanvill," and *De Legibus et Consuetudinibus Angliae* (*On the Laws and Customs of England*, c. 1250), named after its supposed author "Bracton." Both treatises presupposed an intellectual world where the legal framework was that of Roman law, and English law in its origins, appears at first glance to conform to that general framework.[45]

Thus for *Glanvill* English Common law was in source and essence royal legislation (indeed originating in the *Lex Regia*), albeit promulgated "in council, by the advice of magnates and with the concurring of the prince." Though of course *Glanvill* and *Bracton* allowed a place for customary law (as did Roman law), it was relatively neglected, probably because early Common law consisted mainly of knowledge about "writs" the administrative procedures of monarchical government, which depended for the most part on professional technical knowledge by the lawyers, and not on popular custom. In contrast to continental traditions, the Common law thus developed largely in terms of legal procedure – *Glanvill* and *Bracton* being little more than commentaries on various kind of writs. The fact that the source for many laws could not be found in writing, was for *Glanvill* secondary, since the alternative would be the absurdity that the mere fact of writing something down injects it with authority. *Glanvill*, however, had made a seemingly minor departure from Roman law presuppositions, which was to have momentous consequences. He insisted that it would not be absurd to call English custom "leges," though they are unwritten, and justified this assertion

---

[44] See C.B. Schmitt, *John Case and Aristotelianism in Renaissance England* (Montreal: McGill-Queen's University Press, 1983) pp. 19–29, 74–76.

[45] Cromartie *Constitutionalist* pp. 13–15; and E.H. Kantorowicz, *The King's Two Bodies* (Princeton University Press, 1997) pp. 145–147. Indeed, Kantorowicz has pointed out substantial similarities between Bracton and the *Liber Augustalis*, the great collection of Sicilian constitutions published in 1231 by emperor Frederick II in his capacity as King of Sicily, owing to their common reliance on the same Roman law materials.

by paraphrasing a famous statement by Papinian, one of the principal authorities of Roman law, about what law is:

[W]hatever has been rightly decided and approved with the counsel and consent of the magnates and the general agreement of the commonwealth [*communis rei publica sponsio*], with the previous authority of the King or prince, has the force of law.

The significance of *Glanvill*'s paraphrase, lies in his departure from the original Corpus Juris wording, substituting his own "the consent and counsel of the magnates" for what had been in Papinian "the pronouncement of judicious men." In those few words, *Glanvill* replaced a concept of law as the result of princely power (counseled by wise men), with one of law as resulting from cooperation and consent of the king and his subjects. Although the sentence mentions explicitly the consent of only the magnates, their presence transforms the subsequent formulation of "general agreement of the commonwealth" from mere ceremonial acquiescence to top-down government and legislation, to an indication of government and legislation by some kind of ongoing bottom-up consent of the community, of which the magnates are the signatories. *Bracton* in the main followed *Glanvill*'s outlook, including the mention of the *Lex Regia* (and adding a reference to the Digest), but in his case too, employment of Roman law terms and the outward similarities with contemporary legal texts such as the *Liber Augustalis* (the laws collected for Emperor Frederick II, subjecting the ruler's prerogative rights only to the law of nature and reason), conceal the significant differences between his concept of rulership and the imperial one. Although working within the same general system of Romanist politico-legal thought, *Bracton* deduced, many times from passages of the Corpus Juris Civilis, that the king was under the law of the land (while also acknowledging that the monarch's unique position, meant law could not be set in motion against him). Without making too much of such twelfth- and thirteenth-century statements by *Glanvill* and *Bracton*, on their own, the recurrence of the same assumptions about the nature of English government, are evident among those writers as well as in documents of later generations, including the issuing of Magna Carta and the repeated confirmation of it as statute in successive thirteenth-and fourteenth-century Parliaments, so that this approach to law and government, albeit often contested, can nevertheless be seen to persist and inform English political thought for centuries, and is quoted as late as Edmund Burke's *Reflections*, and beyond.[46]

But while English Common law developed its own means of justification and legitimation, distinct from those offered by continental models, it long lacked a fully fledged jurisprudence, a philosophy of law comparable to that formulated by Roman law. Despite influences of Roman and Canon law (always minimized by common lawyers), Common law developed with its

---

[46] Cromartie *Constitutionalist* pp. 13–15; Kantorowicz *Bodies* pp. 145–147; Kelley *Human* pp. 102–103.

own unique jargon and remained largely autonomous of academic jurisprudence until the sixteenth century. In *Glanvill* and *Bracton*, as well as in later medieval treatises like *Fleta* (c. 1290) and *Britton* (c. 1300) one could not find more than suggestions towards a jurisprudence of English law, so that overall it was left to John Fortescue and a generation later Christopher Saint Germain, in the late fifteenth and early sixteenth century, to attempt and show the underlying rationality of the Common law – which they often articulated by (surreptitiously) borrowing from Roman law, at the very same time as they denigrated its principles. To English lawyers, it became self-evident that the Common law acquired its legitimacy through its unique combination of continuity and rationality, which other more rigid systems lacked. Common lawyers from Fortescue on (even to Blackstone) argued that English customary law alone escaped the rigidity of written law, and was derived entirely from popular custom as expressed by the judiciary.[47]

English law was born as, and always remained first and foremost, a law of property, so that the centrality and sanctity of property became its most characteristic trait. From early on, English lawyers made the connection between the exceptional respect assigned to property in the Common law and its role as repository of the rights and liberties of Englishmen. The significant difference in this respect between English and French law (the latter often identified with Roman law), and its connection with political oppression was remarked upon as early as Fortescue. Property indeed was the subject of the most influential legal treatise of Fortescue's age, the *Treatise on Tenures* by Thomas de Littleton (printed c. 1481), commonly known as "Littleton" and described by such later authorities as Camden and Coke as no less than "fundamental" and "perfect." Indeed, it was to a great extent on the basis of the law of private property, as both foundation and extension of personal liberty (an idea which, as we shall see, that Selden too certainly embraced), that the national mythology of the Common law was established, and if anything even intensified in the later sixteenth century.[48]

This self-image developed by English lawyers gradually came to entail a marked and explicit hostility to Roman law (and to legal systems based on it), regarded as its very opposite. This hostility ran very deep, and it can be found already expressed as matter of fact, as early as the fifteenth century, in Sir John Fortescue's writings, where it is identified with the despotic (in both politics and property) law of France. When around 1545, Fortescue's *Laudibus* was first

---

[47] Kelley *Human* pp. 102–103, 169. The English interpretation of French law as Romanist in character was shared by many French lawyers, who held it to be a mark of the superiority of French laws. Thus the eminent layer and scholar Etienne Pasquier, who did not doubt the superiority of French law, asserted in his *L'interpretation des Institutes de Justinian* (written sometimes before 1615, but not published in his lifetime) that French provincial customs were "formed in a largely Roman spirit." See D.R. Kelley, "History, English law and the renaissance" in *Past and Present* 65/1 (November 1974) pp. 29–30.

[48] Kelley *Human* pp. 170–171.

printed (posthumously) the epistle to the reader claimed the book showed how English law excels "not only the constitutions of the Roman Caesars, but also those of every other nation[.]" Similarly, William Lambarde (1536–1601), the antiquary and legal writer, stated as a matter of fact in his works on English legal history that he avoided considerations of Roman law because England was a "peculiar government" whose laws particularly "belong to our nation" and are not "borrowed from the imperial or Roman law," as is the case for most part of the laws of other Christian nations. The reformations' enmity to popery only reinforced this English aversion to Romanist law when in 1535 King Henry VIII ended the teaching of Canon law in English Universities, and its authority in the English Church. Although Henry also instituted the Regius Professorships of Civil Law at Oxford and Cambridge, around 1540, this was regarded not as directed towards English law, but rather as part of an academic program, setting up of other Professorships, of Divinity, Hebrew, Greek and Physics, in order to furnish England with scholars who could repel papal criticism of its policies in church and state. In early 1547, soon after the death of King Henry VIII, students at the Inns of Court petitioned Protector Somerset and the Privy Council against the Lord Chancellor, Thomas Wriothesley, Earl of Southampton, for his having renewed the powers of the Masters in Chancery – who were trained as civil lawyers. Blending the Henrician idea of an independent ("imperial") crown of England with the Fortescuean one of an independent national law, the petitioners declared England to be "a realm imperial, having a law of itself called the common laws of the realm of England, by which law the kings of the same have as imperial governors thereof ruled and governed the people." The petition accused the Masters in Chancery, who were not common lawyers, of daring to "determine weighty causes of this realm according either to the said Law Civil or to their own conscience; which law civil is to the subjects of this realm unknown." The judges and law officers of the crown unanimously justified the petition, declaring that the Lord Chancellor had thus "by common law" forfeited his office and rendered himself liable to such fine and imprisonment as the King should impose. The whole affair undoubtedly reflected in large part power struggles among the ruling circle, but the articulation of the claim and its success undoubtedly bolstered the supremacy of Common law and its rhetoric. Even an eminent English civilian like Sir Thomas Smith (1513–1577), who, with a law degree from Padua University, was from 1543 the first Regius Professor of Civil Law at Cambridge and from 1574 a member of the "Doctors' Commons," the society of civil lawyers practicing in England, nevertheless proudly declared in his *De Republica Anglorum* (*Of the Commonwealth of England*, published posthumously in 1583, but written 1565), that English law was "different from the fashions used either in Fraunce [sic], or in Italy, or in any other place where the Emperors laws and constitutions (called the civill laws) be put in use." By the late sixteenth century anti-Romanist hostility had become very much a defining feature of common lawyers, with civil and Canon law widely regarded as twin Romanist menaces to be held at bay. Prominent Elizabethan common lawyers like William Lambarde and Sir Edward Coke wanted civil and canon lawyers to have nothing at all to do with Common law, arguing that Romanist ignorance of English law meant they could not be either in favor or against it. By this time it must have seemed to most that having extinguished the Romanist threats to its preeminence, the status of English Common law was unassailable. But this perception was soon to change.[49]

The hegemony and prestige enjoyed by the Common law, and its independence from the structures of academic authority, undoubtedly meant for a long time that it did not have to be seriously justified or defended from any significant intellectual challenge. But this very protracted insularity also meant that, being widely accepted as a matter of fact, it also did not need to seriously develop and articulate justifications for its structure and functions. Consequently, when in the later sixteenth century new intellectual winds started to reach the English shores with increasing strength, English lawyers found themselves ill-equipped to defend themselves from proponents of thorough reformation or even outright abolition of the Common law. Such challenges came from without, by such eminent proponents of neo-scholastic and natural right theories as Suarez and Grotius, as well as from within, by such as the naturalized civil lawyer Gentili, the English civilian and canonist Sir Thomas Ridley and even an eminent common lawyer like Bacon, who argued for English law to be brought into line with legal models of the Roman law style. For all their many differences, these various approaches shared a challenge to the legitimation of the Common law's particularistic nature. Instead of a direct subjection to Roman law, such ideas implied rather a Romanization of the principles and structures of the Common law.[50]

---

[49] Kelley "History" pp. 36–37; Kelley *Human* pp. 175–176; Cromartie *Constitutionalist* pp. 100–101; Ferguson *Clio* p. 282. For a different view, arguing that in fact, only when in the early seventeenth century, civilians became aligned with the English political champions of an omnipotent prerogative, did the common lawyers develop an antipathy towards them, see C. Brooks and K. Sharpe, "History, English law and the renaissance" in *Past and Present* 72/1 (August 1976) pp. 137–138.

[50] See discussion in G.L. Mosse, *The Struggle for Sovereignty in England* (East Lansing: Michigan State College Press, 1950) pp. 147–148. Despite resistance from common lawyers, Roman law enjoyed a relative flourishing in sixteenth century England. In 1540 Regius professorships of civil law were established at Cambridge and Oxford, and under Elizabeth there was further a surge in civil law learning, with Francois Hotman even invited to teach it at Oxford, and declining it because of his involvement in Huguenot politics. Although Roman law remained in England for the most part an academic rather than practical occupation, there existed at least since 1511 the "Doctors' Commons" (also known as the College of Civilians), an association of practicing Roman lawyers, which over the next two centuries counted more than two-hundred members, including prominent ones like Bishop Cuthbert Turnstall, Sir Thomas Smith, Sir Julius Caesar, Sir Thomas Ridley and Alberico Gentili. Such lawyers practiced in those particular English courts where Roman rather than Common law was used, such as the Court of Admiralty and the Court of Arches – but even most eminent civilians also practiced at Common law courts

In the seventeenth century, most Englishmen, from simple yeomen to Sir Edward Coke, undoubtedly did believe in an ancient constitution that guaranteed their possessions and liberties, and identified this ancient constitution with the Common law. If anything the Reformation had reinforced this ideal, marginalizing Romanist faith in favor of a national Church, in the same way as English kings were believed to have done to Roman law, extirpated in favor of a national law. This widespread association in English political culture, of political institutions and traditions with the Common law, meant that the challenge to the Common law was often interpreted as partaking of a wider attack against traditional English institutions and liberties.[51]

Not surprisingly, the new challenges to Common law ideas corresponded, to no small degree, with similar developments in political theory. By the early seventeenth century the vast majority of continental works of political theory (both Catholic and Protestant) were readily available to English readers, and discussions about politics and political theory in England were becoming increasingly informed by new political ideas, originating in continental thinkers like Machiavelli, Guicciardini and Bodin. A typical example was Sir William Drake (son of Sir Francis) a common lawyer, man of letters and MP, interested in English law and a user of the Cotton library, who read voraciously, from the classics as well as modern writers like Machiavelli, Guicciardini, Bodin and Francis Bacon. Even prominent defenders of the English Common law like Cotton and Selden were quite familiar with the new continental ideas. Robert Cotton certainly read Machiavelli and Guicciardini, while Selden, we know read Bodin and borrowed in 1622 from Cotton's library Guicciardini's *Sententiae*. The manner in which such eminent defenders of the English political tradition were influenced by these writers is a fascinating and still mostly unexplored question.[52]

A significant factor influencing English political language was the impact of Machiavelli's politics of opportunity and interest as acceptable means by which to advance political power – quickly becoming a source of inspiration as well as of anxiety. His works were certainly studied by many, though few would go as

---

through membership of the Inns of Court: Caesar at the Inner Temple, Gentili at Gray's Inn. See Kelley "History" pp. 41–42; Kelley *Human* pp. 174.

[51] See discussion in Zaller *Legitimacy* p. 268.

[52] Sharpe *Remapping* pp. 307, 337–340; Sommerville *Royalists* pp. 58–59. Another example is Gabriel Harvey (1552–1631), an important scholar and writer in late sixteenth and early seventeenth century England, and literary associate of such as Edmund Spenser and Philip Sydney. He scribbled in a book by Livy that he owned, that there is no "specialist" in politics, economics or ethics "to match Aristotle in his Politics, Oeconomics, Ethics. But how much greater would he have been had he known histories that were so much greater – especially Roman history? Machiavelli certainly outdid Aristotle in observation of this above all, thought he had a weaker foundation in technical rules and philosophical principles. Hence I generally prefer Aristotle's rules, Machiavelli's examples." Quoted in L. Jardine and A. Grafton, "'Studied for Action': How Gabriel Harvey Read his Livy" in *Past and Present* 129/1 (November 1990) pp. 60–61.

far as Bacon in explicitly admitting that in this new way of looking at politics "we are much beholden to Machiavel." For at the very same time, Machiavelli and his politics were also extensively anathemized, so that from the "murderous machiavel" of Shakespeare's *Henry VI*, to the "cunningest of Machiavellians" as a description in 1648 of Henry Ireton (leader of the officers resisting army demands) by Leveller John Lilburne, the very name of the Florentine secretary became a synonym for evil doing and even for the devil, as the "Old Nick" of popular parlance. Consequently, Machiavelli and his ideas were often present in political discussion, but without his name appearing explicitly, especially so in claims made for policies justified by "reason of state" which supposedly overcome bounds of law or even of individual conscience. James I, in his writings as well as in public speeches, explicitly denied the Machiavellian justification of dissimulation in politics, and its division between a good ruler and a good man (instead reasserting the Aristotelian premise that regarded them as one), and in a poem named "The Furies," he explicitly rejected the idea of princes who advance themselves by "false contracts and by unlawfull measures." His son and successor, Charles I, prayed to God in his *Eikon Basilike*: "O never suffer me for reason of state to go against my reason of conscience" – while also acknowledging that at least once, he actually had, when signing Strafford's death warrant. At the same time, as P. Rahe has shown, Hobbes was developing his own theory, owing much to a careful reading of Machiavelli.[53]

Of greater overt impact on English constitutional debate, and certainly much more respectable, were the ideas of the Frenchman Jean Bodin. In his political theory, as articulated in his *République*, the king's sovereignty is understood as the absolute and perpetual power to dictate and change the law. It follows for Bodin that representative bodies in general (and France's Estates Generals in particular), cannot have any legislative authority – the only legitimate power conceded to such bodies by Bodin is the need for their consent to fiscal imposition, deriving from the inviolability of private property that he grounded in natural law. Moreover, Bodin distinguished between law and contract in a way that makes contract irrelevant to political society: while law is regarded as a unilateral act of will depending from the sovereign and obligating only the subjects, a contract is a reciprocal act obligating both sides. Thus, since dictating law without hindrance is the defining attribute of sovereignty, the ruler's abiding by a contract would inevitably undermine and disrupt that very supremacy over the subjects that is the essence of his sovereignty. This leads Bodin to affirm that any obligation by the prince to internal pacts or promises he has made is only that of a private individual (and like one, he is only obliged by just pacts and just promises that are not

---

[53] Collins *Cosmos* p. 114; Underdown *Purge* p. 158; Sharpe *Remapping* pp. 160–161, 169, 189, 436; Rahe *Against* pp. 262–270. Rahe suggests that Hobbes' Machiavellism may date from as early as 1620.

erroneously, fraudulently or violently made), no more and no less, so that essentially a sovereign prince is not obliged to perform any kind of obligation that would impinge on his majesty.[54]

The presence of Bodin and his ideas in English political debate was prominent even in his own lifetime, especially following the publication of the *République* in 1576, which became an instant international success. Hooker, for example, certainly knew the writings of Bodin, although his own constitutionalist position essentially ignored the philosophical issues raised by the Frenchman's idea of sovereignty. By the early seventeenth century, Bodinian ideas were ubiquitous, influencing thinkers as dissimilar as the prolific Presbyterian controversialist William Prynne and the anti-clerical Thomas Hobbes, as well as Filmer, on whose ideas Bodin was probably the thinker who had the greatest influence. Bodin's name and ideas repeatedly surfaced in Parliamentary debates of the 1610s and 1620s, especially so in 1628–1629. Selden certainly read both the *République* and the *Methodus*, and his interest in the collective development of England as a society, suggests that his engagement with Bodin's ideas might be more substantial than the sparse direct quotations of his works suggest.[55]

The impact that such ideas had on English political debate was exacerbated by the impression among Englishmen that their country's retaining of traditional political liberties was becoming definitely anomalous, as these were being extinguished throughout continental Europe. Many were increasingly preoccupied that continental ideas were paving the way for England's succumbing to continental-style despotic politics. As was to be expected, these preoccupations were often voiced within the body universally regarded as repository of English political liberties, Parliament. Concerns about growing absolutist tendencies in European monarchies were expressed in Parliament as early as 1571 by Sir Humphrey Gilbert, who was reported to have warned that lately the King of France, as well as "other kings had absolute power, as Denmark and Portugal, where, as the crown became more free, so are all the subjects thereby rather made slaves." By 1614, as England's Parliament was meeting, across the channel another similar body, roughly as old, the French Estates General, also convened – as it turned out, for the last time in 175 years. Both bodies had had their share of past frictions with the monarchy, but by this time the contrast between the robust constitution of the English Parliament and the feeble condition of the French Estates was unmistakable. The crucial difference between the two bodies was that the French Estates had gradually lost the "power of the purse" – the control of taxation – and thus the

[54] J. Bodin, *Les Six Livres de la République* (Paris, 1576) esp. b1c8–10, and see discussion in Gambino *Politiques* pp. 63–65, 68–69.
[55] Cargill Thompson *Reformation* pp. 173–174; W. Lamont, *Puritanism and Historical Controversy* (UCL Press, 1996) pp. 60–61; J. Daly, *Sir Robert Filmer and English political thought* (Toronto University Press, 1979) pp. 20–22; Woolf *Idea* p. 208.

hold over the monarch's government and his policies. A difference that was certainly not lost either on the vast majority of the 620-odd MPs, members of the House of Lords (both lay and clergy) and the House of Commons, or on most of the 200,000 men who voted the latter in.[56]

If anything, the English political class clung more tenaciously than ever to their traditional control of taxation and legislation, reacting with utmost hostility to any intimation that it might be diluted. Leaders of the 1614 Parliament seem to have been convinced they were the last guardians of the beleaguered ancient rights of Englishmen, some or all of which were in danger of imminent extinction. Christopher Brooke (a lawyer and poet close to the literary circles of which Selden was part) declared that as MPs they must "[n]ot leave our Posterity in worse Case than our Ancestors have left us" and William Hakewill (lawyer, antiquarian and also close to Selden) added that among a House of Commons of about 472 members there were now "above 300 new, not of the last Parliament; whereof divers young" and that it was imperative to educate this next generation of parliamentarians as to the liberties they should defend, so that "they may understand the true State of their Right, to leave it for hereafter to Posterity." It was against this background that the parliamentary leadership made a major constitutional issue of "impositions" – the attempt of the King to raise revenues without prior parliamentary approval. Throughout this short Parliament, the King and his councilors tried desperately to secure agreement to some financial supply, while the Commons repeatedly refused replying that "before these ymposicions were Layed downe if they shoulde graunt the kinge releife it might in after ages be accompted a reall Confirmation of the kinge[s] absolute power of imposinge." Although the King eventually dissolved Parliament and stopped this debate in its tracks, he had failed to secure a parliamentary grant, and even more important, had given the parliamentarians the chance to articulate a coherent case in favor of the subjects' rights and against the "absolute power" of the King's prerogative. When the next Parliament assembled in 1621, many of its members observed that more than six years had passed since the previous one had been dissolved – more than double the pause between any two Parliaments for more than a century, and a worrying sign of the growing royal ability, and perhaps preference, to rule without Parliament. By 1625 Sir Robert Phelips could declare to wide approval in the Commons, with equal measure of pride and apprehension, that: "Wee are, the last monarchy in Christendome that retayne our originall rightes and constitutions."[57]

---

[56] Cromartie *Constitutionalist* pp. 107–108; Zaller *Legitimacy* p. 608; Judson *Crisis* pp. 221, 229. The English House of Lords comprised in the early seventeenth century some 120 members, of whom about 20 were bishops sitting as Lords Spiritual, and the remaining 100 were lay Lords Temporal; while the English House of Commons comprised at the same time of about 500 elected members. See Adamson *Noble* pp. 85, 109.

[57] Cromartie *Constitutionalist* pp. 107–108; Zaller *Legitimacy* p. 608; Judson *Crisis* pp. 221, 229; "18 April 1614" in *Journal of the House of Commons: volume 1: 1547–1629* (1802), pp. 466–468. See also Sharpe *Remapping* p. 289.

It certainly did not help that in 1603, the Tudor dynasty, which especially in its last Queen had come to be so much identified with English exceptionalism, was succeeded by James Stuart, King of Scotland. As James I of England (and VI of Scotland), the new King, who in his person effected the union of the British crowns, also brought with him political practices and ideas which, regardless of his intentions (much debated in today's scholarship), aggravated existing anxieties among many of his new English subjects. Some such ideas were to be found even in works penned by the King's own hand, and indeed I suspect that too little consequence has been assigned in histories of English political thought to the exceptional occurrence of the two English kings reigning in the first half of the seventeenth century, being more than any of their predecessors or successors, serious and attentive readers, as well as writers, of works of political significance. James I's careful and even pedantic reading of works he regarded as touching on his powers in church and state (including of course Selden's *Historie of Tithes*) is well attested. The same is true for his political writings, such as the *The True Law of Free Monarchies* (1598) and *Basilikon Doron* (1599). There is far less awareness of the activities in this sphere of his son and successor, Charles I, who read carefully a wide range of books, many of them with implications for politics, including ones by Tasso, Spenser, Donne, Sandys, Erasmus, Dallington, Beaumont, Fletcher and Harington – and still extant are copies of books carefully annotated by him, such as Aristotle's *On Rhetoric*, Bacon's *Advancement of Learning*, and the *Works* of Shakespeare. Moreover, Charles I was not only a prolific reader but also a successful writer. He wrote and published volumes of prayers, and more significantly later revised in his own hand the translation into English of Robert Sanderson's *De Juramento* (*Of Oaths*, published posthumously in 1655), lectures delivered at Oxford in the 1640s, dealing with promises and obligations. In his final years, Charles I of course composed (solely or jointly with Jeremy Taylor) his most famous and influential work, *Eikon Basilike* (*The Pourtrature of his Sacred Majestie in his Solitudes and Sufferings*, 1649).[58]

Following the Stuart accession to the throne, a number of political developments and judicial decisions were interpreted by many Englishmen as alarums for novel perils facing their traditional system of government. All of these concerns converged early on upon the union of England and Scotland proposed by James I, which became in its many ramifications probably the main

---

[58] Sommerville *Royalists* pp. 107–108; Sharpe *Remapping* pp. 135, 143–147, 191. The *True Law* and *Basilikon Doron* were both written while James was still King of Scotland only, as attempts to counter the theories of government advocated by Buchanan and Knox, by which the deposition of his mother Mary had been justified. The *Eikon Basilike*, published only ten days after Charles' execution, immediately became phenomenally popular and influential, going through 36 editions in 1649 alone. It prompted the Cromwellian regime to commission Milton's rebuttal, *Eikonoklastes*, which attempted to belittle almost all aspects of Charles' work (including the accusations that he stole some prayers in it from Sidney and from Shakespeare) – but ultimately with little success. See Sharpe *Remapping* pp. 149.

political concern of the years 1603–1611 – as parliamentary debates, books and pamphlets from this period amply illustrate. The proposal brought dramatically to the fore the issue of national identity and character, which regardless of modern claims (like Benedict Anderson's) to the opposite, clearly display a widespread and intense public attachment to an English national identity. As early as 1604 the Puritan lawyer Nicholas Fuller presented in Parliament his opposition to the proposed union, on grounds of a basic incompatibility between two different national identities: "God hath made People apt for every Country; some for a cold climate, some for a hot climate, and the several countries he hath fitted for their several Natures and qualities. All grounds be not fit for one kind of grain, some for oats, some for wheat." In other words, it would be against God and nature to try and mix together the wheat-eating English with the oat-eating Scots. In a famous commons speech of 1610, Sir Thomas Hedley reiterated the same concept, only in his account the disposition and qualities of Englishmen were primarily due not to climate or other natural factors, but rather to their laws shaping the wealth and courage that characterize English national identity and character: "[I]t is not the nature of the people or climate, though I know they are not utterly without their operation and influence, that makes this difference; but it is the laws, liberties, and government of this realm." In other words, it was their Common law and constitution which over time made the English what they were; but at the same time, the Common law also adapted to the English in a way that made the two pretty much into one thing: "it is the work of time, which has so adapted and accommodated this law to the kingdom as a garment fitted to the body or a glove to the hand or rather as the skin to the hand, which growth with it." A similar outlook is evident in Selden's "Illustrations" to *Poly-Olbion* (1612) where he stresses that national identity and character are too often discounted: "I am resolved that every land hath its so singular selfe-nature, and individual habitude with celestial influence, that human knowledge, consisting most of all in universality, is not yet furnisht with what is requisite to so particular discoverie."

On the other hand, supporters of the union, while not discounting the existence of two national identities, argued that with time and conviction these could be surmounted. One of these was the anonymous composer of the *Treatise about the Union of England and Scotland* (1604), who believed the process would be both feasible and beneficial, doubting not that "the imposition of one name to both nations" would carry much impression on the population, and "knit together the two people," while from other quarters there were proposals to advance the union by way of creating a Union Flag, combining the English cross of St. George and the Scot cross of St. Andrew.[59]

---

[59] Zaller *Legitimacy* p. 590; McEachern *Poetics* pp. 139–143, 158–160, 181. Nevertheless, elsewhere McEachern describes Selden as regarding the nation as a destructive and divisive ideological force. See, for example, pp. 187, 193.

As early as 1604, James I was explicitly telling Parliament of his hopes for a complete union between England and Scotland, wishing to leave at his death "one worship to God: one kingdom, intirely governed: one uniformity in laws." This vision was not one of a mere technical union of crowns, but instead entailed far-reaching consequences in each of the three areas, that in the public mind were probably most defining of English national identity: religion, political government and the Common law. In church and state, there would be an attempt to conform the Presbyterian Scottish Kirk, for which the King had a strong antipathy, to Anglican-style episcopacy – a move certainly invidious to the not inconsiderable contingent of English Presbyterians and Sectaries. But even among that majority of Englishmen who gladly conformed to the established church, many of the possible beneficial effects of such a move were progressively nullified by the perceived pro-absolutist turn of much of the English clergy, especially in its higher echelons. Elizabethan consensus-based ideas like Hooker's were going out of vogue in the Church, replaced as the orthodox teaching of the early Stuart clergy, by the doctrine that kings derive their powers from God alone. Such positions were undoubtedly a reaction to resistance theories increasingly aired by Catholics as well as Presbyterians, and assuming a religious authority paramount to the political one, but the proposed antidote of sanctifying royal authority had ominous political implications for England, which did not take long to surface. In 1606, the Convocation of the Anglican Church submitted to James I new Canons (ecclesiastical rules) for his approval, the second of which was the following:

If any man shall affirm that men at the first, without all good education and civility, ran up and down the woods and fields, as wild creatures, resting themselves in caves and dens, and acknowledging no superiority one over another, until they were taught by experience the necessity of government; and that thereupon they chose some among themselves to order and rule the rest, giving them power and authority so to do; and that consequently all civil power, jurisdiction and authority was first derived from the people, and disordered multitude; or either is originally still in them, or else is deduced by their consents naturally from them, and is not God's ordinance originally descending from him and depending upon him; he doth greatly err.[60]

The proposed Canon explicitly denied any theory of natural liberty and bottom-up, consensual origin of government, upholding instead a view of government (and of governors) as divinely ordained. Obviously, this section was meaningful only because such theories, positing the first men as "wild creatures" acknowledging "no superiority one over another," were indeed

---

[60] J.P. Kenyon, *The Stuart Constitution 1603–1608 – Documents and Commentary* (Cambridge University Press, 1966) pp. 11–12 – quoting from E. Cardwell, *Synodalia* (Oxford, 1842). See also L. Levy Peck, "Kingship, counsel and law in early Stuart England" in J.G.A. Pocock (ed), *The Varieties of British Political Thought 1500–1800* (Cambridge University Press, 1993) p. 87; see also Collins *Cosmos* p. 110.

circulating. The targets for it, were resistance theories (both Catholic and Presbyterian) which were employing ancient Greek and Roman sources that provided such accounts of the origin of human society. Although essentially agreeing with the ideas expressed in the proposed Canons, King James declined to license them, probably out of a reluctance to needlessly stir a great theoretical controversy of dubious outcome. However, the drift of the whole passage is very much indicative of the new approach emerging within the church to royal authority. Another, connected example of the new Anglican propensities, were claims that church tithes were *jure divino*, and thus independent of political control. First made openly only in 1606 by the clergyman George Carleton, these claims rapidly became the semi-official position of the Church, so that by 1618 Selden was already harshly censured by the King for contesting them. Such attitudes made even many otherwise religiously conforming Englishmen, suspect that the church was becoming merely another tool for introducing political absolutism.[61]

Under Charles I, an even more worrisome development emerged, when some clerical writers, venturing outside of the church confines into unambiguously political territory, began to articulate explicit arguments for a *jure divino* royal authority of extralegal taxation, with two eminent examples being sermons advocating obedience to royal fiscal impositions, published in 1627: Robert Sybthorpe's *Apostolike Obedience* and Roger Maynwaring's *Religion and Allegiance: Two Sermons*. The Parliament of 1628–1629 impeached and imprisoned the two clerics, but many became convinced that their ideas enjoyed royal support when, after the dissolution of Parliament, the two were pardoned and even awarded advancement – Sybthorpe to chaplain in the royal chapel, while Maynwaring who already served as a royal chaplain, was eventually elevated to Bishop of St. David's (in 1635). Significantly, by the late 1620s, complaints about the religious direction of the Church of England were becoming increasingly intertwined with accusations that ecclesiastical authorities were bent upon a policy of subverting the laws in favor of absolute royal rule. Thus the issues of church and state became growingly identified in the minds of many parliamentarians, with the absolutist political threat, a development that by the 1640s was to have explosive consequences. The 1628–1629 sessions of Parliament indicated the coming to the fore of political discourse, of the issue of religion, and its connection to the fears of absolutism. Whereas in previous Parliaments the fear of arbitrary government

[61] The doctrine that kings derive their powers from God alone was officially endorsed by the church convocations of York and Canterbury in 1606. See Sommerville *Royalists* pp. 11–12, 150–151; Zaller *Legitimacy* pp. 59, 317–319; Burgess *Politics* pp. 134–135.

James I held the view that kings were the ones who established states and indeed societies, and not the other way around. "Kings," he wrote, existed before Parliament or any "lawes made," and they were the ones who distributed the land, erected states and as well as devised and established "forms of government" – and from this "it follows of necessitie" that kings made the laws and not laws the kings. See Collins *Cosmos* p. 112.

had been expressed in the main around issues of taxation and imprisonment, religion now came to be seen as yet another gap through which arbitrary government might be introduced. A growing number of voices, of varied religious backgrounds, began to articulate fears that the English church was being transformed into a crypto-Catholic one, especially through the acceptance of "Arminianism" (the position identified with supporters of Duch theologian Jacobus Arminius (Jakob Hermanszoon), aka "Remonstrants," which rejected Calvinist predestination in favor of an unimpaired free will) as a Trojan horse, akin to Romanism, which on top of the spiritual peril it presented, was also naturally attuned to arbitrary government. A pivotal role in securing the connection between religious and political concerns, was played by the 1628–1629 Commons Committee on Religion, chaired by Pym, in which among others Selden and Eliot also sat. Another member of the committee, Sir Francis Rous (Pym's stepbrother, and later a leading Independent and Cromwellian), made the connection between religion and politics most explicit, in a speech of January 1629:

Mr. Speaker, We have of late entered into consideration of the Petition of Right, and the violation of it, and upon good reason; for it concerns our Goods, Liberties, and Laws: But there is a Right of higher nature, that preserves for us far greater things, Eternal life, our Souls, yea, our God himself.

He went on to warn that they were witnessing how "new paintings are laid on the old face of the Whore of Babylon, to make her shew more lovely" while perpetuating the goal of "casting down Kings before Popes." He then made the connection between the danger in religion and in politics explicit, first proposing, "I desire that we may consider the increase of Arminianism, an Error that makes the Grace of God Lackey it after the will of man," then adding "I desire that we may look into the very belly and bowels of this Trojan Horse, to see if there be not men in it ready to open the Gates to Romish Tyranny, and Spanish Monarchy[.]"[62]

In government, the change proposed by James would be mainly symbolic, with an attempt by the King to alter the royal style of his rule to one with a unified name – Great Britain to replace separate England and Scotland – while the political and institutional administration was to remain separate. But the possible disappearance of the name of England from the title of their government was too troubling to most MPs, and Parliament did not approve the change of style. The King resorted (on the advice of Bacon) to issuing a proclamation in October 1604 of his new style in all fields pertaining solely to the royal prerogative, such as treaties, coinage and so on. Albeit of solely symbolic significance, such a unilateral action did nothing to allay the very fears that had made Parliament reject the proposed change of style in the first place. As we shall see much of the anxiety over the threats from union, was channeled

---

[62] Sommerville *Royalists* pp. 111–112; Zaller *Legitimacy* p. 691.

to the legal arena, where many believed they were witnessing attempts to achieve by other means, the same political goals behind the union.[63]

In the legal field, despite James' protestations to the contrary, suspicions abounded of his support for introducing changes that would corrode the integrity of the Common law. Writings by prominent legal authors enjoying royal favor, which proclaimed various deficiencies of Common law, and proposed to amend them by resorting to devices and ideas taken from Roman law, only heightened these suspicions. The problem was that although English civilians tended to treat the Common law respectfully and even tried to argue that it agreed on essential moral points with Roman law, the very assessing of English law not from within it, meant that they found the first principles of law not to be inherent in the Common law, but contained in independently discoverable, rational natural laws. As early as 1601–1602, there had been an effort by the civilian and common lawyer William Fulbecke, in his *A Parallele or Conference of the Civill Law, the Canon Law, and the Common Law of this Realme of England* to harmonize Romanist (both civil and canon) and English law, arguing they should not be "like the two faces of Janus" but rather joined like the three graces. After the accession of James I, similar proposals for legal harmonization gave rise to fears that the King, who in Scotland enjoyed the benefits of Roman law as support for his royal authority, wished to extend the same benefit to England. Regardless of the King's protestations to the contrary, initiatives like the proposed union with Scotland, came to be seen as serious threats to the English legal tradition. It didn't help the proposed union, that many of its prominent supporters were not very tactful when dealing with the English sensibilities towards safeguarding their Common law. Such was the case of the Scottish clergymen Robert Pont, author of the pro-union dialogue *De Unione Britanniæ* (1604), who asserted the essential compatibility of its Roman law-inspired legal system, with the English one, the two being in his view "almost the same in substance" and thus easily reconciled if any differences arise; and a similar view same view was presented by the distinguished English civilian and historian, Sir John Hayward (1560–1627), who in support of the union asserted that to make the two laws into one "the change will not be great." However, by far the majority of the English political establishment was of another opinion, concurring with views like those of Henry Spelman, who believed there could not be anything farther from the truth than any substantial affinity between England and Scotland: the Scottish legal system was fundamentally flawed and alien to the Common law, "liker to France than England" while the Scottish manners were barbarous, for the most part concurring with the "natural Irish."[64]

---

[63] Zaller *Legitimacy* pp. 59, 317–319.

[64] Burgess *Politics* pp. 122–123; McEachern *Poetics* pp. 158–160. Elizabethan and Jacobean Englishmen held the native Irish to be primitive in their law and society, only slightly more advanced than the American Indians. Ferguson *Clio* p. 381.

Probably the most explicit and authoritative attempt to unite the Roman law and Bodinian arguments with James I's policies was made by the prominent civilian, Alberico Gentili, Regius Professor of Civil Law at Oxford, who from about 1590 also practiced at the court of Admiralty in London, and in 1600 was honorifically admitted into Gray's Inn, his academic duties at Oxford being discharged by a deputy. He gained international renown with his *De Iure Belli Libri Tres* of 1589 on international law, but became directly involved in English constitutional issues in 1605, when he published a series of works assembled as *Three Royal Disputations* (*Regales Disputationes Tres*): "Of the absolute power of kings" (De potestate regis absoluta) arguing for absolute royal power of the Bodinian type; "Of the union of the British reigns" (De unione regnorum Britanniae) arguing in favor of the political and legal union of England and Scotland proposed by James I, and "Of civil strife against the king being always unjust" (De vi civium in regem semper iniusta) opposing a right of political resistance.[65]

A more moderate voice was Sir Thomas Ridley (c.1549–1629), an eminent civilian and canonist, practicing in the Court of Admiralty and Court of Arches, who in his *View of the Civile and Ecclesiastical Law* (Oxford, 1607) warned from what he regarded as growing encroachment by the Common law on the ecclesiastic and maritime courts, and rejected the claim for a supreme jurisdiction of the Common law over all legal matters in England. He regarded the theoretical fictions by which the Common law courts were asserting jurisdiction over matters treated in the Court of Admiralty as "*unreasonable*," appealing to the authority of the Bartolist definition of a valid legal fiction. Moreover, Ridley questioned the claim to a general jurisdiction by the Common law, by arguing that matters pertaining to subjects of foreign kings or laws (such as disputes between English and foreign merchants) should not be decided by the laws of one nation, especially as the parties to the suit might be born and live in "countries ordered by the Civil Law."[66]

While Ridley, like Bacon, was among the more moderate voices in favor of a role for Roman law in England, there were those who were willing to go even

---

[65] Kelley *Human* p. 178; D. Panizza, *Alberico Gentili, giurista ideologo nell'Inghilterra Elizabettiana* (Padova: La Garangola, 1981) pp. 158–165. *Iure Belli* is by far Gentili's most famous work, to this day. It originated in three smaller "Commentatio de iure belli," separately published in London during 1588–1589. All three were published together as one work already in 1589 in Hanau (Prussia). See *Alberico Gentili, De Iure Belli Libri Tres* J.C. Rolfe trans. and ed. (Oxford, 1933 – translated from the 1612 edition), in Rolfe's preface. A main point that Gentili stresses throughout *Iure Belli* was as a guiding principle in international law "Pacta servanda sunt" – good faith must be kept and treaties between states must be regarded as law, binding upon successors and even towards those who formerly broke faith. See *Iure Belli*, book 3, ch. 24, and also in G.H.J. van der Molen, *Alberico Gentili and the development of international law* (Leyden: Sijthoff, 1968, 2nd edition) pp. 156–157.

[66] See Sir Thomas Ridley, *View of the civile and ecclesiastical law* (Oxford, 1607); D.R. Coquillette, *The civilian writers of Doctors' Commons, London* (Berlin: Dunker & Humblot, 1988) pp. 116–123.

further than Gentili's theoretical arguments, especially in political matters. One such voice was the aforementioned Sir John Hayward, a supporter of the union with Scotland, who argued in texts like *An Answer to the First Part of a Certaine Conference* (1603) and others in the following decade, that the moral validity of any particular positive law (including English Common law) could be known only by assessing its accordance with natural reason outside it, and that furthermore, in the case of England the Norman conquest completely abrogated the old laws of St. Edward the Confessor, and introduced not only a completely new law but even a new language. He asserted that any claim by William I to be acting on a grant from the Confessor was mere pretense, for the Conqueror had obtained his crown by the sword only, and from this act the royal power had descended to James I. An even more egregious example of such claims was John Cowell (1554–1611), Regius Professor of civil law at Cambridge University, who in his *Institutiones iuris Anglicani ad Methodum et Seriem Institutionum Imperialum Compositae et Degestae* (1605), and even more in his law dictionary named *Interpreter* (1607), stepped into a political minefield when he extolled the royal prerogative and slighted the importance of Parliament. Although he conceded that, in practice, legislation in England was by the King with the consent of the three estates, he nevertheless asserted that in principle since "the king of England is an absolute king," in the final analysis the monarch could quash any law. In the parliamentary session of 1610, Cowell's book was fiercely attacked, but the King succeeded in deflecting possible criticism from himself by joining the censure as an offended party (arguing that as a component of Parliament he had been slighted too). He personally interrogated Cowell, finding the book "in some things too bold with the Common law," and having some mistakes about "the fundamental constitution of the parliament," he added that moreover "it was dangerous to submit the power of a king to definition" – but he then concluded Cowell's offenses were unintended. Thus, while the book was suppressed and burned by order of Parliament, Cowell himself was saved by James from imprisonment, and doubts lingered about the King's true feelings towards the whole affair.[67]

James I's obvious partiality towards Roman law as support for royal authority, and texts extolling such an interpretation, as those of Fulbecke, Hayward, Cowell, Ridley and Gentili, rang to many English ears as alarms about an approaching tyranny. It was becoming a widespread suspicion that James I sought an absolute source for his authority, and found it in Roman law as well as in the divine-right theory which many in the church were adopting. However much he declared his intentions to govern only constitutionally, Parliament increasingly read between the lines of his words and actions, mounting threats to its control of taxing powers and to established property rights. These fears had a major role in the

---

[67] Zaller *Legitimacy* pp. 569–570; Collins *Cosmos* p. 115; Sommerville *Royalists* pp. 67–68; Burgess *Politics* pp. 124–125.

rejection by Parliament of the Anglo-Scottish union proposed in 1603. They emerged again even more explicitly in 1610, when, after some negative comments by MPs to the crown's claim of a royal prerogative to levy extra-parliamentary impositions on goods imported or exported, King James sent message on 11 May, commanding the House of Commons not to dispute his power or prerogative. The Commons reacted by asserting their own ancient prerogative to debate freely in the house, and the King did not further pursue the issue of freedom of debate, but returned to the matters of the purse in a speech of 21 May, in which he reasserted his purported prerogative to levy impositions. A number of prominent MPs, including William Hakewill, Thomas Hedley, Nicholas Fuller and James Whitelocke, regarded this claimed prerogative as endangering the very essence of parliamentary control of supply, and spoke against it in the Commons. They too avoided directly contesting the King by denying the claimed prerogative, instead positing a difference between the power of the King-in-Parliament and that of the King acting alone – asserting that since the former was greater than the latter, parliamentary statutes could in principle overrule the prerogative. To break the constitutional impasse, a "Great Contract" was proposed, that would redefine the financial relationship of King and Parliament, by the crown relinquishing on its part its prerogative rights to nine old feudal revenue-raising powers (such as Purveyance and Wardship), as well as to new impositions, in return for the granting to the crown of a substantial fixed annual income. The matter remained unresolved when James disbanded Parliament in 1611, with the result that it continued to fester in both his own reign and in that of his son. Significantly, both in the case of the proposed union of 1603, and in the debates on impositions of 1610, the actual issues were rapidly overshadowed by what a substantial portion of the Commons perceived as an existential threat to the traditional English "privileges and liberties." In both cases, the Commons drafted constitutional documents intended to be a reassertion of those privileges and liberties: in 1604 it was a proclamation of "Apology and Satisfaction" and in 1610 a petition of right called "Petition of Grievances." Even a brief look at the latter indicates the wider concerns that the issue of impositions was evoking among the Commons. On 23 May 1610 several MPs drafted a petition, touching on the rights and privileges of Parliament which, while not directly contesting James I's claim of a royal prerogative to impositions, argued that Parliament must examine and consider such impositions, and the "reasons" for them, in order that those reasons do not extend to a "general conceit" that might lead "even to the utter ruin of the ancient liberty of this kingdom and of your subjects' right of propriety of their lands and goods." Neither the 1604 proposed proclamation, nor the 1610 proposed petition was ultimately passed by the Commons, but both reflected the growing suspicions and fears of many in Parliament about royal intentions.[68]

In the internal English legal and constitutional sphere, by far the most prominent intellectual effort of the early seventeenth century to counter the increasing aspersions on the Common law, was that by Sir Edward Coke, who attempted to define it as a perfect and hermetic system of law and politics, a literally insular, immemorially ancient constitution, that was so idiosyncratic and self-sufficient as to repel any alien elements which had been attempted to attach to it, over the years. The claim that the Common law was "immemorial" had the added benefit of making the discussions about the origins of power and government irrelevant. The only authorized interpretations of the law and the constitution were for Coke, those of the Common law courts, whose members had achieved mastery of its "artificial reason," which was not apparent to those not privy to such training – including even the King. Reputed the greatest English jurist of his age, who rose to be in succession Solicitor General, Attorney General, Chief Justice of the Common Pleas and Chief Justice of the King's Bench, Coke had several public quarrels with the King about this interpretation of the law, which he upheld in a series of greatly influential volumes of *Reports* and *Institutes* that he composed, as well as in his role as a prominent member of several Parliaments – including in his last one, of 1628–1629, when already 76 years old. Coke's approach and methodology while on the whole quite influential within the internal sphere of Common law jurisprudence, remained extremely vulnerable the moment one lifted his eyes from the confines of English law, towards wider continental standards of scholarship. For there was at the time a flood of continental texts and ideas that were putting serious pressure on the claims of common lawyers, and even in England itself such ideas found serious representatives in the form of prominent resident foreign-born scholars like Gentili, the Flemish Hadrian Saravia, and the Dalmatian Marcantonio de Dominis, as well as native ones, like Fulbecke, Edward Forsett, Sir John Davies, and most prominently Francis Bacon. Such thinkers, drawing explicit inspiration from civil law models tended, much more than usual in the English legal and political tradition, to emphasize the disjunctive nature and origin of politics and to concentrate on the locus and operation of political power. Moreover, following Machiavelli and Bodin, such thinkers regarded the political institutions of a country as the origin of its legal system, and not, as Coke would have it, the other way around.[69]

---

[68] Kelley *Human* p. 177; Zaller *Legitimacy* pp. 28–29, 586–587; J.R. Tanner, *Constitutional Documents of the Reign of James I 1603–1625* (Cambridge, 1930) pp. 245–248. The "Apology and Satisfaction" claimed that James, as a foreign king, was ignorant of the Commons' privileges and liberties that were their "right and due inheritance, no less than our very lands and goods"; the "Petition of Grievances" (actually two, one temporal the other spiritual), focused on financial impositions, regarding them as unlawful practices.

[69] R. Helgerson, *Forms of Nationhood: The Elizabethan Writings of England* (Chicago University Press, 1992) pp. 73–75; Sommerville *Royalists* pp. 150–151, 249–250. On the universalist

Sir John Davies (1569–1626), an eminent common lawyer, antiquary and poet who rose to become Attorney General for Ireland, authored texts with strikingly divergent views on English law. In the preface to his *Irish reports* (1615) he identified the Common law with custom, in the words of J.W. Tubbs, more strongly "than any lawyer before or since." Davies praised English customary law on two separate counts: The first, that law must be appropriate to the nature and disposition of a people, and since English law is so much made out of the wisdom and experience of that people only, that people cannot be ruled by any other; the second, that since custom, by definition, does not become law until tried and approved time out of mind, it necessarily has far fewer defects and inconveniences than any law not thus instituted. These were forceful argument in favor of customary law that, as we shall see, are quite similar to those raised later by Selden (the two were acquainted, frequenting the same literary and legal circles) intriguingly suggesting possible intellectual interactions between them.[70]

However, in a later treatise he composed, *The Question Concerning Impositions, Tonnage, Poundage, Prizage, Customs, &c. ... Dedicated to King James in the Latter End of his Reign* (written c. 1625, published posthumously 1656), supporting the King on the issue of the authority of royal prerogative to levy impositions, Davies presented a very different attitude to the law. In this dispute, about the power of kings to demand forced loans, Davies came down clearly on the side of a royal prerogative unconstrained by English laws. He argued that the King's right in this matter had no relationship to parliamentary authority at all; on the contrary, Parliament had no jurisdiction in such matters, because impositions had their origins not in Common law or statute, but in the "ius gentium, the law of nature

challenges to the Common law in this period, accusing the latter of being "particular, transient and unstable," see also Barbour *Measures* 141–146.

William Fulbecke, for example, in his *Pandects of the Law of Nations* (1602), claimed that in the law of tributes, subsidies and royal prerogatives "all Nations have consented" that every monarch had the right to levy taxes even against the wishes of his subjects, for special causes; Edward Forsett was a justice of the peace, who presented a version of divine-right theory (stressing before Filmer the "natural" justification for monarchy, and witnesses the development of such ideas as response to Catholic resistance theories) in his *A Comparative Discourse of the Bodies Natural and Politique* (1606), and *A Defence of the Right of Kings. Wherein the power of the papacie over princes, is refuted; and the Oath of Allegeance justified* (1624). See Collins *Cosmos* p. 113.

In 1616 James I made a speech directly contesting Coke's idea of the Common law as "artificial" reason. While conceding some use for artificial reason in "many places obscure," James claimed that the overall interpretations of the law must "always subject to common sense and reason." Ultimately, the King asserted: "I will never trust any Interpretation, that agreeth not with my common sense and reason, and trew Logicke: for *Ratio est anima Legis* in all humane Laws, without exception[.]" See Burgess *Absolute* pp. 156–157.

[70] J.W. Tubbs, *The Common Law Mind* (Baltimore: John Hopkins University Press, 2000) pp. 130–132. As we shall see, these two arguments are those which will be raised by Selden in favor of customary law, its "adaptive" and "empirical" functions.

and the law merchant, which pertained to the crown alone." His source for this claim and indeed almost all the authorities he garnered on the question of King's prerogative and its relationship to the laws of England, were from Roman law. Davies justified this apparent contradiction to the supremacy of Common law, by giving his account of the development of political institutions in general. He proposed that at first, by the law of nature, all things were held in common and there was neither King nor subject, then by the establishment of property the law of nature was limited and the law of nations was born, and as the existence of property requires rulers to protect it, all law is merely the King's voluntary creation (like in Roman imperial legal theory). According to this account, the King's powers have been divided by them into two kinds: absolute power (prerogative), not bound by positive law; and power of jurisdiction in which the King may (and often does) bind himself to observe positive law, such as the Common law was.[71]

The starkly differing, almost Jekyll-and-Hyde-like views that Davies presented in his different writings, pose an interesting problem of how he could ever harmonize them. Perhaps he could not, since we know that his text on imposition was composed while he was struggling to get appointed Chief Justice of the King's Bench, after Sir Ranulph Crewe had been removed from that office for having refused to subscribe to a document affirming the legality of forced loans, it might be the case that Davies had decided on a craven effort to sell out his previous principles in order to secure the appointment. Perhaps Davies did have some theoretical model by which he believed the two interpretations could cohabit, and there are indications that he held similar views concerning the financial power of the ruler earlier than this. It is easy to foretell the public furor that would have erupted if the treatise, composed by the paramount figure of the Common law judicial system, had circulated publicly, and it is intriguing to think about what his answers would have been. But in the event we shall never know – Davies was indeed appointed Chief Justice in November of 1626, but his sudden death the following month cut short his accession before he assumed office, and with it the possible fracas about his views.[72]

---

[71] H.S. Pawlisch, "Sir John Davies, the ancient constitution, and civil law" in *The Historical Journal* 23/3 (September 1980) pp. 691–692, 700–701; Sommerville *Royalists* pp. 152–153; Tubbs *Mind* pp. 133–136. Tubbs notes that this distinction of the two powers of English kings, one "royal and absolute" the other "ordinary and legal" by no means originated with Davies. It might be found used by prominent English judges in the early seventeenth century, and even much earlier – in a 1551 description of English monarchy by the Venetian ambassador Daniele Barbaro.

[72] Pawlisch "Davies" pp. 691–692, 700–701; Sharpe *Remapping* p. 308. An indication that the views of the *Impositions* were not a mere opportunistic turn, is supplied by Davies' role in the Case of Mixed Monies (1601), where he had argued that in absence of Common law principles pertinent to the setting of value for money, there exists a prerogative right in this orbit – basing this on a compendium of civil law tracts edited by the sixteenth-century French civilian Guillame Budè (aka Budaeus).

Since Davies' views did not become public in this period, probably the most serious threat to the integrity of the Common law, from one of its own, was that posed by Bacon, who rose to posts of great prestige and influence within the English legal system as Solicitor General in 1607, Attorney General in 1611 and Lord Chancellor in 1618. Bacon attempted to advance a far-reaching reform that would subsume the Common law under the civil law tradition which, he believed, should take precedence to it not only in historical terms but as a matter of actual practice. He proposed the writing down of English law in a shorter and more certain manner, patterned to follow the structure of Justinian's *Corpus Juris* (although not necessarily its contents), and with the King heading the enterprise – thus becoming to a great extent its author. Bacon's views on law were not unconnected to his wider outlook on knowledge and society, which was in some of its aspects proto-Hobbesian.[73]

Not surprisingly, Bacon's program for reforming English law did not, to say the least, meet with Coke's approbation, who wrote about it: "It deserves not to be in schools / But to be fraughted in the ship of fools." Beyond many professional (and personal) differences, the ideological conflict between these two leading legal figures of seventeenth-century England ultimately boiled down to a fundamental disagreement about the nature of English law, with Coke constantly asserting the Law as prior and supreme to the King, and Bacon taking the opposite view.[74]

It is then appropriate to say that the famously insular vision of the common law presented by Coke and most other common lawyers was not a product of ignorance, but rather, in Helgerson's words, an "ideological necessity," part of a self-conscious attempt to preserve the integrity of English law – and as such representing an awareness of foreign legal ideas and the threats they seemed to pose. Coke's awareness of the threat to English law posed by foreign legal ideas was perhaps best articulated in one of his last and most important parliamentary speeches, in March 1628, during a debate on the role of the royal prerogative, he conceded the prerogative was "the supreme part of the laws of the realm" – but not outside of them. Coke then argued this integration

---

[73] Helgerson *Nationhood* pp. 73–75; Zaller *Legitimacy* pp. 314–316; Even as a young man, Bacon had denigrated traditional knowledge as barren of useful manifestations, and added his voice to those denouncing the sterility of scholastic logic. As an antidote he planned a reform of knowledge and a rehabilitation of the mechanical arts. See Collins *Cosmos* p. 143. P. Rahe answers that the intellectual transformation that Bacon initiated is today ill understood, not least because of Bacon's preference for professing orthodoxy while, in Rahe's words, "plotting its demise." Indeed, Rahe regards Bacon as Hobbes' mentor, noting that Aubrey described Hobbes as "beloved" by Bacon, and that Hobbes' *De Cive* was regarded by some as actually based on Baconian fragments. Rahe *Against* pp. 250–253.

[74] Helgerson *Nationhood* pp. 78–79. Bacon wasn't completely consistent in his views on English law, and his attitude to Coke and his work was far less caustic than what the latter reciprocated, remarking that without Coke's *Reports*, the law by the time he was writing (1616), would have become "…almost like a ship without ballast." However, Bacon apparently saw his own work, as the opposite counterbalance needed to keep the "ballast" of the ship of the law.

of the prerogative in within the common law was peculiar to England: "No other state is like this. *Divisos ab orbe Britannos* [the Britons divided from the world]. We have a national appropriate law to this kingdom. If you tell me of other laws, you are gone. I will only speak of the laws of England." The same approach seems to be true of Sir John Davies, in his earlier writings about the common law. Such thinkers were far less insular intellectually than ideologically, thus in effect ideologically "insularist" rather than actually insular – not at all ignorant of continental ideas, but attempting to project a vision that lionized the distinctiveness of the English and their unique destiny, and of the Common law as completely self-referring and impermeable.[75]

However, while Elizabethans like Coke had successfully waived away questions of the origin of government and law with the device of immemoriality and the construct of artificial reason, such positions were progressively being made untenable, by the reception of Machiavellian and Bodinian modes of political analysis, which were sharpening the debate over the distribution of authority, as well as by new methods of critical scholarship which were making possible the tracing of concrete historical origins. Some prominent common lawyers made efforts to locate English law, in Tubbs' words, within a "larger jurisprudential universe," and included in their books substantial sections on general jurisprudence – such were Sir Henry Finch's, *Law, or a Discourse thereof* (1627 – trans. of the original of 1613 in law French) or Sir John Dodderidge's, *The English Lawyer* (1631). But efforts such as these were far from satisfactory, on both the scholarly and intellectual levels, and they did not end up playing any significant legal or constitutional role.[76]

More effective was the new English historical scholarship, loosely linked to aristocratic patrons, such as the Earls of Arundel and Pembroke, which had begun to spread across a wide cultural spectrum, and its fulcrum was with the group of gentlemen-scholars of the Society of Antiquaries. Founded in 1584, the society was forced by James I to disband around about 1605, probably because of the King's recognition of the potentially destabilizing political effects of such scholarship – which became if anything even more marked under Charles I, when the legal papers of Cotton and Coke were indefinitely sealed. Regardless of this formal disbandment, informal network of the antiquaries persisted and their research continued. The new scholarship could certainly be put to the use of different agendas about English law and politics: As a prop for royal authority, showing it to be at the origin of institutions and laws, as emerged

---

[75] Sharpe *Remapping* p. 308; Burgess *Absolute* pp. 203–204; Burgess *Politics* pp. 80–82, 122–123; Helgerson *Nationhood* pp. 71–72; W.T. Murphy, "The oldest social science? The epistemic properties of the common law tradition" in *The Modern Law Review* 54/2 (March 1991) pp. 184–185.

[76] Coke is now regarded as an exceptional figure of his age, whereas other lawyers like Sir John Dodderidge and Sir Henry Finch saw law as mutable and a product of history as much as of reason. See Tubbs *Mind* pp. 167–168; Sharpe *Remapping* p. 310.

from the research of Cotton and Sir Henry Spelman, but also as a restraint on royal power by identifying various institutional and legal precedents limiting royal power, as supplied to Parliament especially in the 1620s, by antiquarians like Cotton (his studies supplying precedents for both sides) and especially Selden, who had placed their talents at its service. When Selden in his *Jure Naturali* castigated inward-looking intellectual tendencies, he may very well also have had in mind the insularistic tendencies of many common lawyers, thereby criticizing,

some kinds of people – more than a few, in fact – are so hemmed in by their education, or their intellectual capacities, or the preconceptions of their particular schools of thought, that they consider it beneath themselves to venture out, like explorers, beyond their own borders. They either rashly deny, or arrogantly refuse to acknowledge, or fail to hope, that there is any truth to be found outside of themselves.

Thus in the face of mounting intellectual and practical threats to traditional English government and law, the simple vision of the law as immemorial and insular came to be seen as patently insufficient.[77]

On top of the new modes of political analysis and the new scholarship, and to some extent building upon them came the additional threat from works justifying royal authority by divine-right arguments. Such arguments trumped both Cokean immemorialism and Camdenian antiquarianism, by asserting monarchy to be divinely and naturally ordained and thus, at least in principle, unconditioned by historical contingencies. Much of this argumentation was originally developed in controversies with those such as Cardinal Bellarmino, who claimed a papal right to depose princes – but once the arguments in favor of divine-right monarchy were available, they could be (and were) easily directed at repelling Presbyterian ideas, as well as to undermining political claims for immemorialist or historical restraints on royal authority.[78]

It is beyond doubt that as the seventeenth century progressed, English politics came to be growingly concerned with claims about an absolutist menace. There is an ongoing debate among historians as to how substantial this alleged menace really was: if, as claimed by the so-called "revisionist" historians, it was a mere phantom menace, the province of only a handful of peripheral eccentrics and disregarded clerics; or if, as was long the accepted account and now newly supported by a cohort of "anti-revisionists," it was a real threat, posed by important and powerful figures (starting with the King), who were seriously

[77] JN b1 Praefatio; Helgerson *Nationhood* pp. 71–72; Zaller *Legitimacy* pp. 326–327; Ferguson *Clio* p. 117; Barbour *Measures* p. 120; Sharpe *Remapping* p. 307 – Sharpe claims Cotton arrived at an understanding of the feudal system before Spelman published his findings in 1626. Sir Robert Cotton's library was sealed in 1629 and Sir Edward Coke's papers were sequestered on his death in 1634 – revealing the perceived authority of legal and historical documents in early Stuart England. Selden's study and library were also sealed for some time after his arrest in 1629. Sharpe *Remapping* pp. 75–76, 325; Zaller *Legitimacy* pp. 40, 248.

[78] Zaller *Legitimacy* p. 327.

attempting to transform the political rules so that they would allow the King to disregard constitutional arrangements, if he deemed it a necessity. Without trying to decide here between the view that there were almost no absolutists of importance and no absolutist agenda in England, and the view that there was a serious scheme with strong intellectual support for establishing absolutism, it is undeniable that English politics really did become increasingly obsessed with an absolutist threat. Even a professed "revisionist" like Burgess, believing there were only very few real absolutists in early seventeenth century, admits that the fears of arbitrary government were indeed (together with popery) "at the core of the nightmares of seventeenth-century Englishmen." Many of those identified as absolutists did allow for theoretical limitations on royal power by natural law or divine laws, as well as advocating in practice the following of existing traditions and forms of government; James I and Charles I, certainly and repeatedly protested they intended to rule only according to established practices. But since the term absolute monarchy had an ambiguous and unstable place in the English political vocabulary, many suspected such royal allowances were merely hiding a design to introduce arbitrary government slowly and by degrees. Evidently there was in England a widespread fear of creeping absolutism, which meant that, irrespective of the intentions behind them, writings, spoken words and political actions were increasingly interpreted as manifestations of this growing threat.[79]

Outside of the world of legal and political theory, there were a number of high-profile incidents, either judicial or parliamentarian, which brought the battle of ideas onto the public stage. One of the most important of these was the Case of the Post-Nati (aka Calvin's Case) of 1608, concerning the right to English nationality of Scottish subjects of King James, like the plaintiff Robert Calvin (actually named Colville), who had been born after (thus, "post-nati") the King of Scotland had also become King of England. Arguing for the plaintiff's demand to be recognized as an English subject was Francis Bacon, who claimed that kings came before law, and in monarchies (especially hereditary ones) "subjection is more natural and simple," only afterward made by laws more formal and perfect. Presenting a narrative of social foundation, he argued that if "a heap of people meet together so near, that they appoint a king, there allegiance is before they have laws proclaimed or

---

[79] Sommerville, for example, lists among "revisionists" C. Russel, P. Christianson, G. Burgess, K. Sharpe and J. Morrill; among "anti-revisionists" J. Salmon and P. Lake as well as himself. See in Sommerville *Royalists* pp. 225–229, 233–234. Burgess claims outright absolutists were, in England, very thin on the ground, but admits "absolutism" was not a complete myth, for there were some – if very few – who indeed advocated it outright, and mentions Gentili, Maynwaring and later Filmer. See Burgess *Absolute* pp. 209–210. But if we recall that James I (the 1606 Canons) and Charles I (*Patriarcha* in 1632) both had to block publication of outright absolutist texts, and we add to these Sybthorpe and Hobbes' *Elements of Law*, we might suspect that the number of advocates of such views, and their prominence (especially in the Church), might not have been so small after all.

prescribed." Thus, he argued, "...you shall find the observation true, and almost general in all states, that their lawgivers were long after their first kings, who governed for a time by natural equity without law." Bacon supported this view from "law of nature" by which all men are "naturalized one towards another," and from biblical sources where men "were all made of one lump of earth" and originally of "one language." He conceded that later came "the curse" of the division of tongues, and of humanity into nations, but he cleverly argued that, from that curse "our present case is excepted" – since English and Scot speak the same language. He was thus not only claiming that the division of humanity into nations was an unnatural curse, but also that the British case, where peoples in several kingdoms share one tongue, means they are providentially excepted from the curse (at least towards each other). Bacon shot an additional blow against English law as expression of a consensual and popular national identity, by asserting that King Edward I was the one who should really be said to be England's "first lawgiver" who brought the law "to some perfection." Thus, in Bacon's interpretation, English law, instead of being a continuing, immemorial and popular source of national identity, became an example of law originating at a certain time, from a king's command, and to be identified with his will and power.[80]

On the opposite side, as one of those arguing against the plaintiff was Sir Edwin Sandys, disciple of Hooker. He presented a view of England (and, by implication, all peoples) possessing a historical national identity independent of their institutions of government. His argument was that since "the world is grown to great distribution of people into places, and to discipline in their government," although in each government people remain generally subject to one head, "the manner of it is locally circumscribed to the places where they are brought forth," and those of one do not, nor should partake of the discipline or birthright of the other, but every one left to his own, "as acquired by the patrimony of their ancestors" upon reasons and circumstances not necessarily now extant, or to be exactly understood. As the case was being judged in Chancery Court, which as court of equity was not bound by the Common law, Sandys was somewhat constrained in making his argument explicitly from common law, or in asserting the immemoriality and continuity of English law. Nevertheless, the frame of his argument, with its references to the "patrimony of their ancestors" and to circumstances not now extant or easily understood, clearly is one of a continuing and customary national law, as an essential part of a national identity.[81]

---

[80] McEachern *Poetics* pp. 150–151; Zaller *Legitimacy* pp. 322–324.
[81] McEachern *Poetics* pp. 149–150. A disciple, friend and executor of Hooker (whom he had assisted in gaining the appointment of Master at the Temple Church), Sandys became a prominent lawyer and an MP tending to oppose the court. Sandys and Selden might possibly have become acquainted early on through legal practice at the Inns of Court (they were respectively members of Middle and Inner Temple), but they certainly knew each other from

The judges in the Case of the Post-Nati, deliberating in Chancery and finding in favor of the plaintiff, nevertheless invested considerable efforts in ensuring their decision about the status of aliens was to be made with reference to English law only, and explicitly pointed out that their decision did not in any way diminish the supremacy and integrity of English law, such as by their referring to a 1351 English statute, Of the Born Over-Seas (De natis Ultra Mare), which recognized as subjects, foreign-born children of the king's subjects. Lord Chancellor Ellesmere, addressed the prosecution's use in its case of non-legal sources such as Plato and Aristotle, and remarked that though "[t]hey were men of singular learning and wisdom," the countries and time they lived in lacked the true learning of the knowledge of God, and that such opinions do not give laws to kings and kingdoms "no more than Sir Thomas More's Utopia" or than such pamphlets as are to be had at every market. Then turning to arguments made from the authority of Roman law, Ellesmere added that he would not suffer an imputation on the judges of England, "that they, or the Common lawe doe not attribute as great power and authoritie to their Soveraignes the kings of England, as the Romane laws did to their Emperours" – thus extolling the common law but incidentally also implying a disturbing view of the possible extent of the royal prerogative. Sir Edward Coke, who sat as another of the judges in the case, was even more explicit in remarking that their arguments for the decision "quoted no foreign laws, produced no alien precedents." He was unperturbed by the fact that no direct precedent could be found in English law for this case, since there being no English judgments, resolutions or rules against it, actually meant for him that it was clearly not prohibited; and the apparent lacuna he overcame by asserting that the "law of nature" was part of English law, as it was part of every equitable law, and thus if the problem could be overcome by an appeal to natural law, that would be regarded as made by English law.[82]

The case can certainly be made (as for instance is done by C. McEachern), that the real debate in the Case of the Post-Nati, as well as in the whole of the union debates, was less one of being for or against the king, for or against constitution, but rather, when it came to questions of law, about whether the universal overrode the local or the other way around. For Sandys the case was about subjection being "locally circumscribed to the places where people are brought forth," while for Bacon it was about local law yielding to natural,

their common activity in the Virginia Company (where Sandys was a leading member and Treasurer until its dissolution in 1624), and their parliamentary activities since the 1621 Parliament in which Sandys was a member and Selden an advisor, as well as in the Parliaments of 1624 and 1626 where both sat as MPs – and of course after being both imprisoned in the Tower for some weeks in 1621, for undisclosed reasons. A generation older than Selden, Sandys (who also knew Paolo Sarpi), might have introduced the younger scholar to Hooker's ideas. Even without any direct intellectual link, many ideas articulated by Sandys find clear parallels in Selden.

[82] Zaller *Legitimacy* pp. 322–324; McEachern *Poetics* p. 153.

universal law, since "[i]t was civil and national law that brought in these differences" of alien and native, and therefore "because they tend to abridge the law of nature, the law favoureth them not." Therefore, according to Bacon, just as in England the "law of the land" overcomes "customs of towns," then "all national laws whatsoever" are to be "taken strictly" in any point where they "derogate from the law of nature." The insistence of the judges in Calvin's case, to base their decision solely on English grounds, indicates they were well aware of this dimension of the debate. Although the Case of the Post-Nati did not directly address issues of sources or limits of royal authority, it crystallized many of the concerns about English identity and law being overwhelmed by foreign influences, and implicitly the powers such foreign ideas ascribe to the monarch.[83]

There were throughout the 1610s and 1620s other examples of judicial confrontation, symbolizing the deepening battle of political ideas, perhaps the most prominent of which was the Case of the Five Knights (aka Darnell's Case) of 1627, in which Selden was counsel for one of five defendants who had refused to pay the forced loan imposed by the King. The defendants claimed that the forced loan, as a financial imposition, was illegal without parliamentary approval; the prosecution claimed such a loan as well as the imprisonment of the accused fell under the authority of the royal prerogative. Attorney General Sir Robert Heath, presented the case for the prosecution in terms guaranteed to raise the apprehension of those fearing an overreaching royal power, when he asserted about the royal prerogative that "sure I am that the first stone of sovereignty was no sooner laid, but this power was given to the sovereign," and that kings should be trusted when they took unusual actions for the common good. Consequently, he argued it should be presumed that when a king imprisons someone without giving cause, "there is great reason of state so to do, or else they would not do it." Besides the obviously tautological argument, the very terms "reason of state" and "sovereignty" were bound to strike those who heard them as distinctly Machiavellian and Bodinian, that is as a foreign terminology threatening to supplant the English traditions (and in Selden's case, reminding him of their use in his own arbitrary imprisonment, a few years earlier). As the judges in this case eventually found in favor of the prosecution, arguing that by common law the court had no jurisdiction over the royal prerogative, all those fearing a growing absolutism under cover of the prerogative, had to conclude that the courts had been proved ineffective in resisting the danger to English liberties, and Parliament now remained as the last line of defense.[84]

Such growing concerns and their consequences are exemplified by the public career of Sir Robert Cotton, Selden's benefactor and friend. A supporter of a strong monarchy and an advisor to the government who nevertheless believed in institutional safeguards for liberty and property against arbitrary rule,

---

[83] McEachern *Poetics* p. 155.   [84] Christianson *Discourse* pp. 120–121.

Cotton's unexceptional views nevertheless gradually brought him into conflict with the court. In 1627 his historical work *A Short View of the Reign of King Henry III* was published, criticizing giddy heads who, seeming to discern blemishes in the existing government, propose to new-fashion the state according to "certaine imaginary and fantastick forms of commonwealths," which would "mould any state to these general rules which in particular application will prove idle." Against the background of the forced loan, the tract was seen to indicate criticism of the royal policies. Cotton was questioned by the Privy Council about the text, and his somewhat disingenuous claims that he had written the *Short View* back in 1614 and that it had been now published without his consent, were accepted by the council; indeed, he was even asked to write a memorandum for the council (which may have had some role in the decision to call the Parliament of 1628). But the whole affair showed how, by this time, a lifelong client of the Howard family with important ties to the court, who had supplied to Stuart governments effective extra-parliamentary financial devices, such as wartime fiscal expedients and the antiquarian resurrection of baronetcies, was gradually being pushed by royal policies, into opposition. Cotton had become a prominent advocate of parliamentary authority as well as a gray eminence of the nascent Caroline opposition, with his home conveniently nestled between the Houses of Parliament, becoming frequent place of informal congregation for the Commons' leadership.[85]

All these suspects and fears came to a head in the first session of the 1628 Parliament, when Sir Benjamin Rudyerd famously articulated in dramatic terms the anxieties of a great many MPs, asserting: "This is the crisis of Parliaments – we shall know by this if Parliament live or die. If we persevere, the King to draw one way, the Parliament another, the Commonwealth must sink in the midst." More ominously prescient was Phelips, when he declared that "we are almost grown like the Turks who send their Janissaries, who placeth his halberd at the doors and there he is master of the house." Immediately on convening, Parliament had set out to confront what it regarded as threats the traditional rights of Englishmen, by initiating a review of the Five Knights' Case, by impeaching, condemning and imprisoning Sybthorpe and Maynwaring, and by attempting to impeach the royal favorite, Buckingham. Selden too indicated the high stakes of the issues involved when he declared that, as he had been in the past a feed counsel defending his clients, so now, "I was sent hither, and trusted with the lives and liberties of them that sent me." He clearly spoke for the vast majority of the Commons, when he stated in the house that "[i]t is the sole distinction of freemen that they cannot be imprisoned at pleasure" – for without this freedom, access to all other rights to life and property was practically negated, making them into empty words.[86]

---

[85] Zaller *Legitimacy* pp. 48–50; Sharpe *Remapping* pp. 321–325, 329–330.
[86] Zaller *Legitimacy* pp. 666–668.

On the matter of imprisonment, the Lords attempted to offer a compromise formula that would address the concerns of the Commons while preserving the prerogative, proposing that in case the King found

> just cause for reason of state to imprison or restrain any man his person, his Majesty would graciously declare that within a convenient time he shall and will express a cause of his commitment or restraint, either general or special, and upon a cause so expressed will leave him immediately to be tried according to the common justice of the kingdom.

This formula must have been especially galling to Selden, who on top of his role in the Five Knights' Case, had also been himself imprisoned for unspecified "reason of state" without trial and without knowledge at what "convenient time" if ever he was to be tried or released. He rose, and scathingly attacked the proposed formula as unacceptable, as well as contradicting Magna Carta and the "fundamental liberties" of Englishmen:

> 'A convenient time'; but [by Magna Carta] every man was to be delivered by law. If they were so wise then to hold it needless, why is it now necessary? And for convenient time, what is convenient time? Who shall judge of it but the judges? And so they now shall have the power of the lords of the Council.

He warned the House of Commons, that the proposed proviso may look as just a little concession, but "[a]t this little gap every man's liberty may in time go out." Selden's view is striking not only for the distrust it displays in the intentions and faith of the crown, but for his equal lack of confidence in the judges. As his own bitter experience of arbitrary imprisonment in 1621, and of others in 1627, had shown him (and his further imprisonment of 1629–1631 would confirm), it was regretfully unrealistic to expect that judges could be the defenders of English liberties; a view he later reiterated more than once in the *Table-Talk*, perhaps most of all in his bitter remark: "The King's Oath is not security enough for our Property, for he swears to Govern according to Law; now the Judges they interpret the Law, and what Judges can be made to do we know." It was a position in which Selden differed starkly from most common lawyers, who followed Coke in viewing the courts and judges as the true bulwark of the English constitution. For Selden it was always and only Parliament who could, in the last resort, defend the "fundamental liberties" of Englishmen.[87]

In the joint conference of the Commons with the Lords, convened to iron out differences between the two houses, Dudley Digges best articulated the

---

[87] *Commons Debates 1628*, Robert C. Johnson et al. eds., (Rochester, NY: Rochester University Press, 1997) vol. iii pp. 96–97; TT "The King" sec. 6. And see in this context James I's assertion that "this oath in the Coronation is the clearest, civill and fundementall Law, whereby the King's office is properly defined," he categorically denied that there is a contract between king and people (he terms it instead a "mutual promise"); King James points out that even if there was a contract, it would still be a meaningless one, for "who should bee judge of the breake"? James I *True* pp. 56–57, 76–80.

argument that the common law as primarily a law of property, regulating what is *meum et tuum* (mine and thine), was in effect the foundation of English liberties and government:

[I]t is an undoubted and fundamental point of this so ancient common law of England, that the subject hath a true property in his goods and possessions, which doth preserve as sacred that *meum et tuum* that is the nurse of industry, and mother of courage, and without which there can be no justice, of which *meum et tuum* is the proper object.

Digges' claims echoed a similar argument made previously by Sir John Eliot in a speech of 22 March, when declaring that he was speaking not only for himself, his county of Cornwall, or even England, but for "the ancient glory of the ancient laws of England," he argued that those laws prohibit extra-parliamentary impositions and exactions:

Yet contrary to those laws, and that common right of the subject, we see notwithstanding how they have been exacted and imposed. Does not this contradict the law, and make it fruitless? Does it not corrupt and stop justice, and all rights depending thereon? Where, then, is property? Where the distinction in which it consists? The *meum* and *tuum*, if this prevails, becomes *nec meum nec tuum*. It falls into the old chaos and confusion, the will and pleasure of the mightier powers.

The rights and privileges which made Englishmen free were in mortal danger, he warned, "[i]f they be not now the more carefully preserved, they will, I fear, render us less free, less worthy than our fathers."[88]

Later on, during the parliamentary discussions of what was to become the Petition of Right, the Lords proposed a number of alterations to the text prepared by the Commons, including the adding of a passage stating:

We present this our humble petition to your Majesty not only with a care of preserving our own liberties, but with a due regard to leave entire that sovereign power, wherewith your Majesty is trusted, for the protection, safety, and happiness of your people.

The passage – turning on the two crucial terms of "sovereign power" and "trusted" – elicited a great debate in the Commons about political terminology and ideology. Old Edward Alford, veteran of many Parliaments (and patron of Selden from his days as a young Sussex scholar), expressed the concerns of most MPs by asking: "What is 'sovereign power'? Bodin says it is that that is free from any condition. By this we shall acknowledge a regal as well as a legal power. Let us give that to the King that the law gives him, and no more." Pym agreed,

---

[88] Christianson *Discourse* pp. 124–129; J. Forster, *Sir John Eliot: A Biography 1592–1632* (1872, 2nd edition) vol. ii pp. 9–10. Another version of the main refrain of Eliot's speech is given as: "Where is law? Where is *meum* and *tuum*? It is fallen into the chaos of a higher power." See Cromartie *Constitutionalist* p. 227. See also discussion in Toomer *Scholarship* p. 319 and Zuckert *Natural* pp. 51–52. Digges' and Eliot's argument was similar to Selden's reported response when shown Sybthorpe's text before publication by Thomas Worral, chaplain to the Bishop of London: "If that book were true, there is no *meum* and *tuum* in England."

saying "[t]his power seems to be another distinct power from the power of the law. I know how to add 'sovereign' to [the King's] person, but not to his power." Sir Edward Coke spoke in similar vein, declaring "I know the prerogative is part of the law, but 'sovereign power' is no parliament word in my opinion. It weakens Magna Carta and all other statutes, for they are absolute without any saving of sovereign power[.]" He stressed that adding such a power to the text, means fatally weakening the foundations of law, after which the whole building must fall, for "[b]y implication we give a sovereign power above all these laws." The implication of 'sovereign power' as something above the law made all the difference to the interpretation of the term 'trusted.' Sir John Glanville advocated rejecting the Lords' proposal outright, based on the distinction between a "trust" that is abstract and general and between a specific trust within common law. He pointed out that there were some cases where the kings of England have a specific trust to dispense with some law, but those laws that were "commands according to the Common lawe and of the nature of the Common lawe, I never heard any trust to dispince [sic] with them." In other words, Glanville was claiming that there was no such thing as a general trust pertaining to government and laws, and certainly not in cases concerning the common law, but only particular instances when a law might contain some dispensing clause. He added that "[t]he word 'trust' is of great latitude and large extent, and therefore out to be well and warily applied and restrained, especially in the case of a king: there is a trust inseparably reposed in the persons of the kings of England, but that trust is regulated by law." Thus, for Glanville, trust was not a term describing some kind of general and unlimited capacity of kings to override laws, but rather it was either a general term defining the moral nature of kingship, or a particular and defined power, regulated by law. Thomas Wentworth (son of Peter, no relation to the future Earl of Strafford), also employing the language of trust, protested that never a House of Parliament trusted the king more, but since they wanted to ensure that the king's goodness "remain to posterity" and since they were "accountable to a public trust," they requested a bill to vindicate a subjects' rights by laying down former laws, with "some modest provision for instruction, performance and execution." Thus in the interpretation implied in the Lords' language, trust was the King's absolute power granted to him by God, to which the subjects must make do with a hope in the good intentions of their monarch; while in the competing interpretation presented by the Commons' leadership, trust is only a specific legal relationship, established by virtue of a contract between king and subjects, and thus bound by the law. In short, for the King's supporters "trust" meant obedience, for the Commons it meant mutually agreed terms.[89]

---

[89] Zaller *Legitimacy* pp. 655–660; Kahn *Wayward* pp. 88–89. Selden agreed with Glanville and Wentworth, in claiming the Common law recognized only a particular and definite trust – while rejecting the idea advocated by Francis Bacon, of a general trust in which men trust the

On May 22, it was Selden's turn to rise in the House of Commons and defend the original text of the petition against the proposed additions, showing that he shared the suspicions of his colleagues in the parliamentary leadership, as to the motives and origins of the House of Lords' text. He decidedly rejected the clause, which if adopted would allow imprisonment without cause or forced loans, even if only by "sovereign power," insisting it was unprecedented in English law, citing a number of historical documents that stated the liberties of the subject, with no such caveat. He then remarked that the use of such a terminology would be at best irrelevant and at worst confusing, ironically asking if "speaking of our own rights, shall we say, We are not to be imprisoned saving, but by the king's 'Sovereign Power'?" He later added that another proposal, one that would allow the king to confiscate inheritances on the suspect of bastardy was clearly of foreign origins: "This project is fetched from beyond the sea. In France, the King has the goods of men interstate that are bastards[.]" It was impossible to miss the drift of Selden's remarks – not only were the proposals self-defeating as well as inimical to the English political tradition and language, but they also bore the ugly marks of the insidious Bodinian ideology, which had sealed France's descent into an absolute monarchy.[90]

However, merely rejecting Machiavellian and Bodinian concepts of political authority was not enough, for there was a need to find some competing conceptual framework, which could serve as firm foundation for government and ensure promises and rights between king and subjects. Sir Francis Seymour, Selden's close parliamentary ally, articulated the problem by asking "how can we think of giving subsidies till we know whether we have anything to give or not?" While Selden himself made the same point more practically, asserting that any "right" to property was meaningless without legal remedies. Thus both Seymour and Selden returned to the idea that property rights represent the foundation of English law and government. Indeed V. Kahn argues convincingly that as the central issue at stake concerned property rights and consent to taxation (in both law courts and Parliament), "the common law notion of an economic contract came to seem the right way to think about the implied contract of Magna Carta" that might make Charles I accountable to Parliament. Speakers like Pym and Robert Mason (who was to serve as counsel to Selden and other MPs arrested soon after the dissolution of this Parliament) made the connection explicit by employing the terminology of contract to address the issue. Pym asserted that Parliament was only demanding the rights established by the contract, the "composition," between William the conqueror and his subjects, while Mason declared that in England the King ruled by

---

conscience of another to dispose as he sees fit of their estate and possessions. See Cromartie *Constitutionalist* p. 188.
[90] Christianson *Discourse* pp. 150, 158; Burgess *Politics* pp. 196–198; Sommerville *Royalists* pp. 159–160.

contract, "ex pacto," the extent and limit of his power depending "on human will and on the ancient agreement or contract between the kings and the kingdom."[91]

In the event, the Commons won this debate, with the Lords abandoning their proposed amendments, and the Petition of Right passed as a traditional restatement of English political ideas and terms. But the vehement upholding of the common law by speakers in the Commons debate, as the completely self-sufficient basis for the government and liberty of Englishmen, while fiercely rejecting any outside arguments and sources as dangerous to the native constitutional fabric – betrayed the manifest realization that such forceful rejections were needed exactly because outside ideas were gaining ground. Thus the 1628 debate around the Petition of Right, was in many ways the swan song of the self-referring "insularistic" common law language. The clash turned on the authority of prerogative to supersede rights explicitly defended by statute, and although the immediate question was that of imprisonment at will, taxation without parliamentary consent was the wider issue of contention. The lawyers behind the Petition of Right were certainly not trying to assert a novel theory of law, and neither to challenge the nature or extent of the prerogative. They were merely attempting to state those of their certified rights which they saw as having been abused, and to gain surety against similar offenses in the future.[92]

This great last stand of the traditional restating of established rights ended in utter failure when, while Parliament was prorogued, Charles I commanded the Clerk of the Parliament to cut off from the parliamentary record of the Petition of Right, the King's formal answer, and to insert in its place the earlier, ambiguous answer (which Parliament had rejected) – and then had the petition and amended answer printed. This was a pure and simple break of faith – arbitrarily and unilaterally nullifying the formal political and legal compact created by his original answer to the petition. Many of those who up to this point had given the King and his intentions the benefit of the doubt now realized with shock that even a statute of Parliament, was not safe from the King's arbitrary will. This was too much to stomach even for most royalists, for it seemed to undermine the whole English legal structure, so that the King's

---

[91] Kahn *Wayward* pp. 84–85, 88–89, 94–95. This debate was eventually sealed many years later, with Charles I's *Answer to the Nineteen Propositions*, where the King adopted the language of mixed constitution, fundamental laws of the kingdom, and even suggested the notion of political contract where the sovereign grants "protection" in exchange for the subjects' "obedience." It immediately produced a new debate, around Henry Parker's language of necessity – the one formerly used by the supporters of absolute monarchy ... A much more Hobbesian view is that presented by Henry Parker, who held that "power must be somewhere supreame" and undivided, in church and state, while denying royal (or indeed any other) authority emanates from God, but only from "pactions and agreements" of political corporations. Collins *Cosmos* pp. 30–31.

[92] Zaller *Legitimacy* pp. 666–668.

supporters would eventually resort to arguing that the Petition was actually no statute. As Parliament reconvened in early 1629, Selden moved on 21 January that a formal search of the official records of the Petition of Right, parliamentary as well as at other courts, should be undertaken. The motion was passed, and it shortly emerged (as Selden knew) that it was the King's rejected first answer to Parliament which had actually been the one officially preserved, instead of the parliamentary approved second one – an obviously craven attempt to deny the Petition legally binding status. Eliot and Selden immediately moved for a committee to inquire into the circumstances of the printing and infringement of the Petition of Right, and got it. The committee was set to work at once, using the Petition as template for a grand inquest into the state of the realm. As Selden declared, under Tunnage and Poundage, goods had been seized illegally by the government: "Next they will take our arms, and then our legs, and so our lives. Let all see that we are sensible of these customs creeping upon us." The new practices must not be allowed to be established as precedent and custom, or the Common law will be lost.[93]

The King would have none of this, and what followed was the chaotic dissolution of Parliament, the arrest of opposition leaders (including Selden) and the 11-year attempt by Charles I at Personal Rule without Parliament, with the infliction of such financial impositions and arbitrary imprisonment as were in direct contravention to both the spirit and the letter of the Petition of Right. This course of events exposed the ineffectiveness of the old ways in the face of resolute royal policies, and it convinced many among the English political class that the time had come for new political ideas and means. The dilemma of loyal subjects exasperated by the misdeeds of their king was articulated by the Bishop of Carlisle, lamenting in a quote from Shakespeare's *Richard III* (4.1.121–129): "What subject can give sentence on his king? And who sits here that is not Richard's subject?" The new political course was to be not only the search for de facto solutions to such old dilemmas, but also for an ideological apparatus that could supply a justification for political actions.[94]

The issues at stake and the search for new directions are best illustrated by the ideas articulated during the 1630s by two central political figures, close allies until the close of the 1620s, whose paths then diverged into completely opposite courses. The first of these was Sir John Eliot, the foremost leader of the Commons in the 1628 Parliament (and close ally and friend of Selden), who was imprisoned in 1629 for his political activities, and would die in the Tower in 1632. While imprisoned, Eliot wrote two pamphlets in which he reiterated many of the themes and preoccupations of the period. In his *De Jure Majestatis* (borrowing heavily from a similarly named work of 1610 by the German thinker Henning Arnisaeus) he attempted to uphold parliamentary rights based on an altered version of Bodinian ideas. The tract was no radical manifesto, actually supporting the notion of an undivided supreme power, since

[93] Zaller *Legitimacy* pp. 665, 689.   [94] Zaller *Legitimacy* p. 424.

a limited one destroys the "nature of order," it also rejected the idea that the people make kings at will, since even if they once did, by having "conferred their right upon another they have deprived themselves of it." But he then went on to argue that kings do not own the property of their subjects, and may alienate any of it only for the public good or extreme necessity, which were not defined, but should be obviously recognized by all, since the king may alienate property only with "the consent of those, who have interest in the propriety, as he hath in the sovereignty." In his second pamphlet *The Monarchy of Man*, although borrowing from Plato and Bodin, to claim that kings should rule according to the laws, Eliot then proceeded to assert what he did not in the first pamphlet, that "Law is the ground of all authority," and that subjects and sovereign bore an equal duty and obligation towards the authority of law. In both writings he was obviously attempting to confront Bodin's ideological apparatus (and showing some surprising similarities to Bacon and Hobbes), while also looking for some principle that could set limits to it. Eliot was evidently struggling to articulate some general political theory in terms that could preserve the integrity of English government and reject a principle of resistance, while at the same time subjecting royal authority to the laws agreed upon in Parliament. We know for a fact that Eliot consulted Selden in these attempts, since the existing copy of Eliot's *The Monarchy of Man*, which he sent to Selden, has added to it a note from Eliot remarking that he amended the text where Selden had thought it "tender and too quick."[95]

The second prominent figure was Thomas Wentworth, later Earl of Strafford, who had been an important opposition leader until late 1628, when he broke with Eliot and his allies over their refusal to explicitly allow for the King to act unchecked in time of special emergency (which Strafford supported). This break heralded Wentworth's complete about-turn to the side of the King, and his then meteoric rise to become the most effective and powerful (and feared) royal servant of the next decade. As early as December 1628, he had accepted a peerage and was Lord President of the North; in his first speech in this capacity he heralded his vision about the necessity for order and efficiency above all, to address multiple crises facing English government. He warned of "distempered minds" endeavouring to divide king and people with "a licentious conception" that denying hierarchy would make "all head or all members," for the "authority of a King is the keystone which closet up the arch of order and government" and keeps all the parts in place, so that if licentious conceptions shake it "all the frame falls together in a confused heap." During the 1630s, as Earl of Strafford, he led a group in government, headed by himself and Archbishop Laud, which increasingly regarded hindrances of royal policies by institutional criticism, delay or precedent as a serious detriment to the good management of the state, and adopted as cure an approach articulated, in the words Laud wrote to Wentworth in 1633: "For the state, indeed my Lord, I am

[95] Collins *Cosmos* pp. 123–125.

for *thorough*." The term "thorough" meant for Wentworth and his supporters in the time of the Personal Rule, a vision of politics that was practically authoritarian, and which, without formally abolishing traditional constitutional politics, sought to ignore and sidestep them for as long as possible. Although Laud and Wentworth seem to have believed such a policy was merely necessary to overcome a temporary crisis, whatever the ultimate goal, its immediate result would be to seriously weaken traditional practices, and indeed Parliament. Soon Wentworth was using the terminology of "reason of state" to argue that in times of emergency, all conventions of government are suspended and the ruler may use whatever means are in his power to resolve the challenges confronting him – and of course it was the ruler who defined what constituted such a time of emergency. Wentworth did not dispense with Parliament altogether, regarding royal rule without it as temporary, only until the time there can be a Parliament "rightly corrected and prepared," but until then, it was "necessary there be a time to forget." Returning to the edifice metaphor he had used to portray royal authority, Strafford now put forward a completely different concept of politics, proposing to Charles I that, with threats to the King's authority in Ireland and Scotland, military force was the "Pillar of your Authority," and in the circumstances extant, its use was "of absolute Necessity." It was not very hard to guess what such a view made of the refusal of the English Parliament to finance military supplies.[96]

The interpretation that the vast majority of the English political class gave to Strafford's policies, was reflected in the eventual Bill of Attainder against him: it claimed that Strafford planned to bring from Ireland the standing army created there to subdue the Irish, over to England, where there was at that time no army, and subdue it militarily. Such policies were regarded as reflecting not some mere opportunistic grab for power, but as representing substantive political ideas, according to which force is the true "pillar" of political authority, and "necessity" can be easily summoned by the ruler to overthrow existing political procedures. In fact these very policies and ideas were indeed introduced into British politics between 1640 and 1660: first by the King's unsuccessful attempts to subdue Scotland by use of an English army and later vice versa to use the Scottish army to defeat his English enemies; later by Parliament's successful subjugation of Ireland and Scotland by its use of the English army and, most successfully, by Cromwell and his New Model Army's eventual subjugation of England as well as Ireland and Scotland. The theory for these policies was supplied in the 1650s by those like Needham and Hobbes who would claim Cromwell's rule to be legitimated by right of conquest and by necessity.

---

[96] C.V. Wedgwood, *Thomas Wentworth First Earl of Strafford 1593–1641 – A Reevaluation* (Phoenix Press, 2000 – reprint of 1961 edition) pp. 68, 73–74, 79, 83–84, 119–120; and A. Milton, "Thomas Wentworth and the Political Thought of the Personal Rule" in J.F. Merrit (ed.), *The Political World of Thomas Wentworth, Earl of Strafford, 1621–1641* (Cambridge University Press, 2003) p. 143. See also Adamson *Noble* pp. 9, 18–19.

It can then be said that by the mid-seventeenth century, in what Zaller has aptly described as the new, "Bodinian climate" of English political discourse, with its constant search for a locus of power, there emerged two alternative conceptions of a binding agent for the laws and government of a country: one was a sovereign power as maker, enforcer and interpreter of law – most naturally this would be a king, but as Hobbes (and the Venetian constitution) showed, some kind of supreme council could also serve the purpose; the second was the concept that Zaller termed "a fundamental framework of law, separate from the law of nature and particular to each nation" which continually guides laws back to their first principles, while historically tempering them, "in short, a constitution." The latter was obviously Selden's view, although he only very rarely employed the term "constitution" to describe the legal character of the state, using instead other terms traditionally employed in England, such as "fundamental laws" and "ancient frame of government." As we shall see, Selden regarded all governments as social constructs which, except for extreme moments of anarchy or conquest, coalesced in virtually all cases into mixed regimes, in which a popular, aristocratic or monarchical element predominated, according to the aptitudes, history and character of each nation.[97]

By 1640, in no small measure as an effect of the decade-long suspension of Parliament and of the circumstances that had brought that suspension about, there was an evident shift in English political discourse from the past-centered idiom of Common law and precedent, to the widespread employment of new ideas and terminologies. In effect the earlier "insularistic" political discourse had to a great degree collapsed, and was replaced by one that was increasingly inclusive of outside arguments and texts. Often the same author would employ several of these idioms, even side by side in the same text, including of course Machiavellian reason of state language and Bodinian sovereignty theory, as well as natural rights ideas of the second scholastics, and Catholic and Presbyterian resistance theories. Moreover, prominent among these new ideas and terminologies were individualistic premises, which increasingly permeated political theory, and in many cases grounded political obligation in self-interest. Within this theoretical free-for-all, as we shall see, some of the most important and coherent political theories, were those put forward by Grotius, Hobbes and Filmer, all of them addressing existing ideas but taking them further towards new theoretical clarity. The same was true for Selden, who from the 1630s onwards attempted to articulate a new, natural law-based legitimation for the English political and legal tradition that would measure up to universal criteria, while also preserving its particularistic character.[98]

---

[97] Zaller *Legitimacy* pp. 331–333.
[98] R. Eccleshall, *Order and Reason in Politics* (Oxford University Press, 1978) pp. 155–156; Burgess *Politics* pp. 224–226. Pocock's view of the speed and extent of this phenomenon has been widely criticized, but I tend to agree with Burgess, that the description is essentially right, if

The shift in political idiom could be, and was indeed, employed in a number of different political directions. We have seen that the supporters of Personal Rule employed it. In other cases it was used to justify a right of resistance, now resting more often than not on arguments and authorities from "natural rights" or religiously based resistance theories, even when these were going against the laws of England. A notable example was offered on 1 September 1640, when a sermon was preached before the muster of the London Artillery Company, by Calybute Downinge, a cleric and protégé of the powerful opposition aristocrat, the Earl of Warwick. The sermon argued that there are circumstances in which it is justified to "take up armes against the King" and significantly, in addition to a biblical source (based on his reading of Deutronomy 25), Downinge also offered as justification for his claim the assertion that in times of extraordinary danger to the people, military resistance to the King's government is legitimate even when strictly against the "Laws of the Land," because these are superseded by the law of nations. That is, he was arguing for a universal authority trouncing that of the Common law. As evidence for this claim, Downinge brought Hugo Grotius, asserting that "...Grotius is clear, that *in gravissimo and certissimo discrimine, lex de non resistendo non obligat*" (in a most grave and certain crisis, the law of non-resistance does not oblige). The sermon certainly gave a justification to a revolt against the King's government, and based it not on the laws of England but on Grotian natural rights, and biblical-based resistance theory.[99]

By December 1641, the struggle was acquiring the character of a Bodinian contest for supreme authority – something inherently contrary to a constitutionalist view of politics. Thus when Sir Arthur Haselrig introduced on 7 December a bill to remove the source of the powers of the Lords General and Admiral from the royal prerogative to the authority of Parliament, Sir John Culpeper commented that the bill took away from the King the power which the law had left him and placed an "unlimited arbitrarie power" elsewhere; only a few days later, on 12 December, Charles I issued a proclamation in which around an ornate opening letter "H" appears a depiction of Hercules about to smite the many-headed Hydra – an image which was used in early-modern Europe, as allegory for royal authority triumphing over rebellion. The increasingly ideological character of the conflict was becoming patent, as is evident, for example, in the *Answer to the Nineteen Propositions*, issued by the King in June 1642, which asserted that while the King wished to protect the laws of England, among his opponents there were "Cabalists of this businesse" plotting to remove the law, in order to make the "Kingdom a Republique"

---

less clear cut and sudden than previously argued. Rather than the simple replacing of Common law discourse with the natural rights one, the former hegemony was replaced by a number of languages – of which that of natural rights was the most prominent.

[99] Adamson *Noble* pp. 68–70. Adamson claims that almost every aspect of what was later to be termed parliamentarism was to be found anticipated within these passages of Downinge.

and to establish "a new Utopia of Religion and Government." The flurry of political pamphleteering that followed, in late 1642 and early 1643, indicated there was some truth to this claim, as terms and ideas hitherto unheard of in English political debates, were publicly broached for the first time. Certainly several pamphlets of this period, mainly by radical clerical writers fearing an accommodation between King and Parliament that would be adverse to their own view of "Religion and Government," raised however tentatively, the possibility of exceeding the bounds of the constitution. Jeremiah Burroughs' printed sermon, *The Glorius Name of God, the Lord of Hosts*, published in 1642, considered the possibility that the Commons might be corrupted by the King into signing an unworthy agreement, and then commented,

in this case whether a Law of Nature would not allow of standing up to defend our selves, yea to re-assume the power they had, and set up some other, I leave to the light of nature to judge.[100]

Other pamphlets in the same vein were, the anonymous *Touching the Fundamental Laws, or Politique Constitution of this Kingdom*, as well as *Scripture and Reason Pleaded for Defensive Arms* (self-described as "Published by divers reverend and learned divines"), both from early 1643. Going further even than these was the anonymously published (but generally attributed to Edward Bowles, chaplain to the Earl of Manchester), *Plain English, or a Discourse Concerning the Accommodation, the Armie, the Association* of January 1643 which, after contemplating the possibility that Parliament would come to an unsatisfactory agreement with the King, proposed the creation of an association of those willing to fight for religion and the laws, even against Parliament. Many years later, when Richard Baxter looked back for the moment when the constitutional conflict turned into a revolution, he identified *Plain English* as the turning point. Clearly, when in 1645 a supporter of Parliament like John Corbet claimed that, unlike previous English internal conflicts, such as the Baron's Wars of the thirteenth century or the Wars of the Roses of the fifteenth century, the conflagration he was currently witnessing was "undertaken upon higher Principles, and carried on to a nobler end, and effects more universal" he was expressing a realization that had by then become widespread.[101]

Probably the point at which the full social and political implications of the conflict reached their most public and potentially explosive moment, were the debates held at the Putney Church, between 28 October and 1 November 1647, when the army officers engaged with several "agitators" (an unwittingly pertinent distortion of 'adjutators'), elected as representatives from various

---

[100] Christianson *Discourse* pp. 299–300; Adamson *Noble* pp. 460–461, 465–466, 519; Jeremiah Burroughs, *The Glorius Name of God, the Lord of Hosts* (4th edition, 1643) pp. 133–134.

[101] Wootton "Rebellion" pp. 654–669, and see especially 662–666; Adamson *Noble* pp. 460–461, 465–466, 519.

army regiments, in a debate about the means and goals that the army should pursue after having won the Civil War. The spokesman for the agitators, Edward Sexby, then a private in the "Ironsides" Horse regiment, who had Leveller connections, addressed the two leading officers present, the Lieutenant-General of the Horse Oliver Cromwell, and his son-in-law, the Commissary-General of the Horse Henry Ireton. Sexby declared the intention of the meeting as: "I desire you will consider those things that shall be offered to you; and, if you see anything of reason, you will join with us, that the kingdom may be eased and our fellow soldiers may be quieted in spirit." The agitators, evidently receiving ideological assistance from Levellers, some of whom, like John Wildman and Maximilian Petty, also participated in the debates, had prepared a proposal, titled *The Case of the Army Truly Stated* (1647), as blueprint for a new English constitution that would replace the old one by jettisoning not only the king but also, in Sexby's words, "Parliament, which consists of a company of rotten members."[102]

In the ensuing public debate, virtually every major strand of the theoretical disputes about political obligation emerged, whether explicitly or implicitly. Although some 30 people are recorded as participating in the debate, the two most dominant speakers by far were Ireton, who became the principal spokesman for retaining the English constitution and laws (albeit with some reforms), and Colonel Thomas Rainsborough, a Leveller sympathizer who was the spokesman for a new constitutional asset based on an equal franchise, implicitly also favoring a redistribution of wealth. Immediately at the opening of the debate Ireton queried if he had understood the wording of the *Case* correctly to imply that "every man that is an inhabitant is to be equally considered, and to have an equal voice in the election of the representers." Rainsborough not only answered in the affirmative but upped the stakes declaring unambiguously:

I think it's clear that every man that is to live under a government ought first by his own consent to put himself under that government; and I do think that the poorest man in England is not at all bound in a strict sense to that government that he has not had a voice to put himself under.

That is, Rainsborough declared his unreserved allegiance to the principle holding legitimate government is to be only based on individual consent, and that those who had not expressed such a consent were not obligated "in a strict sense to that government." Ireton, finding his suspicions justified, no less unambiguously affirmed his total opposition to such a principle, explaining:

---

[102] Sexby (1616–1658), a soldier in Cromwell's own horse regiment, and prominent political activist with connections to the Levellers, later became an army officer, even rising to the rank of colonel. During the interregnum he broke with Cromwell, turning into a leading writer and conspirator against the Protectorate and the Protector's life. After being apprehended he died in jail. On Sexby see D.F. Lawson, *Upon a Dangerous Design: The Public Life of Edward Sexby* (unpublished PhD dissertation, University of Alabama, 2011).

Give me leave to tell you that if you make this the rule, I think you must fly for refuge to an absolute natural right and you must deny all civil right; and I am sure it will come to that in the consequence.

For Ireton, the fundamental problem was clearly that a direct appeal to "absolute natural right" by its very nature, so to speak, overcomes any English law, indeed any law at all, thus in effect destroying the framework upon which political society rests, and collapses constituent and government powers into one. The principal casualty of such approach was for Ireton property – for him the essence of what separated a "natural" existence from a "civil" one. That is, Ireton believed property not to be natural but rather conventional, and therefore regarded the conventions of civil society as the bulwark defending one's property as well as all that attends to it. In a passage (quite similar in tone and content to what Edmund Burke would articulate some 150 years later) he granted the natural birthright of any man to things like "air and place and ground and the freedom of the highways and other things to live amongst us," but denied completely that the same right extends to property or political rights. For Ireton, property and its security, far from being a "natural right" of man, could in effect exist only within political society. More than this, Ireton stated explicitly that in his mind property was the basis for political rights, for the English constitution, indeed for political society in general: "For here is the case of the most fundamental part of the constitution of the kingdom, which if you take away, you take away all by that."[103]

---

[103] A.S.P. Woodhouse (ed.), *Puritanism and Liberty, being the Army Debates* (Chicago University Press, 1951) pp. 53–54. Ireton went on to say: "Truly by birthright there is *thus* much claim. Men may justly have by birthright (by their very being born in England) that we should not seclude them out of England, that we should not refuse to give them air and place and ground and the freedom of the highways and other things to live amongst us – not to any man that is born here, though by his birth there come nothing at all that is part of the permanent interest of this kingdom to him. *That* I think is due to a man by birth. But that by a man's being born here, he shall have a share in that power that shall dispose of the lands here, and of all things here, I do not think it a sufficient ground."

See the similarities to Burke in *Reflections*: "Far am I from denying in theory, full as far is my heart from withholding in practice (if I were of power to give or to withhold) the real rights of men. In denying their false claims of right, I do not mean to injure those which are real, and are such as their pretended rights would totally destroy. If civil society be made for the advantage of man, all the advantages for which it is made become his right. It is an institution of beneficence; and law itself is only beneficence acting by a rule. Men have a right to live by that rule; they have a right to do justice, as between their fellows, whether their fellows are in public function or in ordinary occupation. They have a right to the fruits of their industry and to the means of making their industry fruitful. They have a right to the acquisitions of their parents, to the nourishment and improvement of their offspring, to instruction in life, and to consolation in death. Whatever each man can separately do, without trespassing upon others, he has a right to do for himself; and he has a right to a fair portion of all which society, with all its combinations of skill and force, can do in his favor. In this partnership all men have equal rights, but not to equal things. He that has but five shillings in the partnership has as good a right to it as he that has 500 pounds has to his larger proportion. But he has not a right to an equal dividend in the product of

Behind the vastly differing attitudes to individual consent and absolute natural rights, there was a deep but mostly unarticulated divergence in assumptions between Rainsborough and Ireton, about the tendency and capabilities, of human nature and reason. Rainsborough clearly assumed men to be naturally benevolent and reasonable, so that the sources of their misery lied in obsolete laws and differences of property, that should be removed. In this vein he presented an anti-historical, appeal to reason and nature that was quite Grotian in tone:

I do think that the main cause why Almighty God gave men reason, it was that they should make use of that reason, and that they should improve it for that end and purpose that God gave it them. And truly, I think that half a loaf is better than none if a man be an-hungry. This gift of reason without other property may seem a small thing, yet I think there is nothing that God has given a man that anyone else can take from him. And therefore I say that either it must be the Law of God or the law of man that must prohibit the meanest man in the kingdom to have this benefit as well as the greatest. I do not find anything in the Law of God that a lord shall choose twenty burgesses, and a gentleman but two, or a poor man shall choose none. I find no such thing in the law of nature, nor in the law of nations.[104]

Ireton's approach to political society rested on quite different suppositions about the natural tendencies of men's reason, and the necessity of particular laws to restrain them from grasping at other men's property. He retorted to Rainsborough in a quite Hobbesian description of men's "right of nature" to anything they see:

Now I wish we may all consider of what right you will challenge that all the people should have right to elections. Is it by the right of nature? If you will hold forth that as your ground, then I think you must deny all property too, and this is my reason. For thus: by that same right of nature (whatever it be) that you pretend, by which you can say that one man has an equal right with another to the choosing of him that shall govern him – by the same right of nature he has the same equal right in any goods he sees: meat, drink, clothes, to take and use them for his sustenance. He has a freedom to the land, to take the ground, to exercise it, till it; he has the same freedom to anything that anyone does account himself to have any propriety in.

The obviously pessimistic assumptions in this passage, about men's nature and propensities, as well as their capabilities to govern themselves by "equal

---

the joint stock; and as to the share of power, authority, and direction which each individual ought to have in the management of the state, that I must deny to be amongst the direct original rights of man in civil society; for I have in my contemplation the civil social man, and no other. It is a thing to be settled by convention."

[104] Woodhouse *Puritanism* pp. 54–56. Shortly thereafter Ireton goes on in the very same vein: "if this be allowed (because by the right of nature we are free; we are equal; one man must have as much voice as another), then show me what step or difference there is why I may not by the same right take your property, though not of necessity to sustain nature. It is for my better being, and the better settlement of the kingdom?"

right," were such as both Hobbes and Filmer would have certainly agreed with. The result is for Ireton inescapable: "if you do, paramount to all constitutions, hold up this law of nature, I would fain have any man show me their bounds, where you will end, and why you should not take away all property."[105]

By this point the English debate about political ideas had become popularized and frenzied, and the descent into armed conflict had only exacerbated these trends. While earlier in the conflict, many pamphlets on both sides struggled to claim center ground, presenting themselves as the true defenders of the constitution, now more extreme views and justifications were becoming popular. In the same year the Putney debates presented the more radical views on the parliamentary side, a similar trend was visible on the royalist side, with texts like Michael Hudson's *The Divine Right of Government* (1647), written when its author was in the Tower, it traced the origins of regal authority to Adam's paternity, and brought examples from the natural world to prove the justification of political patterns of inequality; while Robert Grosse's, *Royalty and Loyalty* (1647) based the power of the king on the necessity of preserving national unity, so that this necessity, rather than objective reason had become the measure of legitimate government activity, a justification of arbitrary government radically different from earlier defenses of absolute monarchy.[106]

The traditional and traditionalist political language, already in decline, was now almost completely jettisoned, and in its place an idiom of accusation and vindictiveness rose, dovetailing the events on the ground, increasingly turning on issues of necessity, "de facto" government, and rule of the sword. The execution of the King in 1649 finally turned the traditionalist argument completely on its head, making it in effect a subversive force working against the established regicide regime (although practically, many of its legal and political mechanisms and offices continued to function, throughout the Interregnum). While the new circumstances gave birth to numerous attempts at redefining English political ideas and language, they also made traditionalist positions such as Selden's pretty much irrelevant if not seditious, since to restore the old constitution could only mean overturning the new model government.

The flavor of political debate in this period is best captured in the ideas and writings of two of the most successful pamphleteers of the interregnum era (and significantly, with alternating allegiances to the interregnum governments), Henry Parker and Marchamont Needham. Both writers attempted to justify the parliamentarian and later the Cromwellian position, in the face of traditionalist arguments that had been sized by the royalist side, since Charles

---

[105] Woodhouse *Puritanism* pp. 56–60. Captain William Clarke added: "Yet really properties are the foundation of constitutions; For if so be there were no property, that the Law of Nature does give a principle to have a property of what he has, or may have, which is not another man's: this property is the ground of *meum* and *tuum*."

[106] Eccleshall *Order* pp. 163–164, 170–171.

I's *Answer to the Nineteen Propositions*, had claimed convincingly that the King was defending the established government and constitution of England against those who would destroy them.

Henry Parker was one of the most successful writers of the Civil War period, secretary to Essex as well as to the army from 1642 and to the Commons from 1645; during the 1640s he also published more than thirty pro-parliamentarian pamphlets. One of the earliest of his writings was *The Case of Shipmon[e]y* (1640) presented to the long Parliament on its convening in November, and arguing against the financial imposition. The pamphlet took care not to contest any of the theoretical underpinnings for the claim that "the Sea is part of the Kingdome," which had been famously established by Selden in the *Mare Clausum*, but rather after explicitly declaring "I pray Master *Selden* to pardon me for this transition" went on to argue against the necessity and practicality of actually defending England's maritime claims (and thus raising money for the purpose), since these were not vital to the kingdom, and moreover might embroil it in unnecessary conflict with friends and enemies.[107]

Undoubtedly, Parker's most important pamphlet was the enormously successful *Observations Upon Some of His Majesties Late Answers* (1642, addressing the King's *Answer*), one of the most influential publications of the Civil War period. In this pamphlet, Parker made two main political arguments. The first one, building on Grotius and the French Monarchomachs, was a theory of popular origins of government, which attempted to exchange the terminology used by the royalists, such as "trust" or "conscience," with a contractual and legal one that would make the general "trust" of government into the legal and particular "a trust" and the political relationship a contract; the second one was the appropriation of the formerly royalist language of necessity, imminent danger and emergency, to justify a theory of parliamentary absolutism and reason of state. Thus, although the proper foundation of power for Parker is apparently one of "consent as well as counsel," his insistence that there be some absolute power that judges the interpretation and execution of positive laws, inevitably leads to an arbitrary imposition of sovereignty – and to him the sovereignty of Parliament was preferable to that of the King, being based not on the judgment of one but of several (a standard Aristotelian argument). In effect, Parker introduced the idea of a consent-based contract only to immediately subject it to the unlimited sovereignty necessary for self-preservation and reason of state – melding Grotian and Bodinian ideas into a quite Hobbesian position.[108]

---

[107] Henry Parker, *The Case of SHIPMONY briefly discoursed, ACCORDING TO THE Grounds of Law, Policy, and Conscience. AND MOST HVMBLY PRESENTED TO THE Censure and Correction of the High Court of Parliament, Nov. 3. 1640.* (1640). Unlike all other financial impositions by the crown in this period, which Selden famously opposed as illegal, I have found no evidence that he opposed this one, and in fact he might have supported its legality, at least in principle.

[108] Kahn *Wayward* pp. 96–98. In attempting to differentiate between political contracts, which he regarded as egalitarian and mutual in nature, and between marriage or service contracts, which

Parker's writings effectively expose the dilemma at the heart of so many proponents of consent-based political systems, attempting to reconcile the uncertainty of the individual will with the necessity of clear and reasonable political authority, employing a terminology of contract, but ultimately succumbing to the logic of sovereignty and necessity. In *An Answer to a Printed Book* (1642), a rebuttal of Parker's *Observations*, co-authored by the constitutional royalists Dudley Digges, Lucius Cary Second Viscount Falkland and William Chillingworth (the first two formerly prominent parliamentarians), they employed the language of contract but interpreted it in a fashion completely opposite to Parker's. They denied an interpretation of contract by which the king's authority would be "capable of forfeiture upon a not exact performance of covenant." In their interpretation, the English covenant of government defined Parliament as composed of King, Lords and Commons, so that no one or two parts of it "hath not any power warranted by law to doe what they thinke fit to his prejudice, upon pretence of publique extremity." They point out that acceptance of the principle of a paramount individual consent literally means the dissolution of the bonds of government, by reducing all to "that primitive state, wherein every one had absolute right, to dispose of his own as he pleased." Since this is impossible to practically carry out, the necessity to erect government restrained this "native right by positive Constitutions," so that in the best governed states "the greater part of men were presumed by a *fiction of law*, to handle and approve such things as they never heard of." The ground for this fiction was reasonable, since the people may be said to consent to what their rulers do, since they have "entrusted them with their safety." Significantly, these writers put forward a logic of tacit consent and legal structures, that denies the principle of individual consent and prefers to it a true contractualism, in which individuals are bound to a formalistic and institutional form of consent, which obliges them irrespective of their individual consent. As we shall see, this is a position very close to Selden's.[109]

The important role played by Essex and Selden in the parliamentary politics of the period, as well as their social and professional affinities (Selden was among other things Essex's lawyer), make it quite likely that Parker, serving in this period as secretary to Essex, had frequent and probably close interactions with Selden. The latter was certainly acquainted to some extent with Parker's

---

he regarded as subordinance contracts, Parker, argued that "the wife is inferior in nature, and was created for the assistance of man, and servants are hired for their Lords mere attendance; but it is otherwise in the State betwixt man and man." See Kahn *Wayward* pp. 99–100. Thus Parker, like Grotius and Hobbes, posited a natural subordination of women to men, unlike the apparently less egalitarian Filmer and Selden. The latter gave in the *Table-Talk* discussion on "Contracts," the example of a humorous contract between Lady Kent and Sir Edward Herbert, that let each come and go as they like, regarding it as "Epitome" of all contracts "betwixt man and man, betwixed Prince and Subject." Since Lady Kent was obviously no "man" by gender, it indicates that Selden regarded women as fully legitimate contractors.

[109] Kahn *Wayward* pp. 104–105.

political ideas, since we know for a fact that he presented to Selden at least one of his pamphlets from this period, *The Generall Junto, or the Councell of Union; Chosen Equally out of England, Scotland, and Ireland for the Better Compacting of these Nations into one Monarchy* (1642, signed H.P.). Apparently only fifty copies of this tract were issued, entirely for private circulation, so that this presentation copy means Selden was part of the restricted circle which Parker regarded as relevant for receiving his proposal for a full political union of Britain.[110]

However, Parker's pro-parliamentarian position was being overtaken by events, as the army was becoming the real arbiter of the situation, when finding out that Parliament was unwilling to do its bidding. As early as 1647, an agitator named Francis White had concluded that Parliament (increasingly bent on peace) now imperiled the nation no less than the King, since, as he wrote to Fairfax, God had found a new, more righteous instrument of his will: "the army now at your and His [God's] command in all just things, is the highest power visible in this Kingdome ... there is no superintendent authoritie, but what is exercised by the power and force of the sword." Within two years, Pride's purge and the regicide had carried out this conviction to its logical outcome, and what followed was a decade during which, as various constitutional schemes successively floundered, England was truly ruled by the sword, while various attempts were being made to give this turn of events a theoretical justification. The logic of army rule found a number of defenders, among them John Goodwin and implicitly also Needham and Hobbes. But probably its bluntest expression was in *A Second View of the Army Remonstrance* (1649), written by William Sedgwick, an army chaplain, who argued that "This Army is truly the people of the kingdom, in which the common interest most lies."[111]

In subsequent years, a number of writers published works justifying successive interregnum regimes in terms of reason of state and the "power of the sword." Not surprisingly, many of these writers were merely restating arguments for obedience that had been raised only a few years previously by writers of royalist tendencies, such as the younger Dudley Digges and Thomas Hobbes. In fact, Digges' *The Unlawfulnesse of Subjects Taking up Armes Against their Soveraigne* (1643), was a plagiarizing of arguments from Hobbes' *De Cive*, which had been published in Paris in 1642. Later writers advocating obedience to the Civil War and interregnum regimes similarly formulated Hobbesian-style arguments, sometimes developed in parallel to

---

[110] Among books owned by Selden now held in the Bodleian library, is a copy of Parker's *The Generall Junto, or the Councell of Union* (1642), on which appears the dedication "For the worthy Ho[nora]ble Iohn Selden esq" as well as a list of errata written formally in ink at the end – clearly an author's presentation copy by Parker to Selden. See Sparrow "Documents" p. 271. Incidentally, this pamphlet by Parker seems to be the first proposal for a real union on equal terms between England, Scotland and Ireland.

[111] Zaller *Legitimacy* pp. 705–706; Kahn *Wayward* pp. 132, 257.

Hobbes, at other times directly influenced by his writings. One among these was Sir Francis Rous, as we may recall, formerly a prominent parliamentarian speaker against "Romish Tyranny, and Spanish Monarchy." Rous published after the regicide *The Lawfulness of Obeying the Present Government* (1649), where he proposed that when the question is put, who shall we obey? "[I]t must not be looked at what he is that exerciseth the power, or in what manner he doth dispense it, but only if he hath the power. For if any man do excel in power, it is now out of doubt that he received that power of God." This is a rather Filmerian argument, because there is in it no "Hobbesian" granting of power on consensual or self-preservation grounds, but only a Filmerian-type "mandate of heaven." Another example is Anthony Ascham, who published *A Discourse – What is Particularly Lawful During the Confusions and Revolutions of Governments* (1648), a work full of assumptions and language of a strongly Hobbesian character, but probably developed independently, since Hobbes is neither mentioned nor alluded to; nor is there any sign of Ascham having ever read anything by Hobbes by that time. However, when in 1649 Ascham reissued his book with lengthy additions, renaming it *Of the Confusion and Revolutions of Gover[n]ment*, he now explicitly invoked the authority of Hobbes in the section discussing the state of nature, where he explained the need for a complete subjection to power, as was the "very pertinent and conclusive" supposition of "Mr Hobbes." Later on in the text, he explained that a change of allegiance is automatically permitted in cases when "as Grotius and Mr Hobbes say," there is "a dereliction of command in the person of whom we speak" or if the country is "so subdued that the conquerors can no longer be resisted." Thus Ascham seems to have developed his ideas independently, and only later employed Hobbes (and Grotius), to corroborate them.[112]

However, probably the most effective and consistent writer on these themes during the interregnum, regardless of his several and notorious changes of allegiance, was Marchamont Needham. His *The Case of the Commonwealth of England Stated* (1650) was an influential attempt to address the debate over the political foundations of the English state after the regicide. Although he touched, among others on Machiavelli, Bodin, James I's *Basilikon Doron*, and Salmasius, it is the ideas of Grotius and Hobbes that are most significant to his discussion. In the first edition of the work, Grotius and his ideas are very prominent, and while Hobbesian ideas also appear, the latter's name does not. But in the 2nd edition, appearing later in the same year, a new appendix was added, where Hobbes and his ideas were discussed explicitly and at length.[113]

---

[112] Collins *Cosmos* pp. 30–31; Skinner "ideological" pp. 308–311. Eccleshall *Order* pp. 155–156; P.A. Knachel, "Introduction" in Needham *Case* pp. xii, xxv–xxvii, xxxv, and also Needham *Case* p. 89.

[113] Marchamont Needham, *The Case of the Commonwealth of England Stated* [1650] (Washington: Folger Shakespeare Library, Virginia University Press, 1969) pp. 32, 35, 62, 67, 85, 129–138.

Needham quotes liberally from Grotius' *Jure Belli* as authority for a "*de jure*" duty to submit to new lords after their victory, and for the injunction against private persons meddling in controversies about titles to government, advising them rather to "follow them that are in possession" of power. Perhaps most significant is the employment of Grotius in chapter 4 of Needham's tract, titled "That a Government Erected by a Prevailing Part of the People Is As Valid de jure As If It Had the Ratifying Consent of the Whole." Selden, who Needham knew, and whose *Mare Clausum* he would translate to English in 1652, unlike Grotius or Hobbes, is not mentioned in the work even once, for unlike the others there was nothing in his works which could significantly substantiate Needham's view. However, this chapter devoted to refuting constitutionalist and traditionalist arguments, is also the only one where ideas that might be termed as Seldenian are addressed. Needham's main contention, by which he refutes constitutional and contractual ideas, is that in times of conflict, the authority of natural law and of the law of nations trounces that of established national laws. To substantiate this view, Needham quotes Grotius repeatedly and lengthily: "In a civil war, written laws, that is, the established laws of a nation, are of no force, but those only which are not written, that is which are agreeable to the dictates of nature, or the law and custom of nations" – and then, the only law is that "which shall be declared by the prevailing party" (adding for good measure a quote to similar effect from "the Florentine Secretary," Machiavelli). Needham later uses Grotius to argue that England's new government had acquired by right of conquest "a right to govern the people and even that right also which the people themselves have to government." Another important context of his use of Grotius is when discussing oaths, covenants and faithfulness he quotes Grotius' claim in the *Jure Belli* that: "If one party break[s] a covenant, the other is no longer bound to it. For each particular head of a covenant carries with it the force of a condition." He later adds from the same source that a "covenant, being once at an end, cannot be supposed to be renewed tacitly. For a new obligation is not easily to be presumed, but by such acts as declare it and admit no other construction."[114]

As already mentioned, to the 2nd edition of this work Needham added an appendix of materials from Thomas Hobbes as well as Claude Saumaise, both of whom are dubbed prominent royalists, in order to show how easy it is to "foil our adversaries with weapons of their own approbation" to justify obedience to the new government. His claim that Hobbes' pro-royalist ideas could easily be mustered to justify the regicide regime, were to be spectacularly confirmed less than a year later, when Hobbes himself, who had been a mathematics instructor to Prince Charles, actually came over to England soon after the publication of his *Leviathan*, and formally submitted to the new regime. Accurately identifying

---

[114] Needham *Case* pp. 30–32, 34–35, 39–40, 43–44. See also about private persons not having the right or competence to question those that are in power, so should simply "follow possession" of power; see Needham *Case* pp. 47.

the foundation of Hobbes' theory, Needham notes that a theory according to which (quoting from Hobbes' then recently published *De Copore Politico*) "The cause in general which moveth one man to become subject to another is the fear of not otherwise preserving himself," means that in the current situation in England, submission to the present powers, is the only way to preserve that security and well-being that is supposed to be the general cause for the existence of the state. He brings up Hobbes' argument that since men transfer their right of judgment to the "supreme power," then as long as one "confirms his actions to the laws" promulgated by that authority, he does not sin since these are the judgments of the public power, and the only sins one commits against his private conscience are those which have been left by the laws "to his own liberty." In other words, the transfer of the private right of judgment to the public authority, relieves the individual from his responsibility for public acts.[115]

On top of these explicit Grotian and Hobbesian ideas addressed, we also find in Needham's text a number of ideas that are quite Filmerian (Filmer had already published three political works in 1648, but there is no evidence that Needham ever saw any of them). One of those ideas is the inscrutability of divine intentions in determining the fate of states and dynasties: "a kingdom is translated from one family to another, the causes whereof are locked up in the cabinet of the deity." Needham explicitly links the mysterious cause of such upheavals with the "Divine Providence," and since men are unable to fathom it (except for reporting that the "main cause" recorded for such changes, has been the injustice of rulers), they must willingly accept its decrees. Later on, an account of political society that is very similar to Filmer's version of patriarchalism is put forward by Needham: after the Flood the ills of human society were such that "the *pater familiar* way of government being insufficient" there was need of someone more potent that might restrain them by force, upon which grounds Nimrod was the first to create a "new and arbitrary way of government." Indeed, basing himself on a passage of Salmasius (a thinker with many similarities to Filmer), Needham adopts what was the main Filmerian justification for submission to established power as the supreme Christian principle, when he points out that since Christ "freely and willingly submitted himself" to the rule of the tyrant Tiberius, he by this delivered to his disciples the

---

[115] Needham *Case* pp. 129–132, 135–138, and also P.A. Knachel, "Introduction" in Needham, *Case* pp. xxxiv. Needham also quotes from Salmasius the claim that people submit to the will of others either by forced constraint after victory or by voluntary consent, but in both cases they quit their own natural power and "transfer it irrevocably" to their rulers. This transfer of power, is binding and legitimate even if forced and "though it seem somewhat unjust." As examples he gives the "law royal" by which the Romans purportedly resigned to Augustus all power when they could no longer resist his power; as well as an "old law" by which rape became lawful marriage if the woman gave her subsequent consent to it. He adds that since almost all governments in the world began with some kind of forced conquest, to deny the legitimacy of their origin, would be to make them all illegitimate.

doctrine that he desired not any change of "that form of government" then established.[116]

We have thus followed the descent of English political discourse, from the shared and insularist language of the late Elizabethan age, through the growing divisions and tensions of the first two Stuart monarchs, to the complete chaos and disaggregation of the interregnum. This process found the English increasingly struggling to preserve their political tradition, in the face of the great crisis of scholasticism and the rising tide of new ideas, redefining the landscape of political theory. Throughout this process Selden was a prominent figure, in the theoretical as well as the practical political sphere. We have seen he was part of the effort within Parliament to buttress the crumbling safeguards on traditional English political practices, while at the same time rejecting the attempts to inject Machiavellian and Bodinian ideas into the English constitutional terminology. He was part of the attempt to reassert the traditional political terminologies and mechanisms of Parliament, as he was also privy to the attempts of numerous writers from Cotton to Eliot to address the constitutional crisis and offer a way out of it. After the regicide, he witnessed the eventual attempts by writers like Parker and Needham to construct some kind of new theoretical justification for the new political order. It is against this background that we have to assess the writing of Selden and his contemporaries, attempting to fashion and articulate political ideas that could offer a way out of an overwhelming, many-faceted crisis.

[116] Needham *Case* pp. 9, 15, 133.

3

Selden and the Early-Modern Dispute about the Foundations of Political Order

As we have seen, the early decades of the seventeenth centuries witnessed the full extent of the crisis of scholasticism, bringing in its wake great intellectual ferment in political and legal thought, either from attempts to supersede it completely, by the theories of Machiavelli and of Bodin, or to revamp it, by "neo-scholastics" like Suarez and "neo-civilians" like Gentili. A generation of political thinkers, who came of age at this time, was thus the first to explicitly attempt to fashion comprehensively new theories that would account for the new intellectual landscape. In England too the outlook of medieval origin, that found in Hooker its best expression, disintegrated in the first decades of the seventeenth century, concurrent with the rise of the assumption that political reason was not an attribute of the corporate community but of each individual. Like elsewhere in Europe, new theories came to the fore, stressing rationally defensible interests or concerned with order and accepting arbitrary government as the best means of imposing discipline on society, but in England, such new theories additionally had to consider the role that the Common law should, or should not, have in political society. The common lawyers had been aware for some time of the growing challenges to their perceived role, and though no major Common law thinkers of the sixteenth and early seventeenth centuries composed anything like a systematic theory of English law, the more eminent writers obviously each had his view of a constitutional system whose principles could be individuated through analysis: Saint Germain posited what he called "Maxims" and Coke the idea of "Artificial Reason." But these traditional approaches were seen as insufficient to confront increasing attempts to curtail the reach of the Common law, like James I's assertion of his right to personally determine law in his court (later backed up by several thinkers), and Bacon's proposed codification of English law.[1]

---

[1] Eccleshall *Order* pp. 151–152; Zaller *Legitimacy* p. 353. Zaller's description for the basis of Selden's legal theory is: "law as a community of obligation[.]"

Prominent in this generation were four near contemporaries who offered very distinct and mutually exclusive political theories, that were to have a major impact on the future of political thought as well as on the political events of England. Their lives had some parallels as well as differences, but they all grappled with similar philosophical political concerns.[2]

Indeed, these four thinkers represent in many ways the four principal approaches that were to develop and supply much of the framework for later modern political thought, even to this day. Born within five years of each other, Hugo Grotius (1583–1645), John Selden (1584–1654), Sir Robert Filmer (1588–1653) and Thomas Hobbes (1588–1679), although varying greatly in the remedies they proposed, all directed their efforts at the same challenge: proposing a system of law and politics that would overcome the perceived crisis of the universities' school of thought.[3]

The claims outlined up to this point are not especially controversial. However, surprisingly enough, modern scholarship has not, on the whole, devoted significant efforts to exploring the connection between the philosophical-epistemological crisis and the moral and political one. Although the existence of such multiple crises is widely accepted, as are the many interconnections between them, treatment of the issue usually remains at a generalized level only, or at most is approached at the level of a particular thinker, instead of addressing more comprehensively the connection between

---

[2] The four lived long lives for their time, Grotius to 62 years, Selden to 70, Filmer to 65 and Hobbes spectacularly so, to 91; and were intellectually active to the end (Hobbes a little less). The first three suffered imprisonment for their political views and activities, while Hobbes too left England in 1640 fearing a similar fate. Apparently Hobbes also entertained political ambitions, for in the very same year he had earlier attempted to get elected to the Short Parliament from the Borough of Derby, in the interest of his Cavendish patrons, but the local electorate, probably wisely, wanted absolutely nothing to do with him as their representative. See H. Trevor-Roper, *Catholics, Anglicans and Puritans* (Secker & Warburg, 1987) p. 176 in note.

[3] All four explicitly mentioned in their books as one of the objectives of the work, the exposing of fallacious scholastic ideas. For example, Grotius makes clear he regards his ideas as an attempt to break free from the framework of Aristotelianism, which, in the name of the great man had for some time "degenerated into Tyranny, so that Truth, for the Discovery of which *Aristotle* took so great Pains, is now oppressed by nothing more than the very Name of *Aristotle*." See Hugo Grotius, *Jure Belli ac Pacis* (1625), Prolegomena, sec. 43; Hobbes explicitly and repeatedly accuses the universities' "schoole-men" of spreading incomprehension and confusion through their frequent usage of "insignificant speech." See Thomas Hobbes, *Leviathan* (1651), p1c1; Filmer identifies the object of his work as the refuting of the widespread erroneous belief in a natural liberty of men, asserting that "[t]his tenet was first hatched in the schools." See Sir Robert Filmer, *Patriarcha* (1680), chapter 1 sec. 1; Selden criticizes the "Schooles" for the defective method by which they study *"Morall Philosiphie, or Civill Learning."* See TH (1631) "Preface," not paginated.

On the connection between the epistemological challenges and political ideas in England, see J. Daly, "Cosmic Harmony and Political Thinking in Early Stuart England" in *Transactions of the American Philosophical Society* (NS) 69/7 (1979) pp. 1–41, and especially pp. 31–37. More generally on the crisis of scholasticism and the response to it, see the whole of section IV in Burns and Goldie *History* pp. 477–557.

the new political theories and the crisis of epistemology. The reason for this neglect seems to be a widespread acceptance of the premise that regards the epistemological crisis as somehow distinct from that of moral and political skepticism. Such an approach, viewing social matters as being of a different category than natural ones, can be found among many sixteenth-century thinkers, like Hotman, who wrote that "Philosophy is twofold, natural which turns to the observation of nature, and moral, which turns (as Cicero says) to life and manners." This premise is best articulated in the works of R. Tuck, a prominent scholar of ideas who has had a crucial role in the reevaluation of the significance and impact of early-modern political ideas on the history of political thought. Tuck argues that for early-modern skeptics (like Montaigne and Charron), as well as for skeptics of the ancient world, "the force of their skepticism in ethical matters came simply from their apprehension of the truth of moral relativism." Accordingly, "[i]t thus had a different basis from their skepticism in general epistemological matters, for that rested primarily upon the illusory character of sense experience." Tuck concedes that in both cases the problem was the lack of a criterion with which to distinguish true from false. But he asserts that,

if a *criterion* had become available in the physical sciences, this would have been no remedy for the moral sciences, as no true account of the material world will necessarily resolve fundamental moral disagreements. There was thus an empirical basis to the skeptical doubt in the area of morality: it arose from an observation about the beliefs and practices to be found in different human societies, and not from any general considerations about the nature of ethical thinking.[4]

Although thinkers like Descartes and Galilei attempted to avoid articulating the political or moral consequences of their philosophical theories, there was no shortage of those who spelled these out, mainly as threats to the scholastic-based established moral order of Christendom. But, as I will try to show, among some important political writers of the early-modern period, including all of the four thinkers we will look at, it was very much the attempt to overcome this gap between the epistemological sphere on the one hand, and the moral and political sphere on the other hand, which fueled their theories. That is, they attempted to demonstrate the connection between a true account of the material world and the validity of their moral and political ideas. Indeed, I believe that to a great degree it is exactly the differences between their epistemological premises that account for the differences in their moral and political systems.

A good account of the early-modern awareness to the different epistemological approaches that thinkers could adopt, and of their consequences for the way in which we address the world around us, was articulated (in a text published only

[4] Kelley *Human* p. 212; R. Tuck, "The 'modern' theory of natural law" in A. Pagden (ed.), *The Languages of Political Theory in Early-Modern Europe* (Cambridge University Press, 1990) pp. 109–110.

posthumously) by the Venetian Paolo Sarpi, one of the important European scholars in the generation preceding to the one we will be looking at:

> There are four modes of philosophizing: the first with reason alone, the second with sense alone, the third with reason first and then sense, the fourth beginning with sense and ending with reason. The first is the worst, because from it we know what we would like to be, not what is. The third is bad because we many times distort what is into what we would like, rather than adjusting what we would like to what is. The second is true but crude, permitting us to know little and that rather of things than of their causes. The fourth is the best we can have in this miserable life.[5]

Although I certainly do not wish to claim that any of the four thinkers we will look at exactly and consciously followed one of the modes laid out by Sarpi, we will nevertheless find that the theories of each broadly correspond to one of the modes. Moreover, each of the four followed the same mode both in his treating of epistemological problems as well as of political ones, and did not attempt to separate his approaches towards the two. My work on these four thinkers has convinced me that the two allegedly separate problems of epistemological and of moral uncertainty, were certainly regarded by them as connected, indeed to a great extent as one and the same thing: they all believed that our understanding of how and what individuals know should determine our views of their moral, social and political attributes and capabilities. I hope to show how, as a consequence, their moral, political and legal theories (with varying degrees of articulation) were based on and followed from clear epistemological assumptions they made. Rather than providing a comprehensive account of the theories they developed, the attempt here will be to trace the connection between their epistemological assumptions and the political theories they produced.[6]

I will look at the ideas of Grotius, Hobbes and Filmer, and at the connection between their political thought and their epistemic approach, as well as their relationship with Selden's work, which all of them knew. These four thinkers all developed and articulated their main political ideas between about 1625 and 1632, and had published them by the 1640s (Hobbes and Filmer much later than the other two), dovetailing to no small extent the political fortunes of England in this period. These circumstances will allow us, then, to put Selden's ideas into the context of the early-modern debate on the foundations of the

---

[5] "Pensieri filosofici e scientifici" sec. 146, attributed to the years 1583–1585, in Paolo Sarpi *Pensieri* (Torino, Einaudi, 1976 – G. and L. Cozzi (eds.)) p. 14. The English version is that by W. Bowsma in his *Venice and the Defense of Republican Liberty* (Berkeley, California University Press, 1968), pp. 519–520.

There are many interesting parallels between the ideas of Sarpi and Selden, including on Maritime Law. It is a subject worthy of a separate study, raising many questions – such as Selden's attitude to Sarpi's harsh opposition to the "12 year truce" between Spain and the Netherlands, and the peace policy of Oldenbarnvelt (and Grotius).

[6] See, for example, Gordley *Philosophical* pp. 112–113, 120–123.

political order and to better understand many of the issues that he was addressing.

Before turning to a closer study of the ideas of each thinker, it is useful to have a brief look at the significant intellectual interactions between them. This will show us the extent to which they were all acquainted with, and addressed, similar themes and ideas. There certainly was a measure of interaction between these men, social as well as intellectual: they often moved in similar circles, and there were opportunities for them to meet in person (although, as it turns out, for all we know, they only very seldom did). Grotius visited England for about two months, from March 1613, on occasion of the marriage of Princess Elizabeth, the daughter of King James I, to Prince Fredrick V, Elector Palatine, and he met King James as well as a number of prominent scholars and clergymen. However, we have no reason to suppose that he met either Selden or Filmer (Hobbes was apparently abroad at the time), regardless of their presence in the scholarly circles of the capital at that time.[7] We similarly lack proof positive of any personal acquaintance between Selden and Filmer, although at least a casual one is quite likely because of the many opportunities for their paths to cross in the first three decades of the seventeenth century. Filmer and Selden had many opportunities to get acquainted: at the Inns of Court, where both were students during the first decade of the century, the close geographical vicinity of Cotton's house to Filmer's town house, and their common membership in learned circles of early seventeenth-century London – with at least one close associate of both in Sir Roger Twysden.[8]

---

[7] We know that Grotius dined at the house of the then Bishop of Ely (and later Selden patron), Lancelot Andrewes. Present at the dinner were Isaac Casaubon, one Dr. Steward and another unnamed civilian, as well as Dr. Richardson, Professor of Divinity at Cambridge and another Doctor of that faculty, as well as Archbishop Abbot (who thought Grotius a bit pedantic and overbearing). See W.S.M. Knight *The Life and Works of Hugo Grotius* (1952) pp. 137–149.

[8] Pocock, in a short passage discussing Filmer, suggests that he had been one of the group of scholars who met at Westminster late in James I's reign, and that he not only could quote Cotton, Spelman and Selden, but that he had known them personally. However, no source for this claim is given. See J.G.A. Pocock, *The Ancient Constitution and the Feudal Law* (Cambridge University Press, 1987 – reissue with a retrospect) pp. 154–155.

Sir Roger Twysden (1597–1672) was a Kentish lawyer and scholar as well as an MP who, in the struggle between King and Parliament, held centrist views, at first siding with Parliament, later arguing against the resort to force against the King. Filmer was an early acquaintance of Twysden, and wrote for him around 1625 the short *Quaestio Quodlibetica, or a discourse, whether it may be lawful to take use for money*. Regardless of political differences, the two remained lifelong friends, with Filmer placing the colossal sum of 5000 pounds as bail to release Twysden out of imprisonment during the Civil War, and Twysden bringing the *Quaestio* to print in 1653, a short time before Filmer's death. Twysden was also acquainted with Selden, and the two cooperated in editing and publishing a collection by early English historians *Decem Historiae Anglicana* (to which Selden also wrote the introduction), published in 1652–1653, at the very same time Twysden was putting to print Filmer's *Quaestio*. Earlier Twysden had himself published the rather anti-Filmerian *Certaine Considerations upon the Government of England* (c. 1648),

The same is true of Grotius and Hobbes, who moved in the same Paris intellectual circle around Marin Mersenne during the 1630s and 1640s and could have met there (e.g., in 1636). As to Hobbes and Selden, they had many opportunities to meet, as early as the 1620s, when they both apparently participated in the assemblies of the Virginia Company, but we have a report of their actual substantial acquaintance only from quite late in their lives. Perhaps in their early years they were socially too distinct, Selden rising at an early stage to intellectual, professional and political prominence and enjoying the rewards of financial independence and high social status, while Hobbes remained for most of his life a minor dependent of the Cavendish household, achieving intellectual prominence only in his fifties with *Elements of Law* and *De Cive*, and residing in France for most of the time between 1629 and 1651 (he was in England only during 1632–1635 and 1638–1640). Thus we have no reason to doubt Aubrey's account, previously mentioned, that their significant personal acquaintance occurred only after *Leviathan* was published in 1651, three years before Selden's death. We should however look with more suspicion on Aubrey's claims of close friendship and even intellectual affinity between them, accepted by some modern scholars, which I believe is reading too much into Selden's eminent good nature and toleration – even assistance – to those with ideas different from his own.

Apart from such slight evidence of personal acquaintances, there were far more substantial intellectual interactions and influences between these four contemporaries, with several of them certainly reading and commenting on each other's works, either in private or in public. Grotius was the first among them to gain wide recognition for his work, especially his *Mare Liberum* (1609), and even more the *Jure Belli ac Pacis* (first appeared in 1625), which we know each of his three contemporaries to have read carefully. Indeed, it appears that reading Grotius' *Jure Belli* (1625) caused the transformation of the original early chapters of Selden's *Mare Clausum*, (originally written around 1619 as a rebuttal of *Mare Liberum*) and certainly had some role in the composition of the *Jure Naturali*, which refers to Grotius' work in a number of places (for the most part in order to rebut him). In their turn, Selden's *Mare Clausum* (1635) and *Jure Naturali* (1640) were read by the other three, and the same is true for Hobbes' *De Cive* (completed and widely circulating in manuscript by late 1641, printed in 1642). Filmer, on the other hand, only started publishing political works in 1648, and although a number of these publications followed in close

regarded by Burgess as "a product of the interaction between the common law mind and the political disputes of the 1640s." It is intriguing to consider the possibility that Selden might have been aware of this work and its Filmerian target. See Burgess *Absolute* pp. 142–146. In addition, Twysden was also acquainted with Hobbes and his ideas, since he owned a manuscript copy of the *Elements of Law*, with a handwritten dedication to him from the author. See in *A Catalogue…Also the Very Curious Collection of Manuscripts, of Ancient Chronicles, Monastic History, Charters etc., on Vellum and Paper, Many Finely Illuminated, Collected by Sir Roger Twysden and Mr. E. Lhwyd* [sold at auction] (1807).

succession until his death, as far as we know he was not read by the others, although both Hobbes and Selden could in theory have seen his published works from 1648 onwards (as well as *Patriarcha*, which was circulating in manuscript even earlier), and the latter especially might have been exposed to it through their common friend and literary associate Twysden, whose *Considerations* from that same year answered ideas put forward in Filmer's *Anarchy*. Certainly Filmer did write and comment extensively on the others' works (less on Selden than the other two). Perhaps more suggestively, it appears both Hobbes and Filmer developed and articulated their political theories, to a great extent in response to a combination of the perceived effects of Grotian ideas and of English political developments, in particular the events surrounding the 1628 Petition of Right, of which Selden was a leading drafter. Although the petition's language is wholly that of English tradition and precedent, with nothing allowed to outside terms or authorities, we have seen that its drafting witnessed discussions in the Commons about introducing explicit terminology drawn from "reason of state," Bodinian and natural law theories (including Latin quotes from Suarez). The style and terminology of the petition were an obvious attempt to stem such outside influences, and to anchor political reality in the terms of traditional English political and legal terminology. But the parliamentary proceedings, as well as Hobbes' and Filmer's works addressing the issues, amply display awareness to the wider debate about the nature of society and politics, so that by the mid-1630s all four thinkers had already laid down the main outlines of their theories.[9]

As for recorded intellectual interactions between them, probably the most public one was the *Mare Clausum* in which Selden addressed Grotius' ideas a number of times, and even ended the work on an ironic note by quoting a poem by the Dutchman celebrating the accession of James I to the English throne, in which was included a mention of his lordship over the surrounding seas.[10] Another significant, though less public, intellectual interaction is recorded in an April 1643 letter by Grotius to his brother Willem, where Hugo reports to have read Hobbes' *De Cive* and found that he could not

[9] For the explicit use of Suarez in the House of Commons, by prominent parliamentary leaders, like John Pym, Richard Mason and others, see Sommerville *Royalists* pp. 76–77. For the claim about the impact of Grotius' works on Selden see Christianson *Discourse* pp. 248–249. For Hobbes' careful reading of *Mare Clausum* see P.A. Rahe, *Republics Ancient & Modern* (Chapel Hill: North Carolina University Press, 1994) vol. II pp. 139–140. For the impact of the 1628–1629 parliamentary struggles on Hobbes see Rahe *Against* pp. 280–281; for Selden owning a copy of *De Cive* personally sent to him by Hobbes in 1642 see J. Parkin, *Science, Religion and Politics in Restoration England – Richard Cumberland's De Legibus Naturae* (Woodbridge, Suffolk: The Boydell Press – The Royal Historical Society, 1999) pp. 66–67; for Filmer's careful reading of the other three, see most explicitly his treatment of Hobbes and Grotius in his *Observations Concerning the Originall of Government, upon Mr Hobs Leviathan, Mr Milton Against Salmasius, H. Grotius De Jure Belli* (1652) – where he also amply quotes and discusses ideas from Selden's *Mare Clausum*.
[10] Christianson *Discourse* p. 279.

approve of the "foundations" upon which its arguments rest, like that "by nature there is war between all men," although he did approve of what it says "on behalf of kings," explicitly connecting it with the King's cause in England (which Grotius supported).[11]

Interestingly, Filmer opened his 1652 pamphlet *Observations Concerning the Originall of Government, upon Mr Hobs Leviathan, Mr Milton Against Salmasius, H. Grotius De Jure Belli* with something not unlike Grotius' comment to his brother on Hobbes' ideas:

> With no small content I read Mr. Hobbes's book *De Cive*, and his *Leviathan*, about the rights of sovereignty, which no man, that I know, hath so amply and judiciously handled: I consent with him about the rights of exercising government, but I cannot agree to his means of acquiring it. It may seem strange I should praise his building, and yet mislike his foundation; but so it is, his *Jus Naturae*, and his *Regnum Institutivum*, will not down with me: they appear full of contradiction and impossibilities; a few short notes upon them, I here offer, wishing he would consider whether his building would not stand firmer on the principles of *Regnum Patrimoniale*.[12]

Thus we find both Grotius and Filmer agreeing with Hobbes' argument about the absolute power of the sovereign ruler of the polity (*De Cive*, Part II, chapter 6 sec. 20), while disagreeing on its foundations – Grotius disagreed about the character of human nature and consequently of the state of nature, Filmer about the founding of polity and sovereignty upon individual consent. At the time Grotius and Filmer wrote their comments, the issue was no more a mere theoretical argument, for as both writers acknowledged, it touched directly upon the actual conflict then unfolding in England between King and Parliament – a conflict in which all three evidently sided with the former. Not incidentally, we find John Selden on the opposite side of the dispute, standing, albeit reluctantly, with the parliamentary side. These positions, as we shall see, were no mere expedient born out of opportunistic calculation, but rather the outcome of the fundamental divergence between the purpose of Selden's political thought and that of his three contemporaries. For Grotius, Filmer and Hobbes all held that old-style constitutionalism was dead, and thus that what was needed now was an alternative framework for politics, focusing on the will of the sovereign, while Selden remained a lifelong defender of constitutionalism, and especially of its English version. When all efforts to divert an armed conflict had failed, Selden justified his unenthusiastic but clear siding with the parliamentary side in this conflict, by his assessment that whereas both sides to the conflict had infringed the fundamental laws of the

---

[11] Quoted in Tuck *Philosophy* p. 200. E.H. Kossman claims that in the Netherlands it was being whispered that Grotius had been so much "impressed by [Hobbes'] *De Cive* as to regret having written his own *De Jure Belli ac Pacis.*" See Kossmann "Development" pp. 105–106.

[12] It appears that in this criticism of Hobbes' implicit equation of consent with contract, Filmer also mocked Hobbes, using the latter's own terminology of "consent" and "agree" ironically, to show the incongruence of equating them. See Kahn *Wayward* pp. 3 and 285 note 4.

country, the latter still had the slightly better constitutional justification. During the Civil War he continued to be prominent in the small group in the Commons that was forever trying to find a constitutional settlement acceptable to the parties in the conflict; and in late 1648 when Selden and his allies had apparently succeeded in persuading a majority of MPs to pursue a negotiated settlement, they were abruptly "purged" by the army from Parliament, to prevent such a settlement. Selden's political career ended when England had executed its king and entered a path leading to the establishment of a military-based dictatorship. It is not incidental then, that while Selden's political theory could not ultimately adapt to a despotic political reality, this was not the case with the other three thinkers discussed. Hobbes theory most easily adapted to the new regime ruled by the sword, and the best testimony to this effect is his *Leviathan*, written for this purpose exactly. Filmer strained to extract himself from recognizing the legitimacy of the new regicide regime, but it was probably only his death in 1653 which ultimately averted his having to confront that such a recognition was the inescapable result of his own theory. As for Grotius, since he died in 1645, we do not know how he would have reacted to the interregnum reality, but we certainly find many supporters of the Commonwealth and Protectorate making ample use of Grotius' name and theory to justify those political regimes. The ideas of Hobbes, Filmer and Grotius could be, and were, used to justify royal absolutism as well as the interregnum dictatorship, while those of Selden could not and were not.[13]

Let us turn now to a detailed look at the epistemic foundations, and the political theory stemming from them, of these four contemporaries. In the process, I believe, we will gain the correct perspective for the contexts and concerns of Selden's political thought. As already indicated, whereas most accounts of the transition to distinctly modern political thought (and especially that concerned primarily with individual rights) today regard Hobbes as the seminal figure in the process, I tend to agree with the view, widespread up to the nineteenth century, which regards Grotius' role in this transition as second to none. Hobbes undoubtedly had an important role, especially in spreading the philosophical presupposition of a "state of nature" and in highlighting the role of the passions in deciding human behavior, but it was Grotius who had the pivotal role in defining pre-social individuals as possessing the fundamental authority of political consent, discussing many years previous to Hobbes, such individuals equipped with natural and sovereign rights. Grotius is also more coherent in stressing consent far more than contract (or covenant) as basis for the state, and indeed his theory does without any decisive role to contract. Admittedly, Grotius sometimes did discuss the origin of the state in terms of contract, mentioning for example in the *Jure Belli* that the body politic was formed "from a voluntary compact," but

[13] See R. Tuck, "Grotius and Selden" in Burns and Goldie *History* pp. 528–529; for Selden's position in the conflict between King and Parliament see Berkowitz *Formative* pp. 293–294.

he never considers the state as contractual in its essence. In addressing the origins and principles of political society he only talked of men joining together of their own free will, or of an association of many fathers of families uniting into a single people and state; the point was thus always the superiority of individual consent rather than of any contract.[14]

While this account solved some problems, it created others. Many suspected that individual consent was too unstable a basis upon which to build government. Selden, Filmer and Hobbes were among those who addressed the psychology of consent and its shortcomings as basis for contract: while Selden and Filmer pointed to the inability of a free will to bind itself, Hobbes addressed the unreliable motivation for will in the passions. Grotius himself can be seen to swerve between the twin concerns of rejecting political slavery and discouraging political resistance. He conceded the justification in principle of resisting one's sovereign in cases of "extreme and imminent peril," but then went on to very extensively curtail and qualify this right, as much as he could. On the other hand, while he criticized in harsh words slavery contracts, he did not go as far as denying their validity in principle – he conceded that fear or necessity might bring one to such a contract – but he did not hide his contempt for these motives as base and ultimately irrational (and thus, for him, of suspect legitimacy). In effect, as many of his English readers noticed, Grotius did not ultimately deny a right of resistance to those who had entered a political contract.[15]

As a result in no small part from Grotius' work and the reactions of his contemporaries to it, explicitly crystallizing ideas that had been gaining strength for some time, there emerged in the first decades of the seventeenth century, for the first time, a cultural conversation about the consent of the individual subject as a decisive aspect of political legitimacy.

3.2   GROTIUS

Hugo Grotius was one of the most important figures of seventeenth-century political thought, far more than he is credited with today in most conventional accounts. In England his influence was particularly marked, and it has been convincingly shown that by the mid-seventeenth century, Grotius had become not only "the preeminent modern European influence on English political thought" but later even "dominated seventeenth century Whiggism." Many of his works – not only political but also theatrical and religious – were translated and published in England (some more than once), and his influence is evident in the many writings that either mention him explicitly or make evident use of his ideas and terminology. Some early examples of this influence are prominent Englishmen seeking him out to hear his ideas, when in Paris in the 1630s, among them Robert Sidney, Second Earl of Leicester (who

[14] Hopfl *Contract* pp. 934–935, and see especially note 33.
[15] Kahn *Wayward* pp. 57–58, 62–63.

later recorded his thoughts on the Dutchman's theories), as well as John Milton. We know that in the same period Selden, Filmer and Hobbes were reading Grotius, and the Dutchman's ideas also evidently loom behind some of the debates in the 1628 Parliament.[16]

In the crisis of the following decades, his appeal if anything even increased, as attested by the many attempts to appropriate his authority for various political positions during the 1640s and 1650s. As we have seen, in September 1640, the divine Calybute Downing, while preaching a sermon before the Artillery Company, cited "Rationall Grotius" to affirm his views of a right of resistance of all peoples, in extreme circumstances of *salus populi*. Henry Parker, demonstrated in his *Jus Populi* (1644) the link between the consensual basis of government and the right of resistance, by appropriating elements from the theory of Grotius, while at the same time disparaging him as an assertor (together with Barclay) of "absolute monarchy." An even more radical turn was taken by Edward Sexby in his *Killing Noe Murder* (1657, published under the pseudonym William Allen), which quoted Grotius in building an explicit case for tyrannicide – explicitly targeting Cromwell, as one whose "evangelist" is Machiavelli. These writers all regarded Grotius as a thinker who, while tending to favor monarchy, supplies a theory that in the ultimate analysis allows for a right of resistance. Other English writers attempted to assert that Grotius' ideas deny such a right in practice. Thus the Scottish Presbyterian minister and author Samuel Rutherford stated in the extended title of his popular tract *Lex Rex* (1644), that the work was intended to reject the ideas of such as Barclay, Grotius and "other late anti-magistratical royalists," who deny the right of the people to rise through their lower magistrates against an unjust king – thus highlighting the fact that while Grotius supplied a possible justification for resistance based on a right for individual consent and self-preservation, he at the same time undermined the classic Calvinist claim of a right of resistance through lower magistrates. On the opposite side of the political divide, Dudley Digges' tract, *The Unlawfulnesse of Subjects Taking up Armes Against their Soveraigne* (1643), used Grotian arguments to make its case for the illegitimacy of armed resistance. After the Civil War, Marchamont Needham, in *The Case of the Commonwealth of England Stated* (1650), viewed Grotius favorably, showing he advocated non-resistance to the new regime. There are several more similar examples.[17]

---

[16] See Zuckert *Natural* pp. xvi–xvii, 119–120; Kahn *Wayward* pp. 33–34, 245. Leicester, for example, wrote in his private papers that he believed "as Grotius sayeth, that men, not by the commandment of God, but of their own" mind "gather themselves together into civil societyes [sic] from whence the civile power hath beginning, and is therefore called a humane ordinance."

[17] Kahn *Wayward* pp. 99–100; [Edward Sexby] William Allen, *Killing Noe Murder* (1657) pp. 38–40; Samuel Rutherford, *Lex Rex, or The Law and the Prince; A Dispute for The Just Prerogative of King and People: Containing the Reasons and Causes of the Most Necessary Defensive Wars of the Kingdom of Scotland, and of their Expedition for the Aid and Help of their Dear Brethren of England; in Which their Innocency is Asserted, and a Full Answer is Given*

Grotius' impact was also conspicuous among writers on politics who more prominently incorporated theological concerns in their works, like George Lawson (and through him Locke), Richard Baxter and William Prynne. J. Franklin notes Lawson's frequent reliance on Grotius, in both his *Examination of the Political Part of Mr. Hobbes, his Leviathan* (1657) and *Politica Sacra et Civilis* (1660), and points to the influence of Lawson's writings on, among others, Baxter and Locke. W. Lamont argues convincingly that although Baxter developed an ambivalent attitude to the Dutchman, intellectually his "great mentor was Hugo Grotius." In 1658 Baxter summarized his attitude to Grotius in a pamphlet named *The Grotian Religion Discovered*, and while the goal of the pamphlet is to censure Grotius' proposal for a reconciliation between English Protestantism and Catholicism (which Baxter regarded as designed to deviously re-catholicize England), Baxter's debt to Grotius is nevertheless admitted, among other things, for his insight (which Prynne also pointed to) that "obedience to the magistrate had its self-preservative limits." Prynne too was evidently influenced by Grotius, as shown by the first tracts he wrote on the Civil War, such as his *A Soveraign Antidote...* (1642), *The Soveraigne Power of Parliaments...* (1643), and *The Popish Royall Favourite...* (1643), where he defended resistance to the King by repeatedly referring not to Calvinist resistance theory, but rather to the teachings of Hugo Grotius.[18]

to a *Seditious Pamphlet, Entitled, "SACRO-SANCTA REGUM MAJESTAS,"* or The Sacred and Royal Prerogative of Christian Kings; Under the Name of J. A., but Penned by John Maxwell, the Excommunicate Popish Prelate; with a Scriptural Confutation of the Ruinous Grounds of W. Barclay, H. Grotius, H. Arnisæus, Ant. de Domi. Popish Bishop of Spalato, and of Other Late Anti-Magistratical Royalists, as the Author of Ossorianum, Dr. Ferne, E. Symmons, the Doctors of Aberdeen, etc. In *Forty-four Questions* (1644). Rutherford was one of the four Commissioners sent in 1643 by the Scottish Presbyterians to participate in the Westminster Assembly of Divines, of which Selden was also a member.

[18] J. Franklin, *John Locke and the Theory of Sovereignty* (Cambridge University Press, 1981) pp. 53–86, reiterates claims already made by A.H. McLean, "George Lawson and John Locke" in *Cambridge Historical Journal* 9/1 (1947) pp. 69–77 – who points out that every characteristic claim of Locke's *Second Treatise* is to be found in Lawson, and who quotes Baxter admitting that Lawson's writings "instigating me to the study of politics." But Zuckert *Natural* denies, especially in chapter 4 pp. 95–117, the Grotian and Lawsonian influence on Locke. W. Lamont, "Arminianism: the controversy that never was" in Skinner and Phillipson (eds.), *Political Discourse in Early Modern Britain* (Cambridge University Press, 1993) pp. 7, 68–69; 59–60. It is quite likely that both Baxter and Prynne were drawn to Grotian ideas by their reticence to adopt Calvinist resistance theories, because of their wider theological and political implications. However, Baxter and Prynne, both ferocious anti-Catholics who saw Popish plots and principles everywhere (including among Quakers), developed a theory of creeping crypto-Catholicism dressing in Grotian garb. They conceded that Charles I and Laud rather than being straight Papists, actually subscribed to Grotius' thesis about a possible reconciliation between Rome and the Protestant Churches – Lamont terms this approach as the "French" way of Catholicism (local autonomy and conciliar power) versus the "Italian" way (full submission to the sovereignty of the Pope). In 1659 Baxter published *A Key for Catholicks*, in which he exposed the alleged Grotian plot and Charles I's complicity in it. His conviction that the restored Church had

Although the ostensive goal of Grotius' *Jure Belli* was to systematically elaborate the laws of international conflict, what most impressed his contemporary English readers was his voluntarism and philosophical contractualism as foundations for political thought. The attempts by opposite sides of the English political divide to appropriate his ideas clearly point to the great prestige he enjoyed, as well to obvious difficulties inherent in his theory.[19]

As we shall see below, the characteristics of Hugo Grotius' system as well as the comprehensiveness that he attempted to impart to it, demonstrate that his intent was to present an alternative to the scholastic system. He admitted as much explicitly when he made clear that his ideas should be understood as an attempt to break free from the framework of scholastic Aristotelianism, which, he asserted, in the name of the great man, had for some time "degenerated into Tyranny, so that Truth, for the Discovery of which *Aristotle* took so great Pains, is now oppressed by nothing more than the very Name of *Aristotle*."[20]

Obviously indebted to his scholastic predecessors, on many terminological and conceptual levels, nevertheless his evident goal to establish simple, clear and objective political principles, as well his anxiousness to supply the same criteria for meaning of words, clearly differentiated his work from theirs. To a great extent Grotius succeeded in incorporating into his theory many ideas and terms from the scholastic approach, prominently so the inborn rational and sociable nature of men, while at the same time making them into components of his new naturalist approach. Grotius' great achievement was to successively shift the discussion of collective human behavior to natural terms – joining the scholastic religious doctrine of eternal law with the principle of the social. He employed medieval Aristotelian terms such as "universitas," but transformed them into human (and human-created) collectives.[21]

Grotius' political theory, as presented most cogently in his *Jure Belli*, proposes that the comprehensive system of correct rules for individual, political and international action can be derived from a small number of simple and "natural" principles, with both the identification of the principles and the manner of their implementation performed by the individual's rational capacities.[22]

---

not abandoned its Grotian designs made him refuse the bishopric offered to him at around the same time. pp. 50–51.

[19] Kahn *Wayward* pp. 38–40. See especially Hugo Grotius, *Jure Belli ac Pacis* |1625| F.W. Kelsey trans. (Oxford, 1925) b2c16.

[20] Grotius *Jure Belli* Prolegomena sec. 43. As R. Tuck points out, regardless of his anti-scholastic utterances, Grotius too did not refrain from resorting to combing through Aristotle's writings, in order to muster some passages supporting his very un-Aristotelian thesis. See Sharpe *Remapping* p. 76.

[21] Kelley *Human* pp. 217–218.

[22] The five principles of natural law identified by Grotius are: "the Abstaining from that which is another's, and the Restitution of what we have of another's, or of the Profit we have made by it, the Obligation of fulfilling Promises, the Reparation of a Damage done through our own Default, and the Merit of Punishment among Men." See Grotius *Jure Belli* Prolegomena sec. 8.

Grotius postulated an "impelling desire for society" as a fundamental factor of human motivation, as well, of course, as a paramount desire for self-preservation (but not restricted to humans only). But he made sure to subject these impulses to the rule of reason, by asserting that the source of law is "human intelligence," which draws meaning out of the desires for society and for self-preservation.[23]

From this basis, Grotius then argued, "flows another more extended meaning" of law, by the rational individual's "exercise of judgment," which is subject only to the aforesaid natural law. By that law, the individual has also the right to carry out his judgment, but, since there are unavoidable difficulties with the practical implementation of natural law and judgment, men "consent" to associate into political societies, and these political societies in their turn consent to associate into the "society of states" – however, the foundations for the identification of natural law and the legitimacy of carrying out its judgment always remains in individual reason.[24]

The role of the individual's rational faculty is fundamental for Grotius, since he regards it as not only the source of one's discerning and implementing the law of nature, but also as the basis for obligation. That is, the individual's realization of the law and of the necessity of human cooperation, is supposed to make him submit to its authority as well as to the authority of the political society and magistrates, created to implement its judgments.[25]

The exclusivity of rational understanding and judgment as sole source of obligation, being so important for Grotius, leads him to deny legitimacy from any other possible source of obligation, clearly stressing that the judgment of reason, must not

be corrupted either by Fear, or the Allurements of present Pleasure, nor be carried away violently by blind Passion. And whatsoever is contrary to such a Judgment is likewise understood to be contrary to Natural Right, that is, the Laws of our Nature.

It is in this context that Grotius' notorious statement proposing that his theory would hold true even if "we dare to say" (etiamsi daremus) that "there is no God, or that he takes no Care of human Affairs" becomes clear – for otherwise his theory of law and obligation would become contingent on individual's beliefs instead of their reason, and thus annul the universal natural scope upon which it is predicated. Thus, while Grotius rushes to add that the conviction that God exists and cares has been planted in men "partly by reason, partly by unbroken tradition" and confirmed by various practical

---

[23] Grotius *Jure Belli* Prolegomena sec. 7–8.   [24] Grotius *Jure Belli* Prolegomena sec. 8–10, 16.
[25] Grotius explicitly argues that since it is necessary among men that "there be some method of obligating themselves one to another," and no other "natural method" could be imagined between independent reasonable beings other than "pacts" that is contracts, "the bodies of municipal [that is, political] law have arisen." Grotius *Jure Belli* Prolegomena sec. 15.

proofs, he significantly makes the "free will of God" of secondary importance to his theory – as only "another source of law besides the source in nature[.]"[26]

For Grotius' theory of obligation to function, the rulings of rational judgment that it advocates must be as inevitable and self-evident as mathematical rules, and indeed he explicitly makes the analogy between the two: "For I profess truly, that as Mathematicians consider Figures abstracted from Bodies, so I, in treating of Right, have withdrawn my Mind from all particular Facts."[27] By identifying his theory of law and obligation with mathematical truths requiring no outside validation, Grotius attempts to make it independent and self-contained to the degree that it is insulated not only from objections that might arise as to the existence of a providential deity, but even from the possibility of divine intervention, thus

the Law of Nature is so unalterable, that God himself cannot change it. For tho' the Power of God be infinite, yet we may say, that there are some Things to which this infinite Power does not extend, because they cannot be expressed by Propositions that contain any Sense, but manifestly simply a Contradiction. For Instance then, as God himself cannot effect, that twice two should not be four[.][28]

Grotius is aware that his claim for the truth of his theory being self-evident might be cast into doubt by pointing out that the rational faculty upon which he erects his whole theoretical system, certainly does not seem to be displayed among men to the extent he would hope for. His answer is to argue that indeed there are many men who do not display the full powers of right reason, but that should not bother us too much, for the minds whose reasoning is "more subtle and abstract" can prove what the law of nature is "*à priori*, that is, by Arguments drawn from the very Nature of the Thing," while the less reasonable, "more popular" minds can be brought to comprehend it eventually, "*à posteriori*, that is, by Reasons taken from something external." Grotius is confident that eventually, the unchangeable law of nature can be discerned by all men "who are of a right and sound Mind," and we should not be bothered too much with those who are unable to do so, for they evidently are

---

[26] Grotius *Jure Belli* Prolegomena sec. 9–12. In the first (1625) edition of his *Jure Belli*, Grotius was most unconcerned about God's role in natural law, maintaining that knowledge of the existence of natural law and its content comes only from men's reason and observation of the material universe. Natural right for him is simply a dictate of right reason. He included within this knowledge the conclusion that God has created the natural order, and that what is incongruous with the nature created by God transgresses His law – but belief in the existence of God is not a necessity in this system. In the second edition, of 1631, Grotius made the connection between God and laws more direct: while in 1625 the prolegomena stated that the law was either "proceeding from nature itself or introduced by custom and tacit agreement"; in 1631 the same passage read "proceeding from nature itself, or established by divine laws, or introduced by custom and tacit agreement." According to R. Tuck, there can be no doubt that in the 1631 edition, political pressures brought Grotius to insert some additions about God as law-maker. R. Tuck, *The Rights of War and Peace* (Oxford University Press, 1999) pp. 100–101.

[27] Grotius *Jure Belli* Prolegomena sec. 59 and also sec. 31.   [28] Grotius *Jure Belli* b1 sec. 10.

men of "weak and disturbed Judgments[.]" Indeed, Grotius argues that a perfect polity with perfect laws could in practice be constructed, if only natural lawyers would invest enough concerted efforts in it, so as to cover all aspects of men's life.[29]

Proceeding to cast the political frame that he distills from these epistemological premises, Grotius proposed that, since it was necessary among men that "there be some method of obligating themselves one to another," and no "natural method" could be imaged other than "pacts," it is by them that "the bodies of municipal [that is, political] law have arisen." In other words, he regarded political law as based on a mutual contract between individuals, obligating men "one to another." The forms that such a contract could take, according to him, varied, for men could associate themselves with a group and thus accepting to conform by what should be determined by "the majority," but they could also simply subject themselves to the rule of one or more, in that case promising to abide by decisions of those upon whom they had conferred "authority." But it should be noted that Grotius put each individual's consent (either explicit or implicit) to join with others, as the sole source of men's obedience in all cases. Therefore, for him, even where men subject themselves to a lone ruler, the source of political law is only the obligation arising from "mutual consent." He also made sure to point out that while expediency is certainly an important aspect of political law, it nevertheless could only be "reinforcement" for, and could not replace, the principle of consent. The same principle Grotius held to be true not only between individual men in each state, but also "between all states, or a great many states," and the law arising out of "mutual consent" between states was "the body of law which is maintained between states," that he proposed to term as "the law of nations, whenever we distinguish that term from the law of nature" – upon which was formed "the great society of states." The Grotian system of law and politics can be then schematically viewed as consisting of three levels, each mirroring as well as expanding the previous one: the first level consists of individuals drawing law from nature by exercise of rational "judgment"; the second level consists of rational individuals associating into states by their "consent"; the third level consists of rational states associating by their consent into the "society of states." Or, in Grotius' own amusing image, sociability in "the very nature of man" was "the mother of the law of nature," with the law of nature is in its turn the mother of the obligation rising out of "mutual consent," which finally is the mother of "municipal," political law – thus making human nature "so to say, the great-grand mother of municipal law."[30]

To sum up, Grotius' attempted to replace the scholastic approach to morality and politics with a new theory based upon the individual's use of his reason, to

---

[29] Grotius *Jure Belli* b1 sec. 12 and Prolegomena sec. 21.
[30] Grotius *Jure Belli* Prolegomena sec. 15–17.

identify natural law, to judge its applicability in particular cases, and to execute its verdict, with mathematic-like precision. He also regards the selfsame reasoning faculty in individuals as sufficient basis for generating in them the obligation to submit to the dictates of that law. Evidently, his theory is founded upon the epistemological presupposition that men can gather sufficient knowledge of the world around them by adequate exertion of their faculty to reason, and that this faculty endows them with such a degree of understanding, that they are capable of rightly judging and executing the verdict of the law of nature – including, in cases involving moral issues, even up to the taking of another man's life. Moreover, this personal faculty of individuals is to a great extent the basis for the creation of the political community. Because of the problematic aspects of a man judging in his own case, the political community is created by the selecting of magistrates capable of judging, and by the transferring of the right of punishing enjoyed by every individual in the state of nature, to the agents of the community.

With this avowed supremacy of *a priori* reason, what role is there then in Grotius' system, if at all, to factors that are not strictly rational, like experience or tradition? Ultimately, very little, it seems. Grotius certainly supported the practical use of such instruments as "tradition" or various practical proofs to support belief in the existence of providence; and of "expediency" as "reinforcement" for the political law based on individual rational consent. But such tools were for him ultimately dispensable, in each case supplying only additional or reinforcing support, with reason always delivering the decisive validation. In all cases, as in his use of *a posteriori* arguments to convince "weak" minds, Grotius views the use of *a priori* rational arguments as the true epistemological and political basis for human understanding and obligation, with anything outside it only lending support to the rational foundations (thus following the third of Sarpi's modes, with reason first and then sense).[31]

---

[31] Grotius *Jure Belli* Prolegomena sec. 11, 16–17. It appears that Grotius was aware of the radical consequences of his ideas, for he tried to obfuscate their impact, in successive editions of the *Jure Belli*. In an earlier work he had formulated even more starkly many ideas that were to become mainstays of later liberal thought. His *De Indis* (Of the Indies, aka as *De Jure Praedae* – Of the Law of Booty), written many years previous to the *Jure Belli* but remaining unpublished for centuries – except for the one chapter, which became *Mare Liberum* – articulated a much more voluntarist and radical political theory. For example, he posited in this work that the right of punishment (ius gladii), belonged not only to the state or its representatives but to each and every individual – since every right, including the right to punish, comes to the state from the collective agreement of individuals. As Tuck points out this idea was proposed (independently, for the *Indis* remained unknown until the nineteenth century) by Locke as the "strange doctrine" in his *Two Treatises*. Tuck also notes the similarity to Rousseau's account of men in the state of nature, in the "Prolegomena" of the *Indis* where Grotius articulated a social theory based on the two principles of self-preservation and the preservation of others (the first taking precedence over the second, where they collide), then giving rise to "that brotherhood of man, that world state, commended to us so frequently and so enthusiastically by the ancient philosophers and

3.3 HOBBES

Of all thinkers treated in this chapter, Thomas Hobbes articulated most systematically and explicitly the theory of knowledge on which he based his political thought.[32] Moreover, the developing of his system can be directly connected with the new epistemological claims of his period: it appears that it was from the mid-1630s, influenced by his acquaintance with the ideas of Galileo and Descartes, that Hobbes became interested in philosophical subjects and especially in the new epistemology, and went on to organize his ideas in a tripartite scheme dealing with body (physics and metaphysics), man (epistemology) and citizen (politics). His theory is the most significant attempt to transform raison d'état ideas into a naturalist jurisprudence. With a skeptical epistemology and relativist ethics, he nevertheless constructed what he regarded as a "science" of human conduct which, albeit founded on self-preservation, nevertheless entailed the renouncement of self-judgment into the hands of an all-powerful sovereign.[33]

By late 1640 Hobbes had left England for France, fearing with good reason that the newly assembled English Parliament might penalize the author of the

particularly by the Stoics" (see *De Jure Praedae* (Oxford: Clarendon, 1950) p. 13). In effect, Grotius proposed a vision of men as first existing in a state of nature (though he did not use the term), and then associating into societies. He stressed that civil societies developed "not with the intention of abolishing the society which links all men as a whole, but rather in order to fortify that universal society by a more dependable means of protection, and at the same time, with the purpose of bringing together under a more convenient arrangement the numerous different products of many persons' labor which are required for the uses of human life" (*Jure Praedae* p. 19). He points out that as in entering civil society, individuals agree to subordinate their interests to those of the community, the natural precedence of one's own self-preservation over that of others, does not apply any more. Grotius clearly agreed with Seneca that there exist "two kinds of commonwealth, the world state and the municipal state" (*Jure Praedae* p. 93). But the "world state" was, in Tuck's words, only a "thin version" of human society extending to "commutative justice," such as killing a snake (that might strike any man), while only the "municipal state" supplied "distributive justice." See Tuck *Rights* pp. 81–82, 86–89.

[32] Hobbes was aided in the production of his systematic theory of body, man and politics by the fact that he was almost constantly employed by three successive generations of the Cavendish family, which made him something quite similar to what would today be a tenured academic – and a bachelor at that. Meanwhile, his contemporaries discussed here had to navigate their intellectual activities through economic uncertainties, marriages, and particularly political involvements which landed each of them in jail for some period. Their epistemological assumptions have to be identified from comments scattered through their works. I have adopted here the same approach to Hobbes, excerpting his ideas on the subject from his political works.

[33] N. Malcolm's entry for "Thomas Hobbes" in *The Oxford Dictionary of National Biography* – internet edition (accessed 15 May 2014); Tuck *Philosophy* p. xvii. In Paris Hobbes joined the group around Marin Mersenne, and wrote a critique of Descartes' *Meditations on First Philosophy*, third among the *Objections* (to which are appended "Replies" from Descartes) collected and published by Mersenne in 1641. An additional set of remarks by Hobbes on other works by Descartes only succeeded in ending all correspondence between the two. See Harrison *Masterpiece* p. 39. Hobbes apparently also struck a great friendship with Pierre Gassendi, see Rahe *Against* pp. 296–297.

ideas articulated in the widely circulating manuscript copies of his *Elements of Law Natural and Politic*, completed in May of that year and dedicated to William Cavendish, Earl of Newcastle (one of the more intransigent royalist figures). The text laid out the political consequences of Hobbes' epistemological principles in a manner that was bound to alarm supporters of Parliament. When he posited in his work that "all laws are declarations of the mind," this was a statement which regarded law epistemologically as resulting from motions of the mind, and thus created and knowable by man. He connected this human law with the laws of nature, but in his account the latter are not fixed eternal rules extraneous to man, but rather naturally occurring appetites and aversions, internal within each man. Thus law was mutable and capriciously created by man, rather than eternal and "discovered" as in more traditional views, and as a result (worryingly from the perspective of Parliament), Hobbes' theory undermined customary law, while extolling the lawmaking authority of the sovereign.[34]

As the political conflict in England progressed, Hobbes would go even further in assigning the culpability for all its evils on ideas that would challenge the supremacy of the sovereign. Hobbes' sovereign was to be first and foremost (in Tuck's words) "an epistemic power," able to determine the meaning of words and impose on all a single public language. Consequently, in *Leviathan*, as well as in his later *Behemoth, or The Long Parliament* (composed around 1668, published 1682) he directly blamed the Civil War on ideas impinging on the sovereign's authority, which for him included covenant theology, the Common law, natural rights theory and of course "the schools" – and more generally on the very notion of debating concepts and meanings, an activity which by its very nature impinges on the absolute epistemological and political supremacy of the sovereign.[35]

Hobbes' hostility to scholasticism is one of the most conspicuous features of his work, and in *Leviathan* he attacks, again and again, "the Philosophy-schooles, through all the Universities of Christendome, grounded upon certain Texts of Aristotle" (most often for what he describes as "insignificant Speech"). In later life he was, if anything, even more scathing towards the scholastics (including the later neo-scholastics like Suarez and Vitoria), accusing them in his *Behemoth* of writing "great books of school-divinity, which no man else, nor they themselves are able to understand" and of making the universities to England into "what the wooden horse was to the Trojans." Indeed, he did not hesitate to pour scorn even upon the "babbling philosophy of Aristotle"

---

[34] Kahn *Wayward* p. 171; Collins *Cosmos* p. 35. Hobbes later wrote that soon after the Long Parliament assembled on 3 November 1640, he saw that "words that tended to advance the prerogative of kings began to be examined in Parlament[sic]," and having authored himself the *Elements of Law*, he began to fear for his safety, deciding very suddenly to leave within days, and having departed England by about 15 November. See P. Zagorin, "Thomas Hobbes' Departure from England in 1640: An Unpublished Letter" in *The Historical Journal* 21/1 (1978) pp. 157–160.

[35] Kahn *Wayward* pp. 135–136; Sharpe *Remapping* p. 150.

himself, adding that "none of the ancient philosophers' writings are comparable to those of Aristotle, for their aptness to puzzle and entangle men with words, and to breed disputation."[36]

Hobbes' patent hostility to scholasticism was matched by his rejection of rationalist alternatives to it. To no small extent, the sense-based system that Hobbes developed was directed against the a prioristic, rationalist outlook of Descartes as well as Grotius. Indeed, Tuck even proposes that Hobbes' strong polemic against Descartes might lie behind much of the former's whole philosophical enterprise, which he embarked upon relatively late in life. Thus Hobbes' theory is based on an overtly materialist, sense-based epistemology, which he regarded as alternative to scholastic ideas, and as capable of overcoming what he saw as the failings and the contradictions of more modern theories, based on rational *a priori* reasoning, like those of Descartes and Grotius:

Concerning the thoughts of man, I will consider them first singly, and afterwards in train or dependence upon one another. Singly, they are every one a representation or appearance of some quality, or other accident of a body without us, which is commonly called an object. Which object worketh on the eyes, ears, and other parts of man's body, and by diversity of working produceth diversity of appearances. The original of them all is that which we call sense, (for there is no conception in a man's mind which hath not at first, totally or by parts, been begotten upon the organs of sense). The rest are derived from that original.[37]

Although both the political theory and its epistemological basis are fully articulated in *Leviathan* (1651) – which Filmer read and commented on, and which was presented to Selden by Hobbes personally – the defining features of Hobbes' theory were already evident in his *De Cive*, (circulating in manuscript by 1641, published 1642), which both Grotius and Selden owned. Hobbes' theory starts with a pre-political individual, whose mind and understanding are defined by his sense experience. Some of the defining features ascribed to this

---

[36] Hobbes *Leviathan* p1c1 and c8 (rebuking the ideas of the "Schoole-men" as "Madnesse" and "Absurdity"); Thomas Hobbes, *Behemoth or the Long Parliament* [c. 1668] (Chicago University Press, 1990), Dialogue I, pp. 16–17, 40–42 and Dialogue II p. 95. The neo-scholastic Spaniard, Francisco Vitoria, had asserted in his *On the American Indians* (1532) that unlike what Ovid claims, man is <u>not</u> "a wolf to his fellow men," *homo homini lupis*. It seems plausible that Hobbes used this proverb in his work exactly to address Vitoria's view of human nature. See "On the American Indians," in Francisco Vitoria, *Political Writings*, A. Pagden and J. Lawrance eds. (Cambridge University Press, 1992) p. 280 and note 76. The actual proverb does not in fact appear in Ovid, who has rather a formulation with the same import in his *Tristia* v.8 ("siue homines, uix sunt homines hoc nomine digni, quamque lupi, saeuae plus feritatis habent"). The real origin of the proverb is "lupus est homo homini, non homo" in Plautus' *Asinaria* 495, popularized in renaissance Europe by appearing in Erasmus' *Adagia*.

[37] Hobbes *Leviathan* p1c1. About the background to Hobbes' theory see Tuck *Philosophy* p. 298. Hobbes received a copy of Descartes' *Discourse* as early as late 1637 and read the book carefully. See Rahe *Against* p. 313.

individual are similar to those attributed to him by Grotius, for he is interested in self-preservation, and he is able to reason. However, Hobbes' individual not only seems to lack the Grotian sociable impulse, but in fact his apprehension for his life naturally pushes him in the direction opposite to sociability: he is suspicious and fearful of others. When Hobbes writes in *De Cive* that "men are born unapt for society," he makes a stark epistemological and political statement about society being an artificially constructed concoction, erected in an attempt to bring some order into natural human chaos.[38]

More than this, whereas Grotius thought the rational faculty clearly paramount in men, Hobbes sees it as quite uncertain, most often overwhelmed by passions, and especially prone to distortion by more or less imagined fears for self-preservation. Thus, while Grotius' law of nature is a comprehensive system of layer upon layer of rules, rationally harmonizing a number of principles and interests, Hobbes' law of nature consists of one lone preoccupation:

[T]he *Law of Nature*, that I may define it, is the Dictate of right Reason, conversant about those things which are either to be done, or omitted for the constant preservation of Life, and Members, as much as in us lyes.

This means that, for Hobbes, men's foremost natural obligation, by reason as well as the passions, is first and foremost to himself. It follows then, that, as Hobbes writes in *Leviathan*: there is "no obligation on any man which ariseth not from some act of his own."[39]

How then, from such unpromising premises are men supposed to enter political society and to develop an obligation to it? Hobbes concedes that since all his precepts of nature "are derived by a certain artifice from the single dictate of Reason advising us to look to the preservation, and safeguard of our selves," it is plausible that the deduction of these laws would be so difficult that "it is not to be expected they will be vulgarly known, and therefore neither will they prove obliging." His answer to this problem is to again turn to the principle of individual self-preservation, so that all men, be they however so rude and unlearned, can be expected to understand one simple rule – in effect the precursor to what will become John Rawls' "veil of ignorance": "That when he doubts, whether what he is now doing to another, may be done by the Law of Nature, or not, he conceive himselfe to be in that others stead."[40]

[38] Hobbes *De Cive* chapter 2 sec. 2; Collins *Cosmos* pp. 32–33; and Hobbes *Leviathan* p1c13 where Hobbes explicitly says that: "It may seem strange to some man, that has not well weighted these things; that Nature should thus dissociate, and render men apt to invade and destroy each other" – an obviously anti-Grotian comment if there ever was one.

[39] Hobbes *De Cive* chapter 2 sec. 1; Hobbes *Leviathan* p1c21, and see discussion in Harrison *Masterpiece* p. 105. After 1642 Hobbes abandoned his earlier equivocations about the extent of the right of self-defense, and argued for the impossibility of man to renounce it – revising accordingly his account of the state of nature. See Sharpe *Remapping* p. 82.

[40] Hobbes *De Cive* chapter 3 sec. 26. A similar point is made by Hobbes in *Leviathan*, where he asserts that the "similitude of the thoughts, and Passions of one man, to the thoughts and

Having established to his satisfaction an effective if crude mechanism for men identifying law in the state of nature, Hobbes then goes on to describe an equally minimalist principle justifying the creation of political society and men's obligation to it:

[V]ery often the same man at diverse times, praises, and dispraises the same thing. Whilst thus they doe, necessary it is there should be discord, and strife: They are therefore so long in the state of War, as by reason of the diversity of the present appetites, they mete Good and Evill by diverse measures. All men easily acknowledge this state, as long as they are in it, to be evill, and by consequence that Peace is good."[41]

In other words, men seek peace because of fear for their self-preservation, and are willing to transfer their absolute natural rights to political society and to be bound to it, as the price for maintaining peace between each other. What causes men to seek and find each other and brings them together, what rules them and binds them, is always and only one thing: "Feare of some evill consequence upon the rupture." This is truly the foundation of obligation; for Hobbes, irresistible might is irresistible right, and the reason why dominion of men adheres to those whose power is irresistible. That is also why the word of God should be heeded, not for its moral or true content, but only for His irresistible power. Indeed, Hobbes even suggests that such fear and anxiety from what the future holds constitute the "Natural seed of *Religion.*" Such a religious anxiety is naturally an impediment to the monopoly on fear that Hobbes assigns to his sovereign, and thus requires that within the state political power should control religion. Hobbes goes even further, asserting political power to be more effective than religious sentiments even in regulating basic social behavior; for example, he holds that fear of actual punishment is a better way of ensuring the keeping of contracts than the fear of God, for, he holds, the fear of something visible like the men with swords which will inflict the punishment, is generally stronger than that of "The Power of Spirits Invisible."[42]

Passions of another" means that he who truly looks into himself "shall thereby read and know, what are the thoughts, and Passions of all other men, upon the like occasion." See Hobbes *Leviathan,* in The Introduction.

[41] Hobbes *De Cive,* chapter 3 sec. 31. In *Leviathan* Hobbes also elaborates on this, arguing that men recognize that in the condition of nature when all are equal and all judge of the justness of their fears, there can be no coercive power – and so they create society, by a contract of mutual transfer of all individual rights to society, which then sets a common power over the contractors, with sufficient force to compel them. See Hobbes *Leviathan* p1c14, and see discussion in Harrison *Masterpiece* pp. 46–47.

[42] Hobbes *Leviathan* p1c12 and 14; Kahn *Wayward* pp. 156–157. Hobbes' "anxiety" from the future can be seen as somewhat parallel to the sense of future equity which in Selden's theory brings men to believe in providence and to keep their obligations. But while in Hobbes this is mainly about fear, in Selden it is at least in the same measure, if not more so, about hope (for justice and a good future).

etiamsi - even if, although.
daremus - we give.

In effect, Hobbes too produces his own version of Grotius' "etiamsi daremus," when he writes that his "laws of nature" are really theorems of reason, as in nature there is no one that can command them (since there is not a civil power), and they can be called laws only if "we consider the same Theoremes, as delivered in word of God" – since He has the power to command even in a state of nature. This apparent concession to the word of God, is really irrelevant to Hobbes' wider political theory, since he based the latter on self-preservation as natural right, while making natural law the precept of reason (deduced from natural right). As these laws of nature are only the means to the natural right of self-preservation, it is obvious which of the two should prevail in case they conflict. Moreover, since the only way to ensure keeping of contracts is fear of punishment, which exists only in civil society, and as this leads to the creation of the civil power which can itself create laws and enforce them, any "laws of nature," whether one regards them as theorems of reason or laws of God, are thus anyway extinguished by the creation of political society.[43]

Predictably, like Grotius, Hobbes takes care to protest too much, albeit not very convincingly, of his theory's adherence to theism in general and to Christianity in particular; in truth Hobbes' system has neither the necessity nor the place for a deity or for providence. It is only fear for one's physical life and welfare, both in the immediate and in the more general sense that is the origin, the preserver and the end of Hobbes' political society. The centrality of fear to his whole epistemic and political theory is amusingly illustrated by Hobbes in the autobiography he wrote, in metric Latin, where he mentions the day of his birth as the one in which the Spanish Armada approached England, so that such news (loosely translated) "Which struck so horribly my mother's ear / That she gave birth to twins, myself and fear" (Atque metum tantum concepit tunc mea mater / Ut pareret geminos meque metumque simul).[44]

In current scholarship, Hobbes is regarded as harbinger of so many of the prizes of modernity that his ideas and their implications are often significantly sanitized. His Leviathan is now often suffused with a useful, even benevolent

---

[43] Hobbes *Leviathan* p1c12 and 14; and Kahn *Wayward* p. 163. Samuel Parker, future high church Bishop of Oxford, observed in his *A Discourse of Ecclesiastical Politie* (1670), that even if religion is a cheat, it would be only "the greatest Enemies to Government, that tell the world it is so" because government needs "the Ties of Conscience" upon "those of Secular Interest," for without them kings were noting but "terrible men with long Swords." W. Lamont writes that this was exactly what Hobbes wanted them to be, nothing but men with long swords who could not take up the mantle of God or pry into the souls of their subjects. Lamont *Puritanism* pp. 97–98. After the twentieth century one might very well ask, why wouldn't such men pry even into the souls of men?

[44] From his "Vita carmine expressa" published in *Thomas Hobbesii Malmesburiensis Vita, Authore Seipso* (1679), pp. 1–2. Hobbes would have even promises extracted under duress to be generally obliging, for they are simply a particular instance of the fear which motivates all of men's obligations. See Hobbes *De Cive* chapter 2 sec. 16.

aura, like a powerful but noble whale, being watched at safe distance from a sightseeing ship. Such a rose-tinted view of the Leviathan, besides overlooking the definitely gruesome connotations of dragons and monsters associated with the seventeenth century uses of the term, still apparent two centuries later in the fearsome reputation of Melville's whale – misses the whole point of Hobbes' theory, in which the Leviathan is intended to be a fear-installing, even appalling figure. The Leviathan has to be dreadful, since it is attempting to achieve the double feature of liberating men from their fears and hopes for the fate of their immaterial souls, while at the same time convincing them of the total, even transcendent value, of their fears and hopes in the material world. These connotations resonated in the contemporary public use of the term before its appropriation by Hobbes, such as in 1640, when a clergyman named Cornelius Burges (or Burgess), protégé of the Earl of Warwick, delivered before the House of Commons the first fast sermon commissioned by the house, asking his listeners if England will leave its covenant with God, "Whether is our Condition any whit better now than heretofore, when those *Leviathans* were alive and in their height?" Thus, what Hobbes himself termed the "dreadful Name, LEVIATHAN"' was not some ill-defined large biblical beast, but a metaphor for terrible and loathsome beings, the name of one of the Seven Princes of Hell, the demon mostly associated with the deadly sin of envy, a monster often identified as a dragon. Perhaps not coincidentally, during the interregnum the Commonwealth regime itself was often pictured by its enemies as an all-consuming dragon.[45]

Therefore, while Grotius' rationalist epistemology produces a political society based throughout on rational consent – including grounds for obligation so exclusively rational, that they make him regard any judgment of reason "corrupted" by fear or passion as "contrary to Natural Right, that is, the Laws of our Nature" – Hobbes' unabashedly materialist epistemology,

---

[45] For the ominous resonations of the term Leviathan, and Hobbes' awareness of them, see K.I. Parker, "That 'Dreadful Name, Leviathan': Biblical resonances in the title to Hobbes' famous political work" in *Hebraic Political Studies* 2/4 (2007) pp. 424–447. See also Kahn *Wayward* p. 115. The seven princes of Hell are the seven highest demons in Christian demonology (equivalent to the Seven Archangels), with each demon-prince often corresponding to one of the seven deadly sins. According to the 1589 list composed by the German Jesuit Peter Binsfield, the seven (and their sins) are Lucifer (Pride), Mammon (Greed), Asmodeus (Lust), Satan (Wrath), Beelzebub (Gluttony), Belphegor (Sloth) and Leviathan (Envy). See R. Guiley, *Encyclopedia of Demons and Demonology* (Checkmark Books, 2009) pp. 28–29. During the Civil War and interregnum, royalist prints depicted "The Common wealth ruleing with a standing Army" as a dragon who fed on "Laws," "Customs," "Statutes," "Magna Charta. Prerogative privileges Liberties," "Monarchy," "Episcopacy," "Church Land and tithes," "Nobility and House of peers" "gaine" – while defecating "Taxes," "Excise," "Monthly Assessments," "Loan money," "Oaths of Covenant Ingagements and abjuration." The dragon literally consumes the nation and shackles its people, an image conveying anti-patriotism as well as, by implication, renewing the association of the absent monarch with Saint George. See Sharpe *Remapping* p. 35, and image on p. 244.

produces the very opposite premises for political society, where fear is the very core of community and obligation. It is for this very reason that while Hobbes regards society as founded upon a contract of mutual self-preservation between all individuals, political authority itself is <u>not</u> based on a contract, but on the unconditional handing-over of supreme power to the ruling authority(be it an individual or a council). This principle is necessary, since the very essence of political authority remains the ability to have the unfettered coercive power which instills fear in any who would even consider opposing it. The full scope of such a political theory has only been fully realized in the twentieth century by regimes that endeavored to convince their subjects that religion is false, while at the very same time infusing themselves with transcendent value. The combination has been perhaps most aptly described in a work of fiction, George Orwell's *Nineteen Eighty-Four*, the masterly depiction of the poisoned fruits of English radical thought, where, after the protagonist Winston Smith concedes he does not believe in God, he is then presented by O'Brien, personifying the uninhibited ruling power, with the vision of the future of humanity: "imagine a boot stamping on a human face – for ever."[46]

Hobbes, in attempting to create an epistemology based on sense only, and a political theory following from it, finds that since it is all dependent on the body as repository of the senses, then the beginning and end of such a sense-oriented approach is necessarily the overarching fear of physical destruction (thus following the second of Sarpi's modes, with sense alone).[47]

3.4   FILMER

Unlike the regard long enjoyed by the ideas of his other contemporaries we have looked at, Sir Robert Filmer suffered for more than three centuries from a much-maligned reputation. Thanks in large part to the distortion of his ideas by John Locke, in his *Two Treatises*, Filmer was long caricatured as an unsophisticated and narrow proponent of absurd political notions. Only in recent decades has this distorted picture begun to be corrected and replaced by a more accurate depiction of Filmer's thought – one that, incidentally, can better account for the need felt by thinkers like Locke and Algernon Sidney, to devote significant efforts to refuting his ideas. In truth, Filmer was a serious thinker who possessed unusual critical abilities and did not shirk from thoughtfully challenging even the most widely accepted political assumptions. Certainly, his ideas cannot be regarded as less or more absurd than those of his detractors. In particular, Filmer displayed a remarkable ability to lucidly

---

[46] G. Orwell, *Nineteen Eighty-Four* (1948), chapter 3.

[47] See discussion in Tuck *Philosophy* p. xvii, where Hobbes is regarded as the most convincing example of the transformation of the raison d'état theory into natural jurisprudence; which, by a skeptical epistemology and a relativist ethics, yet attempts to construct a "science" of human conduct on the basis of self-preservation, that entails the renouncement of self-judgment.

discuss foundational issues of political thought, and to starkly expose basic fallacies in the arguments he opposes – especially those pertaining to natural rights, consent and social contract theories.[48]

Filmer's belief that his ideas directly oppose the scholastic outlook emerges in the very opening paragraph of his most important work, *Patriarcha*, where he describes the origin of the outlook he was combating, as the widespread belief in an original absolute self-sovereignty and freedom of individuals. He then goes on to explain that:

> This tenet was first hatched in the schools, and hath been fostered by all succeeding Papists for good divinity. The divines, also, of the Reformed Churches have entertained it, and the common people everywhere tenderly embrace it as being most plausible to flesh and blood, for that it prodigally distributes a portion of liberty to the meanest of the multitude, who magnify liberty as if the height of human felicity were only to be found in it, never remembering that the desire of liberty was the first cause of the fall of Adam.

Filmer regards this idea of a natural human liberty as false as well as absurd, and therefore inevitably conducive to theoretical confusion and political instability. Those who adopt it, he believes, condemn themselves to perpetual unrest and unsettled authority. As evidence of the success of this pernicious idea, he points to the fact that even those of his contemporaries who wrote tracts upholding the absolute rights of kings, usually did so while conceding an original natural freedom – as was the case with Hobbes.[49]

Only relatively recently was it established that *Patriarcha*, thought published posthumously in 1680, had in a previous version been denied permission for publication in early 1632, thus establishing the period of the text's composition to the early 1630s, and its background as the public debate surrounding the 1628–1629 Parliament, the Petition of Right and the subsequent attempt of Charles I to rule without Parliament (the Personal Rule). The time of composition is important, for it points to the context and the intent of the work.[50]

---

[48] C. Cuttica, *Adam… "THE FATHER OF ALL FLESH": An Intellectual History of Sir Robert Filmer (1588–1653) and his Works in Seventeenth-Century European Political Thought* (European University Institute, unpublished PhD thesis, 2007) pp. 44–46. See also W.H. Greenleaf, "Filmer's Patriarchal History" in *The Historical Journal* 9/2 (1966) 157–171, which notes the growing acknowledgment of the "subtlety and learning" with which Filmer deployed his arguments, "in happy contrast to the undiscerning depreciation which had usually characterized discussions of his thought since the mid-seventeenth century." Even Filmer's genealogical argument, Greenleaf asserts, was to contemporaries a perfectly reasonable one.

[49] Filmer *Patriarcha* chapter 1 sec. 1. See above in this essay, the quote from the opening of Filmer's *Observations Concerning the Originall of Government* (1652), criticizing the "foundation" of Hobbes theory in natural liberty, while agreeing with its conclusions about the "rights of sovereignty." See also discussion in G.J. Schochet, *Patriarchalism in Political Thought* (New York: Basic Books, 1975) pp. 37–38, 41–42.

[50] In 1991, Professor David Underdown of Yale noticed a note of February 1632 by G.F. Weckherlin, requesting instructions from Charles I about the request to license for publication a "Discourse" by Filmer "of Government and in praise of Royaltie" – presumably *Patriarcha*; the request was refused. The whole story of the composition and publication of *Patriarcha* is too

Moreover, it appears that, to a great extent, the theoretical framework of all of Filmer's later political works relied to some degree or other on *Patriarcha*, even when these works address ideas by other thinkers. In fact, all of Filmer's political works published in his lifetime, except for the first one, *The Freeholder's Grand Inquest* (1648), were attempts to show the consonance of established thinkers, like Bodin or Aristotle, with his own ideas, or his rebuttal of competing political theories like those of Grotius or Hobbes.[51]

Perhaps the most important, and certainly the least understood, aspect of Filmer's theory is that it is founded on a definite and coherent epistemological approach. This approach combines an absolute metaphysical certainty, with a fundamental skepticism about the material world (indeed a skepticism that was more far-reaching even than Hobbes'). That is, Sir Robert held that men can achieve an absolute knowledge of metaphysical truth while, at the very same time, remaining utterly incapable of attaining any certain knowledge about truth in the physical world surrounding them – certainly so in things concerning political issues. Filmer achieves this unusual combination by taking some traditional Christian notions to their most extreme, if seldom acknowledged, potential conclusions. He brings the principle that the fall of man makes redemption possible only through Christ fully into the realm of political ideas, causing the material world to become one of utter confusion, deception and sin – thus refuting the possibility of individuals ever achieving by their own devices any certain knowledge about it. But, having set up these premises, that were not unheard-of ones in Christian terms, he then goes on a path of his own. Instead of arguing, as is usually done, for the role of faith or of the church in guiding men in this fallen world, he sets up as the cardinal Christian and human virtue – indeed, for him pretty close to the only virtue – the

---

long and convoluted to be fully relayed here, and some aspects of it are still disputed. What we know for certain is that by late 1631 a version of *Patriarcha* was completed (although there are indications that a previous version had been composed even earlier) so that in early 1632 Filmer requested the license for publication. After publication was refused, Filmer continued to work on the text in the next decade (the third part of the treatise apparently did not exist in the earlier version), perhaps hoping to obtain license for publication at a later date. The work did circulate for many years in manuscript form among Filmer acquaintances, but was only published posthumously in 1680. See J.P. Sommerville, "Introduction" in J.P. Sommerville (ed.) *Filmer: Patriarcha and other writings* (Cambridge University Press, 1991), and the broader discussion in Cuttica *Adam* pp. 166–168 and notes 492–493. G. Burgess claims that recent scholarship points to parts of *Patriarcha* possibly having been composed as early as 1606–1614, suggesting a range of intriguing possibilities for the background to it. See Burgess *Absolute* pp. 217–218.

[51] Such are Filmer's *Necessity of the Absolute Power of All Kings* (1648), in effect a selection of excerpts from Bodin's *République; Anarchy of a Limited and Mixed Monarchy* (1648), directed against Philip Hunton's anti-absolutist *A Treatise of Monarchy; Observations Upon Aristotles Politiques Concerning Forms of Government* (1652) presenting Filmer's interpretation of Aristotle's political ideas; and *Observations Concerning the Original of Government upon Mr Hobbes's Leviathan, Mr Milton Against Salmasius, and H. Grotius' De Jure Belli ac Pacis* (1652), whose intent is explicit in the title, and also includes some criticism of Selden's ideas.

absolute obedience to authority. The obedience to paternal authority, of course, and to other duly established authorities too, but first and foremost obedience to the king and his delegates, seems to be the only epistemological tool that men are capable of adequately mastering. Taken to its logical conclusion, such an approach means that obedience takes precedence, indeed is superior, to all other obligations. This is exactly Filmer's view, so that obedience to political authority becomes for him coterminous with obedience to the law of God, and as such takes precedence even over obedience to the teachings of the church or to one's conscience. He puts this idea at its most explicit in an important passage from *Patriarcha* (chapter 3 section 7):

Here is a fit place to examine a question which some have moved, whether it be a sin for a subject to disobey the king if he command [sic] anything contrary to his laws? For satisfaction in this point we must resolve that not only in human laws, but even in divine, a thing may be commanded contrary to law, and yet obedience to such a command is necessary. The sanctifying of the Sabbath is a divine law; yet if a master command his servant not to go to church upon a Sabbath Day, the best divines teach us that the servant must obey this command, though it may be sinful and unlawful in the master; because the servant hath no authority or liberty to examine and judge whether his master sin or no in so commanding; for there may be a just cause for a master to keep his servant from church, as appears Luke xiv. 5. Yet it is not fit to tie the master to acquaint his servant with his secret counsels or present necessity; and in such cases the servant's not going to church becomes the sin of the master, and not of the servant. The like may be said of the king's commanding a man to serve him in the wars: he may not examine whether the war be just or unjust, but must obey, since he hath no commission to judge of the titles of kingdoms or causes of war; nor hath any subject power to condemn his king for breach of his own laws.[52]

That this very issue, of personal moral responsibility versus obedience to royal authority, was present in early seventeenth-century public discourse, is easily illustrated by recalling a quote already referred to above, from Shakespeare's *Henry V* (Act IV scene 1), where a soldier asserts that obedience to the King's order wipes away any moral transgression by the one obeying it: "for we know enough if we know we are the king's subjects. If his cause be wrong, our obedience to the king wipes the crime of it out of us." Although in the play, King Henry dissents from this view, and upholds a personal moral responsibility, the exchange shows that this idea later articulated by Filmer, was not only visible to the public, but indeed regarded as sound and cogent enough to require a serious answer.

While the idea of human fallibility being redeemed only by faith was by no means uncommon, as it undergirds to some degree or other all Christian political and social thought, it is hard to find any thinker willing to go as far as Filmer in justifying such extremes of obedience at any cost. Indeed, as Filmer correctly recognized, the late sixteenth and early seventeenth centuries

---

[52] Filmer *Patriarcha* chapter 3 sec. 7.

witnessed a steep increase in writings, penned by thinkers of both Catholic and Protestant persuasions, actually justifying political disobedience in the name of Christian faith. There are scarce significant precedents to Filmer's theory of absolute obedience, for even most Christian texts urging extensive political obedience, like Romans XIII, or Luther's pamphlets of 1525 *Against the Rioting Peasants* and *An Open Letter on the Harsh Book Against the Peasants*, at most only imply such an extreme form of obedience as Filmer explicitly embraces.[53]

The Protestant doctrine of salvation through faith alone is certainly far more conducive to a political position of extreme obedience than other religious approaches. Among Catholics the doctrine of salvation through works and faith, as well as Thomist philosophy and the very structure of the church, are all potentially opposed, to one degree or other, to extreme political passivity – at least as far as the authority of the church and its principles can be (and were) invoked against the political power; and among adherents of the Calvinist version of Protestantism, the idea of predestination militates against social passivity, because of the need to detect and display it. It is no coincidence, then, that when Filmer opens his attack on those opposed to his doctrine, he identifies them first and foremost as Papists and Calvinists. Lutheranism seems to be the main branch of Western Christianity whose doctrine was least inherently contrary to a Filmerian submission, although even Lutherans who denied that resistance could normally be directed against one's ruler, usually entertained resistance to political authority in some extreme circumstances. Filmer's stance most resembles Luther's early reluctance to allow any kind of active resistance to political authority, even going so far as writing to his ally, the Elector of Wittenberg, that he would be absolved of any sin if he chose to obey the Emperor's instructions as to how to deal with Luther himself (and if the elector would not want to do so, he could at best adopt a passive stance).[54]

---

[53] Filmer *Patriarcha* chapter 3 sec. 3–7. On the affinity of Filmer's theory with Lutheranism see L. Ward, *The Politics of Liberty in England and Revolutionary America* (Cambridge University Press, 2004) pp. 28–29, Cuttica *Adam* pp. 74–75 and Zuckert *Natural* pp. 48–49. Other strands of religious thought leading to similar ideas were Protestant Apocalypticism which could lead to political passivity and even quietism, since God's will could not be fully known, and the subject's only role was to pray for the prince being divinely guided, but even with the prince an apostate, most apocalyptic thought opted for the passive resistance of the Marian martyrs. See Zaller *Legitimacy* pp. 207–208. It is possible to find Catholics too expressing positions close to this – for example, Sir Anthony Tresham as well as the so-called Appellants, English Catholics who opposed resistance theories, and held that it was possible to serve a Catholic conscience and a Protestant ruler together, sometime likening their situation to that of the Christians under the pagan emperors, to whom they rendered their due while their religious duty was to testify to their faith, when they could not enjoy it quietly. See Zaller *Legitimacy* pp. 118–121.

[54] W.D.J. Cargill Thompson makes the convincing argument that Luther spent the quarter-century between his excommunication in 1520 and his death in 1546 trying to avoid declaring a right of resistance of good Christians to properly constituted authority. He repeatedly refuted calls to give blanket support to outbreaks of resistance to Imperial government, and even went as far as

In this sense Filmer's political theory can be said to rest on a kind of extreme neo-Augustinianism. Rejecting the ideas of both Thomistic scholasticism and anti-scholastic "modern" natural right theories, Filmer in effect refurbished Augustinian ideas, which had loomed large in Christian political thought before Aquinas: holding human nature to be too corrupt to allow for the construction of a just political society, a Christian has to abandon all hope of worldly justice and find salvation only in the church. But Filmer's version of Augustinianism was not even the early medieval one, for that version still allowed some kind of positive role to political rulers guided by the church. Filmer's despair of any certainty about constructive political action was so profound, that it can find real counterparts only in the earliest Christian thought, like Tertullian's *Apologeticus* (c. 197 CE), relating to a world governed by non-Christian emperors or by barbarians, where the believer can hope at best to be left alone by his political rulers, at worst to be persecuted and martyred, and in all cases to offer only submission and passive resistance to his tormentors.[55]

Significantly, a number of writings explicitly advocating positions close to Filmer were in fact composed and published in England around the time of the original composition of *Patriarcha*. These were the works of clerical writers, prominent among whom were Sybthorpe and Maynwaring, who in 1627 published sermons supporting Charles I's forced loan, and advocating extreme versions of political obedience, even in the face of the most

---

stating that those who resist will reap damnation, so that if one is ordered by his legitimate ruler to do something that was contrary to divine or natural law, he must content himself at most with passive disobedience and be prepared to suffer the consequences. Under the pressures of events, after the Torgau Declaration of 1530, Luther and his associates, like Melanchton and Jonas, grudgingly allowed a political-juridical right of princes to depose an Emperor, if carried out according to the Imperial constitution, but remained steadfast in this denial of a religiously based right of resistance. By the end of the 1630s, Luther allowed for an additional ground of resistance to the Emperor based on the contention that the latter, by his submission to the papacy, had made himself an agent of the Pope. At this point, Luther's increasingly abrasive depictions of the Pope had reached the point where he was identified as a monster, an all-consuming "Beerwolf" – the Werewolf of Teutonic lore, and in effect the beast foretold in Daniel – and thus something outside of regular schemes of government or even tyranny, a principle of evil that must be resisted. Luther died shortly before the Schmalkaldic war brought his associates, like Melanchton, to formally define what became the basis for Protestant resistance theory: one or both of the twin arguments of resisting the papacy as a monstrosity, and the rights of inter-mediate magistrates. W.D.J. Cargill Thompson, *Studies in the Reformation: Luther to Hooker* (Athlone Press, 1980) pp. 5–8, 13–14, 26–27, 31–36, 37–41.

[55] On political Augustinianism versus Thomism, see in Sommerville *Royalists* pp. 13–18. In the seventeenth century, Catholic quietists in France and Quakers in England developed versions of Christianity that were to some extent similar to elements of Filmer's epistemology, mixing a metaphysical certitude, with an extreme renunciation of the business of the material world. But these approaches implied a detachment from the matters of the world that could (and did) eventually encourage a kind of passive and disinterested resistance to political authority that ran against Filmer's insistence on absolute obedience.

problematic royal decrees. Thus one can find in Sybthorpe's *Apostolike Obedience* (1627) a statement which could as easily have come from Filmer's pen, asserting that,

> if princes command anything which subjects may not performe, because it is against the laws of God, or of nature, or impossible, yet subjects are bound to undergoe the punishment without either resistance or railing and reviling; and so to yeeld a passive obedience, where they cannot exhibit an active one.

Similar, albeit more qualified, statements can be found in Maynwaring's *Religion and Alegiance* (1627), and in the same vein is the import of the 1606 church Canons proposed by Convocation to James I. Although Filmer developed a fuller and more politically sophisticated theory, the evident affinity of his premises about the duty of obedience, to those of such clerical writers, as well as his close's personal and intellectual connections with High Church circles – his wife was daughter of the Bishop of Ely, who had been a member of the 1606 Convocation, and Filmer also was very close to the important clergyman Peter Heylyn who had read *Patriarcha* in manuscript – point to possible sources for background and composition of *Patriarcha*, that seem not as yet to have been adequately looked into.[56]

Obviously, Filmer's political idea of absolute obedience stems from his epistemological claim that men have neither the faculty nor the authority, to judge the decisions of their superiors, and especially of kings. Even leading men, in title or office, whatever their wisdom, have in his view no authority at all to doubt the monarch's decisions. Thus it is the king alone that has the authority and responsibility to wield political power. Intriguingly, Filmer does not invest even the monarch with inherent superiority of judgment, but rather makes clear that his patriarch-king is himself, after all, only an erring mortal, who does not possess as a matter of course any necessary moral or intellectual superiority over others. Thus, even if the king does possess absolute political authority and some knowledge of affairs of state stemming from his practice of them, he in truth does not differ epistemologically from any other man, in his lack of an ability to truly discern God's inscrutable intentions, and as any other man he can only live in hope that his actions are sanctioned by divine will. This idea is most evident when Filmer comes to justify the possession of power as the only criterion for judging the legitimacy of a ruler:

---

[56] Robert Sybthorpe, *Apostolike Obedience* (1627) p. 13. Maynwaring proposed that a subject hazards his soul if he disobeys the command of his king, even if against national and municipal laws – as long as he is not transgressing the laws of God, Nature, Nations and the Gospel. To those faced by royal commands contrary to God's or to Natural law, he advised not to resist but rather that by "patient and meeke suffering of their *Soveraigne's* pleasure, they should become glorious *Martyrs*[.]" See Roger Maynwaring, *Religion and Alegiance* (1627); and see discussion in Christianson *Discourse* p. 115. About Filmer's clerical connections, see Sommerville "Introduction" pp. x–xv.

It skills not which way kings come by their power, whether by election, donation, succession, or by any other means; for it is still the manner of the government by supreme power that makes them properly kings, and not the means of obtaining their crowns.[57]

Filmer endeavored to show that even in the most extraordinary circumstances political power does not really stem from the choice of the subjects – because this would introduce the very liberty to create a government, which he persistently denies. He of course rejected the notion of an original state of natural freedom (or, as Filmer would put it, anarchy), but he did acknowledge that circumstances could, and did, arise in history when for some reason (like the death of a king without heirs) the community finds itself devoid of a natural ruler. In such cases, he argued, the people return to "their first matter" that, to him, is not unconnected individuals, but rather patriarchal families or groups of families under a leader, with these heads of families or groups then determining who is to be the next ruler. But, consistently with his theory, Filmer stresses that even this process is not one of election, but rather one of identification and testimony of the ruler chosen by God – the detecting of the person now enjoying the God-given fatherly right to rule all. It follows that for Filmer, at least theoretically, heredity or selection are not to be preferred over any other method of gaining power, thus making the winning of power by force as legitimate as by any other way. Since the real effecting factor is the divine will, which works in mysterious ways, we must always assume the ruler enjoys divine sanction (ironically bringing Filmer close to Locke's notion of an appeal to heaven...). Consequently, for Filmer, no effective ruler is truly illegitimate, and there really is no such thing as a usurper – the possession of power is very much its own justification.[58]

Filmer's justification for the absolute power of kings is thus a double one. On the one hand stands the moral–religious value he assigns to the individual's obedience to authority, in effect elevating it to the degree of supreme human and Christian principle; on the other hand there is the natural state of subordination to authority to which, according to him, men are born, and must continue in. To rob men of subordination and obedience denies for Filmer their nature and humanity, thus making pretty much any authority better than no authority.

But Filmer did not restrict himself to arguing for the legitimacy and necessity of men's natural subjection and obedience to their rulers. He also put forward serious arguments undermining the theories he opposed, prominent among which were those of Grotius and Hobbes. It was in this context that Filmer tackled one of the most important conceits of modern political thought (not sufficiently addressed even by current scholarship): that most political systems usually described as contract theories are in truth individual consent theories; and that as the true foundation of these theories is the consent of the individual

---

[57] Filmer *Patriarcha* chapter 3 sec. 8.   [58] Filmer *Patriarcha* chapter 1 sec. 9.

will, it ultimately trounces any contract that might oppose it. Filmer pointed explicitly to theories such as Grotius' and Hobbes' employing the idea of a social contract as the apparent basis of political society, while at the same time undermining the value and force of that very contract, by subordinating it to natural rights and to the consent of individuals. He pointed to the logical fallacy of maintaining in parallel the authority of natural rights and consent on the one hand, with the authority of the social contract on the other. In his reading, all forms of government (and property) predicated on an original natural liberty were ultimately based on consent, and thus always leaving with the individuals some residual right to resist their governors. Filmer pointed out that for thinkers like Grotius, the greater the matter at hand, the greater the possible equitable exception against the words of the law, and thus the possibility that some perceived "necessity" could legitimate resistance to the sovereign. Filmer argued (similarly to Selden), that the source of the problem was the impossibility of an individual to bind himself, for it is not enough to have a will to bind without a power to bind – from which it followed that it would be lawful for every man, when he pleased, to dissolve government. Filmer believed that such ideas led England to the dire consequences observed by all in the 1640s.[59]

Filmer thus identified the inherent instability of consent theory based on individual judgment; he convincingly exposed the incoherence of attempting to regard such theories as contractual ones, when consent remains their deciding element; and he seriously challenged the attempts of both Grotius and Hobbes to evade this conflict within their theories. Ironically it was none other than Locke, who a generation later recognized the validity of Filmer's critique, and in his own theory which combines elements from both Grotius and Hobbes, in effect conceded the theoretical point – that in consent theories men could rescind the political setting at will – while arguing only that in practice, since men usually recoil from the dangers and instability of revolutions, such rescinding will occur only seldom and under extremely harsh oppression. As a consequence, the way in which Filmer and Locke justify successful rebellions is quite similar, for in both cases it is an *a posteriori* evaluation of the event – in effect, its success is the justification. For Filmer, a successful usurpation is simply the expression of God's mysterious will, for Locke a popular rebellion is an "appeal to heaven." Both approaches, for all their promise of political stability, retain an inbuilt anarchic tendency.[60]

---

[59] Schochet *Patriarchalism* pp. 9–10; Kahn *Wayward* pp. 40–41, 94. Filmer criticized on similar lines Grotius' two main assumptions about property (that it was naturally common, and that in its current form property is a product of human will), for they amounted to a distinction between law of nature and subsequent human voluntary arrangements, thus making property as well as government dependent on the changeable will of men.

[60] See John Locke, *Second Treatise*, chapter 14, section 168; Filmer, *Observations Concerning the Originall of Government*. See also discussion in Schochet *Patriarchalism* pp. 128–129, 136–137, 252–254).

It is important to recognize that the first principle and engine of Filmer's political theory is the complete identity of the natural with the social and political. They are not similar, or analogous, but rather the very same thing: "If we compare the natural rights of a father with those of a king, we find them all one, without any difference at all but only in the latitude or extent of them." This right and power covers not only the political sphere, but also the familial, the religious and so on. The difference with other political writers identified with absolutism, such as Bodin, James I or Hobbes, is striking. Although King James sometimes used patriarchal images and terms, he explicitly described them as "similitudes," that is, illustrations or analogies; as for Bodin and Hobbes, their absolute sovereignty is a patently artificial structure, distinct from, and superimposed over, natural society, whose natural source of authority is the family. Indeed, the political ideas of James I are overall closer to those of Grotius than to those of Filmer.[61]

Filmer's theory can thus be said to be essentially a naturalistic one, something which becomes even more evident when he addresses the extent to which his theory relies on a biblical justification. Although Filmer certainly upheld the truth of the succession of patriarchal-political power from the descendants of Adam and Noah, he also made it clear that this biblical pedigree of power is not essential to his system. The point is made most unambiguously in his *Originall*, within his "Observations" on Hobbes, where he quotes from chapter 8 of the latter's *De Cive*, the section asking the reader to imagine a scenario in which men at first "as mushrooms they all on a sudden were sprung out of the earth without any obligation one to another." Filmer, while rejecting this account of human origins, makes clear that even if it were true, it would make no difference to his own patriarchal theory, for, by nature, even in such circumstances, each of these first humans would still have had absolute power over his own descendants, having been the source of their natural life.[62]

This extreme monism of Filmer's approach, unique when compared to other absolutist theories (patriarchal and not), begets the truly comprehensive and absolute character of political authority in his theory. While thinkers like Bodin,

---

[61]   Filmer *Patriarcha* chapter 1 sec. 10, and see also Schochet *Patriarchalism* pp. 31–36, 87–88 and Zuckert *Natural* pp. 34–35. L.A. Knafla claims that the ideas underpinning James I's political vision of a Europe where monarchs were absolute in their spheres, Christianity was reunified, and states bound together by the law of nations, mean that had he been a lawyer, his ideas would have made him a precursor to Grotius. See L.A. Knafla, "Britain's Solomon: King James and the Law" in D. Fischlin & M. Fortier (eds.), *Royal Subjects* (Detroit: Wayne State University Press, 2002) pp. 242–243. This however should not disguise the real differences between Grotius and James, for the latter held that there was some original political power held by heads of families from which monarchies derived, a breach with Aristotelian and Grotian thinking, and having the added benefit of denying theories (like those of his tutor George Buchanan), supposing as basis for allegiance and resistance, the terms on which a rational person would voluntarily leave a state of nature. Cromartie *Constitutionalist* pp. 154–155.

[62]   Filmer *Observations Concerning the Originall of Government*; Hobbes *De Cive* chapter 8. See also Schochet *Patriarchalism* pp. 12–13.

James I and Hobbes, for all their profession of upholding absolute sovereignty, ultimately all allowed some principle, of natural law or individual self-defense, which could countermand political authority in extreme cases, Filmer made it unconditional and unbounded. This essential unity of authority, making all power, be it natural, religious, paternal or political ultimately one, leads to some far-reaching, sometimes surprising consequences: the first is that it in effect denies any meaningful autonomous existence outside of the will of the political authority, so that religion, property, self-preservation or even morality have no legitimate existence, as independent of the ruler's will – making the reach of even Hobbes' *Leviathan* appear as political small-fry in comparison; the second consequence is that, since there is no theoretical limit to the practice or disposal of political power, it gives the ruler an unlimited right to do whatever he wishes with it – retain it or give it away, split it or keep it whole, enlarge it or destroy it, just as one would do with his own personal possession; the third consequence, is that making the "right" to political power identical with the possession of it, means there is no difference or even meaning to any distinction between right and might.[63]

The principle of possession of power as the right to it, is the great strength, as well as the greatest weakness, of Filmer's theory, but it has only seldom been subjected to sufficient scrutiny. The strength of the theory is its simplicity, in effect making might into right, even more than Hobbes' approach, which at least ties legitimacy to the ruler's performance of his duty to protect the lives of his subjects. Another significant consequence of Filmer's approach is that it is unusually egalitarian as to the identity of the possessor of supreme power since, after the legitimate Adamic line of succession was lost, there is ultimately nothing in pedigree or personal valor to make someone more or less legitimate a ruler; indeed, this means that it is far easier for Filmer's theory to allow for the rule of a female as perfectly legitimate than, say, the theories of Grotius or Hobbes (who both give the female a naturally subordinate role in the family, which would clash with one of supremacy in politics). However, this same simple principle of possession is also the main weakness of Filmer's theory. For, if only possession of power makes legitimacy, there is no substantial difference between a legitimate ruler and a usurper, so that force and conflict are to a great degree summoned in, every time there is a prospect of political instability. This is in effect a permanent invitation to strife.[64]

---

[63] On identity between patriarchal and political power see Schochet *Patriarchalism* pp. 54–55, 63–64, 146–147; on the principle of possession of political power see Cuttica *Adam* pp. 74–75. J. Daly asserts that Filmer tried to do "what Descartes and Hobbes were doing," creating a whole theory out of one clear and distinct idea, in his case "the need for a single, indivisible, arbitrary sovereign." See Daly *Robert* pp. 155–156.

[64] Schochet *Patriarchalism* pp. 152–155; Cuttica *Adam* pp. 183–184. Whereas Grotius and Hobbes clearly assume the free individuals forming political society to be males, there is nothing of the sort in Filmer since, after the disappearance of the original Adamic pedigree, every ruler possessing power must be assumed to be invested with God's will. In his "Praise of a vertuous

Two serious, self-inflicted contradictions follow directly from Filmer's theory of absolute obedience. The first arises from the tension between the naturalist scope of his theory and his Christian justification for obedience – total obedience in the physical world is predicated on the promise of spiritual, Christian reward. He attempts to claim the two are wholly compatible, but cannot really do so without ultimately disemboweling Christianity from all moral value. Though Filmer claims his approach stems from natural sources of political power, his writings assume that the ruler is at least nominally a Christian, so that even the ruler's errors and misdeeds play out within the framework and values of a Christian society. But if the views held by the ruler are in fact heretical, or if he is not a Christian at all, absolute obedience born to ensure the subject follows the truth of the Christian Gospel may become the instrument destroying that very truth. This problem was certainly not merely theoretical, for England in the century previous to Filmer had already witnessed a succession of rulers with mutually exclusive religious views, who had dragged the kingdom and the subjects into consecutive rounds of intense religious alterations and conflicts – and more were yet to come. The second contradiction within Filmer's theory emerges in periods of political instability, when power is disputed and obedience is demanded from the subject by more than one claimant. In such a case complete passivity is not a viable option, since not only action but even inaction becomes a potential for dangerous disobedience, and the individual is left in an inescapable theoretical quandary – as indeed happened to Filmer himself during England's Civil War and interregnum. In order to counter resistance theories based on claims to an original liberty of individuals, Filmer developed a theory based on an extreme *a priori* reasoned principle only. He identified this principle as the absolute obedience to power owed by nature and preached by Christian Gospel, and followed the principle so completely that his theory did not allow any possibility of experience or contingency to impinge this totality of obedience (thus following Sarpi's first mode, from reason only). But if circumstances arise, where absolute obedience is impossible, or is directly contrary to the

---

wife" (unpublished manuscript dated to the 1640s) Filmer, while upholding inborn differences between men and women, did not ascribe to these differences any moral or intellectual inferiority, implying a possibility of political equality. Accordingly, he conceded that there were occasions when women were equal or superior to men in mental or artistic merit, indeed even in the political arena – as eminently exampled by Queen Elizabeth, under whose rule England achieved such great successes, as to obviously evidence that she enjoyed Divine blessing. While many consent theorists argued or implied an inevitable "natural" political inferiority of women, Sir Robert's anti-naturalist naturalism regarded men and women as equally subject to the authority of the father and king, whose identity could be female (because his test was only possession of power), making her into the patriarch father-king. See Cuttica *Adam* pp. 365–366, 374–375. Thus, contrary to what might appear likely (and much of gender theory), an early-modern thinker like Filmer was far less prone than Grotius or Hobbes (or later Locke), indeed less even than later societies, to enclose women into exclusive gender-archetype political roles. See also Zaller *Legitimacy* p. 723 note 107.

preservation of Christianity, Filmer's theory then becomes plainly self-defeating.[65]

3.5   SELDEN

John Selden was deeply involved in the contemporary intellectual exchanges of his time, epistemological as well as moral and political. He had by 1635 carefully read and commented upon Grotius' *Jure Belli*, was an early owner of Descartes' 1637 *Discourse on the Method*, and by 1643 at the latest owned Hobbes' *De Cive* (his copy of the book is now in the Bodleian). Although there is no record of it, it is also likely that Selden would have had at least some acquaintance with Filmer and his ideas, since they frequented the same social and cultural circles, including mutual acquaintances and intellectual companions, such as the poet George Herbert (brother of Lord Edward), and Sir Roger Twysden.[66] Like his three contemporaries discussed above, Selden too was openly critical (although usually less scathingly so) of many scholastic ideas and methods. We shall encounter more of his critique of scholasticism later on, so here one example will suffice – in the preface to the 1631 edition of his *Titles of Honor*, Selden explicitly attacked the Aristotelian "Schooles" for what he regarded as the defective method by which they studied "*Morall Philosiphie, or Civill Learning*," that is, the moral and political ideas they imparted.[67]

Like many thinkers of his time, Selden's own ideas included elements from the Aristotelian tradition (of the Thomistic-scholastic and of other strands), as well as ideas that were alien and opposed to it (such as Selden's contractarianism). One important element of his thought, coming from a minoritarian Aristotelian strand, which had been rejected by the mainstream scholastic tradition, was the interpretation of the "active intellect," not as an

---

[65] That awareness of problematic theological implications for Christians of absolute non-resistance certainly did exist in this period is indicated by a passage from Richard Baxter's *A Holy Commonwealth* of 1659. The author had gradually moved during the interregnum years from a view allowing a right of political resistance in the individual, to finally denying it completely, even condemning the idea (which, in Lamont's words, he identified as "the poisoned legacy of Hooker") that all civil authority is derived originally from the people, and instead explicitly demanding absolute non-resistance to "even infidel, yea, and even atheist kings." Baxter also opposed the Filmerian and Hobbesian notions that possession of political power gives a right to government, and only allowed a right of resistance in cases in which a king, as he maintained Charles I had, made war upon his own parliament and people, thus effectively ceasing to be king (Selden expressed a somewhat similar view in his *Table-Talk*) – proving the principle by a quote from Grotius about natural law allowing for self-defense. By 1670 Baxter had repudiated even his claim about Charles I. Nevertheless his book, regarded as politically and theologically suspect, was formally condemned and burned by the Oxford Convocation in 1683. See Lamont *Puritanism* pp. 70–71.

[66] For Selden's acquaintance with Descartes' and Hobbes' works, see Tuck *Philosophy* pp. 214–215.

[67] TH (1631) in Preface not paginated.

attribute of the individual (as held by the scholastics following Aquinas) but as an outside illumination of men's mind, pointing to the limitations of the individual's reason (as developed by Averroes, Maimonides and Roger Bacon). Consequently, Selden accepted the argument that men are not able to discern the existence and content of moral principles by the same kind of evidence and certitude with which they perceive the world around them – a view in which he was farther removed from Aristotelian scholasticism, and its concept of ideas as identifiable objects, than were Grotius and thinkers in his tradition.[68]

However, Selden's following of Averroes in his idea of the "active intellect," should not lead one to assume he was necessarily in agreement with other notions of the Averroists, especially so with their notorious attitude to religion. Within Averroes' *The Incoherence of the Incoherence* (c. 1198) there is a section that has come to be known as the "speech concerning the laws," where the author claims that while philosophy can supply directions for happiness to a few intelligent people, philosophers more than anyone else emphasize the afterlife and religion, because nothing more effectively establishes and leads towards morally virtuous actions of the multitude, than the doctrine of afterlife. Such practical considerations already indicate a rather utilitarian view of religion, but elsewhere in the text Averroes goes even further, intimating that religion and religious laws are like Plato's medicinal lies, a drug administered beneficially to the common folk, for whom the stark philosophical truth would be a poison. This approach has been regarded by many (both supporters and opponents), as cover for a philosophical atheism which argues that religion is necessary for keeping the masses in place, but is not really appropriate for serious philosophical minds.[69]

---

[68] Caruso *Miglior* pp. 666–667, 674–675. Caruso argues that Selden's placing the basis for natural law as the will of God (like the early Grotius), is often described as a regression from the later Grotius' rationalism to a premodern, "religious" point of view. It is debatable if a blind faith in "reason" is that different from a "religious" point of view, but in any case Selden did not postulate the will of God as expression of a particular religious faith, but rather as the idea of a deity common to all monotheistic religions as well to ancient Unitarian-polytheists such as Plato and Cicero.

About contractarianism being alien to the Aristotelian tradition see Zuckert *Natural* pp. 49, 149 and Kahn *Wayward* pp. 8–9. Kahn notes that neither Aristotle nor Aquinas accorded any role to contract in establishing and maintaining political society – although both acknowledged the existence of contracts within political associations, their account of politics was based principally on natural sociability and virtue.

[69] Rahe *Against* pp. 65–70. An undoubtedly central role in the introduction of Averroism to Italy and further into Western Europe was played by Jewish scholars and texts, and their Iberian connections. In Italy, Averroes' "speech" and other texts were widely available from the late fifteenth century in manuscript translations, penned by the Jewish author Colonymos ben Colonymos ben Meir, and arguments similar to Averroes' could be found in Maimonides' *Guide of the Perplexed*, which at about the same time had become a much consulted text in Western Europe. More indirect avenues also originating in Jewish connections, were the Venetian scholar Fra Paolo Sarpi (who owned a copy of the *Incoherence* and probably also

Thus, besides positing a stark dichotomy between religious traditions and philosophical understanding (which Selden rejected), Averroists came also to be suspected of atheism – which at least some (but certainly not all) of them indeed were. These suspicions about figures like the philosopher, burned at the stake, Giulio Cesare Vanini (1585–1619), and the thinker he termed approvingly "prince of the atheists" Machiavelli – were popularized in England by the play *The Jew of Malta* (c.1590) by Christopher Marlowe (himself accused of atheism), in which the villainous "Machevill" exclaims the not too subtle ryme: "I count religion but a childish Toy / And hold there is no sinner but Ignorance." There is to this day a debate about the extent to which specific thinkers in the Averroist tradition actually rejected the existence of the deity, or at the least of a providential one. However as for Selden, it is quite clear from his theory of obligation, as well as many comments in other circumstances, that he not only rejected a mere instrumental role for religion, but actually held the opposite view – that a religious foundation was necessary for true morality, and that atheistic opinions were not evidence of a solid mind.[70]

Perhaps the most significant difference between Selden and the three previous thinkers discussed above, was that while they were fashioning their political theories to replace outright what they saw as an exploded old order, Selden was attempting something in the opposite direction. His goal was not to throw away, together with the wreckage of scholasticism, also traditional constitutionalism, but rather to restore and strengthen the latter and its foundations, so that the English legal and political constructions would be solid enough to withstand being swept away with a tide that was overwhelming so many other old intellectual structures. As he believed the Common law tradition worth salvaging, his intention was thus essentially conservative, although he employed some innovative methods to further it. Appreciating the new type of political arguments gaining ground, he recognized that inventive approaches would be necessary to supply legitimacy

read Maimonides), and the Paduan scholar Pietro Pomponazzi (who was apparently acquainted with the Jewish scholar and translator of Averroes, Elia del Medigo). In any event, from 1470 onwards, at the University of Padua (where Averroists abounded), there was started a great publishing project, which took about a century to complete, of printing the works of Aristotle alongside Averroes' commentaries, making the latter easily accessible by the late sixteenth century.

[70] Rahe *Against* pp. 73–75, 85–99, 167. Rahe claims that Averroes' ideas indeed had a role in shaping those of Machiavelli.

For Selden's views, see for example JN b1c8 throughout, and TT "Moral honesty": "…Morality must not be without Religion, for if so, it may change, as I see convenience. Religion must govern it." On this front Locke followed Selden's view: In his *Letter Concerning Toleration*, Locke broke with Hobbes and Grotius, who held obligation to be grounded in right reason and self-interest only. Locke argued instead that atheists should not be regarded as citizens, since an atheist could neither recognize nor accept his divinely ordained moral obligations. See Wootton "Introduction" pp. 41–42; Zuckert *Natural* pp. 188–191, 198, 208–209, 219.

to the old English ways, and set out to develop a method by which he could apply to natural law the same principles with which he addressed English law, making both part of a single intellectual whole. He therefore outlined a theory of law and politics that would address the epistemological challenge as well as supply a coherent justification for regarding customary law as a legal system that was moral, valuable and indeed preferable to the newly fashioned alternatives.[71]

Although one can find occasional discussions of the issues at hand, in works like his *Mare Clausum* (1635) and *Synedriis* (1650–55) as well as the posthumous *Table-Talk* (1689), by far Selden's most extensive and systematic treatment of the connection between the epistemological outlook and the foundations of government and law is to be found in his *Jure Naturali* (1640), and particularly in what has been described as the most "philosophical" of his writings, the first book of the *Jure Naturali*. The (unusually for him) philosophical approach that he adopted in this book, allowed Selden to expound his own theory of natural law while displaying what G.J. Toomer has termed an "astoundingly wide acquaintance" with philosophers, theologians and jurisprudents, from ancient, medieval and modern times, as well as with Jewish ideas, never before addressed to such extent and intensity in Western political thought.[72]

Before proceeding to discuss Selden's ideas at length, it is important to note the marked disinterest that he showed, throughout his intellectual as well as political activity, towards the idea of origins and beginnings of political societies as defining authority within it. Unlike most of his contemporaries, including Grotius, Filmer and Hobbes, who either implicitly or explicitly treated the pre-political origins of political society as determining its defining features (with a potential to resurface in periods of great political crisis), Selden regarded pre-political origins as, at best, starting points in long processes combining change and continuity. His writings do not deal significantly with a pre-political state of nature, either bypassing the issue altogether or at most touching upon it with a noncommittal supposition. A good example of this approach is provided by his comments on the origins of political society in the two editions of his *Titles of Honor*. In the first edition (1614), Chapter I *"The beginning of a* Monarchie*"* gives a brief description of the supposed popular beginning of political societies (which borrows from Aristotle's *Politics*, while also contesting some of its elements), the content of which was

---

[71] Examples of his attacks on the scholastics are in TT "Reason." Tuck asserts that in his rejection of simple innate principles of morality accessible by reason, Selden in many ways only "applied to the question of natural law the principles he had developed to deal with" English law. See Tuck *Philosophy* p. 215.

[72] Toomer proposes that the very origin of the *Jure Naturali* was Selden's wish to address the ideas broached by Grotius. Toomer correctly points out that Selden undoubtedly himself believed the theory of natural law that he described in *Jure Naturali*, for he later reaffirmed it more than once in the *Table-Talk*. See Toomer *Scholarship* pp. 492–493, 506, 825.

succinctly described as, "*Out of Nature and a Democracie, a* Monarchie *derived*": men's "inbred sociablenesse" drove them to congregate in some society larger than families (like Grotius would assume in his *Jure Belli*, at this stage still 11 years in the future), and thus government emerged, popular rather than monarchic in its origins. In the second edition (1631), the account had changed completely, with the contents of the second and third sections of Chapter I, described by Selden as "*The twofold* Originall, *of the Supreme Titles of* King *and* Emperor" and "*Of the first* Kings," now substituting the earlier account of the origins of political societies, with a matter-of-fact description of different kinds of monarchies (conquest, elective and hereditary), without any explicit discussion of the beginning of states or of the original of regimes – but now implying that government began with monarchies (like Hobbes and Filmer assumed). The change between the two editions has sometimes been ascribed to significant changes in Selden's ideas or to his delicate political circumstances in the early 1630s, but without deciding here on the merits of such suppositions, the more significant inference from the change is surely that Selden did not attach that much significance to the origins of societies. This attitude is even more evident in his comment in the dedication to Heyward preceding the work: "*States themselves are from Nature, and the Supreme and Subordinate Powers and Honors in them, from the example of it*[.]" He thus indicated that really there is no natural pre-political condition, for if states are natural, then a pre-political condition is by definition unnatural as well as unimportant in determining the nature of political society. Therefore, in Selden's scheme of things, either account of the origins of political regimes, as democratic or monarchic, was of little consequence, for in his view the point of origin of a political society mattered in the long run far less than its many subsequent political agreements. Similarly, in the *Mare Clausum* (1635), the origin of political society is connected to the division of the earth between the children of Noah, and their settling "themselves as private Lords" in their several territories, while at the same time a freedom of men to create compacts perpetuating those distributions to posterity, is postulated.[73]

Now proceeding to directly address the epistemological foundations of Selden's political theory, as he articulated them in the *Jure Naturali*, we find that he starts by directing his efforts against the idea that human action and society can be based primarily on a principle of pure reasoning. In the first book of his *Jure Naturali* Selden addressed reason-based theory both explicitly and implicitly, and the whole seventh chapter of the book especially, reads like an intentional rebuttal of the foundations for rationalist ideas in general, and for Grotian ones in particular. The starting point for Selden's argument is that

---

[73] TH (1614 and 1631) part 1 ch. 1; *Mare Clausum* b1c4 – Henceforth MC. See also discussion in Sommerville *Royalists* pp. 61–62, and Toomer *Scholarship* p. 130, where Toomer also notes that in the 1614 account, Selden explicitly referred to Machiavelli.

individual reason is neither sufficient for ascertaining what natural law consists of, nor able to obligate the individual to follow that law, even if he could have ascertained it. Selden's contention is that "uncertainty and inconsistency appear in the unrestricted use of pure and simple reason" (Quod ad Incertum atque Inconstantiam, qua laboravit semper liber nudae Rationis ille in hisce usus, spectat), and thus such pure and simple reason cannot serve as the foundation for men's knowledge and understanding of the world. But he goes even further, not sufficing with rejecting pure reason as the foundational epistemic principle, he warns against even circumscribed attempts to derive certainty from pure reason, since the process of arriving at accepted notions by it is "so intrinsically inconsistent and dissimilar among men that it would be better for nothing to be derived from it" (non modo non adeo Certum esse, aut sibi Constantem ac similem apud homines ejusdem in hisce discernendis usum, ut, quid ex eo melius, aut optatius sit, semper satis liqueat). He adds that this basic "uncertainty" in all things arrived at by pure reason, is evident not only among common men in general, but also (and perhaps even more so) among the most learned philosophers, who are ever divided into a plethora of completely opposing disciplines, disagreeing even about the definition of such an essential and basic term as "right reason."[74]

After making short shrift of "pure and simple reason" as the foundation of knowledge, Selden proceeded to argue that regardless of the quality and nature of the knowledge that can be achieved by pure reason, it most certainly cannot serve as the source of obligation. He pointed out that since the workings of reason differ between men, this inevitably creates "a dissimilarity in the cause of obligation," which is a recipe for trouble. Moreover, Selden remarked that, by definition, law is the command of "an authority superior to the one who is commanded. That is what law is" – whereas "pure and simple reason can persuade and prove, but it does not command." He highlighted that reason's inability to obligate was not merely a problem for individuals in their moral

---

[74] JN b1c7. With this view Selden was positioning himself in contrast to the Aristotelian tradition, and in agreement with thinkers like William of Ockham, for whom reason is unable to reveal the real essences of things, so that law is only what is commanded. See Harrison *Masterpiece* pp. 31–32.

  Selden's suspicion about the limitations of men's reason was certainly not new in his thought, for as early as his NL of 1616 he mentioned "the weakness of man's reason" in discerning natural law. See discussion in Burgess *Politics* pp. 38–40. Hobbes' argument against basing human knowledge of laws or political obligation, solely on reason, parallels Selden's on this point: "...But no one mans Reason, nor the Reason of any one number of men, makes the certaintie [sic] ... [a]nd therefore, as when there is a controversy in an account, the parties must by their own accord, set up for the right Reason, the Reason of some Arbitrator, or Judge, to whose sentence they will both stand, or their controversie must either come to blowes, or be undecided, for want of a right Reason constituted by Nature; so is it also in all debates of what kind soever..." Hobbes *Leviathan* p1c5. Filmer too, as seen above, criticized the ideas that pure reason can produce clear rules or obligation for individuals. See Schochet *Patriarchalism* pp. 9–10; Kahn *Wayward* pp. 40–41, 94.

actions; it also posed an insoluble predicament in the political sphere, since placing it at the basis of political obligation would result in a situation where nothing really stands in the way of individuals or groups withdrawing from the civil body, when they do not like its commands. Simply put, the problem with obligation by one's own reason is that it "is not possible for a person to command or prohibit itself."[75]

In order to accentuate the futility of a merely voluntary agreements as basis for obligation, Selden, in a long paragraph that is worth to bring in full, addressed an idea that has since become famous as the "state of nature" – an origin for society in an association of free individuals living in a natural pre-social condition:

> In order that this may be more clearly understood, let us imagine, with some of the ancients, that there was once a time when people roamed the earth like animals, and ate the same food as wild beasts. They did not conduce themselves by their intellectual powers, but relied for the most part upon their physical strength. And let us imagine that the careful use of reason, which was simple and recognized no superior authority, eventually led them to abandon, one by one, the freedom of this bestial existence; and without giving up their equality, they simultaneously agreed to restrain their lives according to the provisions of a legal arrangement called "natural." But what, I ask, does this process, simply understood as in this case, have to do with either the causes or the effects (defined according to the criteria given in the fourth chapter) of a natural obligation or a binding duty, or of a permission? Or with the natural distinction between permitted and illegal?

Selden thus asserted that, even allowing for the hypothesis that there had been some kind of pre-social natural state, and even supposing that it had produced some kind of agreement between individuals as the origin of law and society, all this would still not supply a principle of obligation. The very freedom of association that enabled men to create society, also entailed for them "the same freedom of renunciation." Clearly, even if "at one time every one wanted to obligate themselves for whatever reason, anyone knows that they can properly release themselves" – unless there is some higher authority to maintain them obligated.[76]

---

[75] JN b1c7. That Grotius himself was aware of this problem is made abundantly clear by the significant efforts he devoted in *Jure Belli* b1c3–4 to attempts at circumscribing those cases in which men could, by use of their right reason, resort to their right of resistance and rise against their rulers. But these very attempts prove that his system could not escape individual right reason remaining as the final judge for one's submission or resistance. Tuck describes Grotius' problem, rising from his ultimate reliance on individual right reason, as creating an implausibility of obligation, because stressing "individuality in the area of right, but communality in the area of obligation." See Tuck *Natural* p. 82.

[76] JN b1c7: "Scilicet ut hoc rectius intelfigatur, fingamus cum veteribus aliquot, tempus quoddam fuisse, cum in agris homines passim bestiarum more vagabantur, & sibi victu ferino vitam propagabant nec ratione animi quidquam, sed pleraque viribus corporis administrabant. Atque ferinam hanc vivendi libertarem diligentiori Rationis tandem usu, eoque simplici nec

A little further on, in the text, Selden presents what he regards as the fatal conceit of theories attempting to erect political society upon the "inconsistent reasoning of individuals," in a long passage, which effectively rejects very idea of a reasoned individual consent, serving as basis for any kind of meaningful "social contract":

But let us suppose that they – the entire human people – have in fact been merged into a civil association, and that they have arrived at some arrangement not only for living together but for distributing power, so that now they had rulers in command of subjects, and penalties had been prescribed for transgressors over and above the laws they had created for themselves on the basis of simple reason. It is obvious that we need the addition of some superior authority, and a law superior to any individual's ability to reason. This would preserve the association into which people have entered; make them obey their leaders; guarantee that they abide by their agreements; and finally, tie them all together with a bond more powerful than their individual wills and their weak attempts at reason could achieve. Otherwise, how could there be a natural obligation, that is, one that by its very essence cannot be dissolved by the will or the inconsistent reasoning of individuals, which would keep each of them from abandoning, just as he pleases, agreements, authority, pacts, and prescribed punishments; everything, in essence, to which they have all consented?[77]

Although Selden was treating here mainly pure reason as it pertains to knowledge of natural law and to obligation, he obviously held the same principle, skeptical of *a priori* unaided reasoning, as relevant to all fields of human knowledge. For example, he often criticized what he evidently regarded as the counterpart to the "pure reason" method, in the religious sphere – the claims to religious understanding and knowledge based on individual "spirit" only, which would justify the individual "rashly trusting his unaided eyesight" unassisted by traditions or learning.[78]

superioris autoritatem omnino respiciente sigillatim ductos fingatur eos exuisse, ac unanimes, nectamen ab aequalitate recedentes, vitae secundum Juris qualiacunque, Naturalis nomine, capita formulae in posterum retinendae nomina dedisse. At quid cedo hoc simpliciter ita sumtum ad Naturalis Obligationis seu Officii debitionis non violandae, atque Permissionis sive Causam sive Effectum proprie, juxta capite quarto ostensa, dictum? Aut ad naturalem Liciti atque Illiciti determinationem?"

[77] JN b1c7: "At vero universos illos etiam, id est, totam gentem Humanam in civile corpus fingatur coaluisse, ac de aliqua non solum vivendi, sed etiam imperii formula consensisse, adeo ut jam inter eos, Principes subditis praeessent, paenae insuper jus, quod sic ex nuda natum eis est ratione, violantibus praescriberetur. Certe nisi superior etiam & heic accedat autoritas atque jus, ratione qualicunque singulorum superius, quo fides sic inita servanda, quo Principibus parendum, quo pactis standum, quodemum universi simul, ut vinculo singulorum arbitrio, ac vaga ratione pollentiori, constringantur; qui fieri potest, ut Naturalis aliqua, aut quae a singulis, pro libitu & variante ratione, naturaliter solvi nequeat, Obligatio refragetur, quo minus a fide, imperio, pactis, paenarum praescriptione omnibus tandem in quae sic consenserint, libere quisque & pro arbitrio recedere queat?"

[78] An excellent example is supplied in a letter of June 1646 which Selden wrote to his friend Francis Tayler (1590–1656, a Hebraist scholar and clergyman close to Laud, who translated and published a number of important Jewish texts, including Pirkei Avot, and the Jerusalem

Indeed, Selden's disparagement of unassisted human capacities was part of his wider pessimism about qualities of men in general, not only in the intellectual sphere but in the sentimental, spiritual and moral ones as well. One can find this suspicion towards optimistic assessments of human proclivities repeated in his works through the years, but probably the most direct and concise one is that which he articulated in the dedication to his good friend Heyward, in the first edition of *Titles of Honor* (1614):

And to speake here freely, the speciall worth of your Qualitie and of some more (*luti melioris*) compar'd with that world of Natures infinitely varied by basenesse of Spirit, Daring ignorance, Bewitcht sight, worst of inclination, expressions of scarce more that's not Bestiall then what Clothes and Coffers can, and the like have made me, I confesse, doubt in the Theorie of Nature, whether all known by the name of MAN as the lowest *Species* bee of one *Forme*. So Generous, so Ingenuous, so proportion'd to good, such Fosterers of Vertue, so Industrious, of such Mould are the *Few*: so Inhuman, so Blind, so Dissembling, so Vain, so iustly Nothing, but what's Ill disposition, are the *Most*.[79]

So much for Selden's assessment of the general proclivities of most men. As for his approach to the claims about human reason (and its capability to impose obligation), even among the learned, that is summed up in a terse

Targum), urging him to print his manuscript translation of the Jerusalem Targum of the Pentateuch. Selden justified his proposal in a remarkable passage, where he argued about the said text: "It contains some not inconsiderable records and traces of oriental (or Talmudic) doctrine. Without that [doctrine] the triumphs celebrated by the pretentious and otherwise learned ignorance of many are either ridiculous or dangerous [to us] in the West: these, through utter lack of knowledge of the origins and primal sources of things and practices which are found in the Bible, boldly manufacture dreams for themselves, but dreams which are to their own advantage among men, and cunningly impose these as burdens on others. That is how the Papists often behave; so too do others, who, if anyone opposes them, immediately put forward, the 'new lights' which have as it were risen in the heavens for them. It is true that we believe those 'Starry Messengers' [(alluding to Galileo's *Siderus Nuncius*)] who, having become as keen-sighted as Lynceus by means of the telescopic glass, have taught us about new stars: we are grateful to them and make much of them, as indeed they richly deserve. Not so, if someone, rashly trusting his unaided eyesight, however decayed, proclaims that he perceives I know not how many moons or suns in the heavens, or lions or dragons in the clouds. Once the use of the telescope has been transmitted [to us], we ourselves perceive the very same thing as those Messengers, although otherwise we would be ignorant of it. The same applies to the use of oriental doctrine, whence the whole of Christianity arose: without it, we are often deceived in our judgments of sacred matters, and deceive [others] by guesswork and [by] propagating the monstrous offspring of whatever ingenuity [we possess]." Quoted in Toomer *Scholarship* pp. 845–846.

[79] TH (1614) from the dedication to Edward Heyward, not paginated. See the similar approach from many years later in TT "Difference of Men" sec. 1: "The Difference of Men is very great, you would scarce think them to be of the same Species, and yet it consists more in the Affection than in the Intellect. For as in the Strength of Body, two Men shall be of an equal Strength, yet one shall appear stronger than the other, because he exercises, and puts out his Strength, the other will not stir nor strain himself. So 'tis in the Strength of the Brain, the one endeavours, and strains, and labours, and studies, the other sits still, and is idle, and takes no pains, and therefore he appears so much the inferiour."

comment of his, directed especially against the scholastic employment of the term "right reason," that was recorded in the *Table-Talk*:

> When the School-Men talk of *Recta Ratio* in Morals, either they understand Reason as it is govern'd by a Command from above; or else they say no more than a Woman, when she says a thing is so, because it is so; that is, her Reason perswades her 'tis so. The other Acception has Sense in it. As take a Law of the Land, I must not depopulate, my Reason tells me so. Why? Because if I do, I incur the detriment.[80]

Having demolished to his satisfaction the claims for knowledge and obligation from individual pure reason, which according to him would make men in relation to each other, parallel lines "with nothing at the middle to join them," Selden then proceeded in the *Jure Naturali* to propose an alternative framework of knowledge and obligation. Since his epistemological assumption is that individual reason is insufficient as a tool for identifying and understanding natural law, he has either to give up such knowledge altogether or to propose an alternative path to it. In fact, he presented not one but two such possible paths, at least theoretically: the first path is tradition; the other is the already mentioned concept of the "active intellect" (*intellectus agens*), the more complex of the two, at which we shall look first: we have seen that the concept, originating in Aristotle, was employed by Selden in the version of it that had been strongly rejected by most Aristotelians, both scholastics and not, and embraced only by a dissenting minority which included Averroes, Maimonides and Roger Bacon.[81]

According to this minoritarian interpretation embraced by Selden, the "active intellect" is an intellectual agency existing <u>outside</u> of individuals. In Selden's words, "it is not at all a function or component of the human soul,

---

[80] TT "Reason." It appears that on the limitations of unassisted reason Selden was following Maimonides, see discussion in Barbour *Measures* pp. 210–220.

[81] JN b1c7. That this was understood by contemporaries to be Selden's position, is best illustrated by Nathaniel Culverwel's (1618–1651) posthumously published *An Elegant and Learned Discourse of the Light of Nature* (1652) See discussion in J. Rosenblatt, *Renaissance England's Chief Rabbi: John Selden* (Oxford University Press, 2006) pp. 203–204. See also the excellent discussion of Selden's ideas on human intellectual capabilities, and their impact on later writers in Parkin *Science* pp. 60–66.

It appears Selden regarded Roger Bacon as something of an intellectual precursor, and interestingly they also shared a similar affinity for philology and for the Hebrew language – Bacon had philological proclivities, was quite suspicious of the works of translators and copyists, and displayed great veneration for the Hebrew language, encouraging the learning of it and even attempting to write a Hebrew grammar. Selden was involved in unsuccessful attempts to publish a complete edition of Bacon's works, and he even wrote a "Life of Bacon," which unfortunately has not survived. See G.L. Jones, *The Discovery of Hebrew in Tudor England* (Manchester University Press, 1983) pp. 11–12; S. A. Hirsch, "Early English Hebraists. Roger Bacon and His Predecessors" in *The Jewish Quarterly Review* 12/1 (October 1899), pp. 34–88, and Yael Raizman-Kedar "The Intellect Naturalized: Roger Bacon on the Existence of Corporeal Species within the Intellect" in *Early Science and Medicine* 14/1 (2009) pp. 131–157. See also discussion of Selden's view of the *intellectus agens* in Barbour *Measures* pp. 243–244.

any more than the sun itself is of the eyes" – it is an outside revelation, or at least inspiration, leading to truth. Thus some inspired men have gained access to this illumination in certain circumstances, and some may still, but it is not a constant human faculty present in all. It is impossible to enter here into the full theoretical ramifications of this concept; however, for our purposes it suffices to point out that, since for regular human beings this "active intellect" is at most an uneven and unpredictable ability, it cannot be relied upon to direct the affairs of individuals and societies in a regular way. We may hope for it to appear in some exceptionally gifted persons, and when it does we should heed it, and even record it so that we and others may usufruct of it in the future; but there is absolutely no certainly as to when and how it might appear. The result of the unpredictability of the "active intellect" is that, in the regular course of things, we have a free and regular access only to records of past manifestations of "active intellect," which for Selden amount to the records of actions and ideas of inspired men. Such inspired men were found prominently among the Jewish people, but certainly not solely, as the Hebrews themselves believed "some members of the other nations were given illumination; for they mention that in those days a number of [gentile] prophets served" – although since biblical times that illumination became more rare, so that "it rarely shined thereafter on others besides themselves." Thus, although Selden accepts that some extraordinary men could and did attain without the aid of tradition, some superior intellectual or spiritual understanding, they are exceptions to the rule – just as some men have the ability to draw on their own an exact circle, while most need a compass. Tradition is for him that compass which is necessary for most people, the means by which to reach those truths leading to a better intellectual and spiritual life.[82]

To sum up, the rarity and unforeseeable character of the "active intellect" means that the records of its past manifestations are to be studied, together with the other "uninspired" events and records of human activities, thus becoming one strand, however important, within a wider tradition. It is therefore only through tradition that men can, with any measure of certainty, apprehend the divine light, by their study of historical records, of divinely inspired words and actions, as well as of providential events in history – which he understood as existing not only in the records of biblical revelation, but also through the regular records of the matters of men. In the absence of direct revelation, tradition as accumulated human knowledge, is left as the only effective method by which men can garner truth about fundamental matters, in any regular and consistent way: either through collected records of men's regular past trials and failures, or through the recorded instances of those more

[82] JN b1c9: "Hisce etiam accessisse ex aliis gentibus alios. Nam memorant prophetas aliquot seculo in illo docuisse ... Nimirum raro affulsisse eam postea aliis ptraeter seipsos volunt." See also discussion in Caruso *Miglior* pp. 789–790. Caruso points out that, for Selden, tradition also defines and fosters the separate identities of human groups.

irregular special cases when a higher truth illuminated the path of mankind through direct revelation or more indirectly by way of the "active intellect."[83]

Selden's most sustained and wide-ranging discussion of this epistemic issue is in JN b1c1, where he gathers many different examples and authorities to justify his position, repeatedly using the metaphor of light illuminating the human eye – which he also employed to illustrate the idea of the "active intellect" – to address the function of accumulated knowledge and traditions upon the human understanding. The point is obviously contrasting the notion of a rational self-sufficient knowledge and understanding, with one that is external and acquired. He argued that the "ancients" and even "Aristotle, in his day" (implying modern Aristotelian scholastics did not):

> [B]elieved very strongly in examining, collecting, paying attention to, evaluating, and passing on to posterity other people's ideas (and the arguments which supported them), not only when these resembled their own but even when they were quite different; which is why the more intelligent among our modern scholars will frequently do the same. In this way they could decide which parts of the doctrine they meant to espouse should be adopted, which parts retained, and which rejected; and they could choose ideas for which they could easily and securely provide proof.[84]

He added that the same principle was also valid "in the physical sciences, where we must explore the nature of things that are by turns different and opposite, by considering not only that which is different but that which is opposite[.]" Selden regarded this method as the province of men from many periods and disciplines, but, he claimed, best appreciated by those ancient scholars called "eclectic":

---

[83] The crucial role of the "active intellect" is for Selden in the distinction between the capability of every man to *understand* the principles of natural law, and the *acquiring* of such knowledge. Selden holds that the capability of understanding exists in all men, but that actually acquiring it requires certain circumstances. He connects these circumstances to the concept of the divinely inspired "active intellect" as posited by Averroes. According to this concept, men's eyes can see the truth only when darkness is illuminated by divine light (and the metaphor of the eye that is capable of vision, but sees only when a candle is lighted, is explicitly used by proponents of this theory). To illustrate this point Selden uses the analogy of the discipline of geometry: men know it through learning the principles and explanation of this discipline as brought in Euclides; while if individuals had needed to acquire this knowledge only through their own devices, it is quite probable that more or less no one would be able to do this. This theory also supplies Selden with an answer to the problem of the knowledge of natural law among societies and peoples that have no records of biblical revelation – indeed, he regards the records of activity by exemplary, semi-mythical figures, outside the Judeo-Christian tradition (like the Greek Nymphs or the Roman King Numa) as examples of the action of divine providence among all men. Caruso *Miglior* pp. 718–725.

[84] JN b1c1: "non solum congeneres consimilesque sed & perquam dispares aliorum qualescunque sententias rationesque inservientes impensissime voluisse veteres illos (quos etiam & recentiores, qui simul & cordatiores sunt, non raro imitantur) explorari, congeri, animadverti, perpendi, ad posteros transmitti. Ut feilicet ita quid ipsis scholaeque a se propagandae statuendum, retinendum, rejiciendum foret, dignosceretur & quod seligerent, argumentis fulciretur tum facilius tum securius."

Those excellent scholars were quite correct to realize that the truth, which is often hidden or obscured, is perceived by the human intellect in more or less the same way as the eye tends to perceive objects that are far away or poorly lit, just as our line of sight fails us or is deceived when we see a thing only once, or see it more than once but only vaguely. Though we may try to determine the color, shape, distance, size, location and movement of such an object, when our vision is distorted it is clearly hopeless to depend upon it.[85]

Thus, only by looking at things "from different angles and with careful repetition, as well as frequent changes of position" and while we "compare our observations with other people's" can we reach some kind of true understanding of an object and of an idea. Selden goes on to bring an example from his own life, remarking that in fact he has only recently learned, thanks to the observations of others (referring to Galileo) who have pierced the sun's "depth's with the aid of telescopes" that the sun "has its own cloudy spots which we can see, and which are larger than all of Africa and Asia" – openly admitting that "[u]ntil then I had firmly believed, in accord with a very ancient opinion, that this region of the sun was filthy, and its light spotted." This leads him to conclude that "the serious scholar should not limit himself to ideas that are true, or close to the truth, or coincidentally true; but should embrace even the entirely false ideas of other scholars who have conscientiously tried to make sense of their subjects, however unfortunate the results." For even errors and deceptions, he asserts, can, if treated judiciously, help to lay a "path to the citadel of truth." Therefore, Selden proposes that,

those whom we summon from various ages, countries and disciplines to ask their advice, supply us with more than a few changes in vantage point, which can affect more than anything else the eye's ability to discern color, distance, shape, and size – and with different positions for our (so to speak) intellectual eyes.[86]

---

[85] JN b1c1: "Atque ut in physicis, non solum ex Diverso sed ex Contrario, in Diversi invicem & Contrarii natura exploranda ... Nimirum probe norunt eximii isti indagatores Veritatem saepius sive in abdito sive in obscuro latentem, non aliter ferme ab Intellectu humano capi quam ab Oculo solent Corpora sive longius dissita, sive in luce satis temperata neutiquam posita, aliterve sive primum ac unicum sive indiligenter nimis utcunque iteratum aciei intuitum aut fugentia aut fallentia. De horum alicujus Colore, Figura, distantia, Magnitudine, Loco, Motu, quaeratur. Ubi oculi sunt depravati, res ipsis solis plane in desperato est."

[86] JN b1c1: "At vero ex diligentiori saepiusque tum variato tum accuratius iterato intuitu, crebra item stationum oculique positurae mutatione, comparatisque invicem, quae stationum variatio-nem suppleant, aliorum observationibus (citra quas viri alioquin visu acerrimi ut heic nimium caecutiant necesse est) aut recte tandem de objecto, circa quod tot eveniunt hallucinationes, statuitur, aut undenam res porro fuerit decernenda constat, aut eam non omnino decernendam nec fatis liquere demum reperitur. Quin ne suis quidem Solem ipsum maculis nebulosis, qua nobis visitur, eisque totam Africam ac Asiam ipsam magnitudine superantibus, carere, nuper ex aliorum, qui penitius eum telescopii beneficio introspexere, observatione adjuti didicimus qui defaecatissimam fuisse illam atque omnino immaculatissimam lucis regionem cum vetustate tam diu securi credideramus. Stellas item circa Jovem quatuor ferri quae a rerum conditu ad nostra usque tempora, nunquam, quantum scimus, conspectae sunt aut creditae; ut id genus caetera tam veteris quam nostri seculi exempla tum in Astronomia tum aliis in Artibus ac Scientiis illustria,

Selden clearly recognizes the serious limitations of even the seemingly most reliable traditions. He warns that, even if sometimes "customs and institutions appear to have been received without distortion or interruption even though they are far removed from their origins," in truth "anyone who has carefully consulted the people closest to these origins," understands that actually "such customs and institutions have been skewed a great deal in one direction or another" by the various historical periods, governments, national traits and dispositions which they have encountered. Thus:

> Not only do they not represent a straight line – they often take on an entirely different colour, and a character the opposite of that which they originally had. It is the same as when the sun's rays are refracted as they pass at an angle through a different kind of medium, or colored by passing through a tinted one.[87]

In sum, Selden remarks, there is no doubt that a very many errors originating in the distant past were long willingly accepted as true by entire communities of men, and "adopted without protest, and loaded onto the shoulders of posterity like so much baggage." Nevertheless, for all the aid that can be summoned by the laudable achievements of the moderns, especially in the sciences, it was still up to transmitted knowledge and traditions to supply the best lights by which to illuminate the path of the human intellect. For even the best minds and periods can achieve very little on their own, so that the Egyptian priest was correct when he said to Solon that even "*the Greeks were forever children*" in the face of the great and ancient Eastern wisdom. Therefore, he found the biblical pronouncement "Stand above the roads, and see, and inquire which of the ancient paths is the right one and walk therein, and you shall find rest for your souls" (Jeremiah 6:16), as the best articulation of the correct method to approach tradition, which for Selden means: "All roads must be carefully

---

nec quidem pauca ea, taceamus. Neque tantummodo Verae aut Veris sive prope sive quasi accedentes verum etiam & Falsae adeoque Omnimodae observationes Aliorum qui non indiligenter, utcunque infeliciter, rem assequi tentarunt, rite heic disquirenti adhihendae. Nam ut ex Umbraru ratione de corporis tam Lucidi quam Opaci & figura & magnitudine dijudicatur, ita fere etiam ex Erroribus deceptionibusqe cum judicio animadversis, tutior multo ad Veritatis arcem via saepe sternitur." And "Horum alii rem aliis, sive velut ob distantiam seu medii incommodum, minime perspectam, commodius positi detegunt. Stationem item quasi mutationes (quae in coloribus, distantiis, figuris, magnitudinibus discernendis oculo adeo necessariae sunt, ut fere nihil supra) seu varias oculi, sic dicere liceat, intellectivi posituras, haud parum supplent illi qui aevo, patria, studiis diversi in consilium accersuntur."

[87] JN b1c2: "Quin ubi mores ac instituta aliquot tum continua tum recta, sed ab ipsa origine remotissima, velut linea seu radio, quasi is nullibi, a rigore deflexus distortusve fuisset, recipi (ut saepe nimis) videntur; ea sane, diligentius consultis iis, qui origini proximiores sunt, sive hac sive illac ob diversitatem aliquam medi, id est, secolorum, rerumpublicarum, geniorum, ingeniorumque varietatem, in quam tandem inciderunt, multum inflecti, nec recta protendi, imo & dissimilem omnino colorem statumque plane nonnunquam ei, qui originarius erat, contrarium nancisci ac induere, nemo non deprehendet agnoscetque. Non aliter ac ubi radii etiam solares per medium diversum oblique transeuntes franguntur, aut tinguntur per coloratum." See also JN b1c1.

examined; we must ask about the ancient paths; and only what is truly the best may be chosen."[88]

This crucial role performed by tradition in Selden's epistemology was reiterated by him, in some form or other, throughout his works. It appears repeatedly in the *Table-Talk*, where one can find many of his remarks touching pithily, and often amusingly, on epistemological issues. One such example is when he warns from enquiring after the "reason of a thing" before one is sure what the thing itself is, by recounting an entertaining episode:

'Twas an excellent Question of my Lady *Cotten*, when Sir *Robert Cotten* was magnifying of a Shooe, which was *Moses*'s or *Noah*'s, and wondring at the strange Shape and Fashion of it: *But Mr.* Cotten, says she, *are you sure it is a Shooe.*[89]

Elsewhere in the *Table-Talk*, one can find a more expanded consideration on the issue of knowledge and meaning (again employing Selden's recurring metaphor of sight):

'Tis a great Question how we know Scripture to be Scripture, whether by the Church, or by Man's private Spirit. Let me ask you how I know any thing? how I know this Carpet to be green? First, because somebody told me it was green; that you call the Church in your Way. Then after I have been told it is green, when I see that Colour again, I know it to be green; my own eyes tell me it is green; that you call the private spirit.

For all the difficulties involved in discerning old errors from truths, Selden reiterated countless times, that tradition is indispensable for connecting between words and things, to establish meaningful knowledge.[90]

In other words, for Selden that part of past human experience upon which present men can most of all draw on for guidance, is neither simply the authority of some past ideas or practices in themselves, nor is it in some timeless individual examples. Rather, he regards such experience as primarily tradition-based knowledge, such as living customs and traditions, which are in continuous use and therefore respond to challenges of changing circumstances and times. The interaction between past traditions and current circumstances, creates the tradition-based knowledge he termed in the *Duello* as historical "traditions of use."[91]

Selden's view obviously did not simply amount to the adoption of a nominalist position, by which received knowledge would be absolute and

---

[88] JN b1c1. The very same idea also appears in TT "Truth": "The way to find out the Truth is by others mistakings: For if I was to go to such a place, and one had gone before me on the Right-hand, and he was out; another had gone on the Left-hand, and he was out; this would direct me to keep the middle way, that peradventure would bring me to the place I desir'd to go."

[89] TT "Reason."

[90] TT "Bible, Scripture," see also "Power, State" and "Tradition." In the same vein in "Prayer": "'Tis not the Original Commonprayer-book; why: shew me an original Bible, or an original *Magna Charta*" and section on "Humane invention" ending with "...I am sure the newer the Invention the worse, old Inventions are best."

[91] See discussion in Ferguson *Clio* p. 118.

arbitrary. For this would mean regarding all received traditions as self-justifying, and denying value to any epistemological or moral principle found outside of it – in other words, a position of complete relativism. Nor would he go to the opposite extreme, and deny value to all reality or knowledge originating outside of the individual, such as is suggested by Hobbes' words in his *Elements*: "there is nothing without us really which we call an image or colour." Clearly <u>neither</u> of these was Selden's position, since he maintained the true value of traditions as basis for individual understanding, while at the same time also repeatedly insisting that one should always look out with his own faculties, for errors which had crept into received traditions. He was adamant that not only was there actually such a thing as the "citadel of truth," but also that some kind of natural or universal moral law did exist and that men could be expected to discern it – indeed, this was the whole point of his *Jure Naturali*. His remark quoted above suggests in what manner, by using a combination of received knowledge and their own faculties, in a sense pitting each against the other, men could gradually discern the truth: as, after having been told the carpet is green, he adds – "when I see that Colour again, I know it to be green; my own eyes tell me it is green." That is, to be true, the received meaning of the color "green" has to be consistent with what his "own eyes" tell him – a combination of past traditions and present experience enables one to understand the world surrounding him and advance some more towards the truth. Selden presents an epistemology in which men have to constantly keep looking at the relationship between words and meanings, between traditions and experiences of the world around them, to see what is borne out, and what does not hold up to scrutiny.[92]

Significantly, among the meanings of the word color (usually appearing as "colour") in Selden's time, was one employed especially among lawyers (including Selden himself), as a term describing a plausible claim or proof. Thus I suspect that we should regard his repeated use of "colour" in this context, as implying something that we would term today as plausibility (the first recorded use of "plausibility" is from 1649), and indicating his view about the probabilistic nature of human knowledge.[93]

---

[92] This point is discussed in Berkowitz *Formative* pp. 73–74 and Caruso *Miglior* pp. 492–493, 780–789. Most interesting is Caruso's definition of words in Selden's view as "intersubjective" (intersoggiettivo) and socio-historical – conventional not as an arbitrary invention, but as a convention supported by a tradition. See Caruso *Miglior* pp. 510–511. For Hobbes' position see discussion in Harrison *Masterpiece* p. 63.

[93] See *The Oxford English Dictionary* (2nd edition, Oxford: Clarendon, 1989) vol. III p. 500. Among the many meanings of "colour" described, is one used especially in the law (with examples brought mainly from sixteenth to eighteenth centuries) as "An apparent or *prima facie* right, as in *colour of title*" – that is, a plausible claim to a right or authority (see there also about the first known use of the term "plausibility" in 1649).

Selden was certainly aware of, and sometimes himself used, the term "colour" as synonym for a plausible claim or proof. There are two such examples, where Selden uses the term as plausible claim or proof, in his reply to Dr. Tillesley's attack on the *Historie of Tithes*: first when asserting

What is then for Selden the truth against which tradition is to be measured, and how is it discovered? Selden proposed that there is only one intuition, and a principle following from it, which can be said to be found in all men, completely independent of tradition – and therefore the closest thing in his theory to a truly natural or universal law. This very principle also supplies the source of obligation, which he argued, cannot be gained from reason alone. This intuition existing in all men at some level is, according to Selden, that there is some meaning and order in things, some kind of principle of justice and equity active in the universe – what the more sophisticated human societies have termed as "there is a God and he dispenses recompense." From this metaphysical intuition of equity (that is, the supposition that equity extends beyond the span of an individual's life and time), follows for Selden the one universal principle that all men can be expected to recognize, and can be held to account for breaking: "Fides est servanda" – a promise has to be kept (also appearing as "Pacta sunt servanda" – agreements have to be kept). The need for men to keep their obligations is the obvious linchpin of all societies, since no society can exist without it, but the only natural means of supporting this principle, is the natural intuition men have about metaphysical equity (this, incidentally, seems to imply that fundamentally unjust societies cannot long survive). Thus, Selden, after having established to his satisfaction that reason by itself cannot sustain natural law (first because it is uncertain, second because it cannot impose obligation), proposes that there is nothing to make men observe laws and agreements, except for some outside authority, and for individuals such an authority can only be ultimately founded on the existence of a providential equity, ordaining that one's obligations have to be kept.

that though as any man he might very well err, "yet he that sufficiently shews me colour that I have erred, must be of another manner of brain and learning than this doctor." Again when remarking on an assertion by Tillesley, he asks, "[w]hat colour, what one syllable of colour is there for any such thing in his whole charter of Gundulphus?" (both quotes from *Opera Omnia* vol. 3 tome 2 cols. 1369–1386). Another contemporary example for this use of "colour," is from Henry Finch's, *Law; a Discourse Thereof in Foure Books* (published posthumously, 1636), an English-language version, prepared by the author of the book, originally published in Law French. In book 4, chapter 32 "of Pleas in Barre" pp. 379–381 he writes: "In an assise of novel disseisin and trespass the defenda[n]t pleading a title in barre must give colour of title to the plaintife." There are numerous more such uses of the term.

However, in many cases, especially in court pleading, the word was used (e.g., according to Cowell's *Interpreter*) to describe a plea that was probable but also false. It appears as synonym for false pretext in James I's *The True Law of Free Monarchy*, when discussing men raising their sword against the magistrate with the claim of "relieving the commonwealth out of distress (which is their only excuse and color)[.]" As false pretext the term also appears in the Petition of Right (of which Selden was among the drafters), twice: in the ninth paragraph, "And also sundry grievous offenders, by color thereof claiming an exemption, have escaped the punishments due to them by the laws and statutes of this your realm...," and in the tenth paragraph "...and that hereafter no commissions of like nature may issue forth to any person or persons whatsoever to be executed as aforesaid, lest by color of them any of your Majesty's subjects be destroyed or put to death contrary to the laws and franchise of the land."

In other words, he proposes that the one and only "foundation of natural law is the command of the father of nature."[94]

In a passage of the *Jure Naturali*, Selden puts together concisely the unfeasibility of obligation by simple reason and consent, with his own alternative of obligation by a natural law originating in God's command:

[A]n obligation cannot arise by the simple reason and the consent of men without the authority of a higher being. The source of obligation in these matters is God, a power that is superior to man, and accordingly is the source any of these provisions of the obligative natural law."[95]

Although by far the most extensive discussion of this issue is in the JN, it is also evident in numerous other works by Selden, both implicitly and explicitly. He presented it clearly as early as his *Bona* (1631), while discussing the formula from the Babylonian Talmud (tractate *Bava Metzia* 48a), designed to ensure that one keep his contracts and promises – quoting the original Hebrew:

He who got rid of the men of the flood's generation, and the men of the dispersion's generation, and the men of Sodom and Gomorrah, who washed [Pharaoh and his men] from Egypt into the sea, He will get rid of him who does not stand by his word.[96]

He returned to the very same principle in his *Mare Clausum* (1635), terming it "the *Universal Obligatorie Law*, which provides for the due observation of Compacts and Covenants" (ex *Iure Universali Obligativo*, Quo Pactis Standum

[94] JN b1c7. See also discussion in Toomer *Scholarship* pp. 500–501. Francis Bacon, combining Neoplatonic ideas with materialist ones, reached a conclusion somewhat similar to Selden's about the centrality of keeping faith, although on a different basis. Emphasizing the need to study fables and myths as middle ground between the hidden depths of antiquity and the days of tradition and evidence, he used this approach to read the fable of Styx, as an allegory about treaties and oaths of princes, and asserted in section 5 of "Styx or Treaties" of his *De Sapienta Veterum* (Of the Wisdom of the Ancients, 1609) that the only reason such contracts which secured social order, were adopted, and faith kept, was that: "There is adopted therefore but one true and proper pledge of faith; and it is not any celestial divinity. This is Necessity (the great god of the powerful), and peril of state, and communion of interest." This view supports Selden's position that keeping faith would be a principle naturally self-evident and obvious to all, regardless of their beliefs or background (Bacon discusses Princes, but it seems applicable to all oaths and treaties), while at the same time dissenting from Selden's contention that keeping faith is a principle inevitably connected with a belief in the deity. For Bacon, the principle of keeping faith is only one of necessity, while Selden believes such a basis is too flimsy to withstand pressure, and would crumble with the shifting of interests. See Collins *Cosmos* p. 119.

[95] JN b1c8: "Atqui Obligationem ex simplici hominum ratione & consensu, absque superioris imperio, nasci enquire in ante dictis ostenditur. A Numinis igitur, id est, homine superioris imperio etiam in hisce petendus est obligationis ortus, adeoque ex capitibus aliquibus Juris Naturalis Obligativi." Caruso claims that Selden felt that the problem of social obligation ("obbligazione sociale"), had been inadequately addressed by contemporary theories on natural law, both scholastic and Grotian, and this was the main issue which he set out to overcome in his political theory. See Caruso *Miglior* pp. 659–660.

[96] The Hebrew is: (הוא, מי שפרע מאנשי דור המבול ומאנשי דור הפלגה ומאנשי סדום ועמורה ששטפו ממצרים בים עתידישיפרע ממי שאינו עומד בדיבורו.) and see Rosenblatt *Renaissance* pp. 60–61.

est et Servanda Fides), placing it there as foundation for his discussion of property. In the first volume of *De Synedriis* (1650) he mentions it as the obligation of divine origin, inherent in every human law "requiring us to respect our agreements, pacts, and treaties, along with any conditions or provisos which we may legally add to them, and all the other arrangements we make with one another" (quo scilicet Fides, Pacta, Conventiones, reliquiae omnia, cum conditionibus ac temperamentis suis legitimis, sunt servanda).[97]

As is often the case with Selden, it is in the *Table-Talk* that the issue is articulated in a most concise and direct manner, in the following remark about "Law of Nature":

I cannot fancy to my self what the Law of Nature means, but the Law of God. How should I know I ought not to steal, I ought not to commit Adultery, unless some body had told me so? Surely 'tis because I have been told so? 'Tis not because I think I ought not to do them, nor because you think I ought not; if so, our minds might change, whence then comes the Restraint? from a higher Power, nothing else can bind: I cannot bind my self, for I may untye my self again; nor an equal cannot bind me, for we may untie one another: It must be a superiour Power, even God Almighty. If two of us make a Bargain, why should either of us stand to it? What need you care what you say, or what need I care what I say? Certainly because there is something about me that tells me *Fides est servanda*, and if we after alter our Minds, and make a new Bargain, there's *Fides servanda* there too.[98]

This principle has for Selden the benefit of being derivable from natural law, as well as being obvious from a general view of self-interest, for individuals as well as society as a whole. But, as we have seen, while individuals could clearly recognize the general self-interest of keeping to agreements and obligation, self-interest only could not bind them: even individuals accepting the general principle, would (and do) in particular cases try to avoid keeping their contracts, when it suits them. On a wider societal level, too, all societies certainly accept and try to enforce the rule that men should keep to their obligations, for without this principle society itself could not endure in the long run – but even whole societies nevertheless sometimes attempt to evade keeping their pacts and obligations. Thus, for Selden, although self-interest could make men and societies understand the utility of this principle, the general utility could not really bind them, since there would be nothing to stop them from jettisoning it when convenient, so that ultimately the only sure anchor for obligation was the assumption of metaphysical equity. Thus,

---

[97] MC b1c5. Toomer translates it probably more to the point as "the *universal obligatory law*, by which one must abide by agreements and keep faith," see Toomer *Scholarship* p. 397; *Synedriis* b1c4.

[98] TT "Law of Nature" sec. 1. See also TT "Contracts" sec. 1: "if we once grant we may recede from Contracts upon any inconveniency that may afterwards happen, we shall have no Bargain kept"; and sec. 3 "the Epitome of all the Contracts in the World": "they keep them as long as they like them, and no longer." The issue is discussed in Tuck *Philosophy* pp. 216–217.

Selden remarks, although most men and societies uphold the divine origin of the metaphysical equity, it should be imparted even to those who are not aware of it, and he mentions approvingly that "[a]s I see it, the Hebrews thought that mankind should be made to understand that there was divine judgment, and along with it the expectation of reward or punishment from it, as God would render it."[99]

The supreme principle of keeping agreements made, means for Selden that even ones where fathers bind their progeny are binding, indeed even in the case of a compact of servitude. Moreover, Selden held that the same principle obligates men not only to stand by specific agreements made by individuals or groups, but also to the agreed-upon political order, so that "one must abide by agreements and civilly introduced forms of government" (Pactis ac Regiminum formulis civiliter initis standum) – obviously binding even when the agreement was first entered into by one's remote ancestors. However, Selden's idea of obligation to an agreement is certainly <u>not</u> one of simple non-resistance to established power, for he held that all agreements always have some terms and obligations for both sides to keep, thus binding both, even when one side is far more powerful than the other, like landlord and tenant, or prince and people. Hence, if one party breaks the agreement, the other is justified in endeavoring to make the defaulter fulfill it, rather than simply dissolving it.[100]

From these minimal natural propositions, follows for Selden, the human search for moral precepts one has to live by, in order to fulfill the demands of equity and obligation. Unlike the intuition of equity and the law of obligation, which are natural, and may be expected to be discerned by all men and societies, the moral precepts one has to follow are <u>not</u> natural or self-evident to all. According to Selden, these basic moral precepts were originally imparted by the divinity to all of humankind, first at the creation to Adam, and then again after the flood to Noah and his children. From this latter occurrence, the divine precepts are named by the Jewish tradition "Noahide." Selden contends that while among most human societies the record of the original reception of the rules was long lost, the principles themselves were actually upheld in most places, since the precepts had been embedded in so many traditional laws and practices, although their original was long forgotten. Selden proposed that through diligent search and occasional illumination, these moral precepts

---

[99] JN b7c4: "Ita tamen ut de Divino etiam judicio praemioque ac Poena in eo expectando, seu de eo quod est Deum Renumeratore esse, Persuasionem universis hominibus necessariam esse quantum video, interea existimarent Ebraei."

[100] JN b1c8. See discussion in Toomer *Scholarship* pp. 501–502. Zaller finds Selden's landlord-tenant parallel with the prince-people contract, instructive in several ways: it emphasizes the distinctly contractarian nature of Selden's later thought; it suggests the political contract is not dissimilar from a commercial one; and it implies an essential equality between the contracting parties. Zaller does not mention two other important aspects – the landlord-tenant relationship is the basis for both Feudal Law and for the main part of the Common law. See discussion in Zaller *Legitimacy* pp. 350–351.

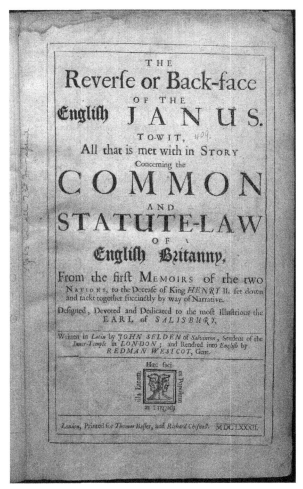

ILLUSTRATION 1: Title page of *The Reverse or Back-face of the English Janus*, the 1682 English translation by Redman Westcot (pseudonym of Adam Littleton) of Selden's first book to be published, *Jani Anglorum Facies Altera* (1610). Note at the bottom of the page the small illustration displaying the two-faced god Janus, surrounded by the cryptic caption, "Haec facies populum spectat; at illa Larem" – literally, "One face looks to the multitude; the other to the household gods." It may be interpreted as "One face looks to the public; the other to the private," or as "One face looks to the political; the other to the spiritual."

Published by kind permission of the Tarlton Law Library, Jamail Center for Legal Research, University of Texas School of Law.

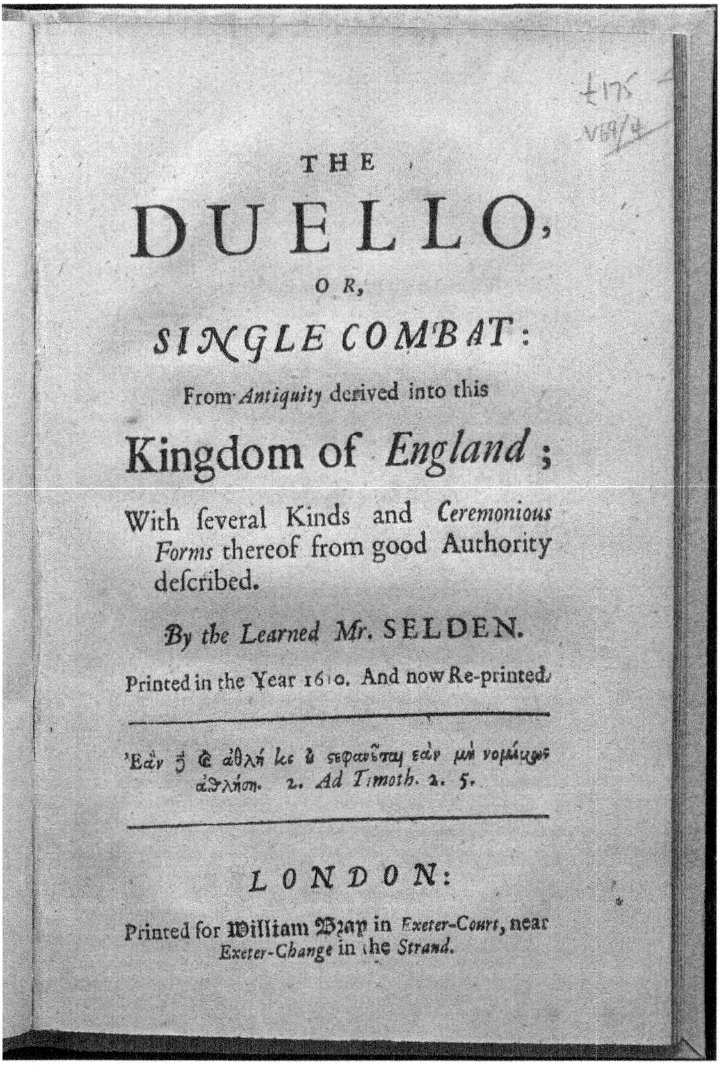

THE

DUELLO,

OR,

SINGLE COMBAT:

From *Antiquity* derived into this

Kingdom of *England*;

With ſeveral Kinds and *Ceremonious Forms* thereof from good Authority deſcribed.

By the Learned Mr. SELDEN.

Printed in the Year 1610. And now Re-printed.

Ἐὰν δὲ καὶ ἀθλῇ τις οὐ στεφανοῦται ἐὰν μὴ νομίμως ἀθλήσῃ. 2. *Ad Timoth.* 2. 5.

LONDON:

Printed for William Bray in *Exeter-Court*, near *Exeter-Change* in the *Strand*.

ILLUSTRATION 2: Title page of the 1711 reprint of *The Duello or Single Combat* (1610). Selden's second book to be published, it established him as the leading authority on the subject.
Published by kind permission of the Tarlton Law Library, Jamail Center for Legal Research, University of Texas School of Law.

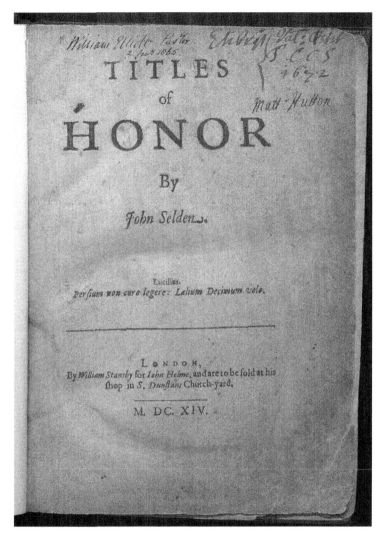

ILLUSTRATION 3: Title page of Selden's *Titles of Honor* (1614), which established him as an expert on issues of succession to titles and honors. Selden assisted Parliament in deciding between contesting claims to some titles. In 1631 he published an expanded and modified second edition.
Published by kind permission of the Tarlton Law Library, Jamail Center for Legal Research, University of Texas School of Law.

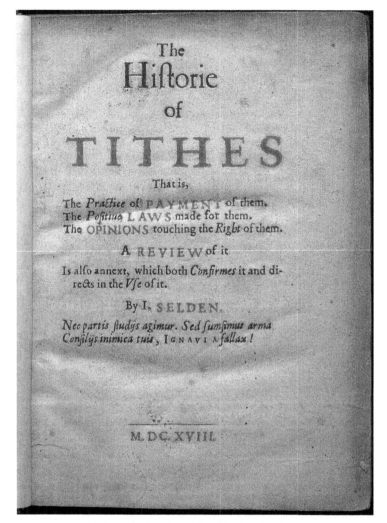

The

Hiſtorie

of

TITHES

That is,

The *Practice* of PAYMENT of them.
The *Poſitiue* LAWS made for them.
The OPINIONS touching the *Right* of them.

A REVIEW of it

Is alſo annext, which both *Confirmes* it and directs in the *Vſe* of it.

By I. SELDEN.

*Nec partis ſtudijs agimur. Sed ſumſimus arma
Conſilijs inimica tuis,* IGNAVI A *fallax!*

M.DC.XVIII

ILLUSTRATION 4: Title page of Selden's *The Historie of Tithes* (1618), certainly his most controversial book, which many clergymen regarded as attacking their divine rights to tithes. Selden was summoned before King James I, who forbade him to reply to critics. Many decades later, Selden enjoyed hearing that his book was used by clergymen to defend their tithes from abolition by the interregnum regime.

Published by kind permission of the Tarlton Law Library, Jamail Center for Legal Research, University of Texas School of Law.

ILLUSTRATION 5: Title page of *Mare Clausum* (1635), in which Selden famously argued for the possibility of nations establishing dominion over tracts of sea, against the position of Hugo Grotius' *Mare Liberum* (1609). Selden's arguments are today being used by countries such as Canada and China in claiming sovereignty over sections of the Arctic Ocean and the South China Sea.

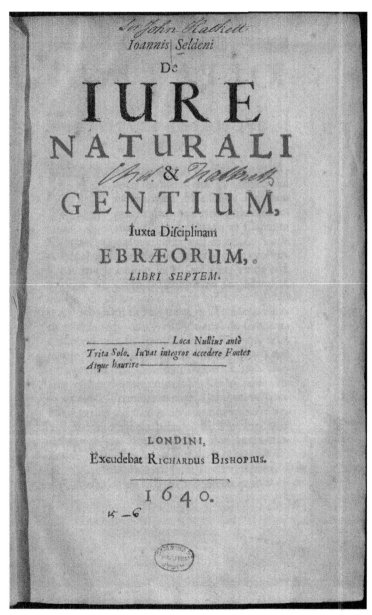

ILLUSTRATION 6: Title page of *De Iure naturali et gentium, juxta disciplinam Ebræorum* (1640), probably Selden's most important and reflective book. Note the motto "Loca Nullius ante Trita Solo. Iuvat integros accedere Fontes Atque haurire," which may be rendered as "Places Never before Trodden by Foot. I love approaching untested springs and drinking" – combining Selden's pride on producing a work that he viewed as unprecedented with his preferred image for learning as drawing water from springs. Published by kind permission of The National Library of Israel, Jerusalem.

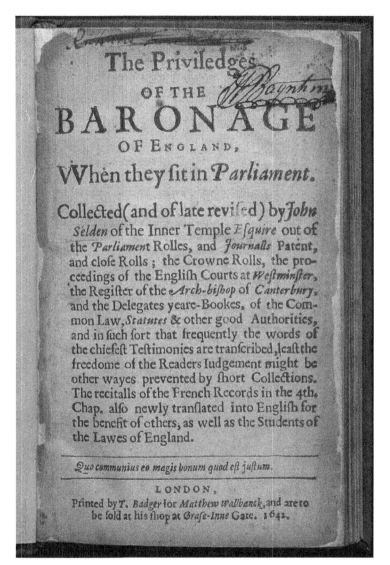

The Priviledges

OF THE

BARONAGE

OF ENGLAND,

VVhen they fit in *Parliament*.

Collected (and of late revised) by *John Selden* of the Inner Temple *Esquire* out of the *Parliament* Rolles, and *Journalls* Patent, and close Rolls ; the Crowne Rolls, the proceedings of the English Courts at *Westminster*, the Regifter of the *Arch-bishop* of *Canterbury*, and the Delegates yeare-Bookes, of the Common Law, *Statutes* & other good Authorities, and in such fort that frequently the words of the chiefeft Teftimonies are tranfcribed, leaft the freedome of the Readers Iudgement might be other wayes prevented by fhort Collections. The recitalls of the French Records in the 4th, Chap. alfo newly tranflated into Englifh for the benefit of others, as well as the Students of the Lawes of England.

Quo communius eo magis bonum quod eft juftum.

LONDON,

Printed by *T. Badger* for *Matthew Wallbanck*, and are to be fold at his fhop at *Grafe-Inne* Gate. 1642.

ILLUSTRATION 7: Title page of *The Priviledges of the Baronage of England When they sit in Parliament* (1642). Originally a Book of Precedents manuscript prepared by Selden in 1621 for the House of Lords, its publication two decades later was apparently an effort to support the retaining of bishops in Parliament, against calls to expel them. Published by kind permission of the Tarlton Law Library, Jamail Center for Legal Research, University of Texas School of Law.

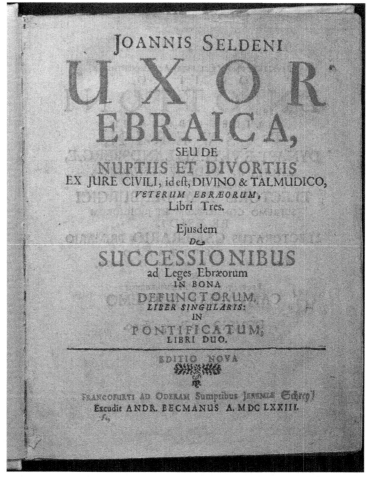

ILLUSTRATION 8: Title page of the 1673 Frankfurt reprint of *Uxor Ebraica* (originally published in 1646), together with two other Selden books, *De successionibus in bona defuncti, seu iure haereditario ad leges Ebraeorum* (originally 1631) and *De successione in pontificatum Ebraeorum* (originally 1636). Combining three of Selden's Hebraist texts, this edition, printed almost two decades after his death, is an example of how his expertise in Jewish legal learning continued to be employed throughout Europe, well into the eighteenth century.

Published by kind permission of the Tarlton Law Library, Jamail Center for Legal Research, University of Texas School of Law.

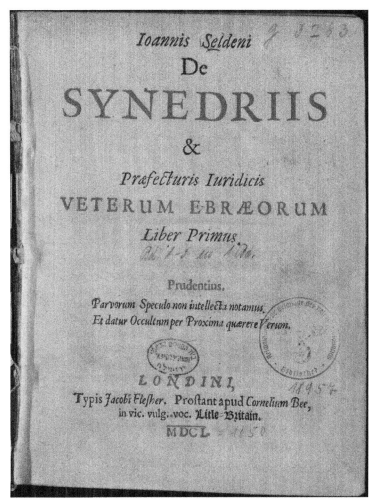

ILLUSTRATION 9: Title page of the first volume of *De Synedriis et Praefecturis Juridicis Veterum Ebraeorum* (1650). Originally conceived as a history of the Jewish great synedrion, it eventually grew to become a massive treatise on the assemblies and offices of the ancient Hebrew state, published in three separate volumes between 1650 and 1655. A principal reason for the change seems to be the fierce 1640s debates on the future of church and state in England, in which Selden was a prominent participant, both in the Westminster Assembly and in Parliament. The preface to the first volume contains a strong and explicit attack on Presbyterians, accusing them of attempting to subvert the traditional frame of church government in England.

Published by kind permission of The National Library of Israel, Jerusalem.

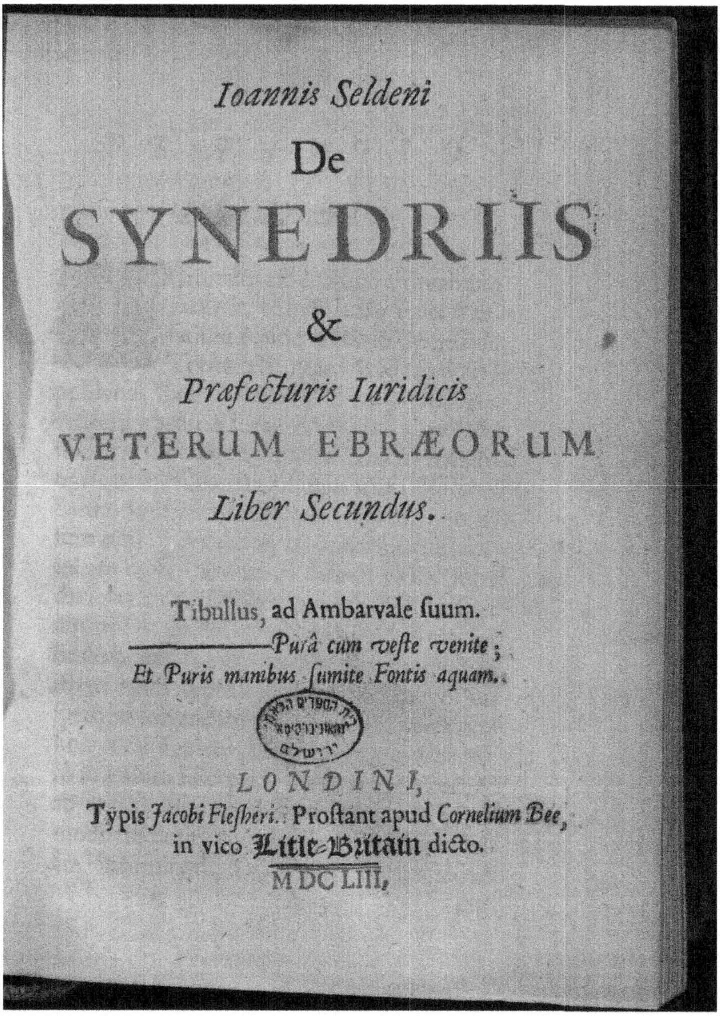

Ioannis Seldeni

De

SYNEDRIIS

&

Præfecturis Iuridicis

VETERUM EBRÆORUM

Liber Secundus.

Tibullus, ad Ambarvale fuum.
———————*Purâ cum vefte venite*;
Et Puris manibus fumite Fontis aquam.

LONDINI,
Typis *Jacobi Flesheri.* Proftant apud *Cornelium Bee,*
in vico 𝕷𝖎𝖙𝖑𝖊-𝕭𝖗𝖎𝖙𝖆𝖎𝖓 dicto.
MDC LIII,

ILLUSTRATION 10: Title page of the second volume of *Synedriis* (1653), the last book Selden published in his lifetime. Note the motto, "Pura cum veste venite; Et Puris manibus sumite Fontis aquam," which might be rendered as "with pure garments approach, and purify your hands with the spring's water" – employing once again Selden's favorite spring image for learning.
Published by kind permission of The National Library of Israel, Jerusalem.

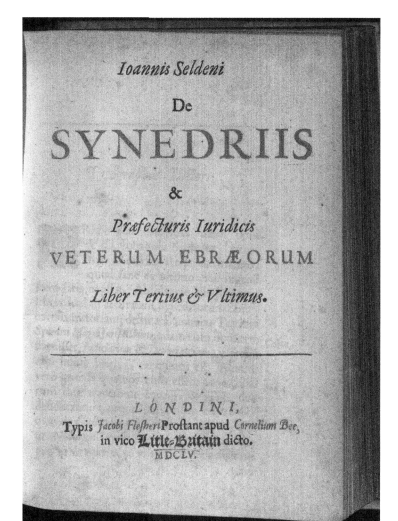

Ioannis Seldeni

De

SYNEDRIIS

&

Præfecturis Iuridicis

VETERUM EBRÆORUM

Liber Tertius & Vltimus.

LONDINI,

Typis *Jacobi Flesheri* Proſtant apud *Cornelium Bee,*
in vico Litle-Britain dicto.
MDCLV.

ILLUSTRATION 11: Title page of the third and last volume of *Synedriis* (1655),
published posthumously. Although Selden had proceeded a long way toward
completing this last great scholarly effort of his, he did not ultimately achieve this goal,
and the volume published a year after his death bears the marks of an incomplete effort,
probably intended to be one-third longer.
Published by kind permission of The National Library of Israel, Jerusalem.

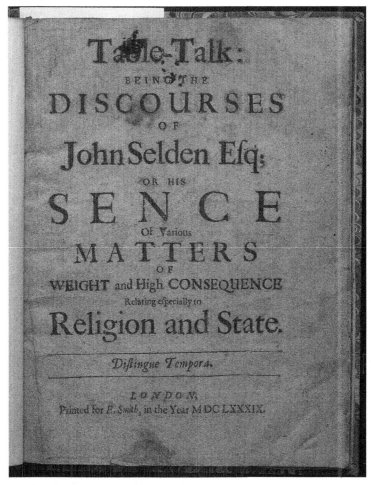

ILLUSTRATION 12: Title page of *Table-Talk* (1689), a collection of sayings from Selden's conversations, for the most part from the last decade of his life, compiled not long after his death by a former member of the household, Richard Milward, but left unpublished at that time. The book was eventually published through joint efforts of Charles Sackville, Sixth Earl of Dorset, and the scholar Thomas Rymer in 1689 – possibly because they believed it could assist efforts to achieve a settlement to the constitutional crisis of that year, as indicated by the title page describing the book as recording discourses of Selden on "MATTERS of WEIGHT and High CONSEQUENCE Relating especially to Religion and State."

Published by kind permission of the Tarlton Law Library, Jamail Center for Legal Research, University of Texas School of Law.

could be recovered, and, according to him, in one case this endeavor had succeeded. Although many philosophers and schools had attempted to define the universal moral rules, it appears that an inconsistence of method and appliance, as well as great divisions of opinions and attitudes, meant that none of them, not even those two great civilizations of the ancient world, the Athenians and Romans, had got close – "except only the Hebrews," who had succeeded in the feat of identifying a coherent set of rules, a "law natural or common to all mankind" which was recognized as distinct and separate, by all Jewish sages.[101]

Selden argued that this corpus identified by the Jewish tradition as the universal moral precepts, the law "natural or common to all mankind" included various provisions, some minor and less known, as well as the major and better known provisions, of which the most important, are seven in number:

Of these there are two that are *bein adam lamaqom*, between man and God, by which the Creator is acknowledged and honored. Four are, *bein adam lekhaveiro*, between man and his fellow, or the reciprocal behavior of men with each other. The seventh prohibits great cruelty to animals. They are customarily listed in this order:

I. *al abodah zarah* On Idolatry
II. *al birchath hashem* On Blaspheming the Holy name or God
III. *al shfikhuth damim* On Shedding blood or Murder
IV. *al gilui arayoth* On Baring Private Parts or Indignity and Forbidden sexual intercourse
V. *al hagezel* On Theft and Robbery
VI. *al hadinim* On Judgments or a System of Courts and Civil Obedience
VII. *al eiver min hakhai* On not eating limbs of a living animal[102]

As Selden explained it, the vagaries of time and human affairs, meant that as particular laws accrued, traditions were broken or discontinued, so that much ancient wisdom, including about the basic moral principles, was lost or

---

[101] JN b1c10.

[102] JN b1c10: "Juris Naturalis seu omnium hominum Communis, juxta eos, Capita sunt alia, ut superius memoratur, Majora atque Illustriora, alia Minora seu Obscuriora. Majora atque Illustriora numero continentur septenario. Horum bina sunt בין אדם למקום seu *inter Hominem & Numen Sanctissimum*; quibius scilicet agnoscatur honoreturque Creator. Quatuor בין אדם לחבירו *inter Hominem & proximam suum*; seu ad hominum inter se invicem mores spectant. Septimum demum immanem erga alia animalia crudelitatem interdicit. Ordine hujusmodi recenseri plerumque solent.

I על עבודה זרה *de Cultu extraneo*.
II על ברכת השם *de Maledictione Nominis Sanctissimi* seu *Numinis*.
III על שפיכות דמים *de Effusione Sanguinis* seu *Homicidio*.
IV על גילוי עריות *de Revelatione Turpitudinum* seu *Turpitudine ex concubitu*.
V על הגזל *de Furto ac Rapina*.
VI על הדינים *de Iudiciis* seu *Regimine forensi ac Obedienta Civili*.
VII על אבר מן החי *de Membro alimalis viventis* non comedendo."

distorted. Thus for Selden, not all traditions were the same, for the oldest continuing ones had the best chance of preserving in some form the most ancient principles and ideas. Accordingly he was to argue that the English political and legal tradition was a particularly ancient continuing one, far older in fact than the "Roman Law" one (and thus certainly not inferior to it). However, even the oldest continuing traditions, had lost much of the ancient wisdom and would have to recover moral principles pretty much by trial and error. Nevertheless, some traditions were different, for having benefited from divine assistance in identifying the moral precepts, either directly by revelation, or by the aid of the "active intellect," which shone more brightly upon them (such as among the progeny of Shem, son of Noah). Therefore, although the tradition of Noahide precepts given to all humanity by God after the flood, was in some form preserved and transmitted through the ages, by most human societies and traditions, there was really one best and oldest continuous tradition of human affairs and divine intervention – the Jewish one. For Selden, this meant that while every society should look within their own tradition for traces of the moral principles, against which their particular tradition is to be judged for its validity, they can be substantially aided in this quest by comparing it to other traditions, and especially to the Jewish legal tradition.[103]

Although Selden treated these matters most extensively in the *Jure Naturali*, what is the most sophisticated and integrated articulation of his approach on this particular issue, is found in another place – the first part of his final great work, *Synedriis*, published from 1650. There, within a few passages, he connects the single universal law of keeping one's obligations, with the divine Noahide precepts (especially the prohibition on theft), as well as with the foundations of all human-created agreements and laws (including of course English Common law), presenting them as different facets of the same whole. To a great extent, he thus weaves the threads of his work on natural law, on the Jewish traditions and on English law, into one theoretical fabric:

Now, the force of obligation which is inherent in every human law (however it may have been introduced) is founded, as I have already pointed out, in the commanded law of God, from which it draws most of its authority. In other words, it is this divine law which requires us to respect our agreements, pacts, and treaties, and all the other arrangements we make with one another, along with any conditions or provisos which we may legally add to them. And it is these agreements which allow us to distinguish, as they generally did in the past, what is mine, what is thine, or his, or someone else's, whether we are talking about property or personal rights.[104]

---

[103] JN b1c9.
[104] *Synedriis* b1c4: "Jam vero Obligationis vis quae juribus ejusmodi Humanis quomodocunque introductis inest, Iure Divino Praeceptivo (uti & ante monitum est) fundatur atque primario eo nititur; quo scilicet Fides, Pacta, Conventiones reliquaque omnia, cum conditionibus ac temperamentis suis legitimis, sunt servanda, quibus Meum, Tuum, Suum, Alienum, sive Res sive Iura intelligas, ab hominibus rite distribuuntur, atque ut plurimum semper distributa sunt."

Selden argues that the divine injunction on keeping one's agreement, the one truly universal law everyone is expected to understand, is not merely the first and most important law, but also the foundation for all other laws touching on property, on personal rights or on other social rules, since all of these, all particular property, all personal rights and all social arrangements, are in fact only conventional agreements between men. He elsewhere in the same book, connects even more explicitly the divine command to keep one's promises and agreements, as well as the foundation of property and thus for him of all human law, with the (fifth) Noahide principle forbidding theft, which, according to him,

...banned theft not only in the common sense of the term, but any agreement to transfer property which violated the law, and any abuse of another person's rights. In other words, it forbade any violation of a trust which had been properly forged between people and the agreements made between them, or of anything which accompanied or resulted from such agreements. Examples of this would be fraud and deception, since a proper understanding of the meaning of 'theft' should leave us in no doubt that it includes all crimes of this kind.[105]

Selden thus displays an approach to human affairs which, except for a core of universally valid moral principles, is dramatically conventionalist. In his view men have by divine law a complete liberty in anything not forbidden by the few basic divine laws: "I am thinking, for example, of our power and liberty where our own persons are concerned; our right to defend ourselves; the right to eat and dress as we chose; and several others which were no less guaranteed than the right to breathe." Nevertheless, for all his granting of such "natural" liberties and rights, these are nothing like the indefeasible natural rights posited by Grotius or Hobbes, for there is also no question in Selden's mind that "all of these rights could legally be diminished or just as readily altered" by human law or the decision of a court. Indeed, any human law making any change relating to people or property "is either giving, or taking away, or modifying the freedoms or other original rights enjoyed by the individuals subjected to this law." People are obligated to accept and respect any such laws properly enacted, "because they have consented to it either directly or indirectly as citizens of their state." This obligation as divine law he regards as resulting from two of the Noahide precepts, "the ban on theft" which for him also "contains a command to preserve the trust given between parties," and the precept "about administering justice," which suggests God ordained that there be judges to conduct trials and inflict penalties. Thus, for Selden, the only non-conventional and indefeasible principles are the divine injunction to keep

---

[105] *De Synedris* b1c2: "...non Furtum solum sic vulgo dictum sed etiam omnimoda rei alienae contrectatio non legitima, omnigena alieni juris usurpatio adeoque fidei rite interpositae ac pactorum violation & quae ex hisce pendent aut cominatur, ut frauds, doli mali, interdicuntur; quae omnia manifesto Furti nomine rite intellect veniunt." See also discussion in Toomer *Scholarship* pp. 694–695.

agreements and the seven Noahide precepts (two of which, as we see, he holds to lend additional support to the keeping of agreements). Except for direct transgressions of these basic principles, people can be restricted or allowed in almost anything, even slavery or polygamy, as long as the agreements and their procedures are properly executed. However, whatever the laws and agreements arrived at are, they have to be respected, and in this sense there is no such thing for Selden as legitimate arbitrary rule; no such thing as a Bodinian or Hobbesian sovereign – for "[t]his force of obligation is of course subject to the provisos which generally make it possible for the law to allow what is mine to be altered or transferred to you, or to him, or to someone else, without the need to commit a theft or injustice."[106]

Selden's repeated identification in *Synedriis*, of the obligation to abide by agreements and of the Noahide prohibition on theft with the creation of private property, the distinction of "what is mine from what is yours" is directly suggesting the pervasive familiar refrain of common lawyers, that the foundation of the English Common law and of personal rights, as ancient as the kingdom itself, is in the law of property, the distinction between "Meum" and "Tuum" (mine and thyne). It directly mirrors fears that royal subversion of the laws of property would herald the destruction of the whole Common law and constitution, an assertion reiterated innumerable times, both implicitly and explicitly, and both within Parliament and without it, especially during the great 1620s debates on impositions by many prominent common lawyers including

---

[106] *Synedriis* b1c4: "veluti Potestas sui ac Libertas, sui Tutela, Victus ratio ac vestitus libera ... alia aliquot non minus atque Spirandi jus[.]" and "Atque ad Legem ejusmodi rite introductam admittendam observandamque ii, in quos introducitur, ob consensum sive expressim sive tacite aut civiliter in eam datum, Obligantur, idque tum ex Divino de Furto seu Alieni raptu interdicto (quo item fidei datae servandae continetur praeceptum) tum ex eo quod de Judiciis est quo Poenas ac Persecutiones forenses praestitui etiam ad invitos coercendos juberi intelligitur, qua de re statim plura. Et manifestum est, post legem sic latam novumque jus, ad modum quo oportet, introductum, adeo tum Reipublicae seu Civilis in quam introducitur societatis tum in ea singulorum interesse ut admittatur observeturque, ut quisquis violaverit, is aut jus alienum plane invaserit aut, quod in idem recidit, alios suo frui omino impediverit: quod Divino illi de Raptu seu Furto interdicto reluctatur. Nec solum in Juribus sic publice introductis Obligatio habetur ex Jure Divino illo Praeceptivo, verum etiam in Pactis ac Conventionibus singulorum contractibusque omnigenis aliisque negotiis quibus, ex Jure Numinis Permissivo, se mutuo per commercia homines commiscent aut Obligationes contrahere dicuntur. Ideo scilicet, quia per consensum sive Personalem seu Naturalem sive Civilem data fides, servanda est ex eo quod in interdicto toties memorato ea de re supponitur; uti & rursus liberanda, aut pro liberata habenda (juxta temperamenta ac conditiones in ejusdem datione sive expressas sive tacitas) ne alienum injuste usurpetur. Etrevera, quemadmodum Veritatis Conclusionis cujusque vis ex Praemissis syllogismi habetur eisque omnino fundatur, seu ut Numerus ex Unitatibus, ita Juris Humani Obligatio ex praemissis illis Juris Divini de Fide servanda nec alieno temerando nascitur; temperamentis semper admissis, quibus Juris Mei, Tui, Sui, Alieni mutationes translationesque legitime seu ex Jure Divino permissivo, non Furti aut injuriae nomine, fieri inde assolent." See discussion in Toomer *Scholarship* pp. 694–696. Caruso points out that Selden's drastic and radical "convenzionalismo" and "anti-essenzialismo" mean that he was much more philosophically revolutionary, than politically so. Selden *Miglior* p. 775.

Selden. In effect, Selden was implying in this text of 1650, and not too subtly at that, that the original cause for the great crisis which had led to the Civil War, the opposition to a royal "transfer of property which violated the law," was completely justified, not only by the English fundamental laws but also by the Noahide principle forbidding theft and the divine injunction that agreements are to be kept.[107]

Selden then can be said to maintain a political and social theory of far-reaching contractarianism. Although there is a divinely ordained morality which must be observed, apart from its very basic core tenets, essentially all social and political rights or obligations are only contractual, or, as he put it pithily in the *Table-Talk*: "Keep your Contracts, so far a Divine goes, but how to make our Contracts is left to our selves[.]" This means that virtually every kind of agreed-upon convention is valid, as long as its terms are kept and it does not infringe the very minimal and broad basic divine principles. While the divine principles serve both as the basis for morality as well as the source of obligation to abide by the agreements.[108]

Selden arrives at a position that while denying anything like *a priori* natural rights, nevertheless is uncompromisingly averse to arbitrary government. The terms of the contract can, and with time do, change, but only by mutual agreement. Rulers have to abide by laws and to set up just courts, and the ruled are totally justified in expecting laws to be respected, to fight and in extreme cases even to rise up, in case of fundamental breach of contract:

To know what Obedience is due to the Prince, you must look into the Contract betwixt him and his People; as if you wou'd know what Rent is due from the Tenant to the Landlord, you must look into the Lease. When the Contract is broken, and there is no

---

[107] Among many examples, we may recall the aforementioned defense of the distinction between "Meum and tuum" as the basis for the Common law, by both Digges and Eliot in the 1628 Parliament, and Selden's similar comment about Laud's chaplain licensing of the books by Sybthorpe and Maynwaring. See discussion in Toomer *Scholarship* p. 319 and Zuckert *Natural* pp. 51–52. Apparently, for Selden (unlike Locke), exactly because property was artificial and conventional, it was mortally endangered by naturalist claims no less than by *jure divino* ones.

In this context it is worthwhile to point out that the extent to which Selden and the common lawyers of his time owed their view of the law being based in "meum and tuum" to Roman law ideas has been as yet largely unexplored. Clearly the root of property (dominium) in Roman law was the difference between meum et tuum, and ever remained the centerpiece of Roman legal thought, and property (private as well as public) a type of "possessive individualism." In Selden's own case there seem to be several more significant parallels: in the "Romano-Byzantine law" of the Corpus Juris Civilis, property was based on a hypothesis of original or natural occupation and use (usucapio), later transferred either by natural family succession or artificial conventional transfer. Moreover, Kelley proposers that as the third component of the Romano-Byzantine legal universe (besides persons and things), "obligation" would be a better description than "action"; depending on individual good faith, "obligations" (which could be natural as well as civil) were the cement of the social order, and like possessions civil obligations were juridically enforceable, as in the obligation to keep compacts "pacta servanda sunt." See Kelley *Human* pp. 51–60.

[108] TT "Contracts" sec. 2.

third Person to judge, the Decision is by Arms. And this is the Case between the Prince and the Subject.

Unlike rebellions based on some universal rights or a reversion to the state of nature, for Selden, social and political conflicts could never be undertaken in the name of abstract or natural individual rights, nor of a general right of resistance (which in his view cannot really exist), but only to defend specific, agreed-upon and law-defined practices that have been violated, to defend the contract and its stipulations. The goal is obviously to restore the contract, but even if the old political and social framework is destroyed, and men are practically free to erect in its place whatever kind of new order they may wish for, he suggests they would be wise to restore one that is as close as possible to their old system, so as to enjoy the benefits of tried ways and laws already adapted to their character. The English, he argued, had repeatedly done exactly this, such as after the Norman conquest and at the time of Magna Carta, as well as during many additional minor conflicts – he strived to achieve a similar outcome in the political conflict of his own days. In a sense, Selden claimed, restorative uprisings had become in England a kind of time-honored tradition, a part of the customary Common law, as he put it explicitly in the *Table-Talk*:

Question. What Law is there to take up Arms against the Prince, in Case he break[s] his Covenant? *Answ*. Though there be no written Law for it, yet there is Custom; which is the best Law of the Kingdom; for in *England* they have always done it.

This approach, that we might term conventional and restorative (upholding traditional conventions and attempting to restore them when breached), informed Selden's political career, and it had great success in later English political though. Alongside the obvious importance of the political ideas that flowed from Grotius, Hobbes and later Locke (who in a way combined the two), approaching political society from the standpoint of universal natural rights and a right of political resistance, we should also recognize Selden as an important figure of a significant approach within English-speaking political thought. The strand of political thought to which Selden belonged was the one that claimed 1660, 1688 and even 1776 and 1787 as "restorations" – rebellions by Englishmen reclaiming their traditionally contracted laws and liberties, rather than the exercise of some universal right of resistance part of a set of abstract natural rights.[109]

Selden's traditionalist epistemology does not necessarily lead to a particular type of political regime, for by itself it tends merely to justify duly established political frameworks, be they monarchical, popular or mixed (and the longer their existence, the better). However, his stress on the keeping of political agreements, not only by subjects but by rulers as well, does not lend itself to any type of arbitrary government, monarchic or popular. Rather, it does lead to

---

[109] TT "War" sec. 5 and 6.

a strictly contractualist interpretation of politics, whatever the type of government. Such an interpretation regards the political order as a framework of precise obligations binding all relevant political actors – what we call today a constitution. His position is one of constitutionalist contractarianism; from such a perspective there are no absolute sovereigns, for every political actor, be he a king, a judge or a Member of Parliament, is obliged to follow the rules regulating his office, and any change to the rules requires the consent of all parties to them.

Selden's principle of obligation thus addresses what he regarded as the fallacy of Grotius' epistemology as well as the Dutchman's theory of obligation by reason only. Moreover, while we have no grounds for assuming that by late 1639, when Selden had completed the *Jure Naturali*, he was acquainted to any degree with either Hobbes' or Filmer's ideas, Selden's theory also undermines the theoretical grounds on which these two thinkers erected their absolutist political systems. Political claims of the Grotian type, from either right reason or individual consent, are unacceptable to Selden's theory, for his traditionalist constitutional approach only allows political claims that are either already sanctioned within the existing constitution, or that are agreed to by all components of the constitutional order. Moreover, Selden's *Jure Naturali*, not only rejects the Grotian pure reason basis for understanding and obligation, but in addition, as Toomer points out, it "must have been obvious to Selden's readers," that his theory founding natural law on God's commands is "in direct contradiction" to the famous passage of the *Jure Belli* where Grotius proposed that the law of nature would remain valid even without God's existence. A similar contradiction would have been equally apparent to those reading Hobbes' works published after the appearance of Selden's *Jure Naturali* – for Hobbes' whole system is ultimately based on the fear for one's here and now – life and safety certainly, but even reputation or honor which are valued by a solely social measure, not a divine one. Such a view directly opposes Selden's postulation of a central role for men's quest for a universal equity (of divine provenance) that would hold true beyond one's life – the exact opposite of Hobbes' self-involved individual. Selden's insistence on the idea of a divine dispensation of justice prior and unconnected to political power, as the source for obligation, directly clashes with Hobbes' materialist epistemology and self-interested obligation. Selden's insistence on the biding character of agreements and on politics as humanly contingent is also a direct rejection of Filmer's patriarchal and fideistic premises, as well as of all theories of absolute sovereignty, of the Filmerian or Hobbesian type – regardless of the sovereign being monarchic or republican. Although Selden's position, allowing even for an authoritarian overweening regime, where contractually agreed upon, is sometimes described as Hobbesian or quasi-Hobbesian, it is essentially anti-Hobbesian (as well as anti-Filmerian). For the whole point of Hobbes' (and Filmer's) sovereign, is that the ruler is <u>not</u> bound by contract, and hence is absolute in power; while for Selden, a ruler, however "absolute" he might be termed, is bound by a historical and contingent contract; in other words, his is a limited government (however minimal the limits). Such a political system, contractual and limited, is the very opposite of all absolute and arbitrary ones.[110]

Selden sought to counter theories that would have done away with England's traditional law and constitution. In the theoretical framework he developed, a traditionalist epistemology supplied the basis for his political theory, of a strictly contractual constitutionalism. We have seen that his definition of the equity intuition common to all men, as connected to the existence of providential justice, supplied a principle of obligation which blocked the possibility of its sliding into relativism, while allowing most matters to be dealt with contractually. Selden's theory, although anti-rationalist, is thus not at all irrational, but rather it integrates rational considerations with other elements crucial to political society. It begins with tradition as past experience, and goes on to test it by use of current sense and reason (thus following Sarpi's fourth mode, beginning with sense and following with reason).

3.6 LEGACIES OF OBLIGATION

The connection made by Selden (as well as by some of his contemporaries) between his epistemic approach and certain principles of political obligation or action, had an evident impact on several thinkers of his own and of later times. Lord Herbert of Cherbury, for example, was a friend and correspondent of Selden, whose development of the idea of religion as a natural human instinct, is possibly connected to Selden's positing a universal intuition of providential equity, although we lack definite proof. John Milton, on the other hand, was explicit in his familiarity with the epistemology that Selden (himself familiar at least with some of Milton's writings) presented in the *Jure Naturali*, and indeed the poet employed this epistemology to justify his support for freedom of the press, when he wrote in his pamphlet *Areopagitica* (1644):

Whereof what better witness can ye expect I should produce, than one of your own now sitting in Parliament, the chief of learned men reputed in this land, Mr. Selden; whose volume of natural and national laws proves, not only by great authorities brought together, but by exquisite reasons and theorems almost mathematically demonstrative, that all opinions, yea errors, known, read, and collated, are of main service and assistance toward the speedy attainment of what is truest.[111]

---

[110] See discussion in Toomer *Scholarship* pp. 490–491 and note 8; and Zaller *Legitimacy* pp. 796–797 note 345.

[111] Herbert's early important work, *De Veritate* (Paris, 1624), proposed a theory of natural religion, as a human natural instinct – obviously parallel to Selden's intuition of providential equity. Hooker has been proposed as an influence, but Selden appears at least as likely

But it appears that the most significant philosophical impression made by Selden's theory of knowledge and obligation was upon two successive generations of English thinkers associated with the "Cambridge Platonists" group of philosophers, mostly of clerical background. These thinkers, most prominent among them Ralph Cudworth (1617–1688), Nathaniel Culverwel (1618–1651) and Jeremy Taylor (1613–1667) as well as, in the next generation, Richard Cumberland (1631–1718) and James Tyrrel (1642–1718), attempted to develop ideas about knowledge and obligation that would overcome the difficulties they identified in theories of Grotian-type rationalism and even more of Hobbesian-type materialism. They engaged with Selden's theory, finding appealing especially his emphasis on the centrality of keeping one's

a candidate – especially since he corresponded with Herbert. According to Herbert there were never real atheists, only men who have refused some forms of religion, thus even such men, according to him, although rejecting rituals, ceremonies and traditions, never doubted qualities like virtue, compassion, and purity of spirit. Later in life Herbert wrote his *De Religione Gentilium* (completed 1645, only published posthumously in 1663, at Amsterdam, by Isaac Vossius), where he delineated the historic progression of the religious idea he had discussed in his earlier book. Although he assigns Judaism a preeminent role as the first to explicitly recognize a unique supreme being, Cherbury argued that pagans (from Egypt to Greece and to Rome) too were worshipping the divinity through the things it created, in effect identifying this realization of the existence of the divine with reason. Herbert also argued that in all religions there were efforts early on to distinguish between false prophets and oracles, and those with divine guidance – the difference being that true ones were not contrary to reason. As proof he pointed to the Talmudic tractate Sanhedrin (vii, 10), and other "non-delusional rabbinic texts" (see *Religione gentilium* pp. 7–8). This certainly seems quite Seldenian. See discussion in D. Lucci, "Ebraismo e antichi paganesimi. Il sincretismo religioso di Herbert di Cherbury e i suoi influssi sugli studi storico-religiosi del seicento" in *La rassegnia mensile di Israel*, 70/1 (April 2004, Roma).

Milton heaped praise on Selden in *Areopagitica* as well as in *The Doctrine and Discipline of Divorce* (1644) pp. 78–79, where he praised Selden's *Jure Naturali* as "a work more useful and more worthy to be perus'd, whosoever studies to be a great man in wisdom, equity, and justice." This should not lead one to assume their overall epistemology is similar. Milton attempts to argue that in articulating "mathematically demonstrative" political ideas he is trying to do what Selden too undertakes. However, although Selden supported the idea that unprejudiced reading aids the attainment of knowledge, this is only a small point in the preface of *Jure Naturali*. In effect Milton distorts Selden's methodology projecting on him his own method in the *Aeropagitica*, in an attempt to integrate the possibility that morality might be mathematically demonstrable, with the question of how humans came to know what is true. See discussion in N. Smith "Areopagitica: voicing contexts, 1643–5" in D. Lowenstein & J.G. Turner (eds.) *Politics, Poetics, and Hermeneutics in Milton's Prose* (Cambridge University Press, 2007) pp. 61–62; and in T. Fulton, "*Areopagitica* and the Roots of Liberal Epistemology" in *English Literary Renaissance* 34/1 (February 2004).

Selden certainly knew of Milton's works, for he owned two of his pamphlets, the *Doctrine and Discipline of Divorce* (1644: the second edition where Milton refers to *Jure Naturali*), and *Colasterion and Tetrachordon* (1645), both obviously bearing on the content of the *Uxor Ebraica* (1646) that Selden was writing at that time. However, there is no sign of any personal contact between them, and Selden does not mention Milton, his pamphlets, or indeed, anything written on the subject in the previous 50 years – clearly an attempt to distance his work from current controversy. See Toomer *Scholarship* pp. 690–691.

obligations, as the basic divine injunction. These thinkers clearly recognized that Selden's theory was primarily reliant on tradition, with a supportive role assigned to the "active intellect," and although they all finally rejected this reliance on tradition (especially of the Jewish sort) in his theory, some of them attempted to develop the "active intellect" concept which he discussed into the primary foundation for their own theories. All of these writers, while criticizing aspects of Selden's theory (in Taylor's case without explicitly mentioning Selden at all), clearly recognized its power as a critique of the shortcomings of rationalistic and materialistic ideas, as well as appreciating his placing of the origin of obligation and action in a divine source.

Cudworth was from 1645 Regius Professor of Hebrew at Cambridge (and father of Damaris Masham a philosopher and close friend of Locke), and frequent correspondent of Selden (who assisted him during the hard times of the interregnum) particularly on scholarly subjects having to do with Jewish learning. He wrote to Selden on 28 November 1643, asserting his high esteem for the *Jure Naturali*, "youre incomparable Discourse, upon ye Precepts of Noah, the Scope and vse whereof is by too many, (I thinke) wch read it, not vnderstood." He especially agreed with Selden's position about the keeping of agreements as the only fundamental natural law: "I cannot Sir, but compromise with your opinion in every thing; but I must confesse I haue a good while since, entertained these thoughts, that vnder ye Christian State, there is scarcely any thing of Ius Divinum besides the Vniversall and Catholick Law of Nature except only the nómos tês pístevs The Law of ffaith." Although Cudworth's anti-Hobbesian magnum opus, *The True Intellectual System of the Universe* (1678) mentions Selden only in passing, his debt to his ideas (especially in the critique of Hobbes' account of obligation) is evident. A close associate of Cudworth and fellow Cambridge man, Nathaniel Culverwel was far less favorable to Selden, but he more extensively and directly engaged with the latter's ideas in *An Elegant and Learned Discourse of the Light of Nature* (1652, composed before 1646), a tract of rational theology which was to have some influence on the philosophy of late-seventeenth-century England. In it he maintained that "there is light enough in the dictates of Reason to display common notions" and attacked those "Divers into the depths of knowledge, who grant a certainty, and yet will not grant it to Reason[.]" He explicitly took issue with a number of Selden's positions, especially attacking both pillars of Selden's epistemology, tradition (in chapter 8, "How the Law of Nature Is Discovered? Not by Tradition") and the "active intellect" (in chapter 9, "The Light of Reason"). Culverwel rejected Selden's idea that Jewish traditions (indeed any tradition) might hold a role in the discovery and authority of natural law. He regarded as an error "remarkable and of larger influence" the opinion reported by Selden in his *Jure Naturali*, of the Jews who hold that the "light of nature" shines primarily upon them and upon gentiles only by way of dependence, as if "these Praecepta Noachidarum had been lockt up and cabinetted in Noahs Ark, and afterwards kept from the prophane touch of a Gentile," so that Gentiles who would participate in it "all must light their candles at the Jewish Lamp." He then asked, where such light of certainty might be found: "I would they would tell us then, where we might hope to finde it; Surely not in an Oriental Tradition, in a Rabinical dream, in a dusty Manuscript, in a Remnant of Antiquity, in a Bundle of Testimonies; and yet this is all you are like to get of them[.]" Culverwel then turned to attempt and show that "the whole Notion of an Intellectus Agens is a meere fancy and superfluity" asserting that though it had been maintained by various serious thinkers, "'tis built upon I know not what Phantasms and false Appearances." Denying Selden's claim of the limitations of men's unaided intellect to discern things clearly enough, Culverwel instead maintained that: "Whereas those Species and colours, those pictures and representations of being that are set before an Intellectual eye, carry such a light and beauty in themselvs as may justly engratiate them with the understanding." He summed up the position he was rejecting, thus: "This is to tell you that men have no Candle of the Lord within them, but only there must be Traditio Lampadis, a General and Publique light, that must go from one hand to another." Although clearly adversarial in tone, Culverwel is quite correct in identifying Selden's position as relaying mainly on traditions rather than upon men's inner enlightenment. A close contemporary of Cudworth and Culverwel was Jeremy Taylor, a scholar and clergyman (and later Bishop of Down and Connor) close to Laud and to Charles I, who was also a possible collaborator on *Eikon Basilike* and whose wife was rumored to be the natural daughter of the King. With an effort separate but parallel to such as Cudworth's and Culverwel's, Taylor attempted to counter skeptical and materialist ideas in his *Ductor Dubitantium* (1660) by developing among other ideas the fear of divine punishment as the basis of obligation from natural law, as well as the concept of the "active intellect." In both he was clearly indebted to Selden, although not mentioning anywhere in his book the latter's role, or even his name.[112]

Among the next generation of English thinkers, Richard Cumberland, Cambridge Platonist and later Bishop of Peterborough, was an influential figure who addressed Selden's ideas repeatedly in his important *De Legibus Naturae* (1672) especially adopting the latter's criticism of Grotius and Hobbes. Grotius' writings about a rationally discernible natural law were phenomenally popular among those who were striving, in the late seventeenth and early eighteenth century, to create a rational concord of philosophy and theology, sometimes termed "rational divines" – but the same writings were also widely held to not have adequately addressed the issue of obligation. Grotius' rational-utilitarian theory, was directed at answering the search for certainty in

---

[112] Jeremy Taylor, *Ductor Dubitantium* (1660). Selden's influence on the *Ductor* is most evident in the Second Book, Chapter I "Of the Law of Nature in General" with sections titled like "The first of greatest band of the Law of Nature is fear of punishment." See discussion of Taylor's debt to Selden in Parkin *Science* pp. 60–66.

epistemological and hence moral inquiry, and there were many who regarded his answers as an adequate response to these challenges – however, even his fervent supporters acknowledged that he failed to supply convincing grounds for obligation. The most available answer to the problem of obligation was Hobbes' view, offering his own utilitarian-only solution, which however supplied obligation by jettisoning traditional morality. Cumberland sought the answer to the problem by relaying on Selden's response to Grotius, sharing Hobbes' critique of the inability of *a priori* rationalism to supply grounds for obligation, but proposing a totally divergent solution to the problem, by a theory of divine obligation based on morality.[113]

Cumberland's *Legibus*, concerned primarily with moral obligation, seized on Selden's answer to the problem and can be seen as an attempt to build upon it. The *Legibus* shared the suspicion, articulated by Selden, that the view of those like Grotius (appropriated from the scholastics), arguing that the conclusions of reason alone could have the force of law, was unconvincing. Cumberland also rejected Hobbes' solution to the problem, the obligation from the power of the sovereign – an answer providing perhaps for political and practical obligation, but altogether precluding any role for moral obligation. Instead Cumberland adopted Selden's solution, calling it his "judicious hint" to moral philosophers, that the existence of God provided the force necessary to make moral judgments into laws, and hence that what was needed was to discern what the precepts of such a law are. Cumberland discussed in the *Legibus* the two means proposed by Selden for discerning the natural law: precepts of the children of Noah, pronounced by God and handed down "to all their posterity by tradition only," and the ill-defined faculty of the "active intellect" by God endowed to "rational Minds" which are therefore capable by "Application of their Understanding" of discovering natural laws and distinguishing them from positive institutions (probably because he was unwilling to blur again the distinction between reason and command). Though acknowledging that Selden "betakes himself wholly" to the former method of tradition, Cumberland dismissed that part of Selden's theory as pertinent at most, to the tradition of one nation, without the power to obligate others. The other solution indicated by Selden, which was only hinted at and lacked much explanation, was the one Cumberland attempted instead to develop. In his account of the "active intellect" Selden had reported that there were two views of this faculty, one which was rejected by scholastics, regarding it as external to the individual intellect, the other was the orthodox Thomist account regarding it as an internal faculty of the rational soul. While Selden clearly opted for the first, external version (among other things because the "active intellect" as an internal faculty, once again blurred the distinction between reason and command), Cumberland recoiling from both the role assigned to the Jews and the problematic aspects of the external origin of the

---

[113] Parkin *Science* pp. 3–5, 56–61.

"active intellect," preferred to attempt and develop the Thomist version of an
inner "active intellect." He did this by claiming that new advances in
philosophy and especially the scientific method, had made it possible to
discern by observation, God's natural scheme of rewards and punishments
in the world.[114]

Another important figure to address Selden's ideas was James Tyrrel,
a barrister and author, Ussher's grandson and close friend of Locke, who
wrote (anonymously) the anti-Filmerian *Patriarcha non Monarcha* (1681), as
well as a series of some 14 dialogues published between 1692 and 1702,
examining Whig political principles, (eventually collected and published in
1718 as *Bibliotheca Politica*), as well as *A Brief Disquisition of the Law of
Nature* (1692), essentially an abridgment of Cumberland's *Legibus*. In his
"Preface" to the latter work, Tyrrel discusses and rejects the ideas of Hobbes
and Grotius, while also clearly but respectfully disagreeing with Selden.
Acknowledging that "the Laws of Nature, as derived from God the
Legislator, are the foundation of all Moral Philosophy and true Politicks" he
deems it worthwhile to "enquire how these Laws may be discovered to proceed
from God as a Legislator." He argues that a number of authors including
"judicious" Puffendorf, Sharrock, "most learned" Selden and "none deserves
greater Commendation" Grotius – "have all deserved very well in their way"
but their work is found wanting. Tyrrell concedes that although the objections
against Grotius' work are not enough to render it completely "useless," yet it is
unable to convince all, so that it is "more useful, as well as more certain, to seek
for a firmer and clearer Demonstration of these Laws, from a strict search and
inquisition into the nature of things, and also of our own selves[.]" He claims
that the strongest objections to Grotius' method of deriving the laws of nature
and their authority from the "Dictates of Right Reason" have been (besides
objections of "some of the Antients"), "Mr. Selden and Mr. Hobbes" although
"upon different Principles, and from different Designs." While Hobbes asserts
that any law, even those of nature, become such only after "a Supreme Civil
Power be instituted, who shall ordain them to be observed as Laws," Selden
"more fairly finds fault with the want of Authority in these Dictates of Reason,"
and asserts they acquire the force of Laws only "because all our knowledge of
them is to be derived from God alone, who when he makes these Rules known to
us, does then (and not before) promulgate them to us as Laws." Tyrrel thinks
Selden is "in the right, and hath well enough corrected our common Moralists,
who are wont to consider these Dictates of Reason as Laws, without any
sufficient proof." However, though the work of Selden "is indeed most
learnedly and judiciously performed," yet it still seems to Tyrrell "that he
hath not sufficiently answered his own Objection concerning Mens Ignorance,
or want of discovering the Lawgiver," for the fact that the "those Traditions
which they call the Precepts of Noah," are believed by the "whole Jewish

[114] Parkin *Science* pp. 56–66.

Nation," cannot be looked upon as a "sufficient promulgation made by God as a Lawgiver, of those Laws or Precepts therein contained and that all those Nations, which have never heard of Adam or Noah, would be condemned for not living according to them[.]" He proposes instead that for demonstrating the "Divine Authority of those Dictates of Right Reason, or Rules of Life, called the Laws of Nature" it is the "best and fittest Method to inquire into their Natural Causes, as well internal as external, remote as near[.]" Referring soon thereafter the reader, to the opinions of the "sagacious Author" of the "*Essay of humane Understanding*" – John Locke.[115]

Cumberland and Tyrrell represent the informed and respectful rejection of the main tenets of Selden's theory by the English "empirical" philosophical and political school, which to a great extent culminated in the thought of Locke. Although clearly taking full benefit from Selden's criticism of Grotian and Hobbesian theories, and admiring his immense learning, these thinkers rejected his epistemic and political reliance on tradition and contract, adopting instead a view that was essentially a combination of what they viewed as the best elements of Grotius and Hobbes, predicated on a combination of *a priori* reasoning with sense-based utilitarian observation of the world.

It was left to another group of writers, of far less philosophical inclinations, but – rather like Selden himself – oriented more towards historical writing as well as direct political activities, to transmit the core of his theory into the later mainstream of English political thought and practice. These were a number of close contemporaries, among the generation after Selden's, who rose to some of the most influential positions in English law and politics and who, by their political or judicial activities, as well as (perhaps even more so) by their writings, significantly influenced the constitutional practice and thought of post-Restoration England, for generations to come. Most prominent among these were Edward Hyde and Matthew Hale, both prominent lawyers and MPs, with a serious scholarly bent, a generation younger than Selden, who regarded themselves as his disciples and friends (the last, also a beneficiary and executor of his will).[116]

---

[115] James Tyrrell, *A Brief Disquisition of the Law of Nature* (1692) "Preface" pp. xv–xxv.

[116] A similar figure is another friend and executor of Selden, Sir John Vaughan (1603–1674), who was a lawyer and MP and rose to become Chief Justice of Common Pleas (1668–1674). Vaughan and his family certainly cherished his friendship with Selden – for the Inner Temple records note the "special admission" to membership in the Inner Temple of one Selden Vaughan, who was son to Edward and grandson to Sir John. However, Sir John did not compose any work similar in scope or purpose to those of Clarendon and Hale. And although Vaughan's son Edward published in 1677 *The Reports and Arguments of that Learned Judge, Sir John Vaughan … Published by his Son, Edward Vaughan* (a corrected 2nd edition was published in 1706), which clearly displays his acquaintance with and appreciation of Selden's work (especially in his consideration of marriage law), his long-term influence was apparently slight. Moreover, as I show elsewhere in this book, Vaughan's ideas were informed by the theories of Grotius and Hobbes no less than Selden's, so that he hardly qualifies as a Seldenian.

Edward Hyde (1609–1674) later First Earl of Clarendon, was a Middle Templar, who while quite young joined the London literary circles and became acquainted with Jonson, Cotton and Selden, as well as later becoming part of the Great Tew circle of intellectuals gathered by Lord Falkland. An MP in the Long Parliament who initially sided with the opposition to the King, he gradually turned towards the royalist side, primarily because of his fears for the Church of England. As the conflict escalated he became one of the closest advisors to Charles I, eventually elevated to the dignity of Chancellor of the Exchequer. As guardian of the Prince of Wales he fled with him abroad, remaining with the exiled court after the regicide, and was eventually appointed by Charles II his Lord Chancellor in 1658. Upon the Restoration, as Lord Chancellor and First Lord of the Treasury, Hyde became by far the most powerful figure in government, exerting a major influence on the character of the constitutional settlement. Raised, in close succession, to the titles of Baron, Viscount and finally Earl of Clarendon, he also became, through the marriage of his daughter Anne to the King's brother James, the father-in-law to the heir apparent, and grandfather to the last two Stuart queens, the future Mary II and Anne. In 1667 the combination of mounting political opposition to his policies and the King's displeasure with him brought about Clarendon's downfall from office, and as he was impeached by Parliament he went again into exile until his death seven years later. Beside his obvious impact on the Restoration settlement, Clarendon also exerted a great influence on generations of Englishmen well into the nineteenth century by way of his multi-volume *History of the Rebellion*, written during his two exiles and published by his sons in 1717. Other significant works which he composed, and which display clear Seldenian traits, are several of his essays, composed in 1670 at Montpellier and published posthumously in 1676: "On Promises" and "On Liberty" – as well as the self-explanatory *A Brief View and Survey of the Dangerous and Pernicious Errors to Church and State, in Mr. Hobbes's Book, Entitled Leviathan*. Clarendon always defended Selden's conduct and ideas, and in his autobiography bestowed on him unqualified praise, writing that "Mr. Hyde was wont to say, that he valued himself upon nothing more than upon having had Mr. Selden's acquaintance from the time he was very young." Clarendon's attitude to Selden has been described as "something approaching hero-worship" and it appears Selden's ideas profoundly influenced Hyde and had an important role in molding his views on constitutional and religious issues.[117]

Sir Matthew Hale (1609–1676), was a studious and successful barrister of Lincoln's Inn, who early on befriended Selden through their common acquaintance, Attorney General William Noy. It seems that it was Selden who encouraged Hale to pursue studies outside the law, (especially in theology, science and legal theory), and who exerted a strong theoretical impact on

[117] Edward Hyde, "The Life of Edward, Earl of Clarendon" in *The History of the Rebellion and Civil Wars in England* (1702–1704) vol. I pp. 923–924; Harris *Clarendon* pp. 8–10.

much of Hale's subsequent thought. Hale earned a reputation for integrity and for non-political upholding of the law, so that before and during the Civil War he was counsel to a number of prominent royalists, including the two most famous ones, Strafford and Laud. This reputation survived the regicide and, despite his royalist precedents, he sat in every one of the interregnum "Parliaments" from the first Protectorate one onwards, as well as being appointed by Cromwell as Judge in the Court of Common Pleas (1653–1659) – which Hale accepted on the condition that he "would not be required to acknowledge the usurper's authority." At the Restoration he rose even higher, honored with being the member of the Convention Parliament who formally proposed the motion to consider Charles II's reinstatement as monarch; he was later appointed by the King as Chief Baron of the Exchequer (1660–1671), and finally as Lord Chief Justice of England (1671–1676). Hale had a decisive role in preserving the integrity of the English legal system through the interregnum, and at the Restoration. Besides his important judiciary work, he influenced later generations through various posthumously published writings, especially *A History and Analysis of the Common Law of England* (1713) and *The History of the Pleas of the Crown* (*Historia placitorum coronae*, published 1736) – both enormously influential on legal education well into the nineteenth century. He also composed additional manuscripts, among them the unpublished *Government in General, its Origin, Alteration and Trials* as well the anti-Hobbesian *Reflections on Hobbes' Dialogue of the Law*, which was discovered and published only in 1835. All of Hale's works exhibit a manifest Seldenian imprint, and it suffices to point out that the latter is the one author most often cited in Hale's *History* of the common law.[118]

Both Hyde and Hale publicly prided themselves on their personal connection with Selden. The first from the inner circle of royalists, the second as grudging but eminent judicial authority of the interregnum regimes, they had crucial roles in fashioning the political and judicial system of the Restoration. It was, however, as historians who composed enormously influential historical accounts of English politics and law, reflecting constitutionalist views that to a great degree followed Selden's, that their long-term impact was greatest. Both were anti-Hobbesian, and opposed as well Grotian and Filmerian ideas of society and politics. Their descriptions of a traditional constitutionalism exercised immense influence over the ideas and terminology of generations of Englishmen well into the nineteenth century.

The place of Selden's ideas in the Glorious Revolution of 1688–1689, has as yet hardly been looked at in historical studies. However, there are indications that they had an important impact on prominent figures like: Sir Robert Atkyns, Chief Baron of the Exchequer, who became Speaker of the Lords in the

---

[118] "Hale, Sir Matthew" in Edward Foss, *Biographia Juridica: A Biographical Dictionary of the Judges of England from the Conquest to the Present Time, 1066–1870* (1870); A. Cromartie, *Sir Matthew Hale 1609–1676* (Cambridge University Press, 1995) pp. 32–39.

Convention Parliament, fulfilled a crucial function in mediating the constitutional settlement, and was among those who drafted the wording of the Declaration of Right; William Atwood, an important lawyer who wrote *Fundamental Constitution of the English Government* (1690), an anti-Lockean tract, denying that in 1688 the contract and government had been dissolved; and William Petyt, Keeper of the Records, who authored books like *The Antient Right of the Commons of England Asserted* (1680), and as MP in the 1688 parliamentary debates about the original contract, mentioned about the terms of government that "In Selden's Titles of honor you had the oath before any did homage."[119]

Selden's ideas continued to impact England and the English-speaking nations' legal and constitutional thinking through both direct and indirect avenues for centuries after his death. In the eighteenth century, Selden's books were still a required component of an educated Englishman's library, far beyond the circle legal practitioners. That the libraries of prominent literary figures such as Dr. Samuel Johnson and James Boswell held several volumes of Selden's works was natural. But that the same is true of political leaders, from Edmund Burke in England to Benjamin Franklin, John Adams and Thomas Jefferson in America, suggests Selden's works might have had a larger impact on ideas and events than is currently recognized. Burke explicitly mentioned Selden in his influential *Reflections of the Revolution in France* (1790) as a major figure of the English political tradition that he was endeavoring to defend. Even William Blackstone's view of law, can be said to be far closer to Selden's and Hale's than to Locke's. Blackstone's *Commentaries on the Laws of England* (1765–1769) became the most influential legal work in the English-speaking world from the latter eighteenth century well into the early twentieth century (and to this day is used by the US Supreme Court, for establishing intentions of the framers of the US constitution). Franklin, as far as we know, owned only one of Selden's works, the minor *The Priviledges of the Baronage of England* (1642), but its subject, reviewing the powers of the upper house of the English Parliament, suggests it might have had some role in deliberations on American constitutional issues. Adams owned a set of the *Opera Omnia*, Selden's collected works of 1726, thus having access to almost everything Selden ever wrote, and the same was true of Jefferson, who in addition to the *Opera* also owned a separate copy of Selden's "Dissertatio historica" on the *Fleta*, as well as two copies of Selden's *Mare clausum* (the original of 1635 as well as a 1663 edition).[120]

---

[119] Pocock *Ancient* pp. 229–231. Atkyns, together with two Selden associates, Thomas Barlow and Sir Matthew Hale, took a prominent part in drawing up two unsuccessful schemes of religious comprehension in October 1667, and February 1668.

[120] For Selden's approach as proto-Burkean, see Ferguson *Clio* pp. 57–59, 117–125, 292–298, and Collins *Cosmos* p. 210 note 30. For the claim that the reference to Locke at the outset of the *Commentaries*, was (intentionally?) misleading, and that "Blackstone's view of law was closer to Selden's and Hale's than Locke's" see M. Lobban, "The Common Law World," ch. 8 of

Another avenue of Seldenian impact over American legal and constitutional thought, which still needs more looking into, is in ideas about the role of the Common law in the US, disseminated through works which built to some degree on Selden's thought, and were ubiquitous in colonial law libraries far more than his own works, like Hale's *History of the Common Law* and Blackstone's *Commentaries*, certainly the most widely read legal text in late eighteenth-century America. These works, with their many Seldenian ideas and images were also employed in derivative works by prominent nineteenth-century US legal writers, such as Joseph Hopkinson and James Wilson – the latter, for example, using sections from Hale almost verbatim). The role and interpretation of the Common law in the US is not only of historical importance, but is currently being debated in both theoretical and practical aspects, by scholars and judges, including among others, recently deceased Supreme Court justice Antonin Scalia.[121]

To these constitutional and legal aspects one might plausibly add several more. One example is the constitutional authority to impeach, still possessed but not practiced by the UK House of Lords, still possessed and practiced (as late as 1998, against the then sitting president) by the US Senate. Another example is the debate in the UK, about the Human Rights Act of 1998, which established the potential jurisdiction of the European Court of Human Rights over British offenses, with several prominent figures, like Law Lord Leonard Hoffmann, and the President of the Queen's Bench, Sir Brian Leveson, criticizing this trend and upholding the supremacy of Parliament rather than EU courts, until the UK 2016 referendum vote to leave the EU made the debate redundant.[122]

E. Pattaro (Gen ed.), *A Treatise of Legal Philosophy and General Jurisprudence* (Dordrecht: Springer, 2007), vol. 8 pp. 99–101.

    Selden's books that American founding fathers owned, seem especially relevant in Franklin's case to his attempts to justify unicameralism, and in Jefferson's case, to his pursuing of a maritime war against North African pirates.

[121] See, for example, B. Meyler, "Towards a Common Law Originalism" in *Stanford Law Review* 59/3 (2006) pp. 551–600.

[122] Among the vocal critics of the Human Rights Act and its supposed subjection of British courts to the jurisdiction of the European Court of Human Rights (ECHR), which they regard as attempting judicial imperialism, British Law Lord Leonard Hoffmann in 2009 argued the European court had been "unable to resist the temptation to aggrandize its jurisdiction and to impose uniform rules on Member States. It considers itself the equivalent of the Supreme Court of the United States, laying down a federal law of Europe"; while Sir Brian Leveson, President of the Queen's Bench, in May 2015 declared he refuses to be "crushed by the European jackboot" when coming to apply the European convention of human rights in British courts, and asserted UK judges were not bound by the decisions of the ECHR, instead being only obliged to take the Strasbourg court's rulings "into consideration." A political debate had been underway for several years in the British Parliament about replacing the European-bound Human Rights Act with a new British Bill of Rights, with Prime Minister Cameron invoking this idea in a speech on the 800th anniversary of Magna Carta.

A thorough examination of these and other avenues through which Selden's ideas were present and influential in later centuries is beyond the scope of this work, but there are grounds to expect that such an effort might yet yield a bountiful harvest.

Before concluding this chapter, it is important to consider the extent to which the early seventeenth century witnessed a widespread intellectual assault on the value of tradition, which in England became an attack on its traditional legal system, the Common law. The assault started on the epistemological front and spread to that of political and legal theory. Tradition is denied authority in political theories predicated on either absolutism or individual reason, as well as in Hobbes' mix of the two. Grotius, we have seen, allowed tradition in his theory a role merely adjunctory and supportive to reason. Hobbes plainly stated that "[w]hen long Use obtaineth the authority of a Law, it is not the Length of time that maketh the Authority, but the Will of the Soveraign signified by his silence[.]" Similarly, Filmer after asserting that in every state the will of the sovereign power is, by definition, above the law, explained that "[c]ustoms at first became lawful only by some superior power which did either command or consent unto their beginning." Now, the identification of the *origin* of customary laws (in both cases with England's Common law clearly intended) as the will of some sovereign power, was not in itself necessarily undermining to the authority of such law, for this argument was shared by several (though not all) common lawyers, including Selden. The point of contention was rather that views like those of Grotius, Hobbes and Filmer upheld the desirability of a permanent and arbitrary power of sovereign will over all political laws. Selden, both in his parliamentary activities as well as in his learned writings, rejected an arbitrary sovereign will, insisting instead that the supreme principle of political society is: commitments made must be mutually kept.[123]

Selden strived, from early on in his career, to defend and justify a coherent worldview upholding the necessary and beneficial role of custom in political society—a position we would today call *traditionalism*. As he witnessed increasing attacks on the English legal and constitutional tradition at the hands of rising absolutist and naturalist theories, Selden found himself compelled to find adequate justification for the constitutional tradition of his nation. He thus embarked on a wide-ranging reflection on the nature of customary political and judicial systems, not only within the English context, but as a generally desirable feature of all political societies. The result was possibly the richest and most impressive defense of political tradition to arise in British thought for generations, informing and influencing the more familiar works of later thinkers who drew on him, such as Hale and Burke.

---

[123] Hobbes *Leviathan* p1c26; Robert Filmer, *Patriachia and Other Writings*, J.P. Sommerville ed. (Cambridge University Press, 1991) pp. 44–46. For Selden see JN b1c8, and also in TT "Law of Nature" and "Power, State."

4

Law "Fitted to the Genius of the Nation": Selden's Theory of National Tradition in Law and Politics

4.1 CONTINUITY THROUGH CHANGE

In a famous passage from his 1616 critical "Notes" to Sir John Fortescue's fifteenth-century *Laudibus*, Selden explicitly claimed that in England, as in other countries, natural laws had been

> limited for the conveniency [sic] of civil society here, and those limitations have been from thence, increased, altered, interpreted, and brought to what now they are; although perhaps, saving the meerly immutable part of nature[.]

According to this passage, all legal systems (or at least, all just ones), have a common natural "immutable" root, upon which each political society "increased, altered, interpreted" to suit its particular needs and circumstances. In short, he presented a theory of law as changing with time while remaining rooted in some fixed natural principles – of continuity through change, of a tradition. Selden returned to this idea in his writings through the years, repeatedly using two familiar images for continuity through change, in the "Notes" as well as elsewhere, comparing English law to the ship or to "the house that's so often repaired, *ut nihil ex pristina materia supersit*, [that no original material remains] which yet, by the civil law, is to be accounted the same still[.]" The image of the ship or house, maintained and restored through the ages rather than torn down and rebuilt from scratch, to represent the traditional English legal and political framework, recurs in his writings, such as his recorded remark in the *Table-Talk*:

> They that would pull down the Bishops and erect a new way of Government, do as he that pulls down an old House, and builds another in another Fashion. There's a great deal of do, and a great deal of trouble: the old rubbish must be carried away, and new materials must be brought: Workmen must be provided, and perhaps the old one would have serv'd as well.

Both the image and its implication were recurrent among English writers in the following centuries, to convey the very same theoretical preferences, neatly illustrating the continuity of such ideas within a central strand of English thought. Often it became fused with the 'ship of state,' another familiar metaphor, favored by many English speakers and writers on political issues, down to those compacting on the Mayflower, to Edmund Burke, and beyond.[1]

However, allowing for such a description of Selden's theory of law as tradition, does not supply an understanding of how it was supposed to function, of how it was justified and of why such a theory was even necessary. Indeed, although the traditional bent of Selden's view of law is often mentioned, there yet has to be offered a satisfactory account for the grounds and purpose of his theory of tradition. We have seen in previous chapters both the general crisis facing political thought in the early seventeenth century, and the more specific problems faced by the accepted account of English law. This was the context for Selden's addressing these issues, but it is now necessary to inquire about why did he not opt for one of the other alternatives available as response to the crisis, either older ones like the appeal to the structure and ideas of Roman law, or the newer assumptions of the modern natural right theories or the new absolutist theories – and in what way he believed his own view was preferable to these. This chapter will make the case that the foundation for Selden's theory was in the centrality he assigned in it to a category of human association relegated by most other contemporary thinkers to a subsidiary role, if at all: the nation.[2]

As detailed in previous chapters, the investigations of Selden and his contemporaries into political and legal theory were born under the sense of great intellectual crisis in philosophical and political ideas. In the realm of political theory, most answers to the crisis during the first half of the seventeenth century proposed a new foundation of authority in politics. This new foundation was either a law of nature, discoverable through individual judgment, or an

---

[1] NL cols. 1891–1892; TT "Bishops out of Parliament." Elsewhere he described "moral teachings and the rules of civic life" (basic political laws) as "the very stout supports to a building," see JN b1c1.

For the ship of state metaphor see Sharpe *Remapping* p. 98.

For the claim that although the ship or house analogy was found in writers before Selden, he "transposed this analogy from the description of corporate entities to one of a legal system in its entirety conceived of separately from particular governments" – see in O.M. Roslak, *John Selden and the Laws of England* (Cambridge, unpublished PhD dissertation, 2000) p. 41.

[2] I have found the connection between Selden's ideas of tradition and of the nation is in many places implied and sometimes touched upon in current research, but I have not found it anywhere directly addressed and discussed. A recent example is Caruso's book, where the author stresses at the outset the value held by custom in Selden's opinion. Caruso remarks that custom in Selden's thought assumed a value that goes beyond mere conservation: even more than merely juridical significances, it has ethical-political ones. Indeed, Caruso mentions that Selden made a deep innovation in the meaning of custom, taking it beyond the meaning of habit (or second nature) of the scholastic teachings to a place where nature and history coincide, for instance, when including in the principled discussion of the breach of constitutional contract peculiar English values, flowing from the "tradizione politica della nazione" (the nation's political tradition). But Caruso does not further develop the issue. See Caruso *Miglior* pp. 3–4. For the meaning of the term "nation" in England of this period see McEachern *Poetics* pp. 1–2.

absolute submission to the sovereign. The view founded on individual judgment was obviously the application to politics of the Protestant argument against the authority of (Catholic) tradition; but as it was employed ingeniously by many Catholic thinkers, especially the Spanish "second scholastics," to rebut Protestant ideas, it overflowed from the confines of confessional controversy to become part of the wider discussion of political ideas (which was, in its turn, never completely devoid of theological considerations).

Indeed, in England such religiously based political ideas had been debated vigorously at least since the contentious successions of Henry VIII's two daughters. Protestant aversion to the Catholic rule of Mary Tudor brought forth authors such as John Ponet, Bishop of Winchester, who composed in exile a *Short Treatise of Political Power* (1556), in which he justified rebellion against a ruler who acts against one's religion and God, and such as the influential Scottish clergyman exiled in England, John Knox, who authored *The First Blast of the Trumpet Against the Monstruous Regiment of Women* (1558), justifying on biblical grounds a right of resistance against female rulers. The succession to the throne of the Protestant Elizabeth produced similarly pro-resistance texts from the Catholic side, such as the pamphlet *A Conference About the Next Succession to the Crown of England* (1594), published by the English Jesuit Robert Parsons under the pseudonym R. Doleman, which argued that a king's power is delegated from the Commonwealth, and is thus a restricted and limited one, that can be rescinded – such as when a king is not in the service of the true religion. In his *True Law of Free Monarchies* (1598) and *Apology for the Oath of Allegiance* (1607), James I replied to ideas such as these with a theory of royal power derived not from the community but from conquest, as a form of divine favor. In turn, one of the answers to King James was by the Spanish neo-scholastic Jesuit Francisco Suarez, who argued in *Defensor Fidei*, that God, as the ultimate but not the proximate source of power, does not grant political power to any peculiar institution or congregation, but rather to the whole body of the community. This debate merged later in the century with the one engendered by the Civil War, with royalists like Digges, Ferne and Filmer explicitly accusing the parliamentarian side of espousing the ideas of the Jesuits.[3]

Thus, while the most prominent seventeenth-century exponent of political theories founded on individual judgment was Hugo Grotius, his was certainly not the only theory on this front, and another important strand was a version of theologically inspired Protestant political thought, also tending to support ideas of law and politics as based on the judgment of individuals, which became

---

[3] Harrison *Masterpiece* pp. 13–23; McEachern *Poetics* pp. 9–10; Collins *Cosmos* pp. 154–156. Not unaware of the destabilizing potential of such a theory, Suarez added that this principle does not necessarily entail a democracy, for once a form of government (ideally, monarchy) has been agreed on, it is binding and irreversible, or in his own words, "firm and perpetual." Selden, on his part, more than once explicitly indicated in his writings that the attempts to advance the idea of a political supremacy of kings originated in a reaction to Catholic claims about the deposing powers of popes. See, for example, TT "Kings of England" sec. 3.

especially marked among the English sectaries coming to the fore during the Civil War and interregnum periods.[4]

Among the products of this version of Protestant though, which gained great prominence in the 1640s and 1650s, there were learned and articulate texts like the aforementioned *Lex Rex* (1644) by Samuel Rutherford; or like *A Declaration, or Representation from his Excellency Sir Thomas Fairfax, and the Army Under his Command* (1647) produced under the direction of Lord General Thomas Fairfax, commander of the parliamentary army.[5]

There were also similarly inspired ideas articulated by those far lower on the class rung, like the Levellers' *Agreement of the People*, submitted to the Army Council and discussed at Putney, in October and November 1647. The *Agreement* demanded political representation to be devised directly "according to the number of the inhabitants," to which, we have seen, Henry Ireton retorted that such a principle would overturn all traditional laws and constitutional rules, and leave a polity built only on "absolute natural right[.]" Another example of this type, is the Christian-communist movement of True Levellers led by Gerrard Winstanley, wishing to erect a social order based on pure reason and love, they came to be known as Diggers because of their communitarian attempts to cultivate common lands on St. George's Hill, Surrey, and later other locations around the country (all of them, the local authorities had crushed by 1651). Winstanley used the world "Reason" in place and in preference to "God," for example, declaring that "In the beginning of time, the great Creator, Reason, made the earth to be a common treasury." He outlined theories of equality and common-ownership, based on a language of natural rights, which explicitly tagged all traditions in both law and church as the true enemy, such as when he asserted "indeed the main work of reformation lies in this, to reform the clergy, lawyers and law; for all the complaints of the land are wrapped up within them three, not in the person of a king" as well as his call to "[b]urn your old Law-Books" because "as your Government must be new, so let the Laws be new." There thus was a convergence of much of the terminology of such authors and groups with Grotius' basing claims of individual judgment on "the Law of Nature and Nations" and "right reason."[6]

---

[4] The background to this strand of English Protestantism and its political stance, has been described in M. Walzer, *The Revolution of the Saints* (Cambridge, Mass.: Harvard University Press, 1965) especially pp. 148–149, 170, 300–301, and for the use of the building metaphor as opposite to Selden's, see pp. 181–182.

[5] See Samuel Rutherford, *Lex Rex* (1644) pp. 1–10, 66, 103. Rutherford proposed the "Union" of men into a "politick body" receives from God the power of making laws "naturally" (refers this to Bodin and Suarez), denied the teachings of the "Brasilians" that "every single man hath the power of the sword to revenge his own injuries" (refers this to Molina), and regarding the covenant between people and king as a "conditionall" one, that can be dissolved.

[6] See *Agreement of the People* (1647) and, for the Putney debates in general and Ireton's reply in particular, see M. Mendle, *The Putney Debates of 1647: The Army, the Levellers and the English State* (Cambridge University Press, 2010 reissue). Published by November 1647, the *Agreement*, which claims to be a proposal from the representatives (agents) of five cavalry regiments in the

As for those advocating absolute political submission there were, aside from Filmer's comprehensive attempt to arrange and present the absolutist theory in a systematic form, several other prominent intellectual figures tending to some version of political absolutism. Such were the attempts by Gentili and Bacon to refashion Roman law ideas and structures so that they would address current political problems, or more often, the attempts of influential clerical figures like Maynwaring and Sybthorpe to advocate a Christian-inspired absolute submission to authority. In addition, especially in the 1640s and 1650s, there were important attempts to combine into one the two types of political argumentation, rationalist and absolutist, by mixing a basis in individual reason and consent with an absolutist politics erected on that basis. Such were the writings of Dudley Digges, Marchamont Needham and, most prominently, of course, Hobbes, all starting with some premise of individual judgment, followed by the impossibility of transforming individual judgments into a stable collective one, and concluding from this the desirability of an absolutist political setting.[7]

New Model Army, was almost certainly drawn up in close consultation with the Leveller leadership. Both agitators and Leveller leaders were present at Putney.

For the ideas of Winstanley and the "True Levellers" see *Light Shining in Buckinghamshire* (1648), *The True Levellers' Standard Advanced* (1649), *A New-Years Gift for the Parliament and Armie* (1650) and *The Law of Freedom in a Platform* (1652). More generally for the ideas and terminology of Levellers, Diggers and various other naturalistic Christian groupings described as Ranters, Familists and Anabaptists (although many times not an organized movement or doctrine), see C. Hill, *The World Turned Upside Down* (Penguin, 1991 – reprint of 1975 edition) pp. 26–27, 66–67, 118–119, 132–133, 141, 339–340, 346–347, and in Eccleshall *Order* pp. 173–175. In the mid-1640s, the Levellers held that political society had broken down, and something like a state of nature existed, where the "sword" (that is, the pro-sectarian army) remains the only authority until political society is legitimately re-founded. The Levellers thus proposed in Hill's words, a "new social contract refounding of the state." For Leveller and Digger texts and ideas see also Burgess *Politics* pp. 226–228.

On the individualist radical political theory connected with Protestantism see Pocock *Ancient* pp. 126–127, and Tuck *Natural* chapter 7.

[7] For the articulation of standard absolutist theories see Bodin's *Six Livres de la République* (1577), James I's *True Law of Free Monarchies* (1598) and Salmasius' *Defensio Regia pro Carolo I* (1649). Filmer's fullest statement of his absolutist theory is of course *Patriarcha* (first composed in early 1630s), but the best example of his extensive attempts to refute Grotius, Hobbes, Selden (and Milton) was his *Observations Concerning the Originall of Government* (1652).

Dudley Digges the younger's *The Unlawfulnesse of Subjects Taking up Armes Against their Soveraigne, in What Case Soever* (1647) is a good example of combining Grotian-style state of nature arguments, Filmer-style Christian terminology and particularly Hobbes-style utilitarian considerations, to reach an absolutist conclusion arguing that the state is born out of individuals having natural "power" which they "voluntarily and upon agreement" give up when they create the "mutual compact." There is then a transfer of power to him (or them) that rule, coterminous with the "contract" or "covenant" that creates the "civill unity" (pp. 3–6). Digges denies this means an abdication of understanding or conscience, but rather that men must trust the better judgment of authority and not actively resist it, although they might passively do so (pp. 10–13). Like Hobbes he distinguishes between law and right of nature (p. 14), and criticizes aristocratic and democratic forms of government as far worse than monarchy (pp. 22–25).

Hobbes' ingenious combination of individualist and sensualist premises with an absolutist political outcome is probably the most famous of the ideological concoctions of the period, but, as already noted, there were many others. Especially instructive for our purpose is the no less inventive combination of sectarian fervor and rationalist politics into one. Albeit originating from quite different perspectives, the Grotian and the sectarian versions of individualist rationalism drew progressively closer, sometimes overlapping in the same individuals, eventually producing that branch of English political thought termed "rational dissent," which went on to inform the thought of figures from Locke to Joseph Priestley and beyond. An instructive example of this convergence and its impact on English politics were the writings of John Rogers (1627–c. 1671), an influential sectarian preacher who in the 1650s adhered to ideas of the "Fifth Monarchists," envisaging an English state invested with an immediate messianic mission. In 1653, after both monarchy and Parliament had been destroyed by the regicide and the dissolution of the Rump "Parliament," ultimate political power lay in the hands of Cromwell and the Independents-led army, so that an English republic adhering to the values of the Independent sectaries seemed a viable outcome from these circumstances. Rogers' period of activity and political significance opened a mere five days after Cromwell's armed dissolution of the Rump, when the preacher issued a broadside proposing the establishing of a new government of saintly figures, composed of a 70-member "Sanhedrin" and a 12-member council of state, all appointed by General Cromwell. A stream of publications followed, advocating a thorough reformation of law and government devised to create a saintly republic, with Rogers not shirking from turning against Cromwell, when it emerged that the latter would not fulfill the hopes invested in him. The measure of Rogers' perceived impact and influence at this period was his repeated harassment and imprisonment by the Protectorate regime during 1654–1658, together with other prominent Fifth Monarchy men such as Major-General Thomas Harrison and MP John Carew. Rogers best presented his ideas in *Sagrir* (1653), a curious mix of apocalyptic language and imagery with learned discussions of various epistemological and political issues. In it, he described England as now being transformed into a new republic with Christ as its notional king, the Fifth Monarchy of the biblical book of Daniel, ushering a new era in which, as predictions made by such as Nostradamus and Joachim of Fiore purportedly show, Rome and the Antichrist were about to be destroyed by a saintly English army. However, alongside such apocalyptic tones, Rogers' pamphlet also makes a closely argued attempt, including ample quotes from, and references to, such as Philo, Suarez and Cicero, to show his political proposals to be first and foremost the result of right reason. Rogers explicitly defines reason as the inner light within men, which enables them to correctly identify the law of nature, bringing as support for this view repeated quotes from Culverwel (who articulated them, we may recall, against Selden), as well as praising "the learned Grotius" for his identification of the law of nature with right reason. Rogers goes on to insist that reason only is the light of nature, the "intellectual lamp" of men, and asserts that:

He is the great *enemy* to common good and *traytor* that can be, that betrayes his *Reason*, and becomes a slave to enforced Forms and Laws of men, that are *tyranny* and *oppression*, and against *Reason*.[8]

It soon transpires that, for Rogers, the source of this tyranny and oppression by "Forms and Laws of men" going against reason, is in two forces that he regards as the greatest enemies of political and moral freedom: The "Tyranny of the Laws and Lawyers as they now are" and "the Antichristian, National Clergy" – in other words, the Common law and the established church. These two institutions are for him clearly the linchpins of the evil old order in England; and for a new order founded on reason and nature to replace it, first there must occur a destruction of those "two Plagues of the Nation rose up both from the bottomless smoke, and are the priests and Lawyers." Arguing that since local and particular laws restricting natural freedoms, are by the laws of God, nature and nations illegitimate, then the so-called English "fundamental laws" are nothing but a "Norman yoke," created by evil William the Conqueror to enslave Englishmen, now at long last to be undone by good "Oliver the Conqueror."[9]

Rogers' writings began to appear only some months before Selden's death, and we have no evidence that the latter ever saw them; but there could hardly be a better illustration for the epistemic and political outlook that Selden was opposed to. Rogers' insistence that his views were a conclusion of right reason only, perfectly illustrated Selden's argument, especially prominent in *Jure Naturali*, about the dangers inherent in claims proceeding solely from individual reason. Grotius and Culverwel would both almost certainly have been horrified to find their arguments in favor of the inner light of individual right reason mustered by Rogers to justify such political views; on his part, Selden would probably have found the situation ironic, but not very surprising, as it perfectly demonstrated his claims about the limitations of individual reason: claims which he had argued against Grotius, and which, in his turn, Culverwel had attempted to rebut. Rogers' tirade, in the name of nature and reason, against English laws and the established church, as false "Forms and Laws of men" demonstrates very much the whole point of Selden's intellectual efforts to defend and justify those very "Forms and Laws." Moreover, it is not

---

[8] John Rogers, *Sagrir or Doomes-day Drawing Nigh* (1653) pp. 32–42, 48–49, 132–133. "Sagrir" and other titles to his pamphlets are in Hebrew, which Rogers often used in his writings.

[9] Rogers *Sagrir* pp. 48–49, 60–61, 108–109. He also repeatedly rails against particular religious or legal institutions, such as the tithes and the Inns of Court, declaring the latter to be created by and carrying out the "will of a tyrant." p. 83. Inconsistently, he nevertheless terms Coke as "that eminent *Oracle* of the Law." Having failed to stem the demise of the Protectorate in 1659, Rogers then left for the Netherlands, but in 1662 submitted to the restored monarchy and returned to England to live quietly afterward, apparently still alive in 1671.

superfluous to point out how much of the political premises and conclusions in Rogers were close to those of Hobbes and Needham. Hobbes would have naturally rejected much in Rogers' work, and in fact would have probably regarded his claim to ground politics on right reason as an excellent proof of the similar dangers he warns of in both *Leviathan* and *Behemoth*. However, as for Rogers' starting point from a natural freedom of the individual, and his finishing point in an absolute sovereign power in a council or a "single person," as well as his contempt for the Common law and the established church, indeed for all traditions as source of authority – all these would perfectly fit Hobbes' own ideas.

Among the Protestant-inspired versions of rational individual judgment, vehement opposition to traditions in general, and to English ones in particular, is very much a defining characteristic. Among sectaries like Winstanley and Rogers, the traditional Common law (and its lawyers), as well as the clergy of the established church, came to be regarded as enslaving "Forms and Laws of men" and enemies of justice and truth, to be extirpated in the name of "Reason." Even among the most practically minded Independents, like the Protector and his son-in law, Major-General Henry Ireton, the constant intellectual struggle between their more conservative personal tendencies and experiences and their individualist and anti-traditionalist religious ideas is evident. Similar anti-traditionalist tendencies were evident also among some of the non-sectarian Puritans such as Henry Marten, MP, an ardent republican who was among the regicide judges of Charles I and who became a leading figure in Cromwell's Council of State. Among Marten's papers there is a 1947 draft, criticizing Selden and others (like Prynne) for the historical arguments they brought in support of the House of Lords (and its precedence to the Commons) – Marten did not deny the accuracy of the historical precedents brought by Selden and Prynne to support the upper house, but rather invoked against them the authority of "right reason."[10]

We may recall that among adherents of the Grotian approach, albeit usually in a far more temperate manner and tone, similar conclusions were reached about rejecting the authority of customary practices and ideas. Structured as level upon level of rational judgment, Grotius' theory had no real need for custom – either as a source of authority (tradition) or as accumulated experience (expediency). In such a theory all acceptable laws and political systems are ultimately founded only on individual reasoned consent. Even the first principle of Grotius' theory, the social impulse, is subsumed by him to the intellect which draws out its meaning. Although both expediency and "unbroken tradition" did appear in Grotius' *Jure Belli* as purportedly supporting his ideas, they were at the same time very much dispensable. In each case he had ensured that their appearance supplied arguments only "partly" (tradition) or as "reinforcement" (expediency), with reason always

---

[10] Lamont *Puritanism* p. 180.

delivering the decisive validation. In short, they embellished his system, perhaps even aided it, but it would not suffer vital problems without them.

As for the absolutist theoreticians, beneath all their evident scorn of both the sectaries as well as the neo-scholastic and Grotian proponents of right reason, as we have seen already, their rejection of tradition was not very different. Views like Hobbes' and Filmer's held the continuing and arbitrary power of sovereign will over all political laws, including the authority of tradition.[11]

The common denominator of Grotian and sectarian political theories, as well as absolutists, of either the Filmerian or the Hobbesian varieties, was their fundamental rejection of tradition as a source of authority in politics. It is this challenge, in its many guises and manifestations, which Selden attempted to confront throughout his career, both in his writings and in his political activities. England's escalating constitutional conflicts, and the later slide into constitutional breakdown and Civil War, followed by regicide and military tyranny in the first half of the seventeenth century, highlighted how much the theoretical struggle at hand had very practical stakes. The self-referential attitude of previous generations of common lawyers had become gradually unsustainable, for besides the patent collapse of many assumptions upon which it was predicated – like the purported immutability and clarity of English law – it also had to deal with the danger of falling prey to accusations of merely relative and instrumental usefulness, that would deny it moral meaning. For those who wanted the traditional English frame of government and its laws to survive and thrive, clearly a new manner of justification was necessary. Selden's challenge as an avowed upholder of that English frame of government and law, with the crucial role played in it by tradition as both method and source of authority, was to find a theoretical framework that could justify the value of such a role. The new model political theories, based on either individual reason or absolute sovereignty, regardless of diverging political conclusions, had in common a denial of a significant political role to tradition. It is not that the past has in them no value, for it is hard to find any writer who denies all merit to experience. But valuing the empirical benefit of knowing the past awards such past no intrinsic authority, so that looking at it is merely another comparative method of acquiring knowledge. Tradition means something else – that the past (or rather some meaningful and continuing aspects of it) contains some kind of authority over the present.[12]

4.2   THE ROLE OF TRADITION

Tradition is denied authority in political theories predicated on either individual reason or absolutism, as well as in Hobbes' mix of the two. Accepting any one of

---

[11] Hobbes *Leviathan* p1c26; Filmer *Patriarchia* pp. 44–46.
[12] On this issue see G. Schochet, "Traditions as politics and the politics of tradition" in M.S. Philips and G. Schochet, *Questions of Tradition* (Toronto University Press, 2004) pp. 296–322.

such theories, be they based on individual consent or on an absolutist principle, entails the abandonment of tradition as a source of intrinsic authority, and in England it would have meant discarding the principle on which both the constitutional frame and the practice of common law were predicated. Selden for one had no intention of doing so. For all his esteem of the *Jure Belli* as "that incomparable work of that great man, Hugo Grotius" (reciprocated by the latter calling Selden "the best of men and a very brave citizen"), Selden set out to contest the Dutchman's ideas, and to present an alternative theory of justice and state that legitimates the authority of tradition. Although Selden touched on many of these ideas in several of his works, he treated them most explicitly and extensively in two of them, the *Mare Clausum* and the *Jure Naturali*.[13]

We have seen that Selden rejected individual reason as an adequate footing, even for the knowledge of – certainly for an obligation by – natural law, remarking "is not possible for a person to command or prohibit itself," and Hobbes aired similar criticism of the attempts to obligate men by reason only. Grotius himself was certainly aware of this very problem, as shown by the significant efforts he devoted, especially in book 1, chapters 3–4 of *Jure Belli* to limit the cases in which men could resort to their right of resistance and rise against their rulers. These very attempts, as well as the many examples brought above, of the uses made of Grotius' authority to justify the rebellion in England, indicate the extent to which his theory could not escape the consequences of individual right reason remaining the final judge for one's submission or resistance. As we shall see, Selden did not fail to point out these consequences.[14]

So much for obligation by reason; and as for Selden's attitude to the absolutist answer to the problem of political obligation, although it appears he never replied directly to Hobbes' or Filmer's writings, the idea of political power as a continuing supreme arbitrary will was obviously incompatible with his own outlook. All his writings and political activities touching on these issues are directed, in one way or another, to reject not only a practically arbitrary political power, but even the very idea of "sovereignty" as embraced by Hobbes and Filmer.

We have seen that Selden's answer to the challenge was to propose a completely different scheme of knowledge and obligation. The first principle of Selden's theory was what we would today call an anthropological one, the

---

[13] JN b1c10; "virum optimum ac civem fortissimum" in a letter from Grotius to Peiresec of September 1630, in Grotius *Briefwisseling* iv (1639) p. 261. Selden consistently showed high regard for Grotius, even when he used the latter's own words to prove an opposite view. See, for example, MC b1c4.

The exact English translation of *Mare Clausum seu de Dominio Maris, Libri Duo* (1635) should be, *Two Books of the Enclosed Sea or of the Dominion of the Sea* – but the title to the English-language translation of the book, published in 1652, while Selden was still alive, at the behest of the Commonwealth Council of State, was *Of the Dominion, or Ownership of the Sea.* All English-language quotes from MC are from this 1652 version, unless otherwise stated.

[14] JN b1c7. As seen above, this view exactly is reiterated by Selden in the TT "Law of Nature."

recognition of an equity (or conscience) intuition found in all men: the idea that the world exists within an order of metaphysical justice. Or, in Selden's own words, it is "a belief that there is a God, and he dispenses recompense." From this human intuition of equity, Selden drew his law of obligation that pledges must be kept, articulated in the saying, *"Fides est servanda"* (faith must be observed): the only "natural" law, strictly speaking, "the unwritten law that has been common to all mankind from the creation of the universe and is in the hearts of all the human race"; the only law that all men, at all times, can be assumed to know and understand solely by their own devices.[15]

However, directly flowing from this principle, for Selden virtually all laws by which the nations of the world abide, are to be seen as comprised in his understanding of the term "natural" and hence binding. This was because of two assumptions that Selden made: the first was that laws were agreements and as such to be abided by; the second was that accepting the equity intuition meant that all laws were to be assumed as attempts to express an idea of justice. Thus, as long as these two assumptions were valid, so was the law. As long as a law did not transgress either the natural law of obligation or a small number of moral precepts, it was allowed by, and therefore became a legitimate extension of, the natural or (as Selden preferred to term it) universal law. Or, in Selden's own words: "Natural law is law that is world wide or universal, and the law of nations is an aspect of it."[16]

It is worth pointing out that the law of nations (*ius gentium*), long understood as a term covering both the various national laws as well as international law, was in this period starting to become terminologically subdivided. The term law of nations was starting to be reserved for the various national laws as well for those laws that were accepted among all (or all civilized) nations, while international law was increasingly termed *ius inter gentes* (inter-nations law) by such as the Spanish jurists Vitoria in his *De Indis* (1632) and the English civilian Richard Zouche, in the title of his book *Iuris et Judicii Faecialis, Sive, Iuris Inter Gentes* (1650). Significantly, Grotius started to use the term *ius inter civitates* (inter-states law) to signify the separation of international law from the national and traditional law of nations. As for

---

[15] JN b1c4. See also in JN b1c7: "It so happens, even in the ancient teaching of pagans, that any obligation to an agreement or promise must be observed, and the gods themselves did not ignore them." See also JN b1c8; MC b1c3; *Uxor Ebraica, seu de Nuptiis et Divortiis ex Jure Civili, id est, Divino et Talmudico, Veterum Ebræorum* (1646) – henceforth abbreviated as *Uxor* b1c1. See also discussion in Caruso *Miglior* pp. 791–793. For his recorded use of *"Fides est servanda"* see, for example, TT "Power, State": *"All Power is of God*, means no more than *Fides est servanda*. When St. *Paul* said this, the People had made *Nero* Emperour. They agree, he to command, they to obey. Then God comes in, and casts a hook upon them, keep your Faith: then comes in, all Power is of God. Never King dropt out of the Clouds. God did not make a new Emperour, as the King makes a Justice of Peace." See also TT "Law of Nature."

[16] JN b1 Praefatio: *"Jus Naturale* ita significat heic quod *Jus Mundi* seu Universale; *Gentium Ius*, id quod Gentibus aliquot peculiar."

Selden, we shall see that he treated the law of nations for the most part as referring to the various national laws as well as laws accepted among all nations, explicitly indicating those cases where he referred also to international law.[17]

In Selden's theory, a law was invalid only in cases where it arbitrarily breached some agreement, or if it went against fundamental justice; in such cases it was void, because it was no law at all. Now the question naturally arises as to how and by whom such law-invalidating transgressions are to be identified. Selden rejected both right reason and arbitrary power as adequate for this task; he instead proposed tradition, and a traditionalist framework, as the best means to reach such a result. This approach is perhaps most evident in his treatment of the seven Noahide principles identified by the Jewish tradition, which he regarded as the closest thing humanity had to basic principles of justice. Selden did not claim the Noahide principles to have been given to the Jewish nation as revelation, and by it preserved since in pristine form. For the Jewish people received as direct revelation only the law particular to their nation, the laws of Moses, and not the Noahide principles for all nations. Although, like all true moral legal systems, the law of Moses contained within it the Noahide principles, these were not immediately and distinctly apparent any more than in English or Roman law. Instead he argued that the principles had been revealed not only to the Hebrews but to all humanity (twice: first at the time of Adam and then of Noah), and since then they had been transmitted to posterity by traditions, sometimes illuminated through the ages by the "active intellect" informing some inspired individuals. In this way, all human societies that were not totally depraved, preserved, however unaware of it, some version or remnants of the original principles. But if this was the case, then in what exactly did the special advantage of the Jewish teachings on this matter consist? This issue is treated more comprehensively in the next chapter; here it suffices to point out that, for Selden, the main advantage of Jewish tradition was the unusually concerted and continuous efforts of the Jewish nation, for generations upon generations, to uncover, record and preserve those universal principles. In other words, it was a tradition of inquiry, discussion and preservation which restored the knowledge of the universal moral principles to the Jewish nation. Selden proposed that the universal principles were indeed pretty much those identified by the Hebrew juridical-politic tradition as the seven Noahide precepts (with some additional minor stipulations). However, this identification was made not because the Jewish tradition recorded an exact revelation about these principles (it admitted openly that it had not), but

---

[17] A good example of the way the term "law of nations" was understood in seventeenth-century England is the 1608 Case of the Post-Nati, where it was among the issues discussed. Sir Christopher Yelverton held the law of nations to be "observed alike in all nations" and the Lord Chancellor Thomas Egerton, Lord Ellesmere, claimed the law of nations was universal and as such also part of the laws of England. See *The Speech of the Lord Chancellor ... Touching the Post Nati* (1609) pp. 31–32. For Grotius' use of the term *ius inter civitates*, see *Jure Belli* "Prolegomena."

because of its efforts to recover it; thus his analysis always retained gradualist and probabilistic elements.[18]

This special excellence granted to the Jewish traditions implied an assumption in favor of traditional knowledge that was in principle applicable to all traditions – being the accumulated moral and legal knowledge of a society, recording its significant events and ideas, including those instances when it profited from inspired men or fortuitous circumstances. Selden did not leave his appreciation for traditional knowledge merely implied; his writings are replete with explicit expression of his high regard for traditional knowledge and practices. However, we have also seen that his preference for traditional knowledge did not make Selden a sanctifier of traditions and customs as such. Indeed, the explicit purpose of most of his works was to establish what was true and what was not, about many traditionally accepted laws and customs, and he acknowledged that, as he put it in *Jure Naturali*, various errors had been accepted in the past as true, and "loaded onto the shoulders of posterity like so much baggage." Such errors persisted where "the evidence of the ancients" was regarded as exempt from outside examination, while he insisted that careful and detailed scrutiny was necessary to discern among old things, the true from the false.[19]

In almost all of Selden's writings, he can be found expressing his annoyance at the misuse of the past or even at reverence of things only because antique. Describing the purpose of his early *The Duello* (1610), he declared that "[h]*istoricall tradition of use*, and *succinct description of ceremony*, are my ends; both deduced from the Auncients, but without proselenique affectation." Elsewhere he ridiculed that scholar who unquestioningly accepts the more flattering "idle traditions of his own Nation." Indeed, fairly typical of his approach is the following passage from the preface to the *Historie of Tithes* (1618):

Nor is any end in it [the *Historie of Tithes*], to teach any Innovation by an imperfect patterne had from the mustie Reliques of former time. Neither is *Antiquitie* related in it to shew barely what hath been (for the sterile part of *Antiquitie* which shews that only & to no further purpose, I value even as slightly as dull Ignorance doth the most precious and usefull part of it) but to give other light to the Practice & doubts of the present. Light, that is cleer & necessarie. Nor could such as haue searcht in the Subiect see at all often, for want of such Light.

Selden did not mince his words on this – "proselenique affectation," "idle traditions," "mustie Reliques," "sterile part of *Antiquitie*" – so that the message

___
[18] For the discussion of the "active intellect" see JN b1c9; on the Noahide principles see especially JN b1c10 and MC b1c3–4; on the advantages of Jewish tradition see JN b1c3.
  On the debate in recent scholarship, about the manner such principles were retrieved by Jewish tradition: J.P. Sommerville, "John Selden, the law of nature and the origins of government" in *Historical Journal* 27, (1984) pp. 439–440; Tuck *Philosophy* pp. 215–216; Tuck *Rights* pp. 117–118.
[19] JN b1c1. As we saw, to uphold his claim Selden quoted the biblical passage in Jeremiah 6:16.

was loud and clear: there is much in the past that is worthless. Even worse than just a waste of time, he argued that having too much to do with worthless things of the past can be detrimental, as "the too studious Affectation of bare and sterile *Antiquitie*, which is nothing els but to be exceeding busie about nothing, may soon descend to a Dotage."[20]

However, for all the evident problems and faults involved in looking at the past, Selden still held it to be indispensable for present understanding. The reason for this is already indicated in the above passage, as to give "light to the Practice & doubts of the present." Close by in the same text, Selden expanded his explanation and remarked that,

the Neglect or only vulgar regard of the fruitfull and precious part of it [antiquity], which gives necessarie light to the *Present* in matter of *State, Law, Historie*, and the *understanding of good Autors*, is but preferring that kind of Ignorant Infancie, which our short life alone allows us, before the many ages of former Experience and Observation, which may so accumulat yeers to us as if we had lived even from the beginning of Time.

The past, or at least its fruitful part, Selden argues time and again, gives "light" to the present. We may recall in this context the uses of the light metaphor by those Grotians who identified it with individual right reason. In the above passages Selden in effects contrasts his own interpretation of the "light" of the past with those rejecting it, pointing out that men's objectively short life allows such as would rely solely on their faculties only an "Ignorant Infancie" while those who properly employ the past may extract benefit from experience as if they had lived "from the beginning of Time."[21]

However, history is not necessarily tradition. Knowing the past certainly gives "Experience and Observation," but as much as it may instruct it is not immediately clear how can it command. For the past to become an obligatory tradition, especially in fields such as law and politics, more is needed. Something of this nature is already hinted at, in the very expression "as if we had lived even from the beginning of Time" – that is, not merely pointing to some added experience, but implying a long continuity of identity and purpose, reminiscent of the image of intransience through change of the house or ship. Selden pointed more explicitly to this aspect of the problem when he proposed, in the second edition of *Titles of Honor* (1631), that concerning "*Things or Persons*" as part of a State,

there is nothing [that] *more conduces to a right iudgement then the carefull examination of* Constitutions and Customes, *their* received Interpretations, *and their* Force, *in the State and Age of which any Civill disquisition is raised. For they are the very Compasse to*

---

[20] *The Duello, or, Single Combat* (1610), in "Notice to the Reader," not paginated. TH (1614), pp. 132–133. *Historie of Tithes* (1618), Preface p. ii, and the dedication, not paginated.

[21] From *Historie of Tithes* (1618), the dedication, not paginated.

direct in all Iudiciall *proceedings; and of singular use also in whatsoever is* Deliberative[22].

In this passage, the "Force" of political and legal structures in a state is connected to their "received Interpretations." That is, meaning (interpretation) as drawn out of temporal conveyance (received), is associated with the power of constitutional and judicial systems. Selden was ever aware that things in the past and the present acquire meaning by a reciprocal and continuing infusion of context. He distinguished, in the passages above, between looking at (and learning from) things past for the sake of erudition, and the continuing existence of meaning that is tradition. But he was also indicating that, in a sense, tradition colors even the most dispassionate attempt at historical inquiry. He was clearly aware that looking at the past – or a piece of it, like a document – in a way that will be completely divorced from the present cannot bring meaning, and is probably also impossible (because, if that would be the case, how could a document be understood or even read? Some kind of tie of meaning with the present is inevitable).

Selden was not blind to the problematic aspects of such an approach to knowledge and authority, for the fact that some ideas or principles are traditional does not make them for him necessarily right. He discussed this problem extensively in the *Mare Clausum*, where he argued, for example, that only very limited knowledge about natural law can be "gather'd from the Customs of several Nations, about things Divine or such as relate unto Divine Worship." The cause for this very limited scope was, he explained, in the character of religious ideas and information:

For, it hath been the common Custom of men, in all Ages and throughout all parts of the known World, to conclude of such mat[t]ers, either without exact and convenient examination, or els for the serving of their own Interests, or els to suit with the humor and disposition of the people whom they are to rule and keep in order[.]

He gave as an example those Athenian philosophers who, contrary to the usual practice and custom of their era, held that although there are among the peoples many gods, there is in truth only one natural God. That is, in such matters as dealing with the divine – perhaps because subject to neither reason nor experience – views common and customary among men, may very well be erroneous. It was for this reason, Selden held, that among both Jews and Christians, "the contemplation or debate of Religious matters" had been "most deservedly" restrained by "set-Maxims, Principles, and Rules" lest "it should wantonize and wander, either into the old Errors of most Ages and Nations, or after the new devices of a rambling phansie."[23]

---

[22] TH (1631) "Preface," not paginated.
[23] MC b1c7. This is an important comment, because going against the widespread tendency among the learned of Selden's time (as well as ours), to regard religious practices as a mere contrivance applied by rulers upon the masses as sedative or narcotic to keep them in

So much for the limitations of human traditions in things exclusively divine; but what about things human which "reflect only upon matters of dutie betwixt man and man"? On such matters, Selden proposed,

that which shall bee permitted by the *Law Natural*, is no less rightly determined by the Laws, Placarts, and received Customs of divers Ages and Nations, both antient and modern, then it may bee collected what every Clime will or will not bear, by the diligent observation of Countries, Shrubs, Trees, Plants, and other things which belong to the bodie of Husbandrie."

This assertion was only apparently a simple and clear-cut one. For on second thought, it becomes apparent that it actually implies a complexity in, and a warning against, simplistic attempts to draw general laws of nature from the laws of different nations. How simple is it in fact to collect from observation of countries or trees, what "every Clime will or will not bear"? Such an exact ability eludes even today's science, let alone that of centuries ago. Selden stressed this point even more directly when he asked: "But where are all Nations? It is not yet discover'd how many there are, much less upon what Customs they have agreed." Moreover, he added, it is known that there also existed upon the world, and may still exist, not only civilized nations but also (quoting Cicero's words): "A rude sort of men, without Laws, without Government, free and dissolute." Selden's conclusion from these patent limitations was that any attempt to construct universal principles by looking at what is common to all men is prone to fail. What he proposed instead was to look into "the more civilized and more eminent Nations of the past and present Age, and of such whose Customs wee are best acquainted with."[24]

Selden was making an intriguing argument about the kind of knowledge to be drawn from men's societies and traditions. On the one hand he rejected the approach according to which a systematic comparative examination of the various human laws and societies may by itself alone yield an exact knowledge of natural law. In effect, he held such an approach to be untenable, because even if an examination of this kind would ever be completed, it could never yield any kind of final moral and political knowledge, having failed to acknowledge the real and significant differences that could and did develop

---

obedience, it conveys a more reciprocal relationship. He certainly accepted that religious traditions were especially apt to distortion because men often dealt with them "without exact and convenient examination" or for "serving of their own Interests," but the third caveat he added "to suit with the humor and disposition of the people whom they are to rule and keep in order" while accepting that rulers employ religious practices to "rule and keep in order" the people, nevertheless indicates a role for the people that is not merely passive. For the real "humor and disposition" of the particular people concerned, have to be considered and suited to – implying a connection between national character and religious disposition, which rulers would ignore at their peril.

[24] MC b1c6–7; see also b1c4. The same argument is made in JN b1c6.

between men, both morally and practically. There was not, nor could ever exist, any moral common ground to be found by comparing civilized nations, to men who lived "free and dissolute." Differences in national character and disposition between societies heavily influenced even moral and political issues, let alone other aspects of human life. Comparative study could help one to understand, and even to better, his own national system, by emphasizing its distinctive features and mechanisms, but it could not lead to an identification of common rules that, stripping various systems of their differences, would create a "pure" natural law able to replace particular ones.

Significantly, when Selden made the analogy between the differences to be collected from laws and customs "of divers Ages and Nations" and those to be gathered from observation of "Shrubs, Trees, Plants, and other things which belong to the bodie of Husbandrie" he was suggesting that to adequately know men and their societies, was to learn their peculiar "disposition" and "Clime" – that is their circumstances. Anyone who knows something about plants understands that even plants belonging to the same species may exist under very different circumstances in different climates. Selden's analogy therefore clearly implies fundamental differences between nations, so that even universal laws ostensibly applying to all men (or plants for that matter), such as that all need water, would be pretty close to useless, without proper context (how much water). Perhaps most importantly, the analogy indicates Selden's general approach to understanding human societies, for this was clearly not some isolated remark by him, and he articulated the same idea in very similar terms in other works too. The source of the analogy, as Selden indicated in his *Titles of Honor*, is Aristotle, who noted that nobility is born in some merit of an ancestor, "[b]ut, says he, as Plants, so men vary from their first Stocke." However, as is evident, unlike Aristotle who applied the image it to individuals and families, Selden applied the analogy to whole societies and nations, and even to their cultural products, such as social customs and legal systems. In Selden's "Notes" to Fortescue's *Laudibus*, published some 20 years before the *Mare Clausum* (but in fact composed around the same time as the original version of the *Mare Clausum*) he put it thus:

Divers nations, as divers men, have their divers collections and inferences; and so make their divers laws to grow to what they are, out of one and the same root.

Slightly further in the same text, the analogy appears even more prominently, in his discussion of the beginning and development of laws: "the beginning of all here being in the first peopling of the land, when men, by nature being civil creatures, grew to plant a common society." This same idea appears yet again in 1640, when in the *Jure Naturali* Selden described the growth of diverse national laws from the original universal one:

And it would not be out of place to suggest that from this same body of law many other kinds have developed and grown here and there, just as the shoots grafted onto a tree grow from the trunk to which they have been attached."[25]

The analogy repeatedly alluded to, by terms like "plants," "grow," "root," and so on, is of society and law as tree-like, ever-changing albeit slowly and gradually, but also retaining unity of identity and purpose throughout these change. It also implies the need for a connection between local circumstances like soil and climate, and the character of legal and social ideas, in order for the latter to thrive. Intriguingly, in the later example, from *Jure Naturali*, another layer of meaning is added to the analogy, as the image is employed not to convey a development that is simply natural and unspoiled, but rather the opposite, pointing to "shoots grafted onto a tree" – that is an openly artificial intervention in the "natural" growth of a tree, attaching to it grafts which may or may not bond with it to bear better fruits. With time those grafts that are successful become part of the tree and grow with it, "naturally" so to speak, although a mark remains in the grafting site, testimony to the disruption. In this manner, Selden integrated gradual and layered growth with the more severe fractures and mends that inevitably occur to a society over time, thereby conveying the complex character of social and legal traditions, which manage to be at the same time both natural and artificial.[26]

---

[25] TH (1631) in the dedication, not paginated; NL cols. 1891–1892; JN b1 Praefatio.

[26] In an even earlier text, his "Illustrations" in Drayton's *Poly-Olbion* (1612), Selden discussed the possible sources of differences between societies and national character. Addressing the attempts to derive differences between nations, including not only physical ones, but also those of aptitudes and character, from circumstances like the distance from the sun or more generally the weather, one can find Selden's comment on line 255 of "The First Song" rejecting simplistic or overtly deterministic notions of the source for national differences like the distance of the sun (or some inbred racial quality). He asserted that: "I referre it no more to the Sunne, then the speciall Horsmanship in our *Northerne men*, the nimble ability of the *Irish*, the fiery motions of the *French*, *Italian* jealousie, *German* liberty, *Spanish* puft up vanity, or those different and perpetuall carriages of state-gouernement, *Haste* and *Delay*, which as inbred qualities, were remarqueable in the two most martiall people of *Greece* [Athenians and Spartans]." He does accept the influence of environmental factors on natural characteristics, but rejects simplistic inferences, stressing that: "The cause of *Aethiopian* blacknesse and curled hair was long since judiciously fetched from the disposition of soile, ayre, water, and singular operations of the heavens; with confutation of those which attribute it to the Sun's distance." Indeed although he indicates that such eminent authors as "*Hippocrates, Ptolemy, Bodin*" have disputed the issue, his own conclusion is that men are very far from fully understanding the causes for such differences arising: "And I am resolved that every land hath its so singular self-nature, and individuall habitude with celestiall influence, that humane knowledge, consisting most of all in universalitie, is not yet furnisht with what is requisite to so particular discoverie[.]" Intriguingly Selden does not share any notions of narrowly deterministic or mechanic-like influences of natural factors on humans, which in later centuries would be used to argue for racial ideas. He rejects the notion that the geographical situation of a country, be it because of its distance from the sun or otherwise depending on weather and temperature, is the main factor determining the character or even the appearance of a people.

Selden's terminology neatly illustrates how his concept of "nature" diverged from so many of his contemporaries, including Grotius, and Hobbes. The term "nature" implied for those contemporaries a kind of unchanging, perfect essence, akin to the mathematical-like precision and clarity of the exact sciences, which men had to grasp and hold on to in order to transcend and combat their multifarious corrupt and decaying surroundings. This outlook is neatly encapsulated in one of Francis Bacon's "Aphorisms" from his *Novum Organum* (1620), an anti-Seldenian statement if ever there was one:

> It is idle to expect any great advancement in science from the superinducing and engrafting of new things upon old. We must begin anew from the very foundations, unless we would revolve forever in a circle with mean and contemptible progress.

Selden's outlook was the very opposite: "nature," and therefore learning, was that very surrounding, indeed often corrupt and decaying but at the very same time also growing and self-repairing, akin to the life-sciences, operating according to universal principles ingrained within them (but never separate), that nevertheless manifest themselves in an inexact, variable array, responding and adapting to circumstances. This divergence effectively continued a very old dispute about nature and convention going back at least to Plato and Aristotle. With the great majority of ancient, medieval and modern opinions preferring the natural as universal and unchanging to the conventional and particular "second nature" – Selden was firmly among the minority who not only rejected the former view as unrealistic, but indeed always regarded convention as the truly natural and preferable condition of human nature and society.[27]

In other words, men and their political societies had the same "natural" root (for Selden, in the equity intuition and in the basic moral principles), but they grew both "naturally" as well as resulting from "grafts" of artificial interventions, to be as diverse as were different plants (or men), which though having a common origin, had adjusted to circumstances and developed distinctive characteristics. Moreover, the view of nations as adjusted to their circumstances also implied a bond of affinity in attitudes and understanding between those sharing similar circumstances or values, thus justifying a discerning discrimination when looking at the moral, legal and political traditions of various nations. According to such a view there was a "natural" affinity between Greeks and Romans since they share so many religious and social features, or between the legal and moral ideas of Christian nations and the Jewish nation, or between those European nations with a common Feudal Law

---

[27] *Novum Organum* (1620), book I, Aphorism xxxi. See discussion in Ferguson *Clio* p. 408; Kelley *Human* pp. 25–27. The conflicting meanings of the term "nature" have been troubling to philosophy, at least since Aristotle's efforts to argue them away. It can refer to nature as universal order, thus with universal reason, perfection, the ideal; on the other hand it can refer to actual nature, and in this sense is connected to animal instincts, material processes (like generation and corruption), and the like.

heritage. A good example of his approach is Selden's discussing the spread of Feudal practices throughout Europe, including England (as well as connecting those to the use of titles like Dux and Comes, originating in Roman offices), as originating in "customes" such as the "use of Feuds" which "for the most part came immediately from those Northern Nations, that about declining the [Roman] Empire *planted* themselves almost throughout it[.]"[28]

Therefore, in Selden's view, a comparative approach to various national laws can be valuable in the main not as an objective tool but as a subjective one, most fruitful when predicated on some commonality of ideas or values. Such are cases with the most civilized and eminent nations we wish to emulate, or with those nations with whose "Customs wee are best acquainted with," because they are those we may best venture to understand. He articulated this approach explicitly in the *Jure Naturali*, where he wrote:

"law of nations" of my title is explained as that which was held in common by the Hebrews and by other nations both near to them and farther away (though not in all times and places), whether by the specific command of God or by imposed agreement or custom.[29]

For Selden then, the fundamental moral principles, termed by the Hebrews as "Noahide" may point to those few cases where a society was truly unnatural in transgressing them, but except for such extreme cases, all law was natural: the universal drive for equity, was as natural as the laws which had developed (one might say "naturally") with time to fit the peculiar circumstances and needs of each nation. We might discuss about a tree in the abstract, but there never was, nor could be, such a thing as a universal tree, only particular trees, as particular nations; within each particular nation, laws *naturali et gentium* were thus the germ and its shoots.

We might say that Selden's theory of traditional law thus combined two separate but mutually re-enforcing supports for its justification: on the one hand was what we may call the epistemic function "internal" to the law, regarding long-tested traditional laws, as enjoying a far better presumption of being properly enacted and morally sound, than laws predicated on either pure reason or arbitrary power; on the other hand was what we may call the epistemic function "external" to the law and in a sense shaping it, regarding traditional law as the result of the adaptation to changing circumstances, indicated in the idea that laws "grow" and change to suit a people's circumstances. Through both these aspects, Selden's outlook tends to create a close identification of legal tradition and national identity, in a sense making

---

[28] Christianson *Discourse* pp. 219–220, 244.

[29] JN b1 Praefatio: "Gentium autem Jus in Titulo accipitur pro eo quod sive ex singulari Numinis Imperio ex Pacto seu Consuetudine Interveniente, ebraeis aliisque Gentibus sive vicinis sive aliis (nec interim universis nec semper) commune habebatur[.]" The same approach of affinity is clearly reflected when Selden writes of the "Law of the Nations of *Europe*" in MC b1c24.

nation and its traditional laws into one thing – as we shall see, He regarded the Jewish nation as the most eminent example of this principle. Such an understanding of what laws and nations are, means that for Selden, nations cannot really be created by a single contracting event or a forced conquest (as in Grotius and Hobbes), although such moments could and did exist in history, their function was for him quite limited. Nations were created by long-timed processes, incorporating many voluntary associations or positive legislations, events and conquests, and then subsuming these into a traditional national law and identity.

4.3 THE UNIVERSALIST MENACE

We have seen Selden's objections to the type of universalist approach to human affairs made by philosophical theories arguing either from individual reasoned consent or from absolute authority. Such theories came to the fore dramatically in the political free-for-all introduced by the Civil War and the regicide. However, in the decades before the Civil War, such philosophical ideas threatened the traditionalist English legal system, only as junior fellow-travelers attached to the far more extensive and established theoretical framework of Roman law. Accordingly, Selden's aversion to the universal claims made for Roman law is one of the most prominent features of his thought, recurring in some form or other in almost all his works, and looking at this aspect of his work is necessary for providing a full picture of his political theory. Significantly, Selden's rejection of Roman law arguments was a sweeping one, strongly objecting not only to assertions (made among others by Gentili) identifying Roman Civil law with the law of nature and nations, but also to more circumscribed and common claims, that merely argued all Christian European states (with the exception of England) were at that time actually governed by Roman law, as found in Justinian's *Institutes*. In the *Mare Clausum*, Selden made a point of observing that:

> For, not to mention, how that not onely very many Decrees, and Custome's introduced in the *Romane-Germane* Empire it self and other places abroad, have extremely alter'd many things conteined in those Books [the *Institutes*]; but also that wee finde divers Kings both of *Spain* and *France* have sometimes heretofore prohibited the use of them in any kinde within their Courts of Justice; there are truly som things in the very Law of the Nations of *Europe* (who receiv those Books, and that upon very good ground, both into their Schools and Courts, so far as the particular Laws of their Kingdoms will permit) I mean in their Law Common, or Intervenient, which are not grounded at all upon the Law of *Justinian*, but have had their original from Customs quite contrarie thereto.[30]

---

[30] MC b1c24. For similar claims see in TH (1614) preface, not paginated; "Review" appended to the *Historie of Tithes*, pp. 477–481. See also discussion in Caruso *Miglior* pp. 810–811, 842–843.

The argument openly made, is that even in continental Europe Roman law was merely one component of a composite system of legislation. Selden emphasized this characteristic both by his terming the empire "*Romane-Germane*" and by noting how the European legal systems were full of laws that had their origins from customs "quite contrarie" to the *Institutes*.

But, it is in the justifications that Selden gave for this resistance to Roman law that one can find its real significance. In his "Notes" on Fortescue's *Laudibus*, Selden's main objection was to the claims of Roman law excellence based on its antiquity. Sir John Fortescue himself had attempted to answer such claims by asserting that the origin of English law predated Roman law. Selden dissented from the view that regards mere antiquity as desirable in itself, observing that excellence in law should be sought not in antiquity but rather in continuity. Since, as seen above, Selden held the best laws to be those fitted to a nation over a long time, a system of law that had been discontinued would stop adapting, and in a sense die. He proposed that this was exactly what had happened to Roman law, when a break occurred in its application in the west for more than 500 years, between the time of Emperor Justinian (483–565) and the days of Emperor Lothair II (1075–1137). He asserted that during this period, the "Body of the Civil Law" in the Western empire was so neglected that "all that time none ever profest [sic] it"; and that only after an old copy of the *Institutes* was found in the city of Amalfi, in the twelfth century, Roman law started to be "professed" at Bologna and from there gradually spread throughout the universities of the west.[31]

Selden drew two conclusions from this account: First, he stressed, the profession of Roman law that had begun in the west under Lothair II was actually wholly "new, and not a Recontinuance of what was in use under *Justinian*." Second, he noted, since the continuous use of Roman law in the West started at the earliest around the middle of the twelfth century, it obviously wasn't earlier than the English Common law, which was in continuous use arguably from Saxon times (the sixth century), indisputably so by William I's conquest of 1066. Selden explicitly considered continuity as a measure of the excellence of laws, and by this measure, the Common law was certainly not second to Roman law. Moreover, Selden made another important point here, by indicating that "Recontinuance" of law *was* possible, that is, that there were circumstances in which the law could be restored after a break. He held that this was not the case with Roman law in the West, if only because a break of some 600 years meant the law was in truth completely new to those taking it up, and could not be seen as a recontinuance in any meaningful sense. But what if the break had been a much shorter one, and a "Recontinuance" of law realized soon after a break? Could such a case be regarded as effective continuity? Selden seems to suggest just that, and the reason is not hard to fathom: according to a view regarding recontinuance

[31] NL cols. 1892–1893.

after a short break as effective continuity, even if William I's conquest of England did cause a practical or even formal abandonment of English Common law for some time, since it was shortly thereafter resumed, it should be viewed as effectively continuous. These were the "grafts" Selden mentioned in his image of the growing law. A final aspect of this issue worth considering, is the question of why the Common law was so successful in creating continuity, and even "Recontinuance," while Roman law was not so. In his words: why were the *Institutes* "so neglected near 600 years" if their excellence "were so beyond others, as is usually said by many"; and, if neglected for so long, why suddenly be adopted in the twelfth century? Selden only hinted at the answer in his analysis, which implies the Common law to be far closer to the lives and concerns of the people than the long-neglected Roman law.[32]

The idea implied in the "Notes" to Fortescue's *Laudibus*, was spelled out clearly by Selden, in later works like the *Historie of Tithes, Mare Clausum* and "Dissertatio historica" upon *Fleta*: Common law was a national law, fitted to the English and as such loved by them; its blend of inheritance and consent made the people adhere to it until the conqueror reinstated it. Roman law was the opposite of national law (for all those who were not Roman), and as such it worked against both inheritance and consent. Selden argued this point addressing two other issues: the status of Roman law in European states and the motivations behind those who attempted to introduce it into national legislations. Regarding the first issue, Selden stressed that there was no real succession of law or power from the Roman state, not only in England but throughout the Christian states of Europe – not even in the Germanic empire called "Roman." All European states, he argued, had for many centuries after Rome's demise preferred their own customs to the Roman laws; and even after Roman law re-entered public discourse in the twelfth century, there remained a widespread opposition to it, that never completely disappeared. Indeed, as he asserted most clearly in the "Review," annexed to *Historie of Tithes*, regardless of its being

pretended usually, that the Body of the *Imperialls*, read and profest in the Universities, is the Civill Law, that governes (as they say) all other States [except England]. But this, howsoever received through lazie Ignorance, is so farre from Truth, that indeed no Nation in the world is governed by them.[33]

---

[32] NL cols. 1892–1893. He added another sarcastic remark, by noting that the *Institutes* were being taught throughout Western Europe against their own authority, which commanded that they should be read and taught only in Rome, Berytus and Constantinople.

[33] "Of the VII Chapter" of the "Review" in *Historie of Tithes* pp. 477–479. See also the "Dissertatio historica" in *Ioannis Seldeni ad Fletam Dissertatio*, [1647] David Ogg trans. (Cambridge, 1925) pp. 49–51; MC b1c24. In TH (1614) "Preface" not paginated, he indicated this had been long been the situation: "*But [in the Western empire] before Lothar, the Gouernment was by the Salique, Lombardian, and Roman Laws (the Roman beeing some piece of what had been vsed in Rome) euerie one liuing according to either of them as hee*

Regarding the second issue, the motivation behind attempts to introduce Roman law into the legislation of European nations, Selden was no less adamant. He conjectured that many European princes and republics (including England) allowed the introduction of Roman law in the twelfth century as a "Bulwark" against the pressure by the Papacy under Innocent II (reigned 1130–1143) to "receive everywhere the Papal Decrees, collected by his Authority, as the only body of Laws." European governments thus introduced civil Roman law as antidote against the incursion of Canon Roman law. However, Selden indicated, whereas the waning of Papal pressure should have meant a similar ebbing of the influence and allure of Roman law, in fact, except for England – where it disappeared almost completely – in most other places Roman law was not abandoned. The reason for this, Selden proposed, was the allure to rulers of the absolutist element ("absoluta Principis potestate") they had found in Roman law, which by the "Lex Regia" made the ruler possessor of all power. He pointed out that the authority of Roman law rested on the alleged irrevocable transfer of "the powers of People and Senate to the Emperor, that occurred at a certain time in the Roman state." In short, accepting the authority of Roman law meant introducing into politics of an absolutist authority totally removed from outside influences or circumstances.[34]

The rejection of Roman law was a staple of English common lawyers, and not a stance peculiar to Selden, but his argumentation for rejection was somewhat different than the typical one. The usual English perspective was to paint a dichotomy between their own love of freedom, expressed in the Common law, and the continental sullen subjection to authority epitomized by the despotic approach of Roman law. While Selden certainly did not abandon this traditional contention as it pertained to national attitudes, his principled rejection of Roman law rested on a somewhat different argument, one that was in line with his theory of national laws. To him, a crucial danger from Roman law was that "no Nation" in the world was governed by it, and being no one's meant that custom or consent could not influence or alter it. To him the very notion of the perfect, codified, universal Roman law was inherently hostile to concepts of particular development and adaptation. In this sense, its universalism and isolation from people or circumstance, the very qualities that made Roman law so appealing to many philosophers of law as product of abstract and *a priori* reasoning, were for Selden the very essence of its shortcomings. Its absolutism that could never politically be regulated or changed, was the very opposite of Selden's argument for traditional national

---

would make choise." On the importance of continuity to Selden and the early Grotius see also Caruso *Miglior* pp. 442–443.

[34] "Dissertatio historica" Ogg pp. 49–51, 135–138, 170–171. Selden claimed that the remains of Roman law influence in the English judicial system were in the ecclesiastical courts, and in some of the King's courts – the Court of Chivalry and the Court of Admiralty. But even in these courts, he argued, Roman law did not dominate alone.

law, in which continuity ensured adaptation and a degree of consent. His argument on this issue was a general one, and related not only to Roman law but to all legal systems that would remove themselves from circumstance and change.[35]

4.4 NATION AND STATE

For Selden then, national tradition was the indispensable agency by which universal principles were made to fit men's laws and politics. How unique was this view in relation to previous or contemporary opinions?

There was obviously nothing new about the idea that nations existed. In England's political tradition, the idea that the English were a nation with a legal and political heritage of their own was both ubiquitous as well as frequently articulated. For examples of such articulations as were certainly known to Selden, one needs to look no further than the text of Fortescue's *Laudibus*, to which Selden composed "Notes," or the preface to Marchamont Needham's English-language edition of the *Mare Clausum*, published in 1652 while Selden was still alive and active (indeed, endeavoring to defend this very work by composing in the same year his *Vindiciae ... pro Mari Clausi*). As a matter of fact, Selden would have had the opportunity to personally witness such language officially employed, when in August 1608, while he was still a student at the Inner Temple, a Letter of Patent was presented by James I, formally granting (after long possession) the Temple Church and the adjacent lands to "...the Inns of the Inner and Middle Temple, London." The King's letter included, as justification of this grant, his statement that as his "Realm of England" had been for so many ages "exceedingly prosperous in the arts of Peace and War" the "great part of its welfare is justly owing to the ancient and proper Laws of the Realm, tried through a long series of ages, and particularly adapted to that populous and warlike nation, and approved by constant experience."[36]

But this kind of approach to the particular laws of England differed from Selden's, in that it was (many times literally) insular and self-referential. As noted before, there were different views in England about the Common law and its development: on the one hand those viewing it as essentially perfect and static, such as Fortescue and in Selden's days, Sir Edward Coke as well as the prominent lawyer Nicholas Fuller who in his *The Argument of Master*

---

[35] For the affinity (and differences) of this claim to the ideas of such thinkers as Bodin and Hotman, see M.A. Ziskind, "John Selden: Criticism and Affirmation of the Common law tradition" in *The American Journal of Legal history*, 19/1 (January 1975) pp. 24–26.

[36] About this tradition in England see Caruso *Miglior* pp. 61–62. For the Letters of Patent from James I for the Temple lands, to the societies of Inner and Middle Temple (issued 13 August 1608), see Inderwich *Calendar* pp. xiii–xv, and the reproduction after the title page there (not paginated). It appears the letter was drafted for the King by Sir Julius Caesar, then Chancellor of the Exchequer, who was a civil as well as a common lawyer.

Nicholas Fuller (1605), described England's laws as "so fitted to this people" that they make a "sweet harmony in the government." And there were those viewing it as adaptive and developing with important proponents of such views being Henry Spelman and Sir John Davies, and it seems also implied in the wording of the King's letter, apparently drafted by Sir Julius Caesar as "tried through a long series of ages, and particularly adapted." But what was common to all these views was that they tended to treat their nation's ancient constitutional tradition as being so different from others that it became *sui generis*, one of a kind, having very little to do with other systems – as famously put by Coke in his parliamentary speech of 25 March 1628, "*Divisos ab orbe Britannos*. We have a national appropriate law to this kingdom. If you tell me of other laws, you are gone. I will only speak of the laws of England."[37]

Whereas earlier writers on the Common law, from Fortescue to Saint. Germain, simply asserted that English customary law was a reflection of the law of reason or of nature, it was Coke who first proposed a way to actually connect English customary law with the wider philosophical framework of reason and nature in the Natural Law tradition. By his idea of "Artificial Reason" transmitting the law of reason into the Common law, he made it in a sense superior even to Parliament, in effect making customary English law into the law of reason, as he best articulated in his *First Institute*:

[T]he Common Law it selfe is nothing else but reason, which is to be understood of an artificiall perfection of reason gotten by long studie, observation and experience and not every mans naturall reason[.][38]

Sir John Davies in the preface to his *Irish Reports*, made on different grounds pretty much the same *sui generi* claims as Coke, arguing that the Common law was "the peculiar invention of this nation" which was indeed "nearest to the law of nature," which has been "delivered over from age to age by Tradition"; that the Norman conquest did not bring about any fundamental change but only in some legal "forms of proceeding"; and that the Common law is "so framed and fitted to the nature and disposition of this people, as we may

---

[37] See Nicholas Fuller, *The Argument of Master Nicholas Fuller, in the Case of Thomas Lad, and Richard Maunsell, his Clients Wherein it is Plainely Proved, that the Ecclesiasticall Commissioners haue no Power, by Vertue of their Commission, to Imprison, to put to the Oath Ex Officio, or to Fine Any of His Maiesties Subiects* (1607) pp. 13–15; G. Burgess *Absolute* pp. 158–159 and pp. 203–204 (quoting Coke). See also discussion in G. Burgess *Politics* pp. 29–32. Burgess stresses that prominent theoreticians of the common law like Fortescue and Saint Germain did not think that the law of reason should be searched outside English law, but within it, so that the entire body of English law was, in one way or another, the law of reason. For another perspective see D. Lieberman, "Law/custom/tradition: Perspectives from the common law" in Philips *Questions of Tradition* (Toronto University Press, 2004) pp. 233–257. By the very same principle, Fortescue had argued, more than a century earlier, that English law could not be exported to France. See Caruso *Miglior* pp. 505–506.

[38] Sir Edward Coke, *The First Institute of the Laws of England, or a Commentary upon Littleton* (1628), 97b, sec. 138; Zaller *Legitimacy* pp. 292, 295–296.

properly say it is connatural to the nation, so as it cannot be ruled by any other law."[39]

However, the English ideas about the ancient constitution were merely one (admittedly exceptionally robust and influential) instance among an European literature on the subject of ancient national constitutions, which flourished in the sixteenth century in England, Scotland, France, the Netherlands and Germany, and which found its most important early exponent in Francois Hotman's *Francogallia* (1573). The common denominator of this literature was the assumption that the customs and laws of a nation were inherently in accord with its peculiar needs. But the ancient constitution literature concentrated in the main on the suitability of their political tradition to that particular nation, without usually attempting to offer a theoretical and universal proposal for the moral value of such an approach. Whereas in the English (and perhaps also the German) case, the ancient constitutional argument was conservative in nature, attempting to preserve current constitutional settings against challenges to it, elsewhere this literature tended to be rebellious (and Calvinist) in character, proposing resistance to current political settings in the name of asserting allegedly old ideals against their current debasement. Grotius, early in his career, was a proponent of such ideas, asserting especially in his *De Antiquitate Republicae Batavicae* (Leiden, 1610) an ancient Dutch national tradition that had withstood Spanish rule, and which he was now proposing as the best form for the newly independent Dutch state – a form fashioned as an aristocracy and leaving most power in the hands of the provinces rather than central authority. Grotius argued the ancient Batavian republican government was the form of government best fit for the Dutch, but he admitted other forms were best for other nations.[40]

Ancient constitutional theories tend to justify the particular over the general, and in works such as Hotman's *Francogallia* and Grotius' *Batavicae* more general political rules applying outside of the particular case treated, are at most implied. Even when the danger of relativism is avoided by regarding the ancient constitution as consistent with natural law, writers in this tradition made little real attempt to explain how exactly the particularist customary law came to supposedly express the law of reason or of nature, or even to present more general rules that would apply not only in their own countries' cases. As we have seen, in England, works on law and politics usually sufficed, with stating a relationship between the local and universal law, and the one attempt to explain how this was effected, by identifying it with the unchanging law of reason, necessarily had to claim English law too as essentially unchanging: something that was less than convincing for a generation increasingly exposed to historical scholarship. Thus, Selden's writings offer by far the most comprehensive and theoretically cogent model of customary national law

---

[39] Davies *Irish* "Preface," unpaginated; Ferguson *Clio* pp. 274–275.
[40] Burgess *Politics* pp. 12–17; M.A. Ziskind "Criticism" pp. 24–26.

within a universal framework than any other that had been proposed before. Selden's innovation, in respect to previous literature on the ancient constitution, was in his attempt to blend ideas extant (many times only implicitly) in writings from many sources, English, European and Jewish, about the suitableness and perfection of ancient constitutions in general, and England's Common law in particular as the national law of the English, from the insular and self-referring sphere, into the one of thought about universals. He thus proposed that the nation was a meaningful and necessary category for the articulation of a universal moral and political theory.

The original aspect of Selden's views becomes clear when compared to the role assigned to nations in the universal political theories developed by his three contemporaries we have looked at: there was none to speak of. That is not to say that Grotius, Hobbes or Filmer attempted to actively deny the existence of nations, but rather that nations were unimportant (or, rather, irrelevant), within their theories of law and politics. In their systems the categories that did matter for considerations of political theory were individuals and states (and perhaps families), so that if nations existed or not was immaterial. Not only nations, but traditions and indeed constitutions effectively stand for nothing and are worth nothing in such theories, because these theories are essentially anti-historical. In the political systems devised by Filmer, Hobbes and Grotius; men stand as it were in a perennial moment of creation ex-nihilo. Moreover, to such theories and their apparatus, the nation as a category of obligation that is not one and the same with the state, was incompatible, even destructive. A national bond existing in parallel to the civil one, indeed potentially superior to it, would demolish the whole contractual superiority of the state, in the theories of such as Grotius and Hobbes, and the authority of father-ruler in Filmer's.[41]

Grotius' ideas serve best to exemplify this point, especially since in his earlier works he did entertain some role to national traditions. In the first decade of the seventeenth century, young Grotius applied himself to the study of ancient constitutions in a number of works such as the *Republica Emendanda* (c.1600), the *Annales et Historiae de Rebus Belgicis* (commissioned by the States of Holland c. 1601, completed by 1612, published only posthumously in 1657) and the *Parallela Reumpublicarum* (c. 1602) – none published in his lifetime – and most significantly his aforementioned *Batavicae* (1610). In the latter he strove to foster what is today called the "Batavian Myth" – to show

[41] Grotius' views are addressed below, while Filmer's rejection of national traditions as conflicting with the absolute authority of the ruler is quite obvious. As for Hobbes, his mortal god, *Leviathan*, as R. Helgerson notes, rather than representing England, represents a political order that could – and, according to Hobbes, should – be instituted anywhere. Thus Leviathan "belongs not to a discourse of the nation but to a discourse of the state." Helgerson proposes the emerging distinction (between nation and state) would "perhaps" have been lost on Hobbes, and would "certainly" have been lost on his Elizabethan predecessors. See R. Helgerson, *Forms of Nationhood* (Chicago University Press, 1992) pp. 295–296.

that the ancient Batavi, alleged forefathers of the Dutch, had been ruled, like other Germanic tribes, not by kings but by an aristocratic republic, and where kings existed they were merely first among equals. Intriguingly, Selden had separately reached the same conclusion by 1607 in his *Analecton*, an account of aristocratic republics among ancient Gauls and Britons, published only in 1615 (in an apparently unauthorized edition which he later disowned). Grotius' account of the resistance by the ancient Batavians against Roman tyranny became the perfect parallel for the Dutch revolt against Spain. Published just as the twelve-year truce between the United Provinces and Spain had been signed, the *Batavicae* was soon translated into the vernacular and often reprinted. It was a clear legitimization of the independent existence of the young republic, and it presented to its readers the exemplary way in which their ancestors had organized their government.[42]

This reading of Grotius' book about the ancient Batavi, was the direct motive for its translation into English in 1649 as *A Treatise of the Antiquity of the Commonwealth of the Battavers Which Is Now the Hollanders*. The time of publication was, of course, not accidental, for as regicide England debated the new regime to replace its monarchy, Grotius' old book claiming that the dispositions, manners and traditional laws of northern peoples dwelling "adjoining unto the Seacoasts" ever have had "an antipathy of the absolute authority of one man onely" was regarded by the translator Thomas Woods as advocating the retaining of traditional English laws with the establishing of an aristocratic-led regime instead of a monarchy. Irrespective of Woods' intentions, Grotius' argument in the book certainly supports traditional national law, and the close affinity of his ideas at the time he composed this book with Selden's is illustrated by the former's use in the book, of the plant analogy often employed by the latter, while explaining the regard customary laws must receive: "For it is with Lawes even as it is with the Plants, there must be of necessity time for the establishing and fastning of the Roots; and contrarily, if they be often removed, they lose their virtue, power and efficacy."[43]

---

[42] Tuck *Philosophy* pp. 165–166, 169–173; Burgess *Politics* pp. 16–17; I. Schoffer, "The Batavian Myth during the Sixteenth and Seventeenth centuries" in J.S. Bromley & E.H. Kossmann (eds.), *Britain and the Netherlands* (The Hague: Martinus Nijhoff, 1975) volume V pp. 78–101. Caruso discusses the parallels (pointed out among others by Tuck, and by L. Campos Boralevi) between Selden's *Analecton* and Grotius' *Batavicae*, claiming they show that in both countries there was at this time an attempt to build up "una coscienza nazional-statale" by a search for the roots of the national community and the state, and the continuity of legal forms, as "*ininterrotte*." See Caruso *Miglior* pp. 442–443.

[43] See *A Treatise of the Antiquity of the Commonwealth of the Battavers Which Is Now the Hollanders* (1649) in the dedicatory epistle, not paginated, and also pp. 146–148. The translator, Thomas Woods, intended to indicate the Netherlands as a model for a post-monarchic England "restoring" its ancient republican liberties in the form of an aristocratic republic. Since he supported retaining existing English laws, Woods proposed not to go too much by "names" for political institutions, since "altering and changing of names and Offices of

However, as early as 1604 Grotius also began working on a different set of issues and ideas that would lead him in an opposite direction from these early historical and humanist works. The work on these later ideas that was eventually to culminate in the publication of the *Jure Belli* in 1625, comes into view already pretty well developed in a text referred to by Grotius himself as *De Indis*, composed around 1604/5 but remaining unpublished until the nineteenth century (and then published as *De Iure Praedae*). One chapter of *De Indis* was published separately, in 1609, becoming the famous *Mare Liberum Sive de Jure quod Batavis Competit ad Indicana Commercia Dissertatio* (*The Freedom of the Seas, or the Right Which Belongs to the Dutch to Take Part in the East Indian Trade, a Dissertation*). The theoretical basis for political association in *De Indis* is already pretty much that of the *Jure Belli*: humans imitate nature when that "considerable group sufficing for self-protection through mutual aid, and for equal acquisition of the necessities of life– is called a common-wealth [*Respublica*]; and the individuals making up the commonwealth are called citizens [*cives*]." In such a scheme of things, every right comes to the state from the collective agreement of individuals. As in his later *Jure Belli*, only men's "natural reason" establishes the rules and justifications for the political and legal superstructure, so that approval of "men of wisdom" and of "nations of the highest repute," cannot serve as validation but only as "confirmation." The most significant difference between *De Indis* and the *Jure Belli*, was that in the earlier text natural reason is anchored in God's will, in the latter the law of nature is independent of His will.[44]

By his composing of *De Indis*, Grotius was creating a theory totally at odds with his earlier assigning of a role to the nation as a source of political or legal obligation. As has been aptly noted by Tuck, while in the *Batavicae* Grotius described the Dutch provinces interchangeably as "Federated Nations" (Federatae Nationes) or as "Republic" (Respublica); in *De Indis* only the latter appellation is used. For some years these conflicting ideas remained largely unseen by outsiders, because the latter text remained for the most part unpublished; indeed, the publication of the *Batavicae* in 1610 still reflected Grotius' earlier attitudes. Perhaps Grotius was still developing his new theory, or was unsure about its repercussions, and we should not divorce his considerations in this respect from his prominent role in Dutch political affairs during this period. Certainly, he refrained from publishing in his

some Magistrates, doth not make presently another Commonwealth" and argued that among the Batavian-Hollanders "Soveraignty [sic] and power of the States" has through long "continuall consequent succession" devolved into the aristocratic government of the Dutch States General.

[44] Hugo Grotius, *De Iure Praedae* [*De Indis*] (Oxford, 1950), pp. 6–7, 19–20. These ideas are considerably explored by Tuck in *Philosophy* pp. 169–176, and Tuck *Rights* pp. 80–82. In the latter, Tuck indicates the similarity between Grotius' theory to the one arrived at independently by John Locke.

lifetime another work in the historical vein, the *Annales et Historiae de Rebus Belgicis*, which had been commissioned as early as 1601 by the Dutch States General, and he had definitely completed by 1612. The publication of the *Mare Liberum* in 1609 was the first hint of the change of direction of thought that would eventually produce the *Iure Belli*.[45]

There is an insurmountable theoretical conflict within Grotius' writings, between his earlier works on national traditions, assuming authority from continuity, and his later theory of political association drawing authority from the natural reason of individuals. Every national political tradition, including the Dutch one, loses its inherent authority if required to conform to Grotius' theory of association by individual natural reason. A national tradition might be a valuable empirical tool for government, but in the political theory developed by Grotius, it can only be subservient to the authority of individual reason and consent.[46]

Selden, in his *Mare Clausum*, explicitly identified this problem within Grotius' theory, and though referring to Grotius as a man of "extraordinarie knowledge in things both Divine and Humane" he did not spare him his criticism. Addressing the Dutchman's main argument concerning the community of human ownership over the seas, Selden remarked that "[h]e hath handled that point in two Books; in his *Mare Liberum*, and in that excellent work *De Jure Belli ac Pacis*" and while finding that in the earlier work Grotius had already equivocated his ideas on a supposed natural and perpetual community of sea ownership, by the later work his ideas had become completely self-contradicting. Selden shows how in the *Jure Belli* Grotius began his argument by founding it on right reason only:

> But at length hee betake's himself to the received Customs of Nations and speaks more then[sic] once concerning the proprietie of private Dominion of the Sea, as a thing sometimes to bee yielded without Controversie.

That is, Selden points out that Grotius veers between two different theoretical groundings, right reason and traditional customs, that are mutually exclusive. Thus, Selden observes, Grotius attempts to hide this fundamental theoretical inconsistency, by abandoning at a certain point his theoretical grounding in right reason, and turning to find recourse for his claims in customs of nations, suddenly arguing "that not by any natural Right or Reason, but by Custom it came to pass, that the Sea was not appropriated, or that it could not lawfully bee entered upon by Right of Occupation[.]" For

---

[45] Caruso *Miglior* pp. 442–443; Tuck *Rights* p. 83 note 11. It might be that, as long as Grotius was politically active in the Netherlands as an ally of Oldenbarnvelt, he did not feel free to fully disclose his views, but after escaping his imprisonment to exile in France, he had no more need to do so.

[46] It seems that Grotius attempted to blur this difficulty by emphasizing the connection between national existence and a state (whereas Selden emphasized culture), because, unlike nations, states could be justified by his theory of individual consent.

Selden it was obvious that a theoretical argumentation from right reason was diametrically opposed to one from national traditions, and there was never any doubt, that he cast his lot firmly with the latter.[47]

The crucial point in the divergence is that Grotian argumentation from right reason, but also Hobbesian or Filmerian theoretical foundations lead inevitably to formation of the political society of the state, while the Seldenian outlook culminates in the nation, for which the state is a political instrument. The state as political association is born out of necessity and calculation, be it fear or self-interest, while the nation belongs to associations born (at least ideally) of affections and attachments, alongside such as the family and religion. That is not to say that no passions or affections could be directed towards the state, or that national or religious identity is totally devoid of calculation and interest. However, clearly, men's inborn inclination to sociability was only ancillary in Grotius' theory, to a supreme reason, and the passions in Hobbes' theory were ruled above all by fear, as the dominant factor directing men's calculation of political allegiance. Conversely, traditional accounts of political society, in England as well as the continent, stressed that legitimate monarchs rule by love and affection, rather than by fear and interest, and that those elements composing one's national identity, such as traditions, language, religious attachment and even customary laws, are all forms of attachment and consent that have little component of calculation in them.[48]

The political crisis of the 1640s, and especially the regicide, sharpened the divergence between various views of politics and gradually identified the royalist side far more with the claims grounding government in "affection" and those supporting the Commonwealth far more with arguments of self-interest. No regime really desires to claim fear and self-interest as the sole basis for allegiance to it, but it is striking how much of the parliamentary controversialist literature, and even more so the supporters of the Cromwell regime, employed primarily arguments of self-interest. While on the other side of the political divide, especially after the regicide, one of the characteristics of Royalists was the rejection by so many among their political and cultural spokesmen, of the principle of fear (so eminently adopted by supporters of the Commonwealth and Protectorate), in favor of a language of love and affection.[49]

---

[47] MC b1c26.

[48] D.R. Kelley "Second nature: The idea of custom in European law, society and culture" in A. Grafton & A. Blair, *The Transmission of Culture in Early Modern Europe* (Philadelphia: University of Pennsylvania Press, 1990) p. 134; Kahn *Wayward* p. 95. A good example is the 1651 dedication to Hobbes, by the poet William Davenant of an unfinished epic poem, named *Gondibert*. Hobbes responded to the poem's praise of love as a positive political power, by addressing to Davenant a critique of romance and of any supernatural machinery. This was in line with Hobbes' view that contract or fear (or both) should replace love as the basis of subjection. Against the majority of contemporaries who believed the sovereign had to appeal to his subjects' affections, Hobbes held love was erratic and subversive. Kahn *Wayward* p. 143.

[49] Adamson *Noble* pp. 244, 272; Digby Thomas *Hero* pp. 36–37.

The divergence between affection and interest as foundation of political society should not be seen as merely one between two kinds of arguments for establishing the origin and the authority of government, but rather standing for two quite different visions of political society. For the polity born out of coercion or necessity, be it even rational necessity, and ultimately sustained on fear and force is always and only a state, and as such it exists only as long as its material attributes do; while, on the other hand, the political community born out of affections, and sustained by such voluntary adherence, is not ultimately a reflection of a state or of formal institutions like government or church; instead it places allegiance in a particular person or nation. Thus, when in Shakespeare's *Henry V*, the King rallies his exhausted troops in order to make one last, desperate effort to take the walled city before them, in the famous "once more into the breach" speech, he certainly does not talk to them of calculations or necessities concerning king, state and church, but rather exhorts their particular affections, to cry out "God for Harry, England and Saint George!"[50]

New political theories, from Machiavelli to Hobbes, openly challenged the traditional account of politics by regarding it as unrealistic and secondary to the real pillars of government: fear and calculation. These new theories put individual self-interest at the center of political allegiance, whether in the menacing version of Machiavelli and Hobbes, or in the more benevolent form of rational calculation of such as Grotius. For these new theories, any other competing allegiances, be they religious, personal or national, form a clear threat to the authority of the state. Hobbes regarded all such allegiances as competing with the sovereign, and reduced them to some type of self-interest. But if he could arguably claim that religious allegiance was based in the fear of otherworldly punishment, the same was not true of personal or national attachments, which were many times based on the very opposite of individual self-interest. On the other hand, the traditional accounts of politics, to be found in such as Bracton and Fortescue, identified custom with Aristotelian "second nature," through the principle of "love" by which use becomes another nature ("usus alteram facit naturam"), while often attempting to neatly reconcile it with rational arguments. Obviously this approach was still potent enough in the

---

Margaret Cavendish's novel *The Contract* (1656) is one such example, describing the lives of a pair of characters who had been betrothed at a very early age, while the woman was a young orphan. It explores the question of the degree to which this contract was valid and in what way, if at all. Her answer is to reject the contract of self-interest and to uphold the contract of love. She connects the marriage contract to the political one, and by implication argues for a more egalitarian contract, spousal as well as political, between men and women. Sir Richard Fanshawe is another example, in a poem and prose appendix to his translation of the Italian poem *Il Pastor Fido* (The Faithful Shepherd), dedicated to the future Charles II, clearly stating that consent predicated on the affections is more binding than coercion or self-interest could ever be. See Kahn *Wayward* pp. 171–173, 178–179, 185, 195.

[50] *Henry V*, Act III scene I.

early seventeenth century for Shakespeare to build around it his account of Henry V, a play completely within this tradition, extolling as it did the love and attachment of the protagonists to their national identity and the person of their king.[51]

4.5 "WHAT ISH MY NATION?" – THE ELEMENTS OF NATIONAL IDENTITY

The centrality of national identity for Selden's legal and political theory requires that we look into what is it that defines a nation. In Selden's day, the issue repeatedly came up because of its relevance to various political issues of the time, especially pertaining to the relationship of England with its British neighbors. For while it was quite easy for an Englishman to identify the Spanish or the French as a separate nation, with their distinct history, geography and culture, the question became much more complicated when one was addressing the Irish or the Scots, which in many ways might seem hardly distinguishable from the English. In the early seventeenth century it was the union of crowns with Scotland and its political repercussions, as well as English rule in Ireland, which occasioned repeated discussion of national identities, while in the 1640s and 1650s it was the spread of civil wars and the uncertainty about the political future that triggered debates on this issue. Usually, the two most widely mentioned components of national identity were "descent of blood" and language. These two components are of course central in the biblical narrative, commonly identifying nations by descent and by language, but they were conventional in all European countries of Selden's time. Nations were often identified by language (e.g., in Italian universities, the students of the German or French "nation" dwelled together based on their language, not the state they came from) and stories of ancient and medieval provenance abounded about alleged national descent from either a single eponymous ancestor or some ancient tribe (such as the Britons from "Brutus" the Dutch from the "Batavi"). However, in the British Isles, the issue was complicated by the fact that neither "blood" nor "language" was of much help in distinguishing national identity. The actual differences in descent among English, the Scots and the Irish were relatively negligible, especially among the heavily Englishized ruling classes of the latter two. All of the populations of Britain and Ireland had a recorded history of influxes of (mainly Germanic) population groups from Frisia, Scandinavia and Normandy, intermingling with native Celtic ones. Although the peripheral areas might contain a larger contingent of native Celtic-speaking populations, in England too the Welsh (themselves sometimes represented as a separate nation, at other times as English) supplied a sizeable contingent on that front

---

[51] See Rahe *Against* pp. 44, 129.

too, while in Ireland a considerable part of the population comprised English and Scottish settlers. This situation was amusingly represented in Shakespeare's *Henry V*, where the division between the four national components (including the Welsh) of the British population is made, but since they were all English speakers, in order to distinguish them from each other, there is a resort to the different national accents – not a very solid basis for national identity, especially as it could equally be employed to highlight differences between Englishmen with accents from, say, Yorkshire and Essex.

As a result of the limitations of upholding national identity within Britain, based on descent or language only, there was often a resort to highlighting two additional distinctive national elements, also of biblical origin: religion and laws. Alongside descent and language, the biblical books also address religion and laws as indicating national identity, most often when making the distinction between the Israelites and other nations. Although closely connected between them and sometimes appearing as one, in the Bible religious worship and laws, at least in the strict sense, are not necessarily identical, certainly so for other nations, and even in some cases for the Israelites themselves – the prophetic later biblical books, in particular, repeatedly address cases where the Israelites, although worshipping the true God of Israel (and not false gods or idolatrous practices), are nevertheless censured for transgressing moral and social laws (such as the book of Micah accusing the leadership of Judea of corruption, dishonesty and oppression of the poor). In Britain, national differences in religion and law could be, and indeed were, employed to define national identity, for the English church and the Common law certainly differed from what went on in these matters in Scotland or Ireland. The vicissitudes of the seventeenth century saw these differences increase and to a great degree impress themselves on popular imagination to this very day, defining the English identity as a moderate middle ground between the Catholic and therefore inherently absolutist Irish on the one hand, and the Presbyterian and therefore inherently rebellious Scots on the other. Indeed, these distinctions were the origin for the English political appellations of Tories and Whigs: slang designations respectively for Irish and Scottish bandits, which became by-words for those faulted with absolutist or rebellious political leanings.

Not surprisingly, throughout the seventeenth century there was no lack of attempts to downplay or augment these national distinctions in religion and law, usually in the service of wider political considerations. In the religious field, for example, neat distinctions were often complicated by the facts on the ground. In Ireland, although a great majority of the population was Catholic, the ruling class was for the most part composed of fervent Protestants (many of them of English or Scottish descent), wishing to bring the whole country over to the reformed religion. In Scotland, Presbyterianism was distinct from English Episcopalianism and later from the Independents (that is, Congregationalists) who dominated the Cromwellian regime – but it was nevertheless a Protestant ally in the greater battle against Catholicism, and in the 1640s a rising English

Presbyterianism made it for a time seem possible to merge the doctrines of the two national Churches.

As for the field of law, the pride and eminence reputed by the English to their Common law should seemingly have made redundant any attempts to downplay its difference from Scottish or Irish law, but as we have seen, in this field too there were such attempts, mainly in pursuit of a political union of Britain. The proposals for a full union of England and Scotland, early in the reign of James I, had been occasion for much debate about national differences and similarities, with supporters of the union minimizing the differences and their import, and opponents naturally taking the reverse course. Robert Cotton (an Englishman of proud Scottish descent), for example, supported the union, and in a tract published within days of Elizabeth's death, he described both kingdoms as being "of one descend in blood," of one language and of one religion. Significantly, Cotton did not claim there was "one law," for this was a far more contentious issue. Other supporters of the union did address the issue of national law, proposing an essential compatibility of English with Scottish law. Not surprisingly, these claims were mostly aired either by Scotsmen such as Robert Pont, who argued that the two laws were "almost the same in substance" and easily reconciled if any differences arise; or else by Civil lawyers specializing in Roman law, such as Gentili and Sir John Hayward, who believed that by making the two laws into one "the change will not be great." Accordingly, common lawyers were for the most part intensely averse to such claims and held them to be absolutely false; they shared the views of the eminent antiquary and common lawyer Sir Henry Spelman, for whom the Scottish legal system was fundamentally alien to the Common law, "liker to France than England" and the Scottish manners for the most part concurring with the (barbaric) "natural Irish." The vast majority of the English political class tended to agree with Spelman, and James I recognized this when he commented that whereas in Scotland (like in France) the fundamental law consisted essentially of the rules governing the succession to the throne, in England the whole of the Common law was fundamental. This remark by James was intended to circumvent the problem of English attachment to the Common law, by proposing that a legal union palatable to the English could be simply achieved by the adoption lock-stock-and-barrel of the English Common law in Scotland (with the exception of the Scottish legal regulation of the succession). However, even such flattering proposals did not suffice to remove English opposition to the union with Scotland, and the project petered out. It revealed that the main obstacle to James' desire to create a single nation out of his kingdoms (as well as to later attempts, like Benedict Anderson's, to deny an early-modern English national identity), was the existence among so many Englishmen of a robust corporate identity embodied in their national customary constitution.[52]

---

[52] See especially Sharpe *Remapping* pp. 318–319; McEachern *Poetics* pp. 158–160; Cromartie *Constitutionalist* p. 153.

As for Selden, while all of the four abovementioned elements of national identity are found in his writings, they are certainly not assigned equal importance. Selden never denied national identity as a mix of descent with cultural factors such as language, religion and law, but he always regarded the latter factors as more important by far. The role of physical descent, in Selden's view of national identity, is neither central nor decisive, and he certainly rejected the idea that any men, even kings, were in any sense born naturally superior to others. Even when discussing hereditary nobility, while he mentioned the claim (made by Aristotle) that "one not like his Parents is, in some sort, a Monster" which might indicate the children of the nobility as naturally superior, Selden effectively neutralized its import by arguing that it merely meant there were *"severall individuating Qualities deriv'd from divers of the neere Ancestors"* which transferred by the parents (both mother or father)*"may be exprest in the Children*[.]" He further minimized the import of physical heredity by pointing out that *"this likenesse is oft times to a remote Ancestor."* The result was that the impact of heredity becomes completely ambiguous and diffuse, pointing more to potentialities than definite traits, and quite wide-ranging, since very many people could find some *"remote"* noble or otherwise eminent ancestor (including Selden's own supposed connection to the knightly Bakers).[53]

In his works, Selden never derived political legitimacy from physical descent only, and always expressed a strong suspicion towards claims of ancient noble descent, made for individuals or nations. Describing the rulers and titles of the Muslim states of northern Africa and of the Ottoman domains, he remarked about "the Princes there being either out of one root and nation, or, at least deriving themselves so." Similarly, he expressed his agreement with a historian "more iudicious, and not flattering the idle traditions of his own Nation" when that writer denied that the current (Capetians) kings of France were actual blood descendants of former (Merovingian and Carolingian) dynasties. Elsewhere he repeatedly heaped scorn on similar attempts made for whole nations, such as those in England who "on purpose to raise the *British* name out of the *Trojan* ashes" claimed its laws and people to have originated with a Trojan named Brutus.[54]

---

[53] TH (1614), in the Preface, not paginated; TT "King." The basis for the discussion of the impact of heredity in the Preface to the TH is directly culled from Aristotle's *On the Generation of Animals*, book 4 chapter 3: "The same causes must be held responsible for the following groups of facts. (1) Some children resemble their parents, while others do not; some being like the father and others like the mother, both in the body as a whole and in each part, male and female offspring resembling father and mother respectively rather than the other way about. (2) They resemble their parents more than remoter ancestors, and resemble those ancestors more than any chance individual. (3) Some, though resembling none of their relations, yet do at any rate resemble a human being, but others are not even like a human being but a monstrosity. For even he who does not resemble his parents is already in a certain sense a monstrosity; for in these cases Nature has in a way departed from the type."

[54] TH (1631) pp. 92–93, 132–133. *The Reverse or Back-face of the English Janus* (1682) – "Redman Westcot" [Adam Littleton] translation of *Jani Anglorum* b1c6. Perhaps a better

As we shall see, for Selden it was the cultural aspects, language in the widest sense (including proverbs), as well as laws (for him both religious and not), with the ideas appended to them, that constituted the principal element of national identity. A concern with language and philology, and an awareness of language as a combination of change and continuity, was a prominent feature of Selden's works. In his early *Jani Anglorum* (1610) his first published book written when aged only 26, Selden quoted verse from the medieval writer Robert of Gloucester, allowing that as an "old fashioned rhyme" it will probably bother the refined tastes of his own age while reminding his readers that even the finest artifice of contemporary "Masters of Expression" will perhaps "in future Ages" seem coarse and unrefined. Later, in the second chapter of his lengthy prolegomena to his *Diis Syriis* (1617) – addressing the relationship between the Hebrew and Phoenician languages – Selden shows he understands languages as changing, being corrupted, thriving or declining (as he claims was the case with the Phoenician language), one can almost say developing. It is the *Table-Talk* which offers the most succinct example of Selden's view of this relationship, using yet another version of the continuity-through-change imagery:

> If you look upon the Language spoken in the *Saxon* Time, and the Language spoken now, you will find the Difference to be just, as if a Man had a Cloak that he wore plain in Queen *Elizabeth*'s Days, and since, here has put in a piece of Red, and there a piece of Blue, and here a piece of Green, and there a piece of Orange-tawny. We borrow Words from the *French, Italian, Latin*, as every Pedantick Man pleases.[55]

Elsewhere, the importance of language to Selden's thought is reported in his pithy remark, appearing in the *Table-Talk*, where he declared that "Syllables govern the World," thus indicating that men can understand the world only through words and speech. Significantly, for Selden, language was (like for William of Ockham and for Hobbes), conventional, with no inherent significance to words. The significance of words was then to be found out by correspondence with the use made of them – not with some assessment of rational adequacy between words and their signification. Caruso has remarked that such a view regards language as inherently unstable, because in constant tension of the opposed pulls from accepted opinion about the meaning of words on the one hand, and human invention creating new, sometimes arbitrary associations, on the other. Within such a scheme, tradition, as established accepted opinion, is an indispensable tool for supplying some stability and continuity in the employment of language and its meaning. Use and tradition are thus not merely revealing of the meaning of words, but in

English rendition of the title is *The Twofold Face of the English Janus*. See also NL cols. 1891–1892.
[55] See McEachern *Poetics* p. 176; *Diis Syriis* (1617) "Prolegomena" and ch. 2; and TT "Language" sec. 3.

a sense produce the things being designated. In short, without tradition, words lose ascertainable meaning, and conversely tradition can be said to a great degree to define reality.[56]

As for Selden's view of the religious component of national identity, we will look at this issue more extensively in a following chapter. Here it suffices to point out that in general Selden was opposed to a neat distinction or separation between church and state, and in England especially he regarded all legislation and regulation of the national Church as subject to Parliament and the Common law. More particularly, Selden opposed the attempts to undermine the traditional practices of the national Church by the "private" readings of the biblical texts, preferred by religious dissidents from the established church. He is recorded as repeatedly criticizing the resort to extempory praying, instead of employing the established book of Common Prayer, and there are several of his saying from the *Table-Talk* where he explicitly directs his disdain towards such attempts, as well as more generally implying the connections of such concerns to epistemic issues and to the role of tradition. He is recorded as arguing:

> Say what you will against *Tradition*; we know the signification of Words by nothing but tradition. You will say the Scripture was written by the Holy *Spirit*, but do you understand that Language 'twas writ in? No. Then for Example, take these words, *In principio erat verbum*. How do you know those words signifie, *In the beginning was the word*, but by Tradition, because some Body has told you so?

In this passage Selden addressed specifically religious traditions (which among many English Protestants of his time had come under a blanket suspicion of popery), pointing out that even the most Puritan Christian anti-traditionalist had to allow for the national tradition if they wished to read the Bible, the point about the significance of words very much in evidence. We might also recall in this context the above discussion about Selden's epistemological views, where we saw that the connection he made between tradition and observation ("how I know this Carpet to be green?") was also uttered within a comment regarding the controversy about the authority of national traditions in Church matters, when he remarked "'Tis a great Question how we know Scripture to be Scripture, whether by the Church, or by Man's private Spirit." In this example again it is the Church which stands for national tradition and the "private Spirit" for irresponsible religious innovations.[57]

It is only natural that the aspect which most concerned Selden, where his work touches on issues of national identity, was the role of the laws. Not surprisingly, he regarded the traditional English laws as, to a great extent, the

---

[56] TT "Power"; Caruso *Miglior* pp. 760–763, 780–784.
[57] See TT "Tradition." See also on "Bible, Scripture"; "Power, State" and "Prayer": "'Tis not the Original Common prayer-book; why: shew me an original Bible, or an original *Magna Charta*." See Selden's stating of his view of church and state, in C. Van Dixhoorn, *The Minutes and Papers of the Westminster Assembly 1643–1652* (Oxford University Press, 2012) vol. II pp. 442–443.

defining element of national identity, certainly far exceeding the importance of factors such as descent or of state authority, even at a time of conquest. This position of his is exemplified in his many discussions, through the years, of the significance of William I's rule in England, and its impact on politics and law. Raising questions of legitimacy, continuity and identity, this was one of the most debated issues of English constitutional history. Already in his 1610 *Jani Anglorum*, Selden denied the view that the Norman conquest was a decisive break with the past, which initiated a totally new political and legal asset. He pointed out that William's claim to legitimate title to the crown, as King Edward's heir, committed him to a continuity in forms. Moreover, Selden argued, the "Norman" understood that it was famously hazardous to attempt new laws in recently acquired possessions,

and the Norman *did warily provide against this danger, by bestowing upon the yielding conquered Nation the requital of their ancient Law: a requital, I say, but more, as it should seem, for shew than use; and rather to curry favour with the people at the present, than in good deed for the advantage of the* English *Name.*

However, he maintained, this "requital," to begin with mainly for show, became with time a real one, when William committed himself to respect Saxon laws (regardless of his having changed some of them). Selden was proposing a view of the tradition of English legislation, distinct, on the one hand from those proponents of an English ancient constitution that regarded it as perfect and unchanging, since its inception and having withstood the conquest essentially untouched; and on the other hand from those who claimed English laws to have been born, essentially with the conquest, out of royal will only. Instead, Selden treated the English of the eleventh century as a nation already possessing a distinct character and law at the time of the conquest, which were preserved by the Norman conquerors, even if mainly for practical considerations. In this context he illustrated the blend of change and continuity, which is so characteristic of his idea of national identity, and later in the same text, he pointed out that:

For the times on this side of the Normans *entrance, are so full of new Laws, especially such as belong to the right of Tenancy or Vassalage; though other Laws have been carefully enough kept up from the time of the Saxons, and perhaps from an earlier date.*

To press this point, Selden also compared the Norman conquest to Henry VIII's religious reformation, proposing both events shared a mixture of persistence and change.[58]

---

[58] *Jani Anglorum*, in the author's preface (not paginated). The original Latin is: "& caute sibi cavit ab hoc periculo Normannus, atque aviti juris obsequentes victos imperativit hostimento, sed perquam, ut videtur, specioso, adque ineundam potius impraesentiarum gratiam, quam reapse in Anglici nominis commodum." Later in book II ch. 19, after describing the development and authority of popular assemblies into Parliament, he writes: "Assemblies do now sit in great State, which with a wonderful harmony of the Three Estates, the *King*, the *Lords* and the *Commons*, or

In *England's Epinomis*, a work in many ways parallel to the *Jani* and composed around the same time (but left unpublished, until printed posthumously in 1681), after making the point that the various Germanic tribes invading Britain, while described as Saxons, Jutes and Angles, in fact "differed more in name than Nation, and are in good Authors but Synonymies of the same Countrey-people," then goes on to consider a somewhat different aspect of the fate of English laws at the Norman conquest, but makes very much the same point of continuity. Selden argued that at the time of William the Conqueror, at first the new King,

> honouring with respect the Northern stock, whence his blood was derived, the Danelage [law of Scandinavian origin] he preferred, as worthier and better for Government than the mere *English*. But seeming at first inexorable, the perswasive remembrance of [the Saxon king Edward the Confessor's] *his* Soul, which bequeathed him the Kingdom, and whose Laws they desired, being, as the best supposed motive, inserted in the Petitions of the conquered, he granted so much,

that since that time, the laws of Edward the Confessor were corroborated and observed in all England.[59]

This is one of the more instructive treatments of the relationship between the claims of blood, culture and popular consent in Selden's works. The passage shows that William I's ties to where his "blood was derived" were not some vague organic or subconscious influence, but rather came out of his "honouring" his origins. However, despite this honoring of Danelage, William eventually conceded a restoration of the old laws of England, because of regard for Edward the Confessor's "Soul," and because the English population so "desired." The national identity of the English, embodied in their traditional laws, eventually overcomes the appeal of blood descent, and in a way conquers the conqueror, making the Norman into English.

The same mix of change and continuity is also evident in Selden's comments about English localities and history in his "Illustrations" to Drayton's *Poly-Olbion* (1612), which opens with a remark about the connection between a land and the national character of its inhabitants: "for anciently both *Jews*, *Gentiles* and *Christians* have supposed to every Country a singular *Genius*."[60]

In his *Analecton Anglobritannicon*, written around 1607, the same point is again made, that the legal changes introduced by the Normans "commingled with ancient practice" (omnia antiquis tametsi immista moribus) to the degree that, as Selden put in an amusing image, new Norman laws and English

---

Deputies of the People, are joyned together, to a most firm security of the publick, and are by a very Learned Man [Camden] in allusion to that made word in *Livy, Panaetolium* from the *Aetolians*, most rightly called *Pananglium*, that is *all England*." He then quotes from Augustine's *City of God* to describe the harmony and concord of the state thus governed.

[59] *England's Epinomis* (1681), ch. 3 p.8 and ch. 4 p. 12.

[60] See discussion in McEachern *Poetics* pp. 187 and Toomer *Scholarship* pp. 99, 121.

customary law could not be told apart, and legal matters all equally "smelled of Norman and Norm" (Normanniam tamen et Normam redolerent).[61]

The *Titles of Honor* (1614) afforded Selden another opportunity for pointing out the legal intermixture of continuity and change, when discussing the nobiliar titles in England. An admixture of Roman (duke, marquess, viscount), Norman (baron) and Danish and Saxon (earl) origins, was a perfect example of the successive adding of varied strands into one national identity. Selden illustrated the idea of continuity through gradual change, connecting it with language, by addressing the nomenclature of the title known in his time as Baron. He noted that the title Baron was introduced at the beginning of the "Norman state" in England, in place of the title Thane that had been used among the Saxons. However, for a time both titles were retained in use, because it was unlikely that "the use of language could have beene so sodainly[sic] altered that the Title of Baron only should have presently expressed it," so that in William I's *Domesday Book* and in Henry I's *Laws* both terms are used interchangeably. He also pointed out the limits of attempting to restore ancient laws after a long time had passed, mentioning that in the *Laws* of Henry I there was an attempt to restore some pre-Conquest laws, but this was more "desired, then truly restored" – the desire nevertheless indicating the English continuing attachment and predisposition towards old laws.[62]

The two editions of the *Titles of Honor* allow us to see that, if anything, the importance Selden assigned to the role of local national traditions only increased with time. In the first edition Selden followed Hotman (and many civilians) in giving a centralized account of the spread of Feudal Law in Europe after the fall of the Roman Empire, as originating among the Franks, then following the conquests of Charlemagne into Germany and Italy, of William I into England, and into the rest of Europe by imitation (an account that could be used to claim a unified Imperial political authority over European kingdoms). Seventeen years later, in the second edition of the *Titles* (1631), the account was markedly different: unitary no more, it was far more attuned to the different national and local realities, which effected various amalgamations of the customs of the "northern nations" with Roman offices. The result was a series of "states," polities with their own national ancient constitutions, each with its own particular customs and distribution of political power, among them the English "state" in which kings, nobles, clergy and freemen had from the very beginning shared power, and the Common law consisted of customs and statutes.[63]

---

[61] *Analecton Anglobritannicon* (1615), book 2 chapter 7. See discussion in Barbour *Measures* pp. 99–101; Toomer *Scholarship* p. 87 and note 110; Cromartie *Hale* pp. 35–36
[62] TH (1631) part 2 ch. 5. See discussion in Christianson *Discourse* p. 232 and Toomer *Scholarship* p. 137 note 79.
[63] See discussion in Christianson *Discourse* pp. 214–215

By the time Selden published his *Historie of Tithes* (1618), the claim that the conquest had not caused a definite breach in the Common law was an established feature of his work. He asserted that "neither were the Laws formerly made, abolisht by that *Conquest*" although the conqueror certainly would have been within his rights to do so, "but also the ancient and former Laws of the Kingdome were confirmed by him." Selden's conclusion is adamant:

But these things prove enough that this *William* seized the Crown of *England*, not as conquerd, but by pretence of gift or adoption, aided and confirmed by neernesse of bloud; and so the *Saxon* Lawes formerly in force could not but continue, and such of them as are now abrogated, were not at all abrogated by his Conquest but either by the Parliaments or Ordinances of his time and of his Successors, or else by non-usage or contrarie custom."[64]

This approach by Selden to national identity can be shown to have been employed by him consistently and coherently throughout his many discussions of English legislative and constitutional history, across more than four decades. It is especially prominent throughout Selden's extensive "Notes" on Fortescue's *Legibus* (1616). Discussing the evolution of English identity and laws he wrote:

As succeeding ages, so new nations (coming in by a conquest, although mixed with a title, as of *Norman* conqueror, is to be affirmed) bring always some alteration. By this well considered, that of the laws of this realm being never changed, will be better understood.

In this passage Selden did not treat the Norman conquest as a mere change of government effected by an invading army, but as the coming into England of a nation – one, however, which eventually blended completely into the English one. In the same text, Selden articulated this idea more generally, and not only as pertaining to the English case. The fact that, as a general rule, he regarded national identity as the determining element in the fashioning of traditional law

---

[64] *Historie of Tithes* pp. 481–484. Selden pointed out that this confirmation of the old law was not only for show, since a perusal of post-conquest texts like *Domesday Book*, attested to the survival of land titles from Saxon times, and "How could such Titles have held if he [William I] had made an absolute conquest of England, wherein a vniversall acquisition of all had been to the Conqueror, and no title could have been deriud but only from under him?" Indeed, Selden indicated that the confirmation of the old law, however much born out of interest and pretense only, needed to be effective for it served the conqueror's interests, both as pertaining to the legitimacy of his title to the crown as well as to the efficacy of his government over the country. Thus, "the *Norman* with his sword & pretence of the sufficiencie & precedence of the gift made to himself, got the Crown as if he had bin a lawfull Successor to the Confessor, and not a vniuersall Conqueror." Later on Selden added that: "For, although the Laws of this Kingdom, and, I think, of all other ciuill States at this day, exclude Bastards (without a subsequent legitimation) from enheritance; yet by the old Laws vsd by his Ancestors & Countrie men, that is, by those of *Norway*, a Princes sonne gotten on a Concubine bond or free, was equally inheritable as any other born in Wedlock; which was, I beleeue, no small reason why he stood at first so much for the Lawes of *Norway* to haue been generally receiud in this Kingdome." See discussion in Toomer *Scholarship* p. 301.

is even more evident in another passage of the same text, where he discussed the claims made by writers about the origins, antiquity and excellence of the laws in different countries. Selden dismissed the idea (also expressed in Fortescue's own text) that the mere antiquity of some law should be construed as proof of its excellence. Instead, Selden remarked,

[b]ut in truth and to speak without perverse affectation, all laws in general are originally equally antient. All were grounded upon nature, and no nation was, that out of it took not their grounds; and nature being the same in all, the beginning of all laws must be the same. As soon as Italy was peopled, this beginning of laws was there, and upon it were grounded the *Roman* laws, which could not have that distinct name indeed till *Rome* was built, yet remained always that they were at first, saving that additions and interpretations, in succeeding ages increased, and somewhat altered them, by making a *determinatio juris naturalis*, which is nothing but the civil law of any nation. For although the law of nature be truly said immutable, yet it is as true, that it is limitable, and limited law of nature is the law now used in every state.[65]

In this manner, traditional national laws were also natural laws: the "civil law of any nation" was grounded on nature, and although "additions and interpretations, in succeeding ages increased, and somewhat altered them," yet through the alterations they preserved their original nature and "remained always that they were at first."

To stress the extent to which circumstances make national laws different, Selden proposed that even if the Britons had received their laws directly from Greece, as the Romans were reputed to have had, with time the two systems would have nevertheless ended up considerably different, because of "interpretations, and additions which by this time would have been put to them here." Thus, Selden clearly indicated that these differences were not only the result of external factors such as circumstances and local conditions, but of deeper inclinations attending nations, in effect of what would be termed today national character (he indicated elsewhere that even climate might have something to do with it). He made this argument explicitly when he compared national differences to those between individuals: "Divers [sic] nations, as divers men, have their divers collections and inferences; and so make their divers laws to grow to what they are, out of one and the same root." At the same time that thinkers like Grotius and Hobbes were developing ideas about society and the state being (at least ideally) products of *a priori* individual choice guided by rational considerations, Selden was arguing for a view very much the opposite – that not only political societies as a whole, but the groups and individuals within them, were themselves products of peculiar characteristics, paramount among which was the national one. Selden did not deny the possibility that individuals might associate to create a society or a state, but

[65] NL cols. 1888, 1891–1892. Selden also seems to have indicated some cross-fertilization of laws (like peoples), when he added that "those customs which have come all out of one fountain, *nature*, thus vary from and cross one another in several common-wealths."

he regarded this element of the political set-up as subsidiary to the character and development of the community. In this vein, when he proposed that the beginning of law and constitution in England, as elsewhere, was "in the first peopling of the land, when men, by nature being civil creatures, grew to plant a common society," he meant that at that time also began the development of the law and identity peculiar to that civil society, "when and in like kind as the laws of all other states, that is, *When there was first a state in that land, which the common law now governs.*" At this stage came his description of the natural law being limited, altered and interpreted for the convenience of that political society. Selden believed this argument should, if "rationally considered," end the "question of those, which would say something against the laws of *England* if they could." To press his point that the value of laws is not in their fitting some abstract model, but in their suitability to particular environments, he added that "[t]hose which best fit the state wherein they are, clearly deserve the name of best laws."[66]

Selden's argument above was directed against claims for the antiquity of laws being proof of their excellence, but it also effectively rejected the value of a law that would deny a central role to particular circumstances and character. The inevitable result of accepting his argument would be that instead of antiquity (or right reason), it is continuity that should be sought out as the important, indeed the legitimizing element of laws – for continuity over time would be the best way to reflect the particular and changing character of a political society.

In the following decades, Selden's writings were directed for the most part towards fields that were quite far from English constitutional history. His political activities involved him in the great constitutional struggles of the 1620s and 1640s (and landed him in prison), and in the 1630s he produced the bulk of his massive Hebraist project. Other preoccupations, possibly mixed with the danger of political repercussions, shifted Selden's writings for the most part into subjects bearing less directly on English constitutional history. However, even in such writings, when issues of national identity bearing on England came up, he reiterated the very same ideas he had presented earlier. His treatment of the subject in the second edition of the *Titles* has already been noted. In his *Mare Clausum* (1635), he also briefly returned to the same point.[67]

But it was in 1647, at the height of his fame and intellectual powers, and still engaged in his wide-ranging Hebraist project, that Selden returned one more time to treat extensively the history and theory of the English constitution, when

---

[66] NL cols. 1891–1892.
[67] MC b2 c10–11. Selden's claim that the English refused to introduce Roman law to England, though well acquainted with it, because of its dangerous ideological implications, is similar to Edmund Burke's claim in the *Reflections*, that Selden and those of his generation, knowingly refused to replace traditional English rights with those based on abstract universal theories about rights of men.

he published his "Dissertatio historica," upon *Fleta*. The "Dissertatio" is Selden's most mature extensive treatment of these matters, and in it his view of English laws, puts national identity at the center, as a compound of tradition and consent, which is the exact opposite of the universalist and authoritarian Roman law. Selden asserts in the book that when Germans overwhelmed the Roman Empire, Britain's "Celtic Nations" (Celticae illae nations) expelled the Roman governors and "constituted according to their own will a kind of Republic[.]" Moreover, even those residues of Roman law which persisted in the Common law for a long time, some even to his day "derive their present Force from the Consent of those who make Use of or moderate them at their pleasure, they not at all, as before, depending on the Authority of the Roman Emperors or Caesars." Describing the (ultimately failed) attempt around 1140 AD to introduce Roman law into England, Selden remarked that for some 700 years previous, while Roman law was not admitted into Britain, various laws of Saxons, Danes and Normans were indeed admitted, clearly indicating the congruity of the latter laws with the English ones. He added that during those 700 years, the Anglo-Saxons, Danes and Normans, were under "one and the same line of Kings," and made use of "their own peculiar Laws, now called by us, the common Law of *England*; though variously, as it must always happen, altered according to the different State of Affairs." Obviously indicating an overall continuity of legal framework, regardless of some contingent alterations, Selden's account points out that the refusal to admit Roman law into England was not the result of ignorance, but of a conscious choice on the part of English learned men, some of whom at least were certainly well acquainted with Roman law.[68]

Selden portrayed this struggle between Britons holding on to their heritage and defending it, even through subsequent changes, against pretensions based on some sort of imperial authority, as characteristic of England's constitutional history. This approach dovetailed nicely with the high regard he had towards old legal texts of the Common law, for in both cases the issue was whether historical changes with time simply superseded the past, or if some kind of continuity persisted through the changes. Clearly, for those who maintain simply that the law changes over the years, a legal text some hundreds of years old could not by itself have authority as to the current state of the law. But Selden clearly disagreed with the many who regarded such old texts as being at most ornamental, bearing no current authority at all.

There was no lack of prominent legal writers who had explicitly declared that old legal text had no authority whatsoever, from the prominent early sixteenth-

---

[68] "Dissertatio historica" Ogg pp. 25–29. In the three decades between 1617 and 1647, the only works Selden published on English constitutional history were very brief pieces like his *Privileges of the Baronage of England* of 1642, as well as touching on these matters in works like the second edition of *Titles of Honor*, the *Mare Clausum* and even *Jure Naturali*, as well as in parliamentary speeches, but only occasionally and relatively briefly.

century judge Sir Anthony Fitzherbert, who thought Bracton "of no authority," to Edward Littleton, who, when counsel for Selden in 1629, defended him from an accusation of "sedition" by arguing that although prominent medieval figures such as Bracton, Hengham and Glanville had mentioned "sedition" among the crimes pertaining to "Laesae majestatis" (high treason), nevertheless "they are obsolete Authors," so that they may be used as "ornament" showing how the law once was, but not to declare what the law is at this day, for later sources like *Britton* do not have the said crime, and even if they did "they are no binding authority." We may forgive Selden for not objecting and pointing out at his trial, that his own opinion differed somewhat from his counsel's on this point. For, as early as his 1616 "Notes" on Hengham's *Summae* (published together with his "Notes" on Fortescue's *Laudibus*), Selden emphasized that although the Common law was continuously developing, the study of old, even obsolete legal texts, such as those by Fortescue and Hengam, is justified by these giving light to the customs and laws of their own times, and to the origin of particular laws, "as though an ancestor of the right line, wee must deduct that of the present." That is, Selden was making the analogy of family ancestry, which supposedly retains over generations some degree of continuity and of characteristic traits. By this analogy, Selden was opposing to a view of historical change that occurs haphazardly and aimlessly, his own idea of the modification of English law (or at least some English laws) over time, which retains throughout some discernible continuity and pattern.[69]

More than 30 years after his 1616 "Notes," in his 1647 "Dissertatio historica," Selden made the same point in the context of another old, classic Common law text. Declaring that even though "the authority of every legist in relation to later times must decrease in proportion to the different nature of subsequent legislation and custom," nevertheless even changes in the law "serve to reveal the original law which is used in interpreting most recent law in a traditional as well as exemplary manner." In his opinion, although the antiquity of the *Fleta* and the many alterations in the law since, meant it did not have sufficient authority to determine judicial decisions by itself, it nevertheless still contained many things relevant as authority on which "the interpretation of the law may depend." This claim clearly suggests the existence and authority of some sort of distinctive approach, a pattern and continuity of purpose and ideas, which remain in place regardless of changes in the law, and thus are significant to current legal deliberations: in other words, what was later to be termed the Spirit of the law.[70]

---

[69] Christianson *Discourse* p. 185; Toomer *Scholarship* pp. 186–190; Ferguson *Clio* p. 294. Selden's view is in effect the epistemic one he articulated in JN, about using even erring sources for ascertaining truth, and it undergirds his view of law and politics: the original law is used to interpret recent law in a "traditional" manner – creating an interpretative tradition which seeks to reconcile the various phases of the law within one continuity of intent.

[70] "Dissertatio historica" Ogg pp. 4–7; Cromartie *Constitutionalist* p. 100; Christianson *Discourse* p. 185.

This approach clearly informs the twofold justification given by Selden in the "Dissertatio historica," for the traditional hostility of the English to the adoption of Roman law principles into the government of their own country. First, he argued, "our ancestors" were averse to Roman law as it "concerns principles of government," that is, they were against its absolutist political implications. Secondly, he claimed, there was the "remarkable esteem in which the English or Common law was held, and our constant faithfulness to it as something immemorially fitted to the genius of the nation." In other words, the English nation's attachment to its legal traditions sprang from a combination of a rejection of political absolutism on the one hand, and affection for laws suited to its national character on the other. Significantly, Selden does not treat this attachment as merely some past historical occurrence, for the passage is clearly about something that is still "our" (nostros) for England of his own days.[71]

However, if their premises are properly considered, both arguments are really the flip sides of one coin. For both the aversion of the English nation to absolutist government, and the national attachment to the Common law, spring in the final analysis, from the traditional law being the expression of a kind of national consent. National common law, consensual because traditional, thus becomes alternative to the absolutist character of a law predicated on universalism (and, according to its supporters, right reason), as was Roman law. In this vein, Selden's remark in the same text, that one of the widespread descriptions of the Common law was "the laws and admitted customs of England" (legibus Angliae et consuetudinibus rectis), should be seen as carrying the implication that the term "rectis" for English customs, indicates that national laws and traditions are the good and right alternative, to those who proposed "right reason" as the foundation of the law.[72]

4.6 "MANKINDE IN GENERAL, THAT IS, ALL NATIONS" – NATION AS TRADITION

As we have seen, Selden's explicit advocacy of traditional national law as the actual foundation for English law, and his implicit suggestion of it as preferable for all nations, is a prominent feature in his work through many decades. But probably the most explicit and extensive exposition of his general ideas touching on national identity is to be found in his *Mare Clausum*. Published in 1635, but with an earlier unpublished version composed almost 20 years earlier, the *Mare Clausum* was a treaty on the legal and moral foundations for

---

[71] "Dissertatio historica" Ogg pp. 164–165.
[72] "Dissertatio historica" Ogg pp. 172–173. See also Selden's observation there that, every time it was attempted to introduce Roman law into England, the English nation and its judges were always extremely tenacious of the customs of their own country and did not accept terms or words from the Imperial law into public records.

property, divisions and boundaries of the sea. It argued for the legitimacy of England's claim of sovereignty over the seas adjacent (and not so adjacent) to it, and against the ideas of Grotius' *Mare Liberum* (1609) denying this very claim. For our purpose, what is most significant in this work is its account of the division of the world into possessions by the posterity of Noah, as quoted by Selden (from the book of Genesis 10:5), to the effect that the Earth was divided to "*everie one after his Tongue, after their Families, in their Nations*; as it is recorded by Moses." Now, it can be clearly seen in this account how nations are supposed to proceed from both descent of progeny (*Families*) and language *(Tongue)*; it epitomizes the approach of the biblical narrative, that consistently offers a double origin for nations: the first by the progeny of Noah, the second by the "confusion of Tongues" after the building of the tower of Babylon. The same account is also valid for the much later emergence of the Israelite nation from both the progeny of Abraham, Isaac and Jacob, as well as their reception of the law at Sinai. Although in the case of the Israelites, it is law rather than tongue which makes them a nation; we have seen that this was an additional biblical element of national identity, which Englishmen, and especially Selden, happily identified with.

Clearly, the abovementioned reference was not some backhand remark on Selden's part, for in the *Mare Clausum* he went on to give a detailed account of political obligation that was consistent with this argument about the beginning of nations. Moreover, four years earlier, in his 1631 edition of the *Titles of Honor*, Selden had used the same argument (and the same passage from Genesis), but added an even clearer connection between this account of the biblical first nations and the origins of political societies. He described the first institution of kingships thus:

> For in the holy memories of that Division among the posteritie of *Noah*, we see that the Earth was so divided that the Heads of Families took their severall parts *according to their Language, and according to the Families in their Nations*. And they which are named there were doubtlesse the Kings or supreme Princes of the Nations of which they were Authors[.][73]

Selden's account of political obligation is important in this context because it clarifies the role of tradition and its place within national identity, especially as distinct from competing accounts of political obligation. Obviously, in an account of obligation that is historical and collective, the source of authority cannot be individual consent (as was Grotius'). But this implied denial of the political supremacy of individual consent did not mean for Selden the adoption of a patriarchal position, where authority simply resides in the heads of families. In his account, both paternal authority and individual consent have a role, but

---

[73] MC b1c4; TH (1631) p. 10. The language of the passage from Genesis differs a little in the two versions, since the first was Needham's rendition of Selden's Latin, while the second was Selden's own English. About the biblical account see also TH (1614) p. 5.

more important than these is another, decisive ingredient, which subsumes both: tradition as multi-generational obligation.[74]

Shortly after relating the beginning of nations, in the *Mare Clausum*, Selden goes on to describe the origin and attributes of property. In his account, private property is not at all a natural condition or right, but rather the result of convention. According to Selden, natural law permits men to order property in whatever kind of manner they wish, private or common, so that any ordered and systematic regulation of property is to be observed as any other human matter agreed upon in accordance with permissive natural law. Selden proposed that the conventional regulation of property had been born out of the wish to prevent endless disputes that would lead to strife and war, and described how the original common interest or ancient right of all men, devolved into particular proprietors with "division of Bounds and Territories." This, he posited, was achieved by "as it were, a consent of the whole bodie or universalitie of mankinde" given "by the mediation of something like a compact, which might binde their posteritie." Significantly, Selden did not go here into what exactly constituted this supposed "consent," whether by the authority individuals (as in the Grotian view) that of the patriarch-kings (as in the Filmerian view), or some other idea, like prescription. Rather he emphasized another point – that the concurrence by which not only property but eventually states too ("Bounds and Territories") were born, could "binde their posteritie." While particular stipulations of property naturally changed over time, the general principle and purpose of the compact remained. That is, Selden offered an interpretation of consent in which later generations are, to a great degree, bound by the decisions of their ancestors, and themselves, by their own actions bind their progeny. This continuing binding of posterity by successive generations, is tradition as an ever-reaffirmed contract.[75]

That Selden in writing this text was aware of – indeed explicitly refuted – Grotius' atemporal and individual understanding of consent is pretty well proved shortly afterward in the text, where Selden returned to the subject as follows:

Therefore (I suppose) it must bee yelded, that som such Compact or Covenant was passed in the very first beginnings of private Dominion or possession, and that it was in full force and virtue transmitted to posteritie by the Fathers, who had the power of distributing possessions after the flood. So that wee may conclude no less concerning distribution by Assignment, then touching Seisure by occupation of things relinquish't at

---

[74] Selden's position seems close to that of thinkers of like Dudley Digges and Henry Spelman, but it appears to me that while they embraced, somewhat inconsistently, both patriarchal *and* consensual obligation, Selden's authority of tradition attempted to overcome this inconsistency. See the discussion of these issues in Schochet *Patriarchalism* pp. 97–109.

[75] MC b1c4, also b1c5. In this context it is interesting to consider the divergence between Selden's premises and those of Locke, since they are sometimes described as arguing the same basic principles. For Selden property is certainly not a natural quality or right, and men are bound by their ancestors' decisions; for Locke the opposite is true in both cases.

pleasure, that a general compact or Agreement was made or ratified, either expressly in words, or implicitly by custom. And truly, the self same thing seem's to bee the opinion of the most excellent Hugo Grotius[.]

Here Selden went on to quote from Grotius' *Jure Belli* (book 2, ch. 2 par. 2), and in reading the passage and the quote, one can hardly refrain from suspecting that Selden in this case (and perhaps others) intentionally reaps praise on Grotius just before delivering the blow to his position – by using the Dutchman's own arguments against him. The most important point here is Selden's reiteration of the argument that the "Compact or Covenant" of private dominion was "transmitted to posteritie by the Fathers, who had the power of distributing possessions after the flood" – future generations are bound by the authority of the founding fathers of their nations.[76]

However, it is significant that not only individual consent but patriarchal political authority as well is refuted by these passages from the *Mare Clausum*. Although a "power" of the "Fathers" explicitly appears, its import is the complete opposite to that suggested by the proponents of patriarchal authority in Selden's days. Patriarchal authority means that the fathers (or those with their power) of every current generation have the absolute authority to dispense possessions even against the wishes of their predecessors, while Selden's passage instead makes clear that the current generation is bound by the covenant made by its ancestors. Indeed, as Filmer himself explicitly recognized in his *The Originall of Government*, where he attacks Selden's claims on this count, this whole line of argumentation is anti-patriarchal, for it supposes that God gave possession of the world to all men (and not only to their patriarch-kings); which is exactly why a general compact for division of property is needed – otherwise all the world would simply have been the possession of the divine-right patriarchs.[77]

Moreover, Selden's binding power of the fathers is not in any way absolute or ultimate. It was certainly a constituent power, but its continuation was also dependent on posterity. Since the covenant and its stipulations were neither a natural human attribute nor a divine decree, but only conventions, they could arguably be changed or even wholly dissolved by posterity. Indeed, this was the reason why change was possible. For the compact to subsist, changed or unchanged, some degree of continuing consent was needed. This continuing general consent was for Selden tradition, the transmission from fathers to sons,

---

[76] MC b1c4. Such an attitude by Selden would be in keeping with his recorded remark in TT "Books, Authors": "To quote a Modern Dutchman, where I may use a Classic Author, is as if I were to justifie my Reputation, and I neglect all Persons of Note and Quality that know me, and bring the Testimonial of the Scullion in the Kitchen."

[77] In *Observations Concerning the Originall of Government*, Filmer attacked as unwarranted the claim for "the general community [of property] between Noah and his sons which Mr Selden will have to be granted them."

In MC b1c4, Selden argued that, as there was explicit testimony of possessions by Adam's children, and of boundaries between Noah's children, even if Adam and Noah *had* been original possessors of the whole world, this situation had changed already in their own lifetime.

in which both have a role, in order for it to subsist. In this way, tradition itself was infused with authority as the expression, not of the rational consent of a self-referring individual, but of a multi-generational continuing general consent. As seen above he even allowed "custom" a possible role in the very creation of the covenant; in the later transmission and binding power of obligation, its role was indispensable. Selden's employment of this principle throughout his career will be detailed below, but, as usual, it is the *Table-Talk* which supplies the most concise and direct formulations. Discussing how knowledge of the "Minds of several Nations" is to be obtained, Selden reportedly recommended the study of national proverbs, since to know the "minds and insides of Men" is to know "what is habitual" to them: "Proverbs are habitual to a Nation, being transmitted from Father to Son." However, the transmission of political obligation from father to son as habitual, is most marked in another passage, where Selden is recorded as arguing:

> It hath ever been the way for Fathers, to bind their Sons, to strengthen this by the Law of the Land: every one at Twelve Years of Age is to take the Oath of Allegiance in Court-Leets, whereby he swears Obedience to the King.

In this example, political obligation and tradition, mutually strengthening each other, become pretty much undistinguishable. The Oath of Allegiance given at age twelve, is a formal act of individual consent to political obligation, but one that is obviously directed and determined by the father and not by the twelve-year-old. Tradition thus transmitted from fathers to sons constitutes obligation over the generations, and more than merely informing the mind of men, it shapes them. In this way, tradition and nation were for Selden fused into one: tradition was the agency through which national identity was created and sustained over time.[78]

It is certainly not the case that Selden thought nations the only possible vehicle for either traditions or political obligations. He can be found discussing regional or religious traditions that were not national ones, as well as treating political obligation both at the sub-national (such as city-states) and supra-national (empires) level.[79]

We should also not assume that Selden necessarily identified state with nation. He certainly did not, for in various places Selden discusses national

---

[78] TT "Proverbs" and "Fathers and Sons." Filmer claimed that binding men to the institutions of their predecessors was an admission of the superior powers and rights of the fathers, but as seen above, Selden escaped this concession by decisively qualifying this very power as subject to the continuing consent of future generations. See discussion of this issue in Schochet *Patriarchalism* pp. 97–98.

[79] For local customs see, for example, his mentioning in *Jani Anglorum* of the ancient Kentish custom, contrary to the law of primogeniture found elsewhere in England. For "Laws and Customs of the *Hebrews* and *Mahomentans*, as well as the *Christians*," and for city-states see MC b1c9–10. For customs of "Empires," see MC b1c8. For the difference between state and national law, see in *Historie of Tithes* pp. 477–481. See also in JN b1 Praefatio.

characteristics that were clearly not those of states, such as where in the *Titles of Honor* (1614) he remarked about ennobling: "*In most other Nations (I think) untill particular ennobling, by the Princes autoritie, came in vse, was a kind of distinction of Nobilitie, and most neer to that in* Greece." Now this passage shows clearly that Selden was discussing a cultural and political aspect of the Greek nation that cannot be regarded as synonym for state, since he knew there never had been an ancient state of "Greece." Moreover, in the *Historie of Tithes* (1618), where Selden discussed the distinction between Canon and secular law, he observed that the former was never received wholly "into practice in any state," but had always been subjected in various areas to "the variety of the secular laws of every state, or to national customs that cross it." Thus, not only are state and nation distinct categories but there is indicated a connection between the latter and the possibility of legally binding national "customs" that in some sense "cross" and are different from the "laws" of states.[80]

That Selden's understanding of nations owed much to the biblical, and especially to the Israelite model, is a prominent feature of his work, perhaps best exemplified in the passage from *Jure Naturali* where he described his own use of the Latin term "Gentes":

> The rest of the nations are more distinctively and simply called [by the Hebrews] *umoth*, that is, "peoples" or "nations," also *umoth haolam*, "the peoples" or "nations of the world" and also *goyyim*, "nations" or "barbarians." Similarly [in Greek] *ta ethnei* or "nations" occurs everywhere in the Bible for people other than the Hebrews just as among the Romans the term *gentes* is equivalent to "people" besides the Quirites [synonym for Romans], although the former term includes them as well.[81]

Indeed, Selden's treatment of the Jewish identity and teachings is perhaps the best example of his distinction between national traditions and the laws of states. For the *Disciplinam Ebraeorum* he is treating in his *Jure Naturali* and elsewhere are for the most part the traditions of the Mishna and later periods – that is, they were composed in the main from Roman times on, when no Jewish state existed. In other words, such Jewish traditions would be regarded as no laws at all by those many (like Grotius, Hobbes and Filmer among others) who deemed human laws to be only the decrees of a sovereign state; certainly so after the Jews had been exiled from their country. Selden was not among these, for, as we shall see, he held the Jewish nation to have obligating traditions, spanning at the very least sixteen centuries, which were very much national traditions

---

[80] TH (1614), preface not paginated; *Historie of Tithes* (1618) in the "Preface." That several states existed within the Greek nation is explicitly mentioned in TH (1631), Preface, not paginated.
[81] JN b1c10. Original language: "Gentes tantum ceteras signantius ita vocare solent, quaemadmodum etiam אומות simpliciter, id est, *populos* seu *gentes* atque אומות העולם *gentes* seu *populos mundi* atque גוים id est *Gentes* seu *Barbaros*; uti etiam in sacris libris ta ethnei [Greek character] seu *Gentes* passim occurrit pro aliis praeter Ebraeos Gentibus, sicut etiam *Gentium* Nomen apud Romanos invaluit pro ceteris praeter Quirites populis, tametsi pariter et hos idem complecteretur."

without being connected to any state. The Jewish traditions were the epitome of continuity through change because of their being unconnected to the usual agencies of state coercion; a national tradition that had persisted through time while experiencing enormous attested changes, from biblical times through the second temple period and the post-exilic phase; changes which the Jewish legal tradition explicitly addressed, while maintaining throughout a narrative of continuity. Indeed, one could say with J. Rosenblatt that in the Jewish legal tradition Selden found a Talmudic equivalent to the analogy of ship, edifice or husbandry as expression of continuity through change. He reported in *Synedriis* the idea articulated by the Jewish sages, that all diverse future interpretations of the Torah had already been revealed by God to Moses at Sinai, the law thus remaining the same throughout all the considerable eventual changes in it.[82]

That Selden viewed the Jewish people as a nation (and not merely as a religious community) after the destruction of their state, even to his own time, is obvious both implicitly and explicitly from many places in his works, as will be discussed in the next chapter. Thus, evidently Selden *could* distinguish between state and nation, though, by and large, he preferred to address the latter, a predilection that seems to be connected to the traditional character of national legislation. Selden seems to have regarded national traditions as the regular – one could say "natural" – form of men's political and cultural identity in the order of things, so that other kinds of arrangements were the exception. Nations are regarded by him as the ordinary outcome of men's associating together; it seems that, for Selden, men's political and legal systems tended "naturally" to develop into nations rather than into empires, cities or tribes. Following the biblical model, in the *Mare Clausum* the extended families of the first men explicitly develop into nations; the same premise is true in both editions of the *Titles of Honor*, regardless of 17 years and great changes in contents and arguments, and it is implicit in the *Jure Naturali* and other works. Throughout his literary output, whether explicitly or implicitly, men are regarded as drawing their identity from, and owing their natural allegiance to, their nation.[83]

Selden's thought thus differed from the vast majority of political and legal theories of his days, from common lawyers and continental humanists who for the most part exalted their national traditions but without proposing a more general theory of obligation and morality; from those universal theories of Roman lawyers or of Grotius, Hobbes and Filmer, in which there was no meaningful place for the authority of nations or their traditions. Selden's view of law and politics attempted to embrace both the universal and the particular, by way of making national traditions the agency through which the principles of obligation and morality can be actuated.

---

[82] See discussion in Rosenblatt *Renaissance* pp. 218–219.

[83] TH (1614) pp. 2–5 (and also in the 1631 edition, pp. 4–5, 10); See also JN b1c6.

Was Selden's theory inspired by his training in English Common law or his humanist learning? There was nothing in his work that broke seriously with either the English constitutional tradition or the humanist one. But he also went further than either, by taking ideas that were only implicitly or slightly touched upon in them, and developing these into a more explicit and cohesive outlook. His debt and contribution to English Common law is not in need of further examples.[84]

As for his preference for the continental historical approach to law, identified as the *mos Gallicum*, against the ahistorical *mos Italicum* (or Bartolism), it too has been touched upon. It is easily illustrated by a passage where he thus contrasts the two approaches in their dealing with historical analysis:

> *Where they* [the Bartolists] *talke of* Meum *and* Tuum, *when their Autoritie is requisit, they deserue to bee heard.* [But] *In things, of this nature, to bee extracted out of Storie and Philologie, they cesse to bee* Doctors, *nay, are scarce* Alphabetarians, *euen the whole Rank of them; untill you come to the most learned* Budè, Alciat, Hotoman, Cuias, Wesenbeck, Brisson, *the* Gentiles, *and some few more of this Age, before whom the Bodie of that Profession was not amisse compard to a faire Robe, of Cloth of Gold, or of Richest Stuff and Fashion,* Qui fust *(saving all mannerly respect to you, Reader)* brodee de Merde.[85]

But Selden's approach was not only indebted to the English juridical tradition and the humanist philological method. There was also an important role for the exegetical method found in Bartolist and in Christian exegetical writings, but featuring most prominently in the approach of the Talmud, of interpreting and reinterpreting the text from several directions, even against the literal meaning, in order to disclose its full meaning. As Caruso points out, in the Talmudic approach this is not merely a method of better discerning meaning, but it is an outlook regarding texts as having a perpetual function of continuing dialogue with the community of interpreters, one that is more temporal than spatial. Thus Selden's approach combined elements from a number of commentary traditions: the English Common law and the historical *mos Gallicum*, certainly, but also elements from the more exegetical and analytical *mos Italicum*, as well as from the Talmudic method and tradition that he variously termed as*Ebraeorum mos* and *disciplinam Ebraeorum*. To the latter he owed much of his thinking of a more general and theoretical nature, which

---

[84] Burgess *Politics* pp. 58–63.
[85] "Qui fust brodee de Merde" (that was embroidered with shit) in TH (1614), "Preface," not paginated. Selden is quoting from Rabelais' *La vie de Gargantua et de Pantagruel* (1634) book 2 chapter 5, where the author potrays the Accursian Gloss, and thus Bartolist *mos Italicum* jurisprudence: "Ainsi vint à Bourges, où estudia bien longtemps, et proffita beaucoup en la faculté des loix, et disoit aulcunesfois que les livres des loix luy sembloyent une belle robbe d'or, triumphante et precieuse à merveilles, qui feust brodée de merde." See also Kelley *Human* pp. 144–145.

cohered into a comprehensive view of particular national tradition that can be justified in universal terms.[86]

For all his keen interest in antiquarian and historical matters, the core of Selden's theory was continuity and local adaptation, not antiquity and universals. As we shall see in the following chapter, the Jewish traditions had for him an especially potent appeal, but Selden stressed this point of view in many other places. One example is his *Titles of Honor* (1631), where he attacked attempts to directly draw a political theory from great works of ancient Greek writers like Plato and Aristotle. Admittedly, such writings were the "chief texts" by which all were being "first bred to civil knowledge" in the west (that is, in the schools) at that time, but he nevertheless warned that,

if any of these great writers of *Greece* were now living again, they would in recognizing and fitting their *politicks* to present use first inform themselves of the several faces and forms of government and the constitutions and customs of the present ages, (as they did of their own times) and of their grounds and reasons, and according to them make instaurations of divers of their precepts and directions, no otherwise than they would new examine the lame astronomy of their ages[.]

This was not merely the familiar renaissance argument favoring "modernity" for the added experience accumulated since ancient times, but also a case for adapting political theories to the "several faces and forms of government" current in this age. In effect, Selden was claiming that the attempt to acquire "civil knowledge" in the abstract, even from the most authoritative ancient texts, was counterproductive. Since men and their societies changed and adapted greatly over time, ancient texts lacking continuity could offer only a "lame" understanding, because "*that, which may be most Convenient or Iust in one State, may be as Iniust and Inconvenient in another; and yet both excellently as well framed as governed*[.]"[87]

The impact of the passage of time on laws is also addressed in Selden's NL, where in the same passage describing human laws growing out of a common root into the diverse laws of "[d]ivers nations" he goes on to assert: "Infinite laws we have now that were not thought on D. [five hundred] years since. Then

---

[86] For Selden terming Jewish traditions as "Ebraeorum mos"; see "Prolegomena" p. iii in *Bona*; while *disciplinam Ebraeorum* is of course from the title of the JN. Caruso describes Selden's method as composed of four parts: ascertaining the most original and integral version of the text, placing the text in its historical context, making a comparative analysis of the text, and ascertaining connected discussions (such as other works by the same author, or by contemporary authors treating the same matters). This was not Selden's invention, but rather the combination of several existing methods into a new whole. See Caruso *Miglior* pp. 519–520.

[87] TH (1631) "Preface," not paginated. Selden proposed that Aristotle would have concurred with this, but he objected to the approach of "Plato, *as* Laertius *sayes of him* [...], medled with no publique employment, though he were made also for Civill businesse, as appears by what he hath written; but the cause was, for that the Customs of the State were wholly different from his learning."

were many that D. [five hundred] years before had no being, and less time forward always produced divers new[.]" His conclusion from these considerations was a view preferring law to adapt through time, place and national character, therefore proposing that "[n]either are laws thus to be compared. Those which best fit the state wherein they are, clearly deserve the name of best laws." Such an approach might easily lead to a completely relativistic view of law, draining it of any general or even moral value, but Selden did not abandon the common root of all laws, instead arguing for a combination of the general and particular; employing yet another analogy for the law which, like the ship, the house and the plant, was the river out of the fountain: "hence it is, that those customs which have come all out of one fountain, *nature*, thus vary from and cross one another in several common-wealths." These images merge the general and the particular into one, a view according to which national law *is* natural law.[88]

As we have seen, Selden's account of a balance between the defining role first principles have in shaping laws and institutions, and the constant adaptations of the laws to changing circumstances, was conveyed in the image of the ship of the laws which retained its shape and identity though losing all its original materials – an image of the spirit of the law. However, this image is less adequate for more complex phenomena of social and intellectual change that he described, like the interaction of Saxon, Danish and Norman laws in the English Common law.[89]

The metaphor of the river, with its many possible additions (an ever-moving entity, with tributaries, merging or splitting, its origin at a spring and so on), could far better address such phenomena, and it apparently became Selden's preferred one. The spring-river image, conveying the idea of continuity through change, I have found to be the most prominent and recurring image used by Selden to describe his main idea of a substantial continuity between the present and the past. As we shall see below, there are at least 11 separate occurrences of this image in his writings (and one more, by Ben Jonson, referring to Selden's work). In most cases, the image appears not as casual comment, but rather is identified with the central purpose of the work, such as the motto or as part of the introduction. As early as his 1612 "Illustrations" notes to Drayton's *Poly-Olbion*, Selden used this image in the prefatory section, to justify the search for the original sources of historical writings: "My thirst compeld mee alwayes seeke the *Fountaines*, and, by that, if meanes grant it, iudge the *Riuers* nature." That is, he indicated in this case,

---

[88] NL cols. 1891–1892.
[89] Zaller *Legitimacy* pp. 340–341. Zaller points out that Selden could have employed Machiavelli's embracing of change in his concept of a periodic reduction to first principles. But while Selden was certainly well acquainted with Machiavelli, he did not embrace his theory and especially not the active role it assigned to the citizen in reforming the state.

that following the "river" to its "fountain" may enable one to identify its "nature."[90]

Even at such early stages of his career, this image had already become identified among his literary friends with Selden's intellectual endeavors, to the degree that Ben Jonson could use it in his 1614 prefatory epistle to Selden's *Titles of Honor* (later appearing also in Jonson's *The Underwood*), where he declared that in his book, Selden:

> [...] "Sought out the fountains, sources, creeks, paths, ways,
> And noted the beginnings and decays!"[91]

---

[90] *"Illustrations"* in Drayton's *Poly-Olbion* (1612) in the prefatory section unpaginated. See also discussion of Selden's use of the image in McEachern *Poetics* p. 177.

The spring and river image, of course was not only used by Selden, but was quite widely employed. However, while most of those using it regarded it as a metaphor for unification, he gave it a more complex and unusual interpretation. James I, for example, used the image to justify the loss of particular identities into a larger one, when he defended the union of his two kingdoms: "For even as little brookes lose their names by their running and fall into great rivers," so by the conjunction of "divers little kingdoms in one" are private differences and questions "swallowed up." Samuel Daniel too employed the metaphor of rivers into the sea to describe unification, when he described the Danish invasions and the Norman Conquest as events that had brought about a process of populations blending, claiming the Danes and Normans had been to the English people "as rivers to the Ocean" that did not change it but were changed into it (quoted in Ferguson *Clio* p. 302). Drayton's *Poly-Olbion* itself most naturally and copiously used the river as one of the central metaphors of the work, which described England and its geographical features. But Drayton's descriptions are neither Selden's continuity through change, nor James' unavoidable union and uniformity, but rather they convey ever-changing, unstable interactions of a land crossed by a mass of rivers continuously coming together, splitting again and reuniting again, celebrating diversity in itself, without any purpose: "I view those wanton Brookes, that waxing still doe wane; That scarcely can conceive, but brought to bed againe; Scarce rising from Spring (that is their natural Mother), To growe into a streame, but buried in another." Another use for rivers by Drayton comes closer to Selden's, when they are repeatedly and explicitly offered as metaphors for national identity, which in the English case is often identified with laws. Perhaps the most interesting example of this is when English rivers boast of the greatness of the Saxons in national terms, as "the nation most unmixt/their language as at first, their ancient customes fixt." If this were not enough, the rivers go on to claim, in effect, that there was no Norman conquest – for since Normans and Saxons were originally of the same stock, no real conquest ever occurred. See McEachern *Poetics* pp. 158, 161–164.

Martin Luther, no friend to the Jewish people, also used the metaphor as justification for scriptural, indeed Hebraist, scholarship: "The Hebrews drink from the spring, the Greeks out of a small stream which flows from the spring, the Latins however drink out of the puddles." See Prior "Hebraism" p. 42.

[91] See in Ben Jonson's prefatory epistle in Selden's TH (1614) – later reprinted in Jonson's collection of poems *The Underwood* 14. Another appearance of the same metaphorical imagery more obliquely connected to Selden, is in Thomas Carew's poem "To my friend G.N. from Wrest." The poem describes the intellectual world of the country residence of the earls of Kent at Wrest Park, during the late 1630s – of which Selden was in many ways the linchpin. Intriguingly, the image of sources and streams appears within the important section of the poem addressing the interplay of nature and artifice, itself very much a Seldenian theme, and one having a place of prominence in the *Jure Naturali*, which Selden was working on in 1638–1639, at the very time the poem was composed:

As seen above, only two years later, in 1616, the image appears yet again, this time in Selden's "Notes" on Fortescue's *Laudibus*, where the image is used to argue that particular and differing customs come "out of one fountain" – nature. This early predilection for the image became pretty much a fixture of Selden's later literary output, especially after he embarked in the early 1630s on his great project of Hebraic scholarship. The image became virtually a recurring epitome for his intellectual outlook, justifying the colossal efforts he invested in Jewish ideas and texts. In the subtitle of Selden's 1631 *Bona*, it occurs where the information in the book is described as coming among others "from Hebrew Legal Sources" (ex Iuris Ebraicis Fontibus), as well as in that work's substantially revised 1636 edition appearing together with his new *Pontificatum*, where in the dedication of the combined book to Archbishop Laud, Selden wrote about the diligent, who – to discern the nature of the rivulets – investigates their sources.[92]

Selden's predilection for the image is probably most evident in his great Hebraist endeavor, the *Jure Naturali* of 1640. The motto for the whole work is: "—Places Never Before Trodden by Foot. I Love Approaching Untested Springs and Drinking –[.]" While in the second chapter of book I, where he describes the reasons behind his undertaking of this massive work, Selden asserts that Greek philosophy once combined with Jewish ideas, but later split from it, so that:

> both the ideas drawn directly from the wellsprings (fontibus) of the Hebrews and those which flowed from them by way of rivulets (rivolorum), so to speak, wound up in an ocean (oceanum) of indistinguishable teachings which mostly took on the same insipid character, instead of retaining any of their own.[93]

> Yet we decline not, all the worke of Art,
> But where more bounteous Nature beares a part
> And guides her Hand-maiden, if she but dispence
> Fit matter, she with care and diligence
> Employes her skill, for where the neighbor sourse
> Powers forth her waters she directs their course,
> And entertaines the flowing streames in deepe
> And spacious channels, where they slowly creepe
> In snakie windings, as the shelving ground
> Leades them in circles, till they twice surround
> This Island Mansion, which i'th' center plac'd[.]
> See Parker "Wrest" pp. 182–183 and 186–188.

[92] "ex Iuris Ebraicis Fontibus" in *Bona* title page; "quam diligentem alias rivuli naturae indagationem Physico cui nec Fontes a quibus" in *Pontificatum* unpaginated dedication to Archbishop Laud.

[93] JN, the motto appears on the title page of the work, the justification in b1c2: "ut tam quae ex ipsis hausta sunt fontibus quam quae velut per rivulorum alveos ab eis deducta sunt, in tam multiplicis disciplinae Oceanum recepta hujus naturam plerumque induerent, suam minime satis servantia." The original of the motto is: [Avia Pieridum peragro] "– Loca Nullius ante Trita Solo. Iuvat integros accedere Fontes Atque haurire" from the Epicurean Roman poet Lucretius' *De rerum natura*, iv, which I have rendered in a very literal English version. Addison translated it (in his "pleasures of imagination") as: "ground untrod before [I devious roam], And deep-enamoured

In his 1642 *Eutychius*, which consists for the most part of a lengthy commentary by Selden upon the text of the eponymous author and a discussion of the early Christian church, it is stated that "veteris judaismi fonte" are employed, asserting that the use of such sources supports the scope of the work. In his next substantial Hebraist work, the 1646 *Uxor Ebraica*, Selden brought in the opening the quote from St. Jerome: "These things we have drunk from the deepest sources (fonte) of the Hebrews, not following the streams (rivulos) of opinions or errors which the whole world is full of, terrified by variety, but desiring to know and teach what is true."[94]

An additional appearance of this image is found in the *Table-Talk*, where comments cannot be dated exactly but are mainly from the last decade of Selden's life. In a passage discussing the division of spiritual and temporal power when England was under the authority of Popes, he adds that things have been amended since the reformation: "But now the temporal and the spiritual power (spiritual so called, because ordain'd to a spiritual end), spring both from one fountain."[95]

In 1650, in the first volume of *Synedriis*, Selden's last great Hebraist work, the same metaphor appears once again when used to explain why he believed it essential to look at ancient Jewish practices when considering later Christian ones, even though the two religions long ago divided, and so many of their common beliefs and practices had changed:

But even though rivulets, streams and offshoots often do diverge and decline in various ways from their origins and sources and from the character of the beginnings from which they started (since these are still identifiable), they will always retain some of the qualities and traces of their original nature.

Three years later, the Latin motto for the second volume of *Synedriis*, the last thing Selden ever published in his lifetime, employs once more the very same spring image: "—with pure garments approach, and purify your hands with the spring's water."[96]

---

into latent springs"; while Toomer as: "treading unexplored soil and drinking from new springs." See also Toomer, *Scholarship* p. 819.

[94] *Eutychii Aegyptii, Patriarchae Orthodoxorum Alexandrini, Scriptoris, ut in Oriente admodum Vetusti ac Illustris, ita in Occidente tum paucissimis Visi tum perraro Auditi, Ecclesia suae Origines* (1642) p. 22; in *Uxor* title page, quote (from *Letters of St. Jerome* 138, "to Marcella") the Latin is: "Haec nos de intimo Hebraeorum fonte libavimus non opinionum rivulos persequentes neque errorum, quibus totus mundus expletus est, varietate perterriti, sed cupientes et scire et docere, quae vera sunt."

[95] TT "Pope" sec. 6.

[96] *Synedriis* b1c8: "Sed ita sane Rivuli, Scaturigines, Propagines, non raro aliter ac aliter ab Originibus suis ac Fontibus atque a causarum primariarum fatisque indubitatarum ratione pariter evadunt diversae & degenerant, qualitatibus nihilominus & naturae primariae reliquiis aliquot ac vestigiis semper servatis;" *Synedriis* b2 title page, quote (from Tibullus' *Elegies* book II), the original Latin is: "—Pura cum veste venite; Et Puris manibus sumite Fontis aquam." For the date of publication: we know the second volume of *Synedriis* was published after

The prominent recurrence of the spring and river image, especially in his Hebraist works, indicates that for Selden this was not some occasional literary quirk, but rather it was intended to convey an overarching idea, especially significant to the whole of his massive and seemingly disparate Hebraist efforts. That idea was his belief that origins and foundations, however far and indirect they might be, had a significant and perhaps determining impact on later developments. In the same way as a river, regardless of innumerable changes and alterations through its long path, was still regarded in some essential way the same one as it had commenced at its spring, and accordingly retained the same name throughout, so ideas, traditions and legal systems retained some essential nature throughout later circumstances and challenges encountered.

With his works on Jewish law, Selden further developed and articulated this vision of natural and national law indissolubly combined, which was already evident in earlier works like the *Titles of Honor* and the "Notes" on Fortescue's *Laudibus*, into a theory of law. This inextricable combination meant that although in the course of things, it would be a commonplace event that, at some time or other, one or more basic natural laws were being executed, this only happened through the agency of particular laws, and any attempt to pry out a "pure" type natural law out of existing legislation was impossible, since the laws natural were

> so much mixed together, rolled up and conjoined into one mass (so to speak) with the civil or positive law and with that imperative or intervenient, that no mortal can separate from them only the use and customs of those nations.[97]

Such an account of human political and legal development meant that attempts to construct a law that is purely universal, be it based on right reason (like Grotius') or on an absolutist principle (like Roman law), are in truth unnatural, because such a law lacks the crucial characteristic necessary for good laws: the capability to adapt and change through time. The agency for this capability, for the combination of change with continuity, is the nation. Selden thus regarded the nation and national laws as the natural condition of men, as expressed in the *Mare Clausum*, where he describes law as concerning "either mankinde in general, that is, all Nations; or not at all." When a law did not concern all nations, it was either the positive *"Common Law of divers Nations"* relating to some common tie or obligation of only some nations (such as an alliance), or the particular law of only one nation. Evidently, for Selden, mankind – even when treated generally – is composed of nations, and not of

---

28 October 1653 – while his *Vindiciae* was signed May 1653, and the third volume of *Synedriis* was published only posthumously in 1655.

[97] JN b1c6: "sed ut Civili seu positivo, atque Imperativo illo, ac Intervenienti adeo immixta & involuta & una (sic dicere liceat) in massa conjuncta, ut haec ab illis secernere ex Gentium ipsarum tantum usu seu moribus, earumque ea de referentiam inde elicere queat mortalium nemo."

the undefined mass so commonly found among his contemporaries. Nations are for him the natural vehicle for the expression of the universal principles of law, as well as of particular configurations of it.[98]

The category of nation was thus indispensable in Selden's account of human laws and politics. Its significance did not rest merely in the empirical added value that long-tested national traditions might add as accumulated experience (such value was allowed by many), but in its being the necessary vehicle for the adaptive function which he regarded as required of all good laws. Thus laws (or at least good laws) adapting through history, circumstances and national character became, to a great extent, undistinguishable from that nation: Nation and its traditional laws essentially becoming one.

---

[98] The passage continues: "That which relate's to the generalitie of mankinde, or *all Nations*, is either *Natural* or *Divine*. That is, either manifested by the light of nature or the use of right reason, being elegantly described by *Tertullian* to bee the *Common Law written throughout the whole world, in the very Books of nature*; and by the Grecians called *the Law of mankinde*, and by the Civilians the *Primitive Law of Nations*; or els [sic] it is declared and set down in those Divine Oracles that have been committed to writing: Both of which may properly bee termed *the universal Law of Nations*, or the *Common Law of mankinde*." MC b1c3. The only place where mankind is discussed as a "commonality" without division into nations is in the account of the division of property, which was supposed to have happened at the time of Noah and his sons; that is, when nations were still to be formed, or were only forming. See MC b1c4.

5

Selden and the "Universal Philosophy of Morals" Drawn from the Hebrew Tradition

5.1 "RABBI SELDEN"

John Selden's commanding proficiency in the Jewish traditions and laws, widely acknowledged as the glory of his learning, was unsurpassed for generations among Christian Hebraists, certainly in England and probably in Europe as well. When in 1641 one Johann Stephanus Rittangl, Extraordinary Professor of Oriental Languages at Konigsberg University, wrote Selden a letter (in Hebrew) asking for assistance in publishing some Karaite literature, he addressed him as· *"morenu harav rav Seldenus"* (our honored teacher and rabbi, rabbi Selden) – the title reserved in rabbinic literature for the most distinguished scholars. Indeed, G.J. Toomer proposes that Selden's writings presented the Talmudic traditions to Christian Europe on a level so far exceeding anything that had been done before or after him, that in England for one he became for a long time the substitute for the actual Talmud.[1]

There were many like Rittangl, Lightfoot and Ussher who displayed unreserved admiration for Selden's proficiency in, and use of, Jewish sources. However, most contemporary learned observers, while acknowledging his unmatched erudition, were either hostile to, or at the least puzzled by, Selden's evident predilection for Jewish ideas – none more so than natural

---

[1] For Selden as "undoubtedly the most erudite Englishman of his day," see Ferguson *Clio* pp. 117–118. For Selden's Talmudic learning see Toomer *Scholarship* p. 819.

D.J. Lasker discovered in 2005 at the Beinecke Library of Yale University (Shelfmark OSB Mss. File S, Folder 14513), that an incorrectly attributed letter dated 29 September 1641 had been written to Selden from Rittangl (aka Rittangel) while the latter resided at Cambridge. See D.J. Lasker, "Karaism and Christian Hebraism: a new document" in *Renaissance Quarterly*, 59/4 (December 2006). Rittangl published translations from Hebrew as well as works attempting to prove that Christian doctrine was supported by traditional Jewish texts.

Two examples of eminent writers relying on Selden for their Jewish materials are Prynne and Harrington, whose quoting of Hebraic sources in their writings consisted at least partially of materials they found in Selden (as well as in Grotius). See Prior "Hebraism" pp. 50–51.

rights theorists such as Cumberland and Pufendorf. Especially perplexing to them was Selden's willingness to trust, and even rely upon, Jewish traditions of the times after the rise of Christianity. For while the use of the Hebrew Bible or of Hellenized Jewish sources more or less contemporary with the birth of Christianity, like Philo and Josephus, was common practice and even regarded as a mark of good learning, Selden's engagement with Talmudic and post-Talmudic Jewish ideas was far more unusual and controversial. Such ideas, originating after the Jewish rejection of Christianity, were inherently suspect of impiety, and when addressed were usually treated with circumspection by Christian scholars. While some slight peppering of one's writings with examples of later Jewish sources would not be objected to, Selden's massive engagement with Jewish texts and ideas had no parallel even among his contemporaries, who created a kind of "Hebrew Republic of Letters" in the early seventeenth century.[2]

Moreover, as D.R. Kelley has pointed out, from an evangelical Christian perspective, the cleaving of Judaism to its legalist and traditionalist character came to epitomize human traditions opposed to revealed or natural law (with the two often equated). Pauline dualism, opposing spirit to law, was worked out by Origen, Tertullian and other early Fathers of the Church into a conceptual sort of antisemitism whereby the "Pharisaical" formalism of the Jews had once and for all been replaced by a spiritual "new law." Thus, for example, when medieval jurists like Baldus argued for interpreting laws by their spirit and not their letter, they warned students against reading the law "Jewishly" (*more Judaeorum*); that is, in a narrow legalistic manner. Selden's willingness not only to treat post-biblical Jewish texts with fairness and respect, but to accord their ideas significance and even authority, indeed to treat them as a kind of "mos Judaeorum," was virtually unheard of. Not surprisingly, through the years both explicit and implicit criticisms were directed against him on this account.[3]

---

[2] During the early seventeenth century, there was created a pan-European Hebraist discussion which we might call a Republic of Hebrew Letters, one which, apart from philologists and theologians, also included several prominent political writers like Bodin, Sigonio, Cunaeus, Grotius, Botero, Althusius, and of course Selden, who was in many ways its pinnacle. Prior "Hebraism" p. 42.

[3] Kelley *Human* pp. 68–69, 132–133; C.W.A. Prior has pointed out that in most cases, seventeenth-century Englishmen disassociated Hebrew texts and ideas from actual Jews, mainly addressing texts from before the Jews had rejected the Christian Gospel. Selden's scholarship was an obvious exception. See Prior "Hebraism" pp. 40–41. Pufendorf for one, criticized Selden's effort to separate positive from natural law within the Jewish legal code, giving three reasons for this: first, Selden devoted too little attention to the question of the origins of natural law. Among the doctrines insufficiently scrutinized Pufendorf listed the nature of moral entities in general, the nature of the principles of human actions, character and affections, the nature and requirements of contracts, the origin and nature of the first societies. Secondly, Selden derived the law of nature from the seven precepts of Noah rather than from a premise all nations could recognize (the reverse of Grotius' error according to Pufendorf), also failing to show how these precepts were

Selden was not unaware of such attitudes, and accordingly when treating Jewish matters which might impinge on Christian beliefs, he took special care to articulate his intentions, and to make his language and conclusions as theologically unobjectionable as possible (sometimes even abstaining from drawing conclusion upon some matters, when these might prove too theologically delicate). Regardless of these efforts, he was on various occasions accused of being suspiciously partial to the Jewish tradition. For example, during the controversy following the publication of his *Historie of Tithes*, some of the attacks on him resorted to the familiar device of alleging he was sympathizing or even abetting Jewish theological views, at the expense of Christian ones. Prevented by King James I from publicly answering criticism of his book, Selden for a time resorted to circulating manuscript reactions among his friends (before the King forbade this too). In one of these, answering the attacks of Sir James Sempil, Selden defended himself from accusations of excessive sympathy to Jewish ideas by dismissing the theological import of his sources while insisting on their factual reliability – "the body of the *Jewish canon law*, and those three most eminent *rabbins*, *Jarchi* [aka Rashi], *Ben Maimon*, and *Mikotzi* [aka Moses of Coucy]," sources that had been ever regarded by "any learned man" as "certain and infallible" in relating the practice of their nation, "however they be full of toys and ridiculous fancies for matters of *divinity*." He went one step further, and turned the implication of heterodoxy against his accusers, first pointing out that since "holy scripture" left no memory of ancient practices but only precept, one who would not accept the testimony of "*Jewish doctors* or *rabbins*, is in meer darkness" on such matters, and concluding that while "I tell my *readers*, what the *fathers*, and *rabbins* have of it," him who attempts to enquire about those ancient matters without "aid of the *antients*, must trust only to his own, and new fancies." Interestingly, while the ideas of his accusers are dubbed as "fancies" (the same term used by him to dismiss Jewish ideas on divinity), he is fortifying his own position by associating the Jewish traditions on which he relies, with the

congruent with essential human nature, and sufficient to guide the whole of human moral decisions. Thirdly, Selden was too respectful towards, and too concerned with, describing the views of the Jewish doctors of the law – and too little concerned with assessing whether such views were acceptable to general *sana ratio*. See discussion in T.J. Hochstrasser, *Natural Law Theories in the Early Enlightenment* (Cambridge University Press, 2000) pp. 66–67.

With the rise of enlightenment, later generations of writers on natural rights were even more censorious towards Selden's interest in the Jewish traditions. An example was the Swiss theologian Jean Leclerc (1657–1736), who argued that "Selden only copies the rabbins, and scarcely ever reasons. His rabbinical principles are founded upon an uncertain supposition of the Jewish tradition that God gave to Noah seven precepts, which all the human race was to observe. If this were denied, the Jews would be much at a loss to prove it. Moreover, his ideas are very imperfect and embarrassed." Aikin defended Selden only in a backhanded manner, arguing he was constrained to follow that method by, "partaking of the barbarism of a people unused to philosophical arrangement." Aikin *Lives* p. 111.

"fathers" (of the early Christian church), and the obvious imprimatur of orthodoxy that such an association entails.[4]

At other times, the accusations against Selden were of a more indirect kind, involving innuendo and allusions, as was the case with Nathaniel Culverwel's *An Elegant and Learned Discourse of the Light of Nature* (1651). In that book, to a quote from Cicero about the beauty of natural law (found by Culverwel in Selden's *Jure Naturali*), a line was added stating: "none must enlarge the Phylacteries of this law, nor must dare to prune off the least branch of it." An attack on Jewish Pharisaism, it is also an oblique but obvious attack on Selden's theory and the latter's basing on his reverence for rabbinical tradition, while rejecting right reason as the ultimate source of legislation.[5]

Selden made sure to refute such attacks and innuendos by repeatedly asserting the legitimacy of his explorations of Jewish learning, as beneficial to Christianity. Such an example was the 1636 reissue of *Bona Defuncti*, in which, besides many additions to the content, he wrote a new dedication to Archbishop Laud, presenting his rationale for the work. In this text Selden distinguished between two kinds of contemporary Christian scholars who were interested in Hebrew studies: the "deserters" (transfugae), who included not only genuine converts to Judaism but also those who would brashly change well-established Christian practices to conform with alleged Jewish practice; and the "explorers" (exploratores), like him, who, while remaining true to their Christian faith, nevertheless, when encountering difficult scriptural passages upon which light might be shed by perusing the traditions of the Jews, do not evade consulting the secrets of that "most noble nation" ("gentis Nobilissimae"), once privileged by direct divine illumination. Selden defends this practice by arguing:

> Hence light has been shed on the correct interpretation of their sacrifices, festivals, calendar and courts, and on the State set up by God and the rationale of the laws he established, without which it is certain that even those who are most learned in other respects must stumble in darkness.[6]

Again, like in his answer to Sempil, Selden accused here those objecting to his inquiries, of stumbling in darkness. But even more significant than the obvious contribution of such inquiries to learning, when he argued that they are shedding light on matters pertaining to "the State set up by God and the

---

[4] See James Sempil's *Sacrilege Sacredly Handled* (1619), a defense of the divine ordination of tithes, to which was appended an attack on the *Historie of Tithes*. Selden's answer was a manuscript named "An Admonition to the Readers of Sir James Sempil's Appendix, For so Much as Concerns Scaliger and Selden" (c. 1619) posthumously published in *Opera Omnia* vol. 3 tome 2 cols. 1350–1352.

[5] For Culverwel's attack, see discussion in Rosenblatt *Renaissance* pp. 220–221.

[6] Toomer *Scholarship* p. 470. Possibly Selden's repeated use of the light analogy for his study of the Jewish sources, with its similarity to his account of the active intellect, implied a notion of the Jewish traditions as a kind of active intellect for the nations.

rationale of the laws he established" the implication was inescapable, that the results of such investigations should inform the "State" and the "laws" of Christian countries. With the years and the growth of his Jewish learning, Selden became more confident and willing to justify the study of Jewish sources, not only as necessary for ascertaining the laws of nature and of nations by means of the Jewish traditions in *Jure Naturali*, but even going as far as identifying in *Synedriis* the Jewish Talmudical traditions with early Christianity, and asserting the latter to have been "truly reformed Judaism[.]" He was thus making an analogy between the practice of contemporary reformed Christians referring to the authority of the Fathers of the Church in order to correct practices corrupted by Catholicism, and between the early Christians of the second temple period referring to the authority of ancient Jewish teachings in order to correct practices corrupted by the priestly establishment of their own day. This was a view that implied far more continuity between Judaism (including Talmudical Judaism) and Christianity (especially reformed Christianity) than most of Selden's contemporaries were willing to concede.[7]

It is no surprise, therefore, that Selden was widely reputed by contemporaries to hold that his immense Jewish learning had real relevance to the England of his own days. The idea that England should (or could) follow the example of the Jewish state, in political matters and especially those pertaining to church and state, was hotly contested especially during the 1640s and 1650s. There was no lack of those who, like Selden, supported the idea that Jewish precedents were pertinent to English political society (and not only to strictly theological issues). As we shall see in the next chapter, some among these were Hooker, Coleman as well as Edmund Bunny (1540–1619), a lawyer who became a clergyman and composed *The Sceptre of Iudah* (1584), dedicated to the students of Gray's Inn, so that they may have recourse to the legal precepts contained in the Hebrew commonwealth and to the "government" God ordained to his people. But there were also many who were sorely opposed to this idea, among them: Prynne, who denied that the English church and state were bound to follow Jewish antecedents, and the anti-Prynne radical separatist John Goodwin, who agreed with him on this point, maintaining in his *Certain Briefe* (1644) that "The Nationall Church of the Jewes cannot be a pattern for us now, because the covenant of the Gospel is not made with any particular nation"; William Fiennes, First Viscount Saye and Sele) and founder of the first colony in what is now New Hampshire, who declared in a speech in the Westminster Assembly that the Hebrew church and state "cannot any way pattern evangelic churches," and Roger Williams, separatist clergyman and founder of Rhode Island, who wrote *The Bloudy Tenent of Persecution* (1644), of which chapter 120 is self-explanatorily titled: "Civil Compulsion was proper in the National Church of the Jews, but Most Improper in the Christian, Which is Not National"; Milton, who argued that delving into the history of the Jews was mere antiquarianism

---

[7] *Synedriis* b1c1: "Christianismum, qui plane Judaismus erat vere reformatus."

? you sure he thought that

and custom is against the simple truths of the New Testament; and the prominent Congregationalist Francis Rous, who asserted in his *Ancient Bounds* (1645) against a union of church and state that "the argument will not hold from *Israel* to *England*." Selden's own position regarding the relevance of his Jewish learning to the politics of his day was obviously opposed to these, and was probably best put in the famous characterization of him by one of his bitter rivals, Robert Baillie, the leading Scottish clerical commissioner at the Westminster Assembly of Divines, who wrote of him that "he avows every where that the Jewish State and Church was all one, and that so in England it must be, that the Parliament is the Church."[8]

Modern scholarship concurs on the whole with such assessments of Selden's views in this respect. It emphasizes Selden's debt to the Jewish tradition in his treatment of legal, religious and political issues, and sometimes even maintains that tradition to have had a crucial role within his scholarship.[9]

Why was it, then, that the Jewish tradition held such an important place in the legal and constitutional thought of this prominent early-modern scholar? Doubtless, Selden's interest in Jewish learning was also fueled by his burning intellectual curiosity, which led him to build up his immense learning in so many disciplines and languages. However, I will argue that a major motive behind his Hebraic learning had very much to do with Selden's other main intellectual concern, the defense of English common law. His inquiries into English law, its nature and the challenges to it, in the intellectual as well as the political and judiciary spheres, brought Selden from very early in his career to reflect on, and search for, the principles of a practical and moral justification of customary law. He eventually found much of the interpretative framework and theoretical underpinnings he was looking for, in the national, continuous and adaptive Jewish legal tradition.

5.2 REJECTING THE UNIVERSALIST "LAWS OF UTOPIA"

As we have seen, the debate about the authority of traditional constitutional arrangements was a central theme of early-modern political though in Western Europe. Alongside the famous discussion about the "ancient constitution" in England, similar claims were also being put forward in France, Scotland and the Netherlands. However, while in the English case the argument was essentially a conservative one, arguing for the preservation of the existing constitutional framework and practice against those who would challenge it, in the other cases the opposite was true. Ancient constitutionalists (and not incidentally, mostly Calvinists), like Francois Hotman in France, George Buchanan in Scotland and

---

[8] Prior "Hebraism" pp. 41–45; Robert Baillie, *Letters and Journals* (Edinburgh, 1841) 3 vols., vol. iii pp. 265–266.

[9] See, for example, Cromartie *Hale* pp. 40–41 and 169–170; Roslak *Selden* pp. 23–24 and note 15; Caruso *Miglior* pp. 519–520.

Hugo Grotius in the Netherlands, came to argue against the current political
and legal settings in their countries, in the name of alleged ancient constitutional
ideals which they wished to revive.[10]

We may identify two main types of arguments which the ancient
constitutional ideas of the early seventeenth century wished to challenge.
The first were the older universalist arguments originating from those of
Roman law, identifying it as supreme over all other national and international
ones, either because of some universal authority purportedly enjoyed by the
Roman emperors, or because it was identified with natural law; the most
prominent proponent of these views in the early seventeenth century was
Alberico Gentili, with his *De Iure Belli* (1589) and later works. The second
type of arguments originated in the new natural rights theories, and among their
prominent proponents were the Spanish second scholastics and Hugo Grotius.
These types of grounds should not however be regarded as too neatly distinct,
for as we shall see they shared some assumptions, and may be easily combined
within one theoretical framework. Although both types of theories could be
(and were) used to justify an absolutist political theory – the Roman law type
more often than the natural rights type – they also could be (and were) used to
argue politics from popular consent. Nevertheless, both types had in common
a rejection of the principles upon which customary national laws were
predicated.[11]

As for Grotius, we have seen previously that he appears among both
supporters and critics of customary law – evidence of his crossing over from
the first camp to the second during his career (while attempting to conceal and
minimize this transformation). The tension between the two views is apparent
in his *Mare Liberum* and even more so in the *Iure Belli*. Selden for one clearly
identified this tension, and as early as his *Mare Clausum* claimed Grotius never
satisfactorily solved it.[12]

---

[10] Burgess *Politics* pp. 12–16. Germany is identified by Burgess as a case possibly more constitutionally akin to the English one.

[11] There is an ongoing debate about the degree to which the intellectual battle about political
absolutism was central to the discussion of constitutional issues in seventeenth-century England.
Burgess, for example, tends overall to downplay the issue, while Caruso maintains the issue's
centrality (see especially Caruso, *Miglior* pp. 848–850). The best recent survey of the constitutional ideas and arguments in England at this time is Sommerville *Royalists*, especially chapters 1
and 3.

[12] Although his account of the Batavian legal and political traditions (in the *Batavicae*, for example)
involved a great degree of far-fetched inference, twisting and wishful thinking, this should not
necessarily be seen as conscious falsification by the young Grotius. His clear disassociating of
himself from these youthful views of Dutch history in later years (e.g., in a 1643 letter to his
brother) seems to point to his having sincerely held them at the time he wrote them. Moreover,
further study might very well show this tension in Grotius' work to be smaller than it first
appears. I. Schoffer suggests that Grotius' version of the Batavian myth did not adopt
a "Teutonic" and anti-Roman view to begin with. In his *Parallelon Rerumpublicarum*, for
example, the account of the development of Batavian law stressed far more the influence of

Indeed, among Selden's works it is the *Mare Clausum* which supplies the most direct and detailed theoretical rejection of the universalist challenge – while in later writings he devoted his efforts more towards building the theoretical justification for customary law. In the *Mare Clausum* he identified most clearly the two-pronged character of the challenge to customary law, and because of its long gestation (published in 1635, some 16 years after an earlier completed version had been blocked from publication by Buckingham), the book answered arguments from both the 1610s, when the case from Roman law was predominant, as well as from the mid-1630s, when the case from natural right was becoming more prominent. Selden opposed these arguments, not only on the basis of what he regarded as their own internal contradictions, but also upon the idea that customary systems of law, like the Jewish and the English ones, had a far better claim to authority than abstract universal ones.

The first type of universalist arguments was identified by Selden as "*taken out of* Antient Lawyers" and eminently raised by "Albericus Gentilis" in his *Iure belli*; the second as the opinions of "modern Lawyers," such as "Fernandus Vasquius" (Fernando Vazquez de Menchaca), and especially "Hugo Grotius."

Addressing the argument from Roman law, Selden wrote:

And here, especial care must bee taken to avoid that which som have presumed to affirm, touching those most excellent Books of *Justinian*, which make up an entire Bodie of the antient Law; *That the Law prescribed in those Books is not the Law onely of a Citie, but even of Nations and nature; and that the whole is so fitted unto nature,* that after the Empire was extinct, *though the Law was a long time buried; yet it rose again, and spread it self through all the world. And therefore that it concern's even Princes, although it was framed by* Justinian *for private persons.* As if the law natural and of Nations were to bee derived onely out of those Books.[13]

The heart of the argument that he was taking directly from Gentili's book, was the proposition that Roman law (in the form it achieved in Justinian's *Institutes*) should be identified with the law "*of Nations and nature*" – because its revival and its adoption throughout Europe, hundreds of years after it had been long "*buried*" and the Empire "extinct," were proof of its being perfectly "*fitted unto nature.*" Selden challenged this claim unequivocally, by disputing its factual validity, bringing examples from the "*Romane-Germane* Empire," as well as France and Spain, that showed how many laws and decrees there were "in their Law Common, or Intervenient, which are not grounded at all upon the Law of *Justinian*, but have had their original from Customs quite contrarie thereto." Not sufficing with an empirical refutation of Gentili's claim that Roman law had been accepted as authoritative in Europe, Selden also indicated that essentially, customary law, the "Law Common" of these

the Batavi from the South (that is, the Romanized Gauls) than those from the East (anti-Roman Germans). See Schoffer "Batavian" pp. 86, 92–93.
[13] MC b1c24. About the circumstances of the book's composition and publication see Toomer *Scholarship* pp. 159–160.

European countries, was the real basis for any current authority for Roman laws. The implication of a battle of authority between Roman and customary law was explicitly spelt out later in the text, where Selden summed up his case by remarking that:

Other instances might bee brought, sufficiently to shew that the Law natural and of Nations is not wholly to be drawn out of such Decrees or Determinations as are found in the Books of *Justinian*; And so that what is there inserted touching a Communitie of the Sea, doth not in any way diminish the Autoritie of the received Customs of so many ages and nations.[14]

Selden's absolute refusal to concede any inherent authority to Roman law (never mind identifying it with natural law), not only in England but in any country, and even in the international sphere, was perhaps the most consistent theme of his works, recurring in one way or another in almost all of them. It is evident as early as his *Historie of Tithes* (1618), where he poured his aspersion on the claim "received through lazie Ignorance" that "the *Civill Law*; that is the old *Roman Imperiall* Law of *Iustinian*" as "read and profest in the Universities" governs the states of Europe. He observed that this "is so farre from Truth, that indeed no Nation in the world is governed by them." Selden conceded that some specific Roman laws had been accepted into the legal systems of various European states (indeed, in England itself, for example, in cases concerning Maritime Law). But his point was that the authority creating this acceptance was not found in Roman law itself, but rather in the laws and customs of the states that had chosen to accept it. To reinforce this point, he made sure to address two practices that were often interpreted as proof of an authority that Roman law carried in Europe: its being studied in all European universities, and its influence on the interpretation of laws throughout continental Europe. Selden dismissed the first practice by a derisive comment about those who "can make no difference betwixt the use of Laws in studie or argument (which might equally happen to the Laws of *Utopia*) and the governing autoritie of them"; the second, by stressing that, although "the Interpretation of those common Laws in most places" had indeed "of late time" been much directed by the "reason" of the Roman laws, this was "only by the reason of them (not by their authoritie) and that also in case when they are not opposite at all to the *common Laws*, but seeme to agree with the Law of *Nations* or *common reason*." Selden's recurring effort in all these cases was to clearly deny any "governing authoritie" to Roman law. It was not incidental that he connected this lack of authority with that law not actually governing any nation (that is, it <u>was</u> the "Laws of *Utopia*" – of no place), and with "reason" not conferring "authoritie."[15]

---

[14] MC b1c24. About Selden's struggle against Roman law throughout his career see Caruso *Miglior* p. 810. See also M.A. Ziskind "Criticism" pp. 36–37.

[15] *Historie of Tithes* pp. 477–481. Barbour mentions that even in his early *Analecton Anglobritannicon*, composed around 1607, Selden pointed to the failure of the 1605 Gunpowder Plot, as evidence of

Almost three decades later, in his 1647 "Dissertatio historica," upon the influential medieval commentary on English law *Fleta*, Selden was still patently at it, warning from claims for an authority of Roman law. In this case he directed his efforts not towards the identification of Roman law with natural law, but rather towards the claim of an actual succession of power – the so-called "translatio imperii" – by which it was alleged that the authority of western European monarchs originated in a devolution of Roman imperial power, into the rulers of the several states succeeding it, when the empire dissolved. That Selden saw the necessity to expressly warn readers from the idea that imperial law had any force or precedence in English law, especially regarding the matter of the royal prerogative, indicates he was coming across such claims even as late as the time the "Dissertatio historica" was being written, during the English Civil War. Selden argued forcefully that neither was there any succession of power or law from the Roman state to England or even to the present "German" Roman Empire, nor was there ever in England or in most of the "Christian" republics throughout Europe anything similar to the transfer of the powers from People and Senate to the Emperor (the "Lex Regia") that had allegedly occurred at a certain time in the Roman state. Indeed, he remarked, all past attempts to introduce Roman law into England (and the strong opposition these eventually encountered) were motivated exactly by its ominously absolutist political implications: "absoluta principis potestate."[16]

Returning to the *Mare Clausum*, before looking at Selden's treatment of arguments against customary law that were based on the "modern" ideas about natural law, it is important to point out that he identified a strong connection between arguments from Roman law and those from "modern" natural law (or right). He believed that in many cases, the latter were rooted to no small degree on ideas, assumptions and inferences from the former. Consequently, returning to his favorite roots-plant image for systems of law, Selden argued:

But as the root being cut, the Tree fall's, so the Autoritie of those antient Lawyers being removed out of the way, all the determinations of the modern which are supported by it, must bee extremely weakned.[17]

God's favor in thwarting yet another Romanist attempt to take over England. Barbour *Measures* pp. 96–97.

[16] "Dissertatio historica" Ogg pp. 170–171. See also Selden's addressing the same claim made on a universal level, some years earlier, when he denied what "Indeed divers civilians, especially of *Italy* and *Germany*, which profess the old laws of *Rome*, tell us that the [German] emperor is at this day of right, *lord of the whole world* or *earth*, as their text also affirms." See "Preface" in TH (1631).

For a discussion of Justinian's explicit decree of his divinely sanctioned imperial office being a universal one, as "lord of the world" (*dominus mundi*), and therefore of his will alone as constituting law, so that what pleases the *princeps* has the force of law (*quod principi placuit legis habet vigorem*), see Canning *Medieval* pp. 7–8.

[17] MC b1c26. Gentili's argumentation is a case in point; for example, his attempt, quoted by Selden, to expand private Roman law so it would bear on international law: "*that it* [Roman law]

Turning then to address the "modern" natural law and natural rights arguments directly, Selden began with making short shrift of Vazquez's argument, that prescription was not a binding principle in international law, by remarking that such an absurdity would simply result in the complete abrogation of "the very intervenient Laws of Nations" – the whole of what is today called international law. Selden then went on to deal with his main target, Hugo Grotius, dissecting his views on "a natural and perpetual Communitie of the Sea," as put forward both in the *Mare Liberum* and in the *Jure Belli ac Pacis.* As mentioned in a previous chapter, Selden first reported the inconsistency of argumentation in *Mare Liberum*, and then turned to the *Jure Belli*, pointing out that since Grotius purported to identify and justify a complete system of law based solely on "natural Right or Reason" (to Grotius synonymous), it was inconsistent for such a theory to make any claims concerning the possibility of appropriation of the sea, based on "Custom" or prescription ("Right of Occupation"). Moreover, as he had done in Gentili's case, Selden – on top of arguing that Grotius failed to make a convincing case from natural right only – also visibly positioned Grotian natural right theory as essentially opposite to, and a negation of, customary law.[18]

We can see now that Selden's efforts to defend customary law from the theories opposed to it focused on one cardinal point – the authority of law. Selden readily conceded that both Roman law and natural rights theories presented many valuable ideas and useful inferences, but he strenuously

concern's even Princes, although it was framed by Justinian *for private persons.*" See MC b1c24. For modern scholarship recognizing Grotius' arguments as based on a "Roman framework," especially his (one could almost say Gentilian) extension of the Roman private right to punish to the public sphere, see B. Straumann, "The Right to punish as just cause of war in Hugo Grotius' Natural Law" in *Studies in the History of Ethics*, 2/2006 (electronic journal at: www .historyofethics.org) pp. 15–16 and note 51.

[18] Addressing the view of "Vasquius," that the sea being *"and ever hath been in common, without the least alteration, as 'tis generally known,"* Selden's reaction is: "Whereas the quite contrarie is most certainly known to those, who have had any insight into the received Laws and Customs of Ages and Nations." And about that "hee would have prescription to cease betwixt Foreigners in relation to each other, and not to take place in the Law of Nations but in the *Civil* onely" Selden reacted that "not any thing can be said or imagined more absurd" since it means pretty much "to abrogate the very intervenient Laws of Nations." See MC b1c26.

For Selden's treatment of Grotius see especially MC b1c26. See sections 11 and 16–17 of the "Prolegomena" to Grotius' *Jure Belli* for examples of the Dutchman's attempts to blunt the dichotomy between reason (and reason-based consent) on the one hand, and tradition (and expediency) on the other. For the claim that the ideas of Vazquez de Menchaca had a "marked influence upon Hugo Grotius," see A. Pagden, "Human rights, natural rights, and Europe's imperial legacy" in *Political Theory* 31/2 (April 2003) pp. 185–186. A. Cromartie has argued that Selden's real target in the *Mare Clausum* was Vazquez's argument against prescription in international law, rather than Grotius' one, with which he supposedly agreed on many points. As is evident from my discussion of this issue, I believe that the extent and character of Selden's objections in the *Mare Clausum*, to Grotius' ideas do not support Cromartie's position. See Cromartie *Hale* pp. 39–40.

rejected all attempts to assert that they had any legal or political authority. Instead, he constantly upheld the authority of customary law, in England as well as abroad. Obviously, Selden's insistence that customary law was authoritative begs the question of the source for such an authority. So we turn now to answering this query.

5.3 DEFENDING THE "COMMON OR SECULAR LAWS OF THEIR OWN NATIONS"

All custom draws its authority from its being a form of common consent, a usage to which no one has successfully objected for time out of memory. It is a consent that resides not in each individual, or in a majority, but rather in the history and institutions of a community. Early-modern advocates of customary law, in attempting to define the source for this authority, emphasized two attributes of customary law in particular: it was continuous and it was national. To properly understand these attributes and their grounds, it is sufficient to consider the characteristics shared by the types of legal systems which the ancient constitutionalists opposed, be these based on Roman law, divine right or natural right: they were ahistorical and universal. To the advocates of customary law, it was these very characteristics that made such systems of law arbitrary and tyrannical.[19]

The effort to display both the long continuity and the national character of customary legal systems is evident in works like Francois Hotman's *Francogallia* (1574), where the author explicitly described his work as treating *"our* Francogallia" and the constitution under which *"it flourished for above a Thousand Years,"* attributing the calamities and misfortunes having since befallen the state to the *"great Blow which our Constitution received* 100 *years ago,"* and proposing that recovery could only come by *"replacing and restoring every Member to its true Position."* A similar tendency informs Grotius' early works, like the already discussed *Batavicae* and *Belgicis.*[20]

While Grotius eventually fell out with the national-continuity argument in favor of developing a theory grounded solely upon universal natural rights,

---

[19] Roman law of course originated in an historical and particular system, however some early-modern proponents like Gentili posited it had transcended those origins and become a universal system. For the common lawyers' arguments against Roman law, see Ferguson *Clio* pp. 231–232, 268–270.

[20] Quotes from "The Author's Preface" in Francois Hotman, *Francogallia* Robert Molesworth trans. (1721, 2nd edition) pp. v–vi. About the influence of the humanist histories on Grotius and his extension of their method from personal to societal virtues, see Burgess *Politics* pp. 16–17. The parallels between Grotius' and Selden's early works have been discussed, among others, by R. Tuck, L. Campos Boralevi, and S. Caruso. The latter points to Grotius and Selden as taking part in the attempts – in both of their countries – to build up "una coscienza nazional-statuale," attempting to show the legal and political continuity of the national community and the state as *"ininterrotte."* See Caruso *Miglior* pp. 442–443.

Selden always retained an unswerving loyalty to the common law. However, Selden also came to recognize that universal legal theories, by their claim to hold the higher moral and intellectual ground, posed a real challenge to customary legal systems: threatening either to relegate the latter to the status of subsidiary and irrelevant curiosities, or, what was even worse, to regard them as lacking a moral foundation. In fact, we might recall that among his contemporaries, there were several prominent English civilians, like William Fulbecke, Sir Thomas Ridley and John Cowell – and of course Gentili – who advocated the introduction of Roman law to England, explicitly because by its universality it seemed to them closer to the law of nature than the Common law – thus assuming the equating of more universal with more natural. Selden devoted considerable intellectual efforts to rejecting exactly such arguments, and to developing a theory that would reconcile authoritative customary law with some kind of universal moral and legal principles; indeed, a theory that would ultimately regard customary law as the only adequate path to a feasible moral order.[21]

Celebrated for his learning in the common law, Selden certainly subscribed to the main tenets of the English common lawyers concerning the national and continuous character of their customary law. In his "Dissertatio historica," for example, he stressed the continuity of English law and the fact that the one serious attempt to introduce Roman law to England (in the twelfth century) had been promoted by men who were not of the "English nation" (non de gente Anglicana).[22]

But Selden's writings also demonstrated, from the earliest stages, a familiarity with and respect for the ideas and methods of the continental historical humanist school, as a passage from the *Historie of Tithes* (1618) illustrates:

> [W]itnesse in *France* those ever honord names, *Bude, Cuiacius, Brisson, Tiraquell, Pithou, Pasquier, Le Thou, Aerault, Berterie, Sauaron,* and others; in the Empire, *Gruter, Freher, Ritterhuse*; in the united Prouinces, *Groot, Heuter,* and the like elsewhere. For these all were or are practicers of the various *common* or *secular Laws* of their own Nations, although they studied the *Imperialls* and *Canons* in the Universitie. [A]nd who of the learned knows not what light these have given out of their studies of *Philologie,* both to their own and other Professions?[23]

---

[21] See discussion in Mosse *Struggle* pp. 147–148. For Selden's main concern throughout his many fields of intellectual endeavor, as making sure that "[t]he law of particular places, created by local consent, was defended against rival codes with universal claims," see Cromartie *Hale* pp. 30–31. For a similar point about Selden's work on natural law and his Judaic studies representing his attempt to "reinvest positive law with a superhuman authority," see Barbour *Measures* 94–95.

[22] "Dissertatio historica" Ogg pp. 170–171. Selden argued that attempts to introduce Roman law to England had failed because of the "absolutist" ("absoluta Principis potestate") element in the "Lex Regia." See also about Selden's relationship to early Stuart common law ideas in Burgess *Politics* p. 58.

[23] *Historie of Tithes* (1618) "Preface" pp. xix–xx. P. Christianson claims that when writing his *Analecton*, having "no elaborate English model to follow, Selden appears to have patterned his

In the passage, on top of expressing his admiration for these continental humanists, Selden also connected them and their historical method – *"Philologie"* – to the defense of the *"common* or *secular Laws* of their own Nations" from the *"Imperialls* and *Canons* in the Universitie" (Catholic canon law, being yet another universal system of laws). Selden's wide exposure, from early on in his career, to the Common law tradition and practice, as well as to the historical arguments of the continental humanist (he was of course, also familiar with the work of the English antiquaries), apparently made him more disposed than most of his insularly minded common lawyer colleagues towards the need for a more systematic answer to theoretical attacks on customary law.[24]

The identification of Roman law with continental political absolutism, and of the Common law with English freedom, was widely established among English lawyers of Selden's day, as it had been for centuries. As mentioned before, one of the early classic formulations of this assumption was of course Fortescue's *Laudibus* (c. 1470), which praised the English Common law by claiming it was in fact natural law. That is, Fortescue defended both the universality of natural law and the locality of the English Common law by making the two into one – however, since natural law was widely assumed to be by definition immutable, Fortescue had to argue the same was true about the Common law. This argument was very much the same one used by Sir Edward Coke, a century and a half later.[25]

___

account upon that famous portrayal of the ancient constitution of France, Francois Hotman's *Francogallia.*" See P. Christianson, "Young John Selden and the Ancient Constitution, c. 1610–1618" in *Proceedings of the American Philosophical Society* 128 (1984) pp. 272–274.

[24] On the tendency of English lawyers of this period to regard the common law as "part of a self-enclosed, natural process which could only be comprehended in its own terms and according to its own logic" and on the discussion of the "insularity" of common lawyers see D.R. Kelley, *Foundations of Modern Historical Scholarship* (New York: Columbia University Press, 1970);

Kelley "History" pp. 24–51; Brooks & Sharpe, "History" and D.R. Kelley, "A rejoinder: History, English law and the renaissance" in *Past and Present* 72/1 (August 1976). In the latter, on p. 146, Selden is described as the "higher luminosity" light of historical insight, among the prevalent English insularity of the period.

For the continuing debate about the character of the common law "mind" of the seventeenth century, and Selden's place, see Burgess *Politics* pp. 58–59.

[25] See Caruso *Miglior* pp. 505–508, and M.A. Ziskind "Criticism" pp. 38–39. See also pp. 26–27, where Ziskind points out that the centers at which Roman law was studied in England, Oxford and Cambridge, struggled to attract more than a few students, even when distinguished civil jurists (such as Gentili) were imported from abroad. In contrast, there was always a keen interest to study the law of England in London's Inns of Court, since to the common lawyers went positions and wealth.

Fortescue's identification of English law as natural law might imply other legal systems like the French one, to be opposed to natural law. He attempted to overcome the problem of squaring an unchanging natural law with the differences in circumstances, by positing something like a reverse-kind adaptation: he proposed the existence of two types of natural political laws, the one "politicum et regale" (political and royal), fit for virtuous peoples, like England's, the other "tantum regale" (only royal), suited for more willful and intractable populations needing a firmer rule, like France's.

Selden's strategy for justifying Common law was the very opposite of the one employed by Fortescue and Coke – he described natural law as consisting of only a small core of immutable general rules, *as well* as all the mutable adaptations and stipulations of particular legal systems – as long as the latter do not infringe on the core general rules. He thus proposed a theory of natural law as traditional national law that, by definition, was changing to suit different times and circumstances. This theory, best articulated in his *Jure Naturali*, was already evident in its essential components almost 25 years earlier, in his "Notes" to Fortescue's *Laudibus*, where, after having posited that "nature being the same in all, the beginning of all laws must be the same," Selden then proposed that on top of the circumscribed "meerly immutable part of nature," came with the changes of time and place,

additions and interpretations, in succeeding ages increased, and somewhat altered them, by making a *determinatio juris naturalis*, which is nothing but the *Civil law* of any nation. For although the law of nature be truly said immutable, yet it is as true, that it is limitable, and limited law of nature is the law now used in every state. All the same may be affirmed of our *British* laws, or *English*, or other whatsoever.[26]

Far from regarding these "additions and interpretations" to the natural law as a problem, Selden saw them as being the normal way by which natural law becomes adapted to particular characters and circumstances. Thus change became for him pretty much the mark for the substantive continuity of law; an unchanging law instead implied for him a progressing detachment of the latter from circumstances, and thus a gradual loss of authority. Selden's most significant and inventive idea was therefore his linking of changes in the law with its continuity, rather than its rupture. He articulated continuity through change, as the essential nature of an adapting law, in effect identifying national customary law with natural law and its authority.[27]

Aside from justifying customary law, this idea, according to which continuous national law is natural law, also has quite unsettling implications for legal theories that are neither national nor continuous. For, if it is natural and desirable for laws to change and adapt according to circumstances, one can hardly resist the conclusion that theories of law which do not possess these qualities are, at least, severely handicapped in authority and practicability, and at worst unnatural and detrimental. Law systems which are by definition unconnected to any specific place or time are thus doubly condemned, as not only what he terms laws of "Utopia" (no place), but also of what we might call

---

[26] NL cols. 1891–1892. See also discussion in Toomer *Scholarship* p. 181.

[27] NL cols. 1891–1892. Other passages in the "Notes" make very much the same point. For the innovative aspect of Selden's linking of the idea of the law's continuity with that of adaptation to changing circumstances, so that adaptation becomes in effect a function of continuity, see Ferguson *Clio* pp. 292–293, 296–297. For a good discussion of Selden's theory of history and its significance see H.D. Hazeltine, "Selden as a legal historian" in *Festschrift Heinrich Brunner* (Weimar, 1910) pp. 588–589.

"Uchronia" (no time), which makes them at all times literally anachronistic. For an adaptive concept of law, static universalist theories, like Roman law or the "modern" natural rights systems, far from being identified with natural law, become to a great extent the things farthest from it.[28]

Selden's ideas of adaptive law certainly had some precedents in English legal though. While Sir Edward Coke's advocacy of the Common law followed Fortescue's approach, which regarded it as essentially unchanging, other significant legal writers, like Christopher Saint Germain, in his *Doctor and Student* (1523), the early legal book most read and cited by common lawyers alongside Fortescue's, and in Selden's own time Sir John Davies, presented arguments in praise of English customary law that were implying a changing and adapting Common law.[29]

However, whereas in English commentators like Saint Germain, Davies and others, the idea of a changing and adaptable common law was mostly implicit and certainly not significantly developed or discussed, with Selden it became a far more explicit and general issue, connected to his efforts to supply a theoretical justification of customary law. For Selden, the supreme confidence exhibited by English common lawyers in the solidity of their legal systems could not suffice. His own extensive familiarity with wider legal ideas and developments, made him early on aware of the onslaught on customary law that was then sweeping Europe. He obviously did not believe that the English Common law could long endure as a totally insular system, without any claim

---

[28] Indeed, Selden was conscious enough of temporal change to himself coin the term "Syncronisme" (in his "Illustrations" in *Poly-Olbion*) to describe the cross-referencing of ancient sources to check their reliability. The *Corpus Juris Civilis* fitted perfectly both the atemporal and the atopographical characteristics: Justinian explicitly decreed his codification to be valid "forever" (*in omne aevum*), and his own divine office to be a universal one, as he was "lord of the world" (*dominus mundi*). See Canning *Medieval* pp. 7–8. On his part, Selden repeatedly stressed that what was called Roman Law in the west was not by any means a continuation of the laws of the ancient Romans (this would make it a type of long-continuing common law, and of longer continuance than English common law). He pointed out that Roman law was in fact abandoned in Western Europe, and "neglected near 600 years," so that its revival in thirteenth-century Europe was not a continuation or even a restoration, but rather a new beginning. See, for example, NL cols. 1892–1893. On the decline and revival of the *Corpus Juris Civilis*' influence in western Europe see Canning *Medieval* pp. 6–7.

[29] Saint Germain was aware that different sources had coalesced into English law, but he linked so closely reason and custom, until they became almost identical. For him the long continuance of customs gave them additional authority, for it showed their good effects and necessity – that is, an empirical argument from experience. Burgess *Politics* pp. 7–8, 34–36, 56–57.

Sir John Davies pursued both empirical and adaptive arguments in his defense of the common law. He suggested that since custom, by definition, does not become law until tried and approved time out of mind, it necessarily has far fewer defects and inconveniences than law not thus instituted. But he also argued that law must be appropriate to the nature and disposition of a people, and that in England the law is so much so, that its people cannot be ruled by any other law. It is so well fitted, because the English have made their own laws out of their own wisdom and experience only. Tubbs *Mind* pp. 131–132.

to address outside legal and moral challenges. Although it appears that as early as the mid-1610s Selden had already formulated important components of his idea of natural law as continuous adaptation, as he briefly outlined it in his "Notes" to Fortescue's *Laudibus*, he clearly needed a far more extensive apparatus of both legal theory and practice by which to support and articulate his concepts. A theory out of tune with so much of the intellectual fashions of the day would need, among other things, to show grounds for obligation, for identification of the immutable part of natural law and for preferring particular legal systems to others. In this quest for a more comprehensive theoretical foundation for the common law as natural law, Selden eventually found what he was looking for, in what he came to regard as by far the most successful example of a customary legal system – the Jewish legal tradition.[30]

5.4 FROM "IEWISH FICTION" TO "TESTIMONIES BEYOND EXCEPTION"

Selden's interest in Jewish texts and ideas was certainly not uncommon in seventeenth-century England, and neither was his assumption that many of these texts and ideas could be relevant for his own days, both in the religious as well as in the political sphere (and in the many cases when the two overlapped). The organized study of Hebrew in England had been instituted as early as 1540, with the establishment of the Regius chairs of Hebrew at Oxford and Cambridge Universities; and it was accorded importance within the educational system, to the extent that at places like St. John's College, Cambridge, students were formally forbidden from carrying on their conversation in the halls, in any language but Latin, Greek or Hebrew. Nevertheless, it still took some time for Hebrew to gain momentum as a subject of serious study, so that, for example, Selden's four-year stay at Oxford's Hart Hall, between the years 1598 and 1602, seems to have left very little mark on his later Hebrew proficiency.[31]

It might be said that, in England, the study of the Hebrew language and sources reached its peak in the seventeenth century not only with scholars active

---

[30] Burgess asserts that it is unclear if Selden's early historical writings owed more to the English common law tradition or to his exposure to continental humanists (like Hotman). See Burgess *Politics* p. 58. Christianson portrays Selden as attempting to present a picture of continuity in English law at least from Anglo-Saxon times, by which he attempted to minimize the disruptive influence on that continuity by such as Roman law, the introduction of Christianity and the Scandinavian and Norman invasions. See Christianson "Young" pp. 277–279. Although it is certainly hard to ascribe particular features of Selden's thought to some influence or another, one may nevertheless venture that the stress on continuity came to Selden more through his common law education, while the stress on national law as a category owed more to the humanist historical tradition.

[31] D.S. Katz, "The Abendana Brothers and the Christian Hebraists of seventeenth century England" in *Journal of Ecclesiastical History* 1/40 (January 1989) pp. 28–58, especially 28–30.

within the universities, like Langbaine, Pococke, Robert Sheringham and the Abendana brothers, but even more so with scholars active mostly outside of the universities, like Ussher, Lightfoot and of course Selden. In the next century, the study of Hebrew, as well as the attitude to Jewish learning more generally, declined steeply, partly because of the general decay of learning in the universities, but also because of changing attitudes to Jewish wisdom and ideas. An eighteenth-century Hebraist like Robert Spearman could complain in 1755 that "the Hebrew tongue, left to the ignorant and vile comments of those who knew nothing of its excellency, is grown contemptible even to a proverb," while Edward Gibbon could write censoriously of Lightfoot's interest in Jewish learning, that the scholar "by constant reading the rabbis, became almost a rabbi himself."[32]

The seventeenth century flourishing of Christian Hebraism in England had several sources, but a central one was the widespread belief that Hebrew learning contained important ideas that had been neglected by Christianity for too long, and could be of immense value to contemporary society. The effects of the reformation, with its return to scripture and its suspicion of official interpretation, also militated in favor of the discovery of truths hidden within original Jewish texts. This tendency is observable not only among the clergy or those employed in theological inquiries, but also among a far wider prism of interests and concerns. A typical example was Izaak Walton (1593–1583), a member of the literary circles around Selden, who in his phenomenally popular *The Complete Angler* (1653) remarked in an aside about the Jews that,

many of those people have many secrets, yet unknown to Christians; secrets that have never yet been written, but have been since the days of their Solomon, who knew the nature of all things, even from the cedar to the shrub, delivered by tradition from the father to the son, and so from generation to generation without writing; or, unless it were casually, without the least communicating them to any other nation or tribe[.][33]

Consequently, Jewish traditions were widely believed to be relevant not merely for theological or scholarly purposes, but for social and political ones as well. It is against this background that the evident rise of interest in the Jews and their ideas, in seventeenth-century England, should be understood. Oliver Cromwell, for one, went even farther than most contemporaries in his welcoming attitude to Jews: when he wrote in November 1643 that he waited and prayed "to see union and right understanding between the godly people – Scots, English, Jews, Gentiles, Presbyterians, Independents, Anabaptists, and all" he was obviously counting the Jews among the "godly" – something he never allowed for Roman Catholics, or apparently even Episcopalians. Cromwell's attitude, eventually culminating in the readmission of Jews to

[32] See Katz *Abendana* pp. 32–37, 51.
[33] Izaak Walton, *The Complete Angler* (1653) chapter 11. See also Katz *Abendana* p. 37.

England, was by no means unique, and while there was no lack of hostile and even virulently anti-Jewish views like those of Purchas and Prynne, there were also prominent examples of attitudes that were far more welcoming, from Sir Thomas Shirley's 1607 proposal (to James I) to settle Jews in Ireland, to Thomas Draxe's, *The Worldes Resurrection, or the General Calling of the Jewes* (1608) asserting Christians should not revile the Jews and proposing that they will be restored to their land after the demise of the Ottoman Turkish empire, to Sir Henry Finch's famous *The Calling of the Jews* (1621), to the petition presented in January of 1649, to the General Council of the Army, proposing the repeal of the "inhumane cruel" banishment of the Jews, and the allowing of their readmission to England on the Dutch model.[34]

Apart from the attitude to the Jews, there was a far more widespread employment of Hebrew terminology and ideas in political discussion, especially in the 1640s and 1650s. These were evident in writings ranging from *Sagrir* and *Ohel, or Beth-Shemesh* by the firebrand Fifth Monarchist revolutionary Rogers, to Hobbes' cerebral and authoritarian *Leviathan* and *Behemoth*, as well as among writers of a much more constitutionalist bent like James Howell, a minor writer of moderate royalist tendencies, who was influenced by Selden's views on Parliament, terming it "that high Synedrion."[35]

Such attitudes were by no means restricted to the troubled times of the interregnum period, for the identification with Israelite terminology and ideas, always present in English culture, was never more prominent than in the seventeenth century. In 1601, in the Case of Darcy vs. Allen, the troublemaker Puritan Nicholas Fuller argued that the laws of Moses were to be regarded as decisive in deciding matters of English law, among other reasons because "we are now the house of God and the people of God, the Jews being cut off to whom God was the lawgiver, and we being engraffed in their stead." At the very opposite religious and political pole, King James I wrote that the ancient Jewish kingdom ought to be "a pattern to all Christian and well founded monarchies." He applied his advice to his own case, when, while discussing the prophet Samuel's biblical warning to the Israelites about the injustice and

[34] Finch's book was regarded as disturbing enough for Laud to ferociously attack it as full of "monstrous opinions," in a Sermon of 19 June 1621, preached before King James I (on occasion of his birthday). The book was suppressed, and both Finch and the publisher, William Gouge, were jailed for a time. For Cromwell see J.R. Tanner, *English Constitutional Conflicts 1603–1689* (1961) pp. 129–130. More generally on seventeenth-century English attitudes to Jews see A. Guibbory, *Christian Identity – Jews & Israel in Seventeenth-Century England* (Oxford University Press, 2010) throughout, but particularly pp. 3–7, 11–14.
[35] James Howell (c.1594–1666), was the brother of the royalist-Puritan Bishop of Bristol Thomas Howell, and a friend of the Earls of Bristol and of Dorset, as well as of Cotton and of Selden. Between 1643–1650 he was jailed in the Fleet prison, where he composed a number of works. He was influenced by Selden's ideas, sent to him several of his writings, and in 1663 published an English translation of *Mare Clausum*. See D.R. Woolf "Conscience, Constancy and Ambition in the Career and writings of James Howell" in J. Morrill, et al. (eds.) *Public Duty and Private Conscience* (Oxford University Press, 1993).

sufferings they will befall out of the hands of their kings, he drew from this warning not the lesson that kings are free to do what they wish (this he denied, demanding from kings to rule according to the good laws of their predecessors), but rather that in such eventuality, subjects must suffer in silence and not rise against their kings – even in such extreme cases such as when the prophet Jeremiah forbade the people from rising against Nebuchadnezzar's cruel rule.[36]

The wide currency of such attitudes meant that they were not relegated to the province of private considerations only, but were often employed as tools of ideological propaganda. James I and Archbishop Bancroft, in their efforts to impose on the English and Scottish anti-episcopalians their own vision of Church and State, comprising three estates of commons, nobles and bishops under the king, encouraged the delivery of sermons describing bishops as the Christian successors of the biblical Jewish priesthood – and thus part of the sacred political order, commanded in the Bible and ordained by Moses and Samuel. On the opposite ideological front, in Downinge's aforementioned sermon of 1640 before the Artillery Company, protestant England was identified with ancient Israel, while describing as "Amalekites" its internal and external enemies, from the king's evil counselors in church and state to Papists and their Jesuit agents. Likewise, Cornelius Burges, when selected as preacher before the commons for Gunpowder day 1641 (convened in the Temple Church, for fear of plague at St. Margaret's), took in his sermon a view explicitly identifying England with biblical Israel, drawing especially on the more historical books of the Hebrew Bible, Joshua, I and II Samuel, I and II Kings, to display God's action in history. Among other things, Burges warned of the precedent of biblical King Rehoboam of Judea who followed into disaster and division the counsels of those "brought up with him" while rejecting the advice of graver men of old. The analogy would be obvious to all: new advisors were swaying the king from the correct path, leading the country to division, and only the leadership of the old nobility could prevent this outcome.[37]

---

[36] Cromartie *Constitutionalist* pp. 152,193. James I recommended to his eldest son, Prince Henry, reading the biblical book of Chronicles as preparation for becoming a king. He applied his reading of the text closely, thus identifying the elders of the Chronicles to the barons and burgesses of his day – that is to Parliament. Indeed, King James' identification with his biblical predecessors, especially with King David, went even further: James himself wrote poetry, and personally translated King David's Psalms into poems that combined a kind of meditation upon scripture with the lessons of that king with which he most identified – published as "Psalmes of his Maiestie" in *Poems* of James VI. See Sharpe *Remapping* p. 165.

[37] M. Mendle, *Dangerous Positions: Mixed Government, the estates of the realm and the making of the answer to the xix propositions* (Alabama University Press, 1985) pp. 108–110; Adamson *Noble* pp. 68, 424–425; Kahn *Wayward* pp. 114–115. However, such attitudes were certainly not universal even among Puritans. Burges' patron and prominent leader of opposition peers in 1640, the Puritan Earl of Bedford, considered England as the "elect nation" chosen by God to defend Protestantism from Spain, but when he looked at alternative constitutional systems that might remedy England's problems, like classical Greece and Rome, or the Venetian and Dutch republics, he apparently never considered the Jewish constitutional model. Adamson *Noble* p. 143.

The growing interest in Jewish ideas and sources in England was somewhat hampered (but perhaps also gained allure) because of the lack of a substantial Jewish presence in the country. This presented a special problem for the acquisition of Hebrew books beyond the Bible, since the vast majority of such books were produced in countries where there was a significant Jewish population. Selden himself nevertheless succeeded in building up a collection of Hebraica which grew to be the largest and richest one in England, comprising at his death more than 700 books and manuscripts, many of them quite rare. Indeed, his feats of scholarship become even more remarkable when one considers that apart from the difficulties of acquiring Hebrew texts or language instruction, for all we know Selden never met a Jew in his life – let alone one which could exchange with him of significant information about Jewish law or about contemporary Jewish practices. A learned Polish Jewish convert named Philip Fernandus, taught in both Oxford and Cambridge in the 1590s, and another convert named James Levita (possibly another name of James Wolfgang) taught Hebrew at Oxford shortly after 1600. Selden studied at Oxford around the turn of the century but it appears at this early stage he did not yet develop an interest in Jewish subjects and his Hebrew proficiency at this time certainly left a lot to be desired. Selden also could have met Jacob Barnet, a well-read Italian Jew who stayed at Oxford University and London (at the house of noted Hebraist Isaac Casaubon) between 1610–1612, until he was jailed on being accused of recanting his intended conversion to Christianity, and then expelled from England; or with one of the handful of learned Jewish converts to Christianity which occasionally arrived in England, like Jacob Wolfgang or Jacob Levy, who were brought (respectively in 1608 and 1612) to Oxford by Sir Thomas Bodley, to help catalogue Hebrew manuscripts in his library, or like Italian Jewish converts Antonio Maria de Verona and Alexander Arniedi who taught Hebrew at Oxford respectively in the 1620s and 1630s. Selden also might have encountered members of the growing London community of crypto-Jews of Iberian extraction, such as the wealthy merchants Antonio Robles and Antonio Fernandez Carvajal, who settled down in London around 1635, but such men in any case kept a low profile pertaining to their religion, outwardly professing themselves Christians while holding clandestine Jewish prayer services around Aldgate, until they were permitted by Cromwell to reside and worship in England as Jews, in 1655, one year after Selden's death. There were other even more shadowy figures, such as Jacob the Jew and Cirques Jobson (both apparently from the Levant), who opened up England's competing first and second coffee-shops, by the early 1650s at Oxford, and which Selden might have come across during his visits to the city. However, we have no evidence at all for any such meeting, and even if one did occur, there is no hint that it gave Selden any real assistance to his learning. Considering that Selden acquired proficiency not only in biblical Hebrew, but also in the highly peculiar Aramaic dialect of the Talmud, and in the techniques of Talmudic discourse, his feats of learning are nothing less than astounding.[38]

It appears that Selden's attitude to Jewish learning and tradition went through a significant transformation, early in his career. His first published works, already displayed an interest and detailed knowledge of foreign legal systems, such as Roman and Canon law, which was to be a constant feature of his writing, and a quite uncommon one among the vast majority of common lawyers. However, in such early works as the *Jani Anglorum* (1610) and the *Analecton Anglobritannicon* (1615) – both composed around 1607–1608 – it is obvious that Selden's knowledge of Hebrew and rabbinics is slight, inexact and derivative (and at that from inaccurate sources such as Reuchlin and Pico).[39]

In the *Jani Anglorum*, the young scholar, while touching on the writers who conjectured the origin of Britons from a mythical Trojan named Brutus, also commented that:

There are some both very Learned and very Judicious persons, who suspect, that that story is patched up out of Bards Songs and Poetick Fictions taken upon trust, like *Talmudical* Traditions, on purpose to raise the *British* name out of the *Trojan* ashes.[40]

In other words, "*Talmudical* Traditions" were offered at this point as synonymous with patently unreliable stories and fictions, to be taken or left based on a "trust" that is suspect, to say the least. At this stage of his career it is unclear if Selden had been exposed to any significant traditional Jewish sources, and if his opinion was in any way informed, or merely reflected conventional attitudes that he had not bothered to explore. Two years later, in his extensive "Illustrations" to Michael Drayton's *Poly-Olbion* (1612), one of the works which made his early reputation, the beginning of a change in attitude can be

---

[38] Toomer *Scholarship* pp. 48, 445. The most plausible candidate for a meaningful meeting of Selden with a knowledgeable Jew is probably Jacob Barnet, an Italian Jew well versed in the Hebrew language as well as Talmudic learning, who was staying in England in 1613, assisting scholars with his Jewish learning at Oxford and some weeks in June at the house of the scholar Isaac Casaubon, in London. Even this encounter could have only been quite brief, for shortly thereafter, following a last-minute retreat from converting, Barnet was arrested and imprisoned in harsh conditions. Casaubon and others, including the Royal librarian Patrick Young (a friend of Selden), pressed the authorities to have him released, and in November he was sent out of England. See A. Grafton & J. Weinberg, "*I have always loved the holy tongue*" – *Isaac Casaubon, The Jews, and a forgotten chapter of renaissance scholarship* (Cambridge, Mass.: Harvard Bellknap Press, 2011) pp. 255–257, 264–266.

[39] Toomer *Scholarship* pp. 81–83, 100. Apparently Selden's Hebrew instruction while a student at Oxford was slight at best. He began to seriously learn it only in 1609, from Ussher. This was certainly an unusual undertaking for someone with no clerical aspirations, who was also training at the Inns of Court for a legal career. See Toomer *Scholarship* p. 23; also Parry *Trophies* p. 114.

[40] *Reverse (Jani Anglorum)* b1c 6. An example of the conventional attitude to the Talmud as synonymous with unreliable and fictitious stories, can be found in Sir Francis Bacon's *Essays* (1597), where in the essay "Of Atheisme," Bacon writes that he would "rather beleeve all the Fables in the legend, and the Talmud, and the Alcoran, then that this universall Frame, is without a Minde." See also Rahe *Against* pp. 258–259.

detected. There still were many cases of disparaging comments towards Jewish traditions. Moreover, his attitude now reflected a greater familiarity with the Hebrew language, as well as some Jewish sources and themes.[41] He thus dismissed the *"Iewish* fiction" about Adam's stature "equalling at first the worlds Diameter" as another one of various unreliable stories about ancient men being much larger than modern ones; he derided the story about the biblical King Og purportedly crushing the Israelites opposing him by thrusting at them an enormous stone, "which the *Iewes* are not asham'd to affirme"; and he was clearly suspicious of attempts to create *"Cabalistique* Concordance of identity's in different words" by the means of establishing an equal numerical value of different words "and by consequent of like interpretation" (the technique known in Jewish tradition as Gematria).[42]

However, in the same work, there emerged alongside such scoffing and dismissive comments another, more thoughtful and balanced attitude. In some cases Selden conceded to the Jewish traditions he treated some degree of significance, as is evident even from his comment on Adam's gigantic stature being an "allegorique greatnes" – thus implying that the *"Iewish* Fiction" on this matter did not in fact reflect blind credulity, but rather some symbolical considerations.[43]

For our purpose, Selden's most significant comments in this work have to do with his increasing theoretical interest in tradition, meaning and transmission. In a number of places in the "Illustrations," while reflecting on the wider question of the credence to be assigned to information that had been traditionally transmitted, Selden included the Jewish tradition in the sources

---

[41] Toomer *Scholarship* pp. 119–121, asserts that by this stage there was a clear improvement of Selden's grasp of the Hebrew language, and he could "certainly read the Hebrew Bible." His knowledge of rabbinical literature however, still depended on secondary sources. For example, his knowledge of the Jewish tradition about Adam's enormous size at creation is, according to Toomer, from Ricius' *De Thalmudica doctrina Epitome*, and not from the original source for Adam's story as well as Og's, the *Pirkei Rabbi Eliezer*, an early "Midrash" (exegetical) text, traditionally attributed to the first century CE sage Eliezer ben Horkenus (modern scholarship views it as a pseudo-epigraphical composition, from about the ninth century CE). See *Pirkei Rabbi Eliezer*, on Adam, Hagiga 12:71; on King Og, Berachot 54:72 – I am grateful to R. Dr. Joseph Isaac Lifshitz for his assistance in individuating this source. Circulated in Latin versions, the story about Adam's gigantic size was quite popular in medieval Christian Europe, where it might have contributed to figurative depictions of the Emperor or Jesus as gigantic in stature. See Kantorowicz *Bodies* pp. 69–70.

[42] "Illustrations" in *Poly-Olbion* pp. 20–21, 50–51, 146–147. Selden was also dismissive of claims about the existence of creatures of some "middle nature," between man and god, "as the *Rabbinique*, conceit upon the creation supposes"; see "Illustrations" in *Poly-Olbion* pp. 84–85.
   About the term "cabalistical" as meaning in the seventeenth century something fictitious and presumptuous, see discussion of Richard Baxter's pamphlet *The Glorious Kingdom of Christ* (1691) in Lamont *Puritanism* 156–157.

[43] See also his weighting of possible philological grounds for identification of the mythical progenitor of the Germans, Tuisco, with the biblical Aschenaz, from whom the Hebrew name for Germany derived in Jewish tradition. See "Illustrations" in *Poly-Olbion* pp. 71, 122–123.

he discussed and assessed. In one instance, after asserting that, except for the rare cases when some report survives from those involved in the politics of their times (like Xenophon, Tacitus or Guicciardini), "no Nationall storie" can justify itself "but by tradition" he then went on to enumerate among traditionally authoritative sources, like the Fathers of the early church and ecclesiastical historians, also the "Rabbins" who take their "highest learning of *Cabala*, but from antique and successive report." In another case, while considering the way in which the learning of the ancient British Druids "was delivered only by word of mouth," and thus needed the aid of "a multitude of Verses and *Pythagorean* precepts" (what would today be termed mnemonic devices), he proposed that this method was identical to that of "the *Cabalists*; which, untill of late time, wrote not, but taught and learned by mouth and diligent hearing of their *Rabbins.*" In both examples, although the tradition of the "*Rabbins*" is pretty much identified with "*Cabala*," and no attempt is made to distinguish the Jewish mystical traditions from the legalistic and philosophical ones, its treatment alongside other valid historical sources – especially traditional national ones – implies that it should not be dismissed in its entirety as unreliable, but rather explored and studied, so that some true information might be retrieved out of the whole.[44]

His next works reflect the trend of growing acquaintance with, and interest in, Jewish sources. In the 1614 *Titles of Honor* Selden's knowledge of Hebrew and rabbinics had clearly progressed (although moderately so), and by this point he could quote directly not only from the Hebrew Bible but also from the Targums (also available from polyglot Bibles) and Rashi (presumably from a rabbinical Bible). Beyond these, for quotations from rabbinic works he still relied on translations or editions accompanied by a Latin translation. By his 1616 "Notes" on Fortescue's *Laudibus*, where he derided the fanciful attempts to trace the source of nations to some famous ancient individual (like Brutus for the British), he refrained from comparing this to "*Talmudical* Traditions," as he had done earlier in the"Illustrations" to *Poly-Olbion*.[45]

Sometimes in the mid-1610s a decisive shift in Selden's attitude to Jewish learning and ideas occurred. No direct testimony as to the causes or circumstance of this change survives, and one can only conjecture that it owed, at least partly, to his observably growing direct acquaintance with the Jewish sources. But it is already evident in Selden's next publication, *De Diis Syriis* (published 1617, but in preparation since at least 1613), among continental contemporaries probably his most famous and admired work.

---

[44] "Illustrations" in *Poly-Olbion* pp. 18–19, 168–169. Though all kinds of Jewish traditions can be (and sometimes are) identified by the term "Cabala" (literally, what is received), it is more often associated with the mystical tradition only, while the legal and philosophical traditions are associated with the "Gemara" or the Sages. It is unclear if Selden himself could do so at this time, as he certainly would later.

[45] See TH (1614) and discussion in Toomer *Scholarship* p. 157; NL cols. 1890–1892.

In this book the discussion of Rabbinic ideas is evidently far more extensive and substantive than before – he is familiar with commentators such as Abraham Ibn Ezra and David Kimchi and their ideas (but not yet directly with the Talmud). Although there are still several comments harshly dismissive of particular Jewish ideas or practices, the general attitude is one of serious consideration and engagement with the rabbinic tradition, and for the most part the discussions of opinions from Jewish authors are to the point, akin to the way other kinds of sources and views are treated, and often Selden even wholly adopts rabbinical explanations, when it suits him. There certainly are examples where Selden ridicules what he regards as patent absurdities found among rabbinical opinions, such as the attempt (in Rashi) to calculate the weight of the Golden Calf from its name by "Gematria", or the story (from Pirkei Rabbi Eliezer – apparently found by way of a Christian commentary) according to which the occurrence of gold-colored beards among Jews results from the descendants of those who drank the pulverized calf's gold mixed with water. Nevertheless, Selden does find at least one Rabbinical figure that certainly commands his respect, Maimonides who he describes as the first of the "Rabbinorum" who did not indulge in idle talk. Although dismissive of other rabbinic sages, the comment is intended to extol Maimonides as a reliable source and commentator. Moreover, the last pages of the work are devoted by Selden to defending "God's chosen people," from accusations by ancient authors, such as Juvenal and Tacitus that they were covert idolaters.[46]

One important point addressed in the *Diis*, and that will have an important role in his later theory of natural law, is Selden's repeated proposing that many myths and cults of the ancient pagan world originated in distorted versions and reminiscences of stories related in the Bible, thus indicating a common origin for all those civilizations and peoples – as related in the biblical account. Accordingly, Selden regarded the widespread practice in the ancient world, of identifying various pagan deities with each other, as a process opposite to an aggregative one of syncretism and convergence, since he claims that it was in fact the result of an earlier dis-aggregative process whereby the single original

---

[46] See, for example, *Diis Syriis* (1617) p. 191. An eight-pages long "Autorum Index" inserted between the Prolegomena and the main text of the book and listing sources used, testifies to the extent of Selden's reliance on rabbinic sources in this work, listing, for example, *Abraham Aben* (sic) *Ezra* 7 times, *David Kimchi* (Radak) 16 times, *Hierosolymitanum* (Jerusalem) *Targum* 3 times, *Ioseph Karo* 1 time, *Levi Ben Gersom* (Gersonides) 2 times, *Moses Ben Maimon* (Maimonides) 16 times, *Moses Gerundensis* (Nahmanides) 1 time, *Moses Mikotzi* 4 times, *Salomon Iarchi* (Rashi) 9 times. Even this list does not do full justice to Selden's use of traditional Jewish sources, for it is incomplete and misses several instances where these and other sources are mentioned.

On the *Diis Syriis*, its composition and contents, see Toomer *Scholarship* pp. 211–212, 251–255. For more on his treatment of Jewish sources see Toomer *Scholarship* pp. 223–228.

deity was gradually assigned various names and attributes by different peoples, as they descended into polytheism.[47]

The only significantly jarring note, in a work by Selden touching on Jews from after 1615, is the apparent credence given to a report of ritual murder by medieval English Jews, found alongside an otherwise relatively balanced treatment in the two-page piece "of the Iewes sometimes living in England" – published by Samuel Purchas within a collection of tracts named *His Pilgrimage* (1617, third edition). However, Selden's offended reaction to the publication should lead us to suspect that it probably did not accurately reflect the author's intentions: the work appeared in adulterated form, without Selden's approval, and caused a quarrel between him and Purchas.[48]

In any event, by 1618, Selden's attitude to Jewish traditions and ideas had been permanently transformed, in both character and content. A book Selden was working on at this period was his *Mare Clausum*, of which an early version was completed by 1617. The long and complex journey of the text from composition to print, with considerable additions, only in 1635, precludes ascertaining exactly what part originated when, but we may note that in its final version it evidences a significant knowledge of, and a favorable attitude to, various Jewish sources, among them Maimonides, Nahmanides, Gersonides, Rashi, Ibn Ezra, R. Moses of Kotzi and many others.[49]

The change in Selden's attitude is certainly evident in his *Historie of Tithes*; and especially so in the "Review" added to the published text at the last moment

---

[47] Toomer *Scholarship* pp. 231–235.

[48] G.J. Toomer writes that the essays' "obvious deficiencies" make credible the claim by William Prynne (a writer that, to say the least, had no delicacy towards the Jews) that Purchas printed a "poor maimed accompt," that was "so different from that delivered him," that upon its publication Selden "was very much offended with Mr. Purchas for abusing him in such a manner." Toomer has little doubt that in the section of the essay dealing with the alleged crimes of the English Jews, the original version sent by Selden to Purchas simply reported without comment what was stated in contemporary accounts like Matthew Paris and judiciary sources, while the introductory (and confused) remark about the report being one about the usual "Iewish crime" was authored by Purchas. Regardless, even without Purchas' maiming, Toomer regards the essay on the whole as a slight performance, notable only for being a first attempt to produce an account of medieval Jewish communities, based on the surviving records. Moreover, Toomer proposes that a long off-topic excursus in the *Marmora Arundelliana* of 1628, whose tone is far more sympathetic towards the Jews than the 1617 one, was quite possibly Selden's attempt to rectify the account of Medieval English Jews printed under his name by Purchas. See Toomer *Scholarship* pp. 168–170, 384–385. About Selden and Purchas see also in Fry "Selden" DNB.

[49] In *Mare Clausum* Selden discusses the precedent of the dominion of the sea assigned to Israel by God. In considering the meaning of the biblical text, Selden brings, at length, a number of rabbinical authorities and their arguments, among them: "an antient and very famous Interpreter of the Law, by name *Rabby Judah*," whose Doctrine is found "in the most antient Digests of the Jewish Law"; "Rabbi *Aben-Ezra*, Rabbi *Bechai*, and others"; "not only out of the more antient *Digests*, or both Volums of the *Talmud*, but also by the Testimonie of those most learned Rabbins, Moses Maimonides and Moses Cotzensis"; and "Solomon Jarchius, Rabbenu Nissim, Obadiah Bartenorius, and others." See MC b1c6.

(in order to answer criticism raised against the book, after advance copies had been circulating).[50] In this work Selden displayed a growing familiarity with several important traditional Jewish texts, an understanding of arguments and disagreements appearing in them, and a respect for the leading thinkers and their learning – indeed, the acceptance of their authority on the issues at hand. Thus, while discussing some identification disputed among various Jewish sources, he berated the opinions of "some *Iews*" (unnamed) with whom he disagreed as "idle and rash fancies" – but these disagreements were no mere exercise in controversy, for he supported his own views against them by the authority of other Jewish sources "both the *Hierosolymitan* (Jerusalem) *Targum*, and that other calld *Ben-Vziels*." Elsewhere, he based his argument on rules concerning tithes on both the "*Misnah* or Text," and "the *Gemara*" commentary parts of "their *Talmud*," as well as on the writings of "*Rabbi Ben-Maimon*." The Jewish authors of the texts he treated were "Talmudici, who are both theologians and jurisconsults" and mostly described by Selden as "their Lawyers" and "their Doctors," a significant shift from the "Cabalists" of a few years earlier (and the term "*Rabbins*," when used, had by now become synonymous with scholars rather than mystics). This would be Selden's consistent attitude in his works from this point onwards, usually describing the Jewish authors he treated as learned jurists ("jurisconsulti," his own title) or teachers ("magistri"), their tradition as a legal one, and even coming as far as comparing in his book on Jewish marriage law, *Uxor Ebraica, seu de nuptiis et divortiis ex Jure Civili, id est, Divino et Talmudico, veterum Ebræorum* (1646) the competing Mishnaic schools of interpretation, the houses of Hillel and of Shammai, to the two prominent juridical schools of ancient Rome, the Proculian and the Sabinian. The terminology was not incidental, for by terming the Jewish sages as lawyers and doctors, he conferred on them the same titles identifying the traditional authorities on Roman and Common law, and thus, by implication, the same status and significance.[51]

Indeed, much of Selden's bold argument (which caused that book to be banned, by order of the King), declaring Church tithes not divine but human

---

[50] Most of the *Historie of Tithes* was apparently written between September 1616 and September 1617 – with the main exception being the section on Jewish tithes (Chapter 2), on which Selden had compiled notes at least three years earlier (that is, 1614), probably originating in a summary and criticism of Scaliger's treatment of the issue. The "Review" was composed between April and November 1618. See Toomer *Scholarship* p. 261.

[51] "Review" pp. 450–451, 453–455; *Uxor* b3c20. See also *John Selden on Jewish marriage law: The Uxor Hebraica*, |1646| J. Ziskind trans. and ed. (Leiden, Brill, 1991) in J. Ziskind's "Introduction" pp. 9–10 and Toomer *Scholarship* pp. 298–299, 442.

However, Selden's attitude to the *Zohar*, the most prominent mystical text of the Jewish tradition, was quite different from the evident respect he accords to legal and philosophical Jewish texts like the Talmud or Maimonides' *Guide*. Without explicitly doubting the *Zohar*'s ancient attribution, his skepticism is evident in places where he describes it as a text "held" to be very ancient, in *Uxor* and *Synedriis*, or comments disparagingly upon its "fables" in *Jure Naturali*. See Toomer *Scholarship* p. 62.

law, was based on his acceptance as authoritative of the Jewish traditions concerning biblical tithes, their meaning and practice as well as their discontinuance. He explicitly asserted the value of what "the great Doctors of the Iewes have delivered in the Talmud and their later Comments" on the practice of tithes, as "testimonies beyond exception, for the practice or historicall part[.]" Indeed in his following of Jewish traditions on tithes, Selden sometimes even rejected interpretations by Church Fathers preferring to them some Jewish one, an approach that was duly censured by critics of the work.[52]

This reliability that he accorded to the Jewish "testimonies" Selden based primarily on the particular motive behind the composition of these writings. For although "Legall Tithing" had not been practiced among the Jews since the destruction of the second Temple:

Yet without doubt, most of them have long since [the destruction of the second Temple] expected a third Temple; otherwise why were they so carefull to have their Laws and speciall cases of first Fruits and Tithing, so copiously deliuered in five whole *Massecheths* of their *Talmud*, or body of their Civill and Canon Law, which was, many yeers after the destruction of the second Temple, made for the direction of the dispersed of their Nation?[53]

Most significant, for our purpose, is his indication that the authority of the "testimonies" of this tradition was connected to (indeed, to a great degree founded on) a continuity of national identity: the very delivering and preserving through the centuries of seemingly irrelevant exact historical and practical information about tithes, was directed at the "dispersed" of the Jewish nation, only because of their continuing common expectation of a future national restoration, and a "third Temple." In short, Selden portrayed the Jewish legal tradition as a "Civill and Canon Law," delivered and commented on by "great Doctors"; moreover, this tradition carried a high degree of reliability and authority about the matters it touched upon, because of the intentions and self-image of the Jewish nation. Perhaps the most important result of his approach was that Selden always regarded the Jewish people as a nation, persisting as such even to his own time, and thus treated ancient and modern Jewish sources indiscriminatingly as parts of one cohesive unit. This is one of the recurring criticisms directed at him by modern scholarship, apparently missing the point that such an approach is inevitable for one who wishes to appeal to the authority of a tradition, be it Jewish of English.[54]

---

[52] "Review" pp. 453–455. See also Toomer *Scholarship* pp. 268–269, where it is pointed out, for example, that Selden continued to pour scorn on the practice of numerology as he had repeatedly done in previous works, but this time also made clear that such "vanities" were practiced not only by Jewish writers, but by Christian ones as well.

[53] "Review" pp. 453–455.

[54] It has been remarked that Selden collapsed any simple distinction between the Jewish nation of his days and ancient Israel, not only by explicit statements but more generally by drawing in his

The above passage from the *Historie of Tithes*, as well as many others that appeared in later writings, such as his explicit assertion in *Jure Naturali* that he is treating "the Hebrew nation and people" of the past as well as of his own days, or his affirmation in the second volume of *Synedriis* (published in 1653), that the Jews have never given up their God-given right to their promised land, and that they expect the Sanhedrin (and thus their legal and political independence) to eventually be restored, show that Selden accepted a persistence of Jewish national identity even when in extended exile with their state no more. In many ways the Jewish case became for him the supreme example of a continuous legal tradition: adaptive but coherent and widely witnessed to go back for thousands of years without a break. Thus, Selden repeatedly refers to the Jewish laws and traditions as national ones, and as continuing (and, to the Jews, binding) to his own days. This attitude displayed by Selden to Jewish learning in the *Historie of Tithes*, would persist and, if anything, strengthen for the remaining 35 and more years of his exceptionally fertile career: an unstinting intellectual respect and fascination that would eventually engender a colossal effort to learn, understand and convey the Jewish tradition, as well as to decipher its intellectual (and often, also practical) implications.[55]

It is important to consider in this context, that Selden's view of the nature and authority of Jewish law, especially the in the post-exilic period, was by no means the conventional one among his contemporaries. Far from it; almost all scholars, including those favorably disposed to learning from the Jewish traditions, did not regard these as in any way authoritative any more, even to the Jews themselves. According to the prevalent view, as long as the Jewish nation dwelled in its land and state, its laws were in force, but since the destruction and exile, without their land and state, the Jews were to be regarded as no more a political society; accordingly, their laws had lost their

---

works wholesale from biblical, Talmudic, medieval and contemporary Jewish sources, and treating these sources as parts of one continuous tradition. See J. Rosenblatt, "Rabbinic ideas in the political thought of John Selden" in G. Schochet, F. Oz-Salzberger, M. Jones (eds.), *Political Hebraism: Judaic Sources in Early Modern Political Thought* (Jerusalem: Shalem Press, 2008) pp. 191–192, and 203 note 2 (drawing upon J. Shapiro, *Shakespeare and the Jews* (New York: Columbia University Press, 1995) p. 174). See also Toomer noting that Selden often used Jewish sources indiscriminately in documenting very old occurrences by quite recent Jewish writers. Toomer *Scholarship* 167.

[55] JN b1 Praefatio; *Synedriis* b2c16. Earlier, in *Synedris* b2c15, Selden had quoted Maimonides about the decline of the Sanhedrin, describing that body's migration from place to place until its demise in the city of Tiberias – reporting as well the tradition, accepted among the Jews, that it will be eventually restored in the very city where it passed away, before then returning to the Temple ("*Quin traditione accepimus, Tiberiade instaurandum posthac fore, atque inde transferendum ad Templum*" – קבלה היא שבטבריא עתידין לחזור תחילה ומשם נעתקין למקדש). See discussion in Toomer *Scholarship* pp. 762–763. Another example of Selden's treating the Jews in their exile as a nation is his remark about, "How the Iewish Nation auoided it [adoration of kings], the story of *Haman & Mordechai* discouers" in TH (1614), pp. 41–42.

force and authority, so that they might serve well for information and illustration of past ideas practices, but nothing more. Grotius, for example, explicitly equated in his *Jure Belli* the destruction of the Jewish state with that of their nationhood, arguing that the Jews "though the fall and devastation of their city, which was destroyed without hope for restoration, ceased to be a people."[56]

A similar view was expressed by Sir John Vaughan, when Lord Chief Justice of the Court of Common Pleas. In a 45-pages-long report of his ruling in the Case of Harrison v. Dr. Burwell (concerning a marriage dispute), in which he discussed at length matters of Jewish law, Vaughan explicitly asserted that, by the destruction of the Jewish state "their laws likewise vanished" as was for him the case when any state is dissolved – the same as if it were the state of England, France or Spain – regardless of that states' law being of human or divine origin. He therefore described the continuing Jewish observance of Mosaic law since the destruction of their state as only "the pleasure of a particular person or persons," since there is no more a "Law Common to that people."[57]

Vaughan was Selden's friend, an executor of his will, and is often described as a disciple, so that their views on this issue are sometimes inferred to be the same. Selden certainly influenced Vaughan, as can be seen, for example, by the latter's explicit and extensive use of his ideas in other parts of the case quoted above. However, this should not lead to assume an identity of views between them, certainly on this issue. In this instance, Vaughan's approach seems to follow not Selden's, but rather that of Grotius (whose work Vaughan also knew and approved of) – both Grotius and Vaughan explicitly assume that the authority of legal systems is to be inherently identified with the formal existence of a state.[58]

---

[56] Grotius *Jure Belli* b1c1 sec. 16: "...Postquam populus ille per excidium urbis & desolacionem praecisam sine spe restitutionis populous esse desiit" – English version from B.W. Kelsey's translation (Oxford, 1927) pp. 47–48. This particular view was completely in line with Grotius' theoretical approach, according to which a people as a separate entity could be destroyed physically such as by war, but also politically by the extinguishing of their distinct juridical existence, as he described in *Jure Belli* b2c9 sec. 5–6.

[57] The decision appears within a collection of reports of cases over which Vaughan presided, posthumously published by his son. See Edward Vaughan (ed.), *The reports and arguments of that learned judge, Sir John Vaughan kt. late Chief Justice of his majesties court of common pleas...* (1677), the quote is from pp. 235–236. See also pp. 239–240.

[58] Vaughan certainly knew and approved of Grotius' work, enough so to repeatedly mention and quote him favorably in the same *Reports* (e.g., pp. 232, 243–244), on various subjects – pretty much to the same extent as he does Selden. Indeed, I believe that the sometime automatic identification of Vaughan's ideas with Selden's should be reconsidered, for Vaughan seems to be at least as much indebted to Grotius, and there is also a report of his admiration for Hobbes' legal ideas. On Vaughan and Selden see Rosenblatt *Renaissance* pp. 226–229. For Vaughan's attitude to Grotius see *Reports* pp. 232, 243–244. About Vaughan's alleged admiration of Hobbes' *De Legibus* an unprinted copy of which he owned, see Aubrey *Lives* p. 155.

The divergence in the attitude to the Jewish nation and its laws, between such as Grotius and Vaughan on the one side and Selden on the other, allows a clearer distinction than is usually evident between two contrasting theories of the source of law and political identity. While for contemporaries like Grotius and Vaughan (and Hobbes) the state is the basis of political authority and laws, for Selden it is the nation that is the basis of identity and authority. Selden held that the Jewish nation, even in exile and dispersion, met his basic requirement for what constitutes a "nation," in that its people submit to laws, pretty much identifying the two – as indicated in a phrase that he quotes approvingly in the *Jure Naturali* from the medieval Byzantine scholar Michael Psellos: *"...the term 'nation' as it is used properly here means 'those peoples who submit to laws.'"*[59]

However, if we recall that Selden defines a law, human or divine, as a permission or prohibition that can be enforced by reward or punishment, the question naturally arises as to how Jews are to be punished for transgression of their law (or rewarded for adherence), in their currently dispersed and politically powerless condition. With a people as dispersed as the Jews were at that time, and obviously lacking a central political authority, the very possibility of punishment or reward seemed to be absent. Now, this problem might be easily solved by positing that reward or punishment will be divinely meted to Jews after they died. But while Selden never denied the existence of such a principle of obligation for the Jews or for all people (indeed, it underpinned his whole legal theory), he always avoided sufficing with it; perhaps because it could imply an antinomian redundancy of current laws, before duties relating to the final divine judgment – there were certainly sects in England embracing exactly such a view in the 1640s and 1650s, and in a sense the same view also underpinned Filmer's political theory. Instead, Selden seemed to have placed the source of authority for Jewish laws, even in their exile, in a more worldly-oriented frame, that is, the persisting hope and expectation professed by the Jewish nation, for their eventual concrete political restoration. For while Grotius' and Vaughan's position, explicitly tied the cessation of Jewish nationhood with the lack of hope for restoration of their commonwealth, Selden's repeated references to exactly such a hope and expectation of an eventual political restoration, point to it as fundamental to the persistence of their national identity and laws. Grotius' and Vaughan's position had for them the double benefit of conforming to Grotius' own theory of law as exercised by states on the basis of right reason (without necessarily requiring the existence of

---

[59] JN b1c6. Selden's Latin (translated from the original Greek): "Scilicet Gentis nomen legitime heic acceptum eas Nationes complectitur que legibus subsunt."
    Although Selden's view was an uncommon one, it appears he was not completely alone in averring it. Richard Cumberland for one, although rejecting Selden's account of the seven Noahide laws as obligating all mankind, nevertheless allowed, in Parkin's words, that "for the Hebrew nation at least there could be laws existing prior to the state." Parkin *Science* p. 64.

a deity), as well as to the Christian doctrine about the hopeless fate of the Jews. Selden's position too conformed to his theory of law, as ultimately founded on the idea of providential equity (and thus directly contradicting Grotius' theory), but ironically, for this very reason, it was also potentially problematic in Christian theological terms, since it could seem to cast doubt over the irrevocability of the Jewish commonwealth's destruction. Selden sidestepped the problem by only referring to the subjective Jewish hope for eventual restoration, without touching in any way on its actual feasibility. But it is perhaps not redundant here to point out the similarity of Selden's description of continuing Jewish hope and adherence to their laws, to the account he gave of the Norman conquest and the medieval intrusion of papal laws in England, as political upheavals which for a time discontinued the formal authority of the Common law, during which the stubborn persistence of the English people's love and attachment to their laws, resulted in these laws' eventual restoration.[60]

Thus, by around 1620 or thereabout, Selden had certainly become conversant with, and appreciative of, the Jewish legal tradition; indeed, he was to go on and achieve an extraordinary grasp of the languages and methodology of this tradition, and a collection of Jewish texts unsurpassed in his day.[61] It was however an unforeseen turn of events which presented him with the opportunity (and perhaps some of the drive) for turning this interest and these proficiencies into what would amount to the principal intellectual endeavor of his life.

5.5 THE "UNIVERSAL HEBREW DOCTRINE"

As a result of Selden's parliamentary activities he was imprisoned in March 1629 without charge or time limit. Initially held in the Tower and denied access to books or writing materials, by July he was eventually allowed to receive 19 numbered and signed sheets of paper on which to take notes, as well a small number of books which had to be individually identified. His choice fell on the Babylonian and Jerusalem Talmuds (as well as on a volume of works by the Hellenistic satirist Lucian of Samosata), comprising the main corpus of the Jewish legal tradition.[62]

---

[60] For Selden's position as directly contradicting Grotius' theory of natural law see Toomer, *Scholarship* pp. 490–491 note 8.

[61] Toomer shows Selden achieved a proficiency which enabled him to quote and translate passages from the Talmud and later commentators, for the most part accurately. This is especially impressive when one considers that the Hebrew of the Mishna and the medieval commentators, and the Aramaic of the Talmud, are quite different from those of the Bible and Targums, and that Selden acquired this knowledge without any known assistance from Jews or converts who might have been familiar with this material. See Toomer *Scholarship* pp. 442–445.

[62] See in Toomer *Scholarship* p. 804, about the still extant note written by Selden on 4 July 1629, while in prison, to Robert Cotton, requesting the latter to borrow for him the Talmud from the library of Westminster Cathedral.

It was in these circumstances that Selden came to plan a number of works on Jewish law. Although, from January 1630 on, the conditions of his imprisonment were gradually eased and he was successively transferred to more congenial surroundings, it was only in May 1631 that he was actually freed from imprisonment (and formally so only in 1635). Selden would later claim that it was while in prison that he formed the plan to embark on the massive study of Jewish law which was eventually to produce *De Successionibus in Bona Defuncti, seu Jure Haereditario ad Leges Ebraeorum* (1631), *De Successione in Pontificatum Ebraeorum* (1636), *De Jure Naturali et Gentium Juxta Disciplinam Ebraeorum* (1640), *De Anno Civili et Calendario Veteris Ecclesiae seu Republicae Judaicae Dissertatio* (1644), *Uxor Ebraica* (1646) and the *De Synedriis et Praefecturis Juridicis Veterum Ebraeorum* (3 vols. 1650–1655). Although it is unclear if he actually formed an exact plan to compose all of these books at this stage, he certainly started to compose some part of *De Synedriis* as well as *Pontificatum* and *Bona*, while imprisoned.[63]

On top of these entirely Hebraist works, one has to add a number of other works by Selden which are significantly indebted to his mature Jewish learning: the second edition of *Titles of Honor*, published in 1631, displays a vast increase in interest and knowledge of rabbinic matters as compared with the 1614 first edition, especially in the later sections of the book; while the *Mare Clausum* (1635) which Selden testified to extensively rewriting previous to publication, relies on rabbinic traditions for some of its crucial premises and arguments. Even the *Table-Talk*, a collection of his aphorisms posthumously published in 1689 by Richard Milward, a member of Selden's household in his later years, is replete with ideas, images and phrases that are evidently culled from Jewish sources – although Milward, as well as later successive editors of the work, lacking acquaintance with Jewish sources, completely failed to notice this aspect of it.[64]

---

[63] See *De Successionibus in Bona Defuncti, seu Jure Haereditario ad Leges Ebraeorum* (1631) in the "Prolegomena" pp. i-ii. For a letter from Sir Henry Bourgchier to Ussher, implying Selden had been working on the *Synedriis* as early as 1629, see Toomer *Scholarship* pp. 692–693. For a more general discussion of the times of conception and composition of the works, and Toomer's claim that Selden's memory later deceived him when he asserted that he had conceived the writing of the *Pontificatum*, the *Jure Naturali* and the *Uxor Ebraica* at the beginning of his imprisonment, see Toomer *Scholarship* pp. 447–448.

[64] Perhaps the greatly different account of the emergence of political societies in the second edition of TH, should also be ascribed to his greater reliance on Jewish sources, whereas the first edition owed more to classical Greek and Roman ones. The second edition account is also far more in line with the biblical version of the emergence of political society, as is the *Mare Clausum*. Toomer proposes that the later section of the 1631 edition, replete with digressions originating in rabbinical literature, was composed about 1629, when Selden was already engaged in writing his works on the Jewish tradition. See Toomer *Scholarship* p. 167.

It appears that the composition of *De Anno Civili* (1644) to a great extent resulted from the visit to England of J.S. Rittangl, sometime in early 1641, in an attempt to get financial support for printing a number of Karaite texts (among the attempts was the letter to Selden, quoted at the beginning of this chapter). Rittangl's attempts to print the texts in England failed, and by the end of the year he had already left the country. However, a number of Karaite texts he left with the

One may only speculate about the degree to which imprisonment reinforced an already extant tendency to express his controversial ideas on issues at the center of contemporary political debate, like legal authority, church and state, and political arrangements, within the framework of his learned dissertations on Jewish law. However, his choice of the Jewish tradition as the vehicle for his reflections was not merely incidental or instrumental, for all evidence points to Selden believing that he had found in the Jewish legal tradition an intellectual framework fitting and justifying his own ideas and propensities.[65]

It is quite evident that by this time he had built up a real regard for Jewish ideas and practices, one that was to grow with time and produce by his later years some assertions in esteem of the Jews, which were for their time and place quite unusual. One such example is a passage where Selden discussed Jewish communities practicing excommunication in the Diaspora for those whom their courts had found grave transgressors of the law, even though all was carried out wholly voluntarily, as those courts had no coercive authority with which to compel anyone to comply:

In any case we can say for certain that it was the Jews' good character, their modesty, and their desire to maintain a spotless reputation among their own people which generally motivated them to submit voluntarily to the traditional practice of excommunication even when they were living in foreign lands.[66]

It should be noted that Selden's improving attitude to the Jews and their ideas was not a mark of a general theological mellowing with the years, or of the adoption of some new principle of toleration, towards other religious positions. For, while his attitude towards the Jewish nation changed alongside his growing acquaintance with their ideas and traditions, Selden continued to articulate views that were quite harsh and even caustic against various religious positions that he opposed, and especially so towards Presbyterians, which he

---

young Cambridge scholar Ralph Cudworth were later employed by Selden in writing *Anno Civili* and *Uxor Ebraica*. Toomer *Scholarship* pp. 626–629.

    As for the *Table-Talk*, the extent of its reliance on Jewish learning will become evident in the new edition Professor Jason Rosenblatt is currently working on.

[65] For Selden's own theory of natural law being very much the same as what he describes as the Jewish view, see Toomer *Scholarship*, pp. 490–493.

    To a great extent, one might consider many of Selden's works treating the Jewish tradition as expanded commentaries on most of the Noahide precepts. The *Jure Naturali* is, of course, a comprehensive treatment of the precepts, and of their central premise – the existence of a universal and providential deity; The early *Diis Syriis*, discusses idolatry; *Mare Clausum* is to some extent a treatise on property, and directly pertinent to the precept against theft; *Uxor Ebraica* considers Jewish and non-Jewish law on marriage and sexual conduct; *De Synedriis* treats the supreme Jewish council, identified by Selden with the precept about courts of justice. Thus, two precepts only were not granted extensive treatment in a separate work, the prohibition on the shedding of blood, and the prohibition of cruelty to animals.

[66] *Synedriis* b1c7: "Sed proculdubio boni mores, pudor, atque inter suos existimationis integrae conservationis desiderium, saepe satis in causa erant, ut recepto Excommunicandi usui sponte alienis in terris se submitterent."

denounced increasingly and relentlessly in his later years. The same is true of his treatment of Islam, which through the years remained always censorious and even scornful, so that he did not shirk from describing Muslims quite disparagingly, as for the most part "apes of the Jews."[67]

By 1640, the year he published the *Jure Naturali*, Selden had already planned and partly written his two remaining major works on Jewish law, *Uxor Ebraica* and *Synedriis*. Thus, although Selden studied and published Hebrew ideas and texts for another 14 years, the *Jure Naturali* is in many ways the culmination of his Jewish learning, certainly so in the theoretical sphere. Accordingly, among Selden's many works on Jewish law and tradition, the one place where he presented most directly and cohesively his own theory of law and how it resembles the Jewish one, is undoubtedly the *Jure Naturali* – especially so book I, rightly defined by Toomer as the most "philosophical" of Selden's writings.[68]

The following passage from the *Jure Naturali* may well serve as epitome for Selden's mature outlook on the ideas of the Jewish tradition. After pointing out that many ideas and doctrines originating in pagan sources have been accepted, after due consideration, as compatible with Christianity, he asserted:

> In just the same way, this universal Hebrew doctrine contains (in accordance with the specific character, customs, abilities, and privileges of that nation) some elements that are more or less suited to Christianity, and others that are quite a bit different. But neither should be rejected or condemned solely on that account – in fact they should be welcomed with open arms, as a means of verifying or explaining a number of ideas already established in Christian thought.

This assessment of the Jewish ideas concerning universal obligations was applied by Selden to the whole of the Jewish tradition, stressing that even ideas deemed to conflict with Christian notions and values should at least be given a leading role in the open investigation of truth and falsehood, "just like the ideas of other philosophers (whether barbarian, Greek or Roman) who are no less frequently at odds with Christian doctrine."[69]

---

[67] See discussion in Toomer *Scholarship* p. 624.

[68] Toomer *Scholarship* pp. 560, 492–493. Toomer proposes that regardless of later claims, when in 1629 Selden embarked on his program of writing works on Jewish law, he did not have the *Jure Naturali* in mind. The first mention of the latter work was in the 1636 edition of *Bona*, where Selden referred to as a book he was is working on, about the Jews' theory about the law of nations. Thus, Toomer thinks that the idea for the *Jure Naturali* came to Selden around 1635, while preparing for publication the *Mare Clausum*, his first work where Grotius' *Jure Belli* is mentioned. This would make Grotius' theory, and Selden's attempt to refute it, a major motive behind the composing of the *Jure Naturali*. See Toomer *Scholarship* pp. 90–91.

[69] JN b1c2: "ita pariter Disciplina haec Ebraeis universalis, pro singulari gentis indole, more, genio, praerogativa, alia atque alia habet Christianismo plerunque consona, alia haud parum dissona, quorum nihilosecius neutra sunt adeo rejicienda contemnendave, quin aut pro receptarum aliquot in Christianismo sententiarum sive Confirmatione sive Explicatione sint meritissimo interdum recipienda, aut singularem saltem in libertima, tum Veritatis, tum Errorum

But in his treatment and understanding of the Jewish legal tradition, Selden went much further than the balanced and practical attitude indicated in the above passage. Through many of his comments about Hebraic ideas and traditions, it is clear that he regarded the Jewish tradition as not only another important intellectual tradition from which one could learn, but rather a tradition of ideas and practices that is very much pertinent for Christian political societies in general, and particularly so for England. This relevance of Jewish ideas to contemporary political ideas had for Selden several justifications, among them the very fact that the Jewish tradition was such a lengthy and rich one, as well as its being the wellspring for Christianity, but perhaps most of all, as we shall see, as a model of a successful legal and moral tradition combining universal values and particular national practices. In other words, Jewish ideas had several points of convergence and relevance with England as a Christian political society that was based on a robust common law tradition. One main aspect of this relevance, the issue of Religion (or Church) and State, will be treated separately and at length in the next chapter. Here I will only point out some additional examples of aspects of the Jewish tradition that Selden thought relevant to English society, and deserve future study.

In his *Anno Civili*, looking at the Jewish calendar and the differences in its reckoning rising from different approaches to biblical text, Selden terms the Jewish rabbinical sages "Masters of Tradition" (baalei hakabala) as against those of the Jewish Karaite school termed "Masters of Scripture" (baalei mikra). This distinction, which he touches upon also in the *Uxor*, is of course a real one, between the rabbinical traditionalist attitude, and the Karaite scripturalist one; however, in the context of seventeenth-century England, it is obvious Selden also made it impossible to miss the parallel between the two Jewish approaches, and the rift inside the English church, between Anglican traditionalists and the various scripturalist groups, be they Puritan, Presbyterian, Congregationalist or Sectaries, who wished to jettison traditional church practices based on their direct reading of the biblical text (sola scriptura). The limitations of the scripturalist approach are made evident by Selden, when he shows that, regardless of all their protestations when facing difficulties in the biblical text, the Karaites have no alternative but to recourse to interpretations and commentaries which end up creating what is no less a tradition than the rabbinical one. The inference to the case of the English church would be inescapable.[70]

---

disquisitione, ac contemplatione, sicut & reliquae philosophorum, sive Barbaricorum, sive Graecorum, sive Latinorum, sententiae aeque non raro Christianismo dissonae, locum qualem-cunque debeant sortiri."

[70] *Anno Civili* (1644), ch. 19, and see discussion in Toomer *Scholarship* pp. 631–632. Another apparent parallel to the English church, Selden's claim in book 2 of *Synedriis* that, although with periods of intermission, the Jewish Sanhedrin and lesser courts existed during most of the period from Moses to the destruction of the Second Temple, and more importantly, there was an

Another important parallel between the Jewish political tradition and the English, one that Selden saw as relevant, was the role of the Sanhedrin, the Jewish Assembly of Elders which he regarded as analogous in various aspects to the English Parliament. Although the Sanhedrin appears in several of Selden's works, it is treated by far most thoughtfully and extensively in *Synedriis* (1650–1655), the massive three-volume work, ultimately incomplete at his death, that Selden devoted to it. Selden's treatment of the Sanhedrin's role as a council that was supreme over both civil and religious matters will be discussed in the next chapter, but in *Synedriis* there were several additional aspects of the Jewish supreme council which Selden employed to make more or less direct inferences to the English case, among them: the confiscation of (and thus authority upon) property was not the King's sole right but involved the Sanhedrin also (book 2 chapter 13); the Sanhedrin instituted the Jewish kings and had the theoretical right to judge them (book 3 chapter 9); the consent of the Sanhedrin was necessary for the state to go to war (book 3 chapter 14).[71]

However, the most important aspect that Selden applied the Jewish legal tradition to, was addressing the issue of justification for customary legal systems. To begin with, he obviously deemed it as a national customary law ("the specific character, customs, abilities, and privileges of that nation"), and as such on a par with the customary laws of European nations – England, of course, included. Such is the effect of his description of the Talmud as a text which,

contains the ancestral and universally accepted teachings, interpretations and decisions of the Hebrews, just as we find Roman law in the digests, the codes, the *novellae*, and the Basilica; or French law in the edicts, constitutions, collections of customs and decisions of the French; or just as the same sources in Spain constitute the Spanish law, and in England the English law.[72]

However, the Jewish legal and political tradition also had some peculiar features that distinguished it from others and made it especially important in Selden's view. The first feature was its unusually lengthy continuity; for if one accepted (as Selden did) even the most modest claims Jewish tradition made about itself, that would mean it to be by far the oldest recorded case of an unbroken continuous national customary law. A second peculiar feature of the Jewish legal tradition was that it was explicitly based on a sacred law – the Pentateuch – that Christianity also deemed of divine origin. The implications of

unbroken succession of "ordination" of elders throughout the period – a direct parallel of the claim by the Anglican church to found its authority upon an unbroken succession of bishops from the time of the Apostles. See Toomer *Scholarship* p. 756.

[71] *Synedriis* b2c13; b3c9 and c14.

[72] JN Praefatio: "quae Ebraeorum de Jure Placita, Interpretationes, Sententiasque Receptas ac avitas fuse exhibent perinde ac Digesta, Codices, Novellae, Basilica, easquae fuere Romanorum; seu, ut Edicta, Constitutiones, Consuetudinum Corpora, ac Decisiones Gallicae, jus Gallicum, aut ejusmodi alia, in Hispaniis Hispanicum jus, in Anglia Anglicanum."

this feature were manifold, on the one hand offering a connection of customary law to divine principles and morality, on the other implying a possible (and problematic) conflict with Christian interpretations of that law. Selden would thread onto this path carefully, stressing repeatedly and explicitly that all his claims and conclusions were subject to the "authority of the Holy Scriptures themselves, and of true Christianity and the values contained within it."[73]

Selden believed that exactly because of these two unique features, its exceptionally lengthy continuity and its origin in a sacred law, the Jewish legal tradition, more than any other, had devoted great efforts over a longer time span and in a more systematic and self-conscious manner, to understanding the nature and scope of universal values, and their relationship with particular legal systems.[74]

As we have seen in preceding chapters, the theoretical justification of national customary laws, by their connection to universal values was a central concern of Selden's thought. He found in the Jewish tradition an example of a living, continuous national law, parallel to common law. However, his studies of the Jewish legal and political traditions brought him to the conclusion that he had found in it not merely another living system of national customary law based on universal principles, but the very theoretical framework which could underpin every such a system. It is to this theory that we now turn.

5.6 THE "CHAIN OF TRADITION"

To appreciate what Selden was looking for, we first have to clarify that there are two different ideas, in some aspects conflicting, about the benefit of tradition: one assigns to it an empirical function, the other an adaptive function. Although both functions find expression in habit, creating what Aristotle called "second nature," they bring it about in opposite ways. In the first, the function of customary law is to provide accumulated experience of success or failure of laws over time; in the second, the function of customary law is that of adapting legal stipulations to changing times and circumstances, and thus draws its authority from its being the law best fitting a particular society. At the most

[73] JN b1c2: "quam ipsa sacrarum literarum verique Christianismi morumque in illum receptorum ratio ac autoritas admiserit statueritve." See also in Praefatio. As already noted earlier in this chapter, regardless of his care in this respect, Selden was on various occasions accused, both directly and indirectly, of being suspiciously partial to the Jewish tradition. See, for example, *Opera Omnia* vol. 3 tome 2 cols. 1350–1352, and Rosenblatt *Renaissance* pp. 220–221.

[74] See JN b1c3, on the Hebrews as the only ones who deal with a whole universal natural law clearly and distinctly with a consistent effort in this direction and one that received common consent from all schools and groups in their society. See JN b1c2, on the validity of the Jewish traditions' chain of transmission from ancient times – also treated in the preface to *Bona* (1631), and in *Synedriis* book 2 (1653). See also *Uxor* b1c1, on the connection to sacred law, where Selden notes that the civil law of the Hebrews was "partly Sacred Law"' commanded in the Torah "and partly ancestral custom and sanctions added by those who were in charge of such matters."

basic level these two ideas are mutually exclusive. For while the adaptive function is all about change, the empirical function requires laws that do not change through time, otherwise much (or all) of the accumulated experience would be made obsolete when a change occurs. That is, to the empirical view, true laws are those which endure unchanged through all challenges, and their long continuance is the proof of their truth, so that they draw their authority from their alleged correspondence to eternal principles. The only way to overcome the mutual exclusivity of experience and adaptability is a model of traditional law that is far more dynamic and interactive, combining overall stability and continuity with specific instances of modifications and adjustments to varying circumstances.[75]

It is hard to find thinkers of any period who do not subscribe, at least to some extent, to the notion that empirical experience in legal and political matters is helpful. As we have seen, thinkers like Gentili and Grotius discussed empirical examples of laws from Roman and latter times in order to illustrate their ideas of natural law. But while such thinkers uphold the empirical function apparent in the survival of old laws, the adaptive function, if they touch upon it at all, is to them of merely technical and subordinate importance. Selden on his part, can be found to have agreed about the empirical importance of accumulated legal experience, but his own emphasis was firmly on the side of the changing and adaptive function of customary laws. Naturally, in many cases, and especially so in early-modern England, the argument for customary law combined to some degree both views (even if at times, self-contradictingly so). Indeed, it has been convincingly argued that a characteristic trait of Renaissance English thought was a widespread assumption of compatibility between the absolutes of a divinely ordered nature and the relativity of human affairs to circumstances of time and place. However, what was mostly lacking was a coherent theoretical underpinning for such an assumption. To be coherent, an argument upholding laws on both the empirical and adaptive justifications would have to find a system of law that is both changing and unchanging. The bridge by which to overcome that gap was convention or general consent as expressed in customary legal systems – so that they draw their force not from their antiquity, but from their widespread, uncalculated and continuous acceptance by the people, the same as happens with languages.

[75] To Aristotle, most laws were matters of convention and opinion rather than immutable truth, so the general assent and obedience to established laws, necessary for the stability and lasting of a form of government, are primarily due to *habit*, and since new laws lack this basis in habit, old laws are preferable. However, Stoic philosophy, and especially Cicero, modified Aristotelian thought in accordance with their preference for grounding laws in premises rather than habit, and developed an alternative rationale for preferring old laws: the accretion of experience. Longevity thus became a measure of the law's wisdom, for it has a greater weight of experience supporting it. In both cases it seems that old unchanged laws, whether justified by habit or by experience, are preferable, so that no change should be made in them through statutory improvement. The *adaptive* rationale for laws, being fitted to the circumstances and character of a people, seems not to fit with either of these; see Siegel "Aristotelian" pp. 40–42.

Intimations of what became Selden's idea of adaptation as the necessary means by which eternal truths are translated into the diversity and changes that are human affairs can be found in Aquinas, Calvin and probably most markedly among some historically minded thinkers closer to Selden's time, primarily in the ideas of Richard Hooker.[76]

Hooker proposed a theory of variations and adaptations according to circumstances, as marks of the history of the church as well as of its relationship with temporal power. He harmonized this theory with the Christian notion of eternal teachings of the Church, by developing the idea of "adiaphora" – things indifferent, to the core teaching of the church, and as such not binding on following generations. Thus he regarded many, perhaps most, of the Christian practices as contingent on time and place, and he moreover even stressed that most of the laws of Moses had been given to a specific people at a specific time – thus positing that God had an eye on the nature of that people and the land where they dwelt. For Hooker this means that elements like national character and geography are what define particular laws and their stipulations, even God-given ones. Indeed, for Hooker, the ever-changing nature of laws meant that in some circumstances even customs devised by heretics, for heretical purposes, might in time grow to be conveniently, even beneficially kept by Christians. Hooker's approach means adopting a probabilistic (rather than necessary) approach to most issues, which is naturally tending to leniency and toleration towards a degree of dissent within the Church. Moreover, he developed a concept of a National church, involving the whole population (aside from the few holding openly heretical opinions about the core Christian unchanging truths), and within which the civil authorities were responsible for church discipline, so that church and state become effectively coterminous.[77]

One particularly suggestive, if mostly overlooked, affinity between Hooker's and Selden's ideas is the former's unusual addressing of the Noahide precepts of the Jewish tradition, which became a central feature of the latter's scholarship. In the fourth volume of his *Laws*, Hooker claimed that the early church Council of Jerusalem, in decreeing the things which Christians of non-Jewish background were bound to observe, based itself primarily on the Jewish tradition of the seven precepts of the sons of Noah:

It was an opinion constantly received among the Jews, that God did deliver unto the sons of Noah seven precepts: namely, first, to live under some form of regiment under public laws; secondly, to serve and call upon the name of God; thirdly, to shun idolatry;

---

[76] See Ferguson *Clio* pp. 71–72, 198–199. On Hooker's rejection of *sola scriptura* in favor of basing church authority on continuity as a process of adaptation of each national church to changing circumstances (arguing that the Puritans, in their attempt to reinstate Mosaic law, forgot that these had been given to a particular people at a particular time) see Ferguson *Clio* pp. 210–214.

[77] Ferguson *Clio* pp. 213–218, and see discussion in the next chapter about Hooker's idea of church and state.

fourthly, not to suffer effusion of blood; fifthly, to abhor all unclean knowledge in the flesh; sixthly, to commit no rapine; seventhly, and finally, not to eat of any living creature whereof the blood was not first let out. If therefore the Gentiles would be exempt from the law of Moses, yet it might seem hard they should also cast off even those things positive which were observed before Moses, and which were not of the same kind with laws that were necessarily to cease. And peradventure hereupon the council saw it expedient to determine, that the Gentiles should, according unto the third, the seventh, and the fifth, of those precepts, abstain from things sacrificed unto idols, from strangled and blood, and from fornication. The rest the Gentiles did of their own accord observe, nature leading them thereto.[78]

Hooker's discussion in this passage raises several interesting issues, but for our purposes we should consider that the source for Selden's knowledge and interest in the issue of the Noahide precepts is today usually ascribed to his reading Grotius (which mentions them in his *Jure Belli*). Selden certainly knew Grotius' treatment of the issue, and in the *Jure Naturali* he also criticizes several theologians of his age (like Balducci and Genebrard) for misunderstanding the issue, while Hooker is not mentioned at all, for good or bad. Selden also mentions the Seder Olam, the Jewish source material for Hooker's knowledge about the Noahide precepts, but again without mentioning Hooker himself. Further study is necessary to establish if Selden simply missed Hooker's writings (which seems unlikely), or had other reasons for not mentioning him, in this context as well as several others in which their ideas concurred.

As we saw, Selden was thinking about this issue at least since his 1616 "Notes" to Fortescue's *Laudibus*, and he eventually found exactly what he was looking for in the Jewish traditions, both in the more circumscribed sphere of particular Jewish law (based on the unchanging Pentateuchal laws, but interpreted through an adaptive post-biblical tradition) and in the universal one of the Jewish concept of the Noahide precepts.[79]

It is important at this point to highlight that, for Selden, the principle of adaptation accounts for two different (though related) qualities of a living law: on the one hand, the inevitable changes wrought by time and circumstances; on the other the continuity, which made such law into a persistent entity throughout all its changes. This combination of change and persistence became an explicit and central component of his thought. Indeed, it appears

---

[78] Richard Hooker, *Of the Laws of Ecclesiastical Polity*, B. Hanbury ed. 3 vols. (1830) book 4, chapter xi, sec. 5–6. The source given by Hooker for this material is "lib. qui Seder Olam inscribitur" – A second-century CE rabbinical commentary on the Bible.

[79] See Ferguson *Clio* pp. 132–133, 207–208. Ferguson argues that the belief of Englishmen in this period in the accommodation between the eternal and the particular was for the most part lacking in preceding generations, and to a great extent was lost in successive ones – when the premise of some kind of compatibility between the two became prey to a growing predilection for more extreme visions of man and society as either completely relative and dynamic, or the newly fashioned rationalistic or scientific absolutes. See also Ferguson *Clio* pp. 62–63.

that for Selden the very authority of customary law derived exactly from this twofold quality of its adaptive character.[80]

We have seen above that already in his "Notes" on Fortescue's *Laudibus*, Selden indicated his adaptive understanding of customary law as growing with "additions and interpretations" except for the "meerly immutable part of nature." But, at that point in his career, he did not yet offer a theory that could explain how or why, throughout all changes, a connection with the universal and moral principles, the "immutable part of nature" could be sustained. Although he would develop his theory fully only in his *Jure Naturali*, he touched on it in a number of other works, for the most part in the context of Jewish learning. As early as the *Historie of Tithes* Selden already identified the Jewish tradition as the common law of the Jewish nation, also ascribing to it ideas touching on a theory of tradition and of its authority. He wrote that:

Touching their Tithing after the second Temple destroyed; although for want of a Temple and a Priesthood at this day, they Tithe not legally, yet among their Aphorismes both divine and morall, they tell us, that as the *Masoreth* is the defence of the Law, so מעשרות סיג לעשר *maighsheroth seag laighsher*, that is, *Tithes paid are the defence of riches.*[81]

This passage proposed that in the Jewish "Aphorismes both divine and morall" it is told that tradition ("*Masoreth*") is the "defence of the Law." The meaning of the statement is further elucidated by comparing it to the parallel comment following it, which asserts that "*Tithes paid are the defence of riches*": since the destruction of the temple there was no formal injunction on Israelites to pay tithes, but the Jewish tradition recommended continuing to pay them voluntarily, since they defend a man's property. The only meaning of this recommendation can be that there is some wider connection (practical or metaphysical, or both) between keeping the tradition of paying tithes and the security of men's property. The analogy with the former dictum is clear: there is a connection between upholding tradition and the security of the law.

Selden subsequently touched on this subject in various works and from different directions. In the *Mare Clausum*, for example, it is the underpinning implied by both the categories into which he divides the law (book 1, chapter 3), as well as the grounding of his treatment of divine law (both the imperative and permissive types) solely on Jewish traditions (book 1, chapter 6). Also in the *Mare Clausum*, one can find Selden returning to the image of persistence through change, when he illustrates that "those things which naturally are thus flitting, do notwithstanding in a Civil sens remain ever the same." In the

---

[80] See Ferguson *Clio* pp. 292–293, 296–297, 330–331.

[81] *Historie of Tithes* (1618) p. 455 – quoting Mishna, Tractate Avot 3:17. The same source is also quoted (using "Mesorah") in Petrus Cunaeus' 1617 *De Republica Hebraeorum*, see in the English translation – *The Hebrew Republic* (Jerusalem: Shalem Press, 2006) pp. 74, 234 (note 245).

Uxor Ebraica, Selden's treatment of the ideas of the literalist approach of the Karaites, reflects his view about the limitations of attempts to base social or political prospects, directly on scriptural terminology, without employing a doctrine of hereditary transmission of traditions. Later on in his *Synedriis*, Selden discusses at length, in the context of the Jewish oral law's "chain of tradition," the idea that law can remain continuous and consistent, despite great accretions and losses through the ages. In the same vein, his acceptance of the Jewish claim that despite some periods of break, the Jewish Sanhedrin existed almost continuously for all the period from Moses to the destruction of the Second Temple, and his stressing that there was an unbroken succession of "ordination" of elders, even in those periods when the Sanhedrin did not sit, is intended to show the unbroken transmission of Jewish traditions.[82]

It was however once again in his *Jure Naturali*, that Selden offered a direct, comprehensive and explicit treatment of the issue, which is in many ways at the heart of that work. He posited that, in effect, the Jewish tradition was the only place where such a "universal philosophy of morals" could be found since:

Nowhere else have the precepts of a nation, or the philosophy, theology and jurisprudence it practices, fixed and defined in such detail the provisions of law that is natural or understood by all mortals, and by general agreement so clearly distinguished it from other kinds of law that it could be made distinct like a single undifferentiated body whose name and function remain always the same, in both the authority it possesses and its control of the people.

That is, Selden held that the Jewish tradition had "fixed and defined" the provisions of a universal theory of moral law, the Noahide precepts, that was not merely intended to justify their own law and tradition, but that effectively offered a justification for all laws and traditions, as long as they did not transgress the basic moral principles.[83]

---

[82] MC b1c3, b1c6 and b1c21; *Uxor* b1c3, this aspect of the work is pointed out in J. Ziskind's "Introduction" pp. 21–22; see especially *Synedriis* b1c16, where Selden renders the Hebrew term "שרשרת הקבלה" as "Traditio illa catenata" discussed in Rosenblatt *Renaissance* pp. 218–219 and in note 39; and *Synedriis* b2 as a whole which gives the history of the Sanhedrin while emphasizing the unbroken transmission of traditions through the ordained elders, discussed in Toomer *Scholarship* p. 756. A similar idea appears in TT "Prayer" sec. 3 and "Tradition" sec. 1.

[83] JN b1c3. The phrase is "philosophia morum universalis" morum also implying a customary dimension. The whole Latin passage is: "Nullibi scilicet ex alius cujuspiam gentis instituto seu Philosophia seu Theologia, seu Jurisprudentia in ea recepta, certa haberi atque subtilius sic definita Juris Naturalis seu omnium mortalium communis Capita, ac seorsim a ceteris sic consensu publico distincta, ut ejusdem veluti Corpus Singulare, Simplex, & perpetuo sibi Simile tum Nomine tum Usu per se tam autoritate dignoscatur quam disciplina publica, & in publica rerum administratione sigillatim ac solum, atque eo nomine a ceteris disterminatum, adhibeatur."

Caruso shows that Selden held the Hebrew Bible to be the peculiar law of the Hebrews (resulting from the contract between God and the Israelites), in which the universal laws given by God to all men (the contracts with Adam and Noah) were only touched upon and not explicitly specified. It was only the exegetical work of the Jewish Talmudic sages, who by reading and

Selden explicitly confronted the two theoretical challenges that such an approach must face, if it is to endure. On the one hand, there was the danger of some simplistic identification of all customary law with moral and natural law; on the other hand was the danger of an attempt to create a natural and moral order which, because of its universality, would altogether jettison customary law.[84]

Selden confronted the first challenge directly, by drawing from Aristotle's notion (in the *Rhetoric*) of second nature, but directing it towards whole nations rather than individuals:

Habit quite often wears the mask of nature, and we are deceived to the point where practices adopted by nations, based solely on custom, frequently come to seem like natural and universal laws of mankind.

In other words, a customary order certainly can deceive as to its universal import, and, although as "custom" it is necessarily adapted to a society or several societies, it might nevertheless contradict the "law of mankind." Implied in Selden's observation is that national law, on top of being adapted to a people, must also conform to some universal moral standards that are relevant to all "mankind."[85]

From this consideration, Selden proceeded to raise the question that all those who studied customary laws, whether they supported or opposed them, had to address:

Let us grant that in ancient times there existed, and there continue to exist, some customs practiced in the same way by all the nations, or by the more familiar or civilized ones, for example in contracts, inheritance, marriage, trials, treaties, and commerce – could customs of this sort ever acquire the force of natural or universal law, and the power to obligate or permit (without which it is pointless to talk about laws at all)?[86]

---

rereading the text, succeeded in reconstructing those universal laws, deriving from it the seven Noahide precepts. In Selden's method – differently from the strict rationalistic derivation of Grotian natural law – philosophy, revelation and history concurred, together and with the help of certain experts such as are the Talmudic sages, in the discovering of the natural law as reasonably inferred ("*abdotti*") rather than logically deduced. See Caruso *Miglior* pp. 684–685.

[84] A prominent critic of customary English law was Thomas Hobbes, who regarded common law as totally divorced from considerations of real equity and justice, arguing, for example, that to justify a man being condemned to death for theft of wood worth a few shillings, the common lawyer could only answer that this had been practiced time out of mind. See discussion in Mosse *Struggle* pp. 177–178.

[85] JN b1c6: "*Nam simulat consuetudo Naturam. Vicinum scilicet est id, quod sape fir, ei quod-semper & Natura quidem ejus est quod semper, consuetudo ejus quod sepe fit.*" – this is Selden's Latin rendition of Aristotle's *Rhetoric* 1370a5–8.

[86] JN b1c6: "*Detur uniformes e seculis priscis fuisse, atque etiamnum esse Gentium, sive Omnium sive Cognitarum, sive Moratiorum pariter mores aliquot, veluti in Contractibus, Successionibus, Conjugiis, Judiciis, Federibus, Commerciis. Anne inde Juris Naturalis seu Universalis vim, atque Obligationis & Permissionis effectum (citra quem frustra de Jure aliquo loquimur) fortiri omnino possent ejusmodi mores?*"

Selden's answer to this question was negative. He proposed that even if one did identify some customs common to all humanity, this universal identification had nothing to do with law – because for humans, law is "the power to obligate or permit." Thus, even if it was found, for example, that nowhere in the world did laws and customs ever sanction marriage between two males, or that nowhere was there human flesh offered for sale in the marketplace, how would such a realization, by itself restrain in any way a society, or even individuals within it, from overturning this seemingly universal and natural law?[87]

This consideration enabled Selden to address the second challenge facing a justification of customary law. The above quote already implied, that searching for *binding* moral and legal principles by means of what we would today call comparative law research, was ultimately futile. However, as we may recall, Selden went further, also explicitly connecting this realization with his additional rejection of claims made for drawing universal laws from reason:

In fact, reason sole and simple, can persuade and demonstrate, but it cannot command or obligate us to perform our duties, unless it possesses an authority superior to the one who is being commanded.[88]

Selden thus rejected both pillars upon which the "modern" natural rights theorists like Grotius were attempting to construct a binding system of universal or natural laws – a justification of natural rights by means of reason only, and a parallel, comparative research of laws, aimed at extracting from them the principles of the natural law observed by all nations. He argued that the Jewish legal tradition had identified this fallacy, and after reviewing the arguments on both sides, he observed that:

[W]e might perhaps be justified in concluding that the Hebrews were quite right to take no account of the behavior and institutions of any, or most nations in their definition of natural law.[89]

---

[87] JN b7c3. Selden brings a Talmudic passage and Rashi's commentary on it, in which the claim is made that there are only three commandments which all the sons of Noah actually observe: they do not draw up a marriage contact for males, they do not bring the flesh of the dead to the market, they show honor to the Tora. These are public aspects of the three most abhorrent sins in the Talmudical tradition: Idolatry, murder and forbidden sexual relations. In his discussion of the passage Selden shows he clearly understands the passage's point that the nations of the world keep these commandments only in public, therefore implying they do not necessarily do so in private. See discussion in Rosenblatt *Renaissance* pp. 240–241.

[88] JN b1c7: "Quin Ratio, quatenus talis solum & simplex, suadet & demonstrat, non jubet aut ad officium, nisi superioris eo, qui iubetur, accedat simul autoritas, obligat." Hobbes expressed a similar argument in his *De Cive* (1642) chapter 14, section 2. Since Hobbes completed his book in 1641, he could certainly have seen the argument in Selden's book, published a year earlier, but there is no indication that he actually did.

[89] JN b1c6: "non imprudenter factum merito forsan dixeris ab Ebraeis, dum in Juris Naturalis designatione, Omniun seu Plurium Gentium morum seu institutirum rationem habent nullam."

Having thus shown to his own satisfaction how the Jewish legal tradition rejected claims for a natural or universal law founded on either unassisted reason or comparative law, Selden then proceeded to propose that the same tradition also supplied a unique approach to combining universal and particular, successfully overcoming the failings of other theoretical methods – an approach which started with the principle of authority, and defined by it what natural and national law was.

Early on in the *Jure Naturali*, Selden addressed this issue thus:

> Before we proceed to the specific provisions of this natural law, I would like the reader to have a proper understanding of just what the Hebrews thought it was, along with the duties shared by every person, by means of a general discussion of these issues. I would also like to avoid the problems that occur whenever people try on their own to distinguish this law, this philosophy and these duties from the Mosaic, or Pentateuchal law.[90]

We have already mentioned that Selden believed the Hebrew tradition identified two essential principles, from which the whole Jewish theory of law proceeded. The first principle was an anthropological claim, to the effect that all men and societies assume there is a principle that might be termed, of metaphysical equity, or in his words, "a belief that there is a God, and he dispenses recompense." Selden stressed that not only in Judaism, Christianity and Islam, but also among the Greeks, Romans and other pagans, there always is a deity (or many in the pagan case) punishing "the violation of the duties and laws that we are bound or obliged to observe." This equity principle enforced the keeping of obligations, which is Selden's second essential principle, in effect the fundamental natural law, or rather a meta-law, since it is the prerequisite for the existence of any coherent legal, social and political system. As already discussed, to a great extent, it could be said that for Selden the keeping of obligations is the *only* natural law, in the strict sense – all men and societies expected to understand and accept it.[91]

Now, allowing for Selden's theory of obligation does not by itself advance us in any way towards identifying particular stipulations of universal moral principles, other than the keeping of one's obligations. Moreover, while Selden certainly thought such moral principles did exist, and indeed had been identified by the Jewish tradition, he nevertheless had to explain why these were

---

[90] JN b1c3: "Ut qualenam Jus illud Naturale ac qualia Officia hominum omnium communia seu Philosophia Morum universalis, quam intelligunt heic Ebraei, fuerit, generali consideratione, antequam ad singularia Capita devenimus, rite capiatur, nec difficultas, qua implicari necesse est quotquot suo Marte Jus hoc, Philosophiam, atque Officia e corpore Juris Mosaici seu Pentateucho secernere contendunt, praetermittatur[.]"

[91] JN b1c4: "Etenim non solum in Christianismo, Judaismo, & Mahumedismo, verum atiam in Theologia, ac Jure Graecorum & Romanorum veterum, (apud quos scilicet viguit illud de Obligatione Naturali,) aliarumque fere gentium, seu in Paganismo, & Numen esse sive Unicum sive Plura, & Numinis vindictam Officii, Jurisque necessario, seu ex vinculo, aut obligatione observandi violationem consequi, id est, Deum esse & remuneratorem, credebatur." See also JN b1c8.

not to be found (at least not obviously so), in the one place where we would expect them to appear, the most moral and Jewish of books, the Hebrew Bible. Selden allowed that the Hebrew Bible, and especially the Pentateuch, as the oldest and most extensive record of divinely sanctioned rules, was an obvious place where one would look for stipulations of the universal law. However, for Selden, the Mosaic corpus was first and foremost a body of laws given to and applicable to the Hebrews only. Thus, as he pointed out, like all particular legal codes that are morally just, the biblical legal code, integrated with the laws particular to the Jews (like the Sabbath) also "the natural or moral laws and duties that are forever binding not just for the Hebrews, but for all humanity." Simply put, the problem was therefore the "separating out the natural law from an integrated code of both natural and civil legislation" in order to isolate only those laws "that are universally binding." This difficulty was patently proved for Selden by the failure of so many later attempts to identify the universal laws contained in the biblical account, such as the claims of some Christians of his own time, that the Decalogue itself was the Universal law – a claim which Selden rejected completely, regarding the Decalogue as the centerpiece only of the Mosaic law, explicitly given solely to the Hebrew nation.[92]

Selden explicitly refused facile equations between the biblical law, or even the Decalogue, and the natural law, instead regarding biblical legislation as merely the laws divinely ordained for the Jews particularly, and as such, like every just and moral legal system, inextricably combining both universal moral principles and particular stipulations binding one nation only. He stressed the difficulties of

finding the best way out of the maze, separating things that are tangled together, navigating the twists and turns that separate truth from falsehood, and drawing conclusions from the external appearances of an idea as to the foundations or principles that lie beneath – such things are very difficult to achieve, almost beyond our grasp, and within the abilities of very few mortals.

He pointed out how so many great men in all philosophical schools, both ancient and modern, had failed over the years in the task of individuating the natural law. He pointed out that the problem of these men, for all their great abilities, was that they had worked with the "ragged scraps of overly disputed

---

[92] JN b1c3: "etiam & Naturalia seu Moralia Jura seu Officia non magis ipsis quam Hominum universitati perpetuo observanda. . .Id quod in quaestione, de Jure Naturali ex Civili aliquo simul & Naturalis Juris corpore secernendo, jam memorata inprimis etiam obtinet." Sir Edward Coke was among those who described the Decalogue as the basis for the "law of God," a phrase used vaguely and supposed to have some kind of vague relationship to the law of nature, so that it could be useful as an appeal against the king's power. See Mosse *Struggle* pp. 149–150. Selden vehemently rejected claims that there is in Jewish law an obligation upon gentiles not dwelling among Israelites to keep the Sabbath, and described as "ravings" allegations by contemporary anti-Jewish writers that Jews believe gentiles suffer in Hell for not keeping the Sabbath. See Toomer *Scholarship* p. 522.

ideas" and approached the problem either alone or at most according to some specific school and doctrine, but received assistance neither from the theologians or the philosophers of their own school of thought, to say nothing of those trained in another doctrine. The result was that nothing even approaching an agreement was ever reached on the issue of natural law, either among whole nations or among schools of thought, indeed not even among single important thinkers – with the one exception of the legal tradition of the Jewish nation.[93]

Selden described how the Jewish tradition long held that beyond the Mosaic precepts and the teaching of the Old Testament that were "their special heritage" there were also in the Bible some "precepts of law and custom, which had their beginnings before there was writing or even letters, let alone Moses," and that all men "were obligated to observe only these precepts." He reported that, acting on this premise, Jewish scholars and jurists had over the years labored to individuate and describe these precepts, as separate from the Mosaic law, eventually identifying them as the seven Noahide precepts.[94]

Selden asserted that the unusual diligence, cohesion and continuity (and probably, it is implied, a measure of providential assistance invited by this very industry) of the efforts by the scholars of the Jewish nation to detect and define the universal laws from within the biblical corpus, eventually resulted in their overcoming the great obstacles before them. It was precisely through its being such a cohesive and continuous national tradition that Jewish customary legal thought alone had achieved such a feat, which was "within the abilities of very few mortals."[95]

The Jewish tradition identified this corpus of laws commanded by God "upon the human race," and called it Mizvot bnei Noah (Selden renders the term in Hebrew characters) – "the precepts or laws of the children or descendants of Noah," seven basic and general rules, six of them setting out prohibitions on idolatry, blasphemy, murder, forbidden sexual relations, theft and eating limbs from a still living animal, while the seventh commands the establishing of a judicial system. These rules were obligatory on all men, and consequently any laws contradicting them were to be regarded as void, societies contravening them beyond the pale.[96]

In Selden's rendition, the Jewish theory of natural law as distinct from the Mosaic law, is a natural law consisting of two components: an "imperative" binding universal basis comprising one primary principle of keeping

---

[93] JN b1c3: "Atque aliis in rebus discernendis simile non raro accidit. Perplexa rite extricare, Confusa invicem distinguere, Veri ac Falsi confinia, horumque sinuosos anfractus satis habere exploratos, & demum ex eis, quae superstruuntur, de Fundamentis seu Principiis recte conjicere, res est perquam ardua, paene inaccessa, & mortalium paucissimorum."

[94] JN b1c1. See S. Caruso's pertinent and insightful comments on Selden's view that in the Talmud he found an explicit and intentional effort to determine and clarify universal legal principles. Caruso *Miglior* pp. 696–697.

[95] JN b1c3. [96] JN Praefatio. See also JN b1c10.

obligations, as well as seven general moral precepts; upon this basis there is a "permissive" or "limited" structure of particular laws, by which each nation then erected its own peculiar legal system. This two-tier edifice, supplied for Selden, the justification for particular and national legal systems – stemming from the obvious inability of basic principles to serve by themselves as a system of law, thus requiring national laws as particular stipulations fitting circumstances and necessities (also implying that abstract non-particular systems of law, were therefore devoid of authority). In his own time, such particular legal systems tended to be in many cases traditional ones, but this was certainly not a necessary prerequisite, for particular laws were legitimate even when not traditional, as long as they did not transgress the basic obligatory principles. However, Selden did believe that traditional legal systems had an advantage over other types, an advantage that we could term as the empirical function of long-lasting systems, and one connected with the fact that indeed, only the Jewish legal system, performing traditionally over a long time, rather than any rational or even inspired individual or group, had successfully recovered the Noahide precepts for all humanity. Selden did not claim the Noahide principles had been given to the Jewish nation as revelation and by it preserved since in pristine form, for the Jewish people had received as direct revelation only the law particular to their nation, the laws of Moses, within which the Noahide precepts were not immediately and distinctly apparent, any more than within English or Roman law. Rather, for Selden the Noahide precepts had been revealed not only to the Hebrews but to all humanity (twice, first to Adam and then to Noah); however, since that time they had been transmitted to posterity by traditions, so that all human societies that were not totally depraved, preserved, although unaware of it, some version or remnant of the original principles. But, if this was the case, and almost every society preserved some version or remnant of the Noahide dispensation, what if any was the special advantage of the Jewish teachings on this matter? Selden allowed that the Jewish nation indeed had the benefit of an unusually large number of inspired individuals within it, but such individuals also existed in other nations, and anyway the vagaries of history meant that the activities and records of inspired men were many times disrupted. Thus, for Selden the principal advantage of Jewish tradition in this respect was another – the unusually continuous and concerted efforts invested by the sages of the Jewish nation, for generations upon generations, in striving to uncover, record and preserve the basic universal principles. In other words, it was first and foremost the Jewish tradition of inquiry, discussion and preservation, which had succeeded in the task in which so many others, including even some of the greatest men who ever lived, had failed – identifying and framing a coherent and accepted set of universal laws. Though certainly aided by their receiving of their own national law by direct divine revelation, and by the unusual numbers of inspired individuals among them, it was, after all, the humanely inspired and practiced traditions of the Jewish nation which, with unique longevity and persistence, exclusively achieved the feat of identifying the provisions of the universal laws of mankind.[97]

Selden proposed that the best shot to be had at identifying universal principles was indeed that labeled by the Hebrew juridical-politic tradition as the Noahide precepts. However, in his view, this identification was not made by the Jewish tradition recording some exact revelation about these principles – that would entail accepting this and other non-biblical Jewish traditions as revelation. Rather the Jewish tradition succeeded in this task specifically because it was such a prolonged and continuous human tradition, which nevertheless was intentionally aimed at recovering and considering traces of providential light, within an acknowledged source of revelation (the Bible). In other words, not the data but the method and approach of the Jewish traditional learning were the decisive elements in this success. Instructively, in describing and analyzing the Noahide principles, Selden never adopted towards them an attitude of unquestionable certainty affected by many writers on such matters. Advocating the principles identified by the Hebrews instead on a combination of high credibility with desirability, his analysis always retained a probabilistic aspect, which assumes future validation by further experience.[98]

Selden's theory of the Noahide precepts as universal foundations of law, meant that all particular laws were to be regarded as equally "natural" (to be kept because of the principle of obligation) as long as they did not contravene the seven general rules. Thus, according to Selden, the laws of pretty much every nation were a mixture of the universal Noahide precepts and particular laws, "mashed into an indistinguishable pulp" in which no mere human being could simply distinguish one from the other, just as was the case of the Mosaic laws to the Hebrews:

[T]he written law was itself partly a reiteration of these [Noahide] precepts, and partly an additional set of laws – those that were particular to the Hebrews – which were added on top of them.[99]

Thus, for Selden, as long as they did not contravene the universal precepts, all national laws consisted of a small core of law common to all humans, on which each nation's system of law added a superstructure of laws particular to it. The universal precepts were: the basic rule of keeping obligations, the only law that was properly speaking natural (since all societies had to uphold it in order

[97] JN b1c3.
[98] For the discussion of the active intellect see JN b1c 9; on the Noahide principles see especially JN b1c10 and MC b1c6–7; on the advantages of Jewish tradition see JN b1c3.
   On the debate in scholarship, about the manner of the principles being retrieved by Jewish tradition according to Selden, see Sommerville "Nature" pp. 439–440; Tuck *Philosophy* pp. 215–216; Tuck *Rights* pp. 117–118.
[99] JN b1c6 and JN b1c3 "ita ut legis scriptae datio partim esset horum iteratio, partim ceterorum, quae ipsis propria, accessio & superstructio."

to exist); and the seven Noahide precepts, which Selden preferred to describe as universal rather than natural, since they obligated all men, but were not innately known.[100]

Now, in this scheme, any law or system of laws that did not conflict with the universal principles, was clearly legitimate and binding – however arrived at. Nevertheless, as seen above, Selden maintained that customary law was vastly preferable to other types of legal systems. He offered two reasons for this, broadly connected with what have been described as the empirical and adaptive aspects of customary law. The first had very much to do with the success of the Jewish tradition in identifying the Noahide precepts, that has been already been discussed above – what can be termed as the empirical function of a long-lasting customary law, and an evidently successful one at that. He explicitly made the connection between the "very great esteem that that philosophy and law of the Hebrews" were deserving of, and the fact that they had survived for such a long time. Indeed, the "philosophy or law of the Hebrews," as the only surviving part of the wisdom of the ancient east (from which the Greeks and the west had learned), was to be assumed also to be the best part of that wisdom:

[I]t would seem that anyone who considers the matter carefully cannot, for the same reasons, help but place the highest possible value on this philosophy or law of the Hebrews as being the best part and sole survivor of a great treasure, i.e. of the sum total of the barbarian philosophies of the East.

One could even say that with this passage, and others like it, Selden in a way inverted the theological Christian notion of testimony, so that the continuing existence of the Jews, notwithstanding all their plights, does not testify to their failure to accept the new divine law, but rather to their success in keeping the old one.[101]

Selden's second rationale for preferring customary law over other systems had to do with its adaptive function. Selden clearly assumed, throughout his works, a division of humanity into nations, and customary law as the standard legal setting for each nation. But in *Jure Naturali* he added to these assumptions

[100] This theory, perhaps most evident in JN b1c7–8, also appears explicitly in *Mare Clausum* b1c7, as well as *Synedriis* b1c4, where he notes that concerning things and actions left to human decision "a free faculty is permitted by God for introducing and enacting other laws besides (provided they do not oppose the chapters of the obligatory divine law). Thus from that permissive divine law, or liberty, conceded or left to men by God, throughout the period now dealt with as always, a faculty existed, as was said before, of introducing additional human laws. Indeed, it was this way [to provide] for the variety of kinds and practices of societies and civil bodies into which men would form themselves." See in Roslak *Selden* p. 30 – the translation into English is Roslak's.

[101] JN b1c2: "Cum, inquam, haec ita se habeant, fieri arbitror non posse, quin recte intuenti summo etiam ex hac ratione habenda fuerit in pretio Philosophia illa, seu Jus Ebraeorum, velut thesauri ingentis, id est, totius ferme Philosiphiae in Oriente Barbaricae, pars optima solum superstes." See also b1c1.

a more ambitious postulation; one to be found implied in almost all that he ever wrote, but best presented in this work: that national law was, to a great extent, what a nation was about. Selden treated the "Hebrews" as a continuous entity, existing from biblical times to his own, with its particular national customary law. He preempted possible claims about Jewish traditions and texts being arbitrary and spurious later inventions by pointing out the manner in which their legal corpus is constructed, as a layered structure of continuous transmission and constant debate:

But if anyone should have his doubts as to whether the Talmud and its writers are sufficiently accurate in their discussion of these sorts of issues; whether, that is, what the Talmud hands down to us bears any resemblance at all to the laws that the ancient Hebrews knew and used, let him rest assured that the text of the Talmud as we now have it, and the other authors who commented on it, come from the time right after the destruction of the Temple and the city. On this you may consult above all the authors who carefully and painstakingly transcribed the text of the Mishna and the Gemara.

Indeed, Selden added, before doubting the reliability of the Jewish legal corpus, one should doubt Justinian's laws or the accounts about many of the early Fathers of the Church, relying as these do on reports about texts from hundreds of years ago, which many times lack any outside corroboration.[102]

However, as already mentioned, there was one additional and very unusual feature about the Jewish customary law: it had developed and survived almost wholly without the usual political or even territorial attributes of nations. The Mishna, Talmud and latter commentaries came from times when the Hebrews did not have an independent state, most of them from when they had been exiled and dispersed. If the corpus of customary Jewish law, the most significant element uniting the Jews in their exile and dispersion, was to be viewed as a national one – as Selden evidently did – it then necessarily became, in itself, pretty much what made and preserved that people as a nation. It is in this sense that the Jewish tradition became the supreme example for those wanting to uphold the merits of adaptive customary law; for in this case, not only had the law been adapted to the nation, but at the very same time it could also be said that the nation itself had become adapted to its law; indeed, to a great extent became defined by it.

---

[102] JN b1c2: "Si cui vero heic dubium forsan occurat, utrum Corpori & Scriptoribus Talmudicis hujusmodi in rebus quatenus historicae sunt, id est, quatenus in eis pro Jure qualicunque Ebraeis veteribus recognito arquensitaro traduntur, fides sit habenda, eo scilicet quod Corpus illud, qua jam habetur contextum, scriptoresque illi ceteri secolurum sunt Templi Urbisque excidio recentiorum (qua de re consulas autores imprimis, qui de Misnarum & Gemararum conscriptione diligentius, & data opera egerunt)[.]" On Selden viewing the Talmud as a venerable ethical–legal tradition, especially interesting in its being structured as continuous layers of comments upon comments on the law, making it structurally similar to the common law, see Caruso *Miglior* pp. 696–697.

The consequence of Selden's approach to Jewish tradition, for his defense of customary law in general, and of English common law in particular, is obvious. It professed to show that a particular customary legal and political tradition could be on the one hand founded on universal moral principles, while on the other hand at the same time it also could fit the specific needs and circumstances of a particular nation. It also points to the crucial role played by national identity in generating continuity and adaptation, rather than change simply bringing about the break-up and dissolution of a system. Moreover, by the resultant condemnation of legal systems based only upon universalist premises and practices as tending to political despotism, Selden was implying that national legal traditions as the Jewish or the English ones, were the best – perhaps the only – path by which to establish and preserve liberty.

The allure of such an approach to someone like Selden, who throughout his career endeavored to defend the English tradition in law and politics, who argued that these traditions persisted through the ages even against the onslaught of the Norman conquest, and who chose "Liberty above all" as his own personal motto inscribed on many of the books he owned – is unmistakable. It is perhaps most apparent in Selden's discussing in *Jure Naturali* the Jewish attitude to slavery, where he pointed out that the Hebrews regarded themselves (unlike other peoples) as being only subject to extrinsic servitude – the loss of civil rights – but never to essential slavery, entailing that one becomes the real and actual property of someone else. Obviously the Jews *were* repeatedly placed in actual bondage during their long history, most famously so in Egypt, so that a belief in their persisting liberty must consist of their refusal to recognize subjection to any human power, acknowledging instead their essential subjection only to their God, and of their concurrent keeping of their national law as mark of this liberty, even when in captivity. Selden indeed proposed this outlook as explanation for the reaction of the Jews who, when Jesus declared "the truth shall set you free" (John 8:32–33) – replied: "We be Abraham's seed, and were never in bondage to any man."[103]

---

[103] JN b6c14, and see discussion in Toomer *Scholarship* p. 552.

A "Single Sword": Selden's Theory of Religion and State

6.1 ERASTIAN, ANTI-CLERICAL, CYNIC – OR DEFENDER OF THE CHURCH?

It is not surprising that, as the leading common lawyer of his generation, a prominent parliamentarian as well as an eminent scholar, reputed the greatest of English Hebraists, Selden's views on religion and state (nowadays more often referred to as "church and state")[1] elicited considerable interest, both in his own time and in later scholarship. This is true of his writings, like the *Historie of Tithes* and *Synedriis*, which addressed contentious issues of church powers, and even more so of his participation in the unprecedented public debates and deliberations about the future of the English church, during the 1640s and 1650s. This chapter will show that Selden had a not inconsiderable influence on the eventual settlement of the established Church of England, and that modern scholarship has for the most part misinterpreted his views on religion and state, as well as the crucial role played those views by his interpretation of the Jewish tradition.

Regardless of his significance in the debate on religion and state in seventeenth century England (or, more probably, because of it), there are widely discordant accounts of Selden's views on this issue. This discord was already evident among Selden's contemporaries. Some of them, especially following his controversial *Historie of Tithes* (1618) regarded him as an inveterate enemy of the established church, or, in the words of Richard

---

[1] The term "church and state," prevalent in English political language from the early nineteenth century following Thomas Jefferson's call for a wall of separation between church and state, replaced the earlier term, "religion and state," common in Selden's day for describing such matters, as it appears, for example, in the extended title of the 1689 *Table-Talk: Being the Discourses of John Selden, Esq; or his Sence of Various Matters of Weight and High Consequence Relating Especially to Religion and State.*

Montagu (1577–1641), Chaplain to James I and later Bishop successively of Chichester and Norwich, in his 1621 *Diatribae* against the *Historie of Tithes*:

[T]he most pernicious underminer of the Church, and of Religion in the Church, that the Prince of darkness hath seth on worke to do mischief many yeeres.[2]

But such characterizations were by no means universal, even among the higher clergy of the established church. Selden was certainly regarded as sympathetic to religion and to the established church by many prominent clergymen, including James Ussher, Archbishop of Armagh and Primate of All Ireland as well as William Laud, Archbishop of Canterbury and Primate of All England.

Among contemporaries of Presbyterian persuasion, such as the prominent English divine Richard Baxter, and the influential Scottish divine Robert Baillie, Selden's views on religion were usually described (and as often decried) as eminently "Erastian." Baxter mentioned Selden among the House of Commons' "Episcopal *Erastians*" who thought episcopacy lawful since the sovereign power may "appoint *Church Government* as he please;" while Baillie, leader of the Scottish clerical commissioners in the Westminster Assembly, most famously characterized Selden as:

This man is the head of the Erastians; his glory is most in the Jewish learning; he avows everywhere that the Jewish state and church was all one, and that so in England it must be, that the parliament is the church[3]

This particular description appears in virtually all studies of Selden's position on religion and state, quoted among others by Cromartie, Rosenblatt, Kaplan, Trevor-Roper and Christianson – but curiously, it is nowadays usually interpreted to mean the very reverse of what Baillie intended. Baillie's passage plainly claims that Selden opposed a separation of church and state, such as was proposed by the Presbyterians of his day, that would assign the church an authority as independent in spiritual matters, as Parliament had in secular matters – instead regarding Parliament as having the final word in both spiritual and secular matters. Virtually all modern readings of the passage, deduce Selden's view thus described to be a simple, very much Hobbesian, assertion of the supremacy of secular authority over spiritual matters. However, Baillie's words about Selden holding that state and church are "all one" and that "parliament is the church" actually indicate a view that is quite distant from a simple assertion of secular superiority, instead pointing to an

---

[2] See discussion in Sommerville *Royalists* pp. 203–204. Montagu was reacting to Selden's claim in the *Historie of Tithes* that the church had always been subject to the civil jurisdiction of the state, and to the implication of this regarding divine-right tithes.

[3] See Richard Baxter, *A Third Defence of the Cause of Peace* (1681) pp. 60–61, 112–113; Robert Baillie, *The Letters and Journals of Robert Baillie, A.M., Principal of the University of Glasgow, 1637–1662* ed. D. Laing, vol. 2 (Edinburgh, 1841) pp. 265–66. For Baxter's and Baillie's views of Selden see also Johnson *Memoirs* pp. 290–291.

assumption that spiritual interests and ideas inherently permeate all political considerations and deliberations – one that would be nothing short of an abomination to Hobbes. This chapter will show that Baillie's comment in fact correctly captured the essence of Selden's ideas on religion and state, and that it is the modern readings that have misinterpreted them.

It appears that an unfortunate combination of hopelessly confused terminology with misguided attempts to associate Selden with certain political or ideological groupings is at the heart of the prevalent misreading of what is meant by his so-called "Erastianism" as well as by his view of church and state being "all one." Selden's views in religion and state are described by some as those of a principled anti-clerical, whose supreme goal was to curb the spiritual claims of the clergy; others depict him as primarily a pragmatist, without dogmatic prejudice about the particulars of the church and state settlement, as long as it worked; still others see him as a cynic on religious matters, concerned only with ensuring the supremacy of the state over religion. This divergence is, if anything, compounded by the frequent employment of terms used by Selden's contemporaries, such as Arminian or Erastian, to describe his views. The problem with such terms is that, on top of inadequately capturing Selden's own position, they are, more often than not, used imprecisely, thus only adding to the confusion.

R. Tuck, probably the one scholar most responsible for sparking the renewed interest in Selden's ideas in the last generation, claims that at least since the *Historie of Tithes* "Selden had been concerned with the threat to free enquiry and the secular way of life posed by an organized and powerful church." The result, according to Tuck, was that Selden, throughout his adult life, "campaigned against ecclesiastical power," an approach that was allegedly epitomized by his comments in the *Table-Talk* favoring state supremacy. Indeed, Tuck sees evidence of increasing radicalism on this issue, over the years, on Selden's part.[4]

However, on closer scrutiny, the picture drawn by Tuck is problematic. For one thing, Selden's own harassment in the wake of the *Historie of Tithes* had actually been carried out by the civil magistrate (in fact, the supreme one, James I), not the ecclesiastical authorities; and Selden would have certainly understood that curtailing clerical authority would do nothing to prevent a similar outcome in the future. Moreover, the list compiled by Selden, of individuals having been persecuted by clergy, to which Tuck and others point as proof of his anti-clericalism, actually consists of individuals who had all suffered under Catholic persecution, and would surely have been interpreted by contemporary readers primarily in an anti-Catholic context, rather as a general anti-clerical indictment that included the Protestant clergy. Indeed, as we have seen, in the 1620s and 1630s, far from being regarded as a campaigner against ecclesiastical power, Selden enjoyed the respect and

---

[4] See, for example, Tuck "Ancient" pp. 154–156.

patronage of several leading Anglican bishops, including Bishop Andrewes and Archbishop Williams, while the head of the English church, Archbishop Laud, described Selden in a letter of 1636 to Vossius, as "doctissimo amico meo."[5]

Tuck himself acknowledges that Selden never became a principled opponent of episcopacy – as is evident from the latter's comments in the *Table-Talk* – even when it would have very much politically expedient to do so. Selden's works show him to have been very pragmatic in his views of the forms of church government, with the only constant a principled rejection of creating an authority in church matters that would be separate from the political one. This principle – of the supremacy of political authority over the church – has been variously regarded as a sign of Selden's so-called "anti-clericalism" or "cynism" or "Erastianism." But in the English context, this was in effect a conservative and legalistic approach; for Selden was merely restating the basic principle of English church government, since its break with Rome under Henry VIII, when by the Act in Restraint of Appeals of 1533, the cornerstone of the English reformation, the King-in-Parliament declared:

Where by divers sundry old authentic histories and chronicles, it is manifestly declared and expressed that this realm of England is an Empire, and so hath been accepted in the world, governed by one Supreme Head and King having the dignity and royal estate of the imperial Crown of the same, unto whom a body politic compact of all sorts and degrees of people divided in terms and by names of Spirituality and Temporal[i]ty, be bounden and owe to bear next to God a natural and humble obedience[.]

By this act the spiritual and secular spheres were declared to be united in one body politic and under one head, producing in essence a national association. This outlook was if anything even more evident in 1559 when, after the short-lived attempt to restore Catholicism under Queen Mary, Parliament declared Queen Elizabeth to be Supreme Governor of the Church, asserting that it was merely "restoring and uniting to the imperial crown of this realm the ancient jurisdictions, authorities, superiorities and preeminences to the same right belonging and appertaining." While over the years there would be no lack of resistance to this official view of religion and state, among English Catholics as well as the growing numbers of Presbyterians and Sectaries, Selden on his part was merely reaffirming the century-old English official view, against the many who came to oppose it in the 1640s and 1650s. Selden's consistent views on these matters had very little to do with "anti-clericalism" or "cynicism," his overriding and consistent principle being instead that there should be no separation of religion and state. Accordingly, while he held that in England episcopacy had traditionally served its purpose well enough, he was also open to consider reforming it in some manner, or even contemplating other means of ensuring preservation of the union of religion and state (e.g., the election of clerical representatives to Parliament). Such an approach is not a sign of radicalism at all, but rather of a desire for stability and continuity within changing circumstances.[6]

The supposed anti-clericalism or Erastianism (not always clearly distinguished among those who make the claims) of Selden does not stand up to scrutiny, even in the cases of those modern studies making claims more modest than Tuck's, and proposing that Selden adopted such positions only during part of his public career. For example, M. Mendle proposes that Selden's view about Episcopal presence in Parliament changed, with his early writings regarding the presence of bishops in Parliament due only to their baronial tenure (that is, as landlords, not as clergy), while by the 1630s and 1640s, Selden's position was that the principle for the presence of bishops was clearly a spiritual right. However, the very opposite trajectory for Selden's views is described by D.R. Woolf, who writes that much "has been made of Selden's 'Erastianism,' which became pronounced during the ecclesiastical debates of the 1640s, as remarks in his widely quoted *Table-Talk* demonstrate" but adds that in the *Historie of Tithes*, Selden had "not yet reached that position" and that his praise of the cooperation of lay and cleric in administrating justice in pre-Conquest England "provides a further caution against considering him an Erastian, or even an anticlerical, at this stage in his career." Thus we have Mendle regarding Selden as rejecting episcopal spiritual right to sit in Parliament early in his career and ending up as a defender of episcopacy by spiritual right in the 1640s; while Woolf describes the opposite trajectory, with Selden starting out as someone who commends past clerical involvement in government but eventually becomes an Erastian and anti-clerical in the 1640s. Obviously, both accounts cannot be correct.[7]

A different claim is made by scholars who view Selden's ideas on church and state as pretty much equivalent to Hobbes'; what T. Fulton describes as proposing to give the state absolute power over the clergy. Even starker is W. Lamont's assessment, describing Selden's as well as Hobbes' views on the place of the clergy in the state as those of the "anti-clerical cynic." Both Fulton and Lamont point to a passage in the *Table-Talk* as the source for their evaluation of Selden's view, where Selden denied bishops to be either *jure divino* (as the Laudians and others claimed) or anti-Christian (as the Presbyterians claimed), arguing instead that "All is as the State likes." However, even based on this one passage, the inference about Selden's ideas is too reductive by far. For one thing, Selden's writings touching on religion and

---

[6] See Prior "Hebraism" pp. 39–40. The formula about European kings to be each "emperor in his kingdom" (rex imperatori in regno suo) was also standard royal doctrine in France and Spain. See Kelley *Human* pp. 121, 129. Selden claimed as much in the TT "Power, State" sec. 7: "The Church is not only subject to the Civil Power with us that are Protestants, but also in *Spain:* if the Church does Excommunicate a Man for what it should not, the Civil Power will take him out of their Hands. So in *France*, the Bishop of *Angiers* alter'd something in the Breviary; they complain'd to the Parliament at *Paris*, that made him alter it again, with a [*comme abuse.*]"

[7] See Mendle *Dangerous* pp. 153–154; Woolf "*Idea*" pp. 222 and 229 note 85.

state convey a tone that is quite far from Hobbes', and is certainly not that of a cynic – instead, his writings and sayings on virtually all issues, not only religious ones, sometime display some sardonic or ironic element, to prove their point. Moreover, Selden not only bases the whole of his moral and political approach on a supposition of belief in providential justice, but also repeatedly argues for the clergy to be represented within the political councils, as based on both justice and utility. As we shall see, Selden's understanding of what is meant by "All is as the state likes," was quite different from what was ascribed to it by those viewing him as a Hobbesian or a complete cynic.[8]

Some scholars do sound a more cautious note about Selden's views on religion and state. D. Smith, for example, while agreeing with Tuck that Selden adopted in the 1640s a growingly Erastian position and conjecturing that this preference must have acted as a powerful motive for his choosing of the Parliamentarian side in the conflict, nevertheless remarks that Selden always remained highly untypical of Parliamentarians in his concern for legalism, his lack of interest in reformation *per se*, and his refusal to assume that the Episcopalians were really covert papists. P. Christianson goes further in rejecting the depictions of Selden as an anti-clerical or cynic on religion and state, asserting that what transpires in the *Historie of Tithes* is Selden's consistent approach to these issues: a markedly Protestant version of Christianity, which envisaged a church governed by the prince and parliaments, integrated into society and enriched by the creative talents of laymen, as well as those of the clergy. Farthest among those rejecting the depiction of Selden as a caricature Erastian is R. Barbour, who views Selden as not only sincerely resolved to devise a successful model for an English "Holy Commonwealth," the seventeenth-century term for "a comprehensively religious society," but even laboring for this goal "monumentally and inventively" against a rising tide of secularism. Such scholars, while correctly identifying Selden's unconventional positions and the seriousness of his contention that clergy and religious ideas have a crucial role to play within the state, nevertheless have not gone nearly far enough in dissipating the confusion in this matter.[9]

Certainly, the attempt to understand the struggles of mid-seventeenth-century England about the future of the established church are greatly impaired by terminological confusion. Terms like Erastian, Presbyterian and Independent are employed, many times inconsistently, not only in the seventeenth century but in later centuries too, to convey different and sometimes conflicting views. Behind this confusion lies the tendency in Selden's days, unfortunately only too often replicated by modern scholars, to use such terms to conflate religious and political disagreements that were not in fact coterminous – sometimes merely

---

[8] See Fulton "Aeropagitica" pp. 75–76; W.M. Lamont, *Godly Rule, Politics and Religion 1603–1606* (Macmillan, 1969) pp. 117–118. For the opposite view see Barbour *Measures* pp. 154–156.

[9] Smith *Constitutional* pp. 103–104; Christianson "Selden" ODNB; Barbour *Measures* pp. 8, 11–12, 19–20.

hurled as abuse, at other times reflecting real terminological disorientation in times of great ideological upheaval.[10]

Indeed, it is important to bear in mind the complex interplay of religious and political concerns in Britain, throughout the seventeenth century and especially during the volatile 1640s and 1650s. For many, perhaps most of the English, the Civil War was primarily a political rather than a religious struggle, while for the Scots (and perhaps for the Irish also), who became deeply involved in the conflict, the opposite seems to have been true. While the Scots tended to subordinate their political considerations in this conflict to their dedication to the religious ideals of Presbyterianism, the English on both sides of the divide, for the most part, had no such dedication to a single prior ideal, certainly not a religious one. One could find among both English Royalists and Parliamentarians those who were religiously Episcopalians or Presbyterians (while Independents and Sectaries were for the most part Parliamentarians), and when push came to shove, many – and perhaps most – of those regarded as English Presbyterians opposed both regicide and republicanism. The failure (or refusal) of the Scottish divines who became so involved in the attempts to find a new church settlement for England to understand that the interplay of religious and political ideas was far more complex in England than in Scotland, had not only practical implications on the ultimate defeat of their hopes, but also an important role in the terminological confusion that ensued.[11]

It appears that there are six main groups identified by both contemporaries and by modern scholarship, as battling out the shape of the English church in 1640s: Episcopalians, English Presbyterians, Scottish Presbyterians, Independents, Erastians and Lawyers (Sectaries might also be added as a seventh group, for although they are usually counted as Independents, many of them were not). "Lawyers" seem to stand out among those groups, because "Lawyer" is apparently not the appellation of a religious position, but actually its inclusion in this list truly reflects the fact that, regardless of the ostensibly religious appellation of the other groups, they all represented positions combining

---

[10] Erastian principles will be discussed below.

   In Presbyterian theory, church officers were appointed not by royal decree but by election – councils of lay elders (Presbyters) were elected in each congregation, who then elected a general council – something the English government and the Episcopalians always opposed. Although Presbyterians denied a power of Presbyters to politically depose kings, they did maintain that the church could enact spiritual sanctions against kings, including outright excommunication. Sommerville *Royalists* pp. 188–190.

   Independency (or Congregationalism), was born in England in the latter sixteenth century when a number of clerics, dissatisfied with the established church, developed a view regarding each congregation as an autonomous entity, where ultimate ecclesiastical authority lay with the congregation as a whole – and not with bishops or the Presbyterian council of congregations. Congregationalism always remained a small minority in Jacobean England. Sommerville *Royalists* pp. 198–199.

[11] L. Kaplan, "English Civil War Politics and the Religious Settlement" in *Church History* 41/3 (1972) pp. 311–315.

religious and political considerations. Moreover, in many cases, appellations regarding the positions towards church settlement did not necessarily correspond to the religious views of those described. Many of those described as Independents and Presbyterians were so in politics, but certainly not in religion, as L. Kaplan, for example, points out: many English "Presbyterians" were in fact very much against what the Scottish understood as Presbyterianism, while the formally defined "Presbyterian system" eventually established by Parliament in the English church in March 1646 offended most of those who held truly Presbyterian theological views, as it was in fact devised by Independents and lawyers to effectively neutralize the authority of Presbyters within the church.[12]

Let us look now to the most problematic of the terms in question, especially as it concerns Selden: Erastian. The term originates in the writings of Thomas Lieber (1524–1582, his name Latinized as Erastus), a Swiss reformed theologian and follower of Zwingly. In 1568 he had composed seventy-five "Theses," against the claims put forward by Presbyterian clergy to have a God-given independent authority of excommunication; that is, to punish sins of congregants by withholding from them the sacraments. The aim of Erastus was to show on scriptural grounds that sins of professing Christians are to be punished by civil authority only. The first seventy-two theses are devoted to particular questions of excommunication, and it is only in the last three that the general relationship of the church to the state is discussed. Of those, the most important is the 73rd, which opens with:

I see not why the Christian magistrate should not nowadays possess the same power as was commanded by God's decree, in the Jewish commonwealth. Can it be that we believe a better constitution of state and Church than that can be established?[13]

Such a view is evidently quite consistent with the thought and practice that had developed in the English Elizabethan church, previously and independently of Erastus, as expressed, for example, in the aforementioned 1559 official restoration of Queen Elizabeth as Supreme Governor of the Church; as well as in the writings of such as Richard Hooker. Thus, when Erastus' ideas were published in 1589, they certainly were in line with the established English practice in religion and state – but there would be no sense in calling the English church "Erastian," for if anything Erastus' ideas were in line with English ideas and practices which preceded the publication of his "Theses" by at least 30 years. This was Selden's point, and on various occasions he furthermore explicitly argued that, although the unitary concept of religion and state was the formal English position since Henry VIII, and certainly so

[12] Kaplan "Settlement" pp. 307–308, 314–315, 324–325.
[13] My rendition of "Non video cur hodie non debeat Magistratus Christianus idem facere, quod in Rep. Iudaeorum facere a Deo iussus est. An putamus nos Reipub. & Ecclesiem formam meliorem costituere posse?" See also E.A. Whitney, "Erastianism and divine right" in *The Huntington Library Quarterly* 2/4 (1939) pp. 379–380.

since Queen Elizabeth, in fact there was never a time when the position, later termed as Erastian, was not the dominant one in England. It was therefore in Selden's view the so-called anti-Erastians who were the innovators on these issues, and to prove this point, he brought at various times documented examples from English history, going back to even before the Norman conquest, showing the civil authority in England encompassed both secular and spiritual matters. His most striking proof that "Erastianism" was in effect following the English established outlook, and not the other way around, came when he revealed in *Synedriis*, that the text of Erastus' "Theses" after circulating for some 20 years in manuscript, and having been printed in 1589 as *Explicatio Gravissimae Quaestionis utrum Excommunicatio, Quatenus Religionem intelligentes & amplexantes, a Sacrementorum vsu, propter admissum facinus arcet; mandato nitatur Divino, an excogitata sit ab hominibus*, purposedly at "Pesclavii" (Poschivio, in the Grigioni Canton of Switzerland), had actually been published in London by the Queen's Printer, on the suggestion of a number of English bishops.[14]

However, in the early seventeenth century, as the monarchy and the church in England became increasingly preoccupied with what James I called "the republicanism of Calvinists and Jesuits," that is, the challenge to political authority (in both church and state) posed by religious ideas of church independence from the authority of the state, the term Erastian started to become associated with the reaction to this challenge – a growing stress on the absolute supremacy of political power over society, that had very little to do with Erastus' original views. There always were contemporaries careful with definitions, who clearly distinguished between followers of Erastus and others with similar views on church and state. One of these was Thomas Barlow (1608–1691), a cleric and academic (who in 1648 retained his Oxford fellowship with the aid of Selden), close to the Tew circle and, after the Restoration, Bishop of Lincoln, who wrote a tract on *Toleration of the Jews in a Christian State* (composed around the time of the debate on readmission in 1655). While presenting in the tract his own belief that in Christian states there should indeed be separate, divinely sanctioned spiritual and temporal powers, Barlow explicitly mentioned that on this issue he disagreed with the opinions of "Erastus," "his followers" (among which he included Hobbes), and of "Selden" in his *Synedriis*, who agree with the Jews that in every Commonwealth there should be only a single divinely sanctioned power over matters both Spiritual and Temporal. However, careful distinctions such as Barlow's were definitely in the minority, as the bulk of writers on such issues simply bundled all opposition to a separate spiritual power under one "Erastian" label.[15]

---

[14] See Whitney "Erastianism" pp. 380–384 and Sommerville *Royalists* p. 94. For the printing of Erastus' "Theses," see Toomer *Scholarship* pp. 713–719.

[15] Barbour *Measures* pp. 364–365.

Thus by the mid-seventeenth century, in English public debates about the shape of the church settlement, the term Erastian came to be applied pretty much indiscriminately to anyone who was not a supporter of a clear separation of church and state. "Erastian" was now used to describe men with widely diverging views: politically absolutists, constitutionalists, or supporters of army rule; and religiously Independents, anti-Calvinists or even moderate Presbyterians (some of these appellations could coexist, others certainly could not). The result was that the only ones who could *not* be covered under this sprawling definition of "Erastians" were Catholics, strict Presbyterians and some (though not all) Sectaries.

The Scottish Presbyterians leaders active in England in this period had a central role in this terminological development. Trying to make sense of the English scene, one of them declared that the "[t]utor which bred up the Erastian error was Arminianism" – that is, they interpreted the set of theological ideas termed "Arminianism," which they identified with Archbishop Laud and his supporters (again wrongly, for in fact a number of prominent supporters of Laud were doctrinally staunch Calvinists), as an exaltation of the political magistrate to the extent of claiming for the King the authority to do without the assent of the clergy if necessary, even in church and spiritual matters. In fact, nothing could have been farther from the truth, for if the group of clergymen associated with Laud had one thing in common, it was their intense pride in the Church as an institution – clearly reflected in their belief in divine-right episcopacy, as well as their emphasis on church independence and on the sacramental functions of church services.[16]

A good example of the problems with the "Erastian" label is William Prynne, a Puritan controversialist and anti-Laudian, as ferocious as there ever was, who nevertheless just as fiercely opposed independent clerical power to suspend from sacrament. Prynne thus could correctly be termed Erastian, in the sense of technically agreeing with Erastus' argument on this issue, but certainly not in what Lamont has aptly termed "the caricature sense of a lay indifference to religious niceties." In Prynne's case "Erastian" is a disciplinarian and strict view of the church, the opposite of the tolerationist or skeptical viewpoint ascribed to others thus labeled.[17]

Moreover, the four commissioners sent to London by the Scottish Presbyterian church as its representatives and agents in England, Robert Baillie, George Gillespie, Samuel Rutherford and Alexander Henderson,

---

[16] Lamont *Godly* pp. 63–64. "Erastian" was not the only misnomer applied by Scottish Presbyterians to the English scene. Finding their chief opposition in the Westminster Assembly coming from religious Independents, they tended to describe their own allies as Presbyterians. The result was that both appellations became after 1645 common not only for the two parties in the Assembly, but also for the two opposing parties in Parliament – very inaccurately so. In reality many of those described as Presbyterians or Independents politically were certainly not so in religion. See Kaplan "Settlement" pp. 312–313.

[17] Lamont *Puritanism* pp. 122–123.

compounded their misleading conflation of Arminianism and Erastianism with a heavily distorted application of the latter term in the 1640s. They attempted to discredit their opponents who advocated the supremacy of the civil power in spiritual matters, by wholesale associating the title of Erastian with a cynical indifference to moral and religious questions. Nevertheless, while much confusion has resulted from their use of the term Erastian as a blanket description covering all who upheld the supremacy of civil power, and implying a simple rejection of theological considerations, it seems that the Scottish commissioners did not let themselves be deceived by their own propaganda. They certainly knew the opposition to their views (and to those of their Independent colleagues) came both from lawyers opposed to clerical supremacy on constitutional grounds as well as from clergymen who had really read Erastus, and were making valid theological arguments – such as Thomas Coleman, the learned Lincolnshire rector who became a scourge to the Scottish Presbyterians in the Westminster Assembly and whose rejection of a clerical authority to excommunicate stemmed from his concern about the church remaining inclusive, rather than any particular preoccupation with the authority of Parliament or with the magistrates and their powers.[18]

The application by the Scottish Commissioners, of terms such as Presbyterians or Independents, was similarly confused and confusing. The unfortunate adoption by most modern scholars of such an inexact use of terminology, results in a hopeless tangle, which puts into one "Erastian" bundle, men as far, politically and religiously, as Selden and Hobbes, Prynne and Lightfoot. It is therefore preferable, when possible, to avoid using the terms "Erastian" and "Erastianism" except when referring directly to professed followers of Erastus and his ideas.[19]

6.2 TWO SWORDS OR ONE?

The idea of a separation between religion and state is a peculiar legacy of Western Christianity. With roots going back to the rise of Christianity as a Jewish sect separated from, and opposed to, the ideals of the Roman state,

---

[18] Lamont, *Godly* pp. 114–116, 120–122; Kaplan "Settlement" pp. 314–315, 324–325; Sommerville *Royalists* pp. 120–121.
[19] Lamont *Godly* pp. 113–114; Whitney "Erastianism" pp. 380–384; Kaplan "Settlement" pp. 312–314, 324–325. Even Kaplan, who is usually very careful with his use of the term, sometimes uses the term Erastians as simply a synonym for anti-clericalism. Recent research on the church and state debate in mid-seventeenth-century England, is increasingly suspicious about the hitherto indiscriminate use of the terms "Erastian" and "Erastianism" to describe views in this period. Such is the conclusion of Barbour's *Measures*, and another recent example is C.W.A. Prior, who based on his reading of relevant texts from the period, claims that the term "Erastianism" obscures the complexity and nuance of argument about religious politics in the Civil War period. See C.W.A. Prior, "Rethinking Church and State during the English Interregnum" in *Historical Research* 87/237 (August 2014) pp. 444–465.

the typical attitude of early Christianity to the state was summed up by New Testament phrases such as "Render unto Caesar the things which are Caesar's, and unto God the things that are God's" (Matthew 22:21), or "My kingdom is not of this world" (John 18:36), and so on.[20]

Even after the adoption of Christianity by Emperor Constantine in 313 CE, the later decline of imperial power in Western Europe meant that, unlike the strong identification of Eastern Christianity with the Byzantine state, the development of Western Christianity under the decaying later empire, and the barbarian kingdoms which followed it, was unusually independent of state power. The theoretical justification for this view was already apparent as early as the time of Pope Gelasius, who in a famous letter of 494 CE titled *Duo sunt* ("Two they are") to the eastern Emperor Anastasius, asserted a distinction between "two powers" in the Christian state – the "sacred authority of priests" and the "royal power." These two powers, the Pope claimed, were to be considered independent in their own spheres of operation. Moreover, while the authority of the emperor is paramount in secular matters, he must bow to the will of the Pope in religious matters. Based on a passage in Luke 22:38, the two authorities, church and state, were often described as "two swords." By the early Middle Ages the Western church had an ideology, hierarchy and administrative apparatus which stressed its separation from state power, while at the same time upholding its theoretical supremacy over it.

This approach informs, to some degree, most of Western Christianity, even to this day. The Catholic Church regards itself as separate and independent in spiritual matters from the authority of the state. Significantly, this separation was developed and upheld by the Church even against the authority of the medieval empire with its claim to universal jurisdiction over Christians; it is all the more adhered to when the Church is dealing with particular states. The reformed churches, born out of the rejection of so many Roman Catholic doctrines, did not for the most part reject this particular one, with Luther developing a doctrine of "two kingdoms" (material and spiritual), and most Calvinists reaching such separatist position either by an *a priori* theory like the Presbyterians, or from more practical considerations, like many of the various Congregationalist and Sectaries Churches.[21]

Although there were and are some exceptions to this separatist view of religion and state in Christianity (especially among Eastern Churches),

---

[20] Selden's take on the use of the "Render unto Caesar" phrase is that divines choose it either in flattery to kings or in order to justify the claims of the church. See TT "King" sec. 5, and Barbour *Measures* p. 244.

[21] Luther held that God appointed "two regiments" (Zwei-Regimente) or orders, through which he governs the world; the spiritual regiment in which he governs men through the Word, and the temporal regiment in which he governs through the Sword. The first is an internal government of the soul, concerned only with its salvation, while the temporal one is an outward government of bodies and lives for maintenance of peace and punishment of sin. The doctrine positing two similar reigns of the Devil, has often led to confusion. See Cargill Thompson *Studies* pp. 46–48.

historically by far the major exception to it in Western Christendom was England. We have seen that the circumstances of the English reformation meant that when Henry VIII broke with the Church of Rome, he also declared himself by the aforementioned Act in Restraint of Appeals of 1533, as Supreme Governor of the English Church, a position reiterated even more clearly in the in 1559 act of Parliament installing Queen Elizabeth as Supreme Governor of the Church. Besides the formal and explicit union into one head of the hitherto separated spiritual and secular spheres, there was also an implied – but in the long run no less significant – consequence of proceeding in this manner: since the Anglican church was formally established by the authority of King-in-Parliament, this very procedure meant that the latter (rather than the King alone) was identified as the supreme authority over spiritual as well as secular matters. As the Elizabethan settlement successfully brought religious stability to England, after the frequent and violent upheavals of the three previous reigns, it managed an uneasy balance between Catholic attempts to bring it back into the papal fold, Protestant "Puritans" demanding further reformation, and a moderate mainstream attempting to avoid both extremes. These religious tensions always had a political dimension that was more marked than elsewhere because of the peculiar feature of the Anglican settlement, which made the monarch also the head of the established church – and they would impact greatly the political upheavals of the 1630s and 1640s.[22]

The unusual asset of church and state in early-modern England was the result of the peculiar circumstances of its reformation, in which a principal motivation were royal and dynastic considerations, rather than theological ones. Henry VIII himself seems to have subscribed, both politically and theologically, to the "one sword" theory of church and state (with him wielding the sword…), but he did not bother too much with the theoretical aspects and the result was that, with little theological forethought, his use of Parliament to extend his royal powers over the English church also simultaneously indicated that Parliament had the authority to extend or limit these powers. After the several violent religious upheavals witnessed under the successive reigns of her brother and her sister, the accession of Queen Elizabeth established the parliamentary supremacy if anything even more firmly, because the act of supremacy passed by Parliament in this circumstance determined not only the religious settlement of the country but also the political one, and indeed intertwined the two: by its assertion that Elizabeth was neither a bastard nor a heretic, the Act of Supremacy became the source for the legitimacy of the Queen's rule over both

---

[22] That Selden acknowledged this character of the English church is shown by the report of his Parliamentary speech of 14 May 1628, which records him as claiming that even under the papacy the English clergy progressively came to be more and more under lay jurisdiction, but that only since Henry VIII "they have been totally." See Barbour *Measures* pp. 161–162. More generally about the character of the English church, see Cargill Thompson *Reformation* pp. 182–183; Cromartie *Constitutionalist* pp. 64–66, 70–75.

state and church. The royal supremacy and the role of Parliament in it, a by-product primarily of political considerations rather than a theological theory, thus supplied for the English Church a basis for consensus that was more institutional than doctrinal, and together with the (not unrelated) relative tolerationist stance of the Elizabethan church, the circumstances were created for the institutions of the English church not being theologically and definitely decided. For a long time no English thinker or institution felt the necessity to supply an explicit and detailed theological justification for this issue, and it remained markedly underdeveloped, so that, while in other Protestant countries the state could address the church as a corps of intellectuals united through an official doctrine, in England this failed to materialize.[23]

The result of these circumstances was that, by the late sixteenth century, competing visions of the church and its relationship with the state developed in England. The failure of a serious English Lutheran option was ensured by Henry's concept of his supremacy and rule over the Church of England. The classic statement of the Lutheran position in England was William Tyndale's *The Obedience of a Christian Man* (1528), which, while emphasizing obedience to the ruler, also showed a marked indifference (typical of the early Luther), to worldly power, as something ordinated by providence merely to take vengeance on evil-doers so that others might fear following them; that is, something that strictly speaking had no relevance at all to the religious lives of proper Christians. Such an approach might be convenient to a ruler interested in discouraging active political participation or action, but for this very reason it could not serve as ideological basis for a state and church mobilized for a struggle against the papacy, such as Henry wanted and worked for, and Elizabeth achieved, the national and virtuous union of church and state which is so apparent a view in this period among the vast majority of Englishmen, whatever their religious persuasions.[24]

The major dynamic within the English church of the early seventeenth century, and in the struggle to determine its direction, was the undoubted

---

[23] Cromartie *Constitutionalist* pp. 70–78. In a collection of anti-clerical materials annotated by Henry VIII in the 1530s, there appears a comment, underlined by Henry, about the state of affairs at the end of the biblical book of Judges, in which each man did which seemed right to him and much evil ensued, because of the absence of a kingly power "by whose sword they might be coerced from vices." See Cromartie *Constitutionalist* pp. 64, 98, 119–121. Selden was certainly aware of the latitudinarian attitude of the Elizabethan church: when in May 1628 there was a proposal in the Commons to return to the presumably more pure state of affairs of the Elizabethan times, Selden pointed out to his fellow MPs that while the Elizabethan dispensation required only subscription to the 39 articles of faith, the Jacobean church had added to these several additional requirements from ministers, such as acknowledging that the monarch only is "Supreme Governor" of the church, and that the Anglican book of common prayer contains nothing against the word of God. Not incidentally, the Jacobean additions that Selden stressed added the political aspect of church government to the theological character of the 39 propositions. See Barbour *Measures* pp. 162–163.
[24] Cromartie *Constitutionalist* pp. 66–68.

growth in its ranks of the numbers of strict Calvinists who came to be known as "Puritans." More than an ideology, Puritanism was an attitude wishing for a further reformation of the English church, which would complete its purification from popish forms and practices that they regarded as having been only partially and laxly executed. Some of the Puritans adopted a Presbyterian ecclesiology as means to this end, while others sought reform within the institutions of an Episcopal church. This commitment of Elizabethan Puritans to a project of national reformation, gave them a strong disciplinarian and anti-sectarian bias, which in turn meant that they were highly critical not only of what they saw as excessive laxity in the church establishment, but also of separatist groups wishing to escape the control of the established church. Moreover, the Puritan wish to further reform the established church necessarily required intensifying the involvement of politics in the church, which militated against the Presbyterian opposition to the political oversight of the state over church affairs. This conflict eventually brought forth a not inconsiderable group of those who might be termed Presbyterian-Puritans, like Prynne and Baxter, who were theologically Presbyterian but came to accept the necessity of an overall political supremacy above the church. Moreover, in the English context, political and religious issues became so entangled that every public discussion of religious matters was immediately read by all for its political ramifications, and vice versa. This would become especially marked after the start of Charles I's reign, when there started to grow the suspicion (believed by many) that the established Church had become a willing tool of the King in his attempt to impose political absolutism.[25]

By the late sixteenth century, Presbyterian writers had begun to challenge the established church with arguments about the need for a more assertive church discipline, including excommunication which, at first implicitly and then explicitly, demanded a freer wielding of the spiritual sword by the clergy. This English development followed a wider one among a new generation of Calvinists, including Theodore Beza, the successor to Calvin as leader of the church in Geneva and the prominent scholar and clergyman Andrew Melville, who became a prominent leader in Scottish Calvinism and who, in contrast to the more relaxed attitude to the role of bishops by Calvin and the previous generation, started to regard episcopacy as a critical hindrance to erecting a strict and effective discipline over society by a church wielding the spiritual sword of excommunication. Although these views had a role in the eventual mid-seventeenth-century debate about episcopacy in the church, their principal importance as to the relationship of religion and state is that they first implied, and later declared openly, an independent clerical "sword" not subject to political authority. By the later part of Elizabeth's reign, prominent figures in the English government, like Lord Chancellor Christopher Hutton, recognized this trend and were warning from the independent power of excommunication

---

[25] Cromartie *Constitutionalist* p. 126.

claimed in "chief presbytery men's books," regarding these as no less dangerous than papists in their denying of "the supremacy of princes." It is important to stress that although this view of independent church authority became identified with the Presbyterians, it was also held by some Puritans whose ecclesiology was not Presbyterian, men such as Francis Knollys and Dr. John Reynolds, who might be defined as Anglicans of moderate-Puritan tendencies.[26]

Not surprisingly, these developments had an impact on the English church establishment. Whereas the early Elizabethan church had been overall content to adhere to St. Jerome's view that episcopacy was a purely human institution, the growing challenges to that institution articulated in late sixteenth century England brought as a reaction, several ecclesiastical writers – among them John Bridges, Dean of Salisbury, Richard Bancroft, Archbishop of Canterbury and Hadrian Saravia, an influential cleric of Flemish extraction who was among the translators of King James' Bible – to claim that episcopacy had been instituted directly by Christ. Ironically, these defenses of episcopacy, although originating in an attempt to rebut the Presbyterian challenge, themselves created a new challenge for the supremacy of political authority, since a *jure divino* episcopacy would be no less independent of political power than a *jure divino* presbytery. Doubly ironically, one of the first to identify and warn against the connection between the new claims to divine-right episcopacy and a challenge to royal authority, was none other than the Puritan Francis Knollys, who in a 1593 letter to Lord Burghley warned that,

the superyoritie of Bysshops is godes own instytucion, which saying dothe Impunge hir Majesties supreme government dyrectlye, & therefore it is to bee retracted playnelye & trulye, ffor chryst playnely confessed yt his kingdome was not of this worlde, and therefore he gave no worldlie rule or prehemynence unto his apostles.[27]

Thus, the late Elizabethan church saw the rise of divine-right claims from supporters of both presbytery and episcopacy, implying a church authority – a "sword" – inherently independent from the political one, even while those who professed this view, in most cases also loudly protested their complete devotion to the Queen and her supremacy. Although episcopacy was among the most important aspects of this debate, it was not the only one, for there were other claims, such as about an independent power of excommunication in the church, or about church tithes being *jure divino*, that were unconnected to the issue of episcopacy or presbytery – indeed in the latter case, many supporters of episcopacy and presbytery, while mutually rejecting each other's claims about church government, were united in asserting church tithes as a divine right.

It appears that the connection of church reform with a threat to the political order, which started to be made in the early seventeenth century, owed most to events in Scotland, and to the succession of a Scottish king to the throne of

---

[26] Cromartie *Constitutionalist* pp. 123–125, 128; Cargill Thompson *Reformation* pp. 100–101.
[27] Cargill Thompson *Reformation* pp. 100–101, 118–119, 128–130.

England. When in 1574 Andrew Melville returned to Scotland from Geneva, where he had imbibed Calvinist Presbyterian ideas from Beza, he soon became leader of a movement for further reform of the Scottish Kirk, including the abolition of episcopacy. Since it was then widely accepted that bishops were an estate of the Scottish Parliament, Melville countered this notion with the idea of the "two kingdoms" – church and state as separate "kingdoms" which institutionally should have nothing to do with each other, thus making clerical representation in Parliament redundant, even disreputable. King James VI resisted these claims, viewing them as rebellious not only towards episcopacy but also towards the monarchy. James later made the connection explicit, when he asserted in his *Basilikon Doron* (1599), that the circumstances of the Scottish reformation had created a dangerous association between rebellious principles of popular government and clerical involvement in politics: "some fiery spirited men in the ministry, got such a guiding of the people at that time of confusion, as finding the gust of government sweet, they begouth to fantasy to themselves a democratic form of government[.]"[28]

These Scottish debates were introduced to England as early as 1584, when Melville and other Scottish Presbyterians fled south from James' pressures and seriously augmented the intellectual firepower of English Presbyterians. The Scottish Presbyterians became involved in the production of the "Martin Marprelate" series of anonymous tracts in 1588–1589, which attacked the existing system of the Anglican Church – with the result that English Presbyterians earned an association with Scotland that they were never again to lose. It was in this context that Thomas Cooper, Bishop of Lincoln and later of Winchester, in controversialist writings against the "Marprelate" tracts, first significantly made the suggestion that not only the church, but also England's civil constitution, would be directly threatened by abolition of the episcopal estate. Arguing that since the laws of England had stood for so long on the authority of three estates, the taking away of one might dangerously destabilize the whole – he in effect implied that eliminating the estate of bishops would mean in a sense to dissolve the whole existing corporation of the kingdom of England, turning it into something else. The "Marprelate" tract *Hay any Work for Cooper* (1588), retorted against Cooper that the act of supremacy on Elizabeth's accession had been passed without bishops in Parliament (for the Marian bishops were opposed to it and did not attend), inferring from this that bishops had no veto power, and thus were no estate. In effect the main arguments that would be employed in the debate about episcopacy of the next decades had already been articulated.[29]

Thus, as early as the 1590s there were in England competing enumerations of the estates, and the issue which had not attracted much attention before, now became significant not only for questions of church and state, but indeed for the

[28] Mendle *Dangerous* pp. 68–69; Cromartie *Constitutionalist* p. 158.
[29] Mendle *Dangerous* pp. 3–4, 34–35, 80–83.

constitutional asset of the English government. The traditional and widespread enumeration of estates in England, at least from the fifteenth century, was Lords spiritual, Lords temporal and Commons – three estates under the king. The competing enumeration, borrowed from the classic formulation of a mixed government by one, few and many, made the three estates into king, nobles and commons, and was progressively adopted by Presbyterians to make their argument that the clergy were no estate – however, the corollary effect of the latter enumeration was to also lower the King to a level of equality with the other two estates. Neither the Scottish nor the English governments missed this inference. In Scotland, James VI declared the opinion that bishops were not an estate to be treason, and in England Elizabeth I's Privy Council declared the same view to be sedition. The immediate result of these decisive governmental proclamations was that, for a time, the debate died out. But it would be revived in Scotland by the covenanters in the 1630s, and in England by the anti-episcopalians of the 1640s.[30]

By the early seventeenth century, the issue of religion and state was increasingly becoming an incendiary one, and it took very little to light up ferocious debates, which also impinged on the issue of the royal supremacy, in the church as well as in the state. The result was that, after his accession to the English throne in 1603 as James I, the King found himself rapidly confronted with heated controversies touching this issue. As early as June 1604 Parliament saw fit to remind the new king, lest he "be misinformed," that for "matters of religion" the kings of England have not "any absolute power in themselves" either to "alter religion" or to "make any laws concerning the same" other than "by the consent of Parliament."[31]

It appears that congregationalism – in this period more commonly known as Independency – in the English church was born in this context of debates about "matters of religion," that is not as a radical departure but rather as a conservative attempt, among Puritans who opposed both Presbyterian and Sectarian calls for full separation from the established church. This was certainly the view of William Bradshaw's *English Puritanisme: Containening the Maine Opinions of the Rigidest Sort of Those That Are Called Puritans in the Realme of England* (1605), protesting to James I the absolute devotion of his Puritan subjects, their anti-separatism and their distance from Presbyterian principles. While more on the establishment side of things, Edwin Sandys, son of the Archbishop of York and Hooker's loyal pupil, who was to become

[30] Mendle *Dangerous* pp. 3–4, 34–35. Intriguingly, Hooker mixed the traditional enumeration of estates with the new one, making in a sense four estates. For while he regarded the King as a parliamentary estate, he also thought of the bishops and the proctors of the lower clergy in Convocation as forming a clerical estate alongside nobles and commons. Consequently, he regarded Convocation as in effect a third House of Parliament, alongside the Houses of Lords and Commons. Mendle *Dangerous* pp. 58, 127.
[31] Zuckert *Natural* pp. 51–52.

Selden's friend and political ally, published *Survey of the State of Religion* (1605) where he criticized the political tendencies of high Calvinism.[32]

But the perceived threat to the established system in church and state was not only from the Presbyterian side. As we have seen, in no small measure as a result of the doctrinal retrenchment prompted by the Presbyterian challenge, there grew voices asserting *jure divino* and political independence on the side of the established church as well. In 1604, a discussion in the House of Commons about the 39 articles provoked a declaration by Convocation, that the Commons had no right to meddle in doctrinal issues. Although the declaration was hastily retracted, it managed to drive some MPs to react by asserting that a church Canon not confirmed by Parliament was no more than a "convocation pamphlet." In this mood, the Commons rejected an act "against innovations in the church" proposed by the bishops, and passed instead an act "against scandalous ministers." In 1606, Convocation drafted a proposal for new church Canons, having a distinctly anti-contractualist flavor, which James I eventually vetoed, assuming (probably correctly) that they would cause political uproar if approved. But the proposed Canons clearly represented ideas that were by then, firmly entrenched among the highest levels of the church hierarchy which had approved them, as it seems that the Canons were drafted by no other than Richard Bancroft, since 1604 Archbishop of Canterbury (who in 1610 would defend his friend Cowell's notorious *Interpreter*). Also in 1606, Sandys attempted to uphold the role of Convocation, with a Hookerian speech in Parliament in which he argued that there should be no alteration of any substantial point of religion "but by parliament, with the advice and consent of the clergy in convocation" otherwise the papist could claim, not unreasonably, that the English "profess only a statute religion."[33]

The concerns and challenges of the Elizabethan church were addressed and, to a great extent epitomized, in the work of one of the seminal figures in its history, Richard Hooker (1554–1600), the man who more than any other might be said to have shaped what came to be "Anglicanism." An anti-Puritan clergyman and controversialist who devoted his later years to writing his massive and influential *Of the Laws of Ecclesiastical Polity*, Hooker as mentioned above was the teacher and friend of Sir Edwin Sandys (who helped fund the publication of *Laws*), and between 1585 and 1591, as Master of the Temple Church, in effect chaplain to the two Templar Inns of Court. Hooker's connections to the Temple and to Sandys, are just two of the more obvious avenues of his possible influence on Selden, especially as it is clear that his time at the Inns of Court, did greatly influence Hooker's ideas about law and tradition. For one, Hooker's quite un-Protestant view that the authority of the church, that is tradition, was the first motive for accepting scripture, has clear

[32] Cromartie *Constitutionalist* pp. 165–166, 240.
[33] Cromartie *Constitutionalist* pp. 165–167, 240.

parallels in Selden's thought. Intriguingly, despite these and other apparent affinities between them, there is little evidence for any direct influence of Hooker on Selden – however this subject has not as yet been significantly studied, and one might suspect that, when given the attention it deserves, it might yield interesting results.[34]

As mentioned in the previous chapter, Hooker fused various previous strands of Anglican thought into an approach based on two central concepts: one was the fundamental distinction between things essential and "adiaphora" (things indifferent) in the church, that is, between matters of faith essential for salvation and the things indifferent that are neither commanded nor prohibited; the other was the central role of the national church in each country, which while remaining part of the universal church, has to a great extent the right to determine its own form of worship and church government according to its particular circumstances. His theory was not completely novel, but rather refined ideas used in the Henrician formulations of the 1530s–1540s, and later employed against the Puritans by eminent figures of the Elizabethan church, such as Archbishops Parker and Whitgift. Hooker's contribution was primarily to make existing arguments more cohesive and sophisticated, by applying to the church, theoretical principles which had been developed to discuss civil societies. What was nevertheless distinctive in Hooker's theory was his extremely comprehensive definition of the membership of the visible church. For him, since true salvation of the soul is known only to God, the visible church should include all those who profess Christianity in the widest possible definition – even heretics and sinners – with only explicit atheism or denial of Christ excluding one from the church. Thus, in a Christian country like England, virtually all members of the commonwealth were, by definition, members of the national church – state and church becoming effectively one, and making membership of the church pretty much coterminous with citizenship.[35]

Hooker's theory of the national church justified the royal supremacy over the church, while rejecting both the papal and the Puritan claims that church and state were two separate societies. Indeed, in a theory maintaining that in England church and state form a single society, there was no reason why the same person could not possess supreme authority over both temporal and spiritual spheres. Hooker gave two basic arguments in support for his theory: first, that as Aristotle proposes, all political societies are also concerned with the care of religion; and second, that in Christian countries, since pretty much the

---

[34] Cromartie *Constitutionalist* pp. 141–142.
[35] Cargill Thompson *Reformation* pp. 142–144, 177–179; Cromartie *Constitutionalist* pp. 68–69. Hooker makes clear that in a state that is not Christian (as Christianity was in its first three centuries), there is no "mutual dependency" between church and state since the population of the state and the church are not the same. It is only in a Christian society that church and state are one. Cargill Thompson *Reformation* pp. 190–191.

same body of people are at the same time both the church and the commonwealth, they therefore do not really form two societies, but one.[36]

Hooker's ideas of "adiaphora" and of a national church resulted in a highly consensual view of both church and state, in which the ultimate authority to make laws for the government of the church belongs neither to clergy nor king alone, but rather to the whole body of the national church, embodied in the supreme lawmaking authority of the state. In the English case the location of that authority is: "the parliament of England together with the convocation annexed thereunto, is that whereupon the very essence of all government within this kingdom doth depend."[37]

The many affinities between Hooker's and Selden's ideas on church and state are evident. Among these are, for example, the marked reticence from assigning *jure divino* status to any particular arrangement in church or state, the viewing of the clergy as a vital element of political society, and the essentially unitary view of church and state (for which both men were accused of Erastianism). But perhaps the most fundamental similarity between their views was the place they assigned to tradition within the framework of natural law. Hooker argued, quite similarly to Selden, that natural law allows for great leeway in things indifferent (what Selden described as "permissive natural law"), and that positive laws derive validity from historical consent – with the goal being the infusing of custom with a higher kind of authority, by being both in accordance with natural law as well as the expression of public consent. Hooker's attitude to custom became the pivotal point, not only of his defense of the national church but of his historical philosophy. He came to see continuity not as the exact perpetuation of a particular system but rather as the process of its historical adaptation to changing circumstances.

Hooker essentially fused the ideas of continuity through change, and of the church being a society, into his justification of tradition. Both he and his Puritan opponents employed the idea that the church is a society, a corporation with its

---

[36] Cargill Thompson *Reformation* pp. 182–185; Ferguson *Clio* p. 250. His argument of identity between church and state had formed a standard part of the Tudor theory of royal supremacy since the 1530s, and had been explicitly articulated as early as 1535 by Gardiner and later by Whitgift – indeed it appears King Henry VIII himself embraced this view. See Cromartie *Constitutionalist* pp. 64–66.

    Cargill Thompson denies any trace of Averroism, that some ascribe to Hooker following from his view of church and state, since the state is for him never only a secular institution, and in the case of Christian commonwealths, it is especially infused with a spiritual dimension by being at the same time a state and a church. Thus Hooker could never envisage a simple subordination of religion to political ends, and he vigorously condemned (in book v) the "wise malignants" who seek to make "a politic use of religion." Hooker was certainly not one of those proposing a pure and simple secular political control of the church in all circumstances. Cargill Thompson *Reformation* pp. 189–190.

[37] Cargill Thompson *Reformation* pp. 186–187, Cromartie *Constitutionalist* p. 145. Hooker regarded Parliament with convocation as "even the body of the whole realm" since it consists of the King and all his subjects either in person or in those they have voluntarily derived their personal right to.

own principles and characteristics – but they drew from this notion quite different inferences. The Puritans stressed corporation as a chartered company, binding the church in perpetuity to rigidly fulfill the terms of its charter; while Hooker took the corporate nature of the church to mean first and foremost that it is capable of ordered change, of adapting to mutable circumstances while retaining its principles and purpose. For Hooker the corporate nature of the church meant above all that, unlike natural men, it could change considerably while retaining its identity, thus becoming immortal custodian of a living tradition:

Wherefore as any man's deed past is good as long as himself continueth; so the act of a public society of men done five hundred years sithence standeth as theirs who presently are of the same societies, because corporations are immortal; we were then alive in our predecessors, and they in their successors do live still.[38]

This adaptive nature means, according to Hooker, that the relationship of the ecclesiastical to the temporal authorities in all states is shaped by particular circumstances: in those Christian states which introduced the authority of the Roman Catholic church, that church remained under its own rules independent of civil magistrates; while in England, even when professing Roman Catholicism and more so after the Reformation, under the laws and customs peculiar to that realm, church and state always constituted one society.[39]

It was in this context that Hooker addressed explicitly, in the eighth and final book of his *Laws*, the "controversy" concerning "the power of supreme jurisdiction, which for distinction's sake we call the power of ecclesiastical dominion." His theory of course denied any claim of *jure divino* independent ecclesiastical authority, and as we have seen above he also argued that the traditions of the English church and state were of a clear supremacy of the civil jurisdiction over both. Moreover, Hooker argued, even as a matter of a church following the best of past practices, the Anglican Church had the best of precedents, in the clear union of civil and religious matters in the ancient Jewish state. He opened the eighth book of the *Laws* with the following statement:

It was not thought fit in the Jews' commonwealth, that the exercise of supremacy ecclesiastical should be denied unto him, to whom the exercise of chiefty civil did appertain; and therefore their kings were invested with both.

---

[38] Richard Hooker, *Of the Laws of Ecclesiastical Polity*, B. Hanbury ed. 3 vols. (1830) book 1 sec. 10. See also Ferguson *Clio* pp. 217–218.

[39] Cargill Thompson *Reformation* pp. 147–148, 175–178; Ferguson *Clio* pp. 210–215, 257. Hooker's view of indifferent outside elements adapted to circumstances, allowed him to argue that the English church followed the pattern of God's old "elect people" while attacking the Puritan claim to exactly reinstate Mosaic law, by arguing that those laws had been given to a particular people at a particular time, with an eye to their national character and the country where they dwelled. Also pointing to the affinity between the ideas of Selden and Hooker on religion and state see Barbour *Measures* pp. 25–26.

Hooker then went on to specify in detail, the manner and circumstances of the said union of state and church among the ancient Israelites, as well as the fact that the English did in fact follow this model exactly for their own state, summing up the issue thus:

In a word, our state is according to the pattern of God's own ancient elect people, which people was not part of them the Common-wealth; and part of them the Church of God; but the self same people whole and entire were both under one Chief Governour, on whose Supream Authority, they did all depend.[40]

It is against this background of Presbyterian and Episcopalian claims for *jure divino* church authority, and attempts by Hooker and others to rebut such claims, by asserting the supremacy of political authority, among other things upon the example of the chosen people, that the Jacobean and Caroline debate on church and state had developed, as Selden entered it.

In this context, Selden's ideas came to have a special role in public debates about church matters. Backed by the formidable combination of unequalled scholarship with a reputation for independence in political and religious matters, his contributions had a significant – indeed many times decisive – effect on the debates he intervened in. Excepting the fracas concerning his *Historie of Tithes* around 1618, Selden became significantly involved in issues of church and state, only in the 1630s and 1640s, first by his treatment of the issue in his Hebraist scholarship, later with his political activities in Parliament and the Westminster Assembly. Especially important was his role in the parliamentary debates of 1641 about the future of episcopacy, and in 1645–1646 about the new settlement of the Church, as well as the 1643–1644 debates in the Westminster Assembly about the nature of a Presbyterian government and the issue of excommunication. In all these instances, Selden's contributions focused on one central question – whether the church possesses a sphere of spiritual authority which is separate from, and independent of, the state – which earned him the oft-repeated, if misleading, label of "Erastian."

Anyone perusing even briefly the *Synedriis* or the *Table-Talk* can witness that Selden's treatment of issues concerning church and state expanded massively in his later years. However, it is also evident that Selden's basic outlook was not shaped by the debates of the early 1640s or of the Civil War – for he can be found to articulate the same opinions, albeit far more briefly, in writings and speeches from the very beginning of his career.

---

[40] The eighth book (like the sixth and seventh) of Hooker's *Laws* was essentially completed but still unpublished at his death, and was printed in mutilated form only in 1648, clearly for its relevance to the debates on church and state that were raging at that time. Intriguingly, it appears that manuscript copies of the unpublished books were held during the early seventeenth century, by two of Selden's closest intellectual counterparts in the Anglican Church, Andrewes and Ussher – opening up another avenue of influence on Selden by Hooker's writings and ideas, especially pertinent in the 1640s.

As early as his *Jani Anglorum* (1610), Selden described a long list of English kings up to Henry II using their authority over ecclesiastical matters by supporting the English church, while at the same time resisting the attempts from Rome to encroach on their authority over religious matters by means of civil and canon laws. Moreover he indicated this tradition as still extant in his own days, by mentioning the then-recent implementation of a medieval law concerning order of appeals, by "the famous Sir Edward Coke" which was directed to "assert and maintain the King[']s ecclesiastical jurisdiction." That this is not simply a case of upholding civil supremacy over religion is shown in several of the cases he treats in his historical review, such as when he mentions that William the Conqueror took steps to protect ecclesiastical jurisdiction from lay encroachment, such as was the case with matters of wills and inheritance which were, according to the "ancient constitution, entrusted to the church by the consent of the king and peers." In his *Duello* of the same year, Selden argued that: "The English customes, never permitted themselves to be subjected" to "Clergy-canons," instead always retaining, under parliamentary correction "whatsoever they have by long use or allowance approved." That is, he was claiming even at the very early stage of his career, that in England, custom and Parliament had always been supreme to Canon law.[41]

Selden's clash with the authorities a few years later, following the publication of the *Historie of Tithes*, should also be seen in this context, since although ostensibly writing a learned historical treatise, the historical controversy he addressed had emerged because of recent clerical claims that tithes were *jure divino* and thus independent of human law or authority. This theory of tithes as God-given to the clergy was obviously directly at odds with the superiority of Parliament over all things in church and state, and Selden's claim in his book that church taxes were mere human law, just as obviously pointed to the subjection of such taxes to political authority. Some years later, during a 1628 debate in the Commons, Selden, by then a leading MP, effectively restated what he had asserted in the *Duello* and implied in *Historie of Tithes*, declaring that: "To subscribe to a canon not confirmed by act of parliament, was like giving way to the destruction of ourselves in our freeholds."[42]

It is moreover instructive to see in the very same Parliament of 1628, in a speech of 16 May, how and why Selden opposed a proposed bill named "An act to restrain some disorders that are or may be in ministers of God's word." Now both before and after this time, Selden was never shy in his criticism of scandalous or disorderly clergy and in his speech on this matter, he was careful to establish that the bill was completely within the authority of Parliament, for although the clergy was granted various liberties by Magna

---

[41] *Reverse (Jani Anglorum)* b1c5; *Duello* p. 21. See also Barbour *Measures* pp. 130–134, and Barbour mentions that Selden brought several examples from Jewish history as analogies with British customs.

[42] Sommerville *Royalists* pp. 201–203.

Carta itself, these had been by many acts of Parliaments circumscribed and varied, and indeed in principle "an act of parliament may alter Magna Carta." Nevertheless, he decidedly opposed the proposed bill, arguing that it was both totally unnecessary and that it singled out the clergy for an unusual and cruel treatment. Selden is reported to have asserted in his speech,

[t]hat ministers and clergymen are already subject to lay jurisdiction and may now be punished by justices of peace. But the reason why he is against the bill is because this is a law without all example; for by this law the minister for being drunk shall lose his benefice, and yet both the justices of peace and the jurymen that are to judge and pass on a clergy shall pay but 5s[hillings] for being drunk, which holds no proportion.

In other words, Selden while affirming the superiority of Parliament over the clergy, refused to demand from that same clergy a higher standard of conduct than the one to be expected from the justices or the jurymen that would try them. Adopting neither the anti-clerical rhetoric that suspects clergymen of being debauched and lazy, nor the Puritan expectation of an exceptionally saintly ministry, Selden obviously regarded clergyman, for all their spiritual concerns, as deserving the same judicial treatment due to any other subjects, not preferential but also not prejudicial.[43]

It was, however, his immersion in Jewish learning during the 1630s which eventually produced Selden's most developed and substantial contributions on the relationship between the religious and civil spheres. Selden's most significant text on religion and state was undoubtedly his *Synedriis*, by definition a work addressing the relationship of political and religious issues, since the subject of the book, the Jewish councils and courts, were institutions which dealt with matters both secular and religious, and indeed were composed of members who were both from within the Jewish priesthood as well as without it – viewed as parallel to Christian clergy and laity. The original plan for the layout of *Synedriis* was with time severely altered, as Selden himself admitted in the preface to the first volume, because of the great accretion of materials on excommunication – evidently the result of this issue becoming a central point of contention in the public debates of his time. It is unclear when exactly Selden started to work extensively on excommunication, but it seems likely that, as Toomer suggests, the book named "On the History of Presbyters and Presbyteries," which in the *Uxor Ebraica* (1646) he promises to publish soon, consisted in the main of material of this sort, which on second thought was eventually inserted into the *Synedriis*.[44]

Selden also touched on issues of church and state in some of his other Hebraist works, although briefly. For example, in his *Pontificatum*, criticizing

---

[43] Johnson *Commons Debate* vol. iii pp. 441–442. See also discussion in Barbour *Measures* pp. 161–162.

[44] Toomer *Scholarship* pp. 692–693. I suspect that at least part of this material also found its way earlier into print, within Selden's commentary to *Eutychius* (1642).

claims by modern authors that the biblical prophets were priests or even the high priests, he proposed that these claims (and especially the one about high priests) were made by those attempting to make the pontificate – that is, the papacy – superior to kingship. Selden also regarded his use of Talmudic and other sources in *Pontificatum* as an illustration of how the ignorance by most Christian writers about such rabbinical sources, had vitiated most accounts of the Hebrew Republic – the 'Jewish State' – in the books treating this subject, that were written by such modern Christian Hebraists as the Italian Sigonius (Carlo Sigonio) and the Dutch Cunaeus (Pieter Van Der Koon). We can see in this context that Selden pointed to two themes that were especially significant to him: the potential relevance of Jewish sources to contemporary issues of religion and state, as well as the attempts to raise clerical authority above the political one. But we can also see that he did so while addressing foreign authors and concerns (the goals of Papist authors, and the writings of Sigonius and Cunaeus) without any sense of local urgency. Obviously such issues did not seem to be very pressing ones for England in the 1630s. In his important and voluminous *Jure Naturali*, completed by 1639, there is overall almost nothing on church and state that would be significantly applicable to the debates of the time, except for a short sections touching on excommunication in book 4 ch 9.[45]

The period of Selden's greatest political activity on the issue of religion and state, were the fierce struggles of the 1640s in Parliament and in the Westminster Assembly, in both of which he played a prominent role. His scholarly output in this decade – between his two great works the *Jure Naturali* (1640) and the first volume of *Synedriis* (1650) – was relatively scant, but in virtually everything that he did publish in this period, there is some reflection of his concerns regarding the English debate about church and state, and in most cases also of his belief of the direct relevance of Jewish traditions and ideas to this debate. As early as his *Eutychius* (1642) Selden put forward his view that early Christianity was clearly a religion still being shaped, with very strong connections to contemporary Judaism. This implied both a view of religion that stressed change and adaptation, and also the necessity to understand Judaism in order to adequately grasp the roots and nature of Christianity. Two years later Selden's *Anno Civili* (1644), a relatively small treatise, written apparently for the most part in 1643, when Selden was most active in the Westminster Assembly, reflects his role in these debates. Even the title of the work, which rendered in English is *The Civil Year and Calendar of the Ancient Jewish Church or State*, downplays the difference between religion and state among the Jews, indicating Selden's view of essential integration between the two in the Jewish commonwealth. Moreover, the work also displays several remarks which seem to reflect, at least in part, Selden's participation in the Assembly debates, such as: about those ignorant, lazy and deceptive persons who claim to apply usages of the ancient Jewish state to Christianity without

---

[45] Toomer *Scholarship* pp. 472–473, 489–490.

knowledge of the Talmud; about those who while rejecting tradition try to distort scripture to follow their own designs; and about those who claimed that the High Priest heading the Sanhedrin supported their claims for supremacy of clergymen (either popish or Presbyterian) over laymen.[46]

Thus, by the mid-1640s Selden had outlined the main features of his contribution to the English debate about church and state, a principled view of essential unity between the two, based upon two main pillars: his belief in the importance of the Jewish roots of Christianity and his opposition to claims of clerical supremacy or even only of independence from the state. The *Uxor Ebraica* (1646) marked an expansion of these themes, especially so in his recurrent assertion that Christianity is a reformed Judaism, that it therefore retains many things from that religion, and that those who neglect this crucial connection are either deceived or deceivers. He made this point copiously in his particular discussion of Jewish marriage laws and their counterparts in other places, where he lashed out at recent "feverish and sometimes fanatic innovators" in this field (Toomer suggests this referred particularly to some Sectaries which at that time were proposing theories of polygamy and free love). He reiterated the same point yet again when more generally attacking those attempting to impose systems of law based on facile and mistaken understanding of Jewish customs, dubbing these "insane cloud-cuckoo-land foundations" (insanae nephelococcygiarum substructiones – alluding to Aristophanes' play *Birds*, ridiculing pie-in-the-sky schemes). The attacks were evidently directed at the current public debates about religion and state, and Selden promised to show in a coming work (obviously *Synedriis*) how a correct analysis of the facts would explode these wild theories. Selden even went one step further when, while discussing Jesus' words about adultery, he cautiously conjectured that the New Testament terminology used on the grounds for divorce, indicated a possible adherence of his to the Jewish sages' school of Shammai – a daring move, setting the ideas not merely of Apostles, but even of Jesus himself, in the particular context of an internal Jewish doctrinal dispute.[47]

A year later, in his "Dissertatio historica" of 1647, Selden returned to issues of church and state, this time not from the perspective of Jewish law, but from that of English law and history. The book is replete with examples of what he regarded as recurring attempts by the clergy to evade subjection to political

[46] Toomer *Scholarship* pp. 613, 628–629. Toomer's translation of the full title is: *A Dissertation by John Selden on the Civil Year and Calendar of the Ancient Jewish Church or State, displaying the doctrine of both the Rabbanites and the Karaites on that matter, which was the very one used both by the Apostles and other early Christians and also by Christ himself.*

[47] Toomer *Scholarship* pp. 662–663, 679–680, 684 note 439, and see pp. 703–704, on Selden's treating this subject in *Synedriis*, and mentioning that the term "Christians" originally simply meant "Messianics" – Jews who believe the Messiah had come. Selden had used the image of Aristophanes' "city of cuckoes in the clouds" before, when he referred in the "Preface" to *Historie of Tithes*, to attempts at drawing inferences about actual practices directly from Canon law. See Barbour *Measures* p. 247.

power. A typical example is his discussion of a passage in the Theodosian Code, making judgments by bishops valid in civil courts – a passage which he asserted was a glaring later insertion "by the usual frauds and deceits practiced by the priestly tribe [generis hieratici], through which they persistently and resourcefully acted to swindle princes and republics out of their authority and legitimate power[.]" An anti-clerical outburst to be sure, albeit directed at Catholic practices, the point of Selden's comment is his assertion of authority and power of political institutions over the church. Moreover, in the same work, Selden also expressed his admiration for earlier generations of clergymen-lawyers (for the most part monks) who, from Bracton onwards, formed the backbone of the early Common law, "and from their number were selected advocates and judges." Clearly Selden had no principled objection to clergymen functioning also as common lawyers, something that was obviously the case also with the Jewish sages he was studying, which were simultaneously judicial and religious figures. His comments on this might actually indicate his thoughts about what England had lost by its past severing of the connection between religious and judicial functions.[48]

However, as already mentioned, it is undoubtedly in *Synedriis* that Selden addressed most comprehensively the theme of religion and state, describing the Jewish model of this relationship, while indicating that he regarded it as a plausible, indeed desirable model for England. It is a unitary model of religion and state to be sure, but not one in which the civil power is simply superior to the religious one (as was the case say in the theories of Hobbes or Filmer). Rather, Selden put forward a model where there is no distinction between religion and state as totally separate entities, but instead there is a single institutional and intellectual framework, dealing with both. In the same manner in which the Jewish sages were, at the same time, both religious figures and legal experts, so the laws and institutions of the Jewish state, are at the same time both religious and civil. He articulated this view most explicitly in the preface (dated October 1653) to book II of *De Synedriis*, where Selden stated his conviction that his account of the ancient Jewish courts will show there was nothing in them corresponding to a distinction between ecclesiastical and civil jurisdictions.[49]

In *Synedriis* and especially so in the first volume, Selden fiercely attacked the Presbyterian view of a divine right in the church to excommunicate independently from the power of the state – to the extent that, unusually for him, he explicitly refers in the scholarly work to the Presbyterians of his own time. He explained that those claiming the power of clerical excommunication

---

[48] Selden seems to imply that when separate, church and state, always attempt to achieve supremacy over the other. See "Dissertatio historica" chapter 6 sec. 5 (p. 137 in 1771 translation). See also discussion in Toomer *Scholarship* p. 203. On Selden's comments about clergymen-lawyers, see also discussion in Barbour *Measures* pp. 152–153.

[49] *Synedriis* b1 Praefatio. See also Toomer *Scholarship* p. 724.

regard it as the "spiritual sword" of the kingdom of Christ on earth, distinct and independent from a "material sword," wielded by the political authority; and remarked that if this contention fails, with it collapses all pretension to clerical authority in such matters. As alternative to this view, he presented the theory according to which there is only one single "sword" – the power of government in every state to enforce laws, be they profane or sacred.[50]

To demonstrate his point, Selden looked at the practice of excommunication among the Jews as well as in Christian countries (and especially England). As for the Jewish part of his discussion, Selden repeatedly returned to his familiar assertion that early "Christianity was truly reformed Judaism" (Christianismum, qui plane Judaismus erat vere reformatus), intended to show that a correct understanding of Jewish terminology, practices and ideas is necessary to determine the issue of an alleged power to excommunicate in Christianity. He determined, in agreement with other commentators (including Grotius) that the inception of the practice of excommunication was at the time of the return of the Jews from their Babylonian exile, when their politico-religious leaders like Ezra and Nehemiah devised it as a method of enforcing their religious laws while they enjoyed only partial self-government. His description showed that excommunication originated in a decree of the political authority, not of the clerical (priestly) one, and certainly not as any kind of divine injunction. It had the added benefit of showing how the Jewish leadership at the time of their national restoration, was composed of persons who possessed simultaneously both religious and political functions.[51]

After having established to his satisfaction the origins and practice of ancient Jewish excommunication, Selden looked at its development in the post-apostolic period, proposing that the practice of Christian excommunication began to differ from the Jewish one mainly because of the growing hostility between the two groups, following the destruction of the Temple, and he asserted that the claim according to which excommunication rests on divine command, only emerged at this later stage of the history of the church. His account demonstrated that the claims of divine-right excommunication were a late and instrumental invention, but it also indicated that excommunication as later practiced in Christian countries was by and large founded on a lie, implying the desirability of restoring it to its original, "Jewish-Christian" character.[52]

Apart from establishing the original and "Jewish" nature of excommunication, Selden also looked to its historical practice in Christian countries, and repeatedly pointed out its fundamental function as a political instrument rather than a religious one, showing how the authority for Catholic bishops exercising it, had originated in the Roman imperial law of the time of Emperor Constantine, and had since then been often employed in strictly

---

[50] Toomer *Scholarship* pp. 693–694. *Synedriis* b1 Praefatio
[51] Toomer *Scholarship* pp. 696, 700–701. [52] Toomer *Scholarship* p. 705.

political matters that had absolutely nothing to do with religious issues – such as when Pope Innocent III notoriously threatened to excommunicate those Englishmen who had asserted their "ancestral liberties" and forced King John to sign the Magna Carta. Selden thus not only established the political nature and practice of excommunication, but also connected its origin in to the tyrannical Imperial Roman law, and its practice to the attempts to extinguish English liberties at the time of Magna Carta – therefore identifying assertions of divine-right excommunication with the past and current threats to English "ancestral law and custom." Indicating explicitly his own position within this scheme of things, he cited among many historical examples of English statutes and legal writers upholding the supremacy of government over the clergy, also Parliament's recent setting of bounds on the "[P]resbyterian excommunication," despite the protest of the "assembly of the ecclesiastical order" – obviously referring to Parliament's passing of the "Ordinance for Church Government" of 1646, and to its rejection of the Westminster Assembly's petition against it, a sequence of events in which Selden had played an important role. As already mentioned, Selden also strongly and explicitly objected to the terming as "Erastian" of the view that excommunication is of human origin, rather than by *jure divino*. Bringing a long list of examples from English history, he showed the civil authority to ever have had the final say on such matters, and that it was those self-defining as "anti-Erastians" who were to be regarded as innovators attempting to challenge established English ways.[53]

Another aspect of the relationship between religion and state, to which Selden returned repeatedly in *Synedriis*, was the alleged scriptural basis for various church offices, which if accepted, would make them *jure divino*, and thus independent of human laws or authority. As seen previously, Selden consistently held episcopacy not to be scripturally commanded (although he supported its continued existence, on the grounds of English laws and traditions), but in his later writings, including *Synedriis*, he invested no lesser efforts in demonstrating that the office of Presbyter in ther church was equally lacking any scriptural basis. While elsewhere he treated the meaning of the term "presbyter" in the New Testament, the *Synedriis'* focus on Jewish traditions allowed him to address claims to find precedents for the Christian Presbyters in the Hebrew Bible. In *Synedriis* I chapter 13, dealing with the early administration of law by Moses and the elders, Selden discussed the meaning of the parallels for the term "Presbyter" in Hebrew and other languages. For example, he argued that the Hebrew synonym for the Greek presbyters, "Zkenim" (elders), was in the Hebrew Bible a term denoting those qualified to serve as judges, and thus as civil magistrates, having in fact nothing at all to do with leading religious communities. Indeed, in this context he harshly criticized Grotius for careless asides on these matters, such as his assuming in his commentary on the New Testament, without any proof whatsoever, the

---

[53] *Synedriis* b1c13. See also Toomer *Scholarship* pp. 708–712, 718–719.

existence of such Christian Presbyteries, as well as his inexact understanding of the Jewish practice of excommunication. The implications of this learned discussion for the debate about a scriptural basis for establishing Presbyterianism in England, were obvious – for if the biblical elders were in fact civil magistrates, they could not serve as basis for establishing an elders-led Presbyterian church independent of civil authority.[54]

Evidently, Selden's claim in *Synedriis* that there was no biblical or otherwise scriptural theological basis to claims for an independent clerical authority was not in itself new with him. But, as Toomer also points out, his returning to the subject again and again in the book, as well as the fact that whereas on most other issues he usually left the readers to draw their own conclusions, while in this case he often explicitly spelled out the expected conclusion, invests the *Synedriis* with an unusual sense of determination and urgency. Probably reacting to the general intellectual crisis and conceptual confusion in English political society of the time, as well as perhaps also sensing his own approaching death, gave this last work of Selden a distinctive character and poignancy.[55]

6.3 "PARLIAMENT IS THE CHURCH"

As already mentioned, parallel to Selden's writings on church and state in his later years, he was also prominently active politically in the 1640s on these issues, both in Parliament and in the Westminster Assembly. His ideas and activities on this front are relatively well documented when compared to his previous political activities, both in parliamentary records and Assembly speeches – as well as in materials from the *Table-Talk*, which include many comments on specific issues he addressed, as well as what seem to be several drafts or headings for speeches to be delivered in both bodies. As the Long Parliament convened in November 1640, complaints about religious issues were already a major part of the political agenda. But while the demand for some kind of change was almost universally shared among the parliamentarians, as for the eventual asset that would replace the current one, there were wildly differing ideas: some merely wanted to end the Laudian excesses, others hoped for a reformed episcopacy, yet others pined for a more godly church, or even worked for a complete overhaul. As to the type of concerns about church and state driving the Parliament men, in later years Richard Baxter aptly described thus the two sorts of men cooperating in the early 1640s for a reformation of religious matters:

One Party made no great matter of these Alterations in the Church; but they said, That if Parliaments were once down, and our Propriety gone, and Arbitrary Government set up, and Law subjected to the Prince's Will, we were then all Slaves, and this they made

---

[54] *Synedriis* b1c13; Toomer *Scholarship* pp. 608, 719–720, 742.
[55] Toomer *Scholarship* p. 787.

a thing intolerable[.] these men were called *Good Commonwealth's Men*; [the other group were] more religious men [caring about political matters too, but] much more sensible of the Interest of Religion.[56]

Thus the first group comprised those (Selden obviously among them) principally concerned with constitutional matters, who regarded the crisis on religious issues as a reflection of the wider political crisis, one of the various arbitrary dangers that had gathered against the liberties and property of Englishmen; while the second group was driven by the attempt to realize a religious idea of a purified church (while widely differing about the actual content of such a purification). Of course, there were also very many among whom the predominance of one concern or another was hard to discern (often even to themselves), or to whom the importance of the religious versus the political changed with the unfolding circumstances of the conflict. As long as the struggle against Laudianism continued, such differences remained for the most part submerged, but after that threat had subsided the path of those who had objected to Laud's policies because they thought them sacrilegious and those who merely thought them contrary to law, gradually diverged, and the groups would eventually correspond, for the most part, to constitutionalists (many of whom chose the royalist side) for the law-minded, and to staunch parliamentarians for those who were primarily religiously motivated.[57]

The political battles of 1641 and 1642 about the presence of bishops in Parliament, were only the prelude to a larger struggle about the future of the church, made urgent by the demands in this direction by the Scottish Presbyterians, as their price for securing an alliance against the royalist armies. Thus, as early as 12 June 1643 an ordinance passed in both Houses of Parliament had decreed the creation of a gathering of clergy which became the Westminster Assembly of Divines, and defined its mandate as "advice and counsel therein to both or either of the said Houses" of Parliament on how "such a government shall be settled in the Church as may be most agreeable to God's Holy Word..." and apt to procure "...nearer agreement with the Church of Scotland." By August an agreement was reached with the Scots about creating a military league and (as its price) a religious covenant, so that on 25 September 1643 a "Solemn League and Covenant" was signed by both Houses of Parliament – in which they pledged themselves to establish in England a Presbyterian Church patterned after the church of Scotland. Four commissioners were sent out from Edinburgh, to represent the Scots within this process.[58]

The Scottish component within the drive to reform the English church had been evident at least since early 1641, when the Scottish commissioners were on

---

[56] Richard Baxter, *Reliquiae Baxterianae* M. Sylvester ed. (1696) i.i pp. 13–18 (paragraphs 17–27) quoted in Paul *Assembly* pp. 52–54; See also Richard Baxter, *A Third Defence of the Cause of Peace* (1681) pp. 112–113.

[57] Smith *Constitutional* pp. 66–67.   [58] Paul *Assembly* pp. 68–69; Tanner *Conflicts* p. 126.

a previous visit to London, and one of them, Alexander Henderson, chose to publicly air his principled opposition to episcopacy, just as that issue was being debated in Parliament. Baillie reported to Scotland that the outburst had hurt their cause, for "diverse of our true friends did think us too rash, and though they loved not the bishops, yet for the honor of their nation, they would keep them up rather than we strangers should put them down." This report points to the degree to which church reform in the Presbyterian style (already very much associated in England with Scotland), became growingly identified with Scottish influence, and therefore as something foreign to the true nature of the English and their church. The attitude of many Englishmen to the Scots always contained thinly veiled (and not so veiled) elements of disdain, which emerged at times when the latter were seen to be encroaching on English national identity. A blunt reflection of this attitude was articulated by Marchamont Needham, who certainly knew how to read and to sway English public opinion, when his *Case of the Commonwealth* (1650) opened the second chapter "Concerning the Scots" with the words: "I AM sorry I must waste paper on this nation[.]" A strong resentment of Scottish influence became an important element hampering the adoption Presbyterianism in England, even among Englishmen of Presbyterian theological views, and contributed to the eventual failure of this effort.[59]

The membership of the Westminster Assembly consisted of a large majority of Presbyterian divines, the result of their numerical predominance on the list of appointed clergy, together with the fact that a not inconsiderable number of members of other ecclesiastical persuasions did not attend. Among the small number of overt Episcopalian clergy appointed, most like Ussher, declined to ever attend the Assembly, and one that did, Dr. Daniel Featley, had by October 1643 already been expelled and imprisoned, for corresponding with Ussher and royalists at Oxford. We might also follow R. Paul in his suspicion that many among the appointed members who never attended the Assembly were what may be termed "Puritan Episcopalians," the like of Richard Baxter (not a member of the Assembly), who while being an anti-Laudian with unimpeachable Puritan credentials, was eventually persuaded by Ussher's scholarly arguments about the existence of a primitive episcopacy in the New Testament.[60]

These developments left the attending membership of the Assembly with a relatively small contingent of members opposed to a strictly Presbyterian church. The largest group among these was of those described by contemporaries as "Dissenting Brethren" who came to be known as Independents or Congregationalists, led by Philip Nye and Thomas Goodwin, who (albeit with great difference of opinion among themselves, and not in principle against some form of Presbyterianism), were opposed to a church

---

[59] Needham *Case* chapter 2; Paul *Assembly* pp. 42–43; Rahe *Against* p. 193.
[60] Paul *Assembly* pp. 105–107.

discipline that would not allow for a large degree of autonomy to individual congregations. Then there was an even smaller contingent of clergymen who although theologically Calvinist, believed that church discipline should not be administered by the clergy (and certainly not by a Presbytery) but rather by the civil power, most prominent among those were two of the most accomplished Hebraists in the Assembly, Thomas Coleman (dubbed "rabbi Coleman" for his Hebraist proficiency) and John Lightfoot – the latter apparently came into the Assembly quite open minded, but was gradually won over by the ideas of Coleman and Selden. Finally there was the non-clerical contingent of the Assembly members, 30 MPs (10 peers and 20 commoners), who for the most part played an insignificant part in the proceedings (William Fiennes, Viscount Saye and Sele was a prominent exception) – except for the small group of prominent lawyers, principally preoccupied with the repercussions of a church settlement over the legal and constitutional primacy of Parliament, most active among whom were Bulstrode Whitelocke, William Pierrepont and, head and shoulders above all, John Selden.[61]

Some Presbyterians had had early hopes for Selden to be aligned on their side, in their efforts to abolish bishops. As it was, he emerged instead as a leading defender of episcopacy, but, as the struggle about bishops in Parliament had been decided in 1642, Presbyterians could hope for Selden to be, if not actively supportive of their cause, at least uninvolved in the following theological debates. They found out otherwise, for Selden's name on the list of MPs that were appointed to the Westminster Assembly indicated his interest and prominence in the proceedings. Selden attended the Assembly fairly regularly in its first months and participated vigorously in many debates. The reason for this involvement, as he confided to the erudite bibliophile John Morris at the time the Westminster Assembly was being created, was that he feared for the liberties of Englishmen, more from such an Assembly and its uninhibited 'spiritual arm' than any army, either royal or parliamentarian. For Selden the problem was with the very creation of a separate "body" of divines, which by its very essence would tend to assume that it had power to determine on its own matters of religion, and that the laity were to be bound by these determinations. He saw no problem in Parliament consulting with divines, and as we have seen he even favored the regular clerical presence within Parliament, as represented by the bishops, but the creating of a body of clerics separate from Parliament was for him to court a conflict of jurisdiction.[62]

Soon, a first intimation of his future role in the Assembly was supplied by his intervention in an early debate, as reported in the royalist newspaper *Mercurius Aulicus* of 23 July 1643, when during a discussion of a clause requiring investigation of Jesus' descent into Hell, Selden scathingly remarked he could

---

[61] Kaplan "Settlement" pp. 318–322; Lamont *Godly* pp. 110–111, 114–116.
[62] Letter by John Morris to Joannes de Laet, 30 May 1643, reported in Toomer *Scholarship* p. 571 note 61; Lamont *Godly* pp. 109–110.

only "wonder, that an Article which had been generally received in the Christian Church 1500 yeares should be doubted of" and mockingly proposed that for the Assembly to be better informed about the matter they might "make a speciall *Committee*, put Dr. [Cornelius] *Burges* in the Chaire" and send them to learn the truth of the matter there, so that from Hell they might "certifie the same to their brethren here." The remark captures what will become some of the more typical traits of Selden's interventions in the Assembly, his sardonic wit, as well as his impatience with clergymen who were dismissive of traditions, while attempting to replace these with dubiously-founded claims of their own. He soon stood out as by far the most active and most effective lay member of the Assembly, who in the debates mostly dominated by clergymen soon came to be identified simply as the "learned gentellman."[63]

There have been many attempts to present a detailed breakdown of Assembly membership along "party lines" of views on church and state, but all such attempts cannot overcome the fact that there was a vast array of issues where the positions of members would not be in line with others of their "party" and not a few cases where individuals were patently grappling with internal conflicts over the issues. Many of those Englishmen in the Assembly regarded as "Presbyterians" were in fact far less doctrinally secure and homogeneous than the relatively disciplined and indoctrinated Scottish commissioners. Among MPs attending, those of Presbyterian sympathies often found themselves in conflict with their beliefs about the role of Parliament, while the Independents, as befits their title, displayed a vast array of positions and beliefs on church and state. However, fairly early on in the life of the Assembly a main divergence emerged around the question of the existence of a *jure divino* sphere of autonomous church authority, against those arguing there was very little *jure divino* about the form of the church and thus preferred the supremacy of Parliament in all things pertaining to church and state. Those adhering to each position came to be dubbed as "Presbyterians" and "Erastians" (sometimes with sub-categories like English Presbyterians, or Lawyers), but as we have seen, both terms were regularly used imprecisely, sometimes intentionally so, and comprised individuals with widely diverging theological views, so that it is better to regard them only as nicknames relating mainly to political maneuvers (just as later, the terms of abuse Tories and Whigs came to denote political groups), and not as necessarily reflecting the actual theological positions of any individual member.[64]

The internal divisions in the Assembly, about the asset of church and state first surfaced substantially on 20–22 September 1643, even before the Solemn

---

[63] Selden in the Assembly quoted in *Mercurius Aulicus* (23 July 1643), reported in Toomer *Scholarship* pp. 571–572; "learned gentellman" see Van Dixhoorn *Minutes* vol. ii pp. 443, 470, and vol. iii p. 394.

[64] Paul *Assembly* pp. 127–128.

League and Covenant had been signed, when after Dr. Thomas Temple had given voice to the widespread antipathy of Assembly members towards antinomianism, the debate turned to how such men should be punished, and by whom. Selden, representing the Commons, spoke in this debate and exposed the problematic implications of the issue by demanding that the Assembly consider what was to be regarded as heresy in English law. He remarked that the aim of the Commons was not "only to make some law & declaration against the opinions [but] to proceed against the persons" yet the Assembly does not give "hint enough hoe to proceed" in such matters. His conclusion was clear:

Unlesse you doe let the House of Commons know that ther be of those things that are direct Herisyes, then they can[not] know how to proceed against them that have already disturbed you.[65]

Following this brief eruption of controversy, discussions in the Assembly returned to a more sedate mode for a number of months, treading in the main on peripheral matters. For some months, the Presbyterians conducted behind-the-scenes maneuvers, attempting to achieve some kind of political deal with the Independents. But fundamental controversies emerged suddenly on 12 December, within a seemingly minor discussion on the scriptural foundation for excommunication, when some speakers claimed for an independent church right of excommunication, exercised by the Christian Fathers of the Church, on the basis of biblical passages describing Jewish laws of Temple worship. These speakers were in effect claiming that there was a biblical divine right of excommunication in the church, that had been translated from Judaism into the Christian church. It was at this point that Selden rose to speak:

The maine question. The word church as now we have it will noe wher be found, nor noe mention of it in that time.
    Church now amongst us is distinguished from the state. But we having received it out of Christian doctrine, will it hould to the Jewish state? State & church are synonyms [...] with relation to them.

The "maine question" at hand was the claim to the existence of a scripturally sanctioned independent authority of the church. In a few terse statements Selden rejected absolutely the main arguments that had been raised to buttress the claim. He argued that the word "church" in the meaning now assigned to it could not be found at the time of the existence of a Jewish state, since with the Jewish laws "State & church are synonyms." Instead, church as "distinguished from the state" is a notion wholly received "out of Christian doctrine" only. In short, if there was any independent church authority, it could certainly not be claimed out of Jewish sources.[66]

---

[65] Van Dixhoorn *Minutes* vol. ii pp. 145–146; Paul *Assembly* p. 178.
[66] Van Dixhoorn *Minutes* vol. ii pp. 442–443. Selden added rhetorically "[w]hat amongst the Jewes was ecclesiasticall?" and went on to examine alleged ecclesiastical jurisdiction drawn by some from the claim that Jewish courts dealing in religious matters were composed of priests and

This intervention by Selden drew harsh responses from Presbyterian clergymen, and this is most likely the source for Baillie's famous assertion about Selden avowing "that the Jewish state and church was all one." The point man in the Presbyterian attack on Selden's view was George Gillespie, a young and scholarly Scottish commissioner, who insisted on the existence (at least implied) of a clear "distinction betwixt the church & state of the Jewes[.]" He went on to point to a passage in the book written by the "learned gentellman" – meaning the *Jure Naturali* – in which he interpreted a mention of excommunication as implying men were separated from "the people & church" while remaining "members of the commonwealth," thus seemingly pointing to a separation of church and state. Gillespie's remark drew from Selden the answer that the passage quoted from his book did not "prove a distinction of church & state" for the "businesse of excommunication" was "never spoken of in the Jewes' state" as a matter separately ecclesiastical. Gillespie retorted that in his view, the very act of excommunication implies a separation of church and state. At this point the debate was cut short, and the Assembly moved to other matters, but the battle lines had been clearly drawn.[67]

The matter resurfaced repeatedly in the following days, as other biblical passages touching on excommunication were discussed by the Assembly. Selden gradually added in his interventions, more and more materials to support his position on excommunication, arguing, for example, that his own reading of this issue in "the Old Testament" was also agreed upon "by the Talmudicall Jewes." His arguments evidently found a sympathetic audience among several members of the Assembly that had been previously swayed by the Presbyterian claims about excommunication, among them the most active of the peers sitting in the Assembly, William Fiennes, Viscount Saye and Sele, who announced his agreement with things spoken on this subject by "that learned gentellman." On 20 December, Selden added to his recurring assertion that among the Jews there was no distinction between church and state, the claim that even if in some Christian countries, a separate church authority to excommunicate did develop, not only that practice had no scriptural basis, but it also did not apply to England, since "[a]mongst us it was perpetually a civil act." The Presbyterians having found that the Assembly might not turn out to be as docile as they expected, signed by late December a truce with the Independents (*Certaine considerations to dis-swade men from further gathering of churches in this present juncture of time*, 1643), and now expecting to have a massive majority in the Assembly, started to strategize about the best manner and context, by which to bring up the issue of a Presbyterian church government.[68]

Levites, the biblical parallels of the Christian clergy. This claim too he rejected saying that "Noe court of Jurisdiction" existed among Jews composed of priests and Levites only, or laymen only.
[67] Van Dixhoorn *Minutes* vol. ii pp. 442–443, 455.
[68] Van Dixhoorn *Minutes* vol. ii pp. 455, 469–470, 485, 488–489; Paul *Assembly* p. 240.

When on 8 January 1644, Selden raised on his own accord the issue of excommunication, proposing a resolution declaring that there is no such thing as a religious excommunication but only by the civil power, the Presbyterians felt they were not yet ready to tackle the issue directly, so that after an inconclusive debate in which some opposed and others supported Selden's view, the matter of "excommunication and censures" was referred to the Assembly's Second Committee. It was on 23 January that Presbyterians were confident that the right time had come, and actively initiated a debate on the issue, when a proposition by George Gillespie came before the Assembly, for ad hoc rules on ordination and censure of the clergy, which the Presbyterians proposed be executed in a manner allegedly based on the authority of the biblical passage from 2 Chronicles 29:34 – a text usually employed by Congregationalists (and thus intended to enlist their support to the Presbyterian proposal). As the debate unfolded, many members, eventually including the Independents, came to regard the proposal as a ploy for creating of a *jure divino* Presbyterian system under another name. Initially the only opposition to the proposal was by a handful of members, quickly dubbed by their enemies "Erastians," – primarily Selden, Coleman and Lightfoot – who denied that the said passage created a scriptural authority for the proposition. Indeed, Selden opposed not only the use of the specific passage, but the very idea of ecclesiastical censures, arguing again that the scriptures only allowed civil ones. Regardless of this vigorous opposition, the proposition passed in the affirmative – but with a majority that the Presbyterians discovered as surprisingly small. When an additional proposal, to use as scriptural authority for this practice two more biblical passages (Numbers 9 and 2 Chronicles 30: 2–5) barely passed the vote, Selden made a motion that hereafter when voting comes to near equality, the scribes of the Assembly should take a count and write down how many affirmatives and negatives there be. One can suppose that on top of confirming that there was indeed a majority in close votes, the writing down of voting numbers might also have been intended to disclose the fact that the overall numbers of actual voters were small as compared to the formal membership of the Assembly. Selden's proposal was again defeated, but it triggered another tense discussion, which exposed the growing degree of hostility between positions and especially an increasing rift between Presbyterian and Independent positions. The Presbyterians discovered that their supposedly vast majority had dissolved, as Selden and his allies had successfully driven a wedge between them and the Independents. Though the Presbyterians had for the time prevailed, they had also discovered that the road ahead was to be a far longer and harder one than they had anticipated. This long and, according to Baillie, cantankerous day of debates opened what was to become the Westminster Assembly's most decisive period of activity pertaining to the relationship of church and state, between January and May of 1644 – the period when the debates raged round the attempt to establish a *jure divino* authority for a Presbyterian system of church government which, as divinely ordained, would by definition be independent of political jurisdiction. Not incidentally, this was also the period of the most intensive activity by John Selden, as a member of the Assembly. In several cases Selden's words in the Assembly exposed and increased divisions among members, and often his interventions were followed by lengthy debates that ended in impasse.[69]

The long day of debates on 23 January in effect broke up the Presbyterian-Independent alliance, and triggered several more similar days in the following weeks, crystallizing into a grand debate between presbytery and its opponents, much of it concerned with identifying the biblical passages upon which the ecclesiological battle was to be fought. Both Presbyterians and Independents, also started to produce pamphlets justifying their positions. The Presbyterians distributed the pamphlets *Church-Government in Scotland Cleered from Some Mmistakes and Prejudices* (1643) and *Congregational Elderships and Classical Presbyteries* (1643), the Independents distributed the pamphlet *Apologeticall Narration* (1643). The debate also involved more substantial publications, prominent among which was Selden's *Anno Civili* of 1644, composed for the most part in 1643, which addressed the issues at hand with its attacks on the ignorant who claim to apply usages of Judaism to Christianity without knowledge of the Talmud, on those who try to distort scripture to follow their own designs, and on those who falsely claim supremacy of ecclesiastics over laymen. In order to answer substantial objections to the Presbyterian positions in both *Anno Civili* as well as the *Jure Naturali* Gillespie published a tract quoting and debating at length from Selden's writings, self-explanatorily titled: *A Late Dialogue Betwixt a Civilian and a Divine, Concerning the Present Condition of the Church of England. In which, Among Other Particulars, these Following are Especially Spoken of. 1 The Sinne and Danger of Delaying Reformation. 2 That There is a Certain Form of Church-Government Jure Divino. 3 That There Was an Ecclesiasticall Excommunication Among the Jews. 4 That Excommunication is an Ordinance in the New Testament. 5 Concerning the Toleration of All Sects and Heresies. 6 Some Answer to a Late Book Come from Oxford.* [1644].

As the debates of January 1644 unfolded, the tactics of those opposing *jure divino* presbytery differed. Many Independents and even Lightfoot, fearing the rising expressions of Sectarianism, were ready to discuss some compromise conceding a Presbyterian church (while refusing to consider it *jure divino*), while Coleman and Selden did not budge, continuing to oppose any concession on this front, tooth and nail. When on 25 January 1644, the Assembly started to discuss the ordination of clergy by ministers, Selden rose and infuriated the Presbyterians with his assertion that "[b]y the laws of England none can ordain but only a Bishop, with some presbyters" and then added that "this law is neither against the law of God, nor nulled yet in our state. And whereas our [solemn league and] covenant swears out the *regimen*

---

[69] Paul *Assembly* pp. 220–222, 240; Dixhoorn *Minutes* vol. ii pp. 488–489.

ecclesiae, this that we have in hand is not *regimen ecclesiae*, and we have sworn to preserve the laws of the kingdom, of which this is one." In other words, Selden was arguing that: 1. The supreme authority concerning ordination of ministers was not the Assembly, but rather the laws of England. 2. By those laws the authority of ordination was still by bishops. 3. They all (including Selden) swore by Solemn League and Covenant to take away the bishops' power of jurisdiction (their sitting in Parliament), which they had, but the power of ordination was something else, and that had not been revoked. Not surprisingly, this position caused much commotion in the Assembly and much consternation among the Presbyterians, who confronted with the debate that erupted upon this issue, saw evaporate their hopes for a speedy establishment of a separate church authority for ordaining.[70]

On the next day, 26 January, the debate on ordination reached a pitch when the Presbyterians threw all they had into the fray, in an all-out attempt to decide the matter through the sheer firepower of their preponderance in numbers. The Scottish commissioner Alexander Henderson fired the opening salvo, followed by speaker after speaker who relentlessly attacked the two leading opponents of Presbyterian ordination, Selden and the prominent Independent theologian Philip Nye (whose growing doubts about a Presbyterian-dominated church were gradually pushing him into an alliance with Selden). The speakers singled out especially Selden's claim that bishops still retained the sole power of ordination, as not only obstructing the setting up of Presbyterian ordination, but seemingly resurrecting an episcopacy that had seemed to them dead and buried. Unperturbed, Selden stood his ground, and delivered a detailed and learned justification of his position. When the debate resumed on the following day, 27 January, it emerged that the dynamics had changed. Several Independents who had stayed silent on the first days of the debate were evidently emboldened by Selden's withstanding of the Presbyterian juggernaut, and they started to speak out against the proposal for Presbyterian ordination, and, discovering it had several inconveniences, "started to cavil at it." The Earls of Pembroke and Salisbury, leading Puritan peers who had been informed that the expected smooth sailing of ordination had been derailed, came into the Assembly, and Pembroke repeatedly intervened in the debate, urging a swift decision of the issue, but to no avail, as this day also ended without resolution. After a Sunday recess, the Assembly reconvened on 29 January, in what was becoming a showdown on the issue of ordination. As the debate resumed, the rising tension produced growing public interest about the proceedings, and Baillie noticed that in the last days of January a growing number of MPs began to crowd into the Jerusalem Chamber the better to closely follow the debates, and a succession of prominent MPs who had never before attended the Assembly started arriving, including Lord Admiral Warwick, Lord General Fairfax, Lords Pembroke, Salisbury, Saye and Sele (the last actually one of the few peers who regularly attended and

---

[70] Paul *Assembly* pp. 220–225.

participated), Howard, Manchester, Northumberland and "some others." Soon those clerical members of the Assembly who had been regularly attending started to complain about the lack of available space for them in these sessions. By the end of January, it was clear that if it came to a formal decision of ordination, while the Presbyterians probably had the numbers to prevail, there was a real prospect of a complete break with the Independents, and the fear of such an outcome finally brought the Assembly to approve, on Friday, 2 February 1644, the proposal of Lord Saye and Sele that the matter of clergy ordination should be "laid aside for the present," and wait for other issues to be settled first. The Presbyterian advance had been blocked.[71]

In a letter from February 1644, Baillie touched on the real heart of the dispute, which reappeared again and again in the various debates about issues of church authority – the source of that authority in scripture. The Presbyterian positions on excommunication, on ordination and on the form of church government, were claimed to be based directly on biblical passages, and thus literally *jure divino*. Selden understood this and his efforts in the Assembly accordingly concentrated primarily on confuting these claims. An example of this is supplied by Baillie's description, in the same letter, of Selden's position on the clerical power of excommunication as "avowing with Erastus, that there was no such censure in Scripture, and what it was, was meerlie civill[.]" On Selden's part, this strategy of his was indicated in a sardonic passage of the *Table-Talk*:

When the queries were sent to the [Westminster] assembly concerning the *jus divinum* of presbytery, their asking time to answer them, was a satire upon themselves; for if it were to be seen in the text, they might quickly turn to the place, and show us it; their delaying to answer makes us think there's no such thing there. They do just as you have seen a fellow do at a tavern-reckoning; when he should come to pay his reckoning, he puts his hands into his pockets, and keeps a grabbling and a fumbling, and shaking, at last tells you he has left his money at home, when all the company knew at first he had no money there, for everyman can quickly find his own money.[72]

By mid-February 1644 as the debates about clerical authority of excommunication and ordination had died down, without the Assembly having reached a concrete decision, a new debate flared up, this time about the terminology appearing in Old and New Testament passages that served as alleged scriptural basis for the form of church government. It turned out that the acceptance of various biblical passages by the Assembly as basis for determining church government, which the Presbyterians had regarded as a decisive victory, was to be nothing of the sort, since the discussion of the passages' terminology rapidly turned into trench warfare about every single word, and the meaning that the words gave to crucial biblical passages. Such, for example, was a debate

---

[71] Paul *Assembly* pp. 227–232; Van Dixhoorn *Minutes* vol. ii pp. 488–489.

[72] Letter to William Spang (18 February 1644) in Baillie *Letters* vol. iii p. 129; TT "Presbytery" sec. 4.

about the meaning of the Hebrew word "Kahal" – if by it the people of Israel or only the elders are meant; or about the Greek word "ecclesia" in Matthew 18 – if by it the Jewish Sanhedrin, or the early Christian church, or something else is meant.[73]

Once again, the Presbyterians attempted to impose their reading of the terminology, by a combination of their clear numerical superiority and the intellectual firepower supplied by the Scottish commissioners, each of their speakers in turn asserting their reading of the passages to be the correct one. The feeble and diverging responses by Independent speakers were clearly no match to the fiery and consistent Presbyterian claims, in what at first appeared to be an unstoppable momentum for adoption of their interpretation. However, on 20 February 1644, Selden rose to speak, and to the dismay of the Presbyterians, by presenting a mass of relevant erudition that could not be ignored, brought about a dramatic change in the direction of the dispute. Selden asserted that Matthew 18, brought as the scriptural proof for a divine right to excommunication by the Presbytery, did not support this contention at all. First he showed that all churches, Presbyterian certainly, but also Catholic, Episcopal and Congregational had appropriated that very same passage to support their claims about independent excommunication, but employed it to justify wildly differing ecclesiologies; then he pointed out that actually, for the first four centuries of Christianity, none of the Church Fathers had ever used the passage to prove a divine authority for church discipline. The claim for the passage to be a sanction for independent ecclesiastic authority was thus shown to be far from a scriptural proof, and rather to the obvious horror of Presbyterians, merely a later self-serving distortion of the text in the service of clerical interests, so typical of unreformed churches. Moreover, Selden declared, the "ecclesia" mentioned in Matthew 18 was in fact neither the whole church nor the Great Sanhedrin, but only the Jewish civil court of Capernaum, where Jesus resided at that time – thus the said passage, rather than endorsing anything like a separate religious jurisdiction, actually justified by scripture the supremacy of the civil authority. After having demolished the claims made upon the specific passage, Selden then went on to address the question at hand more generally, and brought before the Assembly a wealth of Jewish and classical sources, showing excommunication to be a civil form of separation and sentence, and no *jure divino* authority of the church. Selden had patently done his homework since the excommunication debate of December 1643, and now dropped in the lap of the Assembly a mass of materials weighting against a claim to a Presbyterian authority of excommunication. The focus of the whole debate was thus altered – from one between competing visions of church authority and structure, to a debate about the role of civil authority in church matters. Two Presbyterian divines, Herle and Marshall, at once attempted to counter Selden's argument, but it seems they

[73] Paul *Assembly* pp. 266–271.

did so less than convincingly, for Lightfoot who was then wavering upon this issue, recorded in his journal that the words of these two "gave me no satisfaction." The next day, 21 February, the Presbyterians threw in their star performer, George Gillespie, to attack Selden's view, joined in by another of their more articulate spokesmen, Thomas Young. Evidently these two also failed to convince the Assembly, for after them Thomas Coleman weighted in his own considerable erudition on Selden's side. Philip Nye for the Independents, finding all the arguments by his group had been brushed aside, and the Assembly now preoccupied with the issue of civil authority over the church, attempted to add his voice to Selden's side of the argument, although apparently not very convincingly. The supremacy of the civil authority had now been explicitly broached, and it continued to concern the theologians and the politician, both inside the Assembly and out of it, long after this debate – indeed, Selden obviously thought his intervention on this passage worth returning to, years later and at length, when he published in 1650 the first volume of *Synedriis*. Once again, the Presbyterian progress had been unexpectedly bogged down.[74]

On 22 February 1644 there was a new attempt to decide the issue of church government, this time by looking at the example of the earliest church in Jerusalem. As was increasingly happening, the fractiousness of opinions in the Assembly soon made the debate hopelessly confused. Selden censured the muddle the Assembly had put itself in, remarking "you speak of soe many things together" and then proposed that to untangle the confusion, those supporting the proposition that the church of Jerusalem was governed by Presbytery, should clearly prove four things: that there were presbyters, that they formed a presbytery, that there were several congregations under them, and that these congregations were governed by that presbytery. One might suspect this systematic advice on how to proceed was also devised to create an interconnected chain of argument, so that by disproving even one of the four "things" the whole chain would be vitiated. The next day, 23 February, Selden spoke at length to prove that the "church of Christ beginning in Jerusalem" was simply a Jewish sect, whose members did not consider themselves members of a church or religion separate from Judaism, indeed he conjectures that the Jewish sect of "Essens" described by Josephus, actually "might mean to be the Christians." Selden reminded the Assembly that early Christians did not admit

---

[74] Van Dixhoorn *Minutes* vol. ii pp. 488–489, 520; Paul *Assembly* pp. 266–271. In *Synedriis* Selden returned to Matthew 18 at length: "Now, scholars disagree about the exact meaning of the term 'church' in this passage: some think it refers to an ecclesiastical *synedrium* or council of elders, something of the sort which the Jews had in their own state; others to a Jewish *synedrium* or council of elders; others to a Christian council of elders, which did not yet exist but was being foreshadowed here; others to what they call the 'prince of the Church,' i.e., the Supreme Pontiff; others merely to the *rabim* or *majority*, i.e., to a public gathering or meeting which lacked the character of a court; and still others to various other things." He followed this with an exhaustive and very long discussion, showing the term not to mean excommunication. See *Synedriis* b1c9.

members who were not Jews, that they were sticklers for the "law of Moses" and that they even "found fault with Paul, that he should diswade any from walking in the customs of the Jewes." His conclusion was that the early Christian "house[s] of congregation" in Jerusalem, were nothing other than Jewish synagogues of that particular sect, among the many hundreds of other synagogues in that city, whose members, like all Jews also came to worship at the Temple. That is, there was nothing in them conferring any separate authority. A whole week of debates had gone by, and the Presbyterians found they were in a place far worse for them, on the issue of church government, than when they began.[75]

The debates continued in similar manner in the following weeks, so that by late March 1644, Selden and his allies had scored some significant tactical successes, and it was clear the Assembly would not produce a swift and near-unanimous Presbyterian-inspired settlement, as was initially hoped by the latter. But it also became clear, that there was no real chance of breaking the ingrained Presbyterian majority by force of argument and historical evidence; especially as the Independents in the Assembly were proving to be increasingly confused and ineffective. Throughout his activity in the Assembly, relentlessly pressured by the Scottish commissioners and always in a clear minority, Selden, far from being cowed, displayed an implacable opposition to the proposals and views of the Presbyterian majority, and contributed significantly to the differences of opinion on every point discussed, that won the Assembly public notoriety for its slowness. However, it was now also becoming obvious that, sooner or later, the ingrained majority of the Westminster Assembly would decide on a Presbyterian government for the English church, a development that could be obstructed and slowed down for some more time, but not defeated in the Assembly itself. It was about this time that Selden stopped attending the Assembly.[76]

We might suspect that Selden's prominent attendance and participation in the Assembly during the first months of 1644 was also intended to influence the many MPs who showed a marked interest in the Assembly's proceedings during this period – either to draw them to Selden's views, or display the intransigence of the Presbyterian positions on an independent church jurisdiction. Be things as they may, from late March 1644, not only did Selden discontinue his attendance (his last recorded attendance was 22 March 1644) but the overall interest of MPs in the Assembly proceedings also steeply and markedly declined. Although it is not impossible that Selden attended some additional session of the

[75] Van Dixhoorn *Minutes* vol. ii pp. 537–538, 550–552; Paul *Assembly* pp. 282–283; Toomer *Scholarship* p. 573. In early March Selden returned to the issue remarking that a Presbyterian government over many congregations in the early church "must suppose something of *Imperium* and jurisdiction in it" which the early church did not have. See Van Dixhoorn *Minutes* vol. ii pp. 567–568.
[76] Toomer *Scholarship* pp. 572–573 and note 67.

Assembly without speaking or its being recorded, clearly from this time onwards, he did not participate in any notable way in its proceedings; a sudden and evident departure from his previous activity.

However, if the Presbyterians thought that Selden's withdrawing from activity within the Assembly indicated that he was giving up the struggle for the shape of the future settlement of church and state in England, they were soon to discover their mistake. Far from giving up, he merely moved the focus of his activity to his home grounds of Parliament, where he might hope to be more effective in thwarting the triumphal progress of Presbyterianism. In Parliament Selden, Whitelocke and Pierrepont, who had been the most prominent anti-Presbyterian "lawyers" in the Assembly, now joined with a number of MPs – all of them lawyers – representing different theological views but united in their resolve to preserve the parliamentary supremacy over church and state, prominent among whom were Oliver Saint John, Thomas Widdrington (brother-in-law of Lord Fairfax), John Hippisley and John Crew (a Puritan and chairman of the Commons Committee on Religion).[77]

Selden's intentions in Parliament could be gauged as early as 13 March 1644, while he was still also attending the Assembly. When a proposal was put before the Commons to print a letter sent from the Westminster Assembly to foreign Protestant churches together with the answer of the Zealand churches, Selden rose and spoke "earnestlie" against the Zealand letter, showing it claimed church government to be *jure divino*, with which the civil magistrate had nothing to do, "and this he saied was contrarie to the ancient law of England and the use here received[.]" after a short debate, the House of Commons agreed with him, and requested both him and Francis Rous to instruct the Assembly on the proper wording.

In early April 1644, the Assembly handed in to the Commons a proposal for the Ordination of Ministers – an issue on which Selden had had much to say when attending the Assembly's meetings. The proposal was not heard from for a number of months, until in June 1644, Baillie learned to his horror that the Assembly's proposal for the Ordination of Ministers had been extensively altered by the Commons committee preparing it, with the whole doctrinal and scriptural grounds of the Ordination jettisoned. As he reported to Scotland, the parliamentary committee,

had scraped out whatever might displease the Independents, or patrons, or Selden and others, who will have no Discipline at all in any Church *Jure Divino*, but settled only upon the free-will and pleasure of the Parliament.

It is not hard to guess what role Selden had in this outright rejection of *jure divino* church discipline; to Baillie's eyes he had clearly become the chief influence in Parliament working against Presbyterianism. The Assembly sent a group of their members to attempt and sway the Commons committee from

[77] Paul *Assembly* pp. 127–128.

the alterations it wished to introduce, but to no avail. An impasse had been reached between the Assembly supporting a divine-right Presbyterian settlement in church and state, and a Parliament that would have none of it.[78]

In early 1645 the Presbyterians were looking for the opportunity to break the impasse, and found in March 1645 that it seemed to have materialized, as the Independents informed the Assembly they were temporarily withdrawing from it, to form a committee that would formulate their own common principles. The reasons for the Independents absenting themselves remain somewhat unclear; most probably they were outmaneuvered by the Presbyterians, to whom the absence gave free reign in the Assembly. In any case, the Independents gradually found they could not come to an agreed position among themselves, their main dilemma being that to come out for complete religious freedom would alienate their Parliamentary moderate supporters, while to restrict it would bring about a break with their Sectarian allies who were especially strong in the army. The Independents eventually returned to the Assembly only after more than six months of absence, issuing a cowed declaration on 13 October 1645, stating that they had failed to reach an agreement. The period of their absence, between March–October 1645 coincided with the final all-out effort by the Presbyterians to achieve their goals. During this period, the handful of members remaining in the Assembly who opposed *jure divino* Presbitery, were unable to oppose the passage of various Presbyterian measures by the majority – it appeared to the Presbyterian that they were finally within arm's reach of victory. They decided on a course of pushing through a Presbyterian church system first in their stronghold of London, as an example that the rest of the country would follow later.[79]

But this hopeful picture changed very quickly, when already in March 1645 the Presbyterians learned that Selden and his allies had well used the time bought by their delaying tactics: word got out that a majority in Parliament had been convinced to pass a new Ordinance for Church Government, without any conferring or considering of the views of Westminster Assemblymen. The Assembly reacted on 20 March 1645, with a petition protesting Parliament's ignoring them completely, while also censuring the Ordinance as in a number of points contrary to the divine (that is, Presbyterian) dispensation of Church government, and asserting that therefore they could not in conscience submit to it. The Commons created a Grand Committee to consider their response to the petition, with Selden naturally a member, and furious debates ensued, not reaching a resolution even after long days of deliberations. Finally, on 11 April 1645, by a majority of 88 against 76, the House of Commons resolved: "That this petition thus presented by the Assembly of Divines is

---

[78] Letter to Spang (28 June 1644), in Baillie *Letters* vol. iii p. 198; Paul *Assembly* pp. 394–396. "Patrons" were laymen who held some traditional authority to appoint the clergyman in one or more churches – they were of course opposed to a Presbytery appropriating this authority.

[79] Kaplan "Settlement" pp. 319–320.

a breach of privilege of Parliament." On 17 April, the Commons made a further declaration "of their true intentions concerning the ancient and fundamental government of the kingdom" and the government of the Church. The declaration asserted that to concede the demands of the Assembly of Divines for *jure divino* Presbytery and excommunication authority, would grant "an arbitrary and unlimited power and jurisdiction to near ten thousand judicatories to be erected within the kingdom" and thus set aside the fundamental laws which devolve supreme jurisdiction on Parliament only. It added that as Parliament's very unwillingness "to subject themselves and the people of the land to this vast power, hath been a great cause that the government hath not been long since established" they had "the more reason by no means to part with this power out of the hands of the civil magistrate" since, as experience proved "the reformation and purity of religion, and the preservation and protection of the people of God in this kingdom, hath under God been by the Parliament, and their exercise of this power." There was now evidently a decided parliamentary majority – how stable it was yet unknown – for the supremacy of Parliament over the church."[80]

In a letter of 25 April 1645, Baillie was still hopeful that the adverse tide could be turned. He reported that the Presbyterians in the Assembly were on the verge of successfully "setting up Presbyteries and Synods in London" but that this effort also meant "all the ports of hell are opened upon us." He felt they were especially failing to make the intellectual case for the rejection of what he called "Erastianism" – the parliamentary supremacy over the church, which, he was finding out, had in England far greater currency than he had previously suspected. He regarded it as "a mightie neglect" that no one had yet written a learned refutation of Erastus' 75 theses, and urged his Scottish friends to set someone to write down such a refutation in satisfactory and speedy fashion, so to assist their efforts in London, for "[t]he most of the House of Commons are downright Erastians: they are lyke to create us much more woe than all the Sectaries of England." Baillie was especially exasperated at the intellectual activities of Selden, which he regarded as a significant threat to Presbyterianism not only in England, but indeed everywhere. Admitting that Selden's breadth of scholarship, especially in Jewish matters, meant that a refutation would require unusual abilities, he proposed that they might find succor from the famous Dutch scholar Constantijn L'Empereur, who had allegedly "promised to write against Selden, for the Jewish ecclesiastick Sanhedrim, and their excommunication." Baillie was confident that "L'Empereur is well able to beat down the insolent absurditie of the man [Selden], with his own arms; and, if he would doe it quicklie, it were a very good office to us and to all the Reformed churches."[81]

---

[80] *Minutes of the Sessions of the Westminster Assembly of Divines*, A.F. Mitchell & J. Struthers eds. (1874) pp. 209–210, 434–436.

[81] Kaplan "Settlement" pp. 318–322; Lamont, *Godly* pp. 110–111; Letter to Spang (25 April 1645) in Baillie *Letters* vol. iii pp. 265–266. L'Empereur apparently never wrote the tract – if he ever

However, as 1645 progressed, the Assembly discovered to its dismay that there was now a stable Commons majority, bent on rejecting or amending its propositions as it liked. On 13 June 1645, Parliament rejected a paper sent from the Assembly claiming discretionary authority in church offices and courts. Baillie concluded warily that "the Erastian partie in the Parliament is stronger than the Independent, and is lyke to work us much woe," adding bitterly, "Selden is their head." This state of things was manifested even more starkly in the monthly Fast Sermon, delivered to the Commons on 30 July 1645 by Selden's most prominent clerical ally in the Westminster Assembly, Thomas Coleman, a performance which, if not directly engineered by Selden, was certainly supported by him. Coleman was apparently popular with MPs, having already preached before them three times previously, and having had those sermons printed by order of Parliament. Evidently knowing his audience, Coleman gave a combative sermon, in which he deprecated both Presbyterian and Independent attitudes, finding special fault with their claims of *jure divino* for their proposed settlement, and advised the Commons to ignore those, and "establish as few things *jure divino* as well can be." The Commons evidently approved Coleman's words, for they ordered his sermon printed, appearing under the title of *Hopes Deferred and Dashed.*[82]

The Scottish Presbyterians and their English allies sensed Coleman's sermon had crucially damaged the chances of a Presbyterian settlement passing in Parliament, and attempted a counter move. Calculating that they enjoyed more support among the Puritan peers of the upper house, the Presbyterians enlisted the assistance of their supporters there, to secure an invitation to deliver the Fast Sermon to the House of Lords on August 27, for the most articulate and learned of the Scottish clerics, George Gillespie, who had preached a year earlier to the Commons (his *A Sermon Preached Before the Honourable House of Commons at Their Late Solemn Fast, Wednesday March 27, 1644,* published by order of the Commons). In a make-or-break performance, Gillespie devoted almost his entire lecture to an examination of passages from Coleman's sermon of a month earlier, in which he accused the English cleric of being an "Erastian" and of working against the reformation of religion. It appears that in this case, Gillespie incorrectly appraised the ideas and inclinations of his audience, since his sermon certainly did not achieve the hopes invested in it. Far from overturning the opinions of MPs on church

___

intended to. At any event, Selden certainly did not regard him as an adversary, and in fact praised him in *Synedriis* for his commentary on the Talmudic tractate Middoth, writing: "for more on this see the commentary on this tractate by the excellent scholar Constantine L'Empereur." *Synedriis* b1c7.

[82] Paul *Assembly* pp. 492–498; Kaplan "Settlement" pp. 313–315. Coleman's earlier sermons preached before Parliament and later printed by order of the Commons were: *The Christian's Course and Complaint* (30 August 1643); *The Heart's Engagement* (29 September 1643); *God's Unusuall Answer* (12 September 1644).

government, it seems to have been the last sermon invited by Parliament from a Scottish cleric.[83]

The sermons by Coleman and Gillespie before MPs were followed by a furious pamphlet war upon the issue of the authority of Parliament over church matters. After Coleman's sermon had been published by order of the Commons, the Presbyterians published Gillespie's sermon to the Lords *"whereonto is added a brotherly examination of some passages of Mr. Coleman's late printed sermon"* to which Coleman swiftly retorted with *A Brotherly Examination Re-examined*, pointing out in Gillespie's sermons to *"some tenets and principles which intrench upon both the honour and power of the Parliament."* Within one week Gillespie had published *"Nihil Respondens,"* purportedly demonstrating Coleman's *"his abusing of Scripture: his errors in divinity: his abusing of the Parliament, and indangering their authority: his abusing of the Assembly: his calumnies, and namely against the Church of Scotland, and against my selfe: the repugnancy of his doctrin to the solemne League and Covenant[.]"* At this point, the pamphlet war was joined by others, with Adoniram Byfield, a scribe of the Westminster Assembly, anonymously publishing in support of Gillespie *A Brief View of Mr. Coleman His New Modell of Church Government* (1645), while shortly afterward on the opposite side of the debate came William Hussey's, *A Plea for Christian Magistracy, or An Answer to Some Passages in Gillespie's Sermon Against Coleman* (1646). There were two final outbursts in this diatribe: Coleman's, *Male Dicis Maledicis. Or A Brief Reply to Nihil Respondens* (1646) and Gillespie's *Male Audis or An Answer to Mr. Coleman His Malè Dicis* (1646). The exchange then petered out, as it became increasingly evident that Parliament had adopted Coleman's view – although he did not long survive this realization, as his health was rapidly deteriorating, and he was dead by March 1647. Much of this debate turned on the relevance of the example of ancient Israel to the case of English church and state, with Coleman asserting (in *A Brotherly Examination*) "I am sure that the best reformed church that ever was went this way – I mean the church of Israel, which had no distinction of church government and civil government," and Gillespie retorting (in *Nihil Respondens*) "[w]as the Church of Israel better reformed than the apostolicall churches?" Later that year Gillespie published what was intended to be the final word in the controversy, and became his magnum opus (he too was dead soon after, by December 1648), *Aarons Rod Blossoming, or, The Divine Ordinance of Church-Government Vindicated...* (1646). A massive endeavor, of a far more scholarly bent and wider scope than previous publications on this matter, it seriously addressed the ideas of opponents to a Presbyterian church, including of course Selden – but it came too late to make a difference, as the controversy over church

[83] Kaplan "Settlement" pp. 313–314.

government had already been definitely decided by the spring of 1646, on the side of parliamentary supremacy.[84]

During 1645 the Scottish commissioners and their English allies concluded they could not at that time convince the English Parliament to grant presbytery and excommunication *jure divino*, so that they decided to attempt and get these practices established by Parliament at least as regular laws, and wait for the

[84] The sequence and titles of this pamphlet war:

Coleman, *Hopes Deferred and Dashed, Observed in a Sermon to the Honourable House of Commons, in Margarets Westminster: Iuly 30. 1645* (1645)

Gillespie, *A Sermon Preached Before The Right Honourable the House of Lords in the Abbey Church at Westminster, Upon the 27th of August 1645...Whereonto is Added a Brotherly Examination of Some Passages of Mr. Coleman's Late Printed Sermon...* (1645)

Coleman, *A Brotherly Examination Re-examined: or, A Clear Justification of Those Passages in a Sermon Against Which the Reverend and Learned Commissioner, Mr. Gillespy, First in Two Severall Sermons, and Then in Print, Did Preach and Write. And a Short Discovery of Some Tenets and Principles Which Intrench Upon Both the Honour and Power of the Parliament.* [1645]

Gillespie, *Nihil Respondes: or, A Discovery of the Extream Unsatisfactorinesse of Master Colemans Peece, Published Last Weeke Under the Title of A Brotherly Examination Re-examined.: Wherein, His Self-Contradictions: His Yeelding of Some Things, and Not Answering to Other Things Objected Against Him: His Abusing of Scripture: His Errors in Divinity: His Abusing of the Parliament, and Indangering Their Authority: His Abusing of the Assembly: His Calumnies, and Namely Against the Church of Scotland, and Against my Selfe: the Repugnancy of his Doctrin to the Solemne League and Covenant, are Plainly Demonstrated.* (1645)

[Adoniram Byfield], *A Brief View of Mr. Coleman His New Modell of Church Government.* (1645)

Coleman, *Male Dicis Maledicis. Or A Brief Reply to Nihil Respondens. Also, the Brief View, Briefly Viewed. Being Animadversions Upon a Aamelesse Authour in a Book, Called, A Brief View of Mr. Coleman his Nevv Model.* (1646)

William Hussey, *A Plea for Christian Magistracie: or, An Answer to Some Passages in Mr. Gillespies Sermon, Sgainst Mr. Coleman: As Also to the Brotherly Examination of Some Passages of Mr. Colemans Late Printed Sermon, Upon Job 11.20. In Which the Reverend and Learned Commissioner Affirmeth, he hath Endeavoured to Strike at the Root of All Church Government. Wherein the Argumentative Part of the Controversie is Calmely and Mildly, Without any Personall Reflections, Prosecuted.* (1646)

Gillespie, *Male Audis or An Answer to Mr. Coleman his Malè Dicis.: Wherein the Repugnancy of his Erastian Doctrine to the Word of God, to the Solemne League and Covenant, and to the Ordinances of Parliament: Also his Contradictions, Tergiversations, Heterodoxies, Calumnies, and Perverting of Testimonies, are Made More Apparent then Formerly. Together With Some Animadversions Upon Master Hussey his Plea for Christian Magistracy: Shewing, that in Divers of the Afore Mentioned Particulars he hath Miscarried as Much, and in Some Particulars More then Mr. Coleman.* (1646)

Gillespie, *Aarons Rod Blossoming, or, The Divine Ordinance of Church-Government Vindicated so as the Present Erastian Controversie Concerning the Distinction of Civill and Ecclesiasticall Government, Excommunication, and Suspension, is Fully Debated and Discussed, From the Holy Scripture, From the Jewish and Christian Antiquities, From the Consent of Latter Writers, From the True Nature and Rights of Magistracy, and From the Groundlesnesse of the Chief Objections Made Against the Presbyteriall Government in Point of a Domineering Arbitrary Unlimited Power.* (1646)

right circumstances to renew the efforts to base them in divine right. But even this plan miscarried when, in the autumn of 1645, Parliament refused point blank to grant divines the full discretionary powers they demanded to exclude wrong-doers from the sacraments. In October 1645, as the Independents were returning to the Assembly, Parliament passed an ordinance which was a clear defeat for Presbyterians, for while it gave the clergy authority to suspend from the sacraments ignorant and scandalous persons – that is, to excommunicate them – it did so only apparently: it not only granted this power solely as permitted by Parliament (and not as *jure divino*), but also explicitly retained for suspended persons the possibility of appeal to Parliament (unlike in Scotland, where the General Assembly of the Kirk was the final recourse), as well as additionally reasserting the authority of Parliament to change the list of causes for suspension. In effect, Presbyterian authority in this matter had been ultimately neutralized, justifying those who would say (as Kaplan does) that the most Presbyterian feature of this settlement was its name.[85]

Neither the Presbyterians nor their opponents could know that the summer and autumn of 1645, would turn out to have been the high point of attempts to establish a Presbyterian settlement in England. Although Presbyterian efforts in this direction continued, and to many (including probably Selden) it might have looked as if a *jure divino* English Presbyterian church remained a distinct possibility for some time yet, in effect there was never again to be a plausible prospect of Parliament relinquishing its supremacy over all matters of church and state, either before or after the regicide. It appears that the great proliferation of sects and divisions in the church was gradually convincing many Englishmen, including devout Calvinists formerly inclining towards Presbyterianism, that parliamentary supremacy was the only antidote to a complete disintegration of the English church. A good example of this process was Richard Baxter, who in the summer of 1645 had been appointed chaplain of a cavalry regiment in the New Model Army. Discovering to his horror pretty much every conceivable heresy represented among the regiment's ranks, he recorded that the most common error he encountered was the opinion that the civil magistrate had no authority in matters of religion, and therefore that every man had a right to believe and preach as he pleased. This went a long way towards convincing Baxter himself that the opposite was true. Many other Englishmen, including Cromwell, were becoming similarly preoccupied with the theological (and political) excesses that such a stance might produce. Thus, a wide front emerged in Parliament, opposed to an autonomous Presbyterian church, whether *jure divino* or not. Most MPs, of various theological views, and including even some supporters of presbytery (like Prynne), and many independents (like Cromwell), had come to the conclusion that, for godly reasons, the supremacy of Parliament had to be preserved. Although there had been initial hopes of some kind of Presbyterian–Independent settlement,

---

[85] Paul *Assembly* pp. 492–498; Kaplan "Settlement" pp. 314–315, 324–325.

especially considering the reluctance of the latter group to ally with Sectaries, the intransigence of the Scots and some of their English allies, and the fear of overweening clerical discipline, gradually brought the Independents to oppose Presbyterian uniformity outright. These developments eventually produced a stable majority in Parliament that was completely attuned to arguments, such as Selden's, about church and state.[86]

Finally, on 14 March 1646, Parliament formally passed an "Ordinance for Church Government" to "settle matters concerning Religion, and the Worship of Almighty God" in England, in a form which was essentially a restatement of the October 1645 one. The essence of the parliamentary Ordinance was its claim to be laying down "the foundation of a Presbyterial Government in every Congregation, with Subordination to Classical, Provincial, and National Assemblies, and of them all to the Parliament" – that is, a purportedly "Presbyterial Government" that was in fact explicitly subordinate to "Parliament." The ordinance was quite pragmatic in tone, asserting that it settled "the Fundamental and Substantial parts of that Government" of the church, while also allowing that there will probably be "need of Supplyments and Additions, and haply, also of alterations, as experience shall bring to light the necessity thereof" for "it cannot be expected that a present Rule in every particular should be settled all at once[.]" The ordinance, however, acknowledged there was one remaining main point of contention, concerning the suspension of persons guilty of notorious offenses from "the Administration of the Sacrament of the Lord's Supper"; in other words, excommunication. The difficulty, the ordinance claimed, "arising, not so much in the matter itself, as in the Manner how it should be done, and who should be the Judges of the Offence" it came to the heart of the matter – The "Lords and Commons assembled in Parliament":

For the preventing of an indefinite, and unlimited power in the Eldership, they held it fit for the present, That the particular Cases of such scandalous Offences should be specified and enumerated with expresse Declaration, That further provision should be made by Authority of Parliament, for such Cases as were left out of the said enumeration, which, accordingly, having since taken into their serious consideration, and having had several debates thereupon as the difficulty of the Matter required, which hath taken up much time, for the avoiding as far as possible may be all Arbitrary power; and that all such cases wherein persons should be suspended from the Sacrament of the Lords Supper, might be brought to the cognizance, and passe the Judgement of the Parliament, who were bound in Justice as well to take care that none be injuriously detained from that Ordinance, as to give power whereby such may be kept away who are unfit to partake therein[.]

In short, Parliament explicitly declared that it would not grant "an indefinite, and unlimited power in the Eldership" so that it left in its own hands both the determining of the grounds for excommunication, as well as the ultimate actual

---

[86] Tanner *Conflicts* p. 136; Paul *Assembly* p. 123.

judgment of persons accused of it. Not content with this general supervision of church matters, Parliament also decreed that "in every Province persons shall be chosen by the Houses of Parliament, that shall be Commissioners to judge of scandalous offences" – that is appointing parliamentary "Commissioners" to supervise the Presbyterian Elders and the actual judges of excommunication, even before their names are sent to be certified by Parliament. In addition the ordinance made it clear that "any Minister of a Congregation" and "any Elder" may be "suspended from giving or receiving" the sacraments "for the same causes, and in the same manner, and have the like benefit of Appeal as any other person may by any Ordinance of Parliament[.]" The point of this ordinance in general, as well as its particular clauses concerning supervising excommunication of lay and clergy, was unmistakable: "the avoiding as far as possible may be all Arbitrary power." Having successfully fought off what it regarded as arbitrary powers of the pre-Civil War monarchy and church, Parliament was not going to grant those to the church newly established. The interpretation of Selden and his allies as to the unity and supremacy in Parliament of all power concerning church and state had triumphed.[87]

The Westminster Assembly ventured one more feeble attempt to protest the unilateral legislation on Church discipline, by addressing a petition to Parliament against the appointment by Parliament of commissioners judging religious offenses, instead of entrusting the matter to ministers. On 16 March the petition was rebuffed by Parliament, with a further rubbing-in by the appointment of a committee headed by no others than Selden and Vane, to draw up the particulars of the appointment of commissioners. The committee completed its work and conveyed the results to the Assembly on 21 April.[88]

Not surprisingly, Baillie described the new English church as "a lame Erastian Presbytery" and read it as "a trick of the Independents' intervention to enervate and disgrace all our government, in which they have been assisted by the lawyers and the Erastian party." In fact, it appears that overall it was the Independents who followed the lead of the "Erastians" and lawyers in Parliament, among whom Selden had a prominent role. Against the odds, Selden and his small group of allies had achieved what would come to be a definitive victory over the Presbyterian-controlled Assembly. By gradually convincing many of the initially hesitant independents and Puritans, as well as even some of the purported Presbyterians in Parliament, that it was an "ancient and fundamental" (in other words, constitutional) principle of English government, that any church government had to be subject to parliamentary supremacy, a stable majority emerged, opposed to the principle of a church authority independent of political power. The church settlement upon which Parliament eventually agreed in 1646, stipulated the subjection of church judicial and disciplinary powers to the authority of Parliament, thus neutering

---

[87] See "Parliamentary Ordinance of 14 March 1645" (actually 1646 – the official date is Old Style).
[88] Toomer *Scholarship* p. 574.

any independence of Presbyterian discipline, and ensuring the supremacy of political authority. This development also meant the petering out of the Westminster Assembly's energies, so that by the end of 1647 it had stopped dealing with significant matters, although its final plenary session was only held in 22 February 1649.[89]

This victory over Presbyterianism should not make us imagine that Selden was necessarily in tune with his parliamentary colleagues about every matter concerning religion. This was certainly not the case, and one prominent example of his distance from the rest of MPs, came during the parliamentary debates on toleration, on 13–14 October 1647. In these debates it emerged that a large number of MPs of Independent tendencies (including Cromwell) wanted to allow toleration of congregations not wanting to be subject even to the feeble formal Presbyterian organization of the church, but that almost none was prepared to extend this toleration to Roman Catholics. Yet again, Selden rose against virtually the whole House of Commons (apparently the only other supporter of his position was Henry Marten), and advocated that toleration include Roman Catholics too, demanding they be treated as Christians and refuting claims that they were to be regarded as idolaters. His position was amply rejected by his colleagues, and the eventual resolutions which declared a wide-ranging toleration of Protestant congregations – another defeat for Presbyterian discipline – specifically excluded Catholics from such toleration.[90]

In the time that remained to him as MP, until he was purged in December 1648, Selden continued to be involved in debates when issues having to do with church and state relations arose. He could now suffice with playing the defensive side, having only to guard an already-established supremacy of Parliament and a solid majority in favor of it, in the face of weakening attempts by the Assembly to change things. In April 1647, for example, when the Assembly presented a new confession of faith, upon Selden's urging, Parliament required the Assembly to back up each and every claim it made in the new confession, with quotations from scripture.[91]

By early 1649, Pride's purge and the regicide, while destroying Parliament, also finally destroyed the chances of a Presbyterian dominance. Many Presbyterians recoiled in horror at the execution of the King, and became

---

[89] See Mitchell *Minutes* pp. 209–210, 434–436; Toomer *Scholarship* p. 574; Kaplan "Settlement" pp. 314–315, 324–325. Kaplan seems right in thinking that this is a good example of the Scottish misunderstanding of what was going on: an Independent minority followed the lead of the Erastian lawyers who expressed the views of the majority of Parliament. However, Kaplan conflates lawyers and Erastians into one group, which Baillie explicitly gives as separate ones.

[90] Toomer *Scholarship* pp. 574–575. Selden's religious attitudes overall were consistently tolerationalist, but in the case of Catholics an additional motive for his position might have been the exceptional number of Catholics, crypto-Catholics and Catholic sympathizers in his circle of close friends and associates, including Jonson, Arundel, many of the Digbies and Talbots, and probably also Elizabeth Grey.

[91] Toomer *Scholarship* p. 574; Lamont *Godly* pp. 116–117.

ambivalent, to say the least, towards the new regime, while the political predominance of Independents, the Independent-dominated army and the Cromwell clan in the regimes of the next decade, guaranteed there would be no Presbyterian discipline in the English church. As early as September 1650, the Rump "Parliament" passed an act repealing all penalties for those not attending church – to all intent and purpose destroying even the "lame" presbytery that had been erected in 1646.[92]

If, in retrospect, the 1646 "Ordinance for Church Government" signaled the final defeat of an English Presbyterianism, contemporaries could not at the time know the high tide had passed, and it should not be surprising that Selden continued for some time yet to invest intellectual efforts in opposing Presbyterian ideas. To some extent or other, almost all of his significant literary efforts of his last years display his preoccupation with the potential for a renewed Presbyterian threat to parliamentary supremacy: from *Uxor Ebraica*, through the "Dissertatio historica," to the massive *Synedriis*, as well as the *Table-Talk*. Apparently, at least until late 1650, Selden still suspected that a Presbyterian resurgence was possible. However, by late 1653, when he published the second volume of *Synedriis*, Selden must have felt that the specific Presbyterian threat had somewhat receded, for the work lacks the urgency of the first volume, although he obviously still thought the idea of a separation between church and state a corrosive notion that is current enough to be worthy of confuting, lest it raise its ugly head once again; for he criticized the idea of separation in far more general terms than earlier, apportioning the blame for it quite equitably between both Catholics and Protestants (Pontificiis tum Reformatis).

6.4 "IT MAY SEEME STRANGE TO THEM" – DEFENDING TITHES AND EPISCOPACY

Having overviewed Selden's writings and political activities concerning the English debate on religion and state in the first half of the seventeenth century, and particularly his attitude to the issue of a sphere of spiritual church authority, autonomous from the state, I will now look closely at Selden's pronunciations on two additional issues that were connected to this debate, and in which he played a prominent role: the legal basis for church tithes and the justification for episcopacy. Both issues have been mentioned in passing earlier, but it is worthwhile to highlight his views of them in detail, as case studies of how his general views of religion and state informed his stance on specific issues.

We have seen that Selden's *Historie of Tithes* (1618) earned him an early anti-clerical reputation, because in that work he undermined the claim that the clergy were owed tithes by divine biblical law – his central argument was that

[92] Tanner *Conflicts* p. 157.

the divine injunction on tithes bound only the Jews, and even them only when politically independent in their own land. The consequence of this view was that all other tithes, including those paid in England at that time, were to be understood as decreed by only human law, and as such may or may not be levied, pending solely upon the decision of the civil authorities. The book was ferociously attacked by many clergymen, and Selden himself was compelled by King James I to make a retraction of his printing of the book and to abstain from replying to the various tracts attacking his book, although he neither admitted that the book presented false evidence or interpretations, nor retreated from the central thesis that the law of God found enforcement only in the laws of particular jurisdictions.[93]

That the work was composed not merely with a scholarly purpose, but with the intention to address public issues and interests, is explicitly admitted by Selden in a letter of 1618 to Peiresc, in which he gave the reason for his composing of the *Historie of Tithes* in English, rather than Latin, the language of scholarship. Selden explained in the letter that "as it is written in the language of England, so it is as it were dedicated to the name and polity of England" being concerned to a great degree with the English church and with shedding "light on our ancient law (whence also a completely new illumination is kindled from all sides on more recent law)," and that not to have written it in English, "would have been to prevent many people, whose interests are chiefly at stake, from reading it."[94]

It is however worthwhile to keep in mind that for all its anti-clerical reputation, there was much in the *Historie of Tithes* that was actually rather supportive of the necessary role of the church in the state. Aside from Selden's claim, which will be discussed below, that payment of tithes was completely justified when sanctioned by the state, an instructive example of his attitude to religion and state is Selden's criticism of the undesirable effect of the English reformation on Church property – the requisitioning of much of what was monastic property to the benefit of many of England's prominent aristocratic families (among them some of Selden's future political allies), Selden explicitly expresses his view that, for all the excesses of the Catholic clergy, and the fact that much property eventually remained in the reformed church, nevertheless "I doubt not that every good man wishes that at our dissolution of Monasteries both the Lands and Impropriated Tithes and Churches possessed by them" had been bestowed for the advancement of the church, than conferred on those who stood ready to "*devoure what was sanctified.*" His criticism of the way in which the dissolution of monasteries was diverted to benefit political purposes instead of religious ones could not come from a principled cynic or anti-clerical, and in fact puts Selden squarely within a long tradition of English condemnation of the destructive manner of the dissolution, down to Edmund Burke's *Reflections.*[95]

[93] See Christianson "Selden" ODNB; Woolf *Idea* pp. 231–233.
[94] See discussion in Toomer *Scholarship* p. 260.
[95] See *Historie of Tithes* pp. 486–487, and discussion in Barbour *Measures* pp. 248–249.

Selden's early reputation as a principled anti-clerical, and as opposed to tithes, survives to this day among most of those writing on his ideas of religion and state, with some regarding his views on these issues as even hardening with time and ending up close to the position of Hobbes. However, such assessments ignore the evidence, by which his contemporaries had cause to revise his reputation by the 1650s, when the issue of tithes resurfaced, and despite the earlier withering attacks on him by members of the clergy on this very issue, Selden, instead of seizing the opportunity to settle old scores, actually indicated he had no objection at all to his ideas *assisting* the clerical claims to receive tithes, albeit on the grounds of custom and positive law, and indeed he seems to have even enjoyed the irony of the situation. Thus, the evidence points to there being nothing inherently anti-clerical in Selden's view on tithes. His position was that in Christian countries tithes were to be paid by laws that were not divine but human, and which, as established laws, were completely legitimate and useful; his position therefore remained essentially the same throughout – while the frame of the public debate changes.[96]

In the early 1650s the issue of church tithes was again hotly discussed, the renewed debate prompted by the unclear prospects of the new Cromwellian regime, and of the established church within it. Many important voices within the new regime, especially among Sectaries and Independents, supported the complete abolition of compulsory church tithes. Thus, in a letter of 22 August 1653, Gerald Langbaine, Selden's friend, Oxford scholar and Provost of Queen's College, who was a clergyman of Episcopalian opinions, wrote to him:

Upon occasion of the businesse of Tithes now under consideration, some whom it more nerely concernes have bene pleased to enquire of me what might be sayd as to the civill

---

[96] Woolf *Idea* pp. 233–234. The issue of tithes had resurfaced, as early as 1646, to the degree justifying the publication of an anonymous anti-Presbyterian tract, explicitly defending Selden's position on this issue, the self-explanatory and (even for the seventeenth century), exceptionally long-titled: *Tyth-Gatherers, No Gospel Officers. or, Certaine Briefe Observations Concerning the Institution and Paying of Tythes, Whereby it Appears That Men Were Never Compelled to the Payment of Them in the Old Testament, Nor Did Ever Practice it in the New: That the Gospel Contributions Were All Voluntary Accounted as a Free Gift, Not a Debt; the Apostles Themselves, Not Only Choosing to Labour with Their Owne Hands, But Requiring All Their Successours to Doe the Like, That They Might Not Bee Chargeable to Any of Their Disciples. Together with Some Quotations Out of MR. Selden, a Member of the House of Commons, His History of Tythes, for the Writing Whereof He Was Much Troubled by the Episcopall Tythmongers of Those Times, From Whom the Presbyterian Church-Publicans of These Days, Have Learnt to Persecute with Far Greater Violence, All Such as Doe But Speak Against Their Gospel-Taxations . . ., Printed in the hopefull-yeare both of civill and Christian liberty*, 1646.

Even as late as 1685, more than 30 years after Selden had died, and more than 65 after his book had been first published, Thomas Comber, the Precentor of York, published the anti-Seldenian, two-volume *An Historical Vindication of the Divine Right of Tithes . . . Designed to Supply the Omissions, Answer the Objections, and Rectifie the Mistakes of Mr. Selden's History of Tithes* (1685).

right of them, to whom I was not able to give any better direction, then by sending them to your History [of Tithes]; happily it may seeme strange to them, yet I am not out of hopes, but that worke (like Pelias hasta) which was looked upon as a piece that struck deepest against the divine, will afford the strongest argum[en]ts for the the [sic] Civill right; & if that be made the issue, I do not despayre of the cause.[97]

Langbaine thus reports to Selden that some more nearly concerned with the business of tithes "now under consideration" (obviously clergymen of the established church who subsisted on tithes), despairing of upholding tithes as *jure divino*, had approached Langbaine, to enquire about what might be said as to the "civill right of them." Since the deep theological divides between Episcopalians, Presbyterians and Sectaries made any agreement about divine right unlikely, to say the least, the debate about tithes had moved to the political sphere, and arguments in favor of retaining them had to rely on justifications from law and tradition, the very kind of materials previously dismissed with contempt as "rusty Records" – and exactly the stuff Selden's *Historie of Tithes* was replete with. Not surprisingly, Langbaine's recommendation to the clergymen, that they look at that work, seemed to them "strange," considering Selden's reputation as having with that piece "struck deepest against the divine." Langbaine clearly believed that reputation to be completely undeserved, not finding in Selden's works any particularly anti-clerical agenda or proclivity; indeed, if anything, the whole tone of the letter including his using the image of "Pelias hasta" – the mythical spear that had the power both to wound and to heal – indicates that he expected Selden to enjoy not only the irony of the turn of events, but also to approve of his treatise coming to assist the clergy.

Although Selden's letter replying to Langbaine has not survived, his reaction to the affair fortuitously has found its way to the *Table-Talk*, where among a number of reported comments from his later years on the issue of tithes, the following passage is found:

They consulted in Oxford where they might find the best Argument for their Tithes, setting aside the Jus Divinum; they were advised to my History of Tithes, a Book so much cried down by them formerly; in which, I dare boldly say, there are more arguments for them than are extant together any where. Upon this, one writ me word, That my History of Tithes was now become like Pelias Hasta, to Tithes wound and to heal. I told him in my Answer, I thought I could fit him with a better Instance. 'Twas possible it might undergo the same Fate, that Aristotle, Avicen, and Averroes did in France, some five hundred Years ago; which were Excommunicated by Stephen, Bishop of Paris (by that very name, Excommunicated) because that kind of Learning puzzled and troubled their Divinity; but finding themselves at a loss, some Forty Years after (which is much about the time since I writ my History) they were called in again, and so have continued ever since.[98]

---

[97] See Letter of 22 August 1653, in Toomer "Correspondence."   [98] TT "Tithes" sec. 6.

On top of proving that Selden in fact read and overall agreed with Langbaine's letter, the passage reveals a palpable satisfaction on Selden's part, about his much-reviled work turning out to be what he described as the clergy's "best Argument for their Tithes." However, beyond recording his satisfaction as well as his amusement at the irony of his much "cried down" work now becoming the last best hope of the clergy's tithes, the passage also reveals much about Selden's more general attitude to the clergy, which it turns out, was not at all adversarial. Selden actually resists Langbaine's image of the spear that both cuts and heals, obviously because he disagrees with the "cutting" part of it, that is, he does not accept the implication that there was anything in his ideas inherently damaging to the true role and rights of the clergy. This is certainly not the attitude of the convinced anti-clerical, so often attributed to Selden. In fact, the alternative image Selden proposes for the effect of his work – the medieval repeal of the 40 years long excommunication of writings by "Aristotle, Avicen, and Averroes," (which he earlier mentioned in connection with their version of the "active intellect") very much suggests a completely different attitude on his part. Aristotle and his Arab-language commentators had been at first rejected by the medieval church because their "Learning puzzled and troubled their Divinity" – but at length, finding that this exclusion created a theological dead end, the church recognized them as necessary to Christian doctrine, and after being reinstated as theologically reliable authorities, they have so "continued ever since." This account is explicitly offered by Selden as a parallel to his own experience, and he thus indicated his belief that his own ideas are fundamentally beneficial to the clergy, and regards the realization of this by the clergy as a late awakening to the merits, and a vindication, of his position – an attitude completely in line with his claim some 35 years earlier, in the preface to the *Historie of Tithes*, that his exposition of human laws supporting the tithes of clergy was a far surer basis for them, than supposedly divines ones. Indeed, Selden's position was practically proven right by later events, when the Cromwellian regime settled the issue of church tithes: while a Sectarian opt-out from the worship of the established church was allowed, nevertheless the principle of continued payment by all (including Sectaries) of tithes to the established church was upheld, based not on divine right but on English law and custom. Thus the tithes of the English clergy were saved under the interregnum, in no small degree by Selden's much-reviled "rusty Records."[99]

---

[99] Toomer *Scholarship* p. 266. Selden's reaction reported in the *Table-Talk* to the letter and the image of the spear is fully borne out by a later letter of Langbaine, from 5 September 1653, which mentions Selden's disapproval of the spear simile, and his own having profited by it, since "by that occasion I have gained the knowledge of that particular story of the fate of Aristotle and his philosophy, among the Divines of Paris which I must confesse I would not willingly have bene ignorant of[.]" Langbaine however does not repent of his "happy mistake" (Felices errore suo) with the spear image, arguing that: "when I writt that letter some men were of opinion that the greatest wound that ever was given to the (willingly received by them) divine right of Tythes, was by that most learned worke. This I thought they might call Thléfeion traûma as being almost

Selden's position on this issue was, as we have seen, completely in line with his general views of religion and state: rejecting any jurisdiction for spiritual matters that would be completely separated from the so-called lay one, maintaining instead that clergy and laymen both draw their justification, as well as their obligation to follow laws, from God. In another comment on tithes in the *Table-Talk* Selden made this point as clearly as could be:

'Tis ridiculous to say the Tithes are God's Part, and therefore the Clergy must have them. Why, so they are if the Layman has them. 'Tis as if one of my Lady Kent's Maids should be sweeping this Room, and another of them should come and take away the Broom, and tell for a Reason why she should part with it; 'Tis my Lady's Broom: As if it were not my Lady's Broom, which of them soever had it.[100]

Turning now to Selden's ideas on episcopacy, we find perhaps the best illustration of his concept about the role of religion in the state, and it is possible to follow the development of Selden's positions on this issue from his writings and pronouncements, throughout his public career. Selden certainly upheld always the presence of bishops within England's governing structure, but his view of the justification for this presence changed over time. In his early work *Jani Anglorum* (1610) he remarked in passing that Parliament was composed of three "ordines" of kings, magnates and people (thus implying that the bishops were present in Parliament as "magnates" due to their baronial tenure). In the first edition of *Titles of Honor* (1614), there was no mention of orders or estates, but the episcopal presence in Parliament was still described in terms of baronial tenure. In Selden's 1622 long prefatory to Augustine Vincent's *A Discoverie of Errours in the First Edition of the Catalogue of Nobility*, after noting that "a world of Historicall matter both of our Church and State" still lies hidden in the records, he asserts that as far as he had seen, "I finde not that in the elder times, any of those Lords Spirituall, had other originall, of their being constantly Barons of Parliament, then solely from their seisin of Baronies." However, this clear baronial origin of clergymen sitting in the Lords, is mitigated by Selden first by noting that this was the case "especially before the dissolution of Monasteries" (implying that since the reformation things might be different), secondly by repeated referring to the clergy's spiritual role and his mentioning the "Convocation of the Clergy" (indicating a spiritual function of the clergy within the political system). By the reworked second edition of the *Titles of Honor* (1631), perhaps also influenced by Selden's growing immersion in Jewish learning, although not discounting that some of the bishops might also have a baronial tenure, the principle for the episcopal presence in parliaments

---

incureable. But then when I saw they must be forced for the civill right (by which Tythes must either stand or fall) they must be beholden to those (as they would call them) rusty Records which that History is amply fraught with, I did not think it absurd to make use of that simile[.]" Obviously Langbaine too believed the clergy had been mistaken in their depiction of Selden's stance towards the clergy. See Letter of 5 September 1653, in Toomer "Correspondence."

[100] TT "Tithes" sec. 5.

was clearly drawing from some other sort of representation – for he argued that bishops had been present in preconquest public meetings and councils (like the Saxon Witenagemot), that is before the Norman baronial tenures had been established.[101]

Regardless of the growing importance he ascribed to the constitutional role of the clergy within English government, Selden was never tender in his criticism of clerical excesses in general, and of episcopal excesses in particular. He vehemently opposed both general claims about divine-right episcopacy, which purported bishops to be a God-given institution, that men had no power to alter, as well as the specific English claim (prominently supported by Laud) that the episcopal succession was an essential element of an authority of the Church of England that was independent of the state (because drawn from an unbroken succession of bishops going back to the apostles, and not from the king or the community). While Selden obviously respected the learning of bishops such as Andrewes and Ussher, he was most scathing about other clerics who, having not the proclivity or patience for adequate study, made facile claims from an inexact use of scriptural and historical authorities. In the 1626 Parliament, for example, during a debate about a proposed bill against scandalous ministers, he remarked that a better title for the bill would be 'de episcorum ignorantia' (of the ignorance of bishops). In a similar vein was his comment from a later period, recorded in the *Table-Talk*, where he quipped that "Bishops are now unfit to Govern, because of their Learning: they are bred up in another Law; they run to the Text for something done amongst the *Jews* that nothing concerns *England*" – and went on to give several examples of such misapplications. Such comments did create among many the impression that Selden was a principled enemy of episcopacy, who would savor the opportunity to destroy this institution if it presented itself. The truth, they were to discover, was very different.[102]

By the late 1630s the growing identification among the opposition of the established church with fears from arbitrary royal government, brought many moderates in church affairs to views critical towards episcopacy, arguing for the severe curbing or even the outright abolition of bishops. Against these attacks, the supporters of episcopacy raised two different, and to a great extent also contrasting, claims: the first claim, that the bishops representing the clergy were a kind of estate of the realm, was advocated by such as Selden and by Hyde – who, for this reason among others, would object to the claim in the *Answer to*

---

[101] Mendle *Dangerous* pp. 153–154; in Vincent *Discovery*, Selden's prefatory letter, 11-page long, not paginated. Incidentally, the prefatory letter's discussion of the origin of clerical and lay presence in the House of Lords in the possession of baronial tenure, as "auncient reason and Law of this State" is connected by Selden to origin of the English Parliament as is the case "in the most of forreine States the possession of *feuda regalia*."

[102] Cromartie *Hale* pp. 160–161; *Proceedings in Parliament 1626: The House of Commons*, W.D. Bidwell et al. eds. (Rochester, NY: Rochester University Press, 1992) vol. ii pp. 128–129; TT "Bishops in the Parliament" sec. 9.

the Nineteen Propositions, that the King was the first of three estates, which meant eliminating the clergy as an estate distinct from the nobility, something which he regarded as changing for the worse the "frame and constitution of the kingdom." The second claim held that the bishops were sitting in the Lords merely as peers, and therefore that taking them out of Parliament would constitute a first step towards abolishing the upper house – in 1641, Archbishop Laud and his chaplain and confidant Peter Heylyn were assembling material to publicly make this latter case exactly.[103]

The issue resurfaced in all its fury, immediately upon the convening of the Long Parliament, as successive petitions organized by radical ministers (working hand-in-glove with Scottish Presbyterians like Baillie) and signed by thousands, were presented to Parliament in late 1640 and early 1641, for the abolition of the episcopacy "Root and Branch." For a time, both Pym and his patron Bedford attempted to delay a vote on Root and Branch radical reform, fearing it would break the opposition front. For it was becoming gradually clear, that the Parliamentary debates on the role of the episcopacy were not concerned with a reform of its functions (which Selden for one supported), or even with the removal of bishops from Parliament (which Selden opposed), but in fact with the complete abolition of episcopacy in the English church. By early 1641, the chief "Root and Branch" men in the Commons (termed by Peter Heylyn, "the Scotizing English") supporting the total abolition of bishops and deans in the English church, were Nathaniel Fiennes (son of the First Viscount Saye and Sele), Oliver Saint John and Denzil Holles, while Pym and Hampden were gradually moving towards that position, while still preferring to tactically postpone the decision for some time. Those who opposed the "Root and Branch" approach, mostly proposing instead a reformed episcopacy, were Hyde, Falkland, Digby, Colepeper, Hopton, Waller and, surprisingly to many, Selden.[104]

Two crucial debates on episcopacy took place in the Commons on 8 February and 10 March 1641, and Selden participated in both. To the shock of those expecting him to exhibit anti-clerical views, when Selden rose in the Commons to speak on episcopacy, while not ruling out necessary reforms, he on the whole came to the defense of clergy and bishops. Strongly rejecting the claim that the presence of bishops in Parliament was dispensable, he argued instead that it formed an essential component of the English constitution. Employing the "Root and Branch" metaphor, his position may be described as one which proposed some pruning of the branches, and perhaps the grafting of some additions upon them, while leaving all the roots and most branches in place...[105]

[103] Mendle *Dangerous* pp. 148, 152–153, 155.   [104] Tanner *Conflicts* p. 101.
[105] A. Woolrych, *Britain in Revolution 1625–1660* (Oxford University Press, 2002) pp. 169–171; Mendle *Dangerous* pp. 134–135, 148–149.

On 8–9 of February 1641, the simmering tensions about the fate of bishops first flared up, unexpectedly, when a technical motion was followed by eight straight hours of debate on the "Root and Branch" petitions, with some fifty speakers participating, Selden included. In this debate Selden is reported to have asserted that "Root and Branch" abolition of episcopacy would "abolish ecclesiam" since "the clergy are the church." When this assertion was challenged by some speakers, there rose to defend Selden's position, a Mr. Vaughan – most probably John Vaughan, his friend and protégé (and future Chief Justice), since his speech's claim that episcopal writs of summon to Parliament referred specifically to the spiritual role of bishops, was an argument that Selden himself was to put forward a few weeks later when the dispute resurfaced in the Commons. After much inconclusive debate, it was decided that a committee look into the many complaints against the bishops, but with the central question of whether to preserve or abolish episcopacy, reserved to an eventual discussion in the House of Commons itself.[106]

Intriguingly, it was exactly on 9 February 1641, that Selden's friend, the learned and widely respected Archbishop James Ussher, published a proposal for a reform of church government that would create a combination of bishops and presbytery. This proposal, offering a reformed episcopacy was clearly directed at addressing the parliamentary debates, and weakened the case for an outright abolition of bishops "Root and Branch," by offering to many conservative Calvinists the means by which to reform the church, while preserving its traditional forms. We might suspect Selden had a hand in the preparation, and even more in the timing of Ussher's proposal being made public. He certainly subsequently supported Ussher's plan in Parliament. However, the plan did not receive the hoped-for wide support, due to opposition to it not only from the hard-line Presbyterians, but crucially, also from the king who was at this stage opposed to any reform in the church (a position Charles I later regretted).[107]

The widespread expectations at that time, about an impending and irresistible demise of episcopacy, are conveyed in a letter of 28 February 1641 to the presbytery of Irvine by the Scottish Presbyterian Robert Baillie, then reporting from London on the political maneuvers taking place. Remaking with satisfaction that the Commons Committee for Religion, was found to be on the whole in favor of "the rooting out of Episcopacie" except for "Mr. Selden, the avowed proctor for the Bishops[.]" Baillie described with evident delight how, when the matter came to be debated in the Commons, although Digby, Falkland and Rudyerd spoke in favor of keeping a reformed "limited Episcopacie" and "Learned Selden, and a great faction in the house,

---

[106] Woolrych *Britain* pp. 172–173; and see in Mendle *Dangerous* p. 136 and in note 45, where he points out that the similarity in arguments make it very likely the speaker was Selden's friend John Vaughan – one of two members by that surname then sitting in the House of Commons.
[107] Mendle *Dangerous* pp. 141–142, 145.

ran all their way" yet "God carried it against them." Baillie thus was confident of imminent victory, remarking that "let Selden and some few others gnash their teeth as they will" it won't be long until this issue as well as other matters having to do with church policy will be "cast in one bill" and given to the "Higher House" near unanimously. Not for the last time, Baillie underestimated the sharpness and doggedness of Selden's gnashing teeth.[108]

When the issue of abolition returned to the Commons on 10 March, Selden at first held back and did not participate in the debate, probably in order to let others exhaust their arguments, so that his own speech could more comprehensively address them. He joined the debate only after the opponents of bishops in Parliament (prominent among them William Strode) had presented their main arguments: the bishops were sitting in Parliament only in virtue of their baronies (and thus not as representatives of the clergy, or in any other spiritual capacity), and they were not an estate of the realm (and thus were not a necessary component of Parliament, nor could they veto its decisions). Selden then rose to speak, and started by dismissing fears of an alleged veto power of bishops over parliamentary decisions, for precedents clearly showed no such power existed – thus neutralizing one major component of the fear from continued episcopal presence. He then pointed out that, regardless of there not being in the English government a separate house or veto power of the clergy, it was nevertheless certain that the clergy had ever been a part of Parliament. Thus, he argued, as "ancientlie Bishops in Saxon times had voices in making lawes" if Parliament ever considers removing the current clerical participation in it, then it would become necessary that "wee would give the clergie some other voices." He also added the argument made by Vaughan in the February debate – that writs summoning the bishops to attend Parliament explicitly mentioned their spiritual role, and indeed that the bishops in the Lords were formally addressed as "Lords Spiritual" whereas the other peers were "Lords Temporal." In short, Selden was arguing for continued episcopal presence on constitutional grounds: the clergy performs an established spiritual role in the life of the nation, the bishops represent the clergy from ancient times, and if this representation was to be taken away, then some other manner of representing the clergy in Parliament would have to be found – or else a serious subversion of the English "frame of government" would result. Selden also added that to take away the clerical representation, would undermine the very notion of estates in government, implying that it would also essentially remove the legitimacy for the existence of a House of Lords (and we might conjecture if there was at this junction some kind of behind-the-scenes cooperation between Selden and Laud, who as mentioned above was at this time, assembling materials to support this claim exactly).[109]

---

[108] See Baillie *Letters* vol. i pp. 302–303, 307–308.
[109] Woolrych *Britain* pp. 173–174, 182–183; Mendle *Dangerous* pp. 148, 152–153, 155.

The effect of Selden's speech was described by fellow MP Simonds D'Ewes in his *Journal* as having "puzzled the house." In the words of a modern scholar like Mendle, it was a "dazzling performance," which succeeded in neutralizing the political fears of an episcopal veto power if the clergy was recognized as an estate, while at the same time basing the presence of the bishops on the right of the clergy to be represented in the great council and to be part of the constitution. The constitutional aspect of Selden's speech was the most devastating to his opponents, for in a Parliament proclaiming itself the defender of the traditional constitution from its enemies, the argument about the necessity of retaining a representation of the clergy was pretty much impossible to directly deny, without at least conceding in its place some other kind of representation (or else to grant a regular constitutional role to the Convocation of the Clergy). The measure of Selden's success was that there was no real and explicit attempt to directly confute his arguments, either during the March debate or later. Pym, speaking after Selden resorted to quoting Hooker and mentioning Convocation, in an attempt to deflect the issue of clerical representation, but he could not muster much conviction or clarity for an alternative program, and although he and his supporters had beforehand mustered enough numerical support to initiate a bill against the bishops, Selden's arguments had taken too much of the wind out of their sails. The issue was proving far more divisive than Pym and Strode anticipated, so that the bill which eventually received a majority of the Commons on 10 March, sufficed with only attempting to deprive bishops of their legislative and judicial roles (as well as barring them from secular employment) – while desisting at least for the time being, from altogether abolishing them in the church. It was not until 1 May that a bill to exclude bishops from Parliament was sent to the Lords, and there it met with the predictable hostility from a majority of the peers, which had certainly been exacerbated by Selden's arguments – especially the growing conviction that he was correct in claiming that to take bishops away undermined the very idea of estates, and therefore also the legitimacy of an upper house. On 25 May the Lords voted that the bishops should continue to sit in the House, and on 8 June they threw out the exclusion bill. The anti-episcopacy camp in the Commons retorted on 27 June by passing in its first reading a bill to abolish bishops, "Root and Branch." But even this first reading was passed only by a relatively small majority of 139 to 108, indicating it was far from enjoying overwhelming support, and it soon transpired there was no steady majority for outright abolition of episcopacy, so that the attempt to do so petered out at that time. Moreover, after the March 1641 debates the leaders of the parliamentary opposition would only seldom resort to the language of estates, probably fearing it implied the necessary presence of clergy in Parliament.[110]

---

[110] Woolrych *Britain* pp. 173–174, 182–183; Simonds D'Ewes, *The Journal of Sir Simonds D'Ewes*, W. Notenstein ed. (1923) p. 468 and n. 10; Mendle *Dangerous* pp. 140, 149–150, 156–160; Christianson "Selden" ODNB. Selden's argument that the clergy deserve representation in Parliament was in some sense answered in 1663, when the Protectorate practice of taxing

The attempt to exclude the bishops from Parliament was revived only when the run-up to the outbreak of armed conflict had exacerbated positions and changed the composition of Parliament. In October 1641, there were growing reports of a possible deal of the King with the Scottish covenanters, enabling him to raise an army by which he could crush Parliament. Against this background, and with feverish speculations and fears abounding, the Commons ordered guard to be posted on the palace of Westminster night and day, and on 21 October a bill excluding bishops from Parliament was passed, with an attendance so thin that it barely achieved the quorum of 40 members, and so hurriedly that the three readings were completed in two days. But the bill still had to pass the Lords, and there followed weeks of raising tension, with anti-episcopacy mobs making it increasingly difficult for bishops to attend the Lords, and culminating in riots on 27–29 December, that effectively barred episcopal attendance. On 30 December, John Williams, Archbishop of York, the old ally and friend of Selden, who, since Laud's imprisonment on 1 March 1641, was the effective leader of the Anglican church, together with 11 other bishops, formally protested against laws being passed in the Lords, while the bishops were being forcibly excluded from attending by the mobs, and hinted that these might be deemed illegal. The Commons responded by arresting the 12 bishops and sending them to the Tower as traitors – very much ironically in Williams' case, for he had been imprisoned in the Tower by the King in 1637, for not being docile enough, and had been released only in 1640 – as a goodwill gesture towards Parliament. In this atmosphere of impending conflict, and after the King had summoned many of the most loyal peers to attend him at Windsor, thus leaving the upper house in the hands of the opposition, the bill excluding bishops from Parliament finally received the approval of the Lords on 5 February 1642 (the King to cut his losses consented to the bill on 14 February, correctly calculating that with the political issue now gone, most of those opposed to total abolition of episcopacy in the church would come over to his camp).[111]

Intriguingly, soon after the exclusion vote, a version of the House of Lords' *Book of Precedents* (or *Book of Privileges*), prepared by Selden in 1621, was printed as *The Priviledges of the Baronage of England, When They Sit in Parliament Collected (and of Late Revised) by John Selden of the Inner-Temple Esquire* (1642). In its section on bishops it touched on a number of the issues that had been contested in the debate about exclusion. It reiterated

clergy as laity was found convenient by the restoration Parliament, and regularly instituted, rather than returning to the old practice of applying to Convocation for separate clerical grants. The constitutional consequence was that from this time onwards the parochial clergy were permitted to vote for Members of Parliament. The episcopal presence in the Lords however had been restored in 1660, and persists, to this day. Tanner *Conflicts* pp. 222–223.

[111] Woolrych *Britain* pp. 191–192, 216–217; Cromartie *Constitutionalist* pp. 260–261; Mendle *Dangerous* pp. 149–150, 156–160; Christianson "Selden" ODNB. On the friendship of Williams and Selden see Toomer *Scholarship* p. 318.

Selden's view that even the unanimous disapproval of the bishops could not prevent an act of Parliament from passage, and that a Parliament could in practice meet and conduct business without the presence of the Lords Spiritual. Clearly these were the arguments used by the opponents of episcopacy to infer that bishops were not an estate of the realm, and thus not a necessary component of Parliament, so that it would have been quite convenient for Selden to adjust his own view to the new situation, or at least to simply omit the whole discussion. He however chose not to do so, and rejected explicitly the inference that without a veto power bishops were not a necessary component of Parliament, while insisting that irrespective of the lack of a separate episcopal veto power, the clergy were indeed an estate of the realm, that they were represented by the bishops, and that if the Lords Spiritual were abolished, some other spiritual representation in the English Parliament should be established. Thus, although bishops had been successfully ejected from the Lords, it can be said that as for the principled argument Selden had not been bested, since the parliamentarians only succeeded in justifying the ejection out of political expediency, but did not produce a theoretical alternative to Selden's idea of a spiritual representation in Parliament. Moreover, as Selden's warning that exclusion of the bishops from the upper house, would undermine that house's legitimacy to the degree that will lead to its complete demise, was in time fulfilled, the return of bishops to Parliament came to be regarded as an integral part of the eventual Restoration settlement of the English frame of government.[112]

Regardless of the bishops' exclusion from Parliament in February 1642, the outright abolition of episcopacy in the English church had as yet not been decided. As a consequence, a new struggle opened about the future of bishops in the Church, simultaneously on two fronts: the Westminster Assembly and Parliament. Selden again assumed the role of chief advocate for episcopacy, on both fronts. After having published in early 1642 the *Priviledges of the Baronage* with its defense of the traditional parliamentary role of bishops, Selden published in October of the same year another work (on which he had been working since the beginning of that year), with obvious relevance to the role of episcopacy in the church: a book consisting of translated excerpts from the *Stringing of Jewels*, an Arabic-language chronicle by the tenth century CE Greek Orthodox Patriarch of Alexandria, Sa'id ibn Batriq (Latinized as Eutychius) – Selden's only treatment of an Arabic-language text. The published volume, usually referred to by the name of its author, as *Eutychius*, consists of a mere 12 pages of Arabic excerpts from the chronicle translated into Latin, preceded by Selden's 26-page preface, and followed by 169(!) pages of his

---

[112] *The Priviledges of the Baronage of England, When They Sit in Parliament Collected (and of Late Revised) by John Selden of the Inner-Temple Esquire* (1642). Mendle claims that *Priviledges* was certainly composed before the fall of the bishops, perhaps even before the Long Parliament. See Mendle *Dangerous* p. 219.

commentary as well as 14 pages of his textual notes. The chronicle, allowing for a view of early Christian institutions, gave Selden opportunity to present, at length, his own views of the early Christian church, according to which it had a mixed-polity kind of government, combining Episcopal and Presbyterian elements. As indicated by the proportions of the original text to Selden's lengthy preface and comments, the work served primarily a controversialist purpose – one to which Selden explicitly owned to in the preface, asserting that *Eutychius* allows him to correct the many scurrilous claims about episcopacy and presbytery, raised in the current English debate.[113]

In his commentary Selden combined Eutychius' text with considerable Hebraist materials, from the Talmud and Maimonides, to Moses of Coucy and Abraham Zacuto, as well as more contemporary materials from Scaliger and Grotius, in order to present a plausible model for an agreed-upon settlement of a reformed episcopacy in the English Church. The volume was an obvious contribution to the controversy about the role of episcopacy and, as we know, several prominent supporters of episcopacy, including Archbishop Ussher as well as some important English Presbyterians, were inclined to consider such a model of reformed episcopacy, but the intransigence of the Scottish Presbyterians (as well as the King's), who were now part of the debate, made such a compromise impossible.[114]

In the summer of 1643, the main debate about the future of the English church moved for a time to the Westminster Assembly after it had been commissioned by Parliament to advise it on the preferable church settlement. We have seen above that in the Assembly, between late 1643 and the spring of 1644 Selden participated in several debates about the replacement of an Episcopal church government by a Presbyterian one, and engaged within the Assembly in a quite effective rearguard action, aimed at thwarting the installment of a Presbyterian church government. Selden consistently proposed that the actual government of the early church be investigated by thorough inspection of the historical evidence, a suggestion that most clergymen patently resisted. He added insult to injury when he insisted that, since early Christians were actually a Jewish sect, their ideas and actions should be considered with the help of actual Jewish sources – something the vast majority of the members in the Assembly were both unwilling and unable to do.[115]

With the ingrained majority of Presbyterians and Independents in the Assembly, there was never much chance that Selden could completely overturn its projected course. However, it would not have been implausible to hope that he could also engage in some substantive discussion with at least part of the assemblymen. Nevertheless, he found the vast majority of the Assembly's membership uninterested in any historical evidence he might produce, and

---

[113] *Eutychii* Praefatio pp. iii–iv
[114] Toomer *Scholarship* pp. 601–604; Ford *Ussher* pp. 250–254.
[115] Toomer *Scholarship* pp. 569–573.

unwilling to really grapple with the challenges he raised before them. Selden therefore resorted to engaging in various time-consuming tactics to slow down the Presbyterian pushing forward their vision of the English church, until discontinuing his attendance, from the spring of 1644. It is however intriguing to consider the possible influence that his ideas and argument did have on a number of English Calvinist Puritans. Several members of the Assembly, among whom were, for example, Fiennes and Lightfoot, certainly indicated that Selden's argument on some specific issue had convinced them, and the latter came to agree with Selden on many issues. Another member of the Assembly, Thomas Coleman who gradually became Selden's most prominent clerical ally in the Assembly, had earlier favored the complete destruction of episcopacy (and had thus been considered among English "Presbyterians"), but came increasingly to favor some kind of reformed episcopacy. The shift in his views had clearly much to do with recoiling from the spreading Sectarianism, which he witnessed prospering in the absence of a strong church hierarchy. However, a measure of influence from Selden's ideas and analyses, on the development of his views, should not be discounted without further study.[116]

As we have seen above, after ceasing his attendance of the Assembly, in late March 1644, Selden concentrated his efforts in the Commons. But, while his view about the supremacy of Parliament over any Presbyterian system was ultimately adopted by Parliament in the March 1646 "Ordinance for Church Government," Selden's prolonged efforts to save some kind of reformed episcopacy in the church ultimately failed, with the formal passing by Parliament in October 1646 of the "Ordinance for the abolishing of Archbishops and Bishops in England and Wales and for settling their lands and possessions upon Trustees for the use of the Commonwealth." For some two years following the abolition, there were further maneuvers by English and Scottish Presbyterians (not always in concert), exploring the possibility devising a different church settlement, by way of some kind of deal with the King – entailing the possible restoration of some kind of episcopal element in the church. But Pride's Purge and the Regicide put an end to these efforts. In the next decade the fate of the church, as well of the state, would lie solely with the army and the Protector.[117]

Selden's remarks from his later years on religion and state in general, and on episcopacy in particular, as collected in the *Table-Talk*, do not show any significant modification of his ideas from what he had expressed earlier in the 1630s and 1640s. Indeed, if anything, the *Table-Talk* remarks reiterate even more decisively his views as previously expressed. As always with him, in these remarks, Selden treated episcopacy as a human rather than a divine institution; however, as a long-established and successful human institution, it remained for him a plausible and even beneficial element of the spiritual component found in political societies, and in the English case, of the traditional establishment of

[116] Toomer *Scholarship* p. 573; Lamont *Godly* pp. 117–118.
[117] Mitchell *Minutes* pp. 209–210, 434–436.

religion and state. Thus, Selden dismissed with acerbic mockery those who attempted to advance anti-episcopal views based on an alleged propensity particular to bishops to intrude into temporal matters:

You would not have Bishops meddle with Temporal Affairs. Think who you are that say it. If a Papist, they do [so] in your Church; if an English Protestant, they do [so] among you; if a Presbyterian, where you have no Bishops, you mean your Presbyterian Lay-Elders should meddle with Temporal Affairs as well as Spiritual. Besides, all Jurisdiction is Temporal; and in no Church but they have some Jurisdiction or other. The Question then will be reduced to *Magis* and *Minus*; They meddle more in one Church than in another.[118]

Evidently, in Selden's view, some kind of religious establishment is to be envisaged in all political societies, and thus the question of its "meddling" in temporal affairs turns not on the principle, but on the quantity, and perhaps the quality, of meddling by different church establishments. It is implied in the remark that English episcopacy was actually less constitutionally troublesome than the other churches mentioned. Elsewhere, Selden allowed that some bishops indeed "have done ill," but he nevertheless refused to regard the institution itself as at fault, asserting that "'t'was the Men, not the Function." Another remark by Selden indicates the tested usefulness of episcopacy to the English state was a major consideration in his opposition to the removal of bishops from Parliament: "To take away Bishops' Votes, is but the beginning to take them away; for then they can be no longer useful to the King or State[.]" In other words, bishops were politically useful to king and state, and therefore should have remained in Parliament, since other options of clerical representation apparently left much to be desired.[119]

Episcopacy and its presence in Parliament, then, was for Selden a traditional and effective institution, to be preserved even if some reform of it was necessary. He made this preference explicit many times, remarking that other schemes of church government would inevitably stir up "a great deal of trouble," and perhaps episcopacy would serve as well, displaying his marked preference for traditional and tested institutions.[120]

To sum up, Selden's consistent position towards episcopacy regarded it as neither *jure divino* nor anti-Christian, but rather as an overall beneficial institution, which had well served the church and the English nation for so long, that if found wanting in some respects, it would be far better reformed than abolished. Selden believed that like other functional elements of church and state, Parliament had in principle the authority to dispense with episcopacy if it saw fit, although he regarded outright abolition as an unnecessary erosion of

---

[118] TT "Bishops in the Parliament" sec. 5. Incidentally, Selden distinguishes in this comment between what he terms English Protestants and the Presbyterians, regarding the former to be inherently different from the latter – who are thus also implied to be un-English...

[119] TT "Bishops in the Parliament" sec. 10, and "Bishops out of the Parliament" sec. 11. See discussion in Barbour *Measures* pp. 297–298.

[120] TT "Bishops out of the Parliament" sec. 12.

the existing constitutional frame. The same was not true, however, for Selden's belief in the necessity of a spiritual role and representation within government – a principle he never wavered from. He believed episcopacy adequately supplied this function in the English government and that, if abolished, an alternative to it must be set up. Selden therefore opposed arguments against bishops in parliaments, regarding them as veiled attacks against the English political tradition, and indicated that without them – or at least some alternative spiritual representation – the House of Lords, the monarchy and indeed the whole English frame of government would eventually be destroyed. He explicitly and repeatedly indicated his preference for some kind of reformed episcopacy to a Presbyterian settlement. His argument was basically that the representation of the clergy was one of the estates composing English political society time out of mind, and as such was not expendable. It appears that this view was a result of Selden's more general thinking about the development and function of Parliament, which brought him in his later years to increasingly stress its representation and counsel functions. We have seen that, quite early on, Selden came to regard the presence of bishops in Parliament as a function of spiritual representation, even when bishops might also have been sitting by force of an additional baronial tenure. But in later works, like the second edition of *Titles of Honor* (1631) as well as in his remarks in the *Table-Talk*, there are several comments indicating he came to believe that even lay barons sit in Parliament, not by virtue of feudal tenure only. Although he did not deny that temporal peers were originally summoned to the King's council by virtue of personal feudal tenure, he seems also to have concluded that already by the time of Magna Carta, the summon had changed into a public role, having to do with counsel and representation.[121]

6.5 A CHURCH "INTEGRAL"

After having reviewed at length Selden's position within the public church and state controversies concerning tithes, episcopacy and excommunication authority, a common pattern clearly emerges. In all three cases, Selden vehemently and relentlessly rejected divine-right arguments as basis for church institutions and powers, however this rejection did not translate into a denial of validity for such institutions and powers, but rather raised a demand that they be justified like any other human practice, upon principles from law, tradition and national identity. Thus, in all three cases, when the debates turned from *jure divino* arguments to attempts at altogether abolishing traditional religious practices and institutions, Selden, to the surprise of those who believed him to be anti-clerical, was consistently found on the side arguing in favor of retaining them. The reason for what appeared to not a few contemporaries as a contradictory attitude was perhaps the most interesting element of Selden's

---

[121] Toomer *Scholarship* pp. 570–571; Mendle *Dangerous* pp. 150–155.

religion and state theory: the idea that we might term "national religion." He regarded religious ideas and interests as an essential component of political society, both generally and particularly in England, to the extent that a justly-governed state could not do without them. Far from understanding the supremacy of human political institutions over religion, as entailing either a complete disestablishment of religion (like Milton and many Congregationalists and Sectaries came to embrace), or a complete subjugation of religious considerations to political ones (as Hobbes and Filmer advised), Selden regarded this supremacy as warranting the full *integration* of the religious element into the political process. He saw a separation of church and state as morally and politically destructive, and advocated instead integration as a necessary and beneficial component of every political society – in the English case as delivered by the clergy being an estate of Parliament.[122]

Selden believed that the separation between church and state was the poisoned legacy of the period – roughly between the destruction of the second Temple and the rule of Emperor Constantine – during which Christianity gradually separated from the Jewish nation and was engrafted into the Roman state, becoming its official religion. He argued that "the leadership of the various Christian communities of the age we are discussing" borrowed the term "sword" used to describe the civil authority, and applied it to "describe their procedure of excommunication" (a procedure which, Selden stressed, is itself a human invention and not a divine injunction), eventually coming to call it the "spiritual sword."[123]

Although after the adoption of Christianity by the Roman Empire and throughout most of its history, it was clearly the Christian practice to admit the supremacy of the civil power, the precedent of the period of disconnection from civil authority, continued to supply arguments to those like the papists and later some of the Protestant clergy, who for obvious purposes of accumulating power, foster an idea of a divinely inspired separation of "swords." As a result of these efforts, he asserted, there is a strong and widespread notion that power "throughout the Christian world has been split into two: political power, or government by magistrate as it is generally called; and ecclesiastical power,

---

[122] Sergio Caruso, recognizing these traits of Selden's thought, correctly described the two main themes of his attitude to the church throughout his career as its subordination to the state, and "il carattere nazionale della Chiesa d'Inghilterra" (even before the reformation). However, Caruso does not consider enough that these two themes are pretty much one and the same: the very national character of the English church determines to a great degree its subordination to political power. See Caruso *Miglior* p. 526.

[123] *Synedriis* b1c9: "Et quemadmodum in civilis administrationis potestate suprema designanda, Gladii nomen adhiberi est solitum velut instrumenti coercitionis maximi atque eminentissimi adeoque jus vitae necisque & summun imperium satis significantis, ita etiam in Regimine qualicunque hujus quod tractamus temporis Christianorum inter se, Gladii nomen induit eorum Excommunicatio, qui ut ab eo qui in administratione civili is usu erat distingueretur, *Gladius* dici coepit sub Cypriani tempora (floruit ille sub annum Christi 250) *Spiritalis* qui etiam postea *Spiritualis* quemadmodum etiam in tempora nostra dictus."

which is completely separate from it." Selden described this view as absurd, just as "though someone had made two suns" or "allowed more than one soul to take up residence in a human body." He considered this "split" of swords, as not only a false idea, but also as a "wicked" one for ascribing to the will of God various merely human institutions, as well as definitely detrimental, because,

one of the heads or horns of this bifurcated authority must naturally be far more important than the other, just as all the other institutions believed to have been founded upon divine law are correctly considered more powerful than those which come from human law. It would after all be unthinkable for human law to resist in any way the law of God[.][124]

Thus, he warned, the idea of a spiritual order separate from the temporal one should be resisted, for when allowed it creates an "immense abyss on its way to swallowing up all the *Temporal* business of Christians, and all the actions and affairs of the secular world." In Selden's view, a separation of church and state authority, far from advancing either of the two, only serves to create an authority competing with that of the state, and in the long run threatening to swallow it.[125]

To this false notion of a "bifurcated authority," Selden opposed the opinion he supported, that there should be "only one kind of authority and jurisdiction in all of Christendom, one which governs both sacred and secular matters." He stressed that this opinion he supports was an "extremely ancient" one, which had also been widely accepted "as a principle in governing Christian states" (mentioning among others France, Spain and Venice), so that those suggesting that the first proponent of this idea was Thomas Erastus, "must be both extremely arrogant and completely uninformed." For Selden then:

This single institution flows so to speak from a single source, spot and origin, namely the human authority of those who have held various responsibilities in the government of their nations.

From this follows for him that there should not be a separate sword associated with the ecclesiastical order only, any more than there should be

[124] *Synedriis* b1 Praefatio: "Sed & Imperii illius Duplicis Caput seu Cornu alterum ut alteri haud parum antistet nevesse est, non aliter atque alia, quae ex Jure sic nasci Divino credentur, potiora, nec immerito; habentur eis quae ex Humano, cui nefas est, Divino ullatenus reluctari [.]" As an example, Selden mentions his looking at length into the origins and history of excommunication in *Synedriis* "because a number of Catholic scholars, as well as many Protestant ones, have been doggedly seeking the origins" of excommunication in the earliest human times "as though it could be found in some specific provision or regulation of either natural law or that part of divine law which existed even then[.]" He then adds sardonically that "[t]hey seem to believe more or less that we can date the beginnings of excommunication to the very moment that our first ancestors were created."
[125] *Synedriis* b1c10: "Eo spectat quod toties apud summos Effectus hujus poenae assertores occurrit de eo quod est *in Ordine ad Spiritualia* quae abyssus est immanis qua Christianorum *Temporalia* omnimoda omnesque actus ac res humanas devoratum heic eunt."

separate ones for the mercantile, maritime or any other subordinate authority, but only the "Single Sword" (Gladium Unicum) ruling over men and their societies.[126]

Selden musters quite extensively the historical evidence for a unified authority in church and state – but what about the theoretical justification? Why is it the case that there should be only one authority? Selden's own rationale on this is a direct result of his wider theory of law and politics, presented at length in previous chapters. As we may recall, Selden's guiding principle in writing about society and politics was that there was one original "natural" or universal law from which all others followed, resting upon the intuition of providential equity – to keep one's promises (the intuition already pointing to providence as origin of all legal obligations). Upon this intuition, came the seven divine "Noahide" precepts setting up the basic laws for all men and societies, with one of them, the precept against stealing, regarded by Selden as also implying a divine reiteration of the natural intuition to keep one's promises:

> In other words, the source and foundation of the obligation which we associate with human law lies in the divine principle that each person should possess what is his, and our trust in one another should not be betrayed.[127]

We thus see how, even at its most basic level, the keeping of promises, human society and law is understood as an inextricable combination of divine and human elements – creating a seamless fabric of the human and divine components of authority, to the extent that it is impossible to identify a true demarcation between the two. This idea is evident throughout the *Jure Naturali* and even more explicitly in *Synedriis*, especially so in b1c2, where Selden directly connects the unity of authority over all matters, sacred and not, with the Noahide precept to set up courts as well as with the power by which to make

---

[126] *De Synedriis* b1 Praefatio: "Doctissimoque *Thomae Erasto* velut autori ejus primo atque ut novitia a nonnullis tribuitur; certe manifesto satis inde consecuturum videtur, tum perquam impium esse Prioris obtentum (nam velut Majestatis Divinae crimen est, Deo ut legislatori ea quae excogitantur ab Hominibus sic assignare) tum Unicum aut esse aut Jure optimo, nec obstante Divino, esse posse ubique in Christianismo Imperii & Jurisdictionis tam circa Sacra quam Profana Genus, quod velut ab unico Fonte, Angulo, Origine, id est Humano, eorum qui in Regimine public diversimode rebus praefuerint, Instituto manarit, adeoque Gladium Unicum [.]" Later on within the book, Selden mentions a long list of recent texts from Catholic countries, among which are France, and Spain, explicitly stating the supreme jurisdiction of the civil power. He adds (unfortunately without mentioning the specific texts he is referring to): "There is obviously a close kinship between the principles I have been discussing here and the books written by a number of scholars in support of the Venetian Republic's laws about excommunication and interdiction; these books were published some years ago, in the days of Pope Paul V, and they have since become standard references for anyone interested in theories of government." He almost surely means the writings of Paolo Sarpi. See *Synedriis* b1c10.

[127] *Synedriis* b1c2: "Obligationis scilicet quae in Humana agnoscitur origo fundamentum in praecepto Divino de suo cuique tribuendo nec fidem fallendo habetur."

people obey the rulings of the courts, that is political authority. In this scheme, the setting up of human institutions to judge and govern men is a divine injunction – to a great extent THE divine injunction, from which all other depend, for, he makes clear, without courts of justice no other Noahide precept can long survive. Thus the courts of justice are the human reflection of the metaphysical equity intuition which for Selden forms the basis for all human societies. In this way, all just authority, both political and religious, flows from one *jure divino* injunction, and all claims to a separate ecclesiastical authority (or a separate political one for that matter), become void:

So we should obviously understand the Rabbis to mean that the original commandment about appointing judges gave them the authority to pass verdicts about any legitimate cases, whether sacred or secular, which arose in the ages after Creation.[128]

After quoting various additional sources, including Augustine and Cicero, in support of this view, Selden makes sure to articulate his conclusion from these premises and sources, as directly and clearly as he can:

There are many statements like this among scholars who write about the law, both in ancient times and today; and it explains why jurisprudence, which is the source of every standard of trial and judgment, used to be defined as *the knowledge of things divine and human, and an understanding of what is just and unjust*. It is also the reason why courts ever since antiquity have depended for their decisions on a combination of divine and human law.[129]

This integrative vision of church and state, naturally drew much from Selden's Hebraist scholarship, on both the level of general ideas as well as of the specific Jewish traditions which he regarded as particularly apposite to the place of religion in Christian states. This was most evident in *Synedriis* devoted as it to the study of Jewish judicial and political institutions as well as in no lesser measure to rejecting views of those who were arguing for various church powers and institutions to be *jure divino*. Selden articulates both goals, when explaining that the learning of the ancient Jewish institutions in *Synedriis* is necessary to "understand the entire system of government with which ancient Jews administered both their sacred and their secular affairs" as well as for understanding Christianity "the legitimate descendant of early Judaism, which was in a sense its divine parent, and its only offspring; and has often imitated it."[130]

---

[128] *Synedriis* b1c2: "id ita plane capiendum est ut judices ejusmodi, ex ipso de Judiciis constituendis praecepto primario, de causis quibuscunque sive Sacris sive Profanis post rerum conditum[.]" See also discussion in Barbour *Measures* pp. 331–332.

[129] *Synedriis* b1c4: "Obvia sunt apud Scriptores de Legibus veteres recentioresque ejusmodi quamplurima. Atque hinc sane definita olim est Jurisprudentia (unde norma agendi ac judicandi omnimoda) *Divinarum atque Humanarum rerum notitia, justi ac injusti scientia.* Ideoque conjuncta antiquitus Divini juris ac Humani quantum ad usum forensem, cognito."

[130] *Synedriis* b1 Praefatio: "Harum enim cognito, sicut ad Regiminis totius publici tam circa Sacra quam Profana in Judaismo Veteri (cujus, ut Parentis Divini, Christianismus, maxime Primitivus, Legitima & Prophetica Proles est ac Propago unica, nec in paucis Imitator)[.]"

To Selden the affinity of Christianity to Judaism was both a historical and a qualitative one. That is, he held the Judaic origin of Christianity to be not only significant for learning facts about the early stages of the Christian story, and elucidating various concepts, but also to have left a permanent impression on the very character of Christianity. The nature of early Christianity as in effect a Jewish sect among many others (indeed possibly identifiable with the Essenes), was reiterated by Selden in almost all his Hebraist writings, and of course in *Synedriis*, to the point he repeatedly stressed its character as "reformed Judaism" and early Christians as complete and even devout Jews, whose practices (regarding, e.g., excommunication) were at that time "hardly any different" to the extent that "the name and the rights of Jews were shared in those days by both non-believers and believers, meaning Jews who believed in the reformed or true Judaism which all Jews were supposed to adopt (in other words, Christians)." Incidentally, regarding Christians as reformed Jews can hardly fail to imply a significantly tolerant attitude to contemporary Jews, since to a large degree it puts them on a par with the wide array of beliefs, sects and doctrines found within the Christianity of Selden's time – and indeed some Englishmen of that time, including Cromwell, certainly reached the conclusion that the Jews were preferable to several Christian denominations. The common origins of Judaism and Christianity were for Selden not only a matter of historical and scholarly relevance, but also of some still persisting important attributes. For, although many common beliefs and practices certainly had long since changed (using his favorite analogy):

But even though rivulets, streams and offshoots often do diverge and decline in various ways from their origins and sources and from the character of the beginnings from which they started (since these are still identifiable), they will always retain some of the qualities and traces of their original nature.[131]

That what Selden learned from the Jewish traditions about church and state was obviously intended to indicate something about the "original nature" of Christianity, concords completely with his staunch opposition to a religious jurisdiction, separated from the civil jurisdiction. Early on in his career he had started to address the Jewish juridical tradition as not as essentially religious or clerical in character, but rather as legal and political in nature. This is reflected in countless passing references in his works, where he mostly treats the Jewish rabbis not as clerics or theologians, but as legal experts, "jurisconsulti" (jurists) or "magistri" (teachers), whose expertise includes both sacred and profane matters – as well as numerous explicit references to the comprehensiveness of their legal province, such as in *Jure Naturali*, where Selden remarked that in the

---

[131] *Synedriis* b1c8: "Sed de Nominis Jurisque Judaici ejusmodi tunc Communione inter Judaeos Credentes seu qui Judaismum Reformatum seu verum, quem induere debebant Judaei universi, id est Christianos, & non Credentes, plura mox." For Latin of the "rivulets" quote, see Chapter 4.

book he is treating the ideas of the "Talmudici," the "Talmudists, who are both theologians and jurisconsults."[132]

As early as his *Jure Naturali*, Selden had made the argument (which he was later to massively expand on, in *Synedriis*) that Jewish excommunication was a civil penalty not merely a spiritual one, so that papists and Calvinists were both wrong in their assigning such a power to the clergy. By the time of his participation in the Westminster Assembly, Selden had made it an essential element of his more general claim for the necessity of the unity of church and state that this was the arrangement in the ancient Jewish commonwealth and the nature of the Sanhedrin. This claim was raised against the contention of the Presbyterians in the Assembly, that there was in the ancient Jewish state something that could be called a Presbytery, and that its power was independent of the Sanhedrin. Selden' reply was to argue that the Sanhedrin was the sole supreme repository of power in ancient Israel, including of the power to excommunicate.[133]

His last great work, *Synedriis*, deals primarily with the constitution of Jewish courts, including the supreme one, the Great Sanhedrin, which, as Selden noted, was not solely (or even predominantly) priestly in composition. He demolished the claims of those proposing there existed among the institutions of the ancient Jewish state "an ecclesiastical *synedrium* in the sense of a body devoted entirely to the sacred rites or their supervision," concluding that "it is clear that such a body never existed at all." He also demonstrated that matters under the jurisdiction of ecclesiastical courts in England of his own days, were in ancient times decided by Jewish courts that were not separate clerical ones. The obvious implication of the whole work, especially considering the role played by the ancient Jewish commonwealth in the debates of the Westminster Assembly, was that the Sanhedrin was a parallel and model for the English Parliament (which was similarly also considered the highest court in the land). An implication that if anything was only emphasized by Selden's discussion, based on Maimonides, of whether a Sanhedrin could put kings to trial – coming after the execution of Charles I.[134]

---

[132] See Toomer *Scholarship* pp. 505–506; J. Ziskind "Introduction" pp. 9–10. See also pp. 15–16 for Ziskind's claim that the full title of *Anno Civili* (1644) points to Selden's identification of the civil and religious fields as one.

[133] Cromartie *Hale* pp. 160–161. This issue was instructively discussed by Matt Goldish in a paper delivered to the Hebraism colloquium in Jerusalem, August 2004.

Interestingly, in a sermon preached at the opening of the Parliament of 1625 (of which Selden was not a member), Laud employed the model of the "Sanhedrim of the Jews" to illustrate his ideal of a mutual reciprocity between civil government and the church, which nevertheless for him necessitates a division of the civil and religious judicatures – very much the opposite of Selden's view. See Barbour *Measures* pp. 256–257. And in 1637, in a speech before the court of Star Chamber, Laud noted that the elements of "Judaicall worship" could be found throughout the history of the church from "Bethel" and "Jerusalem" to the "*Latine Church*." See Prior "Hebraism" p. 41.

[134] *Synedriis* b1c9: "Ecclesiasticum seu ad Sacra aut Sacrorum cognitionem seorsim tunc attinens Synedrium quod, velut apud Judaeos tunc in usu, ab nonnullis pro Ecclesiae ibi significatu sic obtenditur, nullibi plane apud illos unquam extitit[.]" See also Caruso *Miglior* pp. 750–751;

On top of his general theoretical argument about the mutual interdependence of religion and state, appearing in comments like "[t]he state still makes the religion, and receives into it what will best agree with it," and his drawing about this subject from Jewish and Christian sources, Selden also supported his views about church and state from English history and constitutional practice. He often brought precedents from English history to show his views were upheld in England even from before the conquest (viewing, e.g., the clerical presence in the Anglo-Saxon assemblies, as precedents for what later followed in parliaments). Moreover, it was not just a matter of particular cases but rather that he regarded both clerical presence in Parliament and the concurrent supremacy of Parliament over religious matters as an "ancient and fundamental" component of England's "frame of government" – that is, a defining principle of the English constitution.[135]

Moreover, there are indications that Selden was considering ways for further strengthening the integration of religion and state in England. One example is his comment in the *Table-Talk*, where he advised that the English Courts of Assize could perform a role of inculcating "moral honesty" (which he regarded

J. Ziskind "Introduction" pp. 17–18. Selden returned to the subject in both successive volumes of *Synedriis*. In *Synedriis* b2c14 he discussed the Talmudic dictum that the king cannot be judged, by pointing out that this dictum followed a specific incident when King Yannai faced down the Sanhedrin for summoning him – proving that before this, kings actually could testify and be judged. In *Synedriis* b3c14 Selden returned to the Mishnaic dictum that the king cannot judge or be judged excerpting from Josephus' report, and Grotius' discussion, of the trial in the Sanhedrin of Herod, a servant of King Hyrcanus, but decides this example does not in fact show that kings could be tried. However, he points out that the Talmudic discussion about the Mishnaic passage distinguished between kings of Israel, who may not be judged, and kings of the House of David, who may be. The possible connections of each of these discussions to the "trial" of King Charles are many, but Selden's own position on the issue is somewhat ambiguous. In *Synedriis* b2 he seems on the one hand to regard the trial of a king as in principle legitimate, and Yannai's defense of his servants and his intimidation of the court appear to point to similar practices by Charles I; but on the other hand his account also seems to raise the inescapable problems with practically judging a king, and to the improper manner in which the matter was carried out by the regicide "trial." In *Synedriis* b3 his treatment is if anything even more cautious on the repercussions of this issue on his own days, and avoiding any clear pronouncement of his on the matter, proposing instead to present the various opinions on this and letting everyone draw his own conclusions – he goes on to quote among those maintain that only God may judge a king, opinions by rabbis, Christian Fathers and contemporary scholars, including Salmasius' *Defension Regia* (from which he excerpts long passages), but interestingly, he does not bring the opinions of those on the opposite side, like Milton (nevertheless, Toomer maintains that Selden's opinion differed from Salmasius'). See also Toomer *Scholarship* pp. 754–755, 769–770.

[135] TT "Religion" sec. 8, and also discussion above of comment on "all is as the State likes" (TT "Bishops out of the Parliament" sec. 7), and see discussion in Barbour *Measures* pp. 154–155; Woolrych *Britain* pp. 173–174, 182–183; Notestein *Journal* p. 468 and note 10; Mendle *Dangerous* pp. 140, 149–150, 156–160; Christianson "Selden" ODNB; Mitchell *Minutes* pp. 209–210, 434–436; Paul *Assembly* pp. 492–498; Toomer *Scholarship* p. 574; Kaplan "Settlement" pp. 314–315, 324–325. Hyde was in this respect a follower of Selden when he declared that abolishing bishops as an estate meant changing the "frame and constitution of the kingdom." See Mendle *Dangerous* pp. 148, 155.

as the core doctrine of religion), by a concerted action of the judiciary and clergy. The Assizes were courts periodically held in various towns around the country by traveling judges, and thus displaying judicial proceeding before the public that assembled to watch the trials. On top of the judicial deliberations the Assizes included sermons, in which the clergy obviously directed their listeners to the moral lessons to be drawn from the cases decided by the court. Selden commented that he would have the clergy exhort the people to attend the Assizes in order "to learn their duty towards their neighbor," thus creating an instrument of moral edification for the public, in which the judiciary and clergy cooperated.[136]

Certainly, Selden's view of church and state had many obvious affinities with a long-standing tradition in English political thought. This tradition had many precedents in the Henrician and Elizabethan church (something he repeatedly stressed), including Hooker (something he did not), as well as important successors, including Clarendon, Hale and others, down to Edmund Burke and beyond. The most prominent elements of this tradition were the combination of an established church with a significant "adiaphoric" (and thus tolerationist) attitude to theological disputes, the view of the clergy as an estate of Parliament and, perhaps most important, the idea of the church as integrated with society to the point that they are in effect one. This last idea, which Selden articulated by using the Latin root "integer," appeared in *Synedriis* a number of times as "entire" or "integral" churches (Ecclesias integras/Ecclesiarum integrarum/integrarum Ecclesiarum), denoting what he defined as "communities of believers, *by public law established*" (Coetus fidelium, *publico Iure Constituiti*). This "integral church" was for him pretty much coterminous with those "Christian states" ("statuum Christianorum") which "combined together" (Conflantur) the ecclesiastical estate with the laity – the Christian equivalent to the "whole system of government with which the Jews administered both their sacred and secular affairs."[137]

In effect, "integral church" was Selden's term for what other prominent English writers on religion and state had termed "national church" (Hooker) or "Holy Commonwealth" (Baxter). Richard Baxter (who had an ambiguous attitude to Selden) explicitly indicated, many years after Selden's death, that he believed Selden had understood and supported this very idea: when arguing that as a result of the interregnum the term "commonwealth" had become negatively identified by ignoramuses with democracy, Baxter noted that respected contemporaries of his like Selden and Hale knew what it truly meant. Moreover, Baxter testified that in order to avoid pointless terminological controversy, he had opted to use, instead of the by then provocative "commonwealth," the more established term "National Church," the

[136] TT "Preaching" sec. 10, and see also discussion in Barbour *Measures* pp. 138–139.
[137] *Synedriis* b1c9–10.

meaning of which he outlined in a number of published and unpublished works of 1690–1691.[138]

I hope this study has established that the prevalent view in modern scholarship (Caruso, Cromartie and Barbour are prominent exceptions), tending to regard Selden as an anti-clerical or a cynic in religious matters, set on neutralizing all clerical power by ejecting it from the political realm, is not only erroneous but pretty much the very opposite of his actual view. For not only was Selden a clear and consistent defender of a clerical presence in the political process, but more than this, it is my distinct impression that many of his political interventions and his many exchanges with clergymen about such issues, convey a tone of true conviction in the importance of moral and religious ideas within public discussions. We may suspect that at least some of the failure of scholarship to adequately assess Selden's position results from a lack of familiarity with the content of his studies on the Jewish traditions; but the main culprit seems to be the projection upon Selden of a widely accepted model about the rise of the modern state, in which the dominant ideas about the state supposedly follow a general pattern of secularization and of the supremacy of the state over all. Such a projection tends to make Selden into a harbinger of figures like Hobbes and Spinoza, however, in his case at least, the model is patently inapplicable. Although Selden obviously shared Hobbes' alarm at the dangers of a clerical authority separate from the political one, he shared neither the latter's (or, for that matter, Spinoza's) epistemic and political premises, nor his absolutist antidote. Selden opposed claims of *jure divino* church supremacy to the same extent that he opposed similar claims made for monarchy, or would surely have for democracy. He believed the shape of political societies had very little that was directly *jure divino* in them, but this view was not the result of a cynical or utilitarian view of politics, instead if followed from Selden's belief that the assistance of traditions and institutions is beneficial for the welfare of political societies. In an age that was looking to found political order upon natural rights or sovereignty, Selden always remained an old-school constitutionalist, and a believer in the church as a necessary part of the English constitution.[139]

The issue of religion and state, in which he was interested throughout his career, in effect became the principal field of his political and intellectual

---

[138] Lamont *Puritanism* pp. 116–117; and see also Richard Baxter, *The Nonconformist Plea for Peace* (1679) pp. 251–253. Baxter envisaged the national church as a framework for instilling discipline. Thus, for example, infant baptism became, instead of a ceremony for the infant, one where parents were taught to know what was meant by entering their child into a covenant; while the child's own covenant baptism was to be performed only when reaching adulthood. See in this context Selden's comment about it having ever been the way sons to be bound by their fathers, in TT "Fathers and sons." To his friend John Humfrey, one of the leaders of the Massachusetts colony, Baxter expressed his wish that the world had "more such Nationall Churches as New England is (if a Province may be called a Nation)." See Lamont *Puritanism* p. 118.

[139] Cromartie *Hale* pp. 160–161; Toomer *Scholarship* p. 326 note 112.

activities in the last dozen years of his life. As the English political conflict escalated into all-out confrontation and eventually the Civil War, Selden's political influence declined markedly, since the leading parliamentarian constitutionalist had very little to contribute to the preparations or conduct of armed conflict. Thus the one important exception to his diminishing involvement in politics, regarded the fate of the English church: in Parliament Selden argued vigorously in favor of retaining episcopacy in 1641, and protested its removal from the House of Lords in 1642; between 1643 and 1646 he relentlessly contested a *jure divino* Presbyterian church, first in the Westminster Assembly and later in Parliament; throughout the 1640s virtually everything he published touched to some degree on issues of church and state; even in the 1650s, after being purged from Parliament by the army, and with his health progressively declining, he continued to be active in controversies having to do with church and state matters, by his published writings as well as in private correspondence, on issues such as tithes and church government.[140]

Most modern scholarship, including such as Toomer and Lamont, doubts Selden's efforts either in the Assembly or Parliament had any long-term impact on the religious legislation which emerged. I tend to disagree, for we have seen the leading role Selden had in articulating the arguments which defeated the establishment of a *jure divino* form of church government, as well as (corollary from this) the securing of parliamentary supremacy over church affairs. In addition, testimonies from opposite sides of the ideological divide on church and state, such as Baillie and Whitelocke, point to Selden's leading role, intellectual as well as political, in the struggles of the 1640s, about the shape of English church government. Of course, it is quite tricky to estimate if, or to what extent, events would have taken another course completely without Selden's role, but it is clear that his activities and ideas did play an important part in crystallizing the opposition to a Presbyterian church. As for the longer run, I suspect that further study will reveal Selden's ideas also had a significant role in forming many themes and arguments that shaped the eventual church and state settlement at the Restoration.[141]

The essence of Selden's view about religion and state was that the two should and could be successfully integrated into one system. It was part of his broader constitutionalist outlook regarding religion as an essential component of the English constitution. Looked at from this perspective, Baillie's memorable and oft-quoted comment about Selden avowing "that the Jewish state and church was all one, and that so in England it must be, that the parliament is the church"

---

[140] Fry "Selden" DNB.

[141] See discussion in Toomer *Scholarship* p. 575, and in Lamont *Godly* pp. 112–113. Lamont thinks that the failure of the Westminster Assembly's efforts was due principally to the inability of Presbyterians and Independents to reach some sort of agreement, rather than to the efforts of the "Erastian" opposition. It remains an open question, to what degree the ideas of Selden and of his so-called "Erastian" allies contributed to the resistance of many Independents to the Presbyterian arguments.

does not indicate an intention to subjugate the church or eliminate its political role, but rather a quest to defend its full integration as a necessary and indeed beneficial component of the state. Selden opposed the idea of a separation between church and state, not only on the practical level by which it necessarily leads to a competition about authority that can result only in one triumphing over the other, but also upon a fundamental belief that a state separated from the church (as well as a church separated from the state) are morally and religiously diminished. Significantly, Selden regarded the role of church representatives in the political arena, as not only one of representing the interests of the clergy as a group, but also as representing the spiritual dimension in the government of the nation. In Selden's view, religion is part, even a main part, of the national character that the state should mirror and express. As ancient Israel was not merely a state populated by Jews, but rather a thoroughly Jewish state, without this fact conceding control of its politics to the priesthood, so England is for Selden a "Christian state," within which the church plays a vital role, without however entailing by it a particular primacy for the latter upon political matters.[142]

However, while supporting the integration of religion into the political life of the nation, Selden also vehemently opposed any attempt to establish as divinely ordained, what form this role should take – indeed he regarded divine-right arguments as leading necessarily to a separation of church authority from the state. Selden's denying of a *jure divino* separate church authority, while at the same time demanding a role for the church in the state, meant, as Cromartie has remarked, the lifting of political government and thus of all laws to the level of things divinely sanctioned, resulting in a "sacralisation of secular things."[143]

In the traditional scheme of the estates (clergy, nobility, commons), widespread in western European constitutional practices and institutions, a natural place was assigned to the church in the state. However, a competing political vision was the humanist idea (of classical republican provenance) of mixed government, combining three types of political regime, by one, few and many (or monarchy, aristocracy and democracy), in which there is no specific role for the church. Selden's view offered a model that could combine mixed government with a place for the church. His support for an integral role of the church within government, indeed his regarding it as an estate as well as a structural component, indicates a view of mixed government which includes, in addition to monarchy, aristocracy and democracy, also a fourth

---

[142] *Synedriis* b1c10. See Selden's discussion of "those Christian states" like England "which combined both an ecclesiastical estate and what is usually called 'the laity'." Caruso pertinently discusses this point, claiming that the fact ancient Israel, or Judea, whatever their form of government, appeared to be not only a "state of the Hebrews" ("stato degli Ebrei" – *respublica Hebraeorum*), but to all effects a "Hebrew state" ("stato ebraico" – *respublica Hebraica*), for Selden, was not in itself a good reason to regard it as a model of theocracy. See Caruso *Miglior* p. 751.
[143] Cromartie *Hale* pp. 161–162.

component that we might term as theocracy. Like the other three components, its oppressive potential when it is a lone form of government becomes an asset when mixed with others. Selden found the practical expression of this ideal in many practices of the English political tradition, and its classic expression in the Jewish legal and political tradition.[144]

Overall, Selden's view of church and state was one of an English traditionalist (which for a time in the 1640s and 1650s became something of an endangered species), integrating the church within a system of parliamentary supremacy. This view was by no means a simplistic subordination of clergy to laity, for this would be too absolute a political setting, something Selden was ever opposed to throughout his political activities. He believed that the clergy, as an essential part of political society, cannot be viewed as a separate entity, but rather must be involved in political deliberations. The corollary of this belief was not only that churchmen have to be involved in deliberating about affairs of the whole community, but also that the whole community should in its turn be somehow involved in the determining of religious matters, since the church itself comprised both clergy and laity. Essentially, Selden upheld a model of religion and state that made the two coterminous, the "one sword" that he held had been the case with the Israelites – a model which he termed an "integral church" and, in its more familiar formulation, was a national church.

---

[144] It might then be said that, in a way, Selden, as well as regarding the church as an integral part of political government, also regarded church government within itself as "mixed" – combining "monarchical," "aristocratic" and "democratic" roles to various components of the church government.

7

Conclusion: John Selden and the Tradition of Historical Constitutionalism

In a famous defense of the English political and constitutional tradition against universalist rights theories, Edmund Burke asserted in his *Reflections on the Revolution in France* (1790):

Selden and the other profoundly learned men who drew this Petition of Right were as well acquainted, at least, with all the general theories concerning the 'rights of men' ... [b]ut, for reasons worthy of that practical wisdom which superseded their theoretic science, they preferred this positive, recorded, hereditary title to all which can be dear to the man and the citizen, to that vague speculative right which exposed their sure inheritance to be scrambled for and torn to pieces by every wild, litigious spirit.

As we have seen, in John Selden's case, Burke's claims were observably correct, as pertaining to both proficiencies and preferences. His generation's foremost historian and expert of the Common law, as well as a prominent parliamentarian leader and among the drafters of the Petition of Right, Selden was also eminently knowledgeable on the "general theories" of natural rights, contesting the views of Grotius and the second scholastics, as well as being trusted by both Charles I and Cromwell with making England's case for its rights of ownership over tracts of sea, against the natural law-based arguments which denied those rights.[1]

That Selden "preferred," in Burke's words, "the positive, recorded, hereditary" law to the speculative and abstract, is perhaps the most prominent feature of his work, which, in no small part, consists of an effort to justify customary law in general and English Common law in particular, against varied divine right and "right reason" type of arguments. Selden attempted to justify customary law by subsuming natural law into legal systems that were particular and changing. He employed a number of famous images to illustrate the idea of continuity through change, such as the comparison of the English legal

---

[1] A.L. Rowse, *Four Caroline Portraits* (Duckworth, 1993), p. 141.

system to the ship or "the house that's so often repaired, *ut nihil ex pristina materia supersit*, [that no original material remains] which yet, by the civil law, is to be accounted the same still[.]" Another image he often employed was of "Shrubs, Trees, Plants, and other things which belong to the bodie of Husbandrie" from which by diligent observation "it may bee collected what every Clime will or will not bear[.]" He did not use this as some simple "organic" metaphor, instead employing this image to illustrate the great diversity of societies, and even more so ruptures and changes when "the shoots grafted onto a tree grow from the trunk to which they have been attached."[2]

However, the most prominent and recurring Seldenian image of persistence through change was that of springs, streams and rivers, ever dividing and reuniting in a complex interaction that cannot be untangled. Heraclitus famously stated that its mobile nature means one never can step into the same river twice, yet at the same time, as Selden noted, a river is yet regarded the same regardless of all changes in size and speed, as well as when joining other bodies of water or splitting into several ones, through its course. This image also allowed Selden to justify the place that his historical enquiries into distant origins of ideas and practices had within his thought, arguing that he believed origins of ideas, practices and systems, however ancient, had a role in determining the "nature" of them, so that rivers and streams though far from "their origins and sources," nevertheless "will always retain some of the qualities and traces of their original nature," just as he held the English constitution, to preserve through all its changes some ancient persisting principles and Christianity to still retain certain qualities from its Jewish origins.[3]

The continuity of such ideas within a central strand of English thought, down to Burke and beyond, is easily illustrated in the similar use made of those images throughout the centuries to defend the traditional English constitution against those who would replace it with a newly minted one. In an already quoted remark from *Table-Talk*, Selden compared the abolition of episcopacy in England to "he that pulls down an old House, and builds another in another Fashion," suggesting the uncertainty and trouble involved are unwarranted, for probably "the old one would have serv'd as well." A younger friend and disciple of Selden, who became the prominent common lawyer of his own generation, Matthew Hale, had great influence on the legal and constitutional ideas of future generations through his *History of the Common Law*, and employed the same images as Selden, for the same purpose. He used the images of the old house and the Argonauts' ship to argue that through all evident great changes, English law of his time was nevertheless essentially the same as "600 Years since." Hale also argued, as Selden, for continuity through change by using the very same river imagery, of "those People that were thus intermingled with the ancient *Britains* or

<hr />

[2] NL cols. 1891–1892; JN b1 Praefatio.   [3] *Synedriis* b1c1.

Saxons, [and the respective laws] as rivers continue by the same denomination while having the accession of other streams added."[4]

The same images are also employed by Burke, when making the very same point in favor of retaining traditional constitutional components that revolutionaries of his days wanted jettisoned; for example, when he wrote that,

it is with infinite caution that any man ought to venture upon pulling down an edifice which has answered in any tolerable degree the common purposes of society, or on building it up again, without having models and patterns of approved utility before his eyes.[5]

Much of modern scholarship concurs with Burke's identification of his theoretical debt to Selden. Pocock asserts that "[t]he philosophy of Burke is descended from the concept of custom worked out in the late Renaissance during the first reaction against Roman law, and Hale marks a definite stage in its development." Tuck goes even further, when addressing the above passage from Selden, claiming that in it one can find "already the Burkean theory of English law." The same assessment is shared by I. Hampsher-Monk's survey of modern political thought as well as by Caruso, author of the most wide-ranging recent treatment of Selden's ideas and works.[6]

However, such assessments have for the most part remained at a generalized level, without detailing the components and structure of this theory. At the conclusion of this book, we are now in a position to flesh out more substantially the principles and composition of Selden's theory of law and government, which went on to have a significant influence not only on Hyde, Hale and Burke, but more extensively on the legal and constitutional ideas of the English-speaking countries.

---

[4] Matthew Hale, *History of the Common Law* (second edition, 1716) pp. 57–59, 60–61. And see discussion in Pocock *Ancient* pp. 176–177.

[5] NL cols. 1891–1892. Another example of his use of the house image to describe the English frame of government is TT "Bishops out of Parliament." Elsewhere Selden described the "moral teachings and the rules of civic life" (the basic political laws) as "the very stout supports to a building." See JN b1c1.

For the claim that although the ship or house analogy was found in writers before Selden, he "transposed this analogy from the description of corporate entities to one of a legal system in its entirety, conceived of separately from particular governments." See in Roslak *Selden* p. 41.

For Edmund Burke's use of the image, see *Reflections on the Revolution in France* [1790], C.C. O'Brien ed. (Penguin, 1982) pp. 152–153; see also pp. 280–281, 285–287. A different but related use of the image was made on p. 106.

Burke later described the day when the French natural rights ideology might destroy the British way of artificial representation: "On that day, I fear, there was an end to that narrow scheme of relations called our country, with all its pride, its prejudices and its partial affections. All the little quiet rivulets that watered an humble, a contracted, but not an unfruitful field, are to be lost in the waste expanse, and boundless barren ocean of the homicide philanthropy of France." See Edmund Burke, *A Third Letter on a Regicide Peace* (1797).

[6] Pocock *Ancient* pp. 172–173; Tuck *Natural* pp. 83–84; Hampsher-Monk *History* pp. 46, 270–272 and note 28; Caruso *Miglior* pp. 943–945. See also Ferguson *Clio* pp. 57–59, 117–125, 292–298, and Collins *Cosmos* p. 210 note 30.

We have seen that the background to Selden's developing his ideas was the great intellectual crisis of the early-modern period, in which figures like Descartes, Bacon and Galilei challenged long-established ideas and practices. In England the crisis was exacerbated by the Common law habit of interpreting English politics and society according to the internal assumptions it possessed and not with the aid of any prior or general political and social thought. This relative insularity of the Common law's intellectual development left it with little defense when outside challenges appeared.[7]

The practical effects of the crisis on England are easily illustrated by the fact that while at Selden's birth, in the late sixteenth century, the consensus and self-confidence of the English legal and constitutional system were reflected in Hooker's writings; when Selden died, in the 1650s, not only had the theoretical consensus been shattered, but in practice king-in-parliament had been replaced by a military dictatorship, the constitution lay in ruins and various proposals for erecting a new order in their stead were being put forward on the basis of theories such as those of Grotius, Hobbes or Filmer.

While the main intellectual trend of his age from Machiavelli and Bodin, through Grotius, Hobbes and Filmer to Locke and Spinoza, was towards abstract and universalist systems, Selden's views and proclivities were historical and particular. Accordingly, his life was devoted to defending both intellectually and politically the traditional English "Frame of Government"; what we call today constitutionalism. His own distinctive contribution to this effort was the garnering of innovative arguments and sources, to justify the historical and particular English constitution as being in accordance with universal principles.

I have argued that to adequately assess Selden's place within the history of modern political though, a reconsideration of the terminological framework is necessary, especially as concerns the hopelessly confused employment of terms such as "consent" and "contract." To advance a clearer treatment of the issues involved I have adopted the distinction, drawn by Hopfl and Thompson, between two kind of theories employing the term "contract": on the one hand "philosophical contractarianism," which aims for a general theoretical model and puts in the center terms such as "natural right," "natural liberty," "natural equality," "condition of nature" and "sovereignty"; on the other hand, "constitutional contractarianism," stressing particular institutions and historical inheritances over universal propositions, employing such terms as "fundamental law," "fundamental rights and liberties," "original contract" and "ancient constitution" (or "fundamental constitution"). Although some type of consent is presupposed in all contractarian theories, the consent meant in each of the two models differs crucially: in philosophical contractarian theories, the consent required is fundamentally that of autonomous individuals, which at some level can never wholly relinquish it, the contract

---

[7] JGA Pocock, *Politics, Language and Time* (Methuen, 1972) p. 210

thus becoming a mere technical device within a political society that is ultimately founded on individual consent; while in constitutional contractarian theories, the consent intended is always one of collectives and groups, never of individuals only, therefore it is the contract created by this consent which constitutes identity, obligations and rights within political society, making appeals to what is outside it irrelevant. Writers in the constitutional contractarian tradition put forward a logic of tacit consent and legal structures, which often also include the binding of posterity, effectively denying the principle of a sovereign individual consent while preferring to it a true contractarianism, which is bound to formal and institutional arrangements. As we have seen, this is very much Selden's position.

Selden articulated a theory of constitutional contractarianism, which emerged at least in part as opposition to philosophical contractarian theories of individual consent (such as Grotius' and Hobbes') as well as to absolutist theories of politics (such as Bodin's and Filmer's). For all their many differences, the various approaches Selden was combating shared a challenge to the legitimacy of the Common law's particularistic nature, and to the English constitution founded upon it. Instead the new universalizing theories were proposed, in which the purported confusion and conflict created by particular constitutional governments would be replaced by the unity of purpose and action found in a sovereign will, be it of rational individuals or of the absolute ruler.

Indications of Selden's wider theoretical concerns appear even in his early works. But his efforts to present a complete theory supplying universal foundation and justification for particular political and legal systems, such as England's, were evident especially from the 1630s onwards. Probably this was the result, at least in part, of his own experiences; his parliamentary activities of the 1620s culminating in the hopes of the Petition of Right, which then turned into the dead end of Charles I's Personal Rule, and of his own imprisonment without trial. This turn of events indicated for Selden both the limitations of existing Common law political and ideological concepts, in resisting concerted efforts to undermine them, as well as the considerable theoretical extent of the challenge, as a new terminology of "reason of state" and "sovereignty" gradually infiltrated English constitutional debates.

The theory which Selden developed had as its starting point a universal principle of obligation, upon which a minimal framework of seven divinely inspired "Noahide" universal rules was established. From this point on, all duly instituted laws and polities could be legitimately constructed according to particular proclivities and circumstances, and were so allowed, as long as they did not contravene the basic universal rules. This theory, presented most comprehensively in the *Jure Naturali* but evident in several other works, primarily *Mare Clausum* and *Synedriis*, supplied a universal justification for all particular constitutions not contravening the universal rules, and thus for the English constitution. At the same time, it also implied that legal and political systems lacking a particular and practical dimension, such as Roman law or Natural Rights theories based purely on reason, were to be regarded as deficient.

The prominent place accorded in his theory to particularism was connected to the traditionalistic and probabilistic epistemic approach informing Selden's legal and political outlook. The nature of all human knowledge was for him, by definition, inherently partial and unstable, but it could be significantly augmented by particular experience and accumulated knowledge. The same was valid not only for individuals but also for whole societies, where the experience and accumulation of knowledge became tradition. Conveniently, this role he assigned to tradition as an essential epistemic tool, also supplied the element of consent to Selden's legal and political theory. It was not a consent originating in wholly autonomous individuals, but rather a historical process, expressing the interests and preferences of a community over time, both defining of and defined by, the historical tradition of that particular community.

Following from his advocacy of contractual constitutionalism, and with all the stupendous variety of sources and subjects he treated, a number of main themes recur prominently in his work: the keeping of contracts as basis for society and politics, the limits of self-referring reason, national identity, historical adaptation to circumstances and continuity through change. Not incidentally, these elements were all especially relevant for the English version of traditional constitutionalism.

English Common law was born and always remained first and foremost a law of property, making the centrality and sanctity of property its most characteristic trait. From early on, English lawyers made the connection between the exceptional respect assigned to property in the Common law, and its role as repository of the rights and liberties of Englishmen. The connection between the significant difference in this respect between English law and other legal systems, such as French and Roman law, and the political oppression seen as emblematic of that difference, was remarked upon as early as the fifteenth-century writings of Fortescue. Indeed, it was to a great extent on the basis of the law of private property, as both a foundation and an extension of personal liberty, that the national mythology of the Common law was established, and if anything even intensified from the later sixteenth century. This was the background to the familiar refrain of common lawyers of the early seventeenth century, that the foundation of the English law is in the law of property defining "meum et tuum" (mine and thine), and the fear that royal subversion of the sanctity of private property may herald the destruction of the constitution. As the political issues in contention concerned property rights and consent to taxation, in both law courts and Parliament, the idea of a property contract came to seem to many (as V. Kahn has convincingly argued) the apt way to address *Magna Carta* and latter legislation. Selden certainly embraced such views, remarking about *meum* and *tuum* as basis for English laws and liberties, and declaring in Parliament about goods that had been seized arbitrarily by the government: "Next they will take our arms, and then our legs, and so our lives." It is not hard to see how these concerns informed Selden's writings arguing that property law and the abiding by contracts enjoy a natural and divine sanction, in addition to the self-referential and utilitarian justifications usually given in English political debates. This outlook of his is evident in the prominence he assigned to his repeated identification of the universal first principle of every law and society as the abiding by agreements, "Pacta sunt servanda," as well as in his further connection, especially in *Synedriis*, of both the obligation to abide by agreements and of the Noahide prohibition on theft, to the creation of private property, in the distinction of "what is mine from what is yours or his."[8]

On the central issue of property, as well as on other issues like the duties owed to one's fellow man, on top of those owed to God or on the afterlife and providential retribution, there is an evident affinity between many of Selden's own ideas and similar notions found in the Jewish tradition. It is unclear if this affinity was the result of his extended exposure to Jewish ideas and themes along the years, or rather if to begin with he was drawn to Jewish ideas when finding them congenial to his own previously held views. Probably there was some mix of the two factors, which with the years became impossible to disentangle, resulting in an affinity which often blurred in his writings, the distinction between his own opinions and those of the Jewish sages.

Two issues in particular to which Selden devoted special efforts in his work, and which were prominently connected to his Hebraic studies, were also the most intensely debated ones in the 1640s and 1650s (as well as being interconnected with one another): church and state relations, and the role of the political and judicial assemblies. In religion and state, his positions were characterized more than anything by a consistent opposition to divine-right arguments for a church authority independent from the state, and consequently he was fiercely opposed to a separation of the church from the state. Selden's ideas on this issue have been exhaustively dealt with in the relevant chapter of this book. But it is worthwhile to briefly consider here a corollary consequence of his ideas on wider constitutional concerns – the relevance of the role assigned to the church in Selden's theory to his rejection of absolutism. Since, in his view, it is necessary that there exist a religious interest and authority within the chief deliberative political body, such a component acts as a force that is inherently averse to despotism. It naturally prevents the danger of a religious despotism establishing itself upon the political, but it also prevents political power from doing the same, by denying totality to the political. In other words, it becomes another "mixed" element within a mixed constitution, preventing authority from becoming monolithic and absolute. While many supporters of a separation of church and state authority, such as the Catholic Bellarmine and the Scottish Presbyterians, were by no means absolutists (although Selden

---

[8] *Synedriis*, b1c4 "quibus Juris Mei, Tui Sui."

thought their ideas conducive to political strife, and ultimately to a religious dominance of politics), it is instructive to observe that the most resolute proponents of political absolutism, including those of divine-right monarchists and Hobbesian views, assigned to the church a role that was totally subservient to the political authority, making it into merely another tool of despotism. Selden thus proposed not to take religion out of politics or to make it irrelevant, but rather to incorporate it into the political process, so that it would become a beneficial moral and political power within the state – a view certainly consistent with his description of the ancient Jewish Sanhedrin. Selden's way to oppose a religious tyranny was the very same way by which he opposed political tyranny – not the total victory of one power over the others, be it King or Parliament, be it religious or civil authority, but rather make religion into another power within the state, integrated with and balancing the others, so that it becomes yet another obstacle to the concentration of all power in one place.

Selden brought the same outlook to the second issue to which he devoted special efforts throughout his public career: the role of the political and judicial assemblies in the government of the state. Here, too, rather than the victory of one side over the other, he was looking for a mixed regime as a way to oppose despotism. While in the 1620s Selden was a prominent defender of parliament from what was seen as the encroachments of the constitution by royal power, in the 1640s, although siding with Parliament, he became an untiring proponent of an agreed political solution to the crisis: one that would salvage the constitutional framework. He was never a supporter of unilateral measures or military actions, and relentlessly pursued a policy of reconciliation. Against a background of growing extremism and oft-shifting positions, he stood out as one of the few individuals consistently heard in support of finding a resolution to the conflict that would preclude either side in the conflict from establishing its own arbitrary dominance over politics.

In Selden's political and intellectual activities, these two great issues increasingly came to be combined into his view of what we may call a national government. The traditional constitutional idea of the estates (clergy, nobility, commons), widespread in western European political practices and institutions, assigned a natural place to the church in the state; while the humanist idea of mixed government, combining three types of political regime, by one, few and many, was of classic republican source, and had no place for the church. Selden wanted a political model which could combine the traditional components of mixed government with a place for the church as an important element of society; he found it the Jewish political tradition, where the law was a national one, both religious and civil at the same time, and where the Sanhedrin was a national assembly, socially varied and combining political, judicial and religious functions. In this way, Selden believed the Jewish political tradition had added to the typical version of mixed government, with its "monarchical," "aristocratic" and "democratic" elements in government, also a fourth element that may be termed "theocratic," representing the clerical and even spiritual interests in the government of the nation – duly combined and balanced by with the other three.

Although for most of the 1640s Selden found himself in a small minority (sometimes literally a party of one), his constant and relentless pursuit of his goals, his straightforward constitutional views and his skillful exploiting of tactical opportunities eventually handed him political victories in his two main fields of activity: in the matter of church and state, he had a prominent role in preventing the establishment of a Presbyterian state church of England, and in convincing Parliament that any religious settlement must include the supremacy of civil jurisdiction; in the conflict between King and Parliament, he and his allies ultimately won over the majority of the Long Parliament to their vision of a restored constitution, that would establish a stable balance between King and Parliament, while preserving the reforms of government achieved in 1640–1641.

The military coup and regicide of 1649, which turned England into an 11-year dictatorship, appeared to bring all the efforts of Selden's political life to nothing. However, it was the interregnum and the military rule that were not to last, and in the long run, after the Restoration, Selden's constitutional ideas had an important impact on the shape of things to come. After the mainstream had broken down during the Civil War and dictatorship, Selden's ideas had a significant role in crystallizing the disaffection among key figures of the period, with facile Grotian or Hobbesian recipes for a resolution to the constitutional crisis. Several among both prominent royalist and parliamentarians, who believed some form of eventual reconciliation and restoration desirable, came to look at the ideas that Selden had developed and advocated as the framework for a future settlement.

When Selden died in late 1654, the English constitution he had struggled to defend for all of his adult life seemed irretrievably lost; but in little more than five years the regicide regime had collapsed and Parliament restored the old constitution, declaring that "according to the ancient and fundamental laws of this kingdom, the Government is, and ought to be, by King, Lords and Commons[.]" All things considered, the name of John Selden certainly deserves a place of pride among those responsible for salvaging the English Constitution and the Anglican Church, during their ordeal of Civil War and interregnum. The shape of the Restoration settlement, in state and in church, as well as the intellectual disposition of the English political and legal class for generations to come, owed to Selden's ideas, both directly and indirectly, much more than most knew.[9]

It is now possible to assess the role Selden had within English and western political thought. Following Tuck's studies of early-modern political thought, Selden has been described for some decades as one of the seventeenth-century thinkers who articulated Natural Rights theories, an intermediary figure

---

[9] *Journal of the House of Commons: Volume 8, 1660–1667* (1802) p. 8.

between Grotius and Hobbes. This view has been successfully challenged by such studies as those of Sommerville, Zaller and Toomer, who showed Selden's ideas to be inconsistent with Natural Rights theories. However, such studies concluded from Selden's rejection of Natural Rights theories that he never elaborated any general religious or political ideas of his own, and regard him as a great scholar who added little of importance to political theory.

This book has hopefully shown both of these views of Selden and his ideas to be flawed. Following indications offered by Pocock and Hampsher-Monk, as well as the more substantial studies of such as Caruso and Cromartie, a theoretical framework for Selden's political and legal ideas has been presented. Although certainly not articulating a formal and systematic theoretical apparatus in the manner of Hobbes, Grotius or even Filmer, nevertheless Selden's writings, and especially the *Jure Naturali*, do present the broad outlines of a general theory of man and society. His theory supplies a coherent framework for his scholarly writings (as well as, often, his political activities) in the fields of religion, philosophy, law and politics. In opposition to the Natural Rights theories of his day, which produced a philosophical contractarianism upholding the supremacy of individual consent – Selden articulated his theory, pursuing a traditionalist and constitutionalist contractarianism.[10]

Selden's ideas on the whole ran counter to the obsession typical of his age (and indeed of most modern political thought) with the location and authority of political sovereignty. Whereas political thinkers from Bodin, Grotius, Hobbes and Filmer, to Rousseau, Kant and Schmitt strive to either securely locate sovereignty or else to subsume it within reason or the general will, Selden was patently uninterested in the concept. Indeed, he was among those traditionalists within Parliament who opposed the introduction of sovereignty terminology into the English political system, viewing it as both alien and detrimental to it. But Selden's rejection of the politics of sovereignty and rationalism should not mark him as a relic of scholasticism or as an unthinking follower of established practices, for he was patently neither. In several intellectual fields he was an innovator, and he certainly did not reject new political ideas he was confronted with, out of a merely ignorant or knee-jerk reaction. For Selden understood quite well the drift of sovereignty-based theories, and preferred to them what we call today constitutionalism – guaranteeing the components and the function of the English political system as a whole. His outlook was therefore out of tune with the mainstream of "modern" political thought, but it would be wrong to regard his views as stationary or backward-looking. In many ways, he was far more foresighted than most typical "modern" thinkers, for his views had an important role in shaping and reinforcing the English political tradition,

---

[10] On Selden's style and his philosophical theory, or lack thereof, see Parry, *Trophies* p. 98, and Toomer, *Scholarship* pp. 817–818.

which survived the great upheavals of his times and went on to thrive and diversify, among English-speaking nations and beyond them, to this very day. One of the main features of this political tradition is its combination of preserving customary forms with a great flexibility in function, which enables it to successfully preserve constitutional frameworks over centuries, and indeed regards this very feature as beneficial and defining; whereas other "modern" or "post-modern" political outlooks prize the break with the past and a principled revolutionary nature as essential characteristics. Since the traditionalist and constitutionalist aspects of the English political tradition owe in truth little to Hobbes or Locke, it is necessary to look to Selden and those who followed in his track to adequately consider their nature and resilience. It is a tradition that, as Selden aptly put it in the title of one of his earliest works, the *Jani Anglorum* (1610), is "Janus Faced" – at the very same time both backward-looking and forward-looking; able to securely look to the future exactly because it does not lose sight of its past. Many of the English constitutional ideas and practices of later generations, from Clarendon and Hale to the glorious revolution and into the eighteenth century, to Burke, the American founding fathers and beyond, can be traced to Selden, and there are probably more that have not as yet been identified. In this way, John Selden had a significant, if as yet still relatively unexplored, role in shaping the constitutional and political ideas of England and the English-speaking nations, even to this day.

Bibliography

BIBLIOGRAPHICAL NOTE

Place of publication for all books is London unless otherwise specified.
For pre-1950 books, year and place of publication are noted; for later books, the publisher also.

PRIMARY TEXTS

Selden Texts (further editions appear separately only if revised)

"Carmen potrepticon" in Jonson, Ben, *Volpone* (1607)
The Duello, or Single Combat (1610)
Jani Anglorum Facies Altera (1610)
"Illustrations" in Drayton, Michael, *Poly-Olbion* (1612)
"Laudatory verses" in Browne, William, *Britannia's Pastorals* (1613)
Titles of Honor (1614)
Analecton Anglobritannicon (Frankfurt, 1615); mangled text later disowned
"Notes" to Fortescue, Sir John, *De Laudibus Legum Angliae* & de Hengham, Sir Ralph, *Summae Magna et Parva* (1616)
A Brief Discourse Touching on the Office of Lord Chancellor of England (1617)
"of the Iewes sometimes living in England" in Purchas, Samuel, *His Pilgrimage: or Relations of the World and the Religions Observed in All Ages and Places Discovered, from the Creation unto this Present* (1617, 3rd edition)
De Diis Syriis Syntagmata (1617)
"Commendatory verses" in *Lucani Pharsalia*, Farnaby, Thomas, ed. and trans. (1618)
The Historie of Tithes, That is, The Practice of Payment of Them. The Positive Laws Made for Them. The Opinions Touching the Right of Them. A Review of it is also Annext, which Both Confirmes it and Directs in the Use of it (1618)
"Prefatory letter" in Vincent, Augustine, *Discoverie of Errours in the First Edition of Catalogue of Nobility Published by Ralfe Brooke* (1622)
"Notae" in *Eadmeri Monachi Cantvariensis Historia Novorum*, Selden, John, ed. (1623)

Bibliography

Marmora Arundelliana Sive Saxa Graece Incisa (1628, 2nd edition appeared 1629)
De Diis Syriis Syntagmata (1629, 2nd revised edition)
De Successionibus in Bona Defuncti, Seu Jure Haereditario, ad Leges Ebraeorum, Quae, Florente Olim Eorum Republica, in usu (1631)
Titles of Honor (1631, 2nd revised edition)
Mare Clausum, Seu de Dominio Maris (1635 – three more editions published in 1636, one of them in the Netherlands)
De Successione in Pontificatum Ebraeorum (1636, published together with a revised version of *Bona*)
De Jure Naturali et Gentium Juxta Disciplinam Ebraeorum (1640)
The Priviledges of the Baronage of England, When They Sit in Parliament (1642)
"Commentarius" in *Eutychii Aegyptii, Patriarchae Orthodoxorum Alexandrini, Scriptoris, ut in Oriente Admodum Vetusti ac Illustris, ita in Occidente tum Paucissimis Visi tum Perraro Auditi, Ecclesia suae Origines*, Selden, John, ed. (1642)
De Anno Civili et Calendario Veteris Ecclesiae seu Republicae Judaicae Dissertatio (1644)
Uxor Ebraica, seu de Nuptiis et Divortiis ex Jure Civili, id est, Divino et Talmudico, Veterum Ebræorum (1646)
"Dissertatio historica" annexed to *Fleta, seu Commentarius Juris Anglicani sic Nuncupatus sub Edwardo Rege Primo, seu circa Annos Abhinc CCCXL, ab Anonymo Conscriptus, Atque è Codice Veteri, Autore ipso Aliquantulùm Recentiori, Nunc Primùm Typis Editus*, Selden, John, ed. (1647)
De Synedriis et Praefecturis Juridicis Veterum Ebraeorum, Liber Primus (1650)
Of the Dominion or Ownership of the Sea, Needham, Marchamont, trans. (1652)
"Ad lectorem" in *Historiae Anglicanae Scriptores X*, Twysden, Roger, & Selden, John, eds. (1652)
Vindiciæ Secundùm Integritatem Existimationis Suæ, Per Convitium de Scriptione Maris Clausi, Petulantissimum Mendacissimumque Insolentiùs Læsæ in Vindiciis Maris Liberi Adversùs Petrum Baptistam Burgum, Ligustici Maritimi Dominii Assertorem, Hagæ Comitum Jam Nunc Emissis (1653)
De Synedriis et Praefecturis Juridicis Veterum Ebraeorum, Liber Secundum (1653)

Posthumous Selden Texts – Includes Only Previously Unpublished Pieces or New Translations

De Synedriis et Praefecturis Juridicis Veterum Ebraeorum, Liber Tertius (1655)
Of the Birthday of Our Saviour (1661, one of three short tracts written at James I's orders in 1620)
Mare Clausum; The Right and Dominion of the Seas, Howell, James, trans. (1663)
England's Epinomis (1681)
Tracts Written by John Selden of the Inner-Temple, Esquire; the First Entituled, Jani Anglorvm Facies Altera, Rendred into English, with Large Notes Thereupon, by Redman Westcot, Gent.; the Second, England's Epinomis; the Third, Of the Original of Ecclesiastical Jurisdictions of Testaments; the Fourth, Of the Disposition or Administration of Intestates Goods; the Three Last Never Before Extant, Westcot, Redman, [Littleton, Adam] trans. & notes (1683)

Table-Talk: Being the Discourses of John Selden, Esq; Or his Sence of Various Matters of Weight and High Consequence; Relating Especially to Religion and State, Milward, Richard, ed. (1689)

Joannis Seldeni Jurisconsulti Opera Omnia Tam Edita Quam Inedita, Wilkins, David, ed., 3 vols. (1725) including previously unpublished texts, among which:

  – Two short tracts written in 1620 (together with *Of the Birthday*, published in 1661) to placate James I after he objected to the publication of the *Historie of Tithes*: "Of the passage in the Revelation of St. John touching the number 666"; "Of Calvin's judgement on the Revelation."
  – Four manuscript texts written between 1619 and 1621, to answer objections to his *History of Tithes*: "Letter to the Marquess of Buckingham"; "Of my purpose in writing Historie of Tithes"; "An Admonition to the readers of Sir James Sempil's Appendix, For so much as concerns Scaliger and Selden" manuscript answering James Sempil's *Sacrilege Sacredly Handled* (1619); "To the reader of Dr. Tillesley's animadversions" manuscript answering Tillesley, Richard, *Animadversions upon M. Selden's History of Tithes, and his review thereof. . .* (1621, 2nd edition).
  – Speeches and arguments: "An argument concerning the baronies of Grey and Ruthen"; "In the impeachment against the duke of Buckingham, 1626, May 8"; "Arguments at the king's bench bar upon the Habeas Corpus Novmb. 22 1627"; "An argument concerning the Habeas Corpus 5 Car. I; Of the liberty of the subject 1628. Mar. 27"; "The argument, which by command of the house of commons was made at their first conference with the lords. . . April 7. 1628"; "At the committee about the commission for martial law. April 15, 19, 22, 25. 1628"; "About the five propositions sent from the lords to the house of commons. April 26. 1628"; "At the committe-[e] about the bill for magna charta, and the liberties of the subject. April 28. 1628"; "At the committee about the addition proposed by the lords to be made to the petition of right. May 21 1628"; "About the patent for exchange. June 23. 1628."

The Dissertation of John Selden annexed to his edition of Fleta, [1647] Kelham, Robert, trans. and notes (1771)

Ioannis Seldeni Ad Fletam Dissertatio, [1647] Ogg, David, trans. (Cambridge University Press, 1925)

John Selden on Jewish Marriage Law: The Uxor Hebraica, [1646] Ziskind, J., trans. and ed. (Leiden: Brill, 1991)

"The Correspondence of John Selden (1584–1654)," transcriptions by Toomer, G. J., in *Early Modern Letters Online*, Cultures of Knowledge, http://emlo.bodleian.ox.ac.uk/blog/wp-content/uploads/2015/01/selden-correspondence.pdf.

Other Primary Texts

Pirkei Rabbi Eliezer
The Babylonian Talmud
The Hebrew Bible

The Jerusalem Talmud

The New Testament

"The Case of the Postnati" (1608, aka Calvin's Case) in *A Complete Collection of State Trials and Proceedings*, Howell, T.B., ed., 21 vols. (1816) in vol. 2.

"The Case of Five Knights" (1627, aka Darnell's Case) in *A Complete Collection of State Trials and Proceedings*, Howell, T.B., ed., 21 vols. (1816) in vol. 3.

The Case of Tenures upon the Commission of Defective Titles Argued by All the Judges of Ireland (1637)

"Declaration of both Houses concerning the Commission of Array" (1 July 1642), in *Historical Collections of Private Passages of State: Volume 4, 1640–42*, Browne, D., ed. (1721)

"A second Declaration of both Houses concerning the Commission of Array" (January 1643), in *Historical Collections of Private Passages of State: Volume 4, 1640–42*, Browne, D., ed. (1721)

[Anonymous], *Treatise about the Union of England and Scotland* (1604)

[Anonymous], "Upon the nameinge of the Duke of Buckingham the Remonstrance" (June 1628) in *Proceedings in Parliament 1628*, W.D. Bidwell et al., eds., 6 vols. (Rochester, NY: Rochester University Press, 1991–1996), vol. vi.

[Anonymous], *Touching the Fundamental Laws, or Politique Constitution of this Kingdom* (1643)

[Anonymous] *Scripture and Reason Pleaded for Defensive Arms* (1643)

[Anonymous, perhaps Bowles, Edward], *Plain English, or a Discourse Concerning the Accommodation, the Armie, the Association* (1643)

[Anonymous], *Tyth-Gatherers, No Gospel Officers* (1646)

[Anonymous], *Agreement of the People* (1647)

[Anonymous], *Light Shining in Buckinghamshire* (1648)

[Anonymous], *The True Levellers' Standard Advanced* (1649)

[Anonymous], *A New-Years Gift for the Parliament and Armie* (1650)

[Anonymous], *The Law of Freedom in a Platform* (1652)

Ascham, Anthony, *A Discourse – What Is Particularly Lawful During the Confusions and Revolutions of Governments* (1648)

Ascham, Anthony, *Of the Confusion and Revolutions of Gover[n]ment* (1649)

Bacon, Francis, "Of Atheisme" in his *Essays* (1597)

Bacon, Francis, "Of Styx or Treaties" in his *De Sapienta Veterum* (1609)

Bacon, Francis, *Novum Organum* (1620)

Baillie, Robert, *The Letters and Journals of Robert Baillie*, Laing, D., ed., 3 vols. (Edinburgh, 1841)

Baxter, Richard, *The Grotian Religion Discovered* (1658)

Baxter, Richard, *A Holy Commonwealth* (1659)

Baxter, Richard, *A Key for Catholicks, to Open the Jugling of the Jesuits* (1659)

Baxter, Richard, *The Nonconformist Plea for Peace* (1679)

Baxter, Richard, *A Third Defence of the Cause of Peace* (1681)

Baxter, Richard, *The Glorious Kingdom of Christ* (1691)

Baxter, Richard, *Reliquae Baxterianae*, Sylvester, M., ed. (1696)

Bellarmino, Roberto, *De Transitu Romani Imperii a Graecis ad Francos* (Ghent, 1584)

[Blair, Eric Arthur] Orwell, George, *Nineteen Eighty-Four* (1948)

Bodin, Jean, *Les Six Livres de la République* (Paris, 1576) [de Bracton, Henry] *De Legibus et Consuetudinibus Angliae* (c. 1250) aka *Bracton* after its supposed author

Bridgeman, Orlando, *Sir Orlando Bridgeman's Conveyances* Johnson, T. Page, ed., 2 vols. (1725, 5th edition)

Browne, William, *Britannia's Pastorals* (1613)

"Junius Brutus" [probably de Mornay, Philippe], *Vindiciae Contra Tyrannos* (1579)

Buc, George, "*Third Universitie of England*" in Stow, John, *Annals* (1615)

Buddeus, Johann Franz, "Synopsis juris naturalis et gentium juxta disciplina ebraeorum" *in Institutiones Juris Naturae et Gentium*, Vitriarius, Ph. Reinhard, ed. (Halle, 1695)

Burges, Cornelius, *The First Sermon preached before the House of Commons at their Publique Fast, 17 Nov. 1640* (1641)

Burke, Edmund, *Reflections of the Revolution in France* (1790)

Burke, Edmund, *A Third Letter on a Regicide Peace* (1797)

Burroughs, Jeremiah, *The Glorius Name of God, the Lord of Hosts* (1643, 4th edition)

Burton, William, *A Commentary on Antoninus* (1657)

Cavendish, Margaret, *The Contract* (1656)

Charles I, *Answer to the Nineteen Propositions* (21 June 1642)

Charles I, *His Majesties Gracious Answer to the Different Opinions of the Earles of Bristol and Dorset Concerning Peace and War. Wherein Is Intimated to All His Loyall Subjects the Earnest Desire He Hath of a Faire Attonement Betwixt Himselfe and His High Court of Parliament* (1642)

Charles I, *Eikon Basilike* (1649)

Cleveland, John, *The Works of Mr. John Cleveland*, J. L. and S. D., eds. (1687)

Coke, Edward, *The First Institute of the Laws of England, or a Commentary upon Littleton* (1628)

Comber, Thomas, *An Historical Vindication of the Divine Right of Tithes ... Designed to Supply the Omissions, Answer the Objections, and Rectifie the Mistakes of Mr. Selden's History of Tithes*, 2 vols. (1685)

Cotton, Robert, *A Short View of the Reign of King Henry III* (1627)

Cowell, John, *A Law Dictionary; or, The Interpreter of Words and Terms* (1607)

Culverwel, Nathaniel, *An Elegant and Learned Discourse of the Light of Nature* (1652)

Cunaeus, Petrus, *De Republica Hebraeorum* (Leiden, 1617)

Davies, John, *Les Reports des Cases & Matters en Ley, Resolves & Adjudges en les Courts del Roy en Irland* (Dublin, 1615) aka *Irish Reports*

Davies, John, *The Question Concerning Impositions, Tonnage, Poundage, Prizage, Customs, &c. Fully Stated and Argued, from Reason, Law, and Policy: Dedicated to King James in the Latter End of His Reign* (1656, published posthumously)

D'Ewes, Simonds, *The Journal of Sir Simonds D'Ewes*, Notenstein, W., ed. (1923)

[Digges, Dudley], *An Answer to a Printed Book* (1642)

Digg[le]s, Dudley, *The Unlawfulnesse of Subjects Taking up Armes Against their Soveraigne* (1643)

Donne, John, *The Works of John Donne*, Alford, Henry, ed., 6 vols. (1839)

Downinge, Calybute, *A Sermon Preached to the Renowned Company of the Artillery, 1 September, 1640 Designed to Compose the Present Troubles by Discovering the Enemies of the Peace of the Church and State* (1641).

Dryden, John, "Epistle to Dr. Charleton" in *The Poetical Works of John Dryden*, Gilfillan, George, ed., 2 vols. (1855).

Egerton, Thomas, *The Speech of the Lord Chancellor ... Touching the Post Nati* (1609)

Filmer, Robert, *Anarchy of a Limited and Mixed Monarchy* (1648)

Filmer, Robert, *Necessity of the Absolute Power of All Kings* (1648)

Filmer, Robert, *Observations Upon Aristotle's Politiques Concerning Forms of Government* (1652)

Filmer, Robert, *Observations Concerning the Originall of Government, upon Mr Hobs Leviathan, Mr Milton Against Salmasius, H. Grotius De jure belli* (1652)

Filmer, Robert, *Patriarcha* (1680, published posthumously)

Finch, Henry, *The Calling of the Jews* (1621)

Finch, Henry, *Law; a Discourse Thereof in Foure Books* (1627, English version of original in Law French, named *Nomotexia*)

Fludd, Robert, *Mosaicall Philosophy* (1659)

Forsett, Edward, *A Comparative Discourse of the Bodies Natural and Politique* (1606)

Forsett, Edward, *A Defence of the Right of Kings* (1624)

Fulbecke, William, *A Parallele or Conference of the Civill Law, the Canon Law, and the Common Law of this Realme of England* (1601)

Fulbecke, William, *Pandects of the Law of Nations* (1602)

Fuller, Nicholas, *The Argument of Master Nicholas Fuller, in the Case of Thomas Lad, and Richard Maunsell, his Clients Wherein it is Plainely Proved, that the Ecclesiasticall Commissioners Haue No Power, by Vertue of their Commission, to Imprison, to Put to the Oath Ex Officio, or to Fine Any of his Maiesties Subiects* (1607)

Galilei, Galileo, *Dialogo Sopra i Due Massimi Sistemi del Mondo* (Firenze, 1632)

Galli, Antimo, *Rime di Antimo Galli All'Illustrissima Signora Elizabetta Talbot-Grey* (1609)

Gentili, Alberico, *Alberico Gentili, De Iure Belli Libri Tres* [Hanau, 1589] Rolfe, J.C., ed. & trans. (Oxford: Clarendon, 1933 – translated from 1612 edition)

Gentili, Alberico, *Regales Disputationes Tres* (1605)

[de Glanvill, Ranulph], *Tractatus de Legibus et Consuetudinibus regni Angliae* (c. 1188), aka *Glanvill* after its presumed author

Goldsmith, Oliver, *Retaliation: A Poem* (1774)

Grosse, Robert, *Royalty and Loyalty* (1647)

Grotius, Hugo, *De Jure Belli ac Pacis* [1625], Kelsey, B.W., trans., 2 vols. (Oxford: Clarendon, 1925)

Grotius, Hugo, *A Treatise of the Antiquity of the Commonwealth of the Battavers Which Is Now the Hollanders*, Wood, Thomas, trans. (1649)

Grotius, Hugo, *De Jure Praedae Commentarius* [aka *De Indis*, c. 1604], Williams, G.L., trans., 2 vols. (Oxford: Clarendon, 1950)

Grotius, Hugo, *Briefwisseling Van Hugo Grotius*, Meulenbroeck, B.L., ed., vol. 4 (The Hague: Nijhoff, 1964)

Goodwin, John, *Certain Briefe Observations and Antiquæries* (1644)

Hale, Matthew, *History of the Common Law* (1716, 2nd edition)

Hayward, John, *An Answer to the First Part of a Certaine Conference* (1603)

Herbert, Edward, *De Veritate* (Paris, 1624)

Herbert, Edward, *De Religione Gentilium* (Amsterdam, 1663, published posthumously)

Herrick, Robert, *Hesperides* (1648)

Hudson, Michael, *The Divine Right of Government* (1647)

Hobbes, Thomas, *The Elements of Law Natural and Politic* (1640)

Hobbes, Thomas, *De Cive* (1642)

Hobbes, Thomas, *Leviathan* (1651)

Hobbes, Thomas, *Thomas Hobbesii Malmesburiensis Vita, Authore Seipso* (1679)

Hobbes, Thomas, *Behemoth or the Long Parliament* (1682, published posthumously)

Hooker, Richard, *Of the Laws of Ecclesiastical Polity*, Hanbury, B., ed., 3 vols. (1830)

Hotman, Francois, *Francogallia* [1573], Molesworth, Robert, trans. (1721, 2nd edition)

Hunton, Philip, *A Treatise of Monarchy* (1643)

Hutton, Richard, *The Diary of Sir Richard Hutton 1614–1639*, Prest, W.R., ed. (Selden Society, 1993)

Hyde, Edward, "The Life of Edward, Earl of Clarendon" in *The History of the Rebellion and Civil Wars in England*, 2 vols. (1702–1704, published posthumously)

James VI and I, "Psalmes of his Maiestie" in *The Poems of King James VI of Scotland*, Craigie, James, ed., 2 vols. (Edinburgh: Scottish Text Society, 1955–1958)

James VI and I, *The True Law of Free Monarchies and Basilikon Doron* [1598–1599] Fischlin, D. & Fortier, M., eds. (Toronto: Center for Reformation and Renaissance Studies, 1996)

Jonson, Ben, *The Underwood* (1640 published posthumously)

Lawson, George, *Examination of the Political Part of Mr. Hobbes, his Leviathan* (1657)

Lawson, George, *Politica Sacra et Civilis* (1660)

[Locke, John], *Second Treatise of Government* (1689)

Marlowe, Christopher, *The Jew of Malta* (c. 1590)

Maynwaring, Roger, *Religion and Alegiance* (1627)

Milton, John, *Areopagitica* (1644)

Milton, John, *Doctrine and Discipline of Divorce* (1644, 2nd edition)

Milton, John, *Colasterion and Tetrachordon* (1645)

Milton, John, *Tenure of Kings and Magistrates* (1649)

Milton, John, *Eikonoklastes* (1649)

Modena, Leone, *Riti Ebraici* (1616)

Needham, Marchamont, *The Case of the Commonwealth of England Stated* [1650, 2 editions] (Washington, Folger Shakespeare Library – Virginia University Press, 1969)

Parker, Henry, *The Case of SHIPMONY Briefly Discoursed* (1640)

Parker, Henry, *Observations upon Some of His Majesties Late Answers* (1642)

H.P. [Parker, Henry], *The Generall Junto, or the Councell of Union* (1642)

Pococke, Edward, *Specimen Historiae Arabum* (1649)

Pont, Robert, *De Unione Britanniæ* (1604)

Prynne, William, *A Soveraign Antidote* (1642)

Prynne, William, *The Soveraigne Power of Parliaments* (1643)

Prynne, William, *The Popish Royall Favourite* (1643)

Rabelais, Francois, *La Vie de Gargantua et de Pantagruel* (Lyon, 1532–1564)

Ridley, Thomas, *View of the Civile and Ecclesiastical Law* (Oxford, 1607)

Rogers, John, *Sagrir or Doomes-day Drawing Nigh* (1653)

Rous, Francis, *Ancient Bounds* (1645)

Rous, Francis, *The Lawfulness of Obeying the Present Government* (1649)

Rubens, Peter Paul, *The Letters of Peter Paul Rubens*, Saunders Magurn, R., ed. (Evanston: Northwestern University Press, 1955)

Rutherford, Samuel, *Lex Rex, or The Law and the Prince* (1644).

[Salmasius, Claudius], *Defensio Regia pro Carolo I* (1649)

Sanderson, Robert, *De Juramento* (1655, published posthumously)

Sarpi, Paolo, *Pensieri*, Cozzi, G. & L., eds. (Torino: Einaudi, 1976)
Sedgwick, William, *A Second View of the Army Remonstrance* (1649)
Sempil, James, *Sacrilege Sacredly Handled* (1619)
[Sexby, Edward] Allen, William, *Killing Noe Murder* (1657)
Shakespeare, William, *The Chronicle History of Henry the Fifth* (1600)
Shirley, James, *The Triumph of Peace* (1633 [1634])
Smith, Thomas, *De Republica Anglorum* (1583, published posthumously)
Spelman, Henry, *Archaeologus in Modum Glossarii ad rem Antiqua Posteriore* (1626)
Spelman, Henry, *The Original, Growth, Propagation and Condition of Feuds and Tenures by Knight-Service in England* (1639)
Sybthorpe, Robert, *Apostolike Obedience* (1627)
Taylor, Jeremy, *Ductor Dubitantium* (1660)
Twysden, Roger, *Certaine Considerations upon the Government of England* (c. 1648)
Tyrrell, James, *A Brief Disquisition of the Law of Nature* (1692)
Vaughan, John, *The Reports and Arguments of that Learned Judge, Sir John Vaughan kt. Late Chief Justice of his Majesties Court of Common Pleas...*, Vaughan, Edward, ed. (1677)
Vico, Giambattista, *The New Science [La Scienza Nuova* (1725)]*, Goddard Bergin T. & Fish, M.H., trans. (Ithaca, NY: Cornell University Press, 1984)
Vitoria, Francisco, "On the American Indians" (1532), in *Francisco Vitoria, Political Writings*, Pagden, Anthony and Lawrance, Jeremy, eds. (Cambridge University Press, 1992)
Walton, Izaak, *The Compleat Angler* (1653)
Whitelocke, Bulstrode, *Memorials of the English Affairs...* (1682)
Williams, Roger, *The Bloudy Tenent of Persecution* (1644)

Minutes, Records, Proceedings, Collections, Papers, etc.

Abstract of Proceedings of the Virginia Company, (Richmond, Virginia, 1888)
A Calendar of Inner Temple Records, Inderwich, F.A., ed. (1898)
A catalogue...Also the Very Curious Collection of Manuscripts, of Ancient Chronicles, Monastic History, Charters etc., on Vellum and Paper, Many Finely Illuminated, Collected by Sir Roger Twysden and Mr. E. Lhwyd (auction catalogue, 1807).
Appendiciae et Pertinentiae; Or Parochial Fragments Relating to the Parish of West Tarring... Warter, J.W., ed. (1853)
A Short Collection of the most remarkable passages from the Originall to the Dissolution of the Virginia Company, Woodnoth, Arthur, ed. (1651)
Commons Debates 1628, Johnson, Robert C. et al., eds., 4 vols. (Rochester University Press, 1977–1978)
Dictionary of National Biography, Stephen, Leslie et al., eds., 63 vols. (1885–1900)
Journal of the House of Commons: 1547–1699, 13 vols. (1802–1803)
Minutes of the Sessions of the Westminster Assembly of Divines, Mitchell, A.F. & Struthers, J., eds. (1874)
Oxford Dictionary of National Biography, Matthew, C. & Harrison, B., eds., 60 vols. (Oxford University Press, 2004)
Proceedings in Parliament 1626, Bidwell, W.D. et al., eds., 4 vols. (Rochester University Press, 1991–1996)

Records of the Borough of Nottingham: Being a Series of Extracts from the Archives of the Corporation of Nottingham, Stevenson, W.L. et al., eds., 7 vols. (1882).

Synodalia: A Collection of Articles of Religion, Canons, and Proceedings of Convocations in the Province of Canterbury, from the Year 1547 to the Year 1717, Cardwell, E., ed. (Oxford, 1842)

The History of Parliament: The House of Commons 1604–1629, Thrush, A. and Ferris, J.P., eds. (Cambridge University Press, 2010) www.historyofparliamentonline.org

The Minutes and Papers of the Westminster Assembly 1643–1652, Van Dixhoorn, C., ed., 3 vols. (Oxford University Press, 2012)

The Oxford English Dictionary, 20 vols. (Oxford: Clarendon Press, 1989, 2nd edition)

The Putney Debates of 1647: The Army, the Levellers and the English State, Mendle, M. ed. (Cambridge University Press, 2010 reissue)

The Records of the Virginia Company of London, Kingsbury, S.M., ed., 2 vols. (Washington, 1906)

SECONDARY TEXTS

The Faithful Scout 204 (8 December 1654)

[Anonymous] "Mapping China" in *The Economist* (18 January 2014).

Adamson, J., *The Noble Revolt: The Overthrow of Charles I* (Phoenix, 2009)

Aikin, J., *The Lives of John Selden and Archbishop Usher* (1812)

Aubrey, J., *Brief Lives* [c. 1669–1696], Barber, R., ed. (Boydell, 1982)

Baker, J.H., *The Third University of England – the Inns of Court and the Common Law Tradition* (Selden Society, 1990)

Barbour, R., *John Selden: Measures of the Holy Commonwealth in Seventeenth-Century England* (Toronto University Press, 2003)

Barnes, T.G., *Shaping the Common Law: From Glanvill to Hale, 1188–1688* (Stanford University Press, 2008)

Berkowitz, D.S., *John Selden's Formative Years* (Washington: Folger Shakespeare Library Press, 1988)

Biberman, M., "Milton, Marriage, and a Woman's right to divorce" in *Studies in English Literature 1500–1900*, 39/1 (1999)

Bowsma, W., *Venice and the Defense of Republican Liberty* (Berkeley: California University Press, 1968)

Brook, T., *Mr. Selden's Map of China* (Bloomsbury Press, 2013)

Brooks, C. and K. Sharpe, "History, English law and the renaissance" in *Past and Present* 72/1 (August 1976)

Burgess, G., *The Politics of the Ancient Constitution* (Macmillan, 1992)

Burgess, G., *Absolute Monarchy and the Stuart Constitution* (New Haven: Yale University Press, 1996)

The Cambridge History of Political Thought, 1400–1700, Burns, J.H. and Goldie, M. (eds.) (Cambridge University Press, 1991)

Canning, J., *A History of Medieval Political Thought 300–1450* (Routledge, 1996)

Cargill Thompson, W.D.J., *Studies in the Reformation: Luther to Hooker* (Athlone Press, 1980)

Cartwright, E., *The Parochial Topography of the Rape of Bramber in the Western Division of the County of Sussex* (1830)

Caruso, S., *La Miglior Legge del Regno*, 2 vols. (Milano: Giuffre, 2001)

Christianson, P., "Young John Selden and the Ancient Constitution, c. 1610–1618" in *Proceedings of the American Philosophical Society*, 128 (1984)

Christianson, P., *Discourse on History, Law and Government in the Public Career of John Selden 1610–1635* (Toronto University Press, 1996)

Christianson, P., "Selden, John" in *ODNB*

Clark, G., *A History of the Royal College of Physicians of London* (Oxford: Clarendon, 1964)

Collett-White, J., "The old house at Wrest Park" in *The Bedfordshire Magazine*, vols. 22–23 (1991)

Collins, S.L., *From Divine Cosmos to Sovereign State* (Oxford University Press, 1989)

Considine, J., "Grey, Elizabeth" in *ODNB*

Coquillette, D.R., *The Civilian Writers of Doctors' Commons, London* (Berlin: Dunker & Humblot, 1988)

Craven, W.S., *The Virginia Company of London, 1606–1626* (Williamsburg: Virginia 350th celebration corporation, 1957)

Cromartie, A., *Sir Matthew Hale, 1609–1676* (Cambridge University Press, 1995)

Cromartie, A., *The Constitutionalist Revolution: An Essay on the History of England 1450–1642* (Cambridge University Press, 2006)

Cuttica, C., *Adam... "THE FATHER OF ALL FLESH": An Intellectual History of Sir Robert Filmer (1588–1653) and his Works in Seventeenth-Century European Political Thought* (European University Institute, unpublished PhD thesis, 2007)

Daly, J., "Cosmic Harmony and Political Thinking in Early Stuart England" in *Transactions of the American Philosophical Society* (NS) 69/7 (1979)

Daly, J., *Sir Robert Filmer and English Political Thought* (Toronto University Press, 1979)

Davidson, A., "Phelips, Sir Robert" in *HOPO* (retrieved 6 April 2015)

Davis, K., *Periodization and Sovereignty* (Philadelphia: Pennsylvania University Press, 2008)

Digby Thomas, R., *George Digby: Hero and Villain* (Bloomington, Indiana: Author House Press, 2005)

Eccleshall, R., *Order and Reason in Politics* (Oxford University Press, 1978)

van Eikema Hommes, H., "Grotius' Mathematical Method" *in Netherlands International Law Review* 31/1 (May 1984)

Feingold, M., "John Selden and the nature of 17th century science" in Bienvenu, R.T. & Feingold, M. (eds.) *In the Presence of the Past: Essays in Honor of Frank Manuel* (Dordrecht: Kluwer, 1991)

Ferguson, A.B., *Clio Unbound* (Durham NC: Duke University Press, 1979)

Ford, A., *James Ussher* (Oxford University Press, 2007)

Forster, J., *Sir John Eliot: A Biography 1592–1632* (1872, 2nd edition) vol. ii

Foss, E., "Hale, Sir Matthew" in *Biographia Juridica: A Biographical Dictionary of the Judges of England from the Conquest to the Present Time, 1066–1870* (1870)

Franklin, J., *John Locke and the Theory of Sovereignty* (Cambridge University Press, 1981)

Fry, E., "Selden, John" in *DNB* (1897) vol. 51 pp. 212–224

Fulton, T., "*Areopagitica* and the Roots of Liberal Epistemology" in *English Literary Renaissance* 34/1 (February 2004)

Gambino, L., *I Politiques e l'Idea di Sovranita (1573–1593)* (Milano: Giuffre, 1991)

Gordley, J., *The Philosophical Origins of Modern Contract Doctrine* (Oxford: Clarendon, 1991)

Grafton, A. and Jardine, L., "'Studied for action': How Gabriel Harvey read his Livy" in *Past and Present* 129/1 (November 1990)

Grafton, A. & Weinberg, J., *"I have Always Loved the Holy Tongue" – Isaac Casaubon, The Jews, and a Forgotten Chapter of Renaissance Scholarship* (Cambridge, Mass.: Harvard Bellknap Press, 2011)

Grayling, A.C., *Descartes* (Pocket Books, 2005)

Greenleaf, W.H., "Filmer's Patriarchal History" in *The Historical Journal* 9/2 (1966)

Gregg, P., *King Charles I* (Berkeley: California University Press, 1984)

Grove, S. and Cheng, D., "A National strategy for the South China Sea" *Backgrounder – The Heritage Foundation* (24 April 2014)

Guibbory, A., *Christian Identity – Jews & Israel in Seventeenth-Century England* (Oxford University Press, 2010)

Hampsher-Monk, I., "John Thelwall and the eighteenth-century radical response to political economy" in *Historical Journal* 34/1 (March 1991)

Hampsher-Monk, I., *A History of Modern Political Thought* (Oxford: Blackwell, 1992)

Harris, R.W., *Clarendon and the English Revolution* (Stanford University Press, 1983)

Harrison, R., *Hobbes, Locke and Confusion's Masterpiece* (Cambridge University Press, 2003)

Hazeltine, H.D., "Selden as a legal historian" in *Festschrift Heinrich Brunner* (Weimar, 1910)

Healy, S., "Grey, Sir Henry" in *HOPO* (retrieved 6 April 2015)

Helgerson, R., *Forms of Nationhood: The Elizabethan Writings of England* (Chicago University Press, 1992)

Herford, G.H., *Ben Jonson* (Oxford University Press, 1925)

Hill, C., *The World Turned Upside Down* (Penguin, 1991 – reprint of 1975 edition)

Hirsch, S.A., "Early English Hebraists: Roger Bacon and his predecessors" in *The Jewish Quarterly Review* 12/1 (October 1899)

Hochstrasser, T.J., *Natural Law Theories in the Early Enlightenment* (Cambridge University Press, 2000)

Holmes, J.R., "China's New Naval Theorist" in *The Diplomat* (11 July 2013)

Hopfl, H. and Thompson, M.P., "The History of Contract as a Motif in Political Thought" in *American Historical Review* 84/4 (October 1979)

Hunneyball, P., "Selden, John" in *HOPO* (retrieved 27 October 2014)

Jaffa, H.V., *Thomism and Aristotelianism* (Westport: Greenwood Press, 1979 – reprint of 1952 edition)

Jones, G.L., *The Discovery of Hebrew in Tudor England* (Manchester University Press, 1983)

Johnson, G.W., *Memoirs of John Selden, and Notices of the Political Contest During his Time* (1835)

Johnson, K., "Lord of the Sea" in *Foreign Policy* (16 May 2014)

Johnson Theutenberg, B., "Mare Clausum et Mare Liberum" in *Arctic* 37/4 (December 1984)

Judson, M.A., *The Crisis of the Constitution* (New Brunswick: Rutgers University Press, 1988 – reprint of 1949 edition)

Kahn, V., *Wayward Contracts: The Crisis of Political Obligation in England 1640–1674* (Princeton University Press, 2004)

Kantorowicz, E.H., *The King's Two Bodies* (Princeton University Press, 1997)

Kaplan, L., "English civil war politics and the religious settlement" in *Church History* 41/3 (1972) pp. 311–315

Katz, D.S., "The Abendana brothers and the Christian Hebraists of seventeenth century England" in *Journal of Ecclesiastical History* 1/40 (January 1989)

Keeler, M.F., *The Long Parliament* (Philadelphia: APS, 1954)

Kelley, D.R., *Foundations of Modern Historical Scholarship* (New York: Columbia University Press, 1970)

Kelley, D.R., "History, English law and the renaissance" in *Past and Present* 65/1 (November 1974)

Kelley, D.R., "A rejoinder: History, English law and the renaissance" in *Past and Present*, 72/1 (August 1976)

Kelley, D.R., "Second nature: The idea of custom in European law, society and culture" in Grafton, A. & Blair, A., *The Transmission of Culture in Early Modern Europe* (Philadelphia: University of Pennsylvania Press, 1990)

Kelley, D.R., *The Human Measure: Social Thought in the Western Legal Tradition* (Cambridge, Mass., Harvard University Press, 1990)

Kelley, D.R., *Renaissance Humanism* (Boston: Twayne, 1991)

Kenyon, J.P., *The Stuart Constitution 1603–1608 – Documents and Commentary* (Cambridge University Press, 1966)

Knachel, P.A., "Introduction" in Needham, *Case*

Knafla, L.A., "Britain's Solomon: King James and the Law" in Fischlin, D. & Fortier, M. (eds.), *Royal Subjects* (Detroit: Wayne State University Press, 2002)

Knight, W.S.M., *The Life and Works of Hugo Grotius* (1925)

Kors, A.C., "Theology and atheism in Early Modern France" in Grafton & Blair (eds.), *The Transmission of Culture in Early Modern Europe* (Philadelphia: Pennsylvania University Press, 1990)

Kossmann, E.H., "The development of Dutch political theory in the Seventeenth Century" in Bromley, J.S. and Kossmann, E.H. (eds.) *Britain and the Netherlands* vol. I. (Chatto and Windus, 1960)

Lamont, W.M., *Godly Rule, Politics and Religion 1603–1660* (Macmillan, 1969)

Lamont, W.M., "Arminianism: the controversy that never was" in Skinner and Phillipson (eds.) *Political Discourse in Early Modern Britain* (Cambridge University Press, 1993)

Lamont, W.M., *Puritanism and Historical Controversy* (UCL Press, 1996)

Lasker, D.J., "Karaism and Christian Hebraism: a new document" in *Renaissance Quarterly* 59/4 (December 2006)

Lawson, D.F., *Upon a Dangerous Design: The Public Life of Edward Sexby* (University of Alabama, unpublished PhD dissertation, 2011)

Leith, J.H., *Assembly at Westminster* (Eugene, Oregon: WIP and Stock Publishers, 2008)

Levy Peck, L., "Kingship, counsel and law in early Stuart England" in Pocock, J.G.A. (ed.), *The Varieties of British Political Thought 1500–1800* (Cambridge University Press, 1993)

Lieberman, D., "Law/custom/tradition: Perspectives from the common law" in Philips & Schochet (eds.), *Questions of Tradition* (Toronto University Press, 2004)

Lloyd, H.A., "Constitutionalism" in Burns, J.H. & Goldie, M. (eds.), *The Cambridge History of Political Thought 1450–1700* (Cambridge University Press, 1991)

Lobban, M., "The Common Law World," ch. 8 of E. Pattaro (Gen ed.), *A Treatise of Legal Philosophy and General Jurisprudence* (Dordrecht: Springer, 2007), vol. 8.

Lucci, D., "Ebraismo e antichi paganesimi. Il sincretismo religioso di Herbert di Cherbury e i suoi influssi sugli studi storico-religiosi del seicento" in *La Rassegnia Mensile di Israel* 70/1 (April 2004, Roma)

McEachern, C., *The Poetics of English Nationhood, 1590–1612* (Cambridge University Press, 2007)

McLean, A.H., "George Lawson and John Locke" in *Cambridge Historical Journal* 9/1 (1947)

Malcolm, N., "Hobbes, Sandys and the Virginia Company" in *Historical Journal* 24/2 (1981)

Malcolm, N., "Thomas Hobbes" in *ODNB*

Megarry, J., *Inns Ancient and Modern* (Selden Society, 1972)

Mendle, M., *Dangerous Positions: Mixed Government, the Estates of the Realm and the Making of the Answer to the XIX Propositions* (Birmingham: Alabama University Press, 1985)

Mendle, M., "The Great Council of Parliament and the First Ordinances: The Constitutional Theory of the Civil War" in *Journal of British Studies* 31/2 (April 1992)

Merritt, J.F., *The Social World of Early-Modern Westminster* (Manchester University Press, 2005)

Meyler, B., "Towards a Common Law Originalism" in *Stanford Law Review* 59/3 (2006)

Milton, A., "Thomas Wentworth and the political thought of the personal rule" in Merrit, J.F. (ed.), *The Political World of Thomas Wentworth, Earl of Strafford 1621–1641* (Cambridge University Press, 2003)

van der Molen, G.H.J., *Alberico Gentili and the Development of International Law* (Leyden: Sijthoff, 1968, 2nd edition)

Mosse, G.L., *The Struggle for Sovereignty in England* (East Lansing: Michigan State College Press, 1950)

Murphy, W.T., "The oldest social science? The epistemic properties of the common law tradition" in *The Modern Law Review* 54/2 (March 1991)

Pagden, A., "Human rights, natural rights, and Europe's imperial legacy" in *Political Theory* 31/2 (April 2003).

Panizza, D., *Alberico Gentili, Giurista Ideologo nell'Inghilterra Elizabettiana* (Padova: La Garangola, 1981)

Parker, K.I., "'That 'Dreadful Name, Leviathan': Biblical resonances in the title to Hobbes' famous political work" in *Hebraic Political Studies* 2/4 (2007).

Parker, M.P., "'To my friend G.N. from Wrest': Carew's secular Masque" in Summers, C. J. and Pebworth, T.L. (eds.) *Classic and Cavalier* (Pittsburg University Press, 1982)

Parkin, J., *Science, Religion and Politics in Restoration England – Richard Cumberland's De Legibus Naturae* (Woodbridge, Suffolk: The Boydell Press – The Royal Historical Society, 1999)

Parry, G., *The Trophies of Time* (Oxford University Press, 1995)

Pawlisch, H.S., "Sir John Davies, the ancient constitution, and civil law" in *Historical Journal* 23/3 (September 1980)

Pocock, J.G.A., *The Ancient Constitution and the Feudal Law* (Cambridge University Press, 1987 – reissue with a retrospective)

Pocock, J.G.A., *Politics, Language and Time* (Methuen, 1972)

Prest, R., *The Rise of the Barristers: A Social History of the English Bar 1590–1640* (Oxford University Press, 1986)

Prior, C.W.A., "Hebraism and the problem of church and state in England 1642–1660" in *The Seventeenth Century* 28/1 (2013)

Prior, C.W.A., "Rethinking Church and State during the English Interregnum" in *Historical Research* 87/237 (August 2014)

Raizman-Kedar, Y., "The Intellect Naturalized: Roger Bacon on the Existence of Corporeal Species within the Intellect" in *Early Science and Medicine* 14/1 (2009).

Rahe, P.A., *Republics Ancient & Modern*, 3 vols. (Chapel Hill: North Carolina University Press, 1994).

Rahe, P.A., *Against Throne & Altar – Machiavelli and Political Theory under the English Republic* (Cambridge University Press, 2008)

Reeve, J., "The arguments in King's Bench in 1629 concerning the imprisonment of John Selden and other members of the House of Commons" in *Journal of British Studies* 25/3 (July 1986)

Rex, M.B., *University Representation in England* (G. Allen & Unwin, 1954)

Riley, P., "How coherent is the Social Contract Tradition" in *Journal of the History of Ideas* 34/4 (October–December 1973)

Roberts, C., "The Earl of Bedford and the Coming of the English Revolution" in *Journal of Modern History* 49/4 (1977)

Roberts, C., *Schemes and Undertakings: A Study of English Politics in the Seventeenth Century* (Columbus: Ohio State University Press, 1985)

Roots, I., *Commonwealth and Protectorate* (New York: Schocken, 1966)

Rosenblatt, J., *Renaissance England's Chief Rabbi: John Selden* (Oxford University Press, 2006)

Rosenblatt, J., "Rabbinic ideas in the political thought of John Selden" in Schochet, G., Oz-Salzberger, F., and Jones, M. (eds.), *Political Hebraism: Judaic Sources in Early Modern Political Thought* (Jerusalem: Shalem Press, 2008)

Roslak, O.M., *John Selden and the Laws of England* (Cambridge University, unpublished PhD dissertation, 2000)

Roth, C., "Leone da Modena and England" in *Transactions of the Jewish Historical Society of England* 11 (1928)

Roth, C., "Leone da Modena and his English correspondents" in *Transactions of the Jewish Historical Society of England* 17 (1953)

Rowse, A.L., *Four Caroline Portraits* (Duckworth, 1993)

Schmitt, C.B., *John Case and Aristotelianism in Renaissance England* (Montreal: McGill-Queen's University Press, 1983)

Schochet, G.J., *Patriarchalism in Political Thought* (New York: Basic Books, 1975)

Schochet, G.J., "Traditions as politics and the politics of tradition" in Philips, M.S. and Schochet, G., *Questions of Tradition* (Toronto University Press, 2004)

Schoffer, I., "The Batavian Myth during the Sixteenth and Seventeenth centuries" in Bromley, J.S. & Kossmann, E.H. (eds.), *Britain and the Netherlands* vol. V. (The Hague: Martinus Nijhoff, 1975)

Shapiro, J., *Shakespeare and the Jews* (New York: Columbia University Press, 1995)

Sharpe, K., *Criticism and Compliment* (Cambridge University Press, 1987)

Sharpe, K., *Remapping Early Modern England – The Culture of Seventeenth Century Politics* (Cambridge University Press, 2000)

Siegel, S.A., "The Aristotelian basis of English law" in *New York University Law Review* 56/18 (1981)

Siraisi, N.G., *Avicenna in Renaissance Italy* (Princeton University Press, 1987)

Skinner, Q., *Foundations of Modern Political Thought*, 2 vols. (Cambridge University Press, 1978)

Smith, D.L., "The Fourth Earl of Dorset and the Personal Rule of Charles I" in *Journal of British Studies* 30/3 (July 1991)

Smith, D.L., *Constitutional Royalism and the Search for Settlement c. 1640–1649* (Cambridge University Press, 1994)

Smith, D.L., "Sackville Edward" in *ODNB*

Smith, N., "*Areopagitica*: voicing contexts, 1643–5" in Lowenstein, D. & Turner, J.G. (eds.) *Politics, Poetics, and Hermeneutics in Milton's Prose* (Cambridge University Press, 2007)

Smuts, R.M., "The Puritan Followers of Henrietta Maria in the 1630s" in *English Historical Review* 93/366 (1978) p. 29

Snow, V.F., "The Arundel Case, 1626" in *Historian* 26:4 (1964)

Sommerville, J.P., "John Selden, the law of nature and the origins of government" in *Historical Journal* 27/2 (June 1984)

Sommerville, J.P., "Introduction" in J.P. Sommerville (ed.) *Filmer: Patriarcha and Other Writings* (Cambridge University Press, 1991)

Sommerville, J.P., "Parliament, Privilege, and the Liberties of the Subject" in J.H. Hexter (ed.), *Parliament and Liberty: From the Reign of Elizabeth to the English Civil War* (Stanford: California University Press, 1992)

Sommerville, J.P., *Royalists and Patriots: Politics and Ideology in England 1603–1640* (Longman, 1999, 2nd edition)

Sparrow, J., "Documents and Records – The earlier owners of books in John Selden's library" in *The Bodleian Quarterly Record* 6/70–71 (1931)

Stimson, D., "Ballad of Gresham colledge [sic]" in *Isis* 18/1 (July 1932)

Stoddard Flemion, J., "The struggle for the Petition of Right in the House of Lords: The study of an opposition party victory" in *The Journal of Modern History* 45/2 (1973)

Stone, L., *The Crisis of the Aristocracy, 1558–1641* (Oxford: Clarendon, 1965)

Straumann, B., "The Right to punish as just cause of war in Hugo Grotius' Natural Law" in *Studies in the History of Ethics*, 2/2006 (electronic journal at: www.historyofethics.org)

Tanner, J.R., *Constitutional Documents of the Reign of James I 1603–1625* (Cambridge, 1930)

Tanner, J.R., *English Constitutional Conflicts 1603–1689* (1961)

Tite, C.G.C., "A 'Loan' of printed books from Sir Robert Cotton to John Selden" in *The Bodleian Library Record*, vol. 13/6 (April 1991)

Tomlinson, G., *Monteverdi and the End of the Renaissance* (Los Angeles: UCLA University Press, 1990)

Toomer, J.G., *John Selden: A Life in Scholarship*, 2 vols. (Oxford University Press, 2009)

Trevor-Roper, H., *The Crisis of the Seventeenth Century* (Macmillan, 1967)

Trevor-Roper, H., *Catholics, Anglicans and Puritans* (Secker & Warburg, 1987)

Tubbs, J.W., *The Common Law Mind* (Baltimore: Johns Hopkins University Press, 2000)

Tuck, R., *Natural Rights Theories – Their Origin and Development* (Cambridge University Press, 1979)

Tuck, R., "'The Ancient law of Freedom': John Selden and the English civil war" in Morrill, J. (ed.), *Reactions to the English Civil War 1642–1649* (Macmillan, 1982)

Tuck, R., *Hobbes* (Oxford University Press, 1989)

Tuck, R., "The 'modern' theory of natural law" in A. Pagden (ed.), *The Languages of Political Theory in Early-Modern Europe* (Cambridge University Press, 1990)

Tuck, R., "Grotius and Selden" in Burns, J.H. & Goldie, M., *The Cambridge History of Political Thought 1450–1700* (Cambridge University Press, 1991)

Tuck, R., *Philosophy and Government 1572–1651* (Cambridge University Press, 1993)

Tuck, R., *The Rights of War and Peace* (Oxford University Press, 1999)

Tyacke, N., *Aspects of English Protestantism c. 1530–1700* (Manchester University Press, 2001)

Underdown, D., *Pride's Purge: Politics in the Puritan Revolution* (Oxford: Clarendon, 1971)

Walzer, M., *The Revolution of the Saints* (Cambridge, Mass.: Harvard University Press, 1965)

Ward, L., *The Politics of Liberty in England and Revolutionary America* (Cambridge University Press, 2004)

Watson, P. & Sgroi, R., "May, Humphrey" in *HOPO* (retrieved 27 October 2014)

Wedgwood, C.V., *Thomas Wentworth First Earl of Strafford 1593–1641 – A Reevaluation* (Phoenix Press, 2000 – reprint of 1961 edition)

Whitney, E.A., "Erastianism and divine right" in *The Huntington Library Quarterly* 2/4 (1939)

Wilcher, R., *The Writings of Royalism 1628–1660* (Cambridge University Press, 2001)

Woodhouse, A.S.P. (ed.), *Puritanism and Liberty, Being the Army Debates* (Chicago University Press, 1951)

Woolf, D.R., *The Idea of History in Early Stuart England* (Toronto University Press, 1990)

Woolf, D.R., "Conscience, Constancy and Ambition in the Career and writings of James Howell" in Morrill, J., et al. (eds.) *Public Duty and Private Conscience* (Oxford University Press, 1993)

Woolrych, A., *Britain in Revolution 1625–1660* (Oxford University Press, 2002)

Wootton, D. (ed.), *Divine Right and Democracy* (Harmondsworth: Penguin 1986)

Wootton, D., "From rebellion to revolution: The crisis of the winter of 1642/3 and the origins of civil war radicalism" in *English Historical Review* 105/416 (1990)

Zagorin, P., "Thomas Hobbes' Departure from England in 1640: An Unpublished Letter" in *Historical Journal* 21/1 (1978)

Zaller, R., *The Discourse of Legitimacy in Early Modern England* (Stanford University Press, 2007)

Zaller, R., "Edward Alford" in *ODNB*

Ziskind, M.A., "John Selden: Criticism and affirmation of the common law tradition" in *The American Journal of Legal History* 19/1 (January 1975)

Zuckert, M.P., *Natural Rights and the New Republicanism* (Princeton University Press, 1994)

Index

Printed in Great Britain
by Amazon

21895807R00303